"*The Life of the Vows* is an excellent, detailed presentation of the perennial challenges of the Benedictine vows for anyone who wants to understand them better in order to live them well. A truly helpful study for one in initial formation or as a refresher course for veteran monastics."

—Br. M. Anthony Weber, ocso
Vocation Director
Abbey of the Genesee

"While written prior to Vatican II with an emphasis on external observances, Merton addresses his novices in a refreshingly direct way. His comments on chastity and poverty are still valuable for today and helpful for any newcomer to the life discerning lifetime commitments."

—Br. Placid Morris
Vocation Director
Abbey of New Clairvaux, Vina, California

INITIATION INTO THE MONASTIC TRADITION SERIES

BY

THOMAS MERTON

Cassian and the Fathers:
Initiation into the Monastic Tradition (MW 1)

Pre-Benedictine Monasticism:
Initiation into the Monastic Tradition 2 (MW 9)

An Introduction to Christian Mysticism:
Initiation into the Monastic Tradition 3 (MW 13)

The Rule of St. Benedict:
Initiation into the Monastic Tradition 4 (MW 19)

Monastic Observances:
Initiation into the Monastic Tradition 5 (MW 25)

MONASTIC WISDOM SERIES: NUMBER THIRTY

The Life of the Vows
Initiation into the Monastic Tradition 6

by

Thomas Merton

Edited with an Introduction by
Patrick F. O'Connell

Preface by
Augustine Roberts, ocso

α

Cistercian Publications
www.cistercianpublications.org

LITURGICAL PRESS
Collegeville, Minnesota
www.litpress.org

A Cistercian Publications title published by Liturgical Press

Cistercian Publications
Editorial Offices
Abbey of Gethsemani
3642 Monks Road
Trappist, Kentucky 40051
www.cistercianpublications.org

1   2   3   4   5   6   7   8   9

Library of Congress Cataloging-in-Publication Data

Merton, Thomas, 1915–1968.
  The life of the vows : initiation into the monastic tradition 6 / by
  Thomas Merton ; edited with an introduction by Patrick F. O'Connell ;
  preface by Augustine Roberts.
    p.   cm. — (Monastic wisdom series ; no. 30)
  Includes bibliographical references and index.
  ISBN 978-0-87907-030-4 — ISBN 978-0-87907-793-8 (e-book)
  1. Vows.   2. Monastic and religious life.   3. Benedictines.   4.
Cistercians.   I. O'Connell, Patrick F.   II. Title.

BX2435.M466   2012
255'.01—dc23   2012013342

TABLE OF CONTENTS

PREFACE

It seems that Father Louis, whom most of us know as Thomas Merton, had already begun to think of a plan for more adequate formation of Gethsemani's postulants, novices and simply professed, even before he was named novice master in 1955. He had been in the monastery over thirteen years by that time, the last six as a solemnly professed priest, which was plenty of time for him, with his voracious reading ability, penetrating intellect and teaching experience—not to mention several books already written—to perceive that something was lacking in the abbey's formation program.

One of the results is this present volume on the vowed life, one of several written for young monks in formation. By 1960, when it was completed, Merton was already forty-five and had benefited from four years as master of scholastics, then five more as novice director. It is a moment in life when the creativity of youth crosses with the beginnings of acquired wisdom, and each of these sets of conferences shows such intertwining. Of the texts now published, the present one on the vows is clearly the youngest sister, slightly awkward, yet the one turning out to be the most directly pastoral work Merton ever wrote, and thus one of the most paradoxical ones. Therein lies its special interest for us.

What precisely is this special significance, and where is the paradox? They are to be found primarily in the first half of the volume, sections I–III, where he treats of man and his last end, the states of life and the vows in general. Merton's presentation here of such classic themes of Christian morality as the nature of man and his acts, the importance of justice in relation to the Passion of Christ, to friendship and to love, or self-surrender as the key to grace, prayer and the vowed life—all these pages clearly spring from a committed heart and often flow with the soaring intensity of style that we have come to expect in his more enthusiastic prose.

It seems to me that it is the combination of these three elements—the subjects themselves, the pastoral intensity with which they are treated, and the fact that their author is often thought of in relation to more non-classic themes of interest—that give these first 230-odd pages a certain paradoxical character and at the same time make them a significant contribution to the Merton corpus. Moreover, their interest has been considerably heightened by the work of Professor Patrick O'Connell in identifying and including in the present volume not only the sources of Merton's thought, but also the English translations of many of the original texts he is referring to. Both sources and texts were generally lacking from Merton's typewritten manuscript, which had no footnotes. Generally, Merton simply indicated the authors he had consulted, such as St. John of the Cross, Père Joseph de Guibert, sj, the Benedictines Abbot Anscar Vonier, Olivier Rousseau, Philibert Schmitz, Cuthbert Butler and John Chapman, classic moral theologians like Génicot, Schaefer and Goyneche, and the traditional commentaries on the *Rule* of St. Benedict. What will probably surprise us is his abundant, in-depth use of the *Summa Theologiae* of St. Thomas Aquinas. This is clearly more than just lip service. Merton shows that he has studied the *Summa* and assimilated its inner meaning. We are probably indebted for this to his ongoing familiarity with the works of four outstanding contemporary philosopher-theologians, all of them Catholic laymen: Étienne Gilson, Jacques Maritain, Dietrich von Hildebrand and Josef Pieper. However, Merton's vigorous exposé of traditional themes of moral theology, with the applications he makes to the contemporary situation inside and outside the monastery, gives every indication of being the fruit of personal reflection and sincere conviction.

This first half of the book is probably most akin to the author's *The New Man*,[1] which he was in the process of writing precisely during this period of his life. Yet the present pages have the two advantages of being less than book-length and of not having had to pass through any commercial editing process. It is their spontaneous fervor that gives them added strength, charm and "bite."

The long fourth section, on the contrary, with its treatment of the five particular vows made by Benedictine and Cistercian monks, can interest us for other reasons, not only because of its subject matter, but also for the presence of some outdated, preconciliar features. The latter element is less obvious in the first half of the book, but even there it shows itself in several places where Merton refers to the evangelical counsels—the term traditionally applied to evangelical poverty, chastity and obedience—as adding something to religious life that is lacking in other forms of Christian living. Although such an approach comes from some of the Church Fathers and St. Thomas in his *Summa*,[2] it has had to be rethought after the Second Vatican Council's proclamation that Christian perfection is for "all the faithful of Christ, of whatever rank or status."[3] Since then, the *Catechism of the Catholic Church* applies this teaching to the evangelical counsels and states that the latter were proposed by Christ "in their great variety, to every disciple."[4] During the last twenty years, a deeper reexamination of both religious life and lay spirituality is showing that the counsels, like the Beatitudes they incarnate, belong to the New Law of Christ and so are normative for everyone, here

1. Thomas Merton, *The New Man* (New York: Farrar, Straus and Cudahy, 1961).

2. See *Summa Theologiae, Prima Secundae*, q. 108, art 4, in *Sancti Thomae Aquinatis Doctoris Angelici Ordinis Praedicatorum Opera Omnia, Secundum Impressionem Petri Fiaccadori Parmae 1852–1873 Photolithographice Reimpressa*, 25 vols. (New York: Misurgia, 1948), 2.427–28.

3. Dogmatic Constitution on the Church (*Lumen Gentium*), n. 40, in *The Documents of Vatican II*, ed. Walter M. Abbott, sj (New York: America Press, 1966), 67.

4. *Catechism of the Catholic Church*, n. 915 (Mahwah, NJ: Paulist Press, 1994), 241.

and hereafter—to each person according to the specific state of life he or she is called to.

In the second half of the book, however, there is more to modify. There, Merton's casuistic treatment of the concrete obligations of vowed life strikes our postconciliar ears as one-sided or tendentious, since we are now accustomed to a more biblical approach, one more attuned to the primacy of charity. Merton would surely have preferred such an emphasis, but he felt obliged to give his young monks clear answers to their often unspoken questions, and so gave them detailed determinations of degrees of right and wrong according to the vow in question. Such a method was not uncommon in the pastoral formation of priests and confessors at that time and, of course, was the one his abbot would have expected him to use.

At the same time, there is a deeper motive involved. Implicit in his treatment of these moral obligations and of other aspects of the vows is an ongoing critique of a text to which Merton refers on more than one occasion, the Order's *Spiritual Directory*. This was an official five-hundred-page guide to Trappist life written in detail for all Cistercian monks and nuns in the style characteristic of nineteenth-century Trappist culture. It had been somewhat revised in the first years of the twentieth century at the request of the General Chapter by the well-known abbot of Bricquebec in Normandy, Dom Vital Lehodey. The book's stated purpose was "to include all necessary instructions and present a summary of all the obligations of our holy calling . . . . It is, in fact, a body of rules for directing the good will in its journey towards perfection,"[5] with special attention given to the vows.

The *Spiritual Directory* expressed and fostered a militant moralism, even though somewhat purified of its Jansenistic overtones by Dom Lehodey. Its overwhelming emphasis on moral

---

5. [Vital Lehodey, ocso,] *A Spiritual Directory for Religious*, translated from the original French text, *"Directoire Spirituel à l'Usage des Cisterciens de la Stricte Observance"* by a priest of New Melleray Abbey, Peosta, Iowa (Trappist, KY: Abbey of Our Lady of Gethsemani, 1946), ix.

perfection was weak in an adequate biblical spirituality, where divine mercy plays an important part. It was even more lacking in any integration of contemporary psychology. Merton, of course, was acutely aware of these weaknesses, which explains the pains he took to describe the individual vows in biblical terms and to show their relevance to the human condition today. It also helps us understand his care to distinguish lesser venial sins and imperfections from the extreme gravity of mortal sin and to reinterpret religious duty as an entrance "into the infinite and unending circuit of love that is the very life of the Three Divine Persons" (69).

This major leap forward, beyond and above the *Spiritual Directory*, was probably the chief reason why Merton's mimeographed notes, now published here, were immediately welcomed with gratitude in our English-speaking monasteries, even more so than the other series of mimeographed notes that Gethsemani generously circulated at that time.

Having mentioned this caveat in his presentation of the particular vows, it is equally important to see that in several specific areas Merton explores new ground and brings in considerable new light. Thus the vow of conversion of manners—now usually referred to as "conversion of life" and which he often simply calls "conversion"—is presented not only as a vow to grow in perfection but also as referring to the specifically monastic means to help that growth, that is, as a vow to live as a monk.

In a similar way, poverty is presented not only as personal renunciation or austerity but also more positively as a commitment to accept the purification of our innate possessive instinct and to follow the poor Christ through work and mutual charity, personally and as a community. Obedience, too, is given a beautiful definition as "THE ACT OF A CHILD OF GOD UNITING HIMSELF TO CHRIST IN THE FREE AND LOVING SACRIFICE OF HIS OWN WILL TO GIVE GLORY TO THE FATHER" (248–49). And his pages on the special problems, the asceticism of and the growth in chastity and virginity can be useful for us all.

So as we read his insights on religious and monastic profession, he would doubtless continue to tell us, probably with more verve than ever, "Remember always {that} profession means *first* taking up the Cross to follow Christ, *second* becoming a member of a family which is a supernatural society bound together by ties of love, and then *third*—consecration to God by vow. In other words, charity comes first, even in religious profession—charity towards Christ—leaving all to follow Him; charity towards our brothers; and then *third*—the supreme act of *religion* . . . . Love for God *seeks to determine itself* by definite obligations" (158–59).

Augustine Roberts, ocso
Azul, Argentina

INTRODUCTION

Certainly among the most essential responsibilities of a novice master in a Cistercian monastery is the task of preparing those under his care for profession of the Benedictine vows of obedience, stability and conversion of manners at the conclusion of the two-year period of the novitiate. Thus it is not surprising that Thomas Merton presented weekly, sometimes twice-weekly, conferences on the vows almost continuously from early in his mastership, which began in October 1955, until the very week in which he resigned the position to take up full-time residence in his hermitage on August 20, 1965. Of course it was not exclusively through these group presentations that Merton familiarized his charges with the meaning and purpose of the vows; the individual spiritual direction given regularly to each novice provided an opportunity both to make sure the aspiring monk understood clearly the meaning and purpose of the vows and to engage in a process of discernment that would reveal whether his vocation to monastic life was genuine. But a thorough exposition of the theological, canonical and above all spiritual dimensions of the vows could only be adequately provided through an extensive series of detailed classroom presentations—though Merton's lectures actually turned out to be so extensive that the entire cycle was never completed within any given two-year period, so that more informal personal instruction must have supplemented the group conferences at least for certain crucial points.

The text of these conferences, initially reproduced and distributed in mimeographed form and published in this volume for the first time, is the longest (almost 145,000 words) and most systematically organized of any of numerous series of conferences that Merton presented during the decade of his mastership.[1] It is also arguably the most traditional in content and outlook. No text of Merton, even *The Ascent to Truth*,[2] shows such familiarity with and reliance on the work of Thomas Aquinas—virtually every major section of the work is developed from the Thomistic framework of the *Summa*, and scholastic terminology abounds throughout. There are also copious references to canon law and its commentators. Sin, and the criteria for distinguishing between mortal and venial sins of various categories, are given prominent attention in various places. The intrinsic superiority of religious life to that of the laity is affirmed; the distinction between natural and supernatural planes is assumed; terminology of victimhood, reparation and sacrificial oblation is frequently associated with the monastic state. Part of the reason for this largely traditional perspective is of course that Merton was writing before the Second Vatican Council's call for the renewal of religious life led to a rethinking of many of the commonly held assumptions about the contrasts between Church and world, religious and laity. As former Cistercian Abbot General Bernardo Olivera comments, "These notes, mimeographed and circulated by the Abbey, were obviously pre-conciliar in their tone and content."[3] Yet most of the

1. See the previously published volumes in this series: Thomas Merton, *Cassian and the Fathers: Initiation into the Monastic Tradition*, ed. Patrick F. O'Connell, Monastic Wisdom [MW], vol. 1 (Kalamazoo, MI: Cistercian Publications, 2005); Thomas Merton, *Pre-Benedictine Monasticism: Initiation into the Monastic Tradition* 2, ed. Patrick F. O'Connell, MW 9 (Kalamazoo, MI: Cistercian Publications, 2006); Thomas Merton, *An Introduction to Christian Mysticism: Initiation into the Monastic Tradition* 3, ed. Patrick F. O'Connell, MW 13 (Kalamazoo, MI: Cistercian Publications, 2008); Thomas Merton, *The Rule of Saint Benedict: Initiation into the Monastic Tradition* 4, ed. Patrick F. O'Connell, MW 19 (Collegeville, MN: Cistercian Publications, 2009); Thomas Merton, *Monastic Observances: Initiation into the Monastic Tradition* 5, ed. Patrick F. O'Connell, MW 25 (Collegeville, MN: Cistercian Publications, 2010).

2. Thomas Merton, *The Ascent to Truth* (New York: Harcourt, Brace, 1951).

3. Bernardo Olivera, ocso, Foreword to Augustine Roberts, ocso, *Centered on Christ: A Guide to Monastic Profession*, 3rd ed., MW 5 (Kalamazoo, MI: Cistercian Publications, 2005), xiii.

text, completed in September 1960, was actually composed subsequent to Merton's famous "epiphany" in Louisville in March 1958, when he was forcefully made aware that the "dream of separateness, of spurious self-isolation in a special world, the world of renunciation and supposed holiness" was "a complete illusion: the illusion that by making vows we become a different species of being, pseudoangels, 'spiritual men,' men of interior life, what have you."[4] While his own perception and experience of monastic life was undergoing an evolution, perhaps even a revolution, Merton evidently still felt a responsibility to convey to his novices an understanding and appreciation of the vows that represented not just his own personal views but "the mind of the Order" generally at that point in time. He would also have been quite conscious that the audience for the written text included not just his own novices but formation directors of other American Cistercian houses, to whom the mimeographed notes would be distributed, so that he would have wanted to provide for them a "mainstream" perspective that he would have considered most useful to them for their own work.

But while the more "conservative" elements of the text may be what are most readily noticed by a contemporary reader, especially one familiar with Merton's progressive and often quite critical writings on monastic renewal, a careful reading of these notes will find at least as much continuity as disjunction between those later essays and the present text. The overall orientation of Merton's presentation continually emphasizes the priority of

---

4. This is the revised version of the text as found in Thomas Merton, *Conjectures of a Guilty Bystander* (Garden City, NY: Doubleday, 1966), 140–41, actually rewritten in September 1965 (see Thomas Merton, *Dancing in the Water of Life: Seeking Peace in the Hermitage. Journals, vol. 5: 1963–1965*, ed. Robert E. Daggy [San Francisco: HarperCollins, 1997], 298), but the essential insight that "my vocation does not really make me different from the rest of men or put me in a special category except artificially, juridically" is already present in the original journal entry of March 19, 1958 (Thomas Merton, *A Search for Solitude: Pursuing the Monk's True Life. Journals, vol. 3: 1952–1960*, ed. Lawrence S. Cunningham [San Francisco: HarperCollins, 1996], 182).

lived experience, of personal commitment, over formal categories and juridical regulations. There is a need for those preparing to take vows to have a clear comprehension of moral and canonical obligations, to know exactly what commitment they are making in terms of ecclesiastical law, but Merton constantly stresses that it is more important for them to realize the commitment they are making to a life of Christian discipleship. Monastic profession, he insists, must never be just a matter of following the rules, but of following the person of Jesus, empowered and guided to do so by the Holy Spirit. This focus on spiritual transformation as the only authentic justification for monastic life is evident both in the overall structure of the conferences and in the treatment of the individual vows.

It is not by chance that the full title given to this set of conferences is "An Introduction to the Life of the Vows," rather than simply "An Introduction to the Vows." The vows are not discussed in isolation but set firmly in the context of a broad consideration of the anthropological, moral, soteriological and ecclesial dimensions of human, Christian and monastic life. Merton begins by contrasting a modern pragmatic cult of efficiency that measures success by the fulfillment of material needs and desires with the classic Christian vision of human life as having a transcendent goal of God and life in and with God as the "final end" of the human person. While to some extent the terminology tends toward the abstract and the perspective toward the otherworldly (e.g., "we must get rid of a view that seeks happiness, implicitly, in the present life" [9]), the fundamental orientation is consistent with Merton's contemplative personalism. He writes, "Our job in life is not so much to produce anything, as *to be what we are supposed to be,* to let the divine image come out and manifest itself in our lives by the *way in which we live*" (9). Union with God, ultimately and completely in the beatific vision and proximately in contemplative awareness of the divine presence in this life, is the only authentic self-realization, the only way to become "most completely perfected as a person in the image and likeness of God" (16). Without this recognition, religious vows can easily be misunderstood as a commitment "to a task, to a job" (8) rather than to a Person. On the contrary, the whole purpose of the vows, Merton insists, is "to enable us to *be* someone, not to do something" (9).

Having begun with the end, beatitude, Merton can then investigate in detail the means to that end, outlining and generally following the pattern laid out by St. Thomas in his teaching on the structure of the moral life, though with sufficient flexibility to incorporate material from other sections of the *Summa*, as well as insights from other sources and from his own reflections. He successively considers Thomistic teaching on the passions, the habits (both virtues and vices), the role of law and the working of grace, supplemented by extensive discussion of the significance of justice and the centrality of Christ's Passion for the moral and spiritual life. He continually points out the pertinence of each of these elements to an authentic, mature commitment to monastic vows.

He emphatically rejects all dualistic views that passions are to be regarded as evil and to be suppressed by the will. As "acts of the soul in so far as it informs a body, acts of the sensible appetite" (18), the passions are to be purified and integrated into a life governed by reason, operating according to free will. "It is clear then, that the passions are not to be destroyed but sublimated, and even in the highest and most sublime spiritual state they reclaim their rights" (27), for they are an intrinsic element of incarnate human existence. The purpose of the vows, Merton maintains, is therefore not to eliminate but "to spiritualize the passions in the most effective possible way" (23), especially by the elevation of love, "the most important of all the passions" (22 23), into the virtue of charity, the free choice of the good for its own sake.

As a virtue, charity is, in Thomistic terms, a *habitus*, not an ingrained custom or unconsidered routine as in the modern sense of the word "habit," but a developed orientation of the will and a principle of consistent action—a virtue if directed toward the good, a vice if toward evil. Merton traces Aquinas's various xviii

subdivisions of habits—entitative and operative, acquired and infused—as well as of the virtues—intellectual (speculative and practical), moral, theological—all of which serve as "a source of activity which perfects our *actions*, perfects our *being*, elevates and fulfills our freedom, establishes us in the good, directs us more surely to our last end" (36). He warns against basing religious life on a reductive understanding of *habitus* as habit, discarding "one set of poses, routines, slogans and gestures in order to acquire another set of the same, only this time apparently spiritual" (36).

He also points out that according to St. Thomas, vices operate as *habitus* in an analogous manner and thus "increase the freedom, abandon, spontaneity, permanence with which the soul gives itself over to sin" (38) by making self-love and self-gratification the principle of choice and action. The vows are designed to root out the vices. Too often, Merton observes, attention is focused too narrowly on "how one sins against the vows" (40) rather than on the power of the vows to break the hold of habitual sin by nurturing a life ordered by love. At the same time, gradual detachment from vices is not to be equated, Merton tells his audience, with a disdainful rejection of a sinful world. He cautions, "When we take vows, in this world of ours, it is not in order to wash our hands of all its evils and dissociate ourselves from all responsibility, but rather it is to assume *conscious responsibility* for the evil that is in the world, in the same way that Jesus did. We who have vows do not stand aside in horror and consider ourselves as the sinless members of a sinful race" (41). While this responsibility is still conceived more in terms of penance and reparation than as participation in transforming unjust social structures, as Merton will emphasize in the coming years, the characteristic note of "solidarity with the rest of the human race" (42) is clearly in evidence here.

Merton then follows Aquinas from consideration of the interior principles of human action, virtues and vices, to the exterior principles of law, "norms set down by God to give objective rule for conduct and choice" (17), and grace, exterior in that it does not belong to human nature by right but nevertheless operates within to transform and elevate nature so as to participate in God's own life. Law can be defined as "a divinely sanctioned rule of good conduct which governs our relations with others, with God Himself, and the management of our own life" (44), but ultimately it is simply the expression of the divine will for humanity and for all creation, and therefore it is indistinguishable from love. Only when law is taken "out of context, out of the whole great plan of God, unrelated to the infinite love of God" (45), is it experienced as restrictive and oppressive legalism, as an alien imposition that curtails freedom.

In considering natural law, which directs human nature toward the good and prepares that nature for the reception of grace "for which in fact we were created and without which we cannot be what we are intended to be by God" (45), Merton quite unexpectedly turns to maxims of Confucius on "'human-heartedness' . . . the ability to understand others by realizing that they suffer what we suffer and desire what we desire—to reach out by empathy and put ourselves in their place and act accordingly" (46). This appreciation for Confucian teaching as "a revelation of the depth and wonder of the natural law"[5] (47) is probably Merton's earliest developed citation and commentary on the resources provided by Asian wisdom for moral and spiritual insight.

Divine law clarifies and reinforces natural law and transcends it through the gift of the Holy Spirit that brings about a total conformation to the teaching and example of Christ, who lived only to do the will of His Father. Merton reminds his audience that it is this law, "the law of grace—the law of the Holy Spirit crying out in our hearts, *Abba, Father*," rather than "certain

---

5. See the similar comment in "Classic Chinese Thought," Merton's earliest published essay on Eastern thought: "Confucianism is nothing more or less than natural ethics in a very refined and traditional form: the natural law expressed in a sacred culture" (Thomas Merton, *Mystics and Zen Masters* [New York: Farrar, Straus and Giroux, 1967], 47; originally published in *Jubilee* in January 1961).

exterior prescriptions" (50), that the vows are intended to fulfill.
The obligation of the vows is a strict one, "but it is only an obligation to *love more*, and to follow Christ more closely, that is, to
unite ourselves to Him in Whom the Law is fulfilled" (51). Observance of the law is not a substitute for personal commitment
but an expression of that commitment.

It is only in this context of an accurate perception of law
that the virtue of justice is properly understood, which explains
why Merton (unlike St. Thomas) turns at this point to a detailed
consideration of its nature and purpose: "Formalism, legalism,
etc. are *not* aspects of justice; they are perversions of justice, and
in fact they are rooted in injustice and in the destruction of the
true order of things" (52). Drawing not directly on Aquinas but
on the Thomistic philosopher Josef Pieper, Merton points out that
justice is the highest of the moral virtues because it participates in
God's ordering of creation, "using the light of reason and of faith
to judge as God judges, to act and think as a son of God, to assume
responsibility towards God and towards other men for his own
share in the life of the cosmos" (57). It is the active recognition,
defense and pursuit of the rights due to every human being as
made in the image of God. In this context Merton's developing
social conscience issues a forthright challenge to a comfortable
ecclesial and monastic establishment. He declares that "men who
see nothing but injustice and oppression in those who claim to
be servants of God" are very unlikely to be drawn to the Gospel.
"Charity that does not rest on a firm basis of justice is not true
charity," he continues. "Without a social order that really embodies and preserves true human values willed for man by God, the
Church cannot attain anything but a partial and limited success
in her mission of bringing souls to Christ" (53). This applies even
to monastic orders that are contemplative rather than apostolic,
whose members may renounce personal ownership yet "give
themselves to a life of bourgeois comfort" and thus be "guilty
of injustice, as well as scandal" (53) in a world where millions
are subject to poverty and deprivation. In such circumstances
religious life can easily become "a withdrawal, a burying of our

talents, a sterilization of vital gifts given to us for the good of all" (58). Here can be heard a preliminary articulation both of Merton's prophetic and compassionate identification with the marginalized and of his call for a renewed monasticism that will serve as sacramental witness to Christ's identification with "the least of these."

It is only at the conclusion of this discussion of justice that Merton quotes and explicates St. Thomas's expanded version of the classic definition of justice as giving to each what is due, and in doing so suggests its paradoxical elements. From this perspective, justice is not limited to giving others what they may deserve as a consequence of their own actions, but includes showing them the same unlimited love and mercy that Christ has shown to us: "for a Christian, justice must be sublimated in charity, and for a follower of Christ it is an *injustice* not to try to measure up to the charity of Christ" (63), because to fail to do so "is to refuse to God what is His due" (64), to refuse to love others as God loves them and so repay, however inadequately, the debt owed to God for our salvation.

Rather than following Aquinas directly from a consideration of law to a discussion of grace, Merton uses this exploration of the meaning of justice to move into a reflection on Christ's Passion, an apparent digression that is actually central to this preliminary section of his text. His point of transition is the impossibility of fulfilling the requirement of justice to give to God what is due to God, an impossibility even for humanity in an unfallen state, and incomparably more so after humanity had turned away from God by sin. Only through oneness with Christ, who alone as fully divine and fully human can offer to His Father the perfect honor that is His due, and who alone can rectify the injustice of human sinfulness by His total self-gift to the Father and for His brothers and sisters in complete love and obedience, can the "unimaginable, inconceivable debt of man to God, altogether beyond satisfaction . . . *in fact be paid*" (68–69). In a profound and mysterious way, Christ's gift of Himself on the Cross is an expression in time of the Son's eternal gift of Himself to the Father in response to the Father's eternal gift of Himself to the Son, in the Holy Spirit, the never-ending circumincession of divine love, so that to be united with Christ in the paschal mystery, to die to self and rise with and in and as Christ, is to be drawn into the very love-life of God.

> What God then asks of us is that we give ourselves to Him in Christ, unite our oblation of our lives with the oblation of Christ in His Passion, and then what happens? We receive all back in Him, for in God we receive all. In "paying" our debt we have incurred a further infinite debt, and we repay in kind by giving God back to God, and ourselves with Him, in order to receive God back from God and ourselves in Him.
>
> In other words, true religion is this: to enter into the infinite and unending circuit of love that is the very life of the Three Divine Persons, in which each gives all to the other and receives all again in His gift. (69)

The only condition for sharing this gift is to show to one another the same love that Christ showed toward us in becoming one with us by living and dying with and for us: "This then is supreme justice; this is perfect religion, all in the transcendent charity of the Son Who gave Himself for us on the Cross, in the fire of the Holy Spirit, that God might be perfectly glorified in Him and in us His members" (69). While Merton goes on to examine in detail the teaching of Aquinas on the sufferings of Christ, the necessity, cause and effects of the Passion (which appear much later in the *Summa*), the incandescent heart of his own understanding of the meaning of Christ's sacrifice is here.

When Merton returns to finish his summary of the Thomistic teaching on the moral life by considering the final topic of grace, it is in the context of his own focus on friendship with God. In fact there are no citations from Aquinas on grace in this section at all. After excerpting texts from Jeremiah 31 on the New Covenant and the messianic kingdom, and from the Gospel of John on intimacy with God through Christ, Merton comments:

All that we have said so far in these talks on the life of the vows pales into insignificance in the light of such texts . . . . We have spoken of man, of his passions, of his will, of his habits. We have seen the helps God has given him in the natural order. We have seen something of the meaning of law and justice. But all this is nothing in comparison with the true meaning of our Christian vocation, and the true substance of the perfection to which we are called. This is a LIFE OF INTIMATE FRIENDSHIP WITH GOD, A LIFE TRANS-FORMED IN CHRIST, A LIFE IN WHICH WE BECOME ONE WITH CHRIST AND ARE THUS DIVINIZED AND LIVE AS TRUE SONS OF THE ETERNAL FATHER. (84)

It is by baptismal vows that every Christian is called into this friendship. Religious vows are simply a way "to *intensify the love and the intimacy*" (85) of this relationship that is open to all. In this context, the virtue of charity is now seen as a participation in a mutual relationship, "a love which is *shared* between us and God" (85), in which of course the initiative belongs not to us but to God. It is through sanctifying grace, "the created effect of God's uncreated Love present in our souls" (94), that God draws one into this friendship, a friendship that "means in practice the sharing of His love with our brethren" (98) and that is expressed and nourished above all by prayer, both private and communal, "the greatest and most noble work that a man can perform. . . . the work most characteristic of divine friendship" (105).

Having completed this overview of moral and spiritual principles and practices that apply to all persons in some form, Merton is now ready to focus on the distinctive vocation of the religious life, "the state of perfection." Much of what is found here is the standard, conventional approach of the period, again relying on a Thomistic framework. The distinction between states, orders and offices is explained; the development from beginners to progressives to the perfect is outlined; the practice of the evangelical counsels is described; various works and observances associated with religious life are considered; the characteristics of the active and contemplative lives are delineated;

signs of genuine religious vocations and the means of discerning them are presented. The objective superiority of the religious state to the lay, and of the contemplative life to the active, is accepted on the authority of Aquinas and on the basis of tradition, though it is pointed out, again according to Aquinas, that this is no guarantee that any particular religious is living a more perfect life than a layperson. The "opposition between religion and the world" is recognized, and the advantages of separation from its "distracting influences and its temptations" are noted (106). At the same time, an overly individualized or interiorized conception of the religious life is rejected; a religious vocation is intrinsically and profoundly ecclesial, "dedicated to the life of the Church" (108). Such a life requires existential engagement, not merely juridical or sacramental consecration. Merton continually warns his audience that monastic vows must never be reduced to "a renunciation of responsibility and of risk," settling for a routine of "security and comfort and a pleasant life (which is entirely possible)" (114).

In drawing this section of the text to its conclusion, Merton teaches that the genuine abnegation that is intrinsic to religious life, and especially to monastic life, is simply a way of obeying the Gospel command to leave all, take up one's cross and follow Christ (Mt. 16:24-26). In classic Mertonian terminology, such self-surrender is seen as the only way to authentic self-fulfillment because what is negated is "our false, limited 'self'" that subsists in "the illusion that *we are the whole*. . . . the center" around which all else revolves. True perfection "incorporates and integrates" a person into the Body of Christ, actualizing the divine image that is one's deepest identity, through the power of the Holy Spirit. "Abnegation means the renunciation of all that prevents this perfect integration in the whole Christ," Merton concludes, adding: "This is the true Benedictine outlook" (149). With this declaration he is ready to turn to the vows themselves.

Merton begins this transitional section by clearly indicating that while vows are an essential element of religious profession, they are not the only or even the most important dimension of that profession. First in significance is the commitment to ongoing conversion, to "putting on" Christ, to following Christ, to sharing in the mystery of Christ. Then comes incorporation into the religious community, to be understood not just in a juridical context, as a contractual arrangement, but as participation in a supernatural family that is a manifestation of Trinitarian mutual love. "In this society of love," Merton writes, "what matters is not the assertion of rights and the enforcement of obligations, but *mutual trust and love*" (157), which should then radiate out from the community to embrace the entire Church. Without this family spirit, religious life is reduced to "organized hypocrisy" (158). Consecration to God by vow is thus "but the *third* in importance of the three essential elements of religious profession" (158).

Merton then goes on to consider the nature of religious profession in general and of making vows in particular from both canonical and theological perspectives. The validity of profession depends on the fulfillment of various external factors (age, valid novitiate, explicit public declaration, etc.) but most fundamentally on free and full consent. The theological foundation of profession, traced through the successive diverse acts that constitute consent according to Thomistic analysis, is the will to obligate oneself, the free decision of the entire person, involving intelligence, senses and emotions, and the will. Thus to make a vow is not to renounce one's freedom but to exercise it in an act of worship, the definitive offering of oneself to God. "*Only to such a One can we give our liberty without debasing it. Only to such a One can we give our liberty and become yet more free by doing so*" (185).

Only after considering the religious and spiritual significance of vows does Merton turn to the matter of the specific obligations that are entailed in making religious vows. It is of course essential for one contemplating monastic profession to be aware of exactly what he is binding himself to observe as a professed religious, and Merton provides a detailed explanation of the various obligations shared by clerics and religious (e.g., recitation of the divine office), those pertaining specifically to the religious state, and those unique to monasticism and to Cistercian life, with particular attention to fidelity to the common life, to enclosure and silence, to observance of the Benedictine *Rule* as interpreted by the Cistercian *Constitutions*. The lengthy discussion of the common life moves from its canonical foundation as a consequence of the vow of poverty to its concrete realization in Cistercian life in common prayer, the common dormitory, the common table and common work. This gives Merton the opportunity to consider the texture of community life in all its various manifestations, to point out ways in which the letter of the law may be observed but its spirit violated, to correct distorted ideas of what the common life entails. The great principle he repeatedly appeals to is a sane balance that avoids both inflexibility and laxity, that eschews both a *"Herd Mentality"* (214) and a tendency to isolation, that does not reduce the community of unique individuals with complementary gifts to a regimented institution in which "persons are no longer treated as valuable in themselves" (214) but are valued according to their usefulness and productivity, as "cogs in a machine" (216)—though at the same time he is insistent on the importance of work both as a spiritual discipline and as an essential way of contributing to the life of the community. Ultimately, the common life is not merely a juridical requirement but a spiritual commitment: "Mere observance of obligations and rules, without the attainment of the inner purpose for which they are instituted, is like a body without a soul. *The purpose of the common life* is greater charity, of the individual and of all the members of the community as a whole: it is the glory of God attained by common effort" (210). While the discussion of enclosure is largely taken up with canonical regulations and with local application (e.g., rules on visits), the section on the obligation to keep the rule once again invokes the principle of moderation, recognizing that "the strict obligations and sanctions which exercised such a powerful effect in sanctifying souls in the old days tend to disconcert and confuse souls today" (including St. Thérèse!) (226), but that to go to the opposite extreme and adopt a "lax view" that where rules "do not bind under sin, there is in *no sense any obligation to keep the rule*" (231) is to minimize the importance of the rule in forming a vibrant community. As he will continue to do throughout the rest of the text, Merton proposes a middle way between scrupulosity and superficiality. He concludes: "The important thing then is to keep the rules out of love, not in a spirit of 'conformity,' not trying to show off one's regularity and please others by this external display, but because of their important place in the life which one has embraced out of love for God, and because they are a means of showing our love to God, uniting ourselves to His will, and thus giving Him pleasure" (234).

The pivotal transition point from the general to the particular comes in the short section in which the actual formula of profession is quoted (in Latin) and explained. Here the unique triad of the Benedictine vows is identified, the implicit inclusion of vows of poverty and chastity in the explicit vow of conversion of manners is pointed out, and the concrete nature of the vows is noted, as stability is pledged specifically to a particular community, and the superior before whom the vows are made is mentioned by name. Merton calls attention to the fact that profession is a matter not only of a recitation of the verbal formula but also of a symbolic action: "It is when we read and sign our formula of profession (and lay it on the altar) that we actually make the vows" (236). He also distinguishes between the vows, made to God, and the promise of obedience, made directly to the superior and his successors ("*PATER, PROMITTO TIBI* . . ." [236]). The rationale for exhaustive investigation of every aspect of each of the vows is provided: "we must study them carefully and know precisely what they mean, because they are our most professional concern. Just as a doctor has to know medicine, and a lawyer has to know law, so a religious has to know the meaning of his vows"—though he adds the phrase "and live according to them fully" (234), a reminder that in this context the term "profession" has a much deeper significance than in the case of a career.

In discussing the individual vows, Merton reverses the order found in the formula of profession itself (which corresponds to that found in chapter 58 of the Benedictine *Rule*), treating obedi-

ence first, then *conversio morum* and its corollaries chastity and
poverty, and finally stability. The reason for this alteration is
given at the very outset of the discussion on obedience, which
is called "the first of the Benedictine vows, and for all religious
it is the *most important of the vows*" (237). While not first in the
actual order of profession, it certainly has a primacy in terms of
its centrality to the *Rule*, where it receives extensive discussion,
particularly in the Prologue and in chapter 5, as well as in the
fourth degree of humility in chapter 7.

In this as in subsequent sections, Merton takes pains to incorporate all pertinent information on each particular vow, drawing on theological sources, especially St. Thomas, on canonical
norms, and on the *Rule* and Cistercian regulations and customs;
but in each case his clear intent is to emphasize the centrality of
the spiritual dimension of the vow, its significance in the actual
lived experience of the monk. Thus for obedience, he stresses
above all its intrinsic connection to authentic freedom and its
role in effecting a conformation to Christ, obedient to the Father's
will even to the point of death. He writes: "obedience *is not* simply a blind abdication of our freedom by submission to another
man. . . . By obedience we do not renounce our freedom;
we dedicate it to God; we promise to use it in the service
of God alone and for His honor and glory" (241–42). He
distinguishes religious obedience from the alienated obedience
of a slave, who does the will of another out of coercion, from the
immature obedience of a child, who is not yet ready to make
responsible decisions, and from the functional obedience of a
citizen or employee, who is simply fulfilling an explicit or implicit
contract. *"Our obedience is a union of our will with the will of Christ
dying on the Cross for love.* By obeying we unite ourselves with
the great act of freedom and truth, the supreme manifestation of
love in the world" (249). In so doing, the religious experiences
liberation from excessive concern for insignificant things, from
self-will, from the effects of sin and the influence of the devil,
and finally from the power of death itself. Of these of course the
most immediate is the freedom from self-will through the freely

given submission to the will of another. Merton points out that the source of the superior's authority lies not in his intrinsic wisdom or holiness, nor in his office itself, but in "the fact that I have freely vowed to obey him and to submit to his commands" (258); the same applies to the *Rule*. After outlining the limits of the superior's authority (the power to command according to the rule, the lack of power over interior acts of the will) and the various sins both against the vow of obedience and more broadly against the virtue of obedience, Merton concludes his discussion by focusing on the lifelong process of growth toward perfect obedience, a task that requires faith and humility and that will inevitably involve struggle. Once again he reminds the novices that ultimately the only effective motivation to remain faithful to this arduous commitment is *"out of love for Christ* and in close union with the dispositions with which He obeyed" (273).

Turning to the second vow, conversion of manners, Merton calls it "perhaps the most difficult to understand according to the modern way of looking at it" because it appears "rather vague," with little indication of what specific obligations it might entail (274). The only readily available Cistercian discussion of the vow, in the Trappist *Spiritual Directory*, is seen to be inadequate and misleading in part, not sufficiently rooted in monastic tradition and unfamiliar with the "original and authentic" reading found in the *Rule*—"*conversatio*" rather than "*conversio*" (278). Merton points out that "[f]or St. Benedict the vow of conversion of manners is the vow to *persevere in the monastic state* and *to live and die as a monk*, having left the world, faithful to all the practices that distinguish a monk from the worldling, and especially poverty, chastity, enclosure, austerity, etc." (278), an interpretation supported by the earliest commentators on the *Rule*. "The essence of the vow of conversion of manners {lies in} putting off the world—renouncing one's old ways; putting on Christ—acquiring new ways" (283). Renunciation of the world, of *"everything which creates in the mind a worldly attitude* and keeps *alive a worldly sense of values"* (284), suggests the traditional disjunction between the sacred and the secular, and a good deal of the language Merton uses in this section lends itself to this interpretation; but he eventually points out that this

> renunciation of everything that belongs to this world . . . . must not be taken in the sense that the world is considered "evil"—far from it. But God's creation is unable to help or to sanctify anyone unless the Spirit of God has taken possession of him. Then created things are restored to their original function as means to unite us to God and to awaken love in our hearts at all times. Otherwise, creatures become a snare. The difference lies not in the creatures themselves but in our hearts. If we are full of self-love, then creatures contribute to our ruin. But if we are purified by grace, then creatures help us to love God.[6] (301)

What is at the heart of the vow of conversion of manners, and what is really essential in putting off the world, "is the *renunciation of self* and its correlative, *the love of Christ*" (302), as is clear from chapter 4 of the Benedictine *Rule*. To "put on Christ" (symbolized of course by taking the monastic habit) "means the sincere and generous use of those means which the monastic life provides for our reformation and transformation in Christ" (286), above all penance and prayer, but also the practices of enclosure, silence, fasting, manual labor and living the common life. The spirit of the vow involves seeking God by "prefer[ring] absolutely nothing to Christ," as Benedict proposes in chapter 72 of the *Rule* (296); by a love of renunciation; by a love of good works, specifically those listed by Benedict in chapter 4 of the *Rule*, the celebrated "instruments of good works";[7] and above

6. The language here is quite close to that found in the opening chapter of Thomas Merton, *Seeds of Contemplation* (New York: New Directions, 1949), 22–23, and in slightly revised form in Thomas Merton, *New Seeds of Contemplation* (New York: New Directions, 1961), 25–26.

7. Merton's extensive discussion of chapter 4 of the *Rule* serves to complement the material found in his *Rule of St. Benedict* conferences, where the "instruments of good works" receive little attention, presumably because they have been treated in detail here.

all by the *"ardent desire for transformation in Christ,"* the "desire to die completely to our old life and to our old self, and become new men in Christ, to be made perfectly Christ-like, to have the thoughts, desires, aspirations of Christ, and in a word to 'become Christ'" by sharing in the paschal mystery, as articulated by St. Paul in Galatians 2:19-21 (306–307). Ultimately, "the spirit of our vow of conversion of manners," Merton declares, "is *to aspire to a mystical transformation in Christ, . . .* to generously give ourselves to God's love for us in order that He may fulfill in us what He intends for all men" (309–10). While he has called obedience the most important of the vows, in his explanation of conversion of manners Merton makes clear that when properly understood it is through this vow above all that monastic life becomes an authentic expression of Christian discipleship, a way of following Christ through the Cross to union with God and with God's people.

Merton begins his lengthy discussion of monastic chastity by situating it firmly in the context of the vow of conversion of manners, rejecting the theory that it is to be considered an aspect of obedience, a notion that arises from a narrow and negative conception of chastity simply as "an obligation to abstain from sex pleasure" (312). Recognized as an integral dimension of monastic *conversio,* "chastity means above all a renunciation of partial and limited forms of love to *embrace the perfection of love in a nuptial union with Christ.* This renunciation of earthly love *in order to surrender one's whole being, body and soul, to Christ,* leads in turn *to transformation in Christ"* (312). Renunciation of sexual activity is a necessary but not a sufficient condition for authentic monastic chastity, which must be understood and accepted as "not primarily a negative renunciation of earthly love, and still more crudely a mere renunciation of sex plea-sure—it is primarily and above all a liberation from the bonds of earthly love in order to be free to unite oneself to Christ in spiritual love" (312). Merton goes on to temper this idealistic vision of chastity with practical and realistic commentary on the difficulties involved in a life of continence, but he wants to

impress on his audience at the outset, as he will again at the
conclusion of this section, the profound spiritual significance
of this aspect of self-surrender.

Merton provides a quite comprehensive and detailed survey of scriptural, theological, moral and ascetic considerations
of chastity and virginity. After noting that virginity is the most
ancient element of religious consecration, antedating monasticism itself, he looks at the positive evaluation of sexuality in
the Old Testament and the eschatological character of virginity
in the New Testament, "a preparation and a prefiguring of the
blessed life in heaven . . . because it implies a greater and more
universal capacity for love" (320). He recapitulates in summary
form his earlier discussion of passions and virtues in order to
relate chastity to the virtue of temperance, drawing on Pieper
and on Aquinas to affirm that "chastity is a virtue which can
and must be practiced by *every Christian*, whether in the married
state or out of it" (336), and that within the context of marriage
a "virtuous use of sex naturally allows of passion and pleasure
. . . but the Christian virtue of chastity implies that this pleasure
is subordinate to something higher. . . . to sincere and deep and
mature *human love*" (335), particularized in the marital relationship and universalized in celibate chastity. The moral instruction on sexual purity and impurity is quite traditional, based as
it is on a manual dating from 1905, but its distinction between
sentimentality, sensibility, sensuality and sexuality is helpful in
countering an overly scrupulous approach to a life of chastity.
The obligatory discussion of particular friendships that follows
considers them mainly as manifestations of sentimentality and/
or sensuality, with scarcely a passing reference to actual sexual
activity. Merton goes on to point out that immature relationships
are only one of a number of ways of evading the demands of
authentic chastity: excessive busyness, immoderate concern with
others' spiritual condition, bitterness and chronic impatience,
cultivation of essentially frivolous outside interests, and sentimental and overly emotional devotional practices are all ways in
which erotic energies can be redirected in an unhealthy fashion.

Much of the latter part of this section is taken up with practical advice about aids in living out chastity, beginning with basic instruction about hygiene, cleanliness, sensible health and dietary routines, a proper balance between work and rest, and the need for "a suitable form of mental relaxation" (356). To these natural means must be added "balanced, sane, realistic and humble" (359) ascetic practices as a response to grace: the mortification of the senses, both exterior and interior (imagination and memory), and of the intellect and will. Prayer, meditation, eucharistic piety and devotion to the Blessed Mother are all effective means of supporting chastity, but Merton warns that they "are not to be regarded as magic." They do not work in an automatic fashion but "are means *which we ourselves must use*" to strengthen the will rather than to bypass it (369).

Merton concludes his discussion on chastity with two rather unexpected codas. He provides a ringing endorsement and summary of the major points of Dietrich von Hildebrand's book *In Defense of Purity*, with its "basic theme . . . of *respect for the mystery of sex*" (369), a respect that has disappeared in contemporary eroticized culture with the loss of the sense of mystery and the failure to recognize the symbolic quality of sex as the physical sign of a spiritual self-gift. While the book is not concerned primarily with religious life or with chastity as a vow, it is nonetheless, as Merton would write to a correspondent some years later, "a superbly spiritual treatment of chastity. There is a lot about marriage in it, but I feel the novices ought to appreciate the married state which they are renouncing. What good to renounce it if they do not know its dignity?"[8] As a complement to this broad treatment of purity, Merton closes with a rather lyrical commentary on the text of the rite for the consecration of virgins, largely a historical curiosity at the time, though the rite, if not the traditional text, has been restored in the wake of

8. July 4, 1962, letter to Elaine M. Bane, osf (Thomas Merton, *The School of Charity: Letters on Religious Renewal and Spiritual Direction*, ed. Patrick Hart [New York: Farrar, Straus and Giroux, 1990], 145).

the Second Vatican Council. The emphasis in the ceremony on the close relationship between virginity and contemplation, the "secret and ineffable way" (377) in which the virgin comes to know God, and on the commitment to "love all things in and for God and nothing outside of God" (378) are elements that Merton singles out as constitutive of a sincere and mature practice of religious chastity.

The penultimate section on poverty is in turn the most technical and the most prophetic of the entire volume. Merton immediately indicates that his procedure in discussing this vow will reverse the order found in the preceding sections: "in our treatment of the other vows we have discussed the theological background and history first, in order to come eventually to the actual obligation of the vow," whereas in this case "we will start right out with the actual obligation of the vow" (379). The rationale is not because the "exterior obligations" are more important for this vow, but rather "to dispose of" them first in order to go on "to point out that real religious poverty is actually something much more than the minimum obligation binding under pain of sin" (379). In actual fact, however, he does not proceed directly to the obligation of the vow, extending his prefatory remarks to point out the dangers in affluent America that monastic life will be undermined "because of *the corruption of the spirit and practice of poverty*" (380), that observance of the letter of poverty, renunciation of proprietorship and personal possessions, can too easily coexist with the absence of the spirit of poverty, with a comfortable and conventional standard of living that requires little genuine detachment and inhibits identification with those who are economically deprived. Then follows an exhaustively detailed examination of the canonical obligation of poverty, with particular attention to the status of the novice with regard to ownership prior to taking vows, and to the distinct differences with regard to ownership of property of those under simple, temporary vows, who retain "radical ownership" (398), and those under permanent, solemn vows, who own nothing. Merton wants to make very sure that his novices understand exactly what the laws of the Church are in this area—about to present the effects of the simple vow, he asserts, "this material is important; you should know it thoroughly" (398). He progresses through taking, retaining, borrowing, lending, exchanging, giving, destroying and using beyond permissible limits the common property of the community, and he sums up with a list of sins against the vow and of the principles that extenuate or aggravate the violations.

At this point he turns to *"The Spirit and Practice of Evangelical Poverty"* (409), but even here he devotes considerable space to a rather theoretical consideration of the natural instinct to possess, the inherent human right to possessions, and distorted expressions of the possessive instinct as an exercise of power over others and as an illusory source of security. Such distortions can be found, Merton points out, even when actual ownership is lacking; they can in fact be heightened in the absence of ownership: "It does no good to make 'acts of purity of intention' if in fact we are enslaved to anxieties and needs that flow from the inordinate desire of possessions" (418). An authentic spirit of poverty must be rooted deeply in the Scriptures, in which the poor are revealed to be "a kind of sign and touchstone . . . . an accusation against the unjust rich, against an unjust society, against the falsity and hypocrisy of a society that claims to be just and religious," and "a vindication of the truly religious man who identifies himself with the poor, sharing everything possible with him, because he sees God in the poor man" (418–19). Merton traces this theme through the commandments, the proclamation of jubilee, the writings of the sages and the prophets, the preciousness in God's eyes of the *anawim,* and into the New Testament presentation of Christ as the perfect exemplar of evangelical poverty, the One "Who emptied Himself in death" and "thereby established His title to be the King and Lord of all," for "to be King meant not to dominate but to serve, to give" (432). The obligation to recognize the face of Christ in the poor, in accordance with Matthew 25, has specific and concrete implications for all Christians, monks included: "it would certainly seem," Merton writes, "that Christian charity today, necessarily presupposing Christian justice, brings Christian society face to face with the need for a *social movement*, and therefore a political movement, dedicated to the improvement of conditions for the masses of men, not only spiritually but first and foremost *materially*" (437–38). Merton emphasizes that religious poverty must not be perceived, or lived, in a vacuum, isolated from the situation of the materially poor. It is the responsibility of the community to "share its products with the poor. The monk does not work {only} for his own poor brethren but also for the poor neighbors of the monastery, so that he may help them along also" (441). At the same time as he finds Christ in the least of these, the monk by his vow of poverty is called to identify with Christ in His kenosis. Religious poverty must be both prophetic and contemplative, a radical simplicity that possesses, and is possessed by, Christ alone:

> Interior poverty, based on serious exterior poverty, is an emptying of self and an inner deprivation, a death of self, a disappearance of "I" and "mine." One ceases to be attached to one's desires, opinions, tastes, virtues, spirituality, progress—everything that makes the "I" solid and evident, even in apparently good things. It is better for the "I" to disappear. One should desire to lose this "I," this "self," for the sake of Christ. Thus to lose oneself is to find oneself, and thus to die is to be saved, to live in Christ. This should be our ideal. Without such an ideal, our monastic life will not be solid and we cannot really be happy in the monastery. (446–47)

These concluding words on poverty are perhaps the most eloquent and most characteristic expression in the entire text of Merton's own deepest convictions about the essence of the monastic life in particular and of the Christian life generally.

The last of the vows to be discussed (though the first to be professed) is stability. Merton emphasizes its uniquely Benedictine character as "one of St. Benedict's own characteristic contributions to monastic life" (447), evident from the very first chapter of the *Rule*, in which it is precisely the absence of outward

stability (as with gyrovagues) and inward stability (as with sarabaites) that characterizes failed monks; he also makes clear that
the vocation of the hermit, outside the boundaries of the community, is not a loss of stability but its fulfillment. While Merton
himself calls the obligation of the vow "essentially simple and
uncomplicated" (447), he goes on to quote Dom Cuthbert Butler's claim that "The determination of the meaning and force
of Benedictine stability is . . . perhaps the most difficult point
in the study of Benedictine life" (452), though after considering
the alleged difficulties, he repeats essentially the same definition
he had already provided: "THE CORRECT IDEA OF BENEDICTINE
STABILITY IS THAT THE VOW OBLIGES THE MONK TO LIVE IN THE
COMMUNITY OF HIS PROFESSION ALL HIS LIFE, EVEN UNTIL DEATH"
(454)—that is, not just in the monastic state in general, nor necessarily in the same physical location, but as a member of the
same monastic community. He goes on to consider exceptions,
both apparent and real, such as being sent to a new foundation
or appointed to a position of responsibility in the Order or the
Church, as well as a change of stability for health reasons. He
devotes most attention to the question of a change of stability,
even of one's order, for the sake of a greater spiritual good—of
course a recurring issue throughout his own monastic life—and
comes to the conclusion that while stability does not absolutely
rule out such a change, in most cases "the *vow of stability by its
very nature means a vow to renounce the thought of seeking a greater
good, even a greater spiritual good, in another monastery or order*"
(459). After a brief look at sins against stability, specifically apostasy and flight (which had already been considered at greater
length as violations of conversion of manners), Merton is able to
devote attention to specifically monastic texts on stability, both
from the Desert Fathers (and a Mother, St. Syncletica) and from
the early Cistercians, a "luxury" he hadn't been able to indulge
with the abundance of theological and canonical material to be
incorporated in discussions of the other vows. Thus the tone of
the final pages of this text comes to resemble more closely the
rich monastic ambiance characteristic of the other sets of novitiate

conferences. He concludes with encouragement to live one's
stability not merely by staying put in one's monastery but by
actively yet realistically loving the Order (without *"false idealization"* that degenerates into sterile comparisons and competition
[473]), loving one's own particular community, with charity and
generosity in the face of inevitable imperfections, loving even
"the *place* itself. . . . impregnated with memories and holy associations after years of prayer and sacrifice and work," by which
one becomes "rooted in the land of the monastery" (477–78).
Stability is ultimately the milieu in which all the other vows, observances and responsibilities of the monastic life are grounded.

Having reached the end of this very long exposition, Merton
reminds the novices that it is not pronouncing the vows but living the vows that is paramount: "the important thing is not the
'profession day' but the lifelong fulfillment of our promise to
God" (478). Fidelity to one's vows is an ongoing process requiring deep commitment to prayer, an abiding sense of one's own
poverty and indigence, and dependence on the grace of God. In
good Trappist fashion, he brings his text to an end by counseling
reliance "on the intercession of Our Blessed Lady whose life we
imitate in the monastery" (479), and by repeating one final time
the central message of the conferences as a whole, that the ultimate purpose of the vows is to "bring us deep into the mystery of
the Cross and the Resurrection of the Lord Jesus. Amen" (479–80).

* * * * * * *

All the evidence available points to the likelihood that Merton presented conferences on the vows almost continuously, in
three cycles, throughout most of his tenure as master of novices.
Despite substantial gaps in the documentary record for the earlier
sections of the course the first two times that it was presented,
the overall sequence of the classes can be determined with considerable probability from the abundance of specific information
dating the composition and delivery of the rest of the material.
At the conclusion of his own typescript of the conferences, which
he had in front of him as he taught, Merton notes that it was

completed on the Feast of the Exaltation of the Holy Cross (i.e., September 14), 1960, so that this first round of lectures must have come to an end shortly thereafter. Unfortunately, there is no similar indication of when he began putting them together, and in fact there is no useful information about dating for the first quarter of the typescript. From that point on, however, there is a fairly extensive record indicating the progression of composition that extends over the better part of three years. On the bottom of page 69 of the typescript, shortly before the completion of the section on doubtful or invalid profession,[9] is the penciled notation "12/3"—the first of thirty-six marginal notations, similar to those found in the typescripts of other sets of conferences[10]—made by novices assigned to retype the text of the conferences on stencils for reproduction and distribution. Though no indication of the year is provided, it will become evident from the subsequent series of notations that the typist had reached this point on December 3, 1957.

While there is no necessary correspondence between this date and that either of Merton's own writing of the material or of his class presentation of it, the other type of relevant data suggests that the oral presentation of the text and its retyping on stencils proceeded in fairly close alignment. This second source for dating consists in the brief jottings that Merton often made on the verso sides of his typescript as reminders for the various announcements that usually occupied the first few minutes of the conference period. While these were often cryptic (e.g., "empty milk cans" [4v]) or instructions on proper deportment (e.g., "underwear—leaving things around g. p. [grand parlor]—neatness everywhere" [44v]) and were frequently written in so small a script as to be illegible, on occasion they mention a feast day or some other occasion that provides an indication of the date of delivery of the material it accompanies. The first such notation

9. Page 181 of this edition.
10. See *Cassian and the Fathers*, lviii; *Pre-Benedictine Monasticism*, lxiii; *Rule of Saint Benedict*, xxxvi–xxxviii; *Monastic Observances*, xiv–xvi.

in this set of conferences, on page 55v, is "St. Jerome"—written opposite material on incorporation into a community as the second essential aspect of religious profession,[11] suggesting that this material was discussed on or about September 30, 1957, a bit more than two months previous to the typist's early December notation. There are eight dated typist's notations for the following year, extending from "1/14" (73)[12] through "[December] 2" (121);[13] at one point, Merton's handwritten "July 4" and the typist's date "6/6" are found on facing pages (89v and 90, respectively),[14] indicating that the typing is about a month behind the delivery; but by mid-July the typing seems to have caught up with and perhaps even moved ahead of the conference presentations, as the date "7/18" appears on page 102 of the typescript,[15] while on the verso of the same page there are references to the Feast of Our Lady of the Snows (August 5) as well as to the anniversary of the death of Abbot Frederic Dunne (August 4). Merton's notes indicate that there was evidently a pause in the vows conferences between the end of August and mid-November, as successive pages (111v, 112v)[16] refer to the Feast of St. Rose (August 30) and that of St. Martin (November 11)—this is supported by the fact that the next typist's date after "7/18" is "Nov 20" (114).[17] Mention is made of an exam scheduled for December 19 on the facing page that includes a reference to the pagination of the mimeograph ("begin p. 134a. The Vows in Partic / up to end—Vow of Conv. of Manners."), which indicates that the dittoed pages were being reproduced and distributed as the course was progressing rather than waiting for bound copies of the completed text, still some twenty months from comple-

11. Page 156 of this edition.
12. Page 188 of this edition.
13. Page 287 of this edition; the notation reads "Nov. 2," but this is presumably an error, as a notation seven pages earlier (274 in this edition) reads "Nov 20".
14. Page 223 of this edition.
15. Page 246 of this edition.
16. Pages 265, 267 of this edition.
17. Page 274 of this edition.

tion. The last datable reference for this year comes from Merton's directions as to where to find Christmas trees (124v),[18] presumably from mid-December or later, suggesting that Merton was approximately at the point of discussing the spirit of the vow of conversion of manners by the end of 1958.

There are ten typist's notations for 1959, from "3/9" (128)[19] through "12/31/59" (168),[20] the first date in the entire series to include the year, thus confirming the dating sequence as beginning at the end of 1957. Typist's and delivery dates alternate in taking the lead throughout the year: on 129v[21] Merton mentions that on the following day he will celebrate a Mass for Boris Pasternak, thought (erroneously, as it turned out) to have disappeared; according to his journal,[22] this Mass took place on March 3, while on March 9 the typist was still working on page 128;[23] Pentecost (May 17 that year) is mentioned on page 142v,[24] but the typist is already on page 144[25] three days earlier, and a reference to the Feast of Corpus Christi (May 28) is found on the verso side of the same page; the typist has reached page 153[26] by "6-15," but it is "July 15" before the conference is given on material two pages later; however, the typist has only reached page 163[27] by "Oct 26," while Merton's note on 165v[28] refers to the Feast of the Nativity of the Blessed Virgin, more than six weeks earlier (September 8). References to the Feast of the Immaculate Conception (December 8) and to Abbot James

18. Page 293 of this edition.
19. Page 302 of this edition.
20. Page 383 of this edition.
21. Page 306 of this edition.
22. *Search for Solitude*, 265.
23. Page 302 of this edition.
24. Page 337 of this edition.
25. Page 340 of this edition.
26. Page 354 of this edition (an accompanying reference to the pagination of the mimeograph here provides documentary evidence that these are indeed typist's notes; variation in the style of dating suggests that different typists may have worked on the stencils at various times).
27. Page 373 of this edition.
28. Page 379 of this edition.

Fox's birthday (December 10) on 176v[29] indicate that Merton has reached this point in his presentations, but on the last day of the year the typist is still on page 168[30] of the typescript.

There are eighteen typist's notations for 1960, from "1-12" (169)[31] through "9/13/60" (214)[32]—all but the first including the year as part of the date; the first nine run through January to "2-3-60" (184)[33] and then jump to "6/17/60" (186),[34] followed by two more dates in June, one in July, two in August, and the last three in September. This indicates that there was evidently a hiatus in the conferences through much of the late winter and early spring; a reference on 185v[35] to Blessed Juliana of Mt. Cornillon, whose feast day was in April, on the facing page to one with a typist's dating of "6/17/60", suggests that Merton returned to the conferences sooner than the typist did; he continued to outpace the typist until almost the conclusion of the conferences, as he mentions the anniversary of the Hiroshima bombing (August 6) on 209v,[36] while on the facing page the typist's date is exactly a month later. However, Merton must have slowed down when drawing to a close, as the final typist's date is "9/13/60" on page 214,[37] the day before the Feast of the Holy Cross on which Merton dates the completion of the text, three pages later.

Thus the combined dating evidence gathered from the two series of dates available in the typescript indicates that between the end of September 1957 and mid-September 1960, almost three years later, about three-quarters of the material in the text of the vows conferences was presented; at the same rate, extrapolating backward, Merton would have begun the conferences in early Oc-

29. Page 403 of this edition.
30. Page 383 of this edition.
31. Page 387 of this edition.
32. Page 474 of this edition.
33. Page 415 of this edition.
34. Page 418 of this edition.
35. Page 418 of this edition.
36. Page 467 of this edition.
37. Page 474 of this edition.

tober 1956. While this is at best a rough estimate, since there is no way to be certain, on the basis of the available evidence, that the early vows conferences were given with comparable frequency and progressed at the same pace, it seems safe to suppose that they were begun sometime in the latter half of 1956. This would have allowed Merton sufficient time after assuming the office of master of novices to conceive the overall structure of the text and to have already composed a fairly substantial portion of the first part of the conferences before beginning to present them. But what is especially worthy of note is that he worked on the project for at least four years before bringing it to completion.

The sparse documentary evidence available supports the supposition that the vows conferences did not begin before the latter part of 1956. In an undated letter to Jean Leclercq from the fall of 1956, Merton writes of his novitiate work: "I have spent the year teaching a course on Cassian, on the Cistercian Consuetudines, and now on St. Bernard";[38] presumably, he would have mentioned conferences on the vows as well if they had already started. In the same letter he writes: "I have not attempted anything like a book since I became novice master. But with the inveterate itch of the writer I have turned some novitiate conferences into a pamphlet."[39] This is almost certainly a reference to the booklet *Basic Principles of Monastic Spirituality*, published the following year.[40] It seems likely that the conferences on which this short work was based began soon after Merton became novice master, since it had already been through the censorship process by August 1956.[41] As an introductory overview of the monastic life, it covers, albeit in less detailed and less technical a fashion, much the same ground as would be

38. Thomas Merton and Jean Leclercq, *Survival or Prophecy? The Letters of Thomas Merton and Jean Leclercq*, ed. Brother Patrick Hart (New York: Farrar, Straus and Giroux, 2002), 75.

39. *Survival or Prophecy*, 75.

40. Thomas Merton, *Basic Principles of Monastic Spirituality* (Trappist, KY: Abbey of Gethsemani, 1957); reprinted in Thomas Merton, *The Monastic Journey*, ed. Brother Patrick Hart (Kansas City: Sheed, Andrews & McMeel, 1977), 11–38.

41. See *School of Charity*, 96–98.

considered in the opening sections of *The Life of the Vows*, making it very unlikely that Merton would have been giving the two series of conferences simultaneously. The vows conferences may well have moved into the "slot" previously occupied by the *Basic Principles* classes, though apparently not right away.

There is a gap of almost twenty months between September 14, 1960, the date Merton finished writing the vows text, and April 27, 1962, when Merton's conferences began to be taped so that they could be played for the brothers as they worked.[42] From that point onward, a virtually complete audio record[43] of the vows conferences is available, most of them dated (though not always accurately). When the taping begins, Merton is discussing the early sections on conversion of manners,[44] a bit beyond the halfway point in his text. Thus it seems evident that there could not have been much of an interval between completing the initial series of conferences on the vows in the early fall of 1960 and beginning to present them a second time, though it is impossible to be precise about when the second series began or even if Merton presented the complete series again or only selected sections, as he was to do subsequently.

In the approximately eight months remaining in 1962, Merton gave forty conferences on the vows, seven on conversion of manners (through late May), twenty on chastity (from May 28 through early September), and thirteen on poverty (mid-September through mid-December). The vows conferences were being presented twice weekly until August 10, when Merton announced that they had "caught up" after evidently falling behind at some point before the taping began; from that point the vows classes would regularly take place on Mondays.[45]

42. See *Cassian and the Fathers*, xlvii, for details.

43. See Appendix B (544–48) for a table of correspondences between the taped lectures and the written text.

44. Page 280 of this edition.

45. The other series of conferences being given at this time were on the *Rule* (Wednesdays), on the history of the Order (Fridays), and on the monastic fathers (Saturdays).

Although he had not completed the material on poverty by the end of 1962, Merton began the vows conferences on January 7, 1963 with the first of eleven successive conferences, through April 17, on the vows in general. The reason is that the classes were now being attended not only by the choir novices but also by laybrother novices, since the new year marked the merg-ing of the two novitiates, and by the recently professed monks, or juniors, as part of the newly instituted monastic formation program.[46] Consequently, rather than simply plunge the new members of the class into the midst of the ongoing lectures on poverty, he returned to the section of the course that provided an overview of the vows. When this was completed, however, he did return directly to the poverty material at the point he had left it five months earlier, and he gave nine more conferences on poverty from May 8 through August 14, followed by nine confer-ences on stability from August 21 through December 11, a total of twenty-nine vows conferences for the year.

The stability material is the final section of *The Life of the Vows*, but instead of returning to the introductory material on Christian anthropology or on the states of life, or to the general material on the vows that he had presented at the beginning of the previous year, Merton began the 1964 vows conferences with consideration of the first of the actual Benedictine vows treated in the text, presenting seventeen conferences on obedience be-tween February 5 and August 5, followed by eleven conferences on conversion of manners between August 19 and December 9, thus overlapping material he had been discussing in April 1962 when the recording of conferences began. There were appar-ently few if any conferences on the vows during the first four months of 1965,[47] but Merton presented four more conferences on conversion of manners during May, then eight conferences

---

46. See *Pre-Benedictine Monasticism*, xi–xvi, for details.

47. There are no recorded vows conferences between December 9, 1964 and May 3, 1965, though it is possible that a recording or two may be missing, as there is no indication in the May 3 recording that he is returning to the topic (conversion of manners) after a long gap.

on chastity between June 21 and August 16, four days before he took up permanent residence in the hermitage. Thus the chastity material, like that on conversion of manners, is available in two separate sequences, from mid-1962 and from mid-1965, though the latter series was cut short before reaching the end of the chastity section of the text. Over the course of the forty months that the vows conferences were recorded, then, all the Benedictine vows—obedience, conversion of manners (with chastity and poverty considered as included in this vow) and stability—were thoroughly presented at least once. But other than the eleven conferences in early 1963 on the vows in general, Merton did not return during this period to the opening sections of his text.

* * * * * * *

There are 110 recorded conferences on the vows, over the course of three years and four months, from the very first taped presentation on April 27, 1962 until August 16, 1965, four days before Merton resigned as novice master and took up permanent residence in his hermitage. This represents far and away the most extensive oral record of his teaching,[48] though it includes only sections of the complete course, in two overlapping segments, as already noted above. This recorded material provides an opportunity not only to compare the written text to Merton's actual sessions with the novices, but to consider his successive modifications of at least some of the material as he returns to it repeatedly over the course of his mastership.

As was his usual custom, Merton often began the conferences with various sorts of announcements, which included noting the fact, in the very first of the series, that they were now being taped to be played later in the brothers' workroom, and jokingly warn-

---

48. There are sixty-five recorded conferences on *Pre-Benedictine Monasticism* (see 359–62), sixteen on *The Rule of Saint Benedict* (see 261–62) and fourteen on *Cassian and the Fathers* (see 281–82); the *Christian Mysticism* and *Monastic Observances* conferences were presented before the taping began. Of those novitiate conferences not yet published, none have more than about sixty recorded classes.

ing his audience that therefore no swearing or rebellions would be allowed. Later, on February 11, 1963, he mentions that a new microphone had been installed (unfortunately one that no longer clearly picked up the novices' comments and questions, which are virtually inaudible from this point forward). On July 29, 1964, when he has once again reached the material on conversion of manners that had already been recorded once, he suggests that the taping for the vows conferences could be dispensed with subsequently, but the recordings did in fact continue (and proved to be far from redundant or simply repetitious).

He often used the beginning few minutes to provide "house-keeping" instructions—though these diminished after the beginning of 1963 when the more experienced newly professed monks began attending the conferences as well. He frequently asked for prayers for various intentions, usually sent to him by correspondents. He would note when various novices left the community, usually with a brief comment as to the reason—joining (or re-joining) another religious order, going to college—occasionally with a salutary warning about avoiding strain or scrupulosity. Sometimes there would be explanations of monastic customs or terminology, as on May 4, 1962, with the term "visitation card," the summary evaluation and instructions following the annual visit of a superior from the motherhouse, which was not a "card" at all but a rather extensive written document called in French a *carte*—hence the rather misleading English equivalent. He also conveyed information on pertinent changes in customs ensuing from these visitations, most notably the switch from calling all choir monks, from the novitiate onward, "Father" to distinguish them from the laybrothers (May 8, 1962)—henceforth, all the nonordained were "Brother," an alteration that is quite evident on the recordings themselves from that point. Merton reported on various visitors, such as his friends John Wu in June 1962 and Abraham Heschel in July 1964. He also commented, on occasion at some length, on current events, about which the novices, having no access to newspapers or other media, would otherwise generally know little or nothing. The Cuban missile crisis, the

Kennedy assassination, the murder of three civil rights workers in Mississippi in 1964, and eventually the Vietnam War all received attention at various points during the course of Merton's classes.

Occasionally Merton would include personal details during a conference. Sometimes they were rather peripheral to the topic, as on December 17, 1962, when he mentions seeing Humphrey Bogart on the street and feeling as though he had just encountered a gangster (Bogart's most typical role in the 1930s). But at other times he brought in his own struggles with the vows: in discussing stability, he mentions on December 4, 1963 his own vocational restlessness and emphasizes how glad he is that he didn't transfer to the Camaldolese, where he would have had to spend considerable time in vocal prayers and wouldn't have had the freedom to enjoy solitude in the woods as at Gethsemani. In dealing with obedience, he notes on March 4, 1964 that as a minor superior (i.e., novice master) he has to deal with problems from both sides, as subject and as authority. He comments on June 3, 1964 on his problems with censorship, noting that one censor had recommended that the publication of *The Seven Storey Mountain* be delayed for thirty years, and revealing that his essay "Notes for a Philosophy of Solitude" had to be rewritten about ten times due to censors' objections, which actually resulted, he acknowledges, in a much stronger piece in the end. As with this last example, Merton's purpose in drawing on his own experience is usually to show how, in spite of difficulties, fidelity to the practice and spirit of the vows ultimately strengthens one's monastic identity and more importantly one's relationship with Christ. One biographical detail mentioned twice by Merton in these conferences (October 8, 1962; July 1, 1964) but apparently never recorded in print, by himself or anyone else, is that he had actually taken his initial vows privately after his first (canonical) year of novitiate rather than waiting until he had completed the full two years, a practice that was permissible with the consent of one's abbot, but which Merton himself does not recommend.

As in the text itself, but even more so, Merton in his conferences places the emphasis on the spirit, the inner meaning, of the vows. Yet he also recognizes the need to make certain that the novices are quite clear about the canonical and moral obligations that religious vows entail. Hence he adheres quite closely to the written text for this material, following it point by point in the sections on property arrangements for novices and simple professed, for example, and even scheduling exams to make sure they learned the material thoroughly. This procedure was facilitated by the fact that, unlike the situation with other sets of conferences, where the mimeographed notes would be made available only at the conclusion of the course, the novices already had the complete text available to them when these conferences were given, so that Merton could make reference to specific pages to be studied (and on more than one occasion would even indicate to the novices typographical errors to be corrected in their copies).

Throughout the conferences, Merton highlighted the positive dimensions of the vows, while at the same time providing a more positive evaluation of the world beyond the cloister and its inhabitants than is found in the written text. In discussing conversion of manners on April 27, 1962, he emphasizes that it is a transformation from good to better rather than from bad to good, that the secular world is not simply to be rejected as if the typical layperson did nothing but shoot craps, shoot pool and watch TV. In considering chastity, Merton emphasizes the intrinsic sexual dimension of every human being, and without downplaying the difficulties inherent in celibacy, he is at pains to curb tendencies toward scrupulosity and preoccupation with sexual temptation among his audience. He also stresses the importance of recognizing and appreciating both the joys and the struggles of married life (June 4, 1962), warning against the dangers of pharisaism in a kind of elitist assumption of moral and spiritual superiority among religious. He is moving away from the traditional characterization of the vowed life as intrinsically "better" than that of laypeople that is still quite evident in the written text. The sense of identification and solidarity with people in the world, particularly with one's neighbors, which is already a key element of the section on poverty in the written text, is strongly emphasized in the actual live presentation of the conferences as well,[49] reinforcing Merton's own increasing awareness of connections and continuities between the world and the cloister, without losing a sense of the distinctiveness of the vowed life and its unique contribution to the vitality of the Church as a whole. Here as throughout these and other sets of conferences, Merton relies on humor to make his points in an effective and nonthreatening way: considering the fact that one's secular clothing remains one's own before vows but can be used by others, he jokes on October 22, 1962 that someone's "tartan kilt" could be worn by anyone—even their next-door neighbor, Andy Boone. In a similar context, he quotes Pope John's saying that of the three ways to go broke in Italy—women, gambling and farming—his family had chosen the most boring way (July 10, 1963).

When Merton returns in the course of the conferences to material previously discussed and recorded, he sometimes departs completely from his written text. His first conference on the vows in general after the merging of the novitiates at the beginning of 1963 is spent discussing Dom David Knowles's book on the meaning of monasticism. When he returns to the topic of conversion of manners again, he spends a number of conferences in October and November 1964 drawing on stories and apothegms from the newly published *Collectio Monastica* translated from Ethiopian sources (also used extensively during the same period in his *Pre-Benedictine Monasticism* conferences[50]) rather than repeating material from the text that had already been recorded. On September 16, 1964 he combines insights from monastic letters of the twelfth-century Benedictine Peter of Celles with those taken from a short story of Flannery O'Connor, both exposing the futility of a conventional life of meaningless routine. He also devotes the entire March 11, 1964 conference to discuss-

49. In this context he mentions Webb Bowling on December 3, 1962 and Aidan Nally on August 14, 1963.

50. See *Pre-Benedictine Monasticism*, 254–57, 267–71.

ing an article by the Jesuit patristics scholar Irénée Hausherr, who sees the challenge of young religious to the patterns of conventional religious life as a stimulus to renewal, a position Merton largely endorses. He later considers and commends a similarly progressive article by moral theologian Bernard Häring on the importance of friendship in religious life (July 12, 1965).

This more open attitude is likewise evident in Merton's treatment of chastity in this second series of recorded classes. He emphasizes even more than he had earlier the distinction between sexuality and sensuality, remarking that "necking" (he makes no mention of "petting," the companion term of that era) is not *per se* sexual, but rather sensual, and he declares that sensuality is never a mortal sin in and of itself. Whereas the principle that sexual sin inheres not in the pleasure but in the act itself had initially been cited to convey the traditional position that illicit sexual activity is seriously sinful whether pleasurable or not, Merton now points out that pleasure can be experienced without a willful act and therefore should not be automatically equated with sin. The teaching is the same but the emphasis has changed. Merton warns against a mentality of legalism that asks how far one can go before incurring serious sin, but at the same time counsels the novices not to get into a state of constant, fearful worrying, and he points out that fear itself can be a way of indulging one's sexuality by unhealthy preoccupation. He cites St. Thomas, calling him an extremely sharp and in many ways quite modern moral theologian, on insensibility as a vice. He concludes this final conference on chastity (August 16, 1965), and thus his final conference on the vows, with what he calls the most important practical approach to this and all efforts to live the vows fully—the manifestation of conscience, not "holding it in" but opening oneself to one's spiritual director in freedom and trust, a culminating "word of salvation" that has been central to the monastic tradition since the days of the Desert Fathers, a last piece of evidence indicative of Merton's unusual ability to integrate traditional and contemporary insights in a coherent and convincing way.

* * * * * * *

This series of conferences is of course not Merton's final word on the vows and their significance for monastic life. His evolving understanding of the vows can be traced in writings that span his decade as master of novices and continue through his final years in the hermitage. Already in *Basic Principles of Monastic Spirituality*, the apparent prelude to the vows conferences, he provides a brief epitome of his current understanding of the meaning of the vows: "The whole ascetic life of the monk, in all its aspects both positive and negative, is summed up in his consecration of himself, his whole life, all that he has and all that he is, to God, by his five monastic vows. The life of the monk is the life of the vows."[51] The reference to five vows is of course somewhat inaccurate, and he soon clarifies the fact that poverty and chastity are considered to be included as part of the vow of conversion of manners rather than made the object of distinct vows as in religious orders not in the Benedictine tradition. It is noteworthy that Merton considers the vow of conversion of manners first and presents it as the pivotal vow for monastic life, the commitment "to change one's whole life and all one's attitudes from those of the world to those of the cloister . . . . [to] consecrate our whole life to the service of God as monks, men who have turned their backs on the world, who have substituted the humility, chastity, poverty, renunciation of the cloister for the ambitions, comforts, pleasures, riches and self-satisfaction of the world."[52] The thread connecting this vow with the other two is the element of renunciation, as obedience is characterized as "the renunciation of our own will, in order to carry out in our whole life the will of another who represents God," and stability is defined as "renouncing our freedom to travel about from place to place" by the decision to remain in a particular community for the rest of one's life.[53] But on a deeper level stability is to be recognized as a means, along with the other vows, "to stabilize

51. *Basic Principles*, 24; *Monastic Journey*, 30.
52. *Basic Principles*, 24; *Monastic Journey*, 30–31.
53. *Basic Principles*, 24; *Monastic Journey*, 31.

us in a life of union to the will of God," what the tradition calls "virginity of spirit." Whereas he had initially focused on negation, his brief discussion of the vows concludes with the more positive description of conversion of manners as "orienting our whole life to God in faith and love," as "a vow to live 'in the Spirit.'"[54] Though the predominantly binary language of "world" and "cloister" here still reflects the kind of "world rejection" that characterizes, at least on the surface, much of Merton's early writing on monastic life, he undermines any rigid division by making clear that "an enclosed and penitential life" is no guarantee of genuine spiritual transformation, that without inner silence and peace one "can indeed be more active, more restless and more distracted in the cloister than we would be in the active life," and that the first step in discovering this peace "is the total acceptance of our self, our whole being, as God has willed us to be . . . in the harmony of a balanced and spiritualized personality."[55] The ultimate purpose of the vows, then, is to be understood as the restoration of one's authentic identity as made in the divine image and the unconditional gift of this true self to its Creator.

This focus continues in *Monastic Peace*,[56] the booklet published the year after *Basic Principles*, which discusses the vows in considerably more detail. In reflecting on the notion of monasticism as a penitential life, Merton emphasizes that ascetic practices can easily be distorted into an effort to "earn" salvation by one's works, to elevate "doing" over "being,"[57] and once again highlights the central importance of *conversatio morum*: "The true penance of the monk is essentially and above all in his monastic 'conversion of manners,' the constant and ceaseless effort to make himself over, by God's grace, from a rugged and selfish individualist into a charitable and loving member of Christ."[58] Following St. Bernard,

54. *Basic Principles*, 26; *Monastic Journey*, 32.

55. *Basic Principles*, 25; *Monastic Journey*, 31.

56. Thomas Merton, *Monastic Peace* (Trappist, KY: Abbey of Gethsemani, 1958); reprinted in *Monastic Journey*, 39–84.

57. *Monastic Peace*, 12, *Monastic Journey*, 46.

58. *Monastic Peace*, 13; *Monastic Journey*, 47.

Merton stresses that "mortification of the senses," while important in the monastic life, matters far less than "the mortification of our own will by obedience,"[59] which enables the monk "to seek not his own good but the good of others" and so brings about "the emancipation of the person through his full and mature participation in the common life by self-oblation."[60] The section explicitly devoted to the vows reflects in briefer compass much of what Merton will say in the conferences. He considers the vow of poverty as having a "symbolic, or . . . prophetic significance" in the context of social justice: "It is a silent and implicit condemnation of the misuse of ownership"[61] that testifies to the fact that ultimately all things belong to God and that the right of possessing property is subordinate to the duty to share with others what surpasses one's own needs. For this prophetic witness to be effective, monastic poverty must go beyond the legal renunciation of personal ownership to a commitment that "embraces a state of direct dependence on providence out of love for God, and for the poor,"[62] and that incorporates a communal simplicity and poverty in which "the surplus produced by the monastery is shared with Christ in the poor."[63] While poverty renounces what is external to oneself—possessions—chastity is the renunciation of one's own body; but Merton stresses that to consider the vow simply as "the *refusal to give in* to sexual desires" is to miss the "positive and constructive" heart of chastity, "an interior and fruitful purity, a freedom of spirit which offers itself to God in a higher and more spiritual love in which the lower instinct is sublimated," and spiritual energies are liberated and "channelled into the creative and spiritual activities of the monk's life of prayer."[64] If poverty is surrender of possessions and chastity of the body, obedience can be considered the "greatest of the vows" because it is the surrender of the will, "the

59. *Monastic Peace*, 20; *Monastic Journey*, 53.
60. *Monastic Peace*, 21; *Monastic Journey*, 53.
61. *Monastic Peace*, 31; *Monastic Journey*, 62.
62. *Monastic Peace*, 31; *Monastic Journey*, 63.
63. *Monastic Peace*, 32; *Monastic Journey*, 63.
64. *Monastic Peace*, 32; *Monastic Journey*, 63.

inmost sanctuary of his spirit,"[65] the right to control one's own life. But Merton emphasizes here, as he does in the conferences, that such a commitment is not the extinction or annihilation of one's freedom but rather the responsible exercise of that freedom, the "voluntary assumption of responsibility, a clear-sighted renunciation of private and limited interests in favor of the general good of the community,"[66] as a way of participating in the primordial act of obedience of Christ to the Father, the redemptive sacrifice of the Cross, into which the monk enters "in order to share with Christ the great work of restoring liberty to mankind and of renewing all things in the power and sanctity of the Spirit of God."[67] Finally, stability, the distinctively Benedictine vow, is recognized as a permanent commitment, not so much to a particular place as to a specific community, the concrete group of other human beings with whom one is committed to work out one's salvation and to witness to the presence of the reign of God in a monastery that serves as a "sacrament," a visible and tangible foreshadowing of the ultimate goal to which all its members are drawn.[68] Thus in Merton's view the essence of the vows is not restriction but liberation, not law but grace, not passivity but dynamism, not conformity to juridical regulation but conformation to the person of Christ and openness to the power of the Holy Spirit. "Interior growth is essential to the monastic and spiritual life, and indeed the purpose of the vows is to foster this growth. But to grow interiorly, one must grow in maturity and freedom, in the ability to govern one's own life from within, and not merely to conform to exterior standards. Interior self-government must of course follow the lines laid down by the exterior norm, but it goes far beyond that norm in spontaneity and perfection."[69] This of course is the ideal, which is continuously imperiled on one side by the attractions of an authoritarianism

---

65. *Monastic Peace*, 33; *Monastic Journey*, 64.
66. *Monastic Peace*, 34; *Monastic Journey*, 65.
67. *Monastic Peace*, 35; *Monastic Journey*, 66.
68. *Monastic Peace*, 37; *Monastic Journey*, 68.
69. *Monastic Peace*, 48; *Monastic Journey*, 77.

that removes the risks of mature freedom and on the other by a laissez-faire tendency that reduces freedom to license and laxity. Only by articulating this ideal can the authentic monastic vision be seen and so, however imperfectly, put into practice.

In Merton's subsequent explorations of the significance of the vows he continues to voice this ideal, but he also becomes more aware and more critical of the ways in which monastic structures have often failed to create an environment that draws on the full resources of the vows to lead monks to human and spiritual maturity. Responding to the call of the Second Vatican Council for religious orders to recover the charisms of their founders, Merton repeatedly calls for a genuine renewal and recovery of an authentic monastic spirit rather than merely a reform of structures and observances.

A couple of Merton's writings concerning the vows from the first half of the 1960s are closely connected to the conferences. On August 21, 1963, Merton concludes the first of his conferences on stability in the current cycle by suggesting that, given the growing numbers of simple and even solemnly professed monks seeking dispensations from their vows or just leaving the monastery without being dispensed, there might be a point in modifying the traditional time frame for making vows. He indicates that he would like to see a longer and more flexible period of remaining in simple vows, which could be renewed year by year and could continue indefinitely, perhaps during an entire lifetime for some monks. This would insure, or at least make more likely, that when a monk took solemn vows, he would "stick." Presumably at around the same time, he put together a brief position paper entitled "Monastic Vows: A Memorandum," in which he elaborates essentially the same proposal. This undated article remained unpublished until recently[70] but was reproduced and circulated as a three-page mimeograph. In it Merton points to "the present serious problem of stability" resulting in numer-

---

70. Thomas Merton, "Monastic Vows: A Memorandum," *The Merton Seasonal*, 36.2 (Summer 2011), 3–5.

ous dispensations and defections, and he calls for "very much greater flexibility"[71] than the two years of novitiate followed by three years of temporary profession that had uniformly preceded solemn vows in the Order. He suggests that an abbot, with his chapter or council, should have the authority to adjust the profession schedule to suit individual needs and capacities, and he sets forth a seven-point plan: first, the novitiate could be extended for an additional two years if needed; second, temporary vows should be followed by a period of specifically monastic formation rather than immediately by academic study preparing for ordination, which in any case should be recognized as not essential to the monastic vocation; third, temporary vows should be renewed for an extended period on an annual basis, perhaps to be eventually extended to five-year terms; fourth, solemn vows should be made only after living under temporary vows for twelve or fifteen years, or even longer, and need not be made at all by some monks; fifth, monks could be permitted to hold certain monastic offices while still under simple vows; sixth, a monk under temporary vows could be permitted to live outside the monastery, at a seminary or in another more active religious community, to test his vocation, with the option of returning to the monastery without seeking readmission; lastly, profession of solemn vows would be an expression of "a deeper and more mature commitment to the *contemplative life*,"[72] including the possibility of a more solitary life, not just a prerequisite for major clerical orders or for holding important monastic offices. Rather than being "automatic" (subject to the positive vote of the community), solemn vows would be taken only by "a man of proven maturity with an evident capacity to lead a more deeply contemplative life, or to be a priest in the monastery, or to assume the burdens of the greatest responsibility."[73] Under such a regimen, Merton believed, the life of the vows would reflect more adequately and accurately

71. "Monastic Vows: A Memorandum," 3.
72. "Monastic Vows: A Memorandum," 4.
73. "Monastic Vows: A Memorandum," 4.

the degree of commitment that was evidently being given, and able to be given, by monks in the present religious and cultural climate. It would respect and enhance the seriousness of the vows without imposing a burden that for one reason or another might prove too onerous for some of those making profession.

About a year later, while in the midst of discussing the vow of conversion of manners with the novices, Merton records in a journal entry of September 13, 1964 that he "read the awful article of Dom Lottin in RTAM, 1959. That the vow of *conversatio morum cannot be* anything else but a vow to remain a cenobite and never to go into solitude—'exclusion' of eremitism. Arbitrary and iron-bound logic based on a quasi-mathematical analysis of chapter 1 of the *Rule* in the light of the three vows. Repeated insistence 'no other interpretation is possible.' But indeed many others are not only possible, but far more likely in the light of history!"[74] Merton's response to this article,[75] published three (not five) years earlier but evidently read now in connection with his conferences, was to compose one of his own more scholarly articles, "Conversion of Life,"[76] which provides an overview of the vow, drawn both from the conference notes and from further reading, before engaging with and arguing against Dom Lottin's anti-eremitic interpretation of it. Once again Merton makes clear that he sees conversion of manners as "the essential monastic vow," and he adds that any authentic monastic renewal in the current "age of transition and crisis" depends on "a restoration of the monastic idea of *conversatio morum* in its purity and in its depth, in a way that is timeless, transcends the peculiarities of age and culture, and is therefore able to be as actual and authentic to us in our time as it was to men in the time of St Benedict."[77] As he did in the vows notes, which he closely follows, he points out the general

---

74. *Dancing in the Water of Life*, 145.

75. Odon Lottin, osb, "À Propos du Vœu de 'Conversatio Morum' chez S. Benoît," *Recherches de Théologie Ancienne et Médiévale*, 28 (1961), 154–60.

76. *Monastic Journey*, 107–20; originally published as *"Conversatio Morum"* in *Cistercian Studies*, 1 (1966), 130–44.

77. *Monastic Journey*, 107.

inadequacies of the discussion of the vow in the Cistercian *Spiritual Directory*, provides an overview of the explanations of both early and modern commentators, and associates the vow with the Cistercian description of the *"formula perfectae paenitentiae."*[78] As in the current round of conferences, in the article he draws extensively on texts from the Ethiopian *Collectio Monastica* "that sum up the monastic tradition on this point,"[79] and he even cites the "rich traditional material," albeit "extremely rigorous" in its application, of Abbot de Rancé on monastic *conversio*.[80] Following this overview, he takes up Dom Lottin's contention that the three monastic vows are intended by St. Benedict to exclude the three types of monks other than cenobites mentioned in the first chapter of the *Rule*: stability against the wandering gyrovagues, obedience against the irregular sarabaites, and *conversatio morum* against the solitary hermits. On the contrary, Merton asserts, "to consider the vow of *conversatio morum* nothing more and nothing less than an explicit vow never to become a hermit is to fly in the face of primitive monastic tradition which St Benedict himself, with all his preference for cenobites, accepts without question."[81] Such a rigid interpretation, based on a highly questionable parallelism never explicitly applied by St. Benedict, "would be," Merton asserts, "an arbitrary limitation of the monastic vocation to one of its aspects"[82] and in fact would undermine cenobitic monasticism itself by cutting it off from its historical and spiritual roots in solitude, from the desert ideal central to all monastic life. He supports this position, which is of course of far more than academic interest to him, by considering the meaning of the more authentic term *conversatio* as "rather a more precise view of *conversio* with emphasis on the monastic ascesis or the monastic way of life"[83] that is authentically present in both cenobitic and

78. *Monastic Journey*, 111.
79. *Monastic Journey*, 112.
80. *Monastic Journey*, 114.
81. *Monastic Journey*, 115.
82. *Monastic Journey*, 116.
83. *Monastic Journey*, 119.

eremitic forms of monasticism. While St. Benedict certainly rejects "the inauthentic hermit who throws off the Rule and separates himself from the Abbot and the brethren by an act of his own will," Merton concludes that the purpose of the vow of *conversatio morum* "is certainly not 'the exclusion of all eremitism.'"[84]

In early October 1964, about a month after he had been reading Dom Lottin's article about conversion of manners, Merton participated in a week-long meeting of abbots and novice masters at Gethsemani focused on monastic renewal.[85] Merton originally prepared a presentation entitled "The Identity Crisis and Monastic Vocation,"[86] but he subsequently decided it was "too radical"[87] and substituted another talk that he called "Monastic Vocation and Modern Thought."[88] The original "Identity Crisis" article situates the issue of monastic obedience in the context of a quest for authentic selfhood and particularly of the widespread rebellion against an authority perceived as arbitrary and oppressive by the youth culture of the 1960s, the environment out of which candidates for the monastic life were coming. While recognizing that "there is no real solution to the identity crisis simply in opposing authority" and that such a stance is a sign of immaturity, "a real lack of identity, or a false identity which

---

84. *Monastic Journey*, 120.

85. See *Dancing in the Water of Life*, 152–53 (10/8/64; 10/12/64).

86. Thomas Merton, *Contemplation in a World of Action* (Garden City, NY: Doubleday, 1971), 56–82 (as "The Identity Crisis"); this text circulated in mimeograph but was not published in Merton's lifetime.

87. See Merton's November 1, 1964, letter to Sr. Mary Luke Tobin (*School of Charity*, 251).

88. *Contemplation in a World of Action*, 26–55 (as "Vocation and Modern Thought"); first published under its original title in *Monastic Studies*, 4 (Advent 1966), 17–54. In a journal entry of October 29, 1964, Merton speaks of rewriting it "and trying to deepen it so as to avoid merely repeating platitudes about 'identity crisis' and 'authenticity'" but concludes (at this point at least) that his efforts were "not successful" (*Dancing in the Water of Life*, 159); a year later Merton includes the article on his "to do list" (*Dancing in the Water of Life*, 338), indicating that he continued to rework it before it was sent out for publication.

maintains itself by provoking resistance (attention) rather than by flattering or cajoling authority,"[89] Merton is more concerned with the danger of monastic life inculcating and encouraging—and rewarding—an attitude of passive conformity under the rubric of obedience and hence hindering the process of emotional and spiritual growth:

> But there are others who in actual fact welcome the passivity and irresponsibility that are possible in a strictly controlled and organized life. For these the monastery offers opportunities for a false solution to the identity problem. Their obedience may be an evasion. These persons fear insecurity, and seek security from a well-established and approved system that nobody questions. Rules clearly say what is right and wrong. The monk can turn his back on the world with its problems and forget it. He can simply follow the rules, do what he is told, and have security because everyone around him holds that this is "right" and that to do anything else is "wrong." He no longer has to think. Choices are made for him. Others are responsible. He need not care.[90]

A conception of obedience that fosters such a stunting of the human personality, and reinforces an unhealthy and unreflective conformity, needs to be seen, Merton maintains, as a distortion of the true nature of religious obedience, which must be a free submission of one's own will to God for the sake of the common good of the community, not an abdication of personal responsibility. He insists:

> We must not preach an obedience that is mere passive compliance, a humility that is the glad acceptance of depersonalized abjection, a spirituality that glorifies, as "abnegation," the total abdication of all human worth and all identity. This must be seen for what it is: a debasing of man which gives no glory to God, but is bad theology and false supernaturalism,

89. *Contemplation in a World of Action*, 60.
90. *Contemplation in a World of Action*, 61–62.

and which seriously endangers the faith of those who allow
themselves to be caught in it for a while, only to leave later
disgusted and disillusioned.[91]

These final words seem to reflect the experience of the novice
master who has seen potentially solid vocations lost to the monastery because of these unresolved issues with the nature of authentic obedience; but perhaps it was language such as this that
prompted Merton to consider this presentation "too radical"
for his audience and to replace it with the more descriptive,
less prescriptive survey in "Vocation and Modern Thought" of
cultural and intellectual influences forming the contemporary
consciousness.

When Merton considers the vows in this latter piece, it is
conversion of manners rather than obedience that becomes the
focus: "Once the monk is professed, he must in some way learn
to answer his questions in the monastery, in his vow of *conversatio
morum*. The monastic commitment and consecration does remain
the most deep and authentic solution. But how can he understand
this? He must be formed with such a capacity to understand. The
monastic ideal must consequently be presented in an understandable way, in all its depth, in its existential reality and its demands,
not in formulas of words and slogans."[92] It is not enough to decry
the loss of a sacralized worldview and try to purge those entering
the monastery of the baneful influence of secular life. Attempts
to make the monastery a refuge, a sphere of timeless holiness,
are futile, a mirage that inevitably reduces it to an anachronistic
relic of a dead past. The authentic values of monastic life must
be transmitted in language that resonates with the experience of
contemporary people, which is the reason why those responsible
for formation must be conversant with and even sympathetic to
intellectual and cultural currents that characterize the modern
world. At the same time, a superficial embrace of what passes for

91. *Contemplation in a World of Action*, 74.
92. *Contemplation in a World of Action*, 28.

the latest wisdom risks distorting or trivializing the genuinely contemplative and prophetic role of monasticism to serve as a sign of contradiction to all easy accommodation, in any era, to the fashionable idols of the age. Merton notes, "What is called for today is not a crude modernizing of monastic tradition but a new and sharp perspective on the real values which are latent in the monastic life and tradition and which modern man can reasonably expect to find there. The values are certainly there, but they may be hidden through the lack of attention and sensitivity on the part of those who have hitherto been satisfied with old formulas and conceptions which need to be rethought and seen from a new angle, with greater and more serious concern." He wryly comments, "Need we add: the vows must no longer be regarded in a spirit of vain observance, magic or superstition?"[93] While perhaps less "radical" than the shelved alternative, "Vocation and Modern Thought" nevertheless presents his audience with the challenge to conceive of monastic renewal, including a renewed understanding of the vows, in ways that will foster a distinctly contemporary Christian holiness, a challenge to which he himself will try to respond in a series of subsequent essays spanning the final years of his life.

He returns to the question of obedience in an essay published in September 1965, less than a month after giving the last of his vows conferences, resigning as novice master and taking up residence in the hermitage. His starting point in "The Place of Obedience"[94] is the recognition, already found in *The Life of the Vows*, of the distinctive quality of religious obedience: "The obedience which is vowed by a religious is not the obedience of a child to a parent, nor the obedience of a citizen to civil authority, nor is it properly understood merely as the obedience of a subject to juridically constituted authority, even though this may be within

93. *Contemplation in a World of Action*, 28–29.
94. *Contemplation in a World of Action*, 117–28; first published as "The Place of Obedience in Monastic Renewal" in *American Benedictine Review*, 16 (September 1965), 359–68.

a religious framework. Hence, the renewal of religious obedience will not be accomplished simply by an increase of promptitude and exactness, though these are certainly not to be overlooked."[95] If, as Merton insists and as St. Benedict indicates in the Prologue to the *Rule*, the primary purpose of obedience is to serve as "a means to closer union with God. . . . the chief way by which the monk returns to God," then an exaggerated emphasis on the formal aspects of the vow is largely beside the point: "A merely external and juridical obedience, no matter how exact, is hardly to be prized as an especially efficacious way to union with God."[96] Obedience is less a conformity to rules and observances than a conformation to the incarnate Jesus who emptied himself even to the point of death in obedience to the Father's will, as servant and savior of all humanity. Only in this context does the vow truly make sense: "Monastic obedience is seen by the monk as a way to imitate the obedience and love of Christ his Master. . . . Religious obedience must be seen first of all in this context of love and discipleship. Only then do its formal and juridical aspects fall into the right perspective."[97] Conversely, the superior must likewise recognize the true purpose of obedience and make that the principal aim of his direction of the community: "The Abbot desires not only to get his own will carried out, or to see that the Rule is strictly enforced, or to guarantee that the community is well-disciplined and prosperous, but to help his monks to seek and find God more truly, more sincerely, more intelligently, and more efficaciously."[98] While the treatment of obedience in this article is less critical in tone than in "The Identity Crisis," emphasizing the positive function of the vow in fostering genuine discipleship and a deeply paschal spirituality, the two discussions complement one another in pointing out the inadequacies of an overly juridical approach.

95. *Contemplation in a World of Action*, 118.
96. *Contemplation in a World of Action*, 118.
97. *Contemplation in a World of Action*, 119.
98. *Contemplation in a World of Action*, 119.

It is perhaps initially surprising that Merton's most extensive comments on the need to reexamine the vowed life come in his article "Ecumenism and Renewal," which he was writing in late 1967[99] and which was first published in the spring of 1968.[100] But much of the article is taken up with responding to the Reformation critique of monasticism, particularly of the vows, which Merton acknowledges as having a good deal of validity, at least for the time it was made:

> Before Vatican II it was still possible for monks to ignore the Reformation with its serious charge that the vowed life of the monk, lived under traditional disciplines and devoted to a complex system of pious works, was in fact an evasion of the basic call to discipleship. Instead of responding to the summons of Christ in faith, placing his entire trust in the word and promises of the Risen Savior, seeking salvation, grace and light in the community of those called to confide entirely in the all-merciful Redeemer, the monk took refuge in vows and rites which (in the context of the late Middle Ages) could seriously be seen as a system of more or less superstitious fictions.[101]

It is the more familiar triad of poverty, chastity and obedience (which Luther the Augustinian would have taken), rather than the specifically Benedictine stability and conversion of manners, that are the object of the Reformers' strictures. Poverty was attacked as "a mere hypocritical formality which enabled one to enjoy the goods and comforts of the world without even having to do an honest job of work to get them"; chastity was considered

---

99. In his journal entry of November 22, 1967, Merton writes of the "slow, difficult start" he made on this article, which had been "promised a long time ago to *The Journal of Ecumenical Studies*" (Thomas Merton, *The Other Side of the Mountain: The End of the Journey. Journals, vol. 7: 1967–1968*, ed. Patrick Hart [San Francisco: HarperCollins, 1998], 14).

100. *Contemplation in a World of Action*, 181–97; first published in *The Journal of Ecumenical Studies*, 5 (Spring 1968), 268–83.

101. *Contemplation in a World of Action*, 184.

"a fruitless evasion of the duty of marriage, corrupted perhaps by the most shameful kind of failures"; obedience "became an abdication of mature responsibility and an escape from freedom which could, in extreme cases, turn the monk into a blind instrument of the most nefarious kind of power politics."[102] The entire concept of vows could be, and was, considered a substitute for a response to the free gift of grace, an effort to earn salvation by one's own efforts rather than relying in faith on the redemptive action of Christ. Instead of dismissing this analysis out of hand, as monks and Catholic apologists had been doing for centuries, Merton takes it as an opportunity for serious reflection and a bracing challenge to conventional thinking on the vows, a stimulus to radical monastic self-examination. He asks,

> Is it possible that the whole nature of the vows needs to be theologically re-examined? Does the very ideal of a vow imply the foreclosure of vital future possibilities, the selection of some provisional certitude, that seems ultimate at the moment, for the final and definitive truth? Does the vow, instead of surrendering our liberty to the unpredictable liberty of God, on the contrary seek to bind God's hands and confine Him to the plans we have determined for our own lives—or worse still, to the myopic plans that others, who are not guaranteed to be either prophetic or wise, may impose in His name? Does the very nature of a vow put one in a position where he may be forced to choose for his vow in opposition to God Himself?[103]

These are questions not simply of historical import but that get to the heart of any authentic movement for monastic renewal. Merton's immediate response is not to try to come up with definitive answers but to pose further questions that suggest an alternative reading of the evangelical significance of the vows: "Or is it possible that the true concept of a vow is precisely that of a freedom committed to risk and to the unpredictable, to the

102. *Contemplation in a World of Action*, 184–85.
103. *Contemplation in a World of Action*, 191.

refusal of all bonds to the provisional, to an open-ended newness of life that peels off the 'old man' like a snakeskin which was new last year but is no longer alive and sensitive? Can it be that Luther was mistaken in thinking that the monastic vows and a legalistic existence were necessarily one and the same?"[104] This in turn leads to a third series of questions that raise the issue whether there is an intrinsic, necessary connection between monasticism and religious vows. Can there be a monastic life without vows? Is a monastic life with vows necessarily better and more authentic than one without vows? Is the rigid juridical structure of the dedicated life an obstacle to real renewal? Does the monastic life have to be organized as it is, in such a way that by his vows the monk is incorporated into a complex institutional machine in which his life is subject to very narrow limitations, his movements are all largely predetermined, his capacity for choice and initiative is sometimes at an absolute minimum so that, in practice, the orders with the strictest rules and most stringent obligations, in which everything is regulated for the monk in advance, have been regarded as "the most perfect"?[105]

Thus the Reformation attack on the theory and practice of a vowed life can serve, Merton suggests, as an invitation to a thoroughgoing re-examination of the nature and function of the vows in the context of contemporary monastic renewal. His own response, necessarily tentative and exploratory, includes historical, practical, theological and even personal dimensions. To begin with, he points out that in the early days of desert monasticism "there were no vows, no written rules, and institutional structure was kept at a minimum." The monastic commitment was more personal, and interpersonal, than institutional. The absolute obedience given by a novice monk to his spiritual father was rooted in a trust in the elder's wisdom, spiritual maturity and charismatic authority, rather than in a formal pledge, and the result of formation was to send the monk out to "live on his

104. *Contemplation in a World of Action*, 191.
105. *Contemplation in a World of Action*, 191.

own . . . under the direct guidance of God."[106] Thus the historical evidence does not support the position that the monastic life and the vowed life are necessarily coextensive.

Merton then looks at the contemporary situation in which "the enormous number of professed religious seeking dispensation from their vows—and of others who leave the vowed life without any permission at all—makes the question of vows inescapable." Here Merton revisits the issues confronted in "Monastic Vows: A Memorandum" and comes up with a similar response but extends it by proposing even more open-ended possibilities. He recognizes that there is a need for structure, for "a definite organization, an element of discipline and of rule, of administration and of control," if religious life is to function effectively: "A community cannot exist without its members being reasonably sure of what they can expect of one another from one day to the next. This supposes a certain amount of codification and a formal commitment to elementary obedience." But he goes on to wonder if such structure might not be able to incorporate a greater flexibility and a broader spectrum of connections than is currently available: "It is possible that the taking of vows might be reserved for a minority of monks, and solemn profession might become something analogous to the taking of the 'great habit' in Greek monasticism. Why could there not be monasteries, with a nucleus of permanently dedicated monks, to which others come temporarily for two or three years, for periods of training or for retreat (as for instance in Zen Buddhist monasticism)? Why could not married people participate temporarily, in some way, in monastic life?"[107] Again there are more questions than answers, but Merton implies that such questions need to be raised in the context of the current crisis in monasticism. The model that developed in the Middle Ages might not be adequate for the very different world in which contemporary Christians and contemporary monastics find themselves.

---

106. *Contemplation in a World of Action*, 191–92.
107. *Contemplation in a World of Action*, 192.

Ultimately, the answers to all of these questions, Merton maintains, must arise from a response to the Gospel that is theologically sound and spiritually enriching. For the mature Merton the fundamental truth of the monastic life is its vocation to serve its own members, the wider Church and the world at large as an eschatological sign of God's fidelity to the divine promises of ultimate, definitive participation in the eternal life of Trinitarian love, a participation into which it has already begun to be drawn:

> The monastic community is a covenant community whose gaze . . . is fixed on the definitive eschatological truth: the *emeth* of God, the unfailing promise that is obscurely apprehended by faith as already fulfilled. The vows then are intended simply to bear witness to the monk's completely engaged faith in this fulfillment, this definitive reality made known by God in Christ. They testify that he will seek no other fulfillment, and they remind the monk himself that if he does turn aside and seek fulfillment in something less than the whole, if he abandons the whole in order to put a part in place of it, then he has fissured and severed his own identity by an act of untruth, an infidelity to what he has once experienced as definitive.[108]

Too often in the course of monastic history, Merton suggests, the eschatological has been reduced to the institutional, the following of Christ to the following of rules: "The historical development of the vowed life has more and more institutionalized this radical engagement and has transformed it into an organizational mystique, so that in effect it is the institution itself that becomes definitive. . . . Thus the vows are expressions no longer of an immediate and direct engagement to the definitive truth of God's *emeth*, but of a mediate engagement, the institution itself being taken as practically definitive and as the incarnation of *emeth*."[109] Here Merton touches on the central claim of all his mature writings on monastic renewal, that it cannot be simply a reform of

108. *Contemplation in a World of Action*, 192–93.
109. *Contemplation in a World of Action*, 193.

structures but must be a recovery of the monastic charism to
witness to the hidden presence of God's reign established definitively by the death and resurrection of Christ. Too often the
call to bring the future into the present is replaced by a determination to preserve the past in the present. "Once the institution
itself becomes a completely conservative establishment, the monastic vows become a firm social commitment to ecclesiastical
conservatism. Faith in God's *emeth* is reduced in fact to faith in
the *status quo*, and any criticism of the *status quo* becomes an
act of unbelief, the first step toward apostasy and atheism."[110]
It is this distortion, Merton suggests, that is the real object of
the Reformers' critique, whether they themselves realized it or
not. It is the temptation to which the monastic institution has all
too often succumbed, not the genuine essence of monasticism
itself, "an affirmation of the part (the monastic institution) over
the whole (Christ, Christian unity, the *emeth* of God). As long as
the vowed life is seen exclusively in this distorted perspective,
it will remain a cause of separation and disunity."[111] Echoing
(consciously or unconsciously) the language of his celebrated
"Fourth and Walnut" epiphany,[112] Merton rejects any perception
of the vowed life that fails to situate monasticism in the heart of
the Church and in the midst of the world loved and redeemed
by Christ. Such artificiality and elitism "will simply enable the
monk to affirm himself coldly as a separate kind of human being
and his community as a little, exclusive, perfectly pure and illuminated Church. His fidelity to his vows will confirm him in
this illusion of separateness and exclusive perfection. In so doing
it will short-circuit the personal sincerity of his well-meant faith
and close his Christian love in upon itself in a cloistered ghetto
of pious fantasies. In reality the vows are meant to open wide the
life of faith and love, not to close it in upon itself."[113] The key vow

110. *Contemplation in a World of Action*, 193.
111. *Contemplation in a World of Action*, 194.
112. See *Conjectures of a Guilty Bystander*, 140–42.
113. *Contemplation in a World of Action*, 194.

from this perspective, as Merton reiterates throughout these later essays, is *conversatio morum*, which he terms the "original expression of the Benedictine vows," the call to "a complete *metanoia*, a total conversion of all one's hopes and aspirations to the unfailing promise of God to send His Spirit and give joy and meaning to the ascetic life of the monk by unifying it in the wholeness of love." It is this holistic understanding, and experience, that must mark the life of the vows if they are to retain, or regain, their validity as an expression of authentic Christian discipleship: "The vows then should deliver the monk from fixation upon the partial, the limited, the provisional. They should unify his life in engagement to the definitive, the 'one thing necessary,' God present in His word and in His promise. They orient his life entirely to a wholeness and fulfillment, realized here and now in the darkness of faith."[114] He concludes these reflections with an honest expression of uncertainty as to whether "vows can still mean this to modern man" generally, but with the firm assertion that personally, "I still think they can, or I would not keep mine"[115]—though this in no way negates the possibility considered earlier of a viable monastic life without vows.

While this article is the most detailed and extensive consideration of the vows in the final period of Merton's life, its key insights are echoed and amplified in other essays from his final year. In "Problems and Prospects"[116] he notes that "one of the most disturbing things about the monastic institution for most of those moderns who have come seeking to give themselves to God in solitude, prayer and love, has been the current interpretation of religious vows, especially obedience."[117] Once again he insists that the purpose of vowed obedience is not simply the smooth functioning of an institutional machine but to "guarantee

114. *Contemplation in a World of Action*, 194–95.
115. *Contemplation in a World of Action*, 195.
116. *Contemplation in a World of Action*, 3–25; the first version of this article, which remained unpublished during Merton's lifetime, is dated December 1967.
117. *Contemplation in a World of Action*, 18.

. . . the monk's charismatic inner liberty"[118] by freeing him both from the sterile routines of a superficial society and from the illusions of his own egotism so that he can be drawn into "the lucid and terrible darkness of a contemplation that no tongue can explain and no rationalization can account for."[119] In "Renewal and Discipline"[120] he points out that the traditional "ascesis of virginity" associated with vowed chastity "is not the only formula for monastic ascesis and perfection," citing the Hindu pattern by which the householder takes up the "solitary and ascetic life of prayer" once his or her children have grown up and left home. He suggests that in the Christian tradition as well there could be some who might move from the married state to "a different kind of life, more solitary and disciplined and perhaps in some sense monastic," who precisely because of their life experience "would probably make very good 'monks'—perhaps much better ones than their children."[121]

It is particularly on the vow of *conversatio morum* that Merton reflects, once again, most memorably and most meaningfully at the end of his life. In the seminal late essay "Final Integration,"[122]

118. *Contemplation in a World of Action*, 14.

119. *Contemplation in a World of Action*, 24.

120. *Contemplation in a World of Action*, 98–116; in a journal entry of February 13, 1968, Merton notes that he has finished the first draft of this article but that more remains to be done (*Other Side of the Mountain*, 56). It was first published posthumously as "Renewal and Discipline in the Monastic Life" in *Cistercian Studies*, 5 (1970), 3–18.

121. *Contemplation in a World of Action*, 107–108.

122. *Contemplation in a World of Action*, 205–17; first published as "Final Integration—Toward a 'Monastic Therapy'" in *Monastic Studies*, 6 (1968), 87–99. Merton first proposes a review essay on a book by Reza Arasteh in a letter to *Monastic Studies* editor Basil DePinto on January 22, 1968 (*School of Charity*, 363), noting in his journal the following day that he is reading the book and finds it "very germane to monasticism" (*Other Side of the Mountain*, 45). According to his journal, he wrote the article on March 21, 1968 (*Other Side of the Mountain*, 70); see also Merton's January 26, 1968, and March 22, 1968 letters to Arasteh expressing his appreciation of the book (Thomas Merton, *The Hidden Ground of Love: Letters on Religious Experience and Social Concerns*, ed. William H. Shannon [New York: Farrar, Straus and Giroux, 1985], 42).

drawing on the Persian-American psychoanalyst Reza Arasteh's book of the same title, Merton points out that the "idea of 'rebirth' and of life as a 'new man in Christ, in the Spirit,' of a 'risen life' in the Mystery of Christ or in the Kingdom of God, is fundamental to Christian theology and practice." Not only is it the basis of Christian baptism, but it is "central to that peculiar refinement of the theology of baptism which is the monastic *conversatio*—the vocation to a life especially dedicated to self-renewal, liberation from all sin, and the transformation of one's entire mentality 'in Christ.'"[123] In so far as monastic customs and structures hinder this rebirth, this transformation "to a new and more complete identity, and to a more profoundly fruitful existence in peace, in wisdom, in creativity, in love,"[124] they inhibit the full realization of the vow of conversion of manners. The purpose of any authentic monastic renewal, therefore, must be above all to assist in reaching "the real aim of that monastic *conversatio* which we have not only mentally approved but actually vowed. We have dedicated ourselves to rebirth, to growth, to final maturity and integration. Monastic renewal means a reshaping of structures so that they will not only permit such growth but favor and encourage it in everyone."[125]

This is almost, but not quite, Merton's final word on the true purpose of the vows in general and of *conversatio morum* in particular. In "Marxism and Monastic Perspectives," the talk he gave on the last day of his life, he returns to the topic in the context of his conversations with the Dalai Lama: "He started asking about the vows, and I did not quite know what he was getting at. Then he said: 'Well, to be precise, what do your vows oblige you to do? Do they simply constitute an agreement to stick around for life in the monastery? Or do they imply a commitment to a life of progress up certain mystical stages?' I sort of hemmed and hawed a bit, and said: 'Well, no, that's not quite

123. *Contemplation in a World of Action*, 206–207.
124. *Contemplation in a World of Action*, 208.
125. *Contemplation in a World of Action*, 216.

what the vows are all about.' But it was interesting to see that this is what he thought the vows *should* be about." Merton goes on to imply that it is what he too thinks the vows, and specifically the vow of *conversatio morum*, should be about: "When you stop and think a little bit about St. Benedict's concept of *conversio morum*, that most mysterious of our vows, which is actually the most essential, I believe, it can be interpreted as a commitment to total inner transformation of one sort or another—a commitment to become a completely new man. It seems to me that that could be regarded as the end of the monastic life, and that no matter where one attempts to do this, that remains the essential thing."[126] As he was about to reach the end of his own monastic life, halfway around the world from the monastery where he had attempted to live out, as well as to form others in living out, this process of total inner transformation, in response to a query from a monastic leader of a completely different tradition, Merton gives his audience and his readers an apt and accurate summation, with respect to the vows and the life they define, of what his study and his experience have taught him "remains the essential thing."

* * * * * * *

The text of the conferences on the vows is extant in two complete versions and one partial version. First in importance, and in time, is Merton's own typescript, with extensive handwritten additions and revisions, along with changes made during the original process of composing, which was evidently done directly on the typewriter. This version, preserved in the archives of the Thomas Merton Center at Bellarmine University in Louisville, KY, consists of a total of 233 pages, entitled AN INTRODUCTION TO THE LIFE OF THE VOWS. The main sequence is a series of 221 pages, with consecutive numbering, beginning on page 2 and running through page 217; the discrepancy is accounted for

126. Thomas Merton, *The Asian Journal*, ed. Naomi Burton Stone, Brother Patrick Hart and James Laughlin (New York: New Directions, 1973), 337.

by the fact that two consecutive pages are numbered 202, that the originally unnumbered page following page 37 is given the handwritten number 37a, and that on two other pages duplicate numbers are altered to become 108a and 110a. Of these pages, six (40, 47, 48, 50, 105, 106) are handwritten, all the rest typed. The running heads of the first three numbered pages (2–4) have "life of vows" preceding the number; subsequently, almost all pages read simply "vows" (usually "Vows" from page 54 onward) followed by the number. However, pages 26–32,[127] a section on "THE PASSION OF CHRIST" (perhaps initially composed as an independent conference) originally had a running head of "Passion" followed by its own pagination from 2 through 7, subsequently altered in various ways to fit sequentially with the "vows" pagination preceding and following.[128] The other twelve pages comprise material intended for insertion: 4a, a handwritten page on the nature of the person,[129] and 4b, a typed page on *"The structure of the moral life,"*[130] are additions immediately preceding the section on the passions; 4c, a typed page on patristic and early Cistercian anthropology, continued on its verso side,[131] was inserted shortly after the beginning of the section on the passions in the second version of the text, to be described below; 8a, a typed page on *"The effects of love,"*[132] is marked for insertion by a marginal note on page 8 to replace two cancelled sentences; page 34a,

---

127. Pages 65–80 in this edition.

128. On the first page, originally without a running head, "Vows 26" is written in; on the second, "7" is added after "Passion 2" without further alteration; on the third, "Passion" is enclosed in parentheses and preceded by "Vows," and "28" is added after cancelled "3"; on subsequent pages, the original running head and pagination is cancelled and replaced by "Vows" and the appropriate page number, though originally the fifth page had no running head and the subsequent pages were numbered "5" and "6" then altered by hand to "6" and "7" before being cancelled and replaced by "Vows 31" and "Vows 32".

129. Pages 14–15 in this edition.

130. Pages 16–17 in this edition.

131. Pages 18–21 in this edition.

132. Pages 28–31 in this edition.

a typed page on *"Self-Surrender,"*[133] is clearly an insert because handwritten additions on the verso of page 34 are marked for insertion on page 35 rather than on this page that now faces 34v; after page 53 are found two handwritten, unnumbered pages, the first, headed "(Vocations—cont'd)," on *"The Spirit of Our Order,"*[134] the second, headed *"States of Life Appendix—Contempt for the World";*[135] these in turn are followed by four typed pages forming a separate section entitled "ABNEGATION"[136] with its own running head and pagination on the second through fourth pages; finally, 208a, a handwritten page of quotations from Stoic texts,[137] is marked for insertion by the typed note on page 208: "(Copy here *Stoic Texts on Stability* see p. 208a)".

The second version of the text is the mimeographed copy, entitled *"An Introduction to the Life of the Vows,"* included in volume 14 of "Collected Essays," the 24-volume bound set of published and unpublished materials assembled at the Abbey of Gethsemani and available both there and at the Thomas Merton Center, Bellarmine University, Louisville, KY. It consists of a total of 307 pages: four unnumbered table of contents pages; an unnumbered first page followed by numbered pages 2–72 with the running head "vows" (continued throughout); 72a, "TEXTS FROM ST. THOMAS ON THE STATE OF PERFECTION AND CONTEMPLATION"; 73–77; 77a–77b, on "The Spirit of Our Order"; 77c–77d, "States of Life Appendix—Contempt for the World"; 77e–77j, "Abnegation"; 78–134; 134 (inadvertently repeated)–286; "Appendix to the Vows" [1]–5.

Mention should also be made of a further, partial version of the text. At some point the section from the beginning of "The Vows in Particular" to the conclusion of the material on obedience[138] was retyped on stencils and mimeographed; almost

---

133. Pages 86–88 in this edition.
134. Pages 139–40 in this edition.
135. Pages 141–43 in this edition.
136. Pages 143–51 in this edition.
137. Page 463 in this edition.
138. Pages 234–74 in this edition.

certainly it was copied from the full mimeograph, to which it often corresponds line for line in the early pages (when the later pages of the full mimeo switch from elite to pica type, this correspondence is no longer possible). This version omits the heading "Part II (b)" and the number "2" immediately following and is numbered 1–23, but it is otherwise virtually identical in text to the full mimeo for these pages. The purpose of the reproduction of this section by itself is unknown. It of course has no independent textual authority.

For most of the text, the full mimeograph is simply copied from the typescript, and except for material found only in this version—the table of contents, the appendix (the United States bishops' November 1960 statement on personal responsibility, preceded by Merton's brief preface), and the page of texts from the *Summa* of St. Thomas that is not found in the typescript[139]—it has no independent textual authority. However, in the first part of the mimeograph version, there are more than two hundred additions and alterations, many of which are of substantive significance and can be considered with assurance as authorial. For example, the sentence "This conception has nothing to do with a truly religious outlook on life" on page 3 of the mimeograph[140] is not found in Merton's typescript, one of the numerous additions that must have come from the author himself. These changes disappear around page 65 of the mimeo, when a different typewriter begins to be used.

The explanation for this anomaly is not evident. The simplest explanation would be that Merton began by typing the stencils for the mimeograph himself, making changes as he went along, and that only later did he turn over the typing to novices, his usual procedure in other sets of conferences. However, the textual evidence makes this very unlikely: the typewriter used for mimeo pages 1–64 does not seem to be the same one used for the typescript; the spelling of certain words (e.g., "fulfill" rather

139. Pages 127–30 in this edition.
140. Page 10 in this edition.

than "fulfil"; "indiscreet" rather than "indiscrete") do not reflect
Merton's usual (British-influenced) orthography; and it seems
highly unlikely that Merton himself would have typed "(insert)"
preceding the material on patristic anthropology on page 9 of
the mimeograph[141] or misplaced the insert from page 18v of the
typescript on page 29 of the mimeo.[142] Perhaps the most plausible
explanation is that the novice typist for the early sections worked
not from the ribbon copy of the typescript but from a carbon on
which Merton had made numerous substantive additions and
alterations.[143] Whatever the explanation, the evidence suggests
that the mimeo version of these early pages of the text includes
authorial revisions, and these have been incorporated into the
text of this edition.

However, this does not mean that the mimeograph has become the sole copy text for pages 7 to 114, for it is also evident that
for these pages, as for the rest of the text, Merton subsequently
made numerous, generally minor, alterations, presumably in
the course of presenting the conferences a second time. These
changes are not reflected in the mimeograph, which was not
retyped to incorporate these alterations, but they are included
in the present version. Thus the copy text for this edition of *The
Life of the Vows* varies according to the section: for those pages
found only in the mimeograph, that is the copy text; for the first
114 pages, the copy text is the mimeograph supplemented by
additional handwritten alterations found only in the typescript;
for the rest of the text, the typescript is the copy text.

141. Page 18 in this edition.

142. Page 53 in this edition: "It is especially . . . March 1957)."

143. Another possibility, that the material was typed by Sr. Thérèse Lent-
foehr, who had earlier typed the stencils for Merton's six sets of "Monastic Orientation" notes (dating from 1950 through 1955, the period just prior to and during
his tenure as master of students) and who at about this time would do the same
for his "Liturgical Feasts and Seasons" conferences (see *Cassian and the Fathers,*
lx, n. 63 for details), seems to be ruled out by the fact that there is no reference to
the vows notes in any of Merton's correspondence with Sr. Thérèse.

The textual notes found in Appendix A thus consist of three lists: first, all typescript alterations also found in the mimeograph, including both handwritten changes and on-line corrections made in the process of typing (i.e., cancelling a word or phrase and immediately substituting another); second, all alterations accepted as authorial found in the mimeograph but not in the typescript; third, all alterations present only in the typescript. Thus the interested reader is able to distinguish among the various alterations made by Merton at different stages of the process of composition, incorporated in this edition into a definitive text that is not identical to either of the preceding versions.

All substantive additions made to the text, in order to turn elliptical or fragmentary statements into complete sentences, are included in braces, as are the few emendations incorporated directly into the text, so that the reader can always determine exactly what Merton himself wrote. No effort is made to reproduce Merton's rather inconsistent punctuation, paragraphing, abbreviations and typographical features; a standardized format for these features is established that in the judgment of the editor best represents a synthesis of Merton's own practice and contemporary usage: for example, all Latin passages are italicized unless specific parts of a longer passage are underlined by Merton, in which case the underlined section of the passage is in roman type; all other passages underlined by Merton are italicized; words in upper case in the text are printed in small caps; periods and commas are uniformly included within quotation marks; patterns of abbreviation and capitalization, very inconsistent in the copy text, are regularized. All references to primary and secondary sources are cited in the notes. Untranslated Latin passages in the original text are left in Latin but translated by the editor in the notes. Scriptural citations are taken from the Douai-Rheims-Challoner version of the Bible, the edition Merton himself regularly used.

Also included as a second appendix is a table correlating the written text and the taped lectures, which facilitates comparison of Merton's version of the material as published in this edition with the conferences as actually delivered to the novices. Finally, a list of suggestions for further reading is included as a third appendix, consisting first of other sources in Merton's published works where the subject of this volume is discussed, followed by a list of important recent studies on the same subject, that will provide helpful updating on material discussed by Merton.

* * * * * * *

In conclusion I would like to express my gratitude to all those who have made this volume possible:

- to the Trustees of the Merton Legacy Trust, Peggy Fox, Anne McCormick and Mary Somerville, for permission to publish *The Life of the Vows* conferences;
- to the late Robert E. Daggy, former director of the Thomas Merton Center, Bellarmine College (now University), Louisville, KY, for first alerting me to the project of editing Merton's monastic conferences, and for his encouragement in this and other efforts in Merton studies;
- to Brother Patrick Hart, ocso, the founding editor of the Monastic Wisdom Series, for his friendship and guidance in the publication of this series of volumes of Thomas Merton's monastic conferences;
- to Brother Simeon Leiva, ocso, the present editor of the Monastic Wisdom Series, for his careful editorial guidance and continued encouragement in publishing these conference volumes;
- to Abbot Augustine Roberts, ocso, whose successive editions of *Centered on Christ: A Guide to Monastic Profession* have so beautifully carried the legacy of Thomas Merton's vows conferences up to the present day, for graciously accepting an invitation to provide the preface for this volume;
- to Paul M. Pearson, director and archivist of the Merton Center, and Mark C. Meade, assistant archivist, for their gracious hospitality and valued assistance during my research visits to the Center;

- to Colleen Stiller, production manager at Liturgical Press, for guiding this and previous volumes of Merton's conferences through the publication process with grace and efficiency;
- to the Gannon University Research Committee, which provided a grant that allowed me to pursue research on this project at the Merton Center and at various libraries;
- to Mary Beth Earll of the interlibrary loan department of the Nash Library, Gannon University, for once again providing invaluable assistance by locating and procuring various obscure volumes;
- to library staff of the Hesburgh Library of the University of Notre Dame and the Institute of Cistercian Studies Collection at the Waldo Library, Western Michigan University, especially Neil Chase, for assistance in locating important materials in their collections;
- again and always to my wife, Suzanne and our children for their continual love, support and encouragement in this and other projects.

AN INTRODUCTION
TO THE LIFE OF THE VOWS

INDEX OF CONTENTS

6

The Life of the Vows

AN INTRODUCTION TO THE LIFE OF THE VOWS

{Part I:}

If we want to live our vows well, we must understand them. If we want to understand them, we must recall the basic principles of Christian theology about man and his striving for his last end. If we unconsciously have a view of man's life which is the view of modern materialism, or if our picture of man is too much colored by materialism and pragmatism, we will never really understand the vows, or the life of the vows. This is perhaps one reason for many failures in the religious life.

The modern view of man:

1) The question of finality is ignored. If the notion of God is tolerated, it is left to the subjective choice and needs of individuals. There is no definite conception of the ultimate purpose of man's existence—the world is taken to be eternal, subject to the determinism of blind physical forces. In this world man exists for himself. He dominates and uses the world, yet the question of his real moral freedom is ignored. He too is more or less at the mercy of blind determinism.

2) Speculatively, there exists only the greatest confusion about man, his nature and the reason for his existence. Practically, the answer is usually pragmatic: true and false, good and evil are reduced to what works and what does not work, what serves a purpose here and now and what does not. {There are} no fixed standards of value. Everything fluctuates—how does one judge the value of a man?

What *can he do*? What can he *produce*? How much *is he worth*? In the old-fashioned standards of the nineteenth century, how much money has he been able to make? In modern standards, how necessary is he to an organization, to a business, to society? To what extent is he irreplaceable? To what extent does he possess an efficiency that cannot be duplicated? This "efficiency" in turn is measured by what? by the man's capacity to produce something that everybody needs or wants. We live in a society that wants to be a society of "producers"—in fact, there are in it an enormous number of unproductive persons who have nevertheless made themselves indispensable. But ideally, everything is geared for production—and consumption. In this society man pretends to exist for man—for the sake of humanity—for the sake of a myth of universal well-being to be achieved by scientific techniques of production. In actual fact, man exists for *things*. In our society, we reverence those who seem to *do* the most and *have* the most. There is still a shadow of reverence for personality. In Communist society, everything is centered on man's usefulness as a cog in the machine—the hero is the man who can most approximate the qualities of a machine—tireless efficiency. Man exists for the sake of things, objects, goods, machines. In modern society, when a man ceases to be a producer, he is nothing. In totalitarian states, there is no hesitation on this point. As soon as a person is considered for some reason unproductive, or as soon as his product is not desired—as soon as his contribution is not wanted—he himself can be wiped out. Modern man depends entirely on what he can *do*, on his ability to "put himself across." In this of course there is a large element of hazard too, because the desirability of this or that type, this or that ability, varies with ever-changing conditions and circumstances.

How does the concept of dedication enter into the modern view of man? Is dedication possible with such a view of life? in the strict sense, no! In the strict sense, dedication means the commitment of man's whole life to something ontologically higher than himself. This can only be a person—GOD. But in a diminished sense, yes—modern society encourages man to dedicate himself to *tasks*, to *things*, to spend himself as an instrument of production. In return, he will be surrounded with glamor and will have the choice of the best that is produced.

How can the modern concept pervert the notion of religious dedication? The religious can conceive himself as dedicated to a task, to a job. He makes vows in order to consecrate himself entirely to a certain work. God remains more or less in the background. The vows are made to God, of course, but what matters is turning out a certain result. The religious then values his life not by what he *is* but by what he *does*. Hence the religious tends to measure his value by *what kind of a job* he has in the community—but this is really accidental in so far as the vows are concerned. The vows are to enable us to *be* someone, not to do something. The religious may lose sight of the fact that he lives his vows well if he becomes a man of God, if he *is* not something but someone, and someone who loves God and is loved by Him. What he does must flow from what he is, not vice versa. He does not make himself better by what he produces. God, on the other hand, does not want our works—He wants our love. That is to say, He wants *ourselves*. He does not seek the things we have made, the results of our efforts; He seeks the person that we *are*, in order that we may share His life and His freedom and His love for all eternity. The vows are *orientated to the next life*—we must get rid of a view that seeks happiness, implicitly, in the present life.

What God seeks of us is *His own image in ourselves*. This image is not something that we can produce by our own efforts. Indeed we do not have to produce it. It is already there. It is the simple reality of our true being as sons of God by grace. Our job in life is not so much to produce anything, as *to be what we are supposed to be*, to let the divine image come out and manifest itself in our lives by the *way in which we live*.

The life of the vows is not ordered to producing anything special, or at least not primarily. It is supposed rather to create certain conditions under which we live in a certain way which is most adapted to make us grow in likeness to God. The life of the vows is a life of divine sonship, a life in which we deepen our realization of our kinship with God by deepening our holiness, our likeness to Him, our union with His will.

The concept of man as the image of God is incomprehensible to modern thought. The very idea of God, for modern materialism, is at best a subjective need of man, a sort of illusion that is psychologically necessary for the happiness of some—and hence it can be accepted in so far as it "works"—in so far as it "produces a desirable effect." No question {is raised} as to whether or not religion is "true." This conception has nothing to do with a truly religious outlook on life.

In order to understand the vows, we must look at the Catholic conception of man, and of his activity. We will briefly summarize some basic ideas from St. Thomas.

The principle of finality: instead of trying to ascertain what man is by observing what he does (which is the approach of natural science), theology tries to judge man's actions by their relation to *what man is. Man's being and his activity are only really understandable in the light of his last end.* Man's very being, his freedom, his intelligence, are orientated to some end beyond and above himself, and in attaining this end he becomes fully what he is meant to be. Man does not have all the perfection of being that is necessary for him, here on earth. *He is tending to a greater perfection of being*—he has an appetite for that perfection—he strives for it whether he is conscious of the fact or not. His very acts of volition express his inescapable desire for fulfillment in the good—or rather for a full realization of the good in himself—by union with its objective reality.

Hence, we have in man a power by which reality can be apprehended as true and as valuable (the *intelligence*) and another power by which he can drive onward to union with that reality by "conformity" and, so to speak, by "dedication"—that is to say, by an activity which fully testifies to his union and conformity with what is, causing all the acts of his other faculties to conform to reality. This second faculty is his *free will*.

St. Thomas bases his whole moral theology on the following philosophical principles:

a) *Omnia agentia necesse est agere propter finem* (I-II, q. 1, a. 2).[1] "Everything that acts, acts with an end in view."[2] Agents that are

---

1. Thomas Aquinas, *Summa Theologiae, Prima Secundae* (*Sancti Thomae Aquinatis Doctoris Angelici Ordinis Praedicatorum Opera Omnia, Secundum Impressionem Petri Fiaccadori Parmae 1852–1873 Photolithographice Reimpressa*, 25 vols. [New York: Misurgia, 1948], 2.2).

2. Here and elsewhere the translations from Aquinas are Merton's own.

not free are determined to their end by natural inclination, which in turn is governed by a higher freedom, the will of God, the Author of nature. *Free agents* are masters of their own acts and direct themselves toward their own end. They have the power of choice and the ability to direct their whole lives toward reality or unreality, fulfillment or unfulfillment (READ Ecclesiasticus 18:14-22[3]).

b) Free agents, acting *in view of a good which they choose,* act morally or immorally. Moral action derives its character (*species*) from the end to which it is directed (I-II, q. 1, a. 3–4).[4]

c) There is only one last end for man, and all secondary ends that he seeks are sought in view of that one last end (I-II, q. 1, a. 7).[5] (This is very important in view of the moral anarchy of modern thought. Existentialism, for instance, teaches that man creates his own values and his own ends simply by arbitrarily willing this rather than that. The basic value for existentialism is man's arbitrary freedom—there is no objective norm against which that freedom can be checked; hence there is really no purpose in anything. "Moral" life is simply the purposeless and arbitrary exercise of freedom. {There is} no finality. But the truth is that everyone, no matter how much in error, no matter how perverse, no matter what may be the end he thinks he is seeking, or even if he thinks that he seeks no end at all, is always inevitably seeking the one last end to which we all aspire—there is

---

3. "He hath mercy on him that receiveth the discipline of mercy, and that maketh haste in his judgments. My son, in thy good deeds, make no complaint, and when thou givest any thing, add not grief by an evil word. Shall not the dew assuage the heat? so also the good word is better than the gift. Lo, is not a word better than a gift? but both are with a justified man. A fool will upbraid bitterly: and a gift of one ill taught consumeth the eyes. Before judgment prepare thee justice, and learn before thou speak. Before sickness take a medicine, and before judgment examine thyself, and thou shalt find mercy in the sight of God. Humble thyself before thou art sick, and in the time of sickness shew thy conversation. Let nothing hinder thee from praying always, and be not afraid to be justified even to death: for the reward of God continueth for ever." All Scripture passages are quoted from the Douai-Rheims-Challoner translation, which Merton himself regularly uses.

4. Aquinas, *Opera Omnia*, 2.2–4.

5. Aquinas, *Opera Omnia*, 2.5–6.

no other. Even the sinner seeks God in his sin, without knowing it—and the deviation of sin comes from the fact that the sinner *places the last end in something where it is not.*) The real moral problem is not to get the will of man to tend to its last end *but to tend to it effectively*, TO SEEK THE GOOD WHERE IT IS REALLY TO BE FOUND. There is no problem about getting man to seek the good (subjectively)—basically all seek the good, whether they mean to or not. The problem is to get them to seek the true good, rather than false goods, and to aim for the ultimate good, rather than an intermediate good conceived as an end in itself. Further, the basic problem is to get man to seek *the good willed for him by his God*—and not the good that he wills for himself apart from God. This can never be a true good.

d) *The last end of man is beatitude.* The ultimate end of man, the good willed for him by God, the good that man seeks in everything, either rightly or wrongly, knowingly or unknowingly, is not something that we know merely by our natural reason. "Eye hath not seen, ear hath not heard, nor hath it entered into the heart of man to conceive those things which God hath prepared for those that love Him."[6] Man's supernatural end can only be known to him *if it is revealed by God.* (READ John 17:1-3[7]—eternal life given us in and by Jesus.)

e) *God Himself is our beatitude.* "I am thy reward exceeding great."[8] Objectively, beatitude is God Himself. In us, beatitude is something created—a created participation in the essential beatitude of God (I-II, q. 3, a. 1).[9] This created participation in the divine beatitude is *the ultimate perfection, the ultimate act of man*, the final culminating perfection of his being, in which he fully

6. 1 Cor. 2:9.
7. "These things Jesus spoke, and lifting up his eyes to heaven, he said: Father, the hour is come, glorify thy Son, that thy Son may glorify thee. As thou hast given him power over all flesh, that he may give eternal life to all whom thou hast given him. Now this is eternal life: That they may know thee, the only true God, and Jesus Christ, whom thou hast sent."
8. Gen. 15:1.
9. Aquinas, *Opera Omnia*, 2.12.

and eternally *is*, is perfectly, wholly, completely and indefectibly actualized, not in himself only but above all IN GOD—by being perfectly one with God, by being, as it were, transformed in God so that though the two natures remain distinct, man and God are as fully as possible "one being" by love.

f) *This ultimate perfection of man is union with God by contemplation, in the Beatific Vision.* Contemplation here is used in the supereminent sense, not as it is known here on earth, but far more perfectly—our whole being and our whole life will know God in God by being suffused, as it were, and transformed in God as wood is filled and transformed by flame when it burns.[10] "The intellect of man contemplating the truth of God has all its good in itself and from this good the whole man is perfected and made good through and through" (I-II, q. 3, a. 5, ad. 2).[11]

g) Man himself is not his own ultimate end—he does not seek beatitude for his own perfection and happiness alone— GOD IS MAN'S ULTIMATE END. By union with God, man finds his ultimate fulfillment in the fact that GOD IS PERFECTLY GLORIFIED IN HIM. This is man's true end, the glory of God—not only in us as individuals but in all as members of Christ. The true end of man is not his own individual beatitude alone but the glory of God in the blessedness of the *whole Christ*. What has been said so far of beatitude is still insufficient, for it does not enter into the full perspectives of the mystery of Christ. But it will serve our purpose for the moment.

h) *This ultimate perfection is not possible in the present life.* The end towards which our life and activity is ordered is outside and above the world we live in, and in an altogether different realm. We are here getting further and further away from the context of modern pragmatic thought, which judges things purely and

10. The reference is to St. John of the Cross, *The Dark Night*, Bk. 2, c. 10.1–2 (*The Complete Works of Saint John of the Cross*, ed. and trans. E. Allison Peers, 3 vols. [Westminster, MD: Newman Press, 1946], 1.429–30).

11. "*Sed intellectus speculativus habet bonum in seipso, scilicet contemplationem veritatis; et si illud bonum sit perfectum, ex eo totus homo perficitur, et fit bonus*" (Aquinas, *Opera Omnia*, 2.16).

simply with a view to their usefulness in the present life. For the
Christian, any sacrifice of present and visible things that will help
us to attain God more perfectly in the next life is worthwhile. For
the pragmatist, it is senseless. However, even in the present life
there is possible a certain remote participation in the blessedness
of the saints—and this precisely can be found in contemplation
of the divine truth and in the life of virtue. This fact can be seen
and judged experimentally, and it gives even unbelievers an
indication that faith is "worthwhile."

i) *Beatitude cannot be acquired by natural means, but nevertheless,
though it is a gift of God and depends on His grace, we arrive at it by
our own actions.* That is to say, we merit beatitude by living according to the divine will, which has but one purpose—to bring us to
union with God (I-II, q. 5, a. 7). "God alone possesses beatitude
simply by being Himself without any other operation. For man,
beatitude is reached by many actions, which are called merits."[12]

j) *What are the actions by which man arrives at beatitude? They
must be* HUMAN ACTS, *free acts, more precisely acts of choice, that is
to say, acts of will.* WE ATTAIN OUR LAST END, UNION WITH GOD,
ONLY BY FREELY AND DELIBERATELY CHOOSING (WITH THE AID OF
GRACE) THOSE THINGS WHICH LEAD US TRULY TO OUR LAST END,
i.e., THE THINGS WILLED BY GOD FOR US. Hence, we should look
a little more closely at the action of our will and at our acts of
choice and see by what steps we come to choose one particularly
effective way of attaining union with God—viz., *by religious vows.*

Before we consider the nature of man's acts, let us remember
who it is that acts. It is the PERSON. All substances are *individual.* But
there is in the individual of rational nature a *special perfection of
individuality*, a more perfect kind of individuality—personality—
characterized by the fact that here the individual nature is *free
and intelligent and the master of his own acts.* The concept of person,

---

12. "*Unde solius Dei proprium est quod ad beatitudinem non moveatur per aliquam
operationem praecedentem. . . . homines autem consequuntur ipsam multis motibus
operationum, qui merita dicuntur*" (Aquinas, *Opera Omnia*, 2.28).

then, implies a special value—here is not merely a thing or an animal moved by external forces, determined by instincts—but above all these, self-determining, capable of responsibility. The person is responsible for freely working out his own destiny. But he is held responsible for using the means and aids, given by God, without which his salvation is impossible. Personality—liberty—is a treasure which is given to be increased and developed by union with the Divine Person of the Incarnate Word, Jesus, our Model and Savior. Our personality is a faint reflection of the Person of the Word, the natural Image of the Father.

How does the person act as his own master?

1) His natural endowments equip him for this. Under the direction of his *intelligence*, which sees the good, man's *will* uses his *faculties*, his *organs*, his entire being, and these *carry out* the commands of the will. *Our salvation and fulfillment depend on the use of our faculties, habits, etc., by the will.*

2) His supernatural subjection to grace and to the will of God is, however, necessary for right order, because otherwise he cannot master himself and his acts perfectly. The passions etc. master him, and he is to that extent less a person. To sin is not only to resist God but also to destroy our own true selves and our true destiny as free persons.

3) Only ideally is man fully and perfectly in command of himself in this life. *In fact, this life is given us to acquire mastery* and to fully work out our destiny, becoming the persons we are intended to be.

4) The vows give us the most perfect means of using the talent of personality by consecrating it to Christ—especially obedience, which inserts our liberty into the order decreed by Him. The life of the vows fixes our determination to make the sacrifices demanded by Him. "He that would save his life will lose it; he that would lose his life for my sake shall save it."[13] With our

13. Lk. 9:24; cf. also Mt. 10:39, 16:25; Mk. 8:35.

religious vows, we not only resolve to do this in a moment of fervor, but we bind ourselves to keep this resolution until death.

The Structure of the Moral Life

Man fulfills his destiny by free supernatural acts which lead him to union with God and to the beatific vision in which he is most fully himself, most completely perfected as a person in the image and likeness of God, most capable of giving God all the glory he owes Him. Man does not gain heaven or fulfill his destiny by one or two choices, but by a whole lifetime of right choices. But in living his life, he meets with obstacles within himself and outside himself. Also, he finds helps within himself and receives help from outside. In the present order of things in which we have to work out our salvation, the will does not perform its function in a moral solitude, under perfect conditions, but surrounded by temptations and supported by helps, confronted by enemies and sustained by friends. Moral choice is not always an easy thing; sometimes it is extraordinarily difficult. Our freedom is not sufficient unto itself—it has to be developed and educated—it has to prove itself and mature in interaction with other freedoms. Over all and in all is the providential wisdom of God guiding and educating and forming the freedom of His sons.

Let us outline the structure of the moral life as St. Thomas studies it in the *Prima Secundae*:

1. He studies beatitude and its nature.[14]

2. Then comes the *Treatise on Human Acts*—by which we attain beatitude.

a) First he studies *the will and how it acts*[15]—voluntary acts are those which are human in the strict sense. THE WILL USES ALL THE OTHER FACULTIES.

14. *Prima Secundae*, qq. 1–5 (Aquinas, *Opera Omnia*, 2.1–29).
15. *Prima Secundae*, qq. 6–21 (Aquinas, *Opera Omnia*, 2.29–88).

b) The *passions*[16]—human acts in so far as they are voluntary—proceed from man's soul as the vital principle of his *bodily* life. Passions are acts which man performs in common with other animals, sometimes involuntary—but they are to be ordered to guidance and command of reason and free will.

c) Then follow the *interior principles of human acts*, namely, HABITS:[17] (1) good—virtues; (2) bad—vices. After this we confront the reality of disorder in human activity—SIN—which turns man away from God as his last end to a false end. This in turn requires rectification in *punishment* and *conversion*—penance and reparation, reorientating man to God. The effects of sin weaken our freedom and blind our intelligence, also corrupt the will with malice, perverting the passions with weakness and concupiscence. Good habits or *virtues* must be cultivated by repeated acts of choice, in union with grace, for man to attain his end.

d) Finally, there are *exterior principles of human acts*:[18]

(1) *Laws* or norms set down by God to give objective rule for conduct and choice.

(2) GRACE—a principle from outside our nature but operating within us as a second and higher nature to supernaturalize, divinize and perfect our good choices and to develop our life of virtue on a superhuman level—with infused virtues, gifts of the Holy Ghost, etc.

We will study first of all the passions, which the will must use, then the habits which the will must acquire, the virtues which it must cultivate, the laws which it must follow, the grace which it must receive from God. Then last of all we will consider the choice proposed to some souls by God *of dedicating their life to Him by vow* after having seen in some detail just how the will acts in making a choice.

16. *Prima Secundae*, qq. 22–48 (Aquinas, *Opera Omnia*, 2.88–169).
17. *Prima Secundae*, qq. 49–89 (Aquinas, *Opera Omnia*, 2.169–330).
18. *Prima Secundae*, qq. 90–114 (Aquinas, *Opera Omnia*, 2.330–462).

THE PASSIONS

We have seen that our life is a tending to our last end, union with God, which is to be attained by our *free acts of choice* guided by actual grace and informed by charity. These acts of choice are acts of *will* (their interior principle) moved by *grace* ({their} exterior principle). But we must remember that there are other human acts which are distinct from voluntary acts, which are meant to be ordered to the norms of reason and of faith by our free choice—they are acts which can be controlled by the will but are not themselves acts of the will. They become voluntary by their union with the will. These acts are the *passions*.

If we are to understand fully man's moral activity, we cannot leave out the passions. True human activity is the activity of man as a composite of body and soul. The acts of his spiritual soul are voluntary; those of his animal soul are passions. The acts of man's animal nature are meant, under guidance of reason and free will, to contribute to man's voluntary search for God and to aid him in reaching divine union. *A false view*, {seen in} stoic moralism, Jansenism, etc., {is to} treat the passions as evil and as *per se* obstacles to moral activity—they must be suppressed by the will. {The} only moral activity is voluntary and spiritual. But the passions are *not* diseases of the soul. To regard the passions as essentially evil is heretical. The passions are human acts—acts of the soul in so far as it informs a body, acts of the sensible appetite, informed by sense knowledge. Our nature is inclined to sensible good. This basic inclination is subconscious—{it} is not yet a passion. Nature is inclined to act—by passion it acts.

It might throw some light on our consideration of the passions if we look at the ancient, Patristic notion of man—a notion which corresponds with that of St. Paul, for instance, in the New Testament. Furthermore, it is the view of man held by our Cistercian Fathers, particularly of William of St. Thierry, who got it from the Greek Fathers. The Fathers looked at man's soul from three viewpoints: there is indeed only one soul, but it has three aspects, three ways of being. St. Paul speaks in 1 Thessalonians 5:23 in the following words: "May the God of peace sanctify you in all things, that your whole *spirit* and *soul* and *body* may be preserved blameless in the coming of Our Lord Jesus Christ." The Fathers then distinguish the *anima*—the life principle of the body and the source of the operations of our sense nature, hence, the passions, etc.; {the} *animus*—the principle of freedom and rationality, the seat of thought, the mind; {and the} *spiritus*—the apex of the soul, the soul united with the Holy Spirit, divinized and supernaturalized by grace and love, the soul as the temple of God in which God dwells mystically, moves us to produce divine acts above and beyond our faculties. (?) Hence, to describe man fully, in the state of grace intended for him by God, we have to say he is body, soul and the Holy Ghost. William of St. Thierry distinguishes the three degrees of the spiritual life according to whether one is predominantly: (1) *homo animalis* (*psuchikos*)—led by the passions (dominated by the *anima*); (2) *homo rationalis* (*gnostikos*)—led by reason (dominated by the *animus*); (3) *homo spiritualis* (*pneumatikos*)—led by the Holy Spirit (dominated by the *spiritus* or *pneuma*).[19] The purpose of the spiritual life is to bring us to the perfection of the third category in which all is love, all is moved by the Holy Spirit.

The life of the vows presupposes that one enters the monastery as an *animalis*. The practice of obedience and the submission to rule and authority leads these "animal" men to do good for which they have no spontaneous attraction, since they are more inclined to follow passion and the impressions of the moment. Guided and formed by obedience, the *animalis* becomes a *homo rationalis*, a man of virtue, with an enlightened and reasonable conscience, who is mature and free and in command of his actions and does the right thing according to the light of his reason and of faith. Finally, the Holy Spirit takes over, and the monk

---

19. William of St. Thierry, *Epistola ad Fratres de Monte Dei*, 1.5.12, in J. P. Migne, ed., *Patrologiae Cursus Completus, Series Latina*, 221 vols. (Paris: Garnier, 1844–1865), vol. 184, cols. 315C–316B (subsequently referred to as *PL* in text and notes); ET: *Golden Epistle* (*A Letter to the Brethren at Mont Dieu*), trans. Theodore Berkeley, ocso, Cistercian Fathers Series [CF], vol. 12 (Kalamazoo, MI: Cistercian Publications, 1976), 25.

then is elevated above the level of mere reason and acts by the law of divine love, in so far as he is prompted by the Holy Spirit. He is then in all things fully a child of God, a *homo spiritualis*, a *pneumatikos*.

One must be careful of the danger that confronts many after some time in religion. They grow to the stature of rational men, but afterwards, misguided by their passions and misled by pride and self-conceit, they imagine that the fancies and whims of passion (now more spiritualized) are the promptings of the Holy Ghost, and thus they become once more "animals," but this time in a much more dangerous way—cf. St. Paul: they aspire to whatever is lofty and sublime in the eyes of man, not apprehending the true wisdom of the Spirit which is the wisdom of humility and littleness. READ 1 Corinthians 1:26-31:[20] the foolish things of the world hath God chosen . . . Christ is made unto us wisdom . . . ; *idem* 2:7-9:[21] we speak wisdom among the perfect, yet not the wisdom of the world . . . but the wisdom of God which is hidden; *idem* 2:12-14:[22] we have received not the spirit of this world, but the Spirit that is of God . . . which things we speak

20. "For see your vocation, brethren, that there are not many wise according to the flesh, not many mighty, not many noble: But the foolish things of the world hath God chosen, that he may confound the wise; and the weak things of the world hath God chosen, that he may confound the strong. And the base things of the world, and the things that are contemptible, hath God chosen, and things that are not, that he might bring to nought things that are: That no flesh should glory in his sight. But of him are you in Christ Jesus, who of God is made unto us wisdom, and justice, and sanctification, and redemption; That, as it is written: He that glorieth, may glory in the Lord."

21. "But we speak the wisdom of God in a mystery, a wisdom which is hidden, which God ordained before the world, unto our glory: Which none of the princes of this world knew; for if they had known it, they would never have crucified the Lord of glory. But as it is written: That eye hath not seen, nor ear heard, neither hath it entered into the heart of man, what things God hath prepared for them that love him."

22. "Now we have received not the spirit of this world, but the Spirit that is of God: that we may know the things that are given us from God. Which things also we speak, not in the learned words of human wisdom; but in the doctrine of the Spirit, comparing spiritual things with spiritual. But the sensual man per-

not in the learned words of human wisdom . . . the *sensual man* [*animalis homo*] perceiveth not these things that are of the spirit . . . it is foolishness to him.

How passion acts: {by} *apprehension* of a sensible good by interior and exterior senses {and} "*appreciation*" of the good by {the} instinctive "*vis cogitativa*," an interior sense—like {the} animal "*estimativa*" (instinctive).[23] Modification of passion {takes place} by heredity, temperament, etc. *Regulation* of passion must come from above if it is to be a *human act*, and if it is to *fulfill itself naturally and properly*. (Passion can sometimes be so strong that it inhibits reason and freedom. Then it is not a human act, not free, not imputable unless indirectly voluntary.) If passion acts according to its own arbitrary laws, it is incomplete, unnatural, and will be frustrated in the long run. An involuntary act of passion is *per se* indifferent. *In order to fulfill itself, the act of passion must participate in the higher order of reason.* This participation must be free, not passive subjection to "tyrannical" power—*reason governs passion not as a slave but as a free collaborator*. (Reason and passion, spirit and body, should cooperate like man and wife; the relation is not that of master and slave.) St. Thomas says: "*Ad perfectionem boni*

---

ceiveth not these things that are of the Spirit of God; for it is foolishness to him, and he cannot understand, because it is spiritually examined."

23. See *Pars Prima*, q. 78, a. 4 (Aquinas, *Opera Omnia*, 1.307): "*Nam alia animalia percipiunt hujusmodi intentiones solum naturali quodam instinctu, homo autem per quamdam collationem. Et ideo quae in aliis animalibus dicitur* aestimativa naturalis, *in homine dicitur* cogitativa, *quae per collationem quamdam hujusmodi intentiones adinvenit*" ("For other animals perceive intentions of this sort by means of a certain natural instinct; the human being perceives them through a certain bringing together [of impressions]. And so what is called in other animals the natural estimative [power] is called in the human the cogitative, which discovers such intentions through this type of assembling"); also q. 81, a. 3 (Aquinas, *Opera Omnia*, 1.321): "*Loco autem aestimativae virtutis est in homine, sicut supra dictum est, qu. 78, art. 4, vis cogitativa, qui dicitur a quibusdam* ratio particularis; *eo quod est collativa intentionum individualium*" ("In place of the estimative power, there is in the human being, as was said above (q. 78, a. 4), the cogitative power, which is called by some the particular reason, because it is the bringing together of individual intentions").

moralis pertinet quod homo ad bonum moveatur non solum secundum voluntatem, sed etiam secundum sensitivum appetitum" (I-II, q. 24, a. 3)[24] (cf. St. Benedict, c. 7[25]). Hence, the passions must also play their part—*they must move us* in conquest for God.

How does reason govern passion?

a) by governing the *vis cogitativa* ({the} incarnation of reasonable judgement in a particular and concrete judgement);

b) by spiritualization of instinctive drives through participation in the freedom proper to the will.

In governing the passions, reason must respect them, or they will withdraw from its rule. When the passions act, they bring about a bodily change (respiration, circulation, glandular secretion, nervous reactions). Reason in turn can to some extent modify acts of passion by controlling these physiological factors. How? by mental and physical hygiene ({e.g.} breathing), ritual (cf. especially liturgy), right mortification. Reason should govern the passions from within—by their own immanent logic, not by arbitrary standards from without. If they are governed from within, the passions are fruitful, complete, satisfying, helpful to the soul, productive, joyful, producing peace, aiding virtue and giving glory to God. {Note} *the morality of antecedent and consequent passion*: consequent passion {leads to} joy in virtue {and} increases merit.

All the passions (there are eleven principal passions) are interrelated and united in LOVE, the most important of all the

24. "It belongs to the perfection of the moral good that man should be moved to good not only according to the will but also according to the sensitive appetite" (Aquinas, *Opera Omnia*, 2.95, which reads: ". . . *appetitum sensitivum* . . ."; emphasis added).

25. The reference is evidently to the conclusion of this chapter on the steps of humility, where St. Benedict says that when a monk has ascended to the highest stage of humility, the virtuous activity that was formerly done out of fear and through strenuous effort is now done without labor, as though naturally, according to habit ("*absque ullo labore velut naturaliter ex consuetudine*") (*The Rule of St. Benedict in Latin and English*, ed. and trans. Justin McCann, OSB [London: Burns, Oates, 1952], 48).

passions—concupiscible: LOVE, desire, joy, hate, flight, sorrow; irascible: hope {and} despair (difficult good), daring, fear {and} anger (difficult evil). *Omnes passiones ex amore causantur* (I-II, q. 25, a. 2).[26] Love is the source of all the passions. IF OUR LOVE (passion) IS SPIRITUALIZED BY REASON, GRACE AND THE THEOLOGICAL VIR- TUES, THEN OUR WHOLE LIFE WILL BE SPIRITUALIZED AND ALL OUR AFFECTIVE LIFE AND ALL OUR PASSIONS WILL CONVERGE UPON GOD AND TEND TO OUR LAST END, UNION WITH HIM AND HIS GLORY.

Application: it is already evident that the life of the vows is much concerned with man's affective life, with his passions. If we make certain vows, it is precisely in order to spiritualize the passions in the most effective possible way and make them con- tribute to our consecrated service of God in this life and our union with Him in the next. The success of our religious life depends on a right understanding of our nature and particularly of our passions. To make vows as if we expected that the vows would abolish the acts of the passions is to invite certain failure. (Here {it is} worthwhile {to include} a few remarks on the passion of love and its effects [I-II, q. 26, 27, 28[27]].)

The Passion of LOVE: it is very important to understand the passion of love, the queen of all the passions. St. Augustine said, "*Amor meus pondus meum*":[28] man's destiny is decided by what he

26. "All passions are caused by love" (citing St. Augustine, *De Civitate Dei*, 14.7) (Aquinas, *Opera Omnia*, 2.97).

27. Aquinas, *Opera Omnia*, 2.98–107.

28. Augustine, *Confessions* 13.9 (*PL* 32, col. 849), which reads: "*Pondus meum amor meus*" ("My weight is my love"); see Merton's comments in "The Recovery of Paradise," his part of the dialogue with D. T. Suzuki entitled "Wisdom in Empti- ness" that was originally intended as an introduction to *The Wisdom of the Desert*: "Remember Augustine's dictum, *amor meus, pondus meum*. 'My love is a weight, a gravitational force.' As one loves temporal things, one gains an illusory substan- tiality and a selfhood which gravitates 'downward,' that is to say acquires a *need* for things lower in the scale of being than itself. It depends on these things for its own self-affirmation. In the end this gravitational pull becomes an enslavement to material and temporal cares, and finally to sin. Yet this weight itself is an illu- sion, a result of the 'puffing up' of pride, a 'swelling' without reality. The self that appears to be weighted down by its love and carried away to material things is,

loves. Either he is carried downwards to things below him by disordered passion, or else he is carried upward to spiritual things
and to God by love elevated by reason and grace. But in any case,
man must love. St. Bernard believed that the Cistercian monastery
was a school of love,[29] in which man, guided by the Holy Spirit,
reeducated his innate faculty for loving. It is the power to love
which makes man the image of God, but because this power
has been wasted and squandered on unworthy objects, man has
fallen from likeness to God. Love must be reeducated so that it
returns to God from which it came.

{Note} some phrases from Gilson ({*The*} *Spirit of Medieval
Philosophy*[30]) on the Cistercian theology of love: (1) "Born of love,
the whole universe is penetrated, moved, vivified from within,
by love that circulates through it like life-giving blood through
the body" (p. 276);[31] (2) "Human love, in spite of all its ignorance,
blindness and even downright error, is always a participation in
God's own love for Himself. . . . even in the midst of the low-

---

in fact, an unreal thing" (Thomas Merton, *Zen and the Birds of Appetite* [New York:
New Directions, 1968], 127). This phrase is also cited in Thomas Merton, *Cassian
and the Fathers: Initiation into the Monastic Tradition* 1, ed. Patrick F. O'Connell, Monastic Wisdom [MW], vol. 1 (Kalamazoo, MI: Cistercian Publications, 2005), 235.

29. See Étienne Gilson, *The Mystical Theology of St. Bernard*, trans. A. H. C.
Downes (New York: Sheed & Ward, 1940), chapter 3, "Schola Caritatis" (60–84);
the phrase is taken from William of St. Thierry, *De Natura et Dignitate Amoris*, 9.26:
"*Haec est specialis caritatis schola, hic ejus studia excoluntur, disputationes agitantur,
solutiones non ratiocinationibus tantum, quantum ratione et ipsa rerum veritate et expe-
rientia terminantur*" (231, n. 85; *PL* 184, col. 396D) ("This is a special school of love;
here its studies are perfected, its disputations carried on, its conclusions reached
not so much through abstract reasoning as through an intuitive grasp and direct
experience of the truth of reality"); see also St. Bernard, *De Diversis*, 71 (*PL* 183,
col. 743B): "*In schola Christi sumus, in quo duplici doctrina erudimur; quia aliud per
seipsum ille unus et verus magister docet, aliud per ministros. Per ministros timorem;
per seipsum, dilectionem*" ("We are in the school of Christ, in which we are educated by a twofold teaching, for the one true master teaches one thing by himself,
another through his ministers—through ministers, fear; through himself, love").

30. Étienne Gilson, *The Spirit of Mediaeval Philosophy*, trans. A. H. C. Downes
(New York: Charles Scribner's Sons, 1936).

31. ". . . like the life-giving . . ." in text.

est pleasures, the most abandoned voluptuary is still seeking God" (p. 274);[32] (3) "The question is then not how to acquire the love of God, but rather how to make it fully aware of itself, of its object, and of the way it should bear itself towards its object. In this sense the only difficulty is that of education, or, if you prefer, the re-education of love. *The whole effort of Cistercian mysticism is therefore brought to bear on this point.*"[33]

The whole problem then is to love *truly*. This means loving God with passion, passion ordered by the will and by grace to God, the source and reward of love Who is Himself LOVE. How is this reorientation effected? Pure unregulated passion seeks the nearest concrete object, no matter how unworthy, and seeks it as an end in itself for mere self-satisfaction. In this love frustrates and exhausts itself, and travels far from God in Whom alone is our peace.[34] Narcissistic love {is} not really love at all; {it} loves only self. Every object {is} desired for its effect on the self; {it is} sterile. Altruistic love seeks the good of the one loved and in loving fulfills itself. Passion regulated by the will, elevated by self-denial, spiritualized by grace, contributes to the ardent charity with which the soul is united to God. Charity is never without fear and without desire (says St. Bernard), but the fear and desire are perfectly purified and spiritualized (*De Diligendo Deo*, n. 38).[35] Read St. John of the Cross, *Spiritual Canticle* XIX[36] and *Dark*

---

32. "human love . . . is never anything but a finite participation . . ." in text.

33. "The question, then is not now how. . . . In this sense we might say that the only . . . of the education, . . . prefer it, . . . this precise point" in text (Gilson, *Spirit*, 279–80; emphasis added).

34. The reference is to Dante, *Paradiso*, 3.85: "In His will is our peace" (Dante Alighieri, *The Divine Comedy: Paradiso, I: Italian Text and Translation*, trans. Charles S. Singleton [Princeton, NJ: Princeton University Press, 1975], 30/31).

35. "*Nunquam erit charitas sine timore, sed casto; nunquam sine cupiditate, sed ordinata*" ("There will never be charity without fear, but a chaste fear; never without desire, but an ordered desire") (*PL* 182, col. 998A).

36. *Spiritual Canticle*, 19.3: "By all her possessions she here understands all that pertains to the sensual part of the soul, which things, she says, are employed in His service, even as is the rational or the spiritual part whereof we have just spoken in the last line. In this sensual part is included the body with all its senses

Night II.13,[37] where he speaks of the divinization of the passions in union of love with God. *Spiritual Canticle* XIX shows how by love all the faculties of the soul, spiritual or bodily, including the "four passions," are all dedicated to God and move towards Him as by a superior instinct even in their first movements (see p. 112). *Dark Night* II.13 shows how mystical love operates after the manner of a passion rather than after a fully voluntary manner. Hence mystical love for God is in fact a kind of divinized passion

---

and faculties, both interior and exterior. In this line is understood also all ability of the nature and the reason, as we have said—namely, the four passions, the natural and spiritual desires, and the other possessions of the soul, all of which things, she says, are now employed in his service. For she now orders the body according to God, rules and governs the inward and outward senses according to God and directs their actions towards Him; and all the four passions likewise she keeps bound to God; because she neither has enjoyment save from God, neither has hope save in God, or fears any save God, neither does she grieve save according to God; and likewise her desires are directed wholly to God, with all her cares" (Peers, *Complete Works of Saint John of the Cross*, 2.111–12).

37. *Dark Night*, 2.13.3: "But one question arises here, which is this: Why, since these two faculties are being purged together, are the enkindling and the love of purgative contemplation at first more commonly felt in the will than the intelligence thereof is felt in the understanding? To this it may be answered that this passive love does not now directly strike the will, for the will is free, and this enkindling of love is a passion of love rather than the free act of the will; for this heat of love strikes the substance of the soul and thus moves the affections passively. And thus, this is called passion of love rather than a free act of the will; for this is only called an act of the will in so far as it is free. But since these passions and affections come into the sphere of the will, it is said therefore that if the soul conceives passion with a certain affection, the will conceives passion; and this is indeed so, for in this manner the will is taken captive and loses its liberty, according as the impetus and power of its passion carries it away with it. And therefore we can say that this enkindling of love is in the will—that is, it enkindles the desire of the will; and thus, as we say, this is called passion of love rather than the free work of the will. And because the receptive passion of the understanding can only receive intelligence in a detached and passive way (and this is impossible without its having been purged) therefore until this happens the soul feels the touch of intelligence less frequently than that of the passion of love. For it is not necessary to this end that the will should be so completely purged with respect to the passions, since these very passions help it to feel impassioned love" (Peers, *Complete Works of Saint John of the Cross*, 1.440–41).

in which the whole being, the whole person, in all its spiritual and bodily faculties, moved from within by the Holy Spirit, goes out to God in a passionate and ecstatic love.

It is clear then, that the passions are not to be destroyed but sublimated, and even in the highest and most sublime spiritual state they reclaim their rights. This is necessary because no matter how spiritualized, we will always be (as long as we are fully men) both body and soul, and the *whole person cannot express its love adequately without passion*. This is a most important point which protects us against such deviations as Stoicism, Jansenism, Quietism, etc., etc., and keeps us in our true spiritual tradition.

Now, the life of our vows is given us to unite and integrate all our being in the striving to love God by subjecting ourselves perfectly to His will and His grace. The vows, removing every principal impediment to the love of God, elevate and educate all the passions so that our whole being cooperates with the will and with grace in the constant and perfect love of God.

Let us therefore look, in a little more detail, at St. Thomas's treatment of the passion of love. This is very important for us. In St. Thomas's questions on love as passion, there is some very fine psychology (I-II, q. 26: the nature of love;[38] 27: the cause of love;[39] 28: the effects of love[40]). In brief outline, these questions tell us the following.

Nature of Love: love is man's appetite for the good. Strictly speaking, the passion of love resides in the concupiscible appetite, but St. Thomas also treats of love here in so far as it resides in the will, where the passion of love is lifted up to a higher level to *dilectio* and *caritas* by the power of free choice and the

---

38. "*De Passionibus Animae in Speciali, et Primo de Amore*" ("On the Passions of the Soul in Particular, and First of All on Love") (Aquinas, *Opera Omnia*, 2.98–101).

39. "*De Causa Amoris*" ("On the Cause of Love") (Aquinas, *Opera Omnia*, 2.101–103).

40. "*De Effectibus Amoris*" ("On the Effects of Love") (Aquinas, *Opera Omnia*, 2.103–107).

supernaturalizing work of grace.[41] There are two kinds of *amor* (love): *amor amicitiae*, which loves the good for itself, particularly the good of another person for that person's own sake; {and} *amor concupiscentiae*, {which} is love of the good for our own sakes and is called love only in an improper way, since it is not real love.[42]

Cause of Love: love is caused by a good which is *connatural and proportioned to us*; hence the cause of love is the knowledge of that goodness and an awareness of the *proportion or likeness* between the good and ourselves. The highest love is an appreciation of the value which another has by reason of a good which we can estimate by some kind of participation, since it already exists in ourselves. For example, the love of God is possible because grace gives us some slight taste of the divine goodness and enables us to rejoice that this goodness is infinitely perfect in God Himself. The lesser love comes from desiring a good which we need, for which we feel a lack and a desire. The "likeness" in this case comes from the "emptiness" caused by the need, not by the presence of the same good in ourselves.

Effects of Love: {to consider} *the effects of love*, let us look at St. Thomas's analysis (I-II, q. 28). The first effect of love is *union*.[43] Love brings about union in two ways:

---

41. *Prima Secundae*, q. 26, a. 3: "*Omnis enim dilectio vel charitas est amor, sed non e converso; addit enim* dilectio *supra amorem electionem praecedentem, ut ipsum nomen sonat; unde dilectio non est in concupiscibili, sed in voluntate tantum, et est in sola rationali natura;* charitas *autem addit supra amorem perfectionem quamdam amoris, inquantum id quod amatur, magni pretii aestimatur, ut ipsum nomen designat*" ("For all dilection or charity is love, but not the converse; for dilection adds to love a prior choice, as the sound of the word [*dilectio—electio*] suggests; thus dilection is not in the concupiscible power but only in the will, and it is in the rational nature alone; charity adds to love a certain perfection of love, in as much as what is loved is considered to be of great worth, as the name itself indicates [*carus* = dear, costly]" (Aquinas, *Opera Omnia*, 2.100).

42. *Prima Secundae*, q. 26, a. 4: "love of friendship . . . love of concupiscence" (Aquinas, *Opera Omnia*, 2.100–101).

43. a. 1 (Aquinas, *Opera Omnia*, 2.103–104).

a) *effectively*—it causes the union. Concupiscible love does this by showing that the beloved fills the needs of the lover and {by} striving to bring about this fulfillment. Love of friendship shows that the beloved is the lover's other self.

b) *formally*—in either of the above cases, love itself is the union of the lover and the beloved. In either case it is a different kind of union—and this is most important. In the first, love is an *absorption* in which one or both parties tend to disappear. In the other, love is an *affirmation* which gives more reality, more personal value, to both the lover and the beloved. In the first case, each is diminished by the union; in the second, each is increased. Note the dictum of St. Thomas: *amor est magis unitivus quam cognitio* (ad. 3).[44]

Mutual indwelling {is} the second effect of love:[45]

a) by knowledge, {by} seeking to know the inmost reality of the beloved (again {there are} different ways in which the two kinds of love do this). Note {the} connection between knowledge and connaturality: love *brings out* what the lover finds in the beloved.

b) by affection: love of friendship delights in the good of the beloved as though in its own {and} sorrows at the pain of the beloved as though at its own. *Inquantum quae sunt amati, aestimat sua, amans videtur esse in amato, quasi idem factus amato.*[46]

---

44. "Love is more unitive than knowledge" (Aquinas, *Opera Omnia*, 2.104).

45. a. 2 (Aquinas, *Opera Omnia*, 2.104–105).

46. "In as much as he considers what pertains to his friend as pertaining to himself as well, the lover seems to be in the beloved as if he had become one with the beloved" (". . . *quae sunt amici . . . videatur . . .*" in original) (Aquinas, *Opera Omnia*, 2.104).

Ecstasy {is} a third and divine effect of love.[47] *Divinus amor extasim facit—ipse Deus propter amorem est extasim passus* (Denis).[48] Ecstasy (*extra se poni*) {is} to be out of oneself:[49]

a) in the order of knowledge—to be beyond the level of knowledge proper to oneself. (Love *disposes* for this kind of ecstasy.)

b) in the order of love—love of friendship truly places us out of ourselves in the beloved. Love of concupiscence does so only in a manner of speaking because it terminates in ourselves.

Zeal (*zelus*) {is a fourth effect}. *Zelus ex intensione amoris provenit.*[50] The more powerfully we love, the more powerfully we go against all that is opposed to love.

a) love of concupiscence fights everything that stands in the way of enjoyment of the beloved—zeal here becomes common jealousy.

b) {in} love of friendship, zeal ardently seeks the good of the beloved and opposes everything that is opposed to his good; hence {it} goes against sin in ourselves when there is {the} question of the love of God.

The Perfection of the Lover {is a fifth effect}.[51] This is an important point for us. True love never injures us, in so far as it unites to our true good. Love only injures us when it is love of a false good, or when, directed to our true end, it brings about

47. a. 3 (Aquinas, *Opera Omnia*, 2.105).

48. "Divine love brings about ecstasy. . . . God himself undergoes ecstasy because of love" (quoted from Pseudo-Dionysius, *De Divinis Nominibus*, 4) (Aquinas, *Opera Omnia*, 2.105).

49. "*Respondeo dicendum, quod extasim pati aliquis dicitur, cum extra se ponitur*" ("I answer by saying that someone is said to undergo ecstasy when he is put outside himself") (Aquinas, *Opera Omnia*, 2.105).

50. a. 4: "Zeal arises from the intensity of love" (Aquinas, *Opera Omnia*, 2.105, which includes a brief phrase between "*Zelus*" and "*ex*").

51. a. 5: "*Amor ergo boni convenientis est perfectivus et meliorativus amantis*" ("Thus the love of an appropriate good perfects the lover and makes him better") (Aquinas, *Opera Omnia*, 2.106).

such bodily changes that it harms our health by its excesses. He adds four side effects of love: *liquefactio, fruitio, languor, fervor*[52] (discuss these as signs of true love[53]).

St. Thomas concludes by showing (q. 28, a. 6[54]) that all our actions tend to be acts of love, for everyone who acts, acts for an end, that is to say, out of love. The whole problem of moral life is then the right ordering of our love.

We can now add a few details on the psychology of love, according to St. Thomas:

1. Love is the source of all movement towards the good. All things "love" God in some way or other—the whole universe is penetrated through and through with *amor naturalis*, by which all beings seek Him blindly and unknowingly as their last end. All sensible beings are moved by *amor sensitivus*, and in man this sense love participates in his liberty and intelligence. In man there is *amor rationalis*—a movement based on conscious knowledge, an awareness of the fitness of the good, of our affinity to it. Of course, in us as in all other beings there is *amor naturalis*, which penetrates and impregnates all that we have and all that we are.[55]

2. The passion of love brings about a change in the lover: he *sees* the good and loves it. *Love* is the beginning of movement towards union—*desire* is the movement itself—*fruition* (joy) is the term of the movement, rest in the good to which we are united. In the strict sense, then, the passion of love involves a bodily change in the lover due to the influence of the beloved. In the

---

52. a. 5: "melting, completion, languishing, fervor" (Aquinas, *Opera Omnia*, 2.106).

53. Aquinas points out that liquefaction softens the frozen heart, the presence of the beloved brings fulfillment, the absence of the beloved causes languishing, and the lover is moved by a fervent desire to possess the beloved.

54. Aquinas, *Opera Omnia*, 2.106–107.

55. See *Prima Secundae*, q. 26, a. 1: "sensitive love," "rational love," "natural love" (Aquinas, *Opera Omnia*, 2.99).

sense of *volitional* love, *it is a spiritual transformation* produced by our reaction to a spiritual good.[56]

3. In rational love, the change is not merely passive and instinctive. Of essential importance in the act of rational love and spiritual love is the *act of free choice*, which is our own deliberate response to the good in order to make ourselves more like the value which we have seen, to unite us with it spiritually by sharing and complacency. This is *dilectio*. Charity implies, besides the action of grace, a deeply refined appreciation of spiritual values.[57]

St. Thomas notes (q. 26, a. 3, ad. 4[58]) that when divine love in our souls is raised to a great height, it again becomes passive and mystical and more like a passion in the strict sense of the word, for here it is not so much a matter of our own choice, as the direct transformating action of God producing a supernatural change in our spirit. This throws light on the passages we have read above from St. John of the Cross. As an example of spiritual love which unites two human hearts in the joy of loving God, one might read here the account of the *Vision at Ostia, in St. Augustine's Confessions* (Bk. 9, c. 10). (READ Sheed translation, p. 199–201.[59]) Augustine and Monica are talking of eternal

56. See *Prima Secundae*, q. 26, a. 2 (Aquinas, *Opera Omnia*, 2.100); see also q. 25, a. 2 (Aquinas, *Opera Omnia*, 2.97).

57. See *Prima Secundae*, q. 26, a. 3 (Aquinas, *Opera Omnia*, 2.100).

58. Aquinas, *Opera Omnia*, 2.100.

59. "When the day was approaching on which she was to depart this life—a day that You knew though we did not—it came about, as I believe by Your secret arrangement, that she and I stood alone leaning in a window, which looked inwards to the garden within the house where we were staying, at Ostia on the Tiber; for there we were away from everybody, resting for the sea-voyage from the weariness of our long journey by land. There we talked together, she and I alone, in deep joy; and *forgetting the things that were behind and looking forward to those that were before*, we were discussing in the presence of Truth, which You are, what the eternal life of the saints could be like, *which eye has not seen nor ear heard, nor has it entered into the heart of man*. But with the mouth of our heart we panted for the high waters of Your fountain, the fountain of the life which is with You: that being sprinkled from that fountain according to our capacity, we might in some sense meditate upon so great a matter.

life—the love for truth. Their minds thus become focused on the greatest good, the life of the saints in God. Augustine recognizes that the action of grace produces this kind of knowledge and

---

"And our conversation had brought us to this point, that any pleasure whatsoever of the bodily senses, in any brightness whatsoever of corporeal light, seemed to us not worthy of comparison with the pleasure of that eternal Light, not worthy even of mention. Rising as our love flamed upward towards that Selfsame, we passed in review the various levels of bodily things, up to the heavens themselves, whence sun and moon and stars shine upon this earth. And higher still we soared, thinking in our minds and speaking and marvelling at Your works: and so we came to our own souls, and went beyond them to come at last to that region of richness unending, where You feed Israel forever with the food of truth: and there life is that Wisdom by which all things are made, both the things that have been and the things that are yet to be. But this Wisdom itself is not made: it is as it has ever been, and so it shall be forever: indeed 'has ever been' and 'shall be forever' have no place in it, but it simply is, for it is eternal: whereas 'to have been' and 'to be going to be' are not eternal. And while we were thus talking of His Wisdom and panting for it, with all the effort of our heart we did for one instant attain to touch it; then sighing, and leaving the first fruits of our spirit bound to it, we returned to the sound of our own tongue, in which a word has both beginning and ending. For what is like to your Word, Our Lord, who abides in Himself forever, yet grows not old and makes all things new!

"So we said: If to any man the tumult of the flesh grew silent, silent the images of earth and sea and air: and if the heavens grew silent, and the very soul grew silent to herself and by not thinking of self mounted beyond self: if all dreams and imagined visions grew silent, and every tongue and every sign and whatsoever is transient—for indeed if any man could hear them, he should hear them saying with one voice: We did not make ourselves, but He made us who abides forever: but if, having uttered this and so set us to listening to Him who made them, they all grew silent, and in their silence He alone spoke to us, not by them but by Himself: so that we should hear His word, not by any tongue of flesh nor the voice of an angel nor the sound of thunder nor in the darkness of a parable, but that we should hear Himself whom in all these things we love, should hear Himself and not them: just as we two had but now reached forth and in a flash of the mind attained to touch the eternal Wisdom which abides over all: and if this could continue, and all other visions so different be quite taken away, and this one should so ravish and absorb and wrap the beholder in inward joys that his life should eternally be such as that one moment of understanding for which we had been sighing—would not this be: *Enter Thou into the joy of Thy Lord?* But when shall it be? Shall it be when *we shall all rise again* and *shall not all be changed?*

the consequent desire to enter deeper into the mystery. As they consider the goodness of God, their minds are elevated above every other good. They ascend through the hierarchy of created beings to God Himself, and while they long for the eternal and perfect wisdom of God, "We did for one instant attain to touch it." Then {comes} the beautiful paragraph on silence, the silence of all thought and language and passion that we may rise above created things to the Creator, so as to know and love Him without mediation of any created thing. {This is the} ecstatic character of love. "On that day when we talked of these things the world with all its delights seemed cheap to us in comparison with what we talked of" (p. 201). Thus we see the "change" that takes place in those who experience the highest spiritual love. For a moment there is a touch of the mystical intervention of God—the rest of the experience is *dilectio* and *caritas*. But in it all, they are raised to a higher spiritual level, to an ecstasy of love for God, principally *amor amicitiae*, indeed from which a certain holy and pure desire cannot be absent in the truly Christian heart, since after all we do need God and do aspire to fulfillment in Him. To speak as if we should love God only with pure *amor amicitiae*, without any desire for personal fulfillment, would seem to imply that we were altogether equal to God and had no need of Him. The semiquiet-ists lacked the balance and realism of St. Thomas.

"Such thoughts I uttered, though not in that order or in those actual words; but You know, O Lord, that on that day when we talked of these things the world with all its delights seemed cheap to us in comparison with what we talked of. And my mother said: 'Son, for my own part I no longer find joy in anything in this world. What I am still to do here and why I am here I know not, now that I no longer hope for anything from this world. One thing there was, for which I desired to remain still a little longer in this life, that I should see you a Catholic Christian before I died. This God has granted me in superabundance, in that I now see you His servant to the contempt of all worldly happiness. What then am I doing here?'" (*The Confessions of St. Augustine*, trans. F. J. Sheed [New York: Sheed & Ward, 1943]).

THE VIRTUES

In speaking of the passion of love, and of spiritual love, we have naturally come to talk of charity in its highest form. But we must now emphasize the fact that charity is not a passion, it is a virtue, and a virtue is something quite different from a passion.[60] St. Thomas could talk of certain acts of charity prompted by divine inspiration as if they were acts of passion, because of the close analogy. But in point of fact, these acts of charity do not, like passion, proceed from the *anima* or from the soul in so far as it informs the body. Our acts of charity proceed from the infused habit of charity—not, like passion, from a "natural form" or disposition of our bodily nature but from a supernatural form.

What is a virtue? It is a HABITUS—a habit.[61] But *habitus is something more perfect than habit. Habitus/habit*: habit in our modern sense is a *merely automatic function*. It is the mechanical routine of actions that follows automatically from a disposition acquired by repeated acts. It is a routine, a "custom." For instance, consider the habitual smoker: his smoking is a mechanical act—he smokes not really because he wills to smoke or wants to smoke, but because he is urged to smoke by a kind of routine compulsion. His "habit" of smoking has become something which is more or less beyond the reach of the will or of the consciousness. It is largely unconscious and mechanical. (He is responsible in so far as the routine has been acquired by acts of the will.) *Habit in this sense does not perfect a man's operations*, but rather degrades them, corrupts them, diminishes their efficacy and satisfaction, even if the "habit" is not sinful. Even when we do good things out of routine, we do them less perfectly and less meritoriously because "we" are not in them. We act more like machines than like persons.

Note the overwhelming multitude of those routines which people acquire in modern life—all the poses, façades, routines

---

60. For charity as a theological virtue, see *Prima Secundae*, q. 62 (Aquinas, *Opera Omnia*, 2.215–17); *Secunda Secundae*, q. 23, a. 3 (Aquinas, *Opera Omnia*, 3.83).

61. For virtue as a habit, see *Prima Secundae*, q. 55 (Aquinas, *Opera Omnia*, 2.189–91).

of thought, speech, all the clichés, mannerisms, evasions which empty our life of content—behind these "routines" our soul vanishes into nothingness—we sleep through a life of empty statements, gestures, expressions—never really meaning anything, feeling anything, experiencing anything. DANGER is very considerable when souls thus malformed enter a monastery and simply cast off one set of poses, routines, slogans and gestures in order to acquire another set of the same, only this time apparently spiritual. Their life continues to be hollow, miserable, false. They cannot imagine what is wrong. Eventually the whole "vocation" caves in. Actually, there probably was no vocation in the first place. *You cannot build a religious life on "habits" in the sense of routines. The mere mechanical repetition of acts, even of the very best acts, does not lead to a life of virtue, but to a life of pious automatism and formalism. Consequently, there is no point in emphasizing the quantity or the difficulty of the acts we perform or of the trials we suffer. The mere repetition of acts and sufferings, without inner virtue, dehumanizes and deadens our being.* That is why a person in the contemplative life, after making pious acts over and over again without number, can still end up not only less holy but even less human than someone out in the world with less exalted aspirations. To understand this, we must really grasp the true notion of virtue, as a *habitus* and not as a routine.

The true notion of habitus: a good "*habitus*" is a source of activity which perfects our *actions*, perfects our *being*, elevates and fulfills our freedom, establishes us in the good, directs us more surely to our last end. Without "*habitus*" we will not persevere in good action, we will not develop and grow, we will not find ourselves and order our life as we should toward our last end and consequently we will not attain that end. *Habitus* {is} a principle of action QUO QUIS UTITUR QUANDO VULT.[62] It aids us to do good more constantly, more perfectly, and with greater satisfaction: FIRMITER,

---

62. "that which one uses when one wills": see *Prima Secundae*, q. 50, a. 5, which reads: ". . . *utitur cum voluerit*" (Aquinas, *Opera Omnia*, 2.177).

EXPEDITE, DELECTABILITER OPERARI.[63] Our nature is enriched by *habitus*—we enjoy growth in self-mastery and gain command of our environment. *Firmiter* {means} greater constancy and assurance; *expedite* {means} greater spontaneity—the mastery with which we go directly and without hesitation to the real good; *delectabiliter* {means that} satisfaction comes from the fact that good action has now become second nature. Our being takes a good natural satisfaction in acting well. At times, for supernatural reasons, we have to be content to be without this satisfaction, but on such occasions this is necessary in order to grow in a higher and more supernatural kind of *"habitus"* which ultimately will bear fruit in a more spiritual mode of operation and a more supernatural satisfaction.

There are two kinds of *habitus*: *entitative habits*—dynamic realities, qualities which affect the whole state of our being—for instance, health, sanctifying grace; *operative habits*—virtues which make our faculties capable of repeated good acts.[64] *"Habitus"* reside in the sensible appetite, intelligence or will. In the body there are no real *"habitus,"* but rather mechanical habits which, however, under the government of the will and virtue, make it easier for the will to grow in virtue. The *"habitus"* control the passions and bring them into line with reason and with grace.

With regard to origin, {there is} another division of *"habitus"*: *acquired*—gained by repeated acts;[65] {and} *infused*—gained by infusion of grace.[66] (N.B. there are also natural habits which appear spontaneously—for instance, the habitual knowledge of first

63. "to work firmly, promptly, pleasantly"; see *Quaestiones Disputatae de Virtutibus*, q. 1, a. 1, ad. 13: "*illa quae in sola electione consistent, facile est quod qualitercumque fiant; sed quod debito modo fiant, scilicet expedite, firmiter, et delectabiliter, hoc non est facile; unde ad hoc habitibus virtutum indigemus*" ("it is easy for those things which are a simple matter of choice to happen somehow or other; but it is not easy for them to happen as they should, that is, promptly, firmly and pleasantly; for this we require the habits of virtues") (Aquinas, *Opera Omnia*, 8.547).

64. See *Prima Secundae*, q. 50, a. 1 (Aquinas, *Opera Omnia*, 2.173–74).

65. See *Prima Secundae*, q. 51, aa. 2, 3 (Aquinas, *Opera Omnia*, 2.179–80).

66. See *Prima Secundae*, q. 51, a. 4 (Aquinas, *Opera Omnia*, 2.180).

principles in the order of knowledge or of practical action.[67]) The growth of the habits (*habitus*) {takes place as follows}: *acquired*—by clear-sighted and forceful action; more intense acts dispose for the growth; *infused*—by cooperation with grace; here it is not intensity in the sense of stern application that counts, but rather purity of heart and of love, greater perfection in simplicity and self-renunciation.

Good and bad habitus:[68] vices are bad *"habitus"*—that is, {they entail} not only {a} mechanical propensity to sin, but they increase the freedom, abandon, spontaneity, permanence with which the soul gives itself over to sin. They therefore *increase the evil of our acts*. Passive habits are weaknesses rather than vices ({and so} not properly *"habitus"*).

We can already see, then, that in the life consecrated to God by religious vows, the consecration will reach down into our everyday activity *by the cultivation of good habitus or virtues*. Hence, we must look briefly at the virtues by which, in practice, we offer our actions to God and our whole selves with them and thus fulfill what we have promised.

THE VIRTUES: intellectual {virtues include}: in the speculative intellect—habit of principles (*intellectus, synderesis*), science (*episteme*), wisdom (*sophia*);[69] in the practical intellect—*art* (*techne*), *recta ratio factibilium*;[70] prudence (*phronesis*), *recta ratio agibilium*.[71] These are not virtues in the strict sense of the word, except for *prudence*, which is the most important of the natural virtues and governs all the rest. It is at the same time an intellectual and a moral virtue. Moral (cardinal) {virtues include} prudence, justice, fortitude, temperance.[72] The intellectual and moral

---

67. See *Prima Secundae*, q. 51, a. 1 (Aquinas, *Opera Omnia*, 2.178–79).

68. See *Prima Secundae*, q. 54, a. 3 (Aquinas, *Opera Omnia*, 2.187–88).

69. See *Prima Secundae*, q. 57, a. 2 (Aquinas, *Opera Omnia*, 2.196–97).

70. *Prima Secundae*, q. 57, a. 4: "the right reason of things to be made" (Aquinas, *Opera Omnia*, 2.198).

71. *Prima Secundae*, q. 57, a. 4: "the right reason of things to be done" (Aquinas, *Opera Omnia*, 2.198).

72. See *Prima Secundae*, q. 61 (Aquinas, *Opera Omnia*, 2.211–15).

virtues may be acquired or infused.[73] We will consider *temperance* and *justice* in greater detail later on; they are especially important in the life of the vows. Theological {virtues include} faith, hope, charity.[74]

A virtue in the full sense of the word is an *elective habit*.[75] It implies the guidance of prudence, in making a *choice*, of the good clearly seen, by reason of the connatural appreciation (instinctive affinity for the good) created by the virtue itself. It makes a *right decision* in practice, not merely a theoretical appraisal of value. It goes to the good and is not held back by contrary impulsions of passion, etc. It puts its decision into effect {by} enlisting the support of passion and putting passion to work in the service of reason and of grace. It makes its decision on the basis of *objective norms* (norms of justice—what is right and due) {and} *subjective norms* (norms of prudence—what I ought to do in the circumstances). These norms show it the *just middle between extremes*.

The growth of good habits:[76] in practice, whether we consider the acquired or infused habits of virtue, the growth of habits on our part depends on three things:

1) The placing of *more intense acts* (more fully conscious, deliberate, spontaneous, free, clear-sighted—these acts {are} prompted often by trial, which precipitates choice).

2) The *rhythm of life*—it is utterly useless to expect to be always making more and more intense acts. These intense acts are embedded in a context of less conscious and less intense acts (but not remiss acts). This alternation must be respected; otherwise we will fall into illusion and run the risk of wrecking our vocation.

---

73. See *Prima Secundae*, q. 63, a. 3 (Aquinas, *Opera Omnia*, 2.219).

74. See *Prima Secundae*, q. 62 (Aquinas, *Opera Omnia*, 2.215–17).

75. *Prima Secundae*, q. 65, a. 1: "*Nulla virtus moralis potest sine prudentia haberi, eo quod proprium virtutis moralis est facere electionem rectam, cum sit habitus electivus*" ("No moral virtue can be possessed without prudence, from the fact that making a right decision is proper to moral virtue, since it is an elective habit") (Aquinas, *Opera Omnia*, 2.224).

76. See *Prima Secundae*, q. 52 (Aquinas, *Opera Omnia*, 2.181–83).

3) *Growing capacity for organization*—the development of good habits integrates our activity in an organic whole, {resulting in} greater productivity and scope, reaching out to include our whole life.

The vows aim to foster this moral organization of man's whole life, consecrated to God in worship by the virtue of religion.

SIN:[77] good acts can be habitual. So can bad acts. What is a bad moral act, a sin? What is sinful habit? In studying the vows, we must remember that the vows are aimed against sin, which is the great obstacle to union with God, and the vows are ordered above all to union with God. We should not merely be concerned with knowing "how one sins against the vows," but rather and before all, to realize *what sins the vows protect us against*. A life of religious vows is in fact designed *to protect us against all sin*. If we keep the vows, we will normally be in a position to avoid all offense against God, for the vows remove all the great obstacles to a life of charity, and charity is the fulfillment of the law. Sin, on the other hand, is diametrically opposed to love.

A sin is an act from which LOVE *is missing*. A formal sin is an act which rejects love, which prefers something else to the real good. It despises the real good and embraces a false good which is more pleasing to the disordered love of self. It rejects objective moral values and embraces what is, for some reason or other, subjectively pleasing or convenient. It rebels against God and rejects His holy will in order to gratify self-will. *The seat of sin* is in the depths of man's own soul. It is rooted in the evil of a will that is centered on itself, that prefers malice to wisdom and love, which prefers error to truth because it is "my own." Sin is a distorted, crippled love which prefers "me" and "mine" to everything else and everyone else, including God. No one, however, has to be a sinner. True, we are all born in original sin, subject to malice, concupiscence and error. But we all receive enough grace to turn from evil to God if we so will. Every sinner is so because he

---

77. See *Prima Secundae*, qq. 71–89 (Aquinas, *Opera Omnia*, 250–330).

prefers evil. But there may be reasons why this preference is less voluntary in some than in others. God alone remains the judge of relative culpability. He alone knows who is more guilty and who less, who has more malice and who less. It is not for us to rate sinners according to our own standards. We do not know all the circumstances. "Judge not, that you be not judged."[78]

The roots of sin: the seed of sin is planted in everyone. Baptism sterilizes that seed, but it can be planted again and cultivated. Who plants the seed? the WILL. No one else can plant the seed of sin in our soul. Others can give us the seed to plant, but if we refuse to plant it . . . . Where does the seed come from? the devil, by suggestion or persuasion; other men, by bad example, wrong instruction, etc. What favors the growth of the seed? ignorance {and} error in the intelligence; passion in the sensible soul. This explains the *great evil* of bad education, bad example, scandal. A world which malforms consciences and minds, which warps moral judgement from the beginning, is guilty of a very great evil. In our time, perhaps, many individuals are to a great extent not to be held personally responsible for all the error and deordination in their souls. But *society itself is responsible*, and society itself reaps the consequences in wars, revolutions, etc. Also certain leaders of society may no doubt incur greater guilt, though it is hard to say; God alone knows.

The fact remains that in a society like ours, *all are to some extent guilty*; all are involved in a mutual responsibility. This thought is terrible, and it should move us to a great love of penance in our consecrated life. When we take vows, in this world of ours, it is not in order to wash our hands of all its evils and dissociate ourselves from all responsibility, but rather it is to assume *conscious responsibility* for the evil that is in the world, in the same way that Jesus did. We who have vows do not stand aside in horror and consider ourselves as the sinless members of a sinful race. On the contrary, we are sinners who have received the mercy of God, who have had our eyes opened, to some extent,

78. Mt. 7:1; Lk. 6:37.

to the evils of sin, who recognize the situation, and who take it upon ourselves to cleanse our own hearts gradually and painfully from all sin, to make reparation for our own sins and for those of the entire world, in union with Christ crucified, and to obtain grace for our brothers. For after all, if we have received grace, we owe this to the intervention of other members of the fallen race to which we belong and which has been elevated and sanctified in Christ.

In this way, by our vows, *we recognize in ourselves the effects of sin:*[79] (1) the corruption and defilement of our nature (not in its essence but in its activity); (2) the disfigurement of our soul, made in the image of God; (3) the obligation to undergo punishment and to re-establish order. The life of vows is, therefore, a *life of reparation* in which we consciously and freely assume the obligation, binding the whole race, to repair the disorder caused by sin, to reorient our own souls and all of mankind to God, its last end. Hence, the life of vows is a life of *struggle with sin*. In our solidarity with the rest of the human race, those under vows, who may perhaps be free of personal sin to a great extent, may have to struggle mystically and spiritually with the sins of others. They may have to suffer for others, to bring grace to them, and in doing so they may have to feel in themselves the evil which (though common to all) has been particularly fomented by unrepentant sinners. Hence those who have embraced purity and virginity may in fact have to suffer much not only because of their own concupiscence, but because of the concupiscence of others.

In resumé, sin is the interior principle of evil actions, rooted in all men more or less, encouraged and fomented by the evil that is in the world, part and parcel of the "mystery of evil" which can only be overcome by the Cross of Christ. Our vows unite us to Christ on the Cross and thus give us the victory over the evil that is in the world, which victory is a participation by grace, the theological virtues and the gifts of the Holy Ghost in Christ's death and Resurrection.

79. See *Prima Secundae*, qq. 85–87 (Aquinas, *Opera Omnia*, 2.309–21).

It is true that the vows do not make us impeccable. It is possible for one to violate a vow, and if he does so there is added sin. But this possibility of added sin must be properly understood. The idea of a vow is not to increase sin but to diminish it; and it diminishes sin by bringing our lives into line with the two great exterior principles of human acts: *the Law* (God's will)[80] and *Grace* (God's divine help).[81] We will first consider the notion of law, and in this connection we will also say something of justice, for to make a vow is an act of religion, which comes under the virtue of justice. Justice means giving God and man their due. But there is no way in which we can possibly repay to God all we owe Him as our Creator and Redeemer. The life of the vows, a supreme gift of all that we are and all that we have to God, is the means selected by those who hunger and thirst for justice to give due homage to the Almighty and All-Holy God.

LAW AND JUSTICE: law plays an all-important part in our quest of blessedness in God. It is by manifesting His Holy Will that God shows us the way to union with Him and to Paradise. The whole life of man on earth is then to put his "will in the Law of the Lord and meditate on it day and night" (Psalm 1). Day and night we praise God's Wisdom in the economy of salvation and particularly in the Law, which He has given us to find our way to Him. Psalm 118 is a long panegyric of the Law and is a fervent witness of the joy and peace that are found in the will of God and nowhere else: "Blessed are the undefiled in the way, who walk in the Law of the Lord. Blessed are they that search the testimonies and seek them with their whole heart. . . . O that my ways may be directed to keep Thy justifications. Then shall I not be confounded, when I shall look into all Thy commandments. . . . Thy words have I hidden in my heart, that I may not sin against Thee . . ." (Ps. 118). These are the ardent cries of a soul that *loves the Law of God*, not the letter which killeth, being purely exterior and unable to justify man, but the Spirit, that

80. See *Prima Secundae,* qq. 90–108 (Aquinas, *Opera Omnia,* 2.330–428).
81. See *Prima Secundae,* qq. 109–14 (Aquinas, *Opera Omnia,* 2.428–62).

is to say, the grace and fulfillment which come to the soul that seeks the will of God in Christ, makes Him her law, lives and works in Him and by Him for the glory of the Father. The way, then, to correct our faults, to repair for our sins, to avoid sin for the future, to grow in virtue and charity, to make our lives a life of love, *is to love the will of God and do it with our whole heart. This will is manifested to us by Law.*

What is Law? an exterior principle of good action manifesting the will of God and the way by which we can arrive at union with Him as persons and as members of society. Law is a divinely sanctioned rule of good conduct which governs our relations with others, with God Himself, and the management of our own life. *All law flows from the Eternal Law,*[82] by which God governs His entire creation, all peoples and all beings, ordering them all by His wisdom and love to their final end in Himself. Every particular plan for a creature, for a part of creation, is but a tiny detail of the great eternal law, in which God is not only the Legislator but also the Law itself and the Common Good to which all things are led by the Law. The good of every particular being is found in fulfilling its part in the eternal plan of God. *But no man knows the eternal Law, no creature knows it, and hence the particular plan for each one of us, for each section of God's creation, is not fully realized except in its relation to the whole plan of God, and this plan is unknown to us.* We must never forget this. Too easily we act as if we ought to be expected to know all that God is doing and all that He wills. It is, alas, too easy to go around saying, "God wills this" and "God wills that," as if we were privileged to see His entire plan. On the contrary, the sure manifestations of God's will often completely overthrow what had seemed to be "His Plan."

The heart of the divine plan, its central purpose, is however revealed to us by God. God is LOVE. The eternal Law, the Law by which God rules not only His creation but His own inner life, is LOVE. Hence, every particular dictate of God's will, every legitimate expression of human or divine Law is ordered to the

82. See *Prima Secundae*, q. 93 (Aquinas, *Opera Omnia*, 2.338–42).

fulfillment of *God's Love for us*. Law, seen in its particularity, out of context, out of the whole great plan of God, unrelated to the infinite love of God, is the "letter which killeth"[83]—it is an end in itself—hence futile. Law, seen in relation to God's love, but seen only in the mystery of Divine Charity, therefore in faith and in humility, becomes life-giving Spirit—Christ Himself vivifies and sanctifies us when we do the will of God out of faith in Him.

Natural law[84] is a promulgation of that part of the eternal Law which concerns our nature. It is impressed on our very soul itself; *it is promulgated in our very nature*, in our intelligence, where it reflects the light of God, the wisdom of God. It is known intuitively by every reasonable man—it is the "light which illumines every man coming into the world" (John 1). If we follow the light of the natural law imprinted in us, *we will certainly receive the higher illumination of grace and faith in order to arrive at our end, God*. This is true of everyone—pagan, Jew, Moslem, Red. Ignoring the natural law, man is held guilty for his ignorance of God (Romans 1). It is of no avail to be baptized and to have the faith if we refuse to keep the natural law. *We have to follow the law of our nature in order to be children of God*. He is our Father in the natural order first of all—our Father supernaturally after this. Since, in the actual order established by God, nature is fulfilled and perfected by grace, it is in fact sin that is *against nature* and *virtue that fulfills and elevates nature*, with grace, to the charity for which in fact we were created and without which we cannot be what we are intended to be by God.

The natural law tells us that we must do good and avoid evil. It tells us that children must love and honor their parents, that parents must care for their children, that husbands and wives must love one another and assist one another and particularly work together for the procreation and education of their children. It tells us that we must not hurt others without reason, that we must not do to others what we would not have them do to us, that we must give every man his due.

---

83. 2 Cor. 3:6.
84. See *Prima Secundae*, q. 94 (Aquinas, *Opera Omnia*, 2.342–47).

For instance, {see} the great principle of "human-hearted-ness" which is one of the foundation stones of the ethic of Confucius. It is the ability to understand others by realizing that they suffer what we suffer and desire what we desire—to reach out by empathy and put ourselves in their place and act accordingly. This is one of the very great principles of the natural law, and it also finds its place in St. Bernard—a very central place too.[85] Confucius says:

> If a man be really bent on human-heartedness, there is no wickedness in him[86] . . . . A human-hearted ruler wants security for himself, and so he makes others secure. He wishes to get a wider sphere of influence, and so he extends other people's spheres of influence. The ability to draw parallels from matters very near to oneself may be called the art of human-heartedness.[87] . . . The man bent on public service, if he be human-hearted, will under no circumstances seek to live at the expense of his human-heartedness. There are occasions when he will lay down his life to preserve his human-heartedness.[88]

{This is} a magnificent statement, comparable to Our Lord's own words, "Greater love than this hath no man, than that he lay

85. In *De Diligendo Deo*, VIII.23 (*PL* 182, cols. 987D–988A), on the first degree of love, Bernard points out that carnal love for self becomes social love when it is extended to others: "It is just indeed that he who shares the same nature should not be deprived of the same benefits, especially that benefit which is grafted in that nature. . . . I think you will not find it a burden to share with those of your nature that which you have withheld from the enemy of your soul. Then your love will be sober and just if you do not refuse your brother that which he needs of what you have denied yourself in pleasure" (*On Loving God*, trans. Robert Walton, OSB, *The Works of Bernard of Clairvaux*, vol. 5: *Treatises II*, CF 13 [Washington, DC: Cistercian Publications, 1973], 115–16).

86. Confucius, *Analects*, 4.4, in *Chinese Philosophy in Classical Times*, ed. and trans. E. R. Hughes (London: J. M. Dent, 1942), 19, which reads: ". . . human-heartedness, then there is . . . ."

87. Confucius, *Analects*, 6.28 (Hughes, 19).

88. Confucius, *Analects*, 15.8 (Hughes, 20, which reads: ". . . be the human-hearted kind of man, under no circumstances will he seek . . .").

down his life for his friend."[89] For Confucius, the "man of honor" is the human-hearted man—and the man of principle who realizes that if wealth and high station cannot be obtained without disobeying the law (*Tao*), then they must be relinquished, and that if poverty and low station cannot be avoided without contravention of principle, then they must be accepted.[90] The first thing for the "man of honor" is loyalty and keeping his word. "If he does wrong he will not shirk mending his ways."[91] "Amongst men of honor there is nothing to cause selfish rivalry.[92] {. . .} The man of honor in relation to the Great Society has no private preferences. . . . He sees matters in relation to the right."[93] "The man of true breeding sets his heart on spiritual power in himself: the man of no breeding sets his heart on land."[94] Four characteristics of the man of honor {are} modesty in private, respectfulness in relations with superiors, benevolence in providing for inferiors, justice in the organization of labor.[95] Finally, "Be trustworthy in every respect, devoted to the acquisition of learning, steadfast unto death for the good."[96] These maxims should be to us a revelation of the depth and wonder of the natural law. How sad that by ignoring these depths, imagining ourselves more "supernatural," we are in fact very poor Christians at times. So much for the great importance of the natural law. No one can hope to ignore it and yet become a saint!

Human Law:[97] human legislators merely bring a *further determination* to the natural law. Relatively little of the natural law

---

89. Jn. 15:13.

90. See Confucius, *Analects*, 4.5 (Hughes, 20).

91. Confucius, *Analects*, 1.8 (Hughes, 21).

92. Confucius, *Analects*, 3.7 (Hughes, 21).

93. Confucius, *Analects*, 4.10 (Hughes, 21, which reads: "The true man. . . . He sees these matters . . .").

94. Confucius, *Analects*, 4.11 (Hughes, 21, which reads: "A man . . .").

95. See Confucius, *Analects*, 4.15 (Hughes, 21).

96. Confucius, *Analects*, 8.13 (Hughes, 21, which reads: ". . . respect, be devoted . . . the Good.").

97. See *Prima Secundae*, q. 95 (Aquinas, *Opera Omnia*, 2.347–50).

is fully evident. For the natural law to apply in greater detail, it is necessary that it be interpreted and determined by explicit human laws. Hence, *no human law has any authority except in so far as it accords with the natural law.* {There are} other limitations: human law is concerned with *exterior conduct.* It affects the interior only in so far as it is necessary to carry out an external act. Human law has no power to impose evil. It must not be unjust or useless (but a useless law may still have to be obeyed in order to avoid scandal). Remember that one of the main purposes of human law is to provide security and order, protecting us against the insecurity and disorder that would result if every individual were to interpret the whole natural law and apply it for himself. The modern lack of respect for law is extremely dangerous. Modern man in general has no sense of law, no respect for authority, and he believes he can take it upon himself to judge the law and interpret it according to his own whims and interests "as long as he does not get caught." Even moral theologians encourage this evil by overstressing the theory of "purely penal laws," which "do not bind in conscience except to undergo punishment if one is caught."[98] This theory is *much abused.* It has led to very bad effects. Note also that human law *varies* according to different conditions in different places and evolves from age to age. What might have been just in the sixth century is not necessarily just at the present moment. Conditions have changed.

98. See for example E. Bergh, sj, "Religious Obedience According to the Code of Canon Law," in *Obedience: Being the English Version of "L'Obéissance et la Religieuse d'Aujourd'hui"* (Westminster, MD: Newman Press, 1953): "Many rules, and all the recent constitutions which have adopted article 130 of the *Normae* of 1901, do not directly bind in conscience under pain of sin. What kind of obligation do they therefore entail? The general chapter of the Dominican Order in 1236 regarded these as purely penal laws whose transgression did not entail a moral fault. But one might then ask if the non-fulfilment of the penance imposed for the breach of the law itself constitutes a fault. The majority think it does, but a minority, including names of some eminence—Cajetan and Suárez—held that the penalty was of no greater obligation in conscience than the rule itself" (127).

We must remember the nature of law: it is not an *arbitrary dictate* of authority (although in practice when legal systems degenerate, then they tend more and more to arbitrariness and formalism—a tangle of technicalities which anyone who is smart enough can "get out of"; only the uninitiated and the ones who cannot afford a lawyer eventually get caught). But law should be *an ordinance of practical reason, reflecting the truth, the reality of a certain situation and showing the way to the common good of all who find themselves in that situation.* Law obliges by presenting to us the good, the true, in such a way that we are moved by our reason to see the way to fulfill our own innate aspiration for the good and to embrace the way proposed by the law. In other words, the *obligation of law flows from the relation of the prescribed act to the common good.* This relationship may be evident or inevident, and in the latter case we accept the fact of a relationship to the good on the basis of *submission to competent authority.*

Respect for authority, besides being a virtue in itself (*observantia*), is in practice the work of legal justice and of prudence together. Legal justice inclines us to accept the decisions and dictates of competent authority and to integrate ourselves in the common social striving for the good of all, which is ordered by the law.

Civil law aims to achieve the common temporal good of all. Church law is aimed at the supernatural and eternal good of all. ALL LAW WORTHY OF THE NAME TENDS IN THE LAST ANALYSIS TO BEATITUDE. Supernatural justice gives us a deep realization of this fact and inclines us to order our acts to law, even human law, in a spirit of faith and submission to the supreme authority of God speaking through the legislator.

Divine Law: human law is necessary to supply for the defects in the promulgation of the natural law. But human law itself is imperfect and limited. Above all, neither human nor natural law has any power to lead us to our true goal without the aid of a higher law. This higher law must be supplied by a direct intervention of God. God then promulgates clearly and explicitly, through Jesus the Man-God, in human terms, His divine law, the reflection of His eternal law, in so far as we need to know it and participate in it to arrive at beatitude.

The divine law has two phases:

1. {*The*} *Old Law*[99]—in itself it is only (a) a more clear and explicit formulation of the natural law, given by God Himself, {and} (b) a "pedagogue" and preparation for the New Law. The Old Law is exterior and incomplete. The New Law is spiritual, interior, complete and perfect.

2. *The New Law*[100]—the law of Christ and His Gospel, is the only fully perfect law, given to man for the sure attainment of his true end. It is a truly supernatural law, corresponding to the law of nature in a higher order. *Like the law of nature, the New Law speaks to us from within. It is a law of grace.* To see and keep the New Law, we must be moved by the Holy Spirit living and acting in our hearts. In so far as the New Law is made known to us by words (in the Gospel for instance), it reaches us from without. But unless the Holy Spirit enlightens and moves us from within, the words we hear from without will have no real spiritual effect in our lives.

This interior character of the law of grace is often overlooked by religious, who act as if they had vowed only to keep certain exterior prescriptions. The life of the vows is ordered, on the contrary, to perfect obedience to the law of grace—the law of the Holy Spirit crying out in our hearts, *Abba, Father.*[101] The vow of obedience makes us obey the promptings of the same spirit who made Christ Himself obedient unto death. To really live by our vow, we must then be *attentive to these special interior inspirations* of God. This applies to all our vows. The Benedictine vow of conversion of manners makes this especially clear.

Jesus Himself is the Legislator of the New Law. Living in us by His Spirit, acting upon our hearts, He makes us partici-

99. See *Prima Secundae*, qq. 98–105 (Aquinas, *Opera Omnia*, 2.357–416).
100. See *Prima Secundae*, qq. 106–108 (Aquinas, *Opera Omnia*, 2.416–28).
101. Rom. 8:15; Gal. 4:6.

pate in His own divine life, which He lives in the depths of the Godhead. Since in the Word, God promulgates His eternal Law, when we are united to Jesus in the Holy Spirit, we are united to the eternal law of God, hidden in God Himself. We do not fully see, know or understand that law, which is utterly hidden and incomprehensible to us in itself. But we see and imitate Jesus; we follow the promptings of His grace and do the things He commands: and in so doing we are united to the eternal law in Christ—our life being "hidden with Christ in God."[102] This is the only way in which we can truly and perfectly fulfill the eternal law in our lives, by union with Jesus whose "meat is to do the will of Him that sent me."[103]

The New Law is a law of faith and of grace. It is promulgated in our hearts by baptism, clarified by each increase of grace and especially by our Eucharistic communions, for in the Blessed Eucharist we receive Christ Himself; we follow out the divine command to love Him with our whole heart and soul and mind and strength. We are united to His love for us and His love for the Father. We are united to His love for the brethren. It is most of all as a fruit of Holy Communion that we *learn of Him* the ways of humility, charity, self-denial, obedience, etc., which are the ways of the New Law.

By our vows, we consecrate all our efforts and all our lives to the perfect fulfillment of the New Law by observing in the most perfect possible way the counsels given us by Christ. These counsels of renunciation and obedience enable us to *follow Him most closely* and not only to fulfill His law but to *pattern ourselves most perfectly on His own fulfillment of His Father's will*. By our vows, things which do not bind others become for us a "law," a further strict obligation, but it is only an obligation to *love more* and to follow Christ more closely, that is, to unite ourselves to Him in Whom the Law is fulfilled and from Whom we receive the love

102. Col. 3:3.
103. Jn. 4:34.

that is the *plenitudo Legis*.[104] Our whole "law" is to cling to Him, and His love fulfills everything in us. The life of the vows is the highest expression of fidelity to the New Law.

JUSTICE: *the importance of the virtue of justice in the religious life*: at first sight, the virtue of justice may seem to have little to do with our life consecrated to God. One might argue that everything in this life begins and ends with charity, and to look at it all from the point of view of justice would merely be narrowing it down to naturalism and formalism. Indeed, one might perhaps be tempted to insist that emphasis on justice would reduce our religious life to petty legalism. All these objections flow from a misunderstanding of the true nature of justice. Formalism, legalism, etc. are *not* aspects of justice; they are perversions of justice, and in fact they are rooted in injustice and in the destruction of the true order of things.

To study the virtue of justice in theology is something quite different from the study of civil or canon law. It is a study of man's voluntary acts in so far as they fit into *a structure of social relationships* by which the totality of human society is orientated toward God as its last end. Grace builds on nature, and justice is the keystone of the structure of moral virtue which makes man truly reasonable and makes his conduct as a member of society shine with the light of reason. Justice bases man's social life on the solid foundation of right, which reflects the reality of man's nature and rests firmly on the real order established by God. True Christian justice is not mere exterior conformity to a code of law; it is full and complete interior conformity to the will of God, not only by conduct that accords with right reason and the dictates of natural and positive law, but also by the supernatural life of faith and charity infused into our souls by the merits of the Passion of Christ. In the fullest sense, Christian justice is conformity to Christ—conformity of the individual and conformity of the Mystical Body to its Head. More precisely, it is *conformity to Christ crucified in His total sacrifice for the sins of the world*. When

104. "fulfillment of the law" (Rom. 13:10).

we reflect that the sacrifice of the Incarnate Word was a perfect act of obedience and of charity, it is easy to see that the life of the vows conforms us to Christ crucified and to his perfect justice. The infused moral virtue of justice comes to us in union with charity to supernaturalize our social relations and enable us to advance, in union with other men, in a well-ordered and just society (the Body of Christ), to union with God.

Social order and justice have a tremendous importance in the salvation of souls. You cannot preach the Gospel to men who are starving to death. You cannot convert to God men who see nothing but injustice and oppression in those who claim to be servants of God. To serve and love Christ means to work at the same time for the salvation of our own soul and for the salvation of our brother. But the salvation of our brother is not a matter of charity without justice, of charity considered as somehow completely divorced from justice. Charity that does not rest on a firm basis of justice is not true charity. Without a social order that really embodies and preserves true human values willed for man by God, the Church cannot attain anything but a partial and limited success in her mission of bringing souls to Christ. It is especially important to note that religious can in fact be objectively guilty of very great injustice merely by living too well and too comfortably on the wealth of which others are deprived. In a world of poverty and suffering, religious who give themselves to a life of bourgeois comfort, *even though they can do so without violating the vows*, are nevertheless guilty of injustice, as well as scandal. Abbé Pierre points out that even though the "mystique" of poverty has revived in the religious life, there is no longer any *sociological effect* to religious poverty—it is no longer a witness because religious live better than the poor (cf. *Vie Spirituelle*: March 1957[105]).

105. Abbé Pierre, "La Vocation Monastique et la Misère du Monde," *La Vie Spirituelle*, 39.3 [#426] (March 1957), 288–300; see 290: "Non pas qu'on ne pratique pas une pauvreté d'intention, d'obéissance intérieure, mais *la portée sociologique* de ces vertus a disparu. La portée mystique subsiste" ("It is not that poverty of intention, of interior obedience, is not practiced, but the sociological significance of these virtues has disappeared. The mystical significance remains").

Justice orders the whole life of virtue to God in so far as it integrates all our acts of virtue into the social context of a group
striving for union with God. But more than that, *some of the most
important virtues of the religious life come under justice.* Justice governs not only the rights of men to bodily health and life, to property, to just judgement and equality before the law, but also other
rights which interest us particularly: the right to a good repu-
tation, the right to know the truth. MOST IMPORTANT is the fact
that the virtue of RELIGION is a potential part of justice; PRAYER is
before all an act of justice (religion); *religious obedience* and *reverence for superiors* come under justice, and finally, most crucial of
all, A VOW IS AN ACT OF JUSTICE (under the virtue of religion). *If we
are not just men* and have no connatural appreciation of the values
of justice, we are not fit to make religious vows or to lead lives of
obedience and give ourselves to prayer and the worship of God!

What is Justice? To the mind that has no conception of justice,
justice means nothing more than conformity to a set of rules,
without any special reason except that they are rules and ought
to be kept. *An immature and superficial view of man's moral life*—alas
all too common among religious—might be sketched out in the
following broad lines: Christian perfection is a matter of doing
your duty. Duty is marked out by the rule. You keep the rule
because it is the rule—it is willed by God, Who is a just God and
demands that you do your duty. He has given you a rule for no
special purpose, other than that by keeping it, you do your duty.
This is justice. If you keep the rule, you are just. If you do not, you
are unjust. The little enclosed life in which you live has no special
relation to the rest of society; you have no other obligations in
justice than to keep your rule and carry out your religious duties.
More important than justice (in this purblind view) are fortitude
and temperance. Fortitude is the most important of the moral
virtues because our great task as religious is to suffer. God wants
us to suffer because perfection is attained only through suffering.
Then too, by suffering we undergo punishment which is rightly
meted out upon a world in which, generally speaking, men do
not devote themselves to duty. Most important is the virtue of

temperance. The whole field of morality and duty seems, at times, to be narrowed down to the sixth commandment. "Immorality" is then synonymous with unchastity or incontinence. A "tender conscience" is one that is practically obsessed with sex and wages a constant and hectic battle against impure thoughts and first movements of sensuality or impurity.

What is wrong with this outlook? It represents a completely wrong perspective. There are in it certain elements of truth. The flesh is indeed weak, and man is faced with a constant struggle to guard against inordinate movements of carnal passion. It is impossible to get to heaven without carrying the Cross, quite true, and we must embrace the sufferings willed for us by God—we must accept them with uncompromising fortitude and generosity. But the false view above is upside down, and because of its lack of perspective, *it ends by disorienting the whole moral life.*

a) Emphasizing unduly the control of passion beyond and above all else, it becomes absorbed in subjectivity, knows of no virtue that is not a matter of the movements within one's own soul. Hence it bends back on the self and engages in interminable self-analysis and minute or even scrupulous investigation of the thoughts that pass through one's mind.

b) Emphasizing unduly the necessity to suffer, *it becomes a cult of suffering*, or dolorism, and the exercise of fortitude degenerates into morbid self-preoccupation and self-pity, which ends in abject weakness. Here again, the attention tends to become more and more concentrated on self, and the person becomes narrow and egotistical and small.

c) The concept of justice that results is *hollow and false*. It is a mere matter of *conformity*. It has no inner, spiritual content, no real vital reference to others, to society, to real rights. It is a mere shadow of justice and can easily become the cloak *for very serious injustice.*

In a word, with this wrong moral outlook, the conscience is in fact insensitive to the most important moral values. In such a situation, an apparently "good" and "pious" person can (with a subjectively good conscience) *lead a life that is objectively evil and immoral.* That life can be penetrated through and through with injustice and uncharitableness, and its effects may be disastrous for others and for the Church! (Note: the above picture is necessarily a caricature and must be considered with due discretion.)

Let us now turn to the *true concept of justice*:

1. Of the three virtues which are in the strict sense moral virtues (i.e., temperance, fortitude and justice), *justice is the highest and most important.* Justice is so truly the keystone of the entire structure of man's moral life (in so far as he is a man) that it is absolutely fundamental to all the other moral virtues. Without justice, man's temperance and fortitude tend to be evil rather than good. As St. Ambrose says, "Fortitude without justice is a source of evil."[106] (It leads to tyranny and oppression and ill-directed aggression.) This has been made all too clear in the history of the twentieth century. "Man reveals his true being in its greatest purity when he is just" (Josef Pieper[107]). The good man is not so much the strong man, or the temperate man, as the *just* man (*id.*[108]).

2. Why is justice higher than the other moral virtues?

a) Man is subject to justice in so far as he is a *spiritual* being (in so far as he has a body, he is subject to the other moral virtues).

b) The other moral virtues *safeguard* the good; prudence and justice *orient man directly towards the good.* This is an important point because after all, our lives are happy in proportion as we attain to the true and lasting good, which is something outside and beyond ourselves, and the ordering of our own being within

---

106. *"Fortitudo sine justitia iniquitatis materia est"* (*De Officiis Ministrorum*, 1.35 [*PL* 16, col. 34C], quoted in Josef Pieper, *Justice*, trans. Lawrence E. Lynch [New York: Pantheon Books, 1955], 41).

107. Pieper, *Justice*, 40, citing Aquinas, *Summa Theologiae, Secunda Secundae*, q. 58, a. 3 (Aquinas, *Opera Omnia*, 3.215).

108. "Justice is the highest of the three moral (in the strict sense) virtues; justice, fortitude, and temperance. The good man is above all the just man" (Pieper, *Justice*, 40).

itself is *only a preparation* for this reaching out to objective good and for sure possession of it.

c) The inordinate use of *reason* appears more in vices which are opposed to justice than in the vices opposed to fortitude and temperance (inordinate sensuality causes these acts). But "the good of reason shines more brightly in justice than in the other moral virtues."[109]

3. Justice is a divine attribute by which God orders all things rightly in His universe. Human justice reflects the justice of God in so far as man enters consciously and deliberately into the plan of God by his own cooperation, using the light of reason and of faith *to judge as God judges*, to act and think as a son of God, to assume *responsibility* towards God and towards other men for his own share in the life of the cosmos. In other words, justice presupposes that a man takes mature cognizance of who he is and of his place in the cosmos and assumes responsibility for certain functions in that cosmos *which depend on his own free will and judgement*. The great beauty of justice then begins to appear more clearly when we understand that it means:

a) Conscious conformity with the will of God as ruler and master of the universe—thus a fulfillment of one of the reasons for man's creation, that he should be God's viceroy in the material world. A spirituality which is incapable of appreciating this sublime vocation of human nature will be a negative and defeatist spirituality which will make man not a son of God but less than a man. *We must take an active and creative share in the life of the cosmos*, not only in the sense that we obediently follow a set of hard and fast rules laid down for us, but also in the sense that we *assume responsibility for a certain creative contribution of our own*. (This is clear from the parable of the talents:[110] the man with one

---

109. Pieper, *Justice*, 44 (which reads: ". . . than in any of the other . . ."), citing Aquinas, *Summa Theologiae, Prima Secundae*, q. 66, a. 4 (Aquinas, *Opera Omnia*, 2.229–30).

110. Mt. 25:14-30; cf. Lk. 19:11-27, which has the detail about the napkin.

talent who hid it away in a napkin did not think he was doing God the Creator of the world an injustice, but he was. For God expected him to *use his own initiative* and bring greater good out of the good he had received.) God has created man and placed him in the world as an administrator and a builder and a creator, not only to keep what is there and take care of it, but also to develop what has been given into his charge. This applies to our life as members of society, as workers, as citizens, etc. Man will be held responsible for his misuse of creative opportunities in every field—politics, work, art, religion, etc. It is very important to see that all this is implied by a true Christian concept of justice, and we may, perhaps, receive the grace to wake up and see that our religious life may, when wrongly lived and wrongly understood, represent a *calamitous diminution* of a very great good, a withdrawal, a burying of our talents, a sterilization of vital gifts given to us for the good of all. Hence, we must understand what we are about and appreciate the virtue of justice.

b) Justice also means the perfection of man as a *social being*, enabling him to attain his end precisely as a member of society, that is to say, in union with others. In other words, the acts of a just man lead not only to his own salvation but to the salvation of those with whom he lives and deals. They lead not only to his own happiness but to the happiness and better order of society, which, by virtue of his justice, becomes {a} better and more effective means for the salvation of those who will come after him. (On the other hand, *all injustice, whether conscious or not, deliberate or not*, makes it harder for man to be saved himself, harder for him to be happy himself, and harder for others to be saved or happy. Objective injustice, no matter what may be the subjective intentions of the one who commits it, always corrupts society and lessens its efficacy as a means of bringing men to their last end easily and happily.) Failure to realize these things makes people unwilling to take an interest in the vitally important subject of justice. Because they are fundamentally unjust, they fail to realize that it is to their interest to act disinterestedly and to think of the good of others and of society as well as of their own—the two being correlative.

4. *The Objectivity of Justice*: the most important characteristic of the virtue of justice is its objectivity. Temperance and fortitude depend on our own subjective dispositions. Justice as such has nothing to do with how we feel about the act, or even with our interior willingness to perform the act. A just act is one by which we render to another what is due to him, not one by which we "feel well-disposed" or "feel inclined to be good" to him. (Note, however, in some cases justice demands that we think well of others, but in that event, the thought is something objectively owed to the other, and not the source of the value of our just act. It is the *object* of that act, not its form.) "The 'other person' is not affected by my subjective disposition, by what I intend, think, feel or will, *but only by what I do. Only by an external act* will another receive what is his due" (*Pieper*[111]). This objectivity of justice is a condition of *security*; it guarantees a constant and stable contact with reality. *The values of justice are what they are, and my thought and feeling about them can do nothing to change them.* If I owe a man twenty dollars, it will do no good for me to have the most devoted thoughts about him, to say the nicest things about him, to give him twenty slaps on the back—none of these things will make me just: I have to pay him twenty dollars. This may seem an obvious and trite observation, and yet in our day we have gradually come to act as if it was sufficient to feel well-disposed towards the poor, to have a great respect for labor, to revere the law, to esteem holy obedience—and then we can, without noticing it and without feeling the slightest pang of conscience, neglect the poor, cheat the laborer, get around the law and do our own will whenever we please.

Once again, it is most important to remember this in connection with our vows. To make a vow is to take on a strict obligation in justice. What is then required is *that we keep our vow* and not just that we have a high theoretical esteem for the life of the vows. This is a source of real infidelities. A religious imagines

111. Pieper, *Justice*, 34, which reads: ". . . will the other receive what is *his*, his due" (emphasis added).

that because he has a high ideal of the religious life (in theory), he is beyond faults against his vows, and in fact he may keep them very badly (v.g., stability and conversion of manners). He may unconsciously be living in a spirit of injustice and neglecting the fidelity which he owes to the obligation he has assumed. The same thing applies to religious obedience. Obedience is *due in justice* to one's legitimate superior. The obligation is *objective* and not merely a matter of cultivating certain interior dispositions. Some religious seem to think that obedience consists in permitting the superior to give a command and accepting the command in a "good spirit"—with a kind of "sportsmanship." But they do not take care to *carry out the order.* For them obedience is not objective, but only a subjective matter of *not showing displeasure or resentment* at the orders of another. They have no real conception of doing the will of another.

Hence justice has a great value in that it keeps us in contact with the truth and delivers us from subjective delusions. "In the realm of justice good and evil are judged purely on the basis of the deed itself, regardless of the interior dispositions of the doer; the point is NOT HOW THE DEED ACCORDS WITH THE DOER, BUT RATHER, HOW IT AFFECTS 'THE OTHER PERSON'" (Pieper[112]). One must be *mature* to make religious vows; but without justice, our moral life does not bear the stamp of maturity.

5. *Justice and Personalism*: justice is not concerned merely with things, but with *rights*. The concept of right is meaningless unless it is based on an appreciation of what it means to be a *person*. Only a person can have rights (in the strict sense of the word). To recognize the rights of another is to recognize him as a person. To recognize him as a person is to pay reverence to the creative act and will and love of God which keeps him in being as an individual, as an image of God. To render to another person

---

112. Pieper, *Justice*, 34, which reads: ". . . disposition of . . ." (emphasis added), citing Aquinas, *Summa Theologiae, Prima Secundae*, q. 60, a. 2: "*secundum rationem commensurationis ad alterum*" ("according to the reason of their effect on another") (Aquinas, *Opera Omnia*, 2.208).

what is his right is to pay reverence to the image of God in man, to do homage to the creative act of God and to God's own designs for man. In rendering to another his right, I am cooperating in God's plan for him.

To deny to another his rights, (a) is to depreciate him as a person; (b) to depreciate the idea of personality itself; (c) to refuse reverence to God, Who is imaged in the human person; (d) to despise the plan of God for others and for ourselves; (e) ultimately, to be unjust is to put ourselves in the place of God and to live by our own "providence," which is a supreme disorder. (The systematic injustice of totalitarian states flows from a philosophy which has completely lost contact with reality and with truth. In such states, the question of rights of persons have become equally irrelevant. Everything is judged by purely opportunistic standards—the immediate *apparent* good of the state; all the basic values of reason and of humanity are set aside. Man degrades and dehumanizes himself and his fellow creatures. The systematic injustice practiced by totalitarian regimes is the most destructive agency at work in the world today. If it continues to work unchecked, the world will be reduced to complete barbarism and chaos within a hundred years.)

"'That something belongs to a man inalienably means this: the man who does not give a person what belongs to him . . . *is really doing harm to himself*" (Pieper[113]). This shows the deep inner meaning of justice—it is always more than mere conformity to an external dictate. In the last analysis, our injustice to men flows from our injustice towards God. The greatest harm that man can do to himself is to ignore his debt to God. This being ignored, he cannot possibly pay his debts to other men, because he has put himself in the place of God and in so doing has distorted all standards of value.

6. *Justice and Prudence*: it should be remarked that justice and prudence are always in fact inseparable. "The act of justice not only presupposes that act through which a man comes to

113. Pieper, *Justice*, 16 (emphasis added).

have what is his due; it also presupposes the act of prudence, *which means that the truth of real things is transposed into a decision"* (Pieper[114]). Without prudence we cannot rightly assess the obligation we must meet and determine how to meet it properly. Justice is concerned with the right itself; prudence also examines the circumstances of the particular case, which might change the obligation, and *not only considers but also decides* by what means the obligation is to be fulfilled. All this, as we shall see later, is very important when one comes to make a vow. For instance, an imprudent person may conceive that before he makes his vow he has a hard and fast obligation to make that vow, even though there may be definite indications that the vow should not be made in his case. He may approach his religious vows with a misconception of what he is doing and indeed make his vows invalidly, or make vows he is unable to keep. Thus, through lack of prudence, he would also commit an injustice.

7. *The definition of Justice*: we have now seen all the elements that enter into the virtue of justice. The classic definition of that virtue is PERPETUA ET CONSTANS VOLUNTAS JUS SUUM UNICUIQUE TRIBUENDI.[115]

a) It is a *voluntas*—it is free and voluntary, spontaneous, mature. It is not a mere hazy velleity, a romantic theory that "men ought" to have certain goods. St. Thomas says: *Justitia est habitus qua quis recte operatur et vult* (II-II, q. 58, a. 1, ad. 2).[116]

b) *perpetua et constans*—it perdures; {it} is not a mere flash of enthusiasm. It is something solid and reliable. It applies in all cases, not in some cases only (favoritism {is} injustice).

c) *tribuendi*—to *give* something even with considerable cost to ourselves. Justice can in certain cases demand even the sacrifice of our life itself.

---

114. Pieper, *Justice*, 23, which reads: ". . . have his due; . . ." (emphasis added).
115. "the perpetual and constant will to render to each his right" (Aquinas, *Summa Theologiae, Secunda Secundae*, q. 58, a. 1 [Aquinas, *Opera Omnia*, 3.213], cited in Pieper, *Justice*, 110, n. 9).
116. "Justice is the habit by which each acts and wills rightly" (Aquinas, *Opera Omnia*, 3.214, which reads: "*est enim habitus secundum quem aliquis . . .*").

d) *unicuique*—to each person, in every case (cf. above).

e) *jus suum*—*his* objective right.

8. *Conclusion*: this should be enough on the important topic of justice. But man finds himself faced with certain debts that cannot be paid in full. For these debts—for instance, to our parents and to God—there are special virtues, parts of the virtue of justice—virtues like religion and piety—in which virtue consists not in meeting a strictly determined measure but in *going beyond strict calculation*. "In order to keep the world going, we must be prepared to give what is not in the strict sense obligatory" (Pieper[117]). There is in fact a time when to remain just, we must give others *what is not due to them*. This is all the more true when we see what Christ demands of His followers. "For I tell you that unless your justice abound more than that of the scribes and Pharisees you shall not enter into the Kingdom of Heaven" (Matt. 5:20). Hence, for a Christian, justice must be sublimated in charity, and for a follower of Christ it is an *injustice* not to try to measure up to the charity of Christ. We no longer have any right to be angry with our brother, to hate our brother in our hearts, even if he has done us serious injury. READ Matthew 5:38 to the end:[118] we must be perfect as our heavenly Father is perfect—that

---

117. Pieper, *Justice*, 104, which reads: ". . . strictest sense . . ."

118. "You have heard that it hath been said, An eye for an eye, and a tooth for a tooth. But I say to you not to resist evil: but if one strike thee on thy right cheek, turn to him also the other: And if a man will contend with thee in judgment, and take away thy coat, let go thy cloak also unto him. And whosoever will force thee one mile, go with him other two. Give to him that asketh of thee, and from him that would borrow of thee turn not away. You have heard that it hath been said, Thou shalt love thy neighbour, and hate thy enemy. But I say to you, Love your enemies: do good to them that hate you: and pray for them that persecute and calumniate you: That you may be the children of your Father who is in heaven, who maketh his sun to rise upon the good, and bad, and raineth upon the just and the unjust. For if you love them that love you, what reward shall you have? do not even the publicans this? And if you salute your brethren only, what do you more? do not also the heathens this? Be you therefore perfect, as also your heavenly Father is perfect."

is to say, we are obliged to seek as perfect a resemblance with Him as possible, by selfless charity. Not to seek this is to refuse to God what is His due.

But now we reach the paradox: how is it possible for anyone to keep such an obligation? We may see the beauty of the Law of God and desire to fulfill its obligations, but when we try, we find that we are unable to do so and that instead of doing the good we desire, we sin and fall into injustice and evil. READ Romans 7:15 to the end.[119] Paul gives the only answer. Who shall deliver us from slavery to injustice? "the grace of God by our Lord Jesus Christ." In order that we may be just, we first have to pay off an infinite debt we have contracted to God as sinners, and then live on a level above our own nature. In order that we might be able to do this, Jesus Himself died on the Cross, to become our "justice and sanctification and redemption" (1 Cor. 1:30). True justice, for a Christian, is simply Christ's justice in us. Cf. St. Bernard, *Sermo 22 in Cantica*, n. 11:

> What virtue is there for those who do not know Christ, the power ["*virtus*"] of God? Where is there true prudence but in the doctrine of Christ? *Where is there true justice but in the mercy of Christ?* Where is there temperance but in the life of Christ? Where true fortitude but in the Passion of Christ? They alone are to be called prudent who are steeped in His

---

119. "For that which I work, I understand not. For I do not that good which I will; but the evil which I hate, that I do. If then I do that which I will not, I consent to the law, that it is good. Now then it is no more I that do it, but sin that dwelleth in me. For I know that there dwelleth not in me, that is to say, in my flesh, that which is good. For to will is present with me; but to accomplish that which is good, I find not. For the good which I will, I do not; but the evil which I will not, that I do. Now if I do that which I will not, it is no more I that do it, but sin that dwelleth in me. I find then a law, that when I have a will to do good, evil is present with me. For I am delighted with the law of God, according to the inward man: But I see another law in my members, fighting against the law of my mind, and captivating me in the law of sin, that is in my members. Unhappy man that I am, who shall deliver me from the body of this death? The grace of God, by Jesus Christ our Lord. Therefore, I myself, with the mind serve the law of God; but with the flesh the law of sin."

doctrine. *They alone are just who by His mercy have received pardon for their sins.* They alone temperate who apply themselves to the imitation of His life; they alone are strong who cling firmly to the memory of His sufferings in time of trial. Vainly does he labor for virtue who seeks it somewhere else than in the Lord of Virtues.[120]

This puts Christian justice in its true light: in its relation to the mercy of God. In St. Bernard's doctrine, justice is inseparable from mercy, not only in the relations of man with God but also in the relations of man with man.

To sum it all up, we must love one another as Christ has loved us, and this is the summary of that "justice" which is demanded of the Christian and which consists in conformity to Jesus crucified. In the light of this, it is evident that the New Testament concept of justice is not merely that of fulfilling obligations which, once fulfilled, leave us free to do what we like. For the Christian, duty is not something merely exterior, to be "gotten out of the way" so that one is no longer burdened with an obligation, and the fulfillment of duty is not merely casting off an unpleasant pressure. To do a duty is to enter into communication with the God we love, and to approach the sources of life and light.

THE PASSION OF CHRIST

The Paradox of Justice: there is implanted in man's very nature a law that demands that he give to other men and to God that which is just; and what is "just" in regard to God, the supreme worship due to Him, surpasses infinitely the capacity of human

---

120. "*Quid vobis cum virtutibus, qui Dei virtutem Christum ignoratis? Ubinam, quaeso, vera prudentia, nisi in Christi doctrina? Unde vera justitia, nisi de Christi misericordia? Ubi vera temperantia, nisi in Christi vita? Ubi vera fortitudo, nisi in Christi passione? Soli ergo qui ejus doctrina imbuti sunt, prudentes dicendi sunt; soli justi, qui de ejus misericordia veniam peccatorum consecuti sunt; soli temperantes, qui ejus vitam imitari student; soli fortes, qui ejus patientiae documenta fortiter in adversis tenent. Incassum proinde quis laborat in acquisitione virtutum, si aliunde eas sperandas putat, quam a Domino virtutum*" (PL 183, cols. 883D–884A).

nature to give. Hence, even in the natural order, the virtue of religion does not concern itself with the payment of an ordinary debt—as if there were some ritual acts which were capable of satisfying our obligation towards God. Religion finds itself confronted with an obligation too great to be resolved, *a debt too great to be paid*. What, indeed, can we give to God in return for creating us and maintaining us in being at every moment and giving us all that we need for life? The mere fact that He gives us existence and then does with us what He wills (whether it be pleasing or not to ourselves) is already an immense favor beyond all our capacity for repayment in kind. But that He also gives us so many temporal and spiritual gifts and shows us the way to happiness (even prescinding from perfect beatitude—for we are dealing with the natural order alone)—all this establishes a relation of indebtedness which is altogether unique. Furthermore, this relationship is the most fundamental of all those in which a man can find himself. It is bound up with his very life and existence. Hence, by the very fact that man *is* and *lives*, he is already obliged to a debt of gratitude which cannot be paid in full. No matter what he may do to pay it, he is a useless servant.

The virtue of religion is then a virtue which accepts this situation and deals with it, and thus of its very nature it *perfects justice* by going beyond the limits of strict equality. Religion meets an impossible obligation. How? by a certain *excess* that goes beyond the strict norms of reason because in our debt to God there are no limits. Strict justice (in the sense of seeking to make an "adequate compensation") would be in fact a perversion and an injustice in the sphere of religion. (This was the error of the Pharisees, who were able to weigh and measure everything in their gifts to God. They placed exact limits everywhere and knew precisely what was pleasing to God and for what reason and how much. Everything had its price. But in our relations with God we come to realize that we cannot deal with Him on equal terms except, precisely, when we enter into the realm of the "excessive," in the sense of going beyond the mere norms of human justice. In the fullest sense, we will see that the *excess* that truly pleases

God is the "ecstasy" of pure love, which takes us out of ourselves and delivers us entirely over to His good pleasure.)

Now, this *excess* is the very heart of our consecration to God by vow. It is also of the very nature of sacrifice and *latria*, the supreme act of religion. It belongs likewise to the virtue of penance, not in the sense that penance goes beyond the limits of true prudence—for then it is displeasing to God—but in the sense that no amount of penance can ever be taken, of itself, as a full satisfaction for sin. Our worship and penance have this note of *excess* when they are based on the *true realization of the holiness of God*.

All that has been said so far applies merely to the natural order—assuming that man had not fallen into a state in which his nature is oriented away from God by sin. But the fact of sin makes an even greater difference. The fact that we have offended God, and have deliberately refused Him the service we owe Him, is an infinite injustice which, added to the fact that it separates us completely from Him, makes it absolutely impossible for us *either to please Him or make satisfaction in any way* by our own natural powers. If no amount of sacrifice could be adequate homage to God even if it came from a nature that had not fallen, from a sinful race sacrifice is not only inadequate but even *displeasing* to God in so far as it comes from those who are His enemies.

> To what purpose do you offer me the multitude of your victims, saith the Lord? I am full, I desire not holocausts of rams, and fat of fatlings, and blood of calves, and lambs and buck goats. When you came to appear before me, who required these things at your hands, that you should walk in my courts? Offer sacrifices no more in vain: incense is an abomination to me. The new moons, and the sabbaths, and other festivals I will not abide, your assemblies are wicked. My soul hateth your new moons, and your solemnities: they are become troublesome to me, I am weary of bearing them. And when you stretch forth your hands, I will turn away my eyes from you: And when you multiply prayer, I will not hear: for your hands are full of blood. (Isaias 1:11-15)

(In point of fact, however, the sacrifices of pagans and of Jews before the coming of Christ were pleasing to God to the extent that they were figures of the one true sacrifice and were united to a good moral life.) Hence, in the actual dealings of the human race with God, neither religion nor justice can be of any real help unless they are elevated to a higher plane. But this is precisely what is done by the charity of God, in Christ.

1. God elevates man above his nature, for the flesh profiteth nothing. He sends His Son into the world that all who receive Him may have the power "to be born not of blood nor of the will of the flesh nor of the will of man but of God" (John 1:13). For "unless a man be born again of water and the Holy Ghost he cannot enter into the Kingdom of God" (*id.* 3:3).

2. As a result of this elevation of man's nature by union with the Incarnate Word, man's religious acts become not only pleasing to God, but they merit everlasting life, for all who are given to Christ by the Father enter with Him into the Kingdom of the Father: "No man hath ascended into heaven but he that descended from heaven, the Son of Man who is in heaven . . . that whosoever believeth in Him may not perish, but have life everlasting" (*id.* 13-15).

3. But this is attained *only by the power of the Passion of Christ by which we* pass from death to life, since all who are united to Him in His death share the life of charity which He, as Head of the Church, grants to every one of His members as a share in His risen life, enthroned at the right hand of the Father. "So must the Son of *Man be lifted up* [i.e., on the Cross] that whosoever believeth in Him may not perish. . . . For God *so loved the world* as to give His only begotten Son, ... God sent not His Son into the world to judge the world, but that the world may be saved by Him" (*id.* 14ff.).

These lines, seen in their context of the third chapter of St. John, tell us all about the situation of the Christian with regard to God and his "religious obligations." The unimaginable, inconceivable debt of man to God, altogether beyond satisfaction, *can in fact be paid.* Here is the supreme excess, a divine excess, an excess of love that could come from God alone. Our supreme religious duty is then to enter into the divine excess, the "ecstasy" of divine charity beyond all limits, beyond all belief, in which God has given us His own Son to be a propitiation for our sins, a mediator between ourselves and Him, but more than that, our very union with Him. What God then asks of us is that we give ourselves to Him in Christ, unite our oblation of our lives with the oblation of Christ in His Passion, and then what happens? We receive all back in Him, for in God we receive all. In "paying" our debt we have incurred a further infinite debt, and we repay in kind by giving God back to God, and ourselves with Him, in order to receive God back from God and ourselves in Him.

In other words, true religion is this: to enter into the infinite and unending circuit of love that is the very life of the Three Divine Persons, in which each gives all to the other and receives all again in His gift. And God has willed to make this simple and easy for us, showing us that the proof of our union with Christ in His sacrifice *is our love for one another.* This then is supreme justice; this is perfect religion, all in the transcendent charity of the Son Who gave Himself for us on the Cross, in the fire of the Holy Spirit, that God might be perfectly glorified in Him and in us His members. This explains why the Church says (in the blessing of the palms on Palm Sunday) that true justice is to love God above all: *Deus, quem diligere et amare justitia est.*[121] This is the paradox of Christian justice.

In order to understand more of this, we must look at God's love for us in the Passion of Christ and see with what supreme wisdom the love of God has triumphed over the evil of sin in order to save us and unite us to Himself.

---

121. "God, to cherish and to love Whom is justice" (*Missale Romanum: Ex Decreto Sacrosancti Concilii Tridentini Restitutum: S. Pii V, Pontificis Maximi, Jussu Editum: Aliorum Pontificum Cura Recognitum: a Pio X Reformatum et Benedicti XV Auctoritate Vulgatum,* 4th ed. [New York: Benziger, 1944], 139).

The Glory of the Cross: in the great High Priestly Prayer which is the quintessence of the prayer of Christ and of His Church, expressing the whole meaning of the sacrifice of the Incarnate Word on Calvary and in the Mass, we see that *the dominant note is that of victory and glory.* The Cross is the glory of the Father and of the Son, because it is the supreme expression of God's love for men and (in Christ) of man's love for God elevated to a divine level. "Father the hour has come, glorify Thy Son. . . . that Thy Son may glorify Thee. . . . Glorify me Father with Thyself, the glory which I had before the beginning of the world, with Thee. . . . The glory which Thou hast given to me I have given to them [in His word, and in the sacrament of the Eucharist] that they may be one as we also are one" (John 17). This supreme manifestation of the glory of God is in the union of all the faithful in one Body, in Christ, with the Father, through the power of the Holy Spirit, the mystery of Christ, the "restoration" of all in Christ. This is brought about by the sacred Passion and the glorious Resurrection of the Savior.

There are *innumerable* aspects to this one glory: the aspect of merit, of satisfaction, of redemption, of salvation, of sacrifice, of victory. Vonier points out (in *The Victory of Christ*[122]) how the Cross is a glorious victory over death, the devil, evil itself—how this sense of victory is the most essential note of the true Christian spirit. "Christ's glorification is the one article of the Creed that is to be held responsible for the Christian temperament" (vol. 1, p. 240). "The glorification of Christ is the justification of the Christian religion even more than that religion's inward merit and perfection" (p. 241).[123] Our liturgy is "exclusively a Liturgy of victory" (246). He summarizes: "A people that considers it to be a historic fact, transcending all other events, that Christ has delivered it and is delivering it from its sins, has within itself a fount of perennial joy which no amount of material wealth can ever replace. Worship of that great Redeemer naturally becomes

---

122. Anscar Vonier, osb, *The Victory of Christ* (1934), in *The Collected Works of Abbot Vonier*, 3 vols. (Westminster, MD: Newman Press, 1952–53), 1.237–325.
    123. Text reads: "Glorification . . ."

the primary task of such a people, and its power of suffering adversity in temporal matters is well nigh inexhaustible" (261). He adds, significantly: "Not by believing in the wickedness of man, but by believing in Christ's power to overcome all wickedness are we saved" (277).[124]

Again we see how God's justice and mercy, working together in a mystery of infinite wisdom and love, have enabled us to pay the impossible debt we owe to the Father, by uniting ourselves, through faith and the sacraments, in the victory of His Son. Justice demands that by our faith the power of the Cross may triumph in our lives, in order that Jesus Himself may become our justice and our worship and our love of the Father: "That no flesh should glory in His sight, but of Him are you in Christ Jesus Who is made to us wisdom and justice and sanctification and redemption, that, as it is written, he that glorieth may glory in the Lord" (1 Cor. 1:29-31). Our supreme worship of God is then to "glory in the Lord," which is precisely what we do as a Body in the liturgy when we unite ourselves with the sacrifice of Christ and acclaim the glory of God in union with the heavenly hosts, joining in the eternal song of thanksgiving and praise which is intoned forever in heaven by the Redeemer and *Choregos*[125] Who saves us and unites us to Him in His worship of the Father. It is for this reason that the sign of the Cross will be seen in heaven on the great day of glory when the *Presence* (Parousia) of the glory of Him Who stands in our midst as one we know not will finally burst forth and be seen by all.

St. Thomas and his teaching on the Passion:[126] St. Thomas, with his usual serene clarity and wisdom, answers some perplexing questions about the Passion of Our Lord and in doing so gives us the sane and Catholic view of this great mystery—a view which enables us truly to live the mystery of the Cross and Resurrection of the Son of God without falling into pious eccentricities.

124. Text reads: ". . . of men, but . . ."
125. "chorus leader."
126. *Pars Tertia*, qq. 46–49 (Aquinas, *Opera Omnia*, 4.198–221).

Since the mystery of the Cross is the very heart of the Christian faith and life, it is essential that we have a true and well-balanced understanding of what it implies, in order to follow Christ to eternal glory. In the mystery of the Cross we find the Christian answer to the great questions concerning the basic realities of man's existence: life and death, good and evil, joy and suffering, the purpose of our existence, sin, punishment, forgiveness, merit, beatitude. If we do not solve these problems in the light of the Cross, we are not Christians: for a Christ Who is not crucified is not Christ. And since Christianity is not only a doctrine but a mystery, that is to say a *fact*, we must not only study the Passion but enter into it mystically through faith and the sacraments. If we do not grasp the actual belief of the Church on this great mystery, we will certainly deviate very far from her spirit and from the guidance of Christ Himself. Let us follow St. Thomas step by step in his study of the Passion:

1. *The Passion of Christ was necessary*. Christ had to suffer—not in the sense that once He had become incarnate it was a foregone conclusion that all the pent-up anger of God "had to" pour itself out on Him, whether He willed it or not, but rather in the sense that *He freely embraced the Cross* as an act of love for us and for His Father, and by this act he merited for Himself a glory above all other. The briefest answer to the question, "Why did Christ have to suffer for us?" is, "In order to pay a debt which we were incapable of paying—in order to redeem us, a thing which He alone could accomplish." In order to understand St. Thomas's full meaning, we note that he makes the following statements. *It was not absolutely necessary that someone satisfy for man's sin.* Since God is the supreme Judge, there is no denial of His justice if He forgives sin without demanding any satisfaction (III, q. 46, a. 2, ad. 3).[127] In remitting sin without satisfaction, He would be acting mercifully instead of justly, and He is perfectly free to do this, just as any human prince is free to do the same. But if God

127. Aquinas, *Opera Omnia*, 4.199.

did in fact ask that the sin of man be satisfied for, this was not out of stricter justice but out of greater mercy: *hoc fuit abundantius misericordiae quam si peccata absque satisfactione dimisisset* (III, q. 46, a. 1, ad. {3}).[128] The Passion of Christ was necessary, then, not by some blind compulsion of injured rage or outraged justice that *had to be* satisfied, but by the demands of the infinite mercy of God for men. Christ freely embraced this necessity out of love. In so doing, as Image of the Father, he gave a perfect reflection of the love (the glory) of the Father (Father, glorify Thy Son![129]).

2. *The Cross was an especially appropriate means for redeeming man.* First of all, it was an overwhelmingly clear demonstration of God's love for us (*sic Deus dilexit mundum!*[130]), and therefore a means of awakening our own love, to give ourselves in return, since *love is our salvation* (*Per hoc provocatur homo ad diligendum, in quo perfectio humanae salutis consistit* [III, q. 46, a. 3, corp.][131]). It is also an example of obedience, which is essential to love. It is then, too, a greater deterrent from sin. Notice here how the love of God works: instead of taking vengeance for sin on us and crushing us, God visits all the consequences of sin upon Himself in order to show us how to avoid these consequences by avoiding their cause. The final reason given by St. Thomas is the most admirable of all: the Cross was most fitting because *hoc ad majorem dignitatem hominis cessit,*[132] since it is a man who dies on the Cross and thus overcomes the devil and defeats death. Another insight into the glory of the Cross—which is the glory of divine mercy and divine love—is gained in the laconic remark of the Angelic

128. "This entailed more abundant mercy than if He had absolved sins without satisfaction" (Aquinas, *Opera Omnia*, 4.198–99, which reads: ". . . *abundantioris* . . ."; text reads: "ad. 1").

129. Cf. Jn. 17:1.

130. "God so loved the world" (Jn. 3:16).

131. "In this way man is stirred up to love, in which the perfection of human salvation consists" (Aquinas, *Opera Omnia*, 4.200, which reads: ". . . *provocatur ad eum diligendum* [to love Him] . . .").

132. "This accorded with the greater dignity of man" (Aquinas, *Opera Omnia*, 4.200).

Doctor that Christ on the Cross died as a holocaust consumed not in the flames of outraged justice but in the charity of the Holy Spirit: *Loco materialis ignis fuit in holocausto Christi ignis charitatis* (q. 46, a. 4, ad. 1).[133] So too in the life of the vows—this same fire of charity, the fire of the divine Spirit of Love, must consume our lives. Otherwise, the sacrifice cannot be pleasing to God—it is a mere destruction of the victim without acceptation on the part of Him to Whom it was offered.

3. *The Sufferings of Christ*: in the following articles (q. 46, aa. 5, 6, 7, 8),[134] St. Thomas surveys the totality and the intensity of Christ's sufferings. He suffered from every possible source in every possible way, descended to the final depths of humiliation. Indeed, just as by His glory He excels all other beings, so in His Passion He descended into an abyss of humiliation beyond any other being (a. 5, ad. 2).[135] There can be no minimizing of the sufferings of Christ in any way: on all sides, from every point of view, they were the greatest possible. *Dolor in Christo fuit maximus inter dolores hujus vitae.*[136] He suffered the most painful possible kind of death. In the interior of His soul He suffered an intolerable agony, whose magnitude is beyond our conception, burdened as He was under the sins and iniquities of the whole world. All these sufferings were heightened by the special sensitivity of Christ Himself. (But we must not exaggerate His sensitivity to the point where it becomes morbid, for His was a *perfect* human nature, and it is a sickness and a perversion of human nature to feel acute suffering in what is normally healthy and pleasurable.) Christ suffered in His whole soul, *secundum totam suam animam* (a. 7),[137] that is to say, in its essence and in all its faculties, yet St.

---

133. "In place of material fire, there was in Christ's holocaust the fire of charity" (Aquinas, *Opera Omnia*, 4.201, which reads: "*Loco autem materialis . . .*").

134. Aquinas, *Opera Omnia*, 4:201–205.

135. Aquinas, *Opera Omnia*, 4.202.

136. a. 6: "In Christ suffering was the greatest among the sufferings of this life" (Aquinas, *Opera Omnia*, 4.203, which reads: ". . . *praesentis vitae* [of the present life]").

137. Aquinas, *Opera Omnia*, 4.204, which reads: "*secundum totam animam.*"

Thomas is careful to add that the object of these faculties, God, was not to Him a cause of pain. Indeed, he even goes on to point out that in the very summit of His soul, Jesus still enjoyed the Beatific Vision during the Passion—*superior pars animae perfecte fruebatur Christo patiente* (a. 8).[138] But this did not bring joy to his soul, either directly or indirectly. Even in the higher part of Christ's soul, where the vision of God persisted undisturbed, there was also pure suffering together with the vision of God. How was this possible? The simple act of vision remained, but the totality of the subject, Christ, Who had the vision, was filled with suffering, so that He drew no consolation from it. (We can perhaps understand this a little better when we think that a man can suffer bitterly in every part of his being and yet have unfelt peace of perfect charity in the summit of his soul.) This is one of the most frightening mysteries of the Passion of Christ, again something utterly beyond our grasp. It is important to remember this correct statement of the issue and not erroneously assert that Christ in His Passion was "deprived of the Beatific Vision" and utterly cut off from His divinity, which would be in fact an impossibility, savoring of Nestorianism, and would at the same time make the Passion much less awesome a mystery. We always tend to forget the fact that Christ is God, and in the sufferings of Christ it is God Who suffers, not indeed as God, but in the humanity hypostatically united to His Divine Person (a. 12).[139]

4. *The Cause of the Passion*: first of all, the main cause of the Passion is the obedience of the Son of God. Here we see how St. Thomas, with his unerring instinct, hits upon the most essential point without difficulty—and in this we see how strikingly his teaching is confirmed by the liturgy. *Christus factus est obediens usque ad mortem*[140]—this constant refrain stresses the main theme

---

138. "While Christ was suffering, the higher part of his soul had perfect delight" (Aquinas, *Opera Omnia*, 4.205).

139. Aquinas, *Opera Omnia*, 4.208.

140. "Christ became obedient even unto unto death" (Phil. 2:8), cited in somewhat different form in q. 47, a. 2 (Aquinas, *Opera Omnia*, 4.209).

of Holy Week. By His obedience in the Passion, Christ fulfilled
the entire law: all the moral precepts being founded on charity
were fulfilled by this supreme act of love. All the ceremonial precepts were fulfilled in this great act of *latria* in which the typical
rites and sacrifices of the Old Law were fulfilled. All the judicial
precepts of the Law were fulfilled by this act of justice which
perfectly paid man's debt to God—by a divine excess which is
beyond the power of man to reach. If Jesus delivered Himself
to death out of obedience, this does not mean that He Himself
was the cause of His own death. He was killed by the Romans
and the Jews, but He freely permitted them to commit this crime
upon His Person, and besides that, the violence wrought upon
Him had its effect on His Body only when and as much as He
Himself allowed (q. 47, a. 1 corp., ad. 3).[141]

St. Thomas then asks in what sense the Father (i.e., strictly
speaking, the Holy Trinity) delivered Jesus up to death.

(1) First of all, we must understand that Christ is the Word
of God Incarnate. As Word, His divine will to suffer is identical
with the Father's will that He should suffer. It is one and the
same will (a. 3, ad. 2).[142]

(2) This divine will, identical in the Father and the Son, has
nothing but good in view; it is nothing but love. There is in it no
cruelty and no hatred (ad. 3).[143]

(3) As far as the human will of Christ is concerned, it would
have been cruelty and violence if the Father had delivered Jesus
up to death against His (human) will and in spite of Him. But
precisely one of the ways in which the Father is said to have delivered Jesus to death was by *inspiring Him and filling Him with
the divine charity* towards men and towards Himself, which made
Him freely embrace the Cross out of love (a. 3, corp. and ad. 1).[144]

---

141. Aquinas, *Opera Omnia*, 4.209.
142. Aquinas, *Opera Omnia*, 4.210.
143. Aquinas, *Opera Omnia*, 4.210.
144. Aquinas, *Opera Omnia*, 4.210.

(4) In the Passion of Christ we see indeed the severity of the Father towards sin, but at the same time His goodness in giving us a Redeemer to make satisfaction for our sins, which to us would have been impossible otherwise (a. 3, ad. 1).[145]

(5) Finally, the Father delivered Christ up to death in the sense that the divine will had preordained the Passion and did not prevent the Passion from taking place. St. Thomas takes the words of Jesus on the Cross, "My God, why hast Thou forsaken me?"[146] in this sense, that God had left Him completely at the mercy of His persecutors, and not that God had somehow completely withdrawn from Jesus ontologically speaking, which would be impossible.

Other sidelights on the cause of the Passion (q. 47, a. 4):[147] St. Thomas remarks that it was right for Christ to be done to death by the Gentiles as well as the Jews because the effects of His Passion, namely man's salvation, reached first of all the Jews and then the Gentiles. Here again we see the same astounding emphasis on the superabundant charity of Christ—for salvation of His persecutors was something He particularly prayed for on the Cross, and He "wanted some Gentiles to be there," says St. Thomas in so many words, to gain the effect of this prayer (see ad. 1). Nevertheless (aa. 5 and 6),[148] the crime of those who crucified Jesus was the most terrible of all crimes, chiefly on the part of the Princes and Priests of the Jews who knew, or ought to have known, Who He was. In the Jewish rank and file, and the pagans, the crime was less grave because excusable by ignorance.

5. *The Effects of the Passion*: q. 48, a. 1[149] is a commentary of the central thought of the epistle of Holy Thursday[150]—because of

145. Aquinas, *Opera Omnia*, 4.210.

146. Mt. 27:46; Mk. 15:34.

147. Aquinas, *Opera Omnia*, 4.211.

148. Aquinas, *Opera Omnia*, 4.211–12.

149. Aquinas, *Opera Omnia*, 4.213.

150. 1 Cor. 11:20-32 (*Missale Romanum*, 166–67; *Missale Cisterciense* [Westmalle: Ex Typographia Ordinis Cist. Strict. Obs., 1951], 147–48).

His humility and obedience, Christ was glorified. But, St. Thomas points out, Christ after His Passion was *glorified not only in Himself but also in His members.* The glory of the members is a necessary consequence of the Passion and Resurrection of the Head, for "grace was given to Christ not only as to an individual but as to the Head of the Church, in such a way that it might overflow on to all other members of the Church."[151] Hence, he goes on, the works of Christ have the same fruit in His members as they had in Him. Thus by His Passion He merited for them salvation. True, through all His other works He also merited for us, but in His Passion above all He *saved* us because of the superabundant love with which He suffered, which arouses great love in us, and because the manner of His death was most proper to remove impediments to grace in our souls. One of the great fruits of the Cross, and one of the signal effects of that grace in our souls, is the desire to conform ourselves to Christ crucified by a life in the cloister under religious vows. This indeed is one of the most perfect ways of uniting ourselves to Christ on the Cross and allowing Him to live in us.

{In} a. 2,[152] St. Thomas, once again raising the question of satisfaction, points out that the obedience and charity of Christ were so great in His Passion that He gave to God far more than would have been required by all the sins of man. Because of the perfect love with which Christ suffered, because of the dignity of His Divine Person, and because of the greatness and over-whelming totality of His sufferings, the value of His death was so great that it was not only sufficient but superabundant—so that no matter what sins may be committed by men until the end of time, all will have been wiped out in advance by the charity of Christ—provided only that men avail themselves of it.

We note also that the charity of Christ was infinitely greater than the malice of those who crucified Him (ad. 2).[153] It would

---

151. "*Christo data est gratia non solum sicut singulari personae, sed inquantum est caput Ecclesiae, ut scilicet ab ipso redundaret ad membra*" (Aquinas, *Opera Omnia*, 4.213).

152. Aquinas, *Opera Omnia*, 4.213–14.

153. Aquinas, *Opera Omnia*, 4.214.

seem that God could hardly have allowed the Passion to take place otherwise. This also gives us insight into the reason why God permits evil to happen to the Church and His saints: in order that it may be overcome by good. By the same tokens as above, the suffering and death of Christ was a perfect sacrifice most acceptable to God (a. 3).[154] In stating this, St. Thomas bases himself on an interesting definition of sacrifice from St. Augustine (*De Civitate Dei*, x.6): "A true sacrifice is any work which is performed in order that we may be united to God in holy fellowship [*ut sancta societate inhaereamus Deo*], related to that end of good which will make us truly blessed."[155] This enables us to integrate our notion of sacrifice and of the Passion in our study of the life of the vows, which in their turn are a true sacrifice in the above sense—they unite us to God, in union with the sacrifice of Christ, in a "holy society"—the union of the faithful in charity in His Mystical Body, that we may possess true blessedness, the vision of God in Christ for all eternity. Through the sacrifice of the Cross, to which we are united by our vows, we attain to eternal glory.

The sacrifice of the Cross is also our *redemption* (a. 4).[156] To redeem someone is to ransom him from slavery and captivity. Without the Cross, we were in a double slavery—to sin and to punishment. "His Passion was, as it were, a price by which we were released from this twofold servitude."[157] Someone advances the argument that we could not be redeemed because we belonged to God anyway. St. Thomas replies (ad. l):[158] true, we belong to Him always as Creator, but not always by *charity*. God so loves us, so desires our love, our wills, our union with Him, that He was willing to give Himself to redeem us from captivity to another.

---

154. Aquinas, *Opera Omnia*, 4.214.

155. "*Verum sacrificium est omne opus quod agitur, ut sancta societate inhaereamus Deo, relatum scilicet ad illum finem boni, quo veraciter beati esse possumus.*"

156. Aquinas, *Opera Omnia*, 4.214–15.

157. "*Ejus passio fuit quasi quoddam pretium, per quod liberati sumus ab utraque oblatione*" (Aquinas, *Opera Omnia*, 4.215).

158. Aquinas, *Opera Omnia*, 4.215.

But to whom was the price paid? By sin man had become the slave of the devil. But the price of our redemption, the Precious Blood of Jesus, was certainly not paid to the devil, but to the justice of God. Slavery to the devil and to sin is the just punishment of sin, and God permitted the devil to seize and torment men in order that man might be punished, but the devil had seized man unjustly, and therefore no "ransom" was due to him. The ransom was paid to the divine justice itself, and this means to say that in fact the mercy and charity of God wiped out everything.

The whole Trinity was the first cause of this redemption of man, but Christ as Man was the immediate and instrumental cause. He willed to assume this role freely, out of love (a. 5).[159] Again {there is} the same emphasis, always: because of the hypostatic union, Christ was the instrumental cause of our salvation (a. 6).[160] By the Passion, then, we are liberated from *sin* (q. 49, a. 1),[161] from the power of the devil (a. 2),[162] from punishment for sin (a. 3).[163] For we must realize that in the Passion of Christ *all the debt for sin has been paid*, if we but avail ourselves, by charity, of His merits (*per fidem et charitatem, et fidei sacramenta* [ad. 1];[164] by baptism and penance [ad. 2]). "The satisfaction of Christ has its effect in us in so far as we are incorporated in Him as members to our Head. But a member should be *conformed* to the Head. . . . Hence we receive the spirit of adoption of sons though still in this mortal flesh, and then, configured to the Passion and death of Christ, we pass into His glory."[165] The application of this to the life of the vows is quite obvious.

159. Aquinas, *Opera Omnia*, 4.215–16.

160. Aquinas, *Opera Omnia*, 4.216.

161. Aquinas, *Opera Omnia*, 4.216–17.

162. Aquinas, *Opera Omnia*, 4.217–18.

163. Aquinas, *Opera Omnia*, 4.218.

164. "through faith and charity and the sacraments of faith" (Aquinas, *Opera Omnia*, 4.218, which reads: ". . . *per fidei sacramenta*").

165. ad. 3: "*Satisfactio Christi habet effectum in nobis, inquantum incorporamur ei, ut membra suo capiti . . . . Membra autem oportet capiti conformari. . . . Recipiamus in anima spiritum adoptionis filiorum . . . adhuc corpus passibile et mortale ha-*

FRIENDSHIP WITH GOD

The death of Jesus on the Cross is the supreme proof of God's love for us.

> The Lord hath appeared from afar to me. Yea, I have loved thee with an everlasting love, therefore have I drawn thee, taking pity on thee. . . . They shall come with weeping and I will bring them back in mercy, and I will bring them through the torrents of waters in the right way, and they shall not stumble in it: for I am a Father to Israel, and Ephraim is my firstborn. . . . For the Lord hath redeemed Jacob and delivered him out of the hand of one that was mightier than he. . . . Behold the days shall come, saith the Lord, and I will make a new covenant with the house of Israel and with the house of Juda, not according to the covenant which I made with their fathers. . . . But I will give my law in their bowels and I will write it in their heart and I will be their God and they shall be my people, and they shall teach no more every man his neighbour and every man his brother, saying: Know the Lord, for *all shall know me from the least to the greatest of them, saith the Lord*, for I will forgive their iniquity, and I will remember their sin no more. (from Jeremias 31)

READ especially Jeremias 31:2-9:[166] God's love for Israel, the Church—drawing all the faithful together in one charity; 31:10-

---

bentes; postmodum vero configurati passionibus, et morti Christi, in gloriam immortalem perducimur."

166. "Thus saith the Lord: The people that were left and escaped from the sword, found grace in the desert: Israel shall go to his rest. The Lord hath appeared from afar to me. Yea I have loved thee with an everlasting love, therefore have I drawn thee, taking pity on thee. And I will build thee again, and thou shalt be built, O virgin of Israel: thou shalt again be adorned with thy timbrels, and shalt go forth in the dances of them that make merry. Thou shalt yet plant vineyards in the mountains of Samaria: the planters shall plant, and they shall not gather the vintage before the time. For there shall be a day, in which the watchmen on mount Ephraim, shall cry: Arise, and let us go up to Sion to the Lord our God. For thus saith the Lord: Rejoice ye in the joy of Jacob, and neigh before

14:[167] the joy of the messianic kingdom; 31:17-20:[168] the tender love of the Lord for Ephraim his penitent son (cf. {the} parable of the Prodigal[169]); 31:23-28:[170] again, the consolations of the messianic

---

the head of the Gentiles: shout ye, and sing, and say: Save, O Lord, thy people, the remnant of Israel. Behold I will bring them from the north country, and will gather them from the ends of the earth: and among them shall be the blind, and the lame, the woman with child, and she that is bringing forth, together, a great company of them returning hither. They shall come with weeping: and I will bring them back in mercy: and I will bring them through the torrents of waters in a right way, and they shall not stumble in it: for I am a father to Israel, and Ephraim is my firstborn."

167. "Hear the word of the Lord, O ye nations, and declare it in the islands that are afar off, and say: He that scattered Israel will gather him: and he will keep him as the shepherd doth his flock. For the Lord hath redeemed Jacob, and delivered him out of the hand of one that was mightier than he. And they shall come, and shall give praise in mount Sion: and they shall flow together to the good things of the Lord, for the corn, and wine, and oil, and the increase of cattle and herds, and their soul shall be as a watered garden, and they shall be hungry no more. Then shall the virgin rejoice in the dance, the young men and old men together: and I will turn their mourning into joy, and will comfort them, and make them joyful after their sorrow. And I will fill the soul of the priests with fatness: and my people shall be filled with my good things, saith the Lord."

168. "And there is hope for thy last end, saith the Lord: and the children shall return to their own borders. Hearing I heard Ephraim when he went into captivity: thou hast chastised me, and I was instructed, as a young bullock unaccustomed to the yoke. Convert me, and I shall be converted, for thou art the Lord my God. For after thou didst convert me, I did penance: and after thou didst shew unto me, I struck my thigh: I am confounded and ashamed, because I have borne the reproach of my youth. Surely Ephraim is an honourable son to me, surely he is a tender child: for since I spoke of him, I will still remember him. Therefore are my bowels troubled for him: pitying I will pity him, saith the Lord."

169. Lk. 15:11-32.

170. "Thus saith the Lord of hosts, the God of Israel: As yet shall they say this word in the land of Juda, and in the cities thereof, when I shall bring back their captivity: The Lord bless thee, the beauty of justice, the holy mountain. And Juda and all his cities shall dwell therein together: the husbandmen and they that drive the flocks. For I have inebriated the weary soul: and I have filled every hungry soul. Upon this I was as it were awaked out of a sleep, and I saw, and my sleep was sweet to me. Behold the days come, saith the Lord: and I will sow the house of Israel and the house of Juda with the seed of men, and with

age; 31:31-35[171]: the new covenant—every man will know the Lord. In these typical Old Testament passages on the messianic kingdom we already have a clear picture of God's love for His people and a promise that He will dwell with them in mercy and holiness and justice, and they shall be consoled by His intimate friendship—not only that, but He will teach them and instruct them (by His Spirit) and they will all have intimate knowledge of Him. What is this but to say that God wills to dwell with us in intimate communion and holy friendship surpassing in intimacy and love any created friendship? This then is our vocation.

The New Testament makes it even clearer. John 1: God comes into "His own," desiring to be "received" by them with love—those who receive Him become the "sons of God, born not of blood, nor of the will of the flesh nor of the will of man, but of God."[172] John 3: the Lord comes to give us new life in His Spirit—God so loved the world *as to give His only begotten Son* that whosoever believeth in Him may not perish but may have life everlasting (14-15). This, then, is the true message of the crucifix. How can we be deaf to such a message? John 6:44-47: no one can

---

the seed of beasts. And as I have watched over them, to pluck up, and to throw down, and to scatter, and destroy, and afflict: so will I watch over them, to build up, and to plant them, saith the Lord."

171. "Behold the days shall come, saith the Lord, and I will make a new covenant with the house of Israel, and with the house of Juda: Not according to the covenant which I made with their fathers, in the day that I took them by the hand to bring them out of the land of Egypt: the covenant which they made void, and I had dominion over them, saith the Lord. But this shall be the covenant that I will make with the house of Israel, after those days, saith the Lord: I will give my law in their bowels, and I will write it in their heart: and I will be their God, and they shall be my people. And they shall teach no more every man his neighbour, and every man his brother, saying: Know the Lord: for all shall know me from the least of them even to the greatest, saith the Lord: for I will forgive their iniquity, and I will remember their sin no more. Thus saith the Lord, who giveth the sun for the light of the day, the order of the moon and of the stars, for the light of the night: who stirreth up the sea and the waves thereof roar, the Lord of hosts is his name."

172. Jn. 1:12-13.

come to me unless the Father draw him—they shall all be taught of God; he that believeth in me hath life everlasting; *id*. 54-59: the living Bread—he that eateth my flesh hath everlasting life; as I live by the Father, he that eateth me the same shall live by me. John 14:15-26: the promise of the Holy Spirit—those who love Jesus do His will and abide in Him and He in them; the Spirit teaches us all things. John 15:4-14: abiding in Christ the vine, by love—loving Him, loving the Father, loving one another. John 17:23-24: the supreme communion—participation in the divine life and circumincession of the Divine Persons: "I in them and Thou in me that they may be made perfect in one."

All that we have said so far in these talks on the life of the vows pales into insignificance in the light of such texts from the Scriptures. We have spoken of man, of his passions, of his will, of his habits. We have seen the helps God has given him in the natural order. We have seen something of the meaning of law and justice. But all this is nothing in comparison with the true meaning of our Christian vocation, and the true substance of the perfection to which we are called. This is a LIFE OF INTIMATE FRIENDSHIP WITH GOD, A LIFE TRANSFORMED IN CHRIST, A LIFE IN WHICH WE BECOME ONE WITH CHRIST AND ARE THUS DIVIN-IZED AND LIVE AS TRUE SONS OF THE ETERNAL FATHER. This life of divine sonship is the life of *charity*, a life lived entirely in Christ, beyond and above the level of nature and of this world, and yet still immersed in the problems and difficulties and also in the natural conditions of mortal life.

This life is the *life of the Holy Spirit* in us. It is the *life of grace*. It is the *life of the Church*. We enter this life of grace by a *sacramental consecration* at baptism. In this sacrament of illumination our souls are sealed with the Spirit of promise; Jesus takes possession of them by His Spirit. Our wills and minds and bodies and all that we have and are become His possession, and all the use we make of our faculties belongs to Him. Our *baptismal vows* guarantee this permanent possession of our whole being by God. Hence every Christian lives in fact under the most serious vows, and to break these vows is spiritual death. The life of grace depends on the generosity with which we keep our baptismal vows. The greater our fidelity, the greater will be the intimacy with God in our souls.

In order to increase this life of charity, to make this intimacy with God more perfect, in order to multiply occasions of fidelity and generosity by setting aside distraction and other obstacles to a life given totally to God, we make *religious vows*. The whole purpose of these vows is to *intensify the love and the intimacy of our friendship with God*. In order to understand this better, we must now consider the *mystery of charity and divine grace*.

I. CHARITY: charity is friendship with God. Therefore, it *cannot be explained merely as a virtue by which we love God*. Friendship is two-sided. It always takes two to make a friendship. Charity is not only a love which we cultivate for God, but it is the effect of God's love for us. Charity is a love by which we love God and are loved by Him, a love which is *shared* between us and God, a love by which God gives Himself to us and we give ourselves to Him. Charity is the result of the *creative action* of God's love for us. It is the fruit of a divine love which wills to be loved in return because God knows that love itself is the supreme gift and the perfection of life (cf. St. Bernard[173]). It is the crown of all God's gifts. It is a communication of God's own inner life. It is the sharing of a divine secret, the mystery of God Himself. God opens our hearts to His love in order to give us what is most secret and most intimate and most personal in Himself. By charity, God gives us what cannot be given in any other way. He reveals

---

173. See Gilson's discussion of the influence of 1 John 4 on St. Bernard's thought (*Mystical Theology of St. Bernard*, 22–25); he writes, "If God is charity, and if charity must needs be in us if we are to know God, then charity must of necessity be given by God. There we have the origin of the distinction, so important in St. Bernard, between the Charity which is God, and the charity which in us is the 'gift' of God. This distinction is suggested by the verse that declares that charity comes from God: 'Caritas ex Deo est' (I *John*, IV, 7)" (22); he adds, "No one has ever seen God, but if charity dwells in us, then, since it is the gift of God, God dwells in us, and then our love for Him is perfect. In default, therefore of a vision of God which is not vouchsafed us here below, there is a presence of God in the soul which marks the point of perfection of charity in us" (citing 1 Jn. 4:12, 16) (23).

what cannot be revealed in any other way. And in return, we give to God what cannot be given in any other way—the perfection of charity *is the ultimate and total surrender of our inmost self*. Only in this total surrender can we ever reach perfect peace; short of it our lives will always be narrow and incomplete. The supreme secret of the spiritual life is the secret of this surrender, and this secret can be learned only from God Himself, Who is love: we must *first receive the full outpouring of His mercy* before we can perfectly respond with the *outpouring of our whole self in gratitude*.

Self-surrender: it is not sufficient to have a word here and a phrase there—a few slogans—a few catchwords. These end up by misleading us unless they are fitted into a *coherent body of doctrine* with a *definite orientation*. As soon as we speak of self-surrender, we speak of the mystery of the divine will. To surrender our inmost self to God is to abandon ourselves to the supreme reality which is His will in and through all things. But *what does He will*? Are all the different manifestations of His will ordered to some special end?

There are different degrees in our surrender, which constitutes the perfection of our friendship with God. In proportion as we surrender ourselves to Him we become free; we are able to love in His love. In the beginning, we submit without quite understanding. There may be more or less repugnance. We may have to go against our own deepest feelings and convictions to surrender to God in the beginning.

A. The initial surrender is the act of faith by which the soul abandons the guidance of its own lights in order to accept the light of God in darkness. John 6:28-29: This is the work of God, that you believe in Him whom He hath sent. John 1:12: To as many as received Him He gave the power to become the sons of God . . . who believed in His Name.

B. To "receive" Christ is to receive His *Word*. But this reception of the word implies an interior change of heart (*metanoia*), a lasting conversion which makes us live in Him, "bring forth fruit in patience"[174] (Parable of the Sower). This means in fact *bearing*

174. Lk. 8:15.

with the purification sent by the Father. John 15:2: Every branch that beareth fruit, He will purge it that it may bring forth more fruit; cf. Luke 8:13-15: Those who hear the word with joy but have no roots—those who bring forth fruit in patience. It also means above all *denying ourselves* to take our Cross and follow Him.

C. It is by doing the Father's will that we become united to the Son—for, as He says, it is His meat to do the will of the Father. John 4:34: My meat is to do the will of Him that sent me, that I may *perfect His work.* John 5:30: I cannot of myself do anything. . . . As I hear, so I judge. . . . I seek not my own will but the will of Him that sent me.

D. As the Father has sent Jesus into the world, so Jesus has sent His disciples into the world (John 17:18). To these, Jesus says (Luke 10:16): He that heareth you heareth me; he that despiseth you despiseth me, and he that despiseth me despiseth Him that sent me. Hence, to prove our friendship with God, we must receive Him in those who represent Him. Here, too, we find again the basic "work of God"—to "believe in Him whom He sends"[175]—to see Christ in His Church.

E. The great work of God is the "building up of the Body of Christ"[176] (see St. Paul *passim*). This work replaces the works of the Old Law so that His mercy may be manifest to the world in the Mystical Christ (cf. Ephesians 2:4-13, 4:1-16).

F. Consequently, the great commandment is the commandment of charity. It is in fulfilling this commandment that we fulfill all the will of God and the whole law, for it is thus that we abandon ourselves fully and truly to the Holy Spirit, the one Who both makes known to us the will of God and gives us power to carry out that will, and in fact moves us to fulfill that will, and then, finally, when we have done the will of God, it is the Holy Spirit Who rewards us by uniting us more closely in the bonds of love which are the union of the Three Divine Persons themselves, manifested in the mystery of the Church.

175. Jn. 6:29.
176. Eph. 4:12.

In these few lines we see something of the true Christian perspectives of self-surrender. It is not a matter of merely carrying out a lot of prescriptions which we do not understand and do not particularly like—things we "have to do" because they are more or less "arbitrarily" willed by God. No, it is a matter of entering clear-sightedly into God's plan and freely carrying out His will in order *to accomplish His work*, which is also the desire of our own hearts. Then ultimately, as the Psalmist says (Ps. 144:19), VOLUNTATEM TIMENTIUM SE FACIET.[177] Yes, so great is the sharing of love that God even does "the will" of those who love Him (explain). Hence, the whole question of self-surrender is one of *charity* and incorporation in the Mystical Christ.

How do we give ourselves to God by charity? The answer to this question is the whole moral theology of the New Testament, summed up: "A new commandment I give you, that you love one another as I have loved you, that you also love one another. *By this shall all men know that you are my disciples, if you have love one for another*" (John 13:34-35). "The love of our neighbor worketh no evil. Love therefore is the fulfillment of the Law" (Romans 13:10; READ also {in the} same chapter {vv.} 8-10:[178] the context explains).

St. Maximus the Confessor says: "Although the commandments are numerous we can sum them all up in one sentence: Thou shalt love the Lord thy God with thy whole heart and all thy mind and all thy strength, and thy neighbor as thyself; he who struggles to put this into effect *thus carries out all the commandments*" (*Liber Asceticus* [PG 90.916][179]). For St. Maximus, love implies the *mastery of all the passions*, and the way of charity is the

---

177. "He will do the will of them that fear him."

178. "Owe no man any thing, but to love one another. For he that loveth his neighbour, hath fulfilled the law. For thou shalt not commit adultery: Thou shalt not kill: Thou shalt not steal, Thou shalt not bear false witness: Thou shalt not covet: and if there be any other commandment, it is comprised in this word, Thou shalt love thy neighbour as thyself. The love of our neighbour worketh no evil. Love therefore is the fulfilling of the law."

179. J. P. Migne, ed., *Patrologiae Cursus Completus, Series Graeca* [PG], 161 vols. (Paris: Garnier, 1857–66).

perfection of all sane asceticism, but above all it carries out God's plan for man, restoring the *unity of mankind in one brotherhood*. The charity by which we love God is measured by the charity with which we love our brother in God, but this charity in turn must be based on a knowledge of the Mystical Christ. It is by loving our brother *in Christ* that we fulfill the law, intensify our union with God, purify our hearts, abandon ourselves to God. The charity of Christ is the life of a *visible* but Mystical Body, the Church. Union with the other members of the Church in one faith, one discipline, one worship is the only fully reliable sign of union with Christ. The charity by which we are united with God is then nourished and communicated to us in the Church, particularly in the liturgy of the Church, at Holy Mass, and in our participation in the sacrifice of the Church and of the Son of God. The life of charity is therefore not a merely interior and affective life; it is also exterior and effective. The interior and the exterior work together. Both together reach their highest expression in the *mystery of the Eucharist*. All other aspects of charity radiate from this central point—kindness, almsgiving, self-sacrifice, cooperation with others in labor, etc., etc. Our life is a life of *sharing* both burdens and consolations in Christ. This notion of solidarity is most important to give our idea of charity a correct and genuinely Christian orientation. If we merely think of charity as an "affective" and interior thing, we will tend to cultivate a delusion. The affective charity which is indeed most important is measured by and nourished by exterior and effective charity, and all depends on union with Christ in His Mystical Body, the Church.

The life of love in Christ implies:

1) A deepening realization of our common sharing in Christ's love for us.

2) A deepening need to help one another fulfill in our lives God's loving plan in our regard—ardently desiring the spiritual and temporal good of our brother as we desire our own.

3) Desiring *everything* that in *any* way is for the good of my brother and of the Church—and of mankind as a whole.

4) Desiring the salvation of enemies of God and of the Church.

5) In all and above all, resting in the supreme love of God, desiring God to be all in all—satisfied that *He is God*—seeking His glory in all things.

Other details about the life of perfection, and our giving of ourselves to God by charity, will be taken up later. The basic idea is that of communion, sharing, the gift of self; and this implies (to sum up) *communion and sharing with our brethren* in effective charity in order to have *communion with God interiorly and spiritually*, all summed up and nourished by our *liturgical participation in the great mystery of God's love for us, the Eucharist.*

It is easy to see from this how one who wishes to dedicate himself to God by religious vows will naturally seek to intensify his participation in the life of the Church by entering into a religious community and embracing that common life which is the great *school of charity* and which provides innumerable opportunities for giving ourselves, for sharing the burdens and the joys of others and deepening our common participation in the life of the Mystical Christ. In order to understand this life of charity in Christ, this *work* by which we are "builded together into one dwelling of God in the Spirit," let us READ a few lines from St. Paul—Ephesians 4:1-16.[180] This sums up all we want

---

180. "I therefore, a prisoner in the Lord, beseech you that you walk worthy of the vocation in which you are called, With all humility and mildness, with patience, supporting one another in charity. Careful to keep the unity of the Spirit in the bond of peace. One body and one Spirit; as you are called in one hope of your calling. One Lord, one faith, one baptism. One God and Father of all, who is above all, and through all, and in us all. But to every one of us is given grace, according to the measure of the giving of Christ. Wherefore he saith: Ascending on high, he led captivity captive; he gave gifts to men. Now that he ascended, what is it, but because he also descended first into the lower parts of the earth? He that descended is the same also that ascended above all the heavens, that he might fill all things. And he gave some apostles, and some prophets, and other some evangelists, and other some pastors and doctors, For the perfecting of the saints, for the work of the ministry, for the edifying of the body of Christ: Until we all meet into the unity of faith, and of the knowledge of the Son of God, unto a perfect man, unto the measure

to say—the idea of the vocation to union with God, fulfilled by generous efforts to live in unity with our brethren, that God may be "through all and in us all"—each one, however, carrying out his own personal part, for there is diversity in unity, and the end in view is that we should all "meet into one perfect man," the maturity and "fullness" of Christ—that "doing the truth in charity, we may in all things grow up in Him who is the Head, even Christ."

Our vows must always be seen against this background of the great "common work" (liturgy) which is the building up of the Mystical Christ. Our obedience unites us to the visible community in which Christ lives. Our chastity is the sacrifice of those pleasures which most tend to center a man upon himself and his own satisfaction. Our poverty renounces all those goods which the greed of man takes to itself, thus depriving others. Christian poverty is never merely a negative giving up, but also a positive giving *to*. What we renounce should be given to those who have not, shared with the poor, in whom Christ lives most truly. Our stability unites us for life to one visible "monastic Church" to which we are, as it were, "married." Our fidelity in this respect has a stabilizing influence on the whole Church and wins graces of fidelity for many others in their respective vocations. Our conversion of manners includes all that has been said about poverty and chastity, as well as the purification of our love in the eschatological waiting for the coming of Christ. The purity of our life, the purity of our hope, is as it were, part of the vigilance of the whole Church waiting for the coming of the Redeemer. We are the watchmen on the walls of the heavenly Jerusalem, waiting for the coming of the Bridegroom.

---

of the age of the fulness of Christ; That henceforth we be no more children tossed to and fro, and carried about with every wind of doctrine by the wickedness of men, by cunning craftiness, by which they lie in wait to deceive. But doing the truth in charity, we may in all things grow up in him who is the head, even Christ: From whom the whole body, being compacted and fitly joined together, by what every joint supplieth, according to the operation in the measure of every part, maketh increase of the body, unto the edifying of itself in charity."

Charity in this sense is the crown and perfection of the whole life of virtue—it is in the fullest sense Christian justice, sanctity—it is Christ living and acting in us. All the other virtues prepare the way for this charity. They all depend on it for their own existence. *Without this love of all in Christ, this ardent self-surrender that Christ may be all in all,* the other virtues tend to be only exterior and incomplete. Finally and above all, this charity gives our whole moral life that unity without which it would not be a "life" at all. It is not sufficient to make spasmodic, disconnected acts of virtue, even though they may be heroic. Christian perfection depends not first of all on what we do but on *what we are*—or rather who we are. And unless our life is integrated in Christ by charity, unless we are a "new creature" in Him, all efforts and virtues are more or less useless and bound to ultimate frustration. That was why St. Paul rejected the ceremonies and practices of the Old Law as insufficient and "fleshly": For in Christ Jesus neither circumcision availeth anything nor uncircumcision, *but a new creature* (READ Galatians 6:12-16[181]).

The object of charity: we love first of all and above all God Himself. Then we love ourselves out of charity—our souls and even our bodies. After that comes love of neighbor out of charity, with preference given to those who are closest to God (if we know) and for those closest to ourselves. This love of neighbors reaches out to all men and angels. We love charity itself out of charity; and finally our charity reaches out to the whole cosmic order in which we see mysteriously evident the infinite wisdom of God's plan for the redemption of the world and the recapitulation of all things in Christ. Charity seeks every possible way to

---

181. "For as many as desire to please in the flesh, they constrain you to be circumcised, only that they may not suffer the persecution of the cross of Christ. For neither they themselves who are circumcised, keep the law; but they will have you to be circumcised, that they may glory in your flesh. But God forbid that I should glory, save in the cross of our Lord Jesus Christ; by whom the world is crucified to me, and I to the world. For in Christ Jesus neither circumcision availeth any thing, nor uncircumcision, but a new creature. And whosoever shall follow this rule, peace on them, and mercy, and upon the Israel of God."

manifest itself, even in little things, perhaps especially in little things: for the delicacy and sincerity of love is proved most of all by attention to small things which will please the beloved or will bring about a greater good for him. In general, all the works of charity tend to share with others the good things of heaven and of earth, and the sins against charity tend to block the neighbor out and exclude him from some of these good things, which we take exclusively to ourselves. To cultivate charity we must then open our hearts, develop a spirituality that is open and broad and universal and far-reaching. We must have wide horizons, be very humble and generous; we must have warm and understanding hearts; we must resist all temptations to exclusivism and segregationism, all forms of contempt and rash judgement, all drives to set ourselves above others and consider ourselves "not as other men."[182] We must be willing to sacrifice our feelings, not be sensitive, not bear grudges, not be sulky or demanding. All this is learned in community life.

II. DIVINE GRACE: we have said that our life of friendship with God is a life of charity, a sharing of God's charity towards us. We have spoken a little of the *virtue* of charity. This virtue of charity is a *habitus* by which we respond to God's love for us and make Him a return of love, both in Himself directly and in our brethren. It is the *life* of the Son of God in us, manifesting itself and uniting us to God in His Church, which is, as it were, a continued incarnation of charity, a blazing hearth of divine love in which the love of God for men and the love of men for God form one great and eternal flame. Underlying this *virtue of charity* is the charity of God for us, and in us, which we call *sanctifying grace*.

Sometimes, particularly in the writings of the Fathers, there is no clear distinction made between charity as a theological virtue and charity in the sense of sanctifying grace. The distinction is this: grace is the effect of God's love in us, the dynamic and transforming love of God in our own being. Charity is the

182. Lk. 18:11.

response of our faculties to God's love, returning to Him a love which comes from Him, the fruit of our transformation. Charity and grace go together so that they seem to form but one reality, the reality of love. As in breathing we inhale and exhale, so in the life of love we inhale (receiving grace) and exhale (in works of love). But this image is imperfect, since the reception of grace is not something intermittent: grace is the permanent presence of God's love in us—or to be more concise, grace is the presence in us of God Who is love. Grace is the created effect of God's uncreated Love present in our souls. Grace is the created participation, by our souls, in the uncreated Love of God. Grace is God in us. To possess grace is to be possessed by God, *to be possessed by love. Habere est haberi* (St. Bonaventure[183]).

Grace is the embrace by which God takes our soul to Himself and holds us in His own heart. Grace is the embrace by which the Holy Spirit unites us to the Father in the Son. Grace is the indwelling of the Three Divine Persons in us, not merely as static and passive "objects" but as dynamic and active principles of love and life, conforming our souls to their own relations so that the Word in us reflects the glory and splendor of the Father (by faith) and the Holy Spirit unites us to the Father in the Son as a result of the love that flows from this glory that is given to us in the Word.

All the above statements are contained, it would seem to us, in these three quotations from Scripture:

1. "Charity is of God, and everyone that loveth is born of God, and knoweth God. He that loveth not, knoweth not God, for God is charity. By this hath the charity of God appeared towards us, for God hath sent His only begotten Son into the world that we may live by Him. . . . *In this we know that we abide in Him and He in us, because He hath given us of His Spirit.* And we have known

183. "To possess [a habit] is to be possessed [by God]," a compressed version of Bonaventure's discussion of the *"habitus deiformis"* in *Breviloquium,* V.1 (*Sancti Bonaventurae Opera Omnia,* ed. PP. Collegii S. Bonaventurae, 10 vols. [Quaracchi: Collegium Sancti Bonaventurae, 1882–1902], 5.253a).

and have believed in the charity which God hath to us: and he that abideth in charity abideth in God and God in Him" (1 John 4). Here we see the two realities—the "birth from God" which is divine grace, the presence of His Son living in us that we may live by Him, the sending of the Spirit by Whom we know the Son living in ourselves, by Whom we know the love of God for us, and by Whom we respond to God's love by loving Him and loving our brethren—thus increasing the intimacy with which our souls are possessed by the love of God.

2. "The charity of God is poured forth in our hearts by the Holy Ghost Who is given to us."[184] (The presence of the Holy Ghost, as an uncreated gift of love, results in charity, the created "state" of one loved and possessed by God, and moves us to works of love.)

3. St. Peter sums it all up: we are sanctified by the divine power given to us through the knowledge of Christ and making us "PARTAKERS OF THE DIVINE NATURE" (2 Peter 1:4).

In a word, God Who is present in all things by His power, presence and essence, makes Himself present to us in a very special way "by grace." This presence of God is a presence in which the *Three Divine Persons dwell in us.* The Triune God makes Himself known to us and in us, as the object of love, sharing with us His own love, which establishes the relations of the Persons among themselves. Grace is the sharing, by a created spirit, in the uncreated relations of the Divine Persons, so that the image of the Son in us is united with the Father in the love of the Holy Spirit. Furthermore, by grace we are united to all the others who are caught up in the same sanctifying and transforming action of God's love, so that we all form one "Son of God" in one love of the Holy Spirit, for the one Father Who is in us all.

Special Cautions:

1. In speaking of grace, we must avoid regarding it as a "thing" or an "object" or a commodity. Too glib a use of the formulas and

184. Rom. 5:5.

metaphors used by certain spiritual writers will lead to a complete incomprehension of the reality of grace. For instance, St. Bernard's comparison of the "canals" and "reservoirs"[185] in order to stress the importance of the *fullness of charity* makes us too readily think of charity as something that fills us quantitatively like water or gasoline. Grace is then something of which we need a "big supply," and we concentrate on the "quantity" of grace we have, etc. Grace is not a *thing*, not an *object*. It is not something that stands between us and God, a kind of link or medium between us and God. Grace is a "quality" of the soul that is *immediately* united with God and possessed by His love.

2. It would be a perversion to become so obsessed with the idea of the "state of grace" as to forget that the state of grace is simply the presence of the Holy Spirit in us, or at least the effect of that presence. To be in the state of grace is not to be furnished with something which will enable the Spirit to come to us—like a diving suit which would permit us to descend into the depths of God. The "state of grace" is not a kind of "protection" that will enable us to bear the holiness and justice of God (this would be arrived at from too human and literalistic an interpretation of the "wedding garment" of the Gospel[186]). The state of grace is the state of one who is in the friendship of God and is embraced by God's love—rather than a purely juridical condition like that of, say, American citizenship. Do not think of the state of grace too much in terms of whether or not one is guilty or not guilty—whether one has or has not his proper passports and identifications when confronted by the police. This falsifies our relations with God and creates distrust and fear when in fact He asks confidence and abandonment of ourselves to His love

185. See *Sermones in Cantica*, 18.3 (*PL* 183, col. 860AD), in which Bernard says the wise man who teaches others only what he has learned and practiced himself is more like a reservoir, which shares the overflow of its fullness, than a canal, which immediately lets pass what it receives; one should not presume to pass on what one has not adequately grasped oneself.

186. Mt. 22:11-14.

and His will. (Needless to say, of course, at times when a "state of grace" is required for the reception of a sacrament, there are juridical considerations that *must* be kept in mind, and without these there can be no friendship with God. But the whole concept of the state of grace will be distorted if we think of it *only* or *primarily* in terms of this kind of situation.)

3. Don't become so involved in subjective reflections on grace as "something we have" and forget that grace is really the evidence of something that we *are* as a result of the presence of the Three Divine Persons in supernatural love and friendship in our souls. Do not concentrate on your degree of grace (which no one knows but God). Do not try to measure what cannot be measured by man—turn to God and love Him: that is why He has come to you.

4. *Grace is simply the will of God translated into transforming action in the depths of our being*, making us His friends. Grace is the effect of a divine *fiat*, a creative command of God's love, *by which He "looks upon us and loves us" and in so doing produces His own love in the inmost depths of our own being*, like the sun shining into the inmost depths of a diamond and reflecting Himself therein. *Increase in grace* is simply the intensification of this light and this impression of the divine will in our own being, a more intimate embrace, an entering into a "deeper center" in God, a greater purity of love, a greater alienation from self and from all that is opposed to love, a greater readiness to be acted upon by the Holy Spirit and to abandon oneself to the action of the divine will (cf. St. John of the Cross[187]).

---

187. See *Living Flame of Love*, especially the commentary on stanza 1 (Peers, *Complete Works of Saint John of the Cross*, 3.18–40 [first recension], 3.118–40 [second recension]), in which the Holy Spirit is identified with the flame of God's love that wounds the soul in its "deepest centre" (23–27, 122–27) and leads to divine union in which "the will and desire are to such an extent united with God that the soul regards it as its glory that it should fulfil the will of God in it" (33, 133).

III. PRAYER: we have seen two important aspects of our life of friendship with God: the "grace" by which God, present to us as our Father and our friend, takes possession of our souls; the charity by which we respond to God's love and *share His love*. We have seen that this sharing of love with God means in practice the sharing of His love with our brethren—desiring them to love Him as He loves both us and them. But now, what of the even more important consideration: our love for God in Himself? How does our love for Him seek to express itself in this life of friendship with Him?

Love first of all seeks the person and presence of the beloved. In the mystery of fraternal charity we have realized that we enter more deeply into communion with God. But there is also necessary, even more necessary, a solitary and personal communion in which the *soul is alone with Him and surrenders itself to Him in silence and recollection*. Wherever there is grace, wherever there is the "presence" of God, the soul responds to that presence with *awareness and desire for communion*. This is the deepest and most fundamental and most noble desire of man's soul.

It is true that grace can be present in a soul that is seldom vividly aware of God; but it is normal for a soul that is in the friendship of God *to think of Him and seek intimacy with Him*—hence the need for solitude and prayer, which is one of the signs of divine grace in the soul. We do not here speak of a need for absolute and continual solitude, which is a rare and special vocation. Every child of God is normally aware of a need for a certain amount of interior solitude and personal prayer. Pope Pius XII, in *Mediator Dei*,[188] condemned the error of those who held that because common liturgical public prayer was by its nature *superior* to private prayer, that it therefore *ruled out and excluded* all private prayer. There is in fact no contradiction between public and pri-

---

188. *Encyclical Letter of His Holiness Pius XII on the Sacred Liturgy* (Vatican Library Translation) (Washington: National Catholic Welfare Conference, 1948), 13–18 (#28–37).

vate prayer. Both require a certain amount of interior solitude and recollection, though in different ways and different degrees.

Even in public prayer the soul seeks intimacy with God in the secrecy of its own heart. (But note that this is perfectly compatible with public prayer—one does not have to "block out" and "exclude" the presence of others in order to be recollected. One can at the same time be perfectly united with others and united with God in the intimacy of his deepest self—indeed, the nature of the Church is such that when we are more closely united to others in the Holy Spirit, we are also paradoxically more intimately united to God in the secrecy of our own hearts. It is not a matter of opposition at all, but of a solution which *transcends an apparent opposition*.)

What we shall say here about prayer will therefore ignore any distinction between public and private prayer: for the principles given will apply equally to both. In *all* prayer worthy of the name, the soul is *seeking the face of God*, seeking a genuine contact with Him, a true and personal communion with Him, in order to pour out its heart before Him *and to open its inmost self to Him* and abandon itself to His holy will as the expression of the most sincere and total love. Prayer without such dispositions as these is not yet true prayer. But even the humblest prayer of petition, made in such a way, is an act of true friendship and love for God and will indeed be much more perfect and more supernatural than some other apparently "higher" form of prayer which is entered into without any real, sincere attention to God or desire for surrender to Him (for instance, in the case of one who might be enclosing himself in his own interior silence merely because he is bored and irritated with what is going on around him and withdraws from it in a spirit of negation and contempt).

Essential to all true prayer, whether public or private, is this expression of friendship for God, this need for His presence and the need to surrender oneself to Him. We pray with the deepest and most noble part of ourselves. For want of a better term we call it "the heart." Of course, the form taken by this seeking of the face of God will vary greatly according to the dispositions and condition of the one praying. One who is conscious above all of his unworthiness will approach God in an attitude of humble supplication and will think more of his need for the mercy of God. Another, more conscious that he has received mercy, will rest in peace and confidence and will rejoice in the company of a loving Friend and Savior. Yet another will be moved to jubilant praise. Another still, concerned with the needs of others more than with his own, will plead for them before God with ardent charity, which is very pleasing to God and unites us closely to Him.

Basic to all these approaches to prayer is the need to love God, the need for His presence, the desire to be with Him, to "see" Him, to commune with Him—*and to commune with His reality by approaching Him as we ourselves really are.* THIS DESIRE IS BASIC IN THE RELIGIOUS LIFE. A PERSON WHO EMBRACES THE RELIGIOUS LIFE WITHOUT A NEED FOR SOME KIND OF INTIMACY WITH GOD IN PRAYER IS MAKING A GREAT MISTAKE. But this does not mean that all should imagine that a religious vocation is necessarily a vocation to the higher degrees of contemplative prayer. The fact remains, we have come to the monastery to seek God, and the chief, the most obvious way in which we seek God is in prayer—so much so that if we do not have a spirit of prayer in some way or other, we do not really have a religious vocation. (Caution: in the Father's house there are *many mansions*.[189] The inability to adjust oneself completely to the liturgical life, and especially the inability to get anywhere at formal meditations made in community, *is not necessarily a sign that one lacks the spirit of prayer.* But one must be able to find God somewhere, somehow. There are many who pray better working quietly in the fields than they do in choir. Others pray best when quietly meditating and reading during the *lectio divina*.[190] *Freedom and spontaneity* are very important in the life of prayer. God wants *your* heart. He wants to commune

---

189. Jn. 14:2.

190. "divine reading": see the discussion in Thomas Merton, *Monastic Observances: Initiation into the Monastic Tradition 5*, ed. Patrick F. O'Connell, MW 25 (Collegeville, MN: Cistercian Publications, 2010), 149–83.

with you—therefore, you have to be yourself with Him, above all. This means never say anything to Him that you do not really mean. Or—in the case of liturgical prayer—would *like to* mean.)

Let us consider a few practical points about the life of prayer, illustrating them from the Scriptures.

1. Seeking God in prayer {involves} the need to express our love for Him, to abandon ourselves to His love with our whole heart, although we do not see Him—yet as we know we can *obscurely experience His presence by love* which is illuminated by faith. We find Him in the depths of our own being, and we must somehow declare His presence and praise Him for His great goodness to us—whether in words or not makes little difference. Silence is at times the most perfect praise we can offer Him—the silence of loving adoration, pure prayer. READ Psalm 17:1-21[191]

191. "I will love thee, O Lord, my strength: The Lord is my firmament, my refuge, and my deliverer. My God is my helper, and in him will I put my trust. My protector and the horn of my salvation, and my support. Praising I will call upon the Lord: and I shall be saved from my enemies. The sorrows of death surrounded me: and the torrents of iniquity troubled me. The sorrows of hell encompassed me: and the snares of death prevented me. In my affliction I called upon the Lord, and I cried to my God: And he heard my voice from his holy temple: and my cry before him came into his ears. The earth shook and trembled: the foundations of the mountains were troubled and were moved, because he was angry with them. There went up a smoke in his wrath: and a fire flamed from his face: coals were kindled by it. He bowed the heavens, and came down: and darkness was under his feet. And he ascended upon the cherubim, and he flew; he flew upon the wings of the winds. And he made darkness his covert, his pavilion round about him: dark waters in the clouds of the air. At the brightness that was before him the clouds passed, hail and coals of fire. And the Lord thundered from heaven, and the highest gave his voice: hail and coals of fire. And he sent forth his arrows, and he scattered them: he multiplied lightnings, and troubled them. Then the fountains of waters appeared, and the foundations of the world were discovered: At thy rebuke, O Lord, at the blast of the spirit of thy wrath. He sent from on high, and took me: and received me out of many waters. He delivered me from my strongest enemies, and from them that hated me: for they were too strong for me. They prevented me in the day of my affliction: and the Lord became my protector. And he brought me forth into a large place: he saved me, because he

as a model of prayer: I will love Thee O Lord my strength. . . .
Praising I will call upon the Lord and I shall be saved from my
enemies. . . . In my affliction I called upon the Lord, and I cried
to my God, and He heard my voice from His holy temple. . . .
He bowed the heavens and came down, and darkness was under
His feet. . . . He sent from on high and took me and received me
out of many waters, etc. Note that *these* concrete images used by
Scripture express the reality of our relation with God *more perfectly* than "scientific" and abstract terms—"the Absolute Being"
or even *"Actus Purissimus."*[192] Poetic expression is best suited
for religious truths because poetic and religious experience are
closely related—have much the same deep and intuitive character. {This is} a magnificent psalm, in which David praises the
Lord and at the same time gives us a deep insight into the meaning of communion with God in prayer. Who is this God Who is
our friend? He is the Almighty Lord, Who dwells in heaven. But
He hears our cry. He comes to us in darkness and secrecy, yet
with effects of great power, transforming our lives and turning
them upside down and renewing them completely, as it were,
in a new creation, for the coming of God to the soul by grace
is more wonderful and more awesome than the creation of the
world, and it is always something magnificent and new, for God
is not another being like ourselves: He is beyond all imagining
and all defining; He cannot be contained within the limits of
our concepts and He is infinite and all-holy, totally "other" from
anything or anyone we know, yet more close to us than we are
to ourselves. And His "coming" to us is a work of great mercy
and love and condescension, but also of simplicity and perfect
friendship. Who are we that He should make us His friends? And
yet He has. What a glorious mystery.

------

was well pleased with me. And the Lord will reward me according to my justice;
and will repay me according to the cleanness of my hands."

192. "absolutely pure act": see Aquinas, *Summa Theologiae, Pars Prima*, q. 3,
a. 2: "*Deus est purus actus, non habens aliquid de potentialitate*" ("God is pure act,
having nothing of potentiality") (Aquinas, *Opera Omnia*, 1.11).

2. Psalm 72:21-28: {this is} a wonderful example of the *meta-noia*—the inner change—that belongs to all true prayer: the compunction that makes us see that we are nothing and God is all. *Ad nihil redactus sum, et nescivi*[193]—{note the} application made of this by mystical writers. *Voluntate tua deduxisti me*[194]—our greatest consolation {is} to realize that we have indeed surrendered to the will of God. God is our all, and true prayer declares this with intense conviction. The same holds good even when God is *absent*. Read Psalm 129 (*De Profundis*):[195] here we declare our need of Him, our absolute dependence on Him, just as in Psalm 72. Note how strong and profound is the language of real love in prayer. Go over these psalms slowly in meditation. This intensity is not merely human and literary. There is in it the grace and power of the Holy Spirit (cf. {the} boldness and confidence in the intimacy of love with God: Exodus 33—esp. v. 11).

3. God is pleased with simple prayer of petition, because it is full of the *truth* of our relations with Him—our need not only of Him but of His gifts. Our love for Him is inseparable from our total dependence on Him. Note that He Himself has urged us over and over again in the strongest terms to ask of Him. He wants us to "bother" Him—like the man who woke up his friend in the

---

193. "I am brought to nothing, and I knew not" (v. 22).

194. "By thy will thou hast conducted me" (v. 24).

195. "Out of the depth I have cried to thee, O Lord: Lord, hear my voice. Let thy ears be attentive to the voice of my supplication. If thou, O Lord, wilt mark iniquities: Lord, who shall stand it. For with thee there is merciful forgiveness: and by reason of thy law, I have waited for thee, O Lord. My soul hath relied on his word: my soul hath hoped in the Lord. From the morning watch even until night, let Israel hope in the Lord. Because with the Lord there is mercy: and with him plentiful redemption. And he shall redeem Israel from all his iniquities."

middle of the night.[196] READ III Kings 3:5-15;[197] Luke 11:5-13[198]

196. Lk. 11:5-8.

197. "And the Lord appeared to Solomon in a dream by night, saying: Ask what thou wilt that I should give thee. And Solomon said: Thou hast shewn great mercy to thy servant David my father, even as he walked before thee in truth, and justice, and an upright heart with thee: and thou hast kept thy great mercy for him, and hast given him a son to sit on his throne, as it is this day. And now, O Lord God, thou hast made thy servant king instead of David my father: and I am but a child, and know not how to go out and come in. And thy servant is in the midst of the people which thou hast chosen, an immense people, which cannot be numbered nor counted for multitude. Give therefore to thy servant an understanding heart, to judge thy people, and discern between good and evil. For who shall be able to judge this people, thy people which is so numerous? And the word was pleasing to the Lord that Solomon had asked such a thing. And the Lord said to Solomon: Because thou hast asked this thing, and hast not asked for thyself long life or riches, nor the lives of thy enemies, but hast asked for thyself wisdom to discern judgment, Behold I have done for thee according to thy words, and have given thee a wise and understanding heart, insomuch that there hath been no one like thee before thee, nor shall arise after thee. Yea and the things also which thou didst not ask, I have given thee: to wit, riches and glory, so that no one hath been like thee among the kings in all days heretofore. And if thou wilt walk in my ways, and keep my precepts, and my commandments, as thy father walked, I will lengthen thy days. And Solomon awaked, and perceived that it was a dream: and when he was come to Jerusalem, he stood before the ark of the covenant of the Lord, and offered holocausts, and sacrificed victims of peace offerings, and made a great feast for all his servants."

198. "And he said to them: Which of you shall have a friend, and shall go to him at midnight, and shall say to him: Friend, lend me three loaves, Because a friend of mine is come off his journey to me, and I have not what to set before him. And he from within should answer, and say: Trouble me not, the door is now shut, and my children are with me in bed; I cannot rise and give thee. Yet if he shall continue knocking, I say to you, although he will not rise and give him, because he is his friend; yet, because of his importunity, he will rise, and give him as many as he needeth. And I say to you, Ask, and it shall be given you: seek, and you shall find: knock, and it shall be opened to you. For every one that asketh, receiveth: and he that seeketh, findeth; and to him that knocketh, it shall be opened. And which of you, if he ask his father bread, will he give him a stone? or a fish, will he for a fish give him a serpent? Or if he shall ask an egg, will he reach him a scorpion? If you then, being evil, know how to give good gifts to your children, how much more will your Father from heaven give the good Spirit to them that ask him?"

(gospel of the Mass of Rogation Days[199]).

In summary, prayer is the greatest and most noble work that a man can perform. It is the work most characteristic of divine friendship. *Perfect prayer* {is exemplified in} John 17—the High Priestly Prayer of Jesus. Note how the structure of the canon of the Mass corresponds to the structure of Jesus' Sacerdotal Prayer (cf. Gassner, *The Canon of the Mass*[200]).

{Part II:}

STATES OF LIFE: *The State of Perfection*

Having now considered man, the structure of the moral life, the passions and habits which man must use in order to love God, the justice on which his moral life is built, the laws which he must follow, the grace by which he is helped and brought to his last end, having reached the conclusion that man's life should be nothing else but a friendship with God, a communion in the divine nature, a divinization by grace, we now come to the *consideration of the religious state*. The religious state offers itself to those who are called by God to spend their entire life in a more intimate friendship with Him. It is a way of life in which everything else is set aside or subordinated to the one great occupation of loving God. Those who are called to the religious life are the objects of a special love and election on the part of God. They receive very special graces. He makes Himself more accessible to them. He wants them to love more, and consequently He acts more continuously in their souls by His Holy Spirit. He reveals His inmost heart to them, and it is those who are called to the religious and priestly states who are in all truth the friends of

---

199. Rogation Days, set aside for penitential acts, were April 25 and the three days preceding the Feast of the Ascension.

200. Jerome Gassner, OSB, *The Canon of the Mass: Its History, Theology, and Art* (St. Louis: B. Herder, 1949), 20–25: "The High-Priestly Prayer, a Model of the Canon"; see also 218–19, 225–26.

God. "I will not call you servants but friends—all things which the Father has revealed I have made known to you."[201]

a) They are called to know God better because they are called to realize more intimately the love He has for them. They in a very special way receive the Holy Ghost because they devote themselves more exclusively to pleasing God and doing His will.

b) They are able to know Him better because they are called apart from the world and from its distracting influences and its temptations. Purified of sin and of evil desires, they are able to receive the Holy Spirit Whom the world cannot receive. Note that we can never be too grateful for the wonderful grace of our vocation. We have been called out of the confusion and the very great dangers of the world, as men saved from shipwreck in a stormy sea and placed in a safe harbor. We are perhaps too ready to underestimate this grace, and then we neglect it and fail to cooperate. Never forget how easily souls are lost in the world and how easily they are saved in the monastery. Cultivate a deep realization of the vanity and triviality of the things of this world which turn us away from God.

c) Religious may have to pay for their privileged position by meeting the incomprehension of the world. They must consolidate their union with God by a closer union with one another. READ John 15:14-21.[202] It is important to stress from the outset

201. Jn. 15:15.
202. "You are my friends, if you do the things that I command you. I will not now call you servants: for the servant knoweth not what his lord doth. But I have called you friends: because all things whatsoever I have heard of my Father, I have made known to you. You have not chosen me: but I have chosen you: and have appointed you, that you should go, and should bring forth fruit; and your fruit should remain: that whatsoever you shall ask of the Father in my name, he may give it you. These things I command you, that you love one another. If the world hate you, know ye, that it hath hated me before you. If you had been of the world, the world would love its own: but because you are not of the world, but I have chosen you out of the world, therefore the world hateth you. Remember my word that I said to you: The servant is not greater than his master. If they have persecuted me, they will also persecute you: if they have kept my word,

the opposition between religion and the world, so strong in the Gospels.

In summary, the religious state is one in which men and women give themselves exclusively to the love and service of God, in lives totally impregnated with prayer and sacrifice. There are many different kinds of religious observance—some active, some contemplative, some apostolic; all have this in common— that they are consecrated to God exclusively and permanently and that this consecration is offered predominantly in a spirit of sacrifice and prayer, and the ones who are thus called seek to make themselves perfect in the friendship of God by love.

Let us now consider the theology of the religious life, particularly as it is taught us by St. Thomas.

Offices and States of Life: having considered in the abstract and in general the means given to man to fulfill his vocation as a son of God, we are now concerned with the *concrete situation of the Christian in the Mystical Body of Christ*. Not only are we called to union with the Father, in the Son, through the Holy Ghost, but if we are called "in Christ," then we are called to occupy a certain definite place and fulfill a certain function in the Mystical Body of Christ. We must always see the question of vocation from this "ecclesiological" point of view. We are called not for ourselves only but for the beauty and sanctity of the Church. We are called not in view of our own sanctification alone, but for the good of all, for the graces that profit us in our vocation also profit all the elect.

Our sanctification is not to be conceived merely as a purely personal and interior thing, without relation to other souls. We are sanctified not just by acts of love for Jesus considered as the guest of our souls, *but by a fully integrated life in Christ*: a prayer life that is not just our own, but the prayer of the "whole Christ" (hence liturgy, Eucharistic sacrifice, communion); an action that is not just our own and for our own growth in virtue, but is

---

they will keep yours also. But all these things they will do to you for my name's sake: because they know not him that sent me."

integrated in the growth of the whole Christ; sacrifices that perfect not only our own souls, but help others to live more fully "in Christ." The religious *lives more fully* this life in Christ. He is more perfectly and completely dedicated to the life of the Church. He lives for God and he lives also for the Church, exclusively, totally. His life, entirely consecrated to God, is also a life totally removed from the world and inserted into the Mystical Body of Christ. His life is not divided between temporal and spiritual concerns: all in his life is spiritual; all is the concern of the Church; all is worship. READ Ephesians 4:1-7, 10-16:[203] {with} humility, {a} spirit of unity, fulfilling our duties of state, and doing our job in the Church, we make others firm in their vocation; we build up the Body of Christ. {See also} 1 Corinthians 12:4-22:[204] the need of different members to complete the Mystical Body. The diversity

---

203. See above, n. 180.

204. "Now there are diversities of graces, but the same Spirit; And there are diversities of ministries, but the same Lord; And there are diversities of operations, but the same God, who worketh all in all. And the manifestation of the Spirit is given to every man unto profit. To one indeed, by the Spirit, is given the word of wisdom: and to another, the word of knowledge, according to the same Spirit; To another, faith in the same spirit; to another, the grace of healing in one Spirit: To another, the working of miracles; to another, prophecy; to another, the discerning of spirits; to another, diverse kinds of tongues; to another, interpretation of speeches. But all these things one and the same Spirit worketh, dividing to every one according as he will. For as the body is one, and hath many members; and all the members of the body, whereas they are many, yet are one body, so also is Christ. For in one Spirit were we all baptized into one body, whether Jews or Gentiles, whether bond or free; and in one Spirit we have all been made to drink. For the body also is not one member, but many. If the foot should say, because I am not the hand, I am not of the body; is it therefore not of the body? And if the ear should say, because I am not the eye, I am not of the body; is it therefore not of the body? If the whole body were the eye, where would be the hearing? If the whole were hearing, where would be the smelling? But now God hath set the members every one of them in the body as it hath pleased him. And if they all were one member, where would be the body? But now there are many members indeed, yet one body. And the eye cannot say to the hand: I need not thy help; nor again the head to the feet: I have no need of you. Yea, much more those that seem to be the more feeble members of the body, are more necessary."

of functions contributes to the vitality and beauty and holiness of the Church.

The diversity of functions in the Church can be divided as follows: *offices*—such as that of judge, preacher, superior; *states*—conditions of stability in liberty or servitude; *orders*—degrees of elevation within a state. Hence, for example, we have:

the lay state—that of "the people" in general. They are Christians, bound to serve Christ by their baptismal vows; they praise and worship Him under the leadership of the priests. Some of the laypeople may be as yet catechumens. Some may be penitents—some may even be in a state of servitude to sin. Some may be married, thus bound by special obligations, and showing forth in their lives the mystery of the union of Christ and His Church.

the clerical state—one becomes a cleric by *tonsure*: see the rite.[205] READ Psalm 15,[206] especially verse 5: "The Lord is the portion of my inheritance." {The cleric is} permanently deputed to the service and praise of God. Here there are diverse *orders*, minor and major—from porter to bishop. Yet all clerics are not by that fact removed from the *secular* state—there is the secular

---

205. *Pontificale Romanum Summorum Pontificum Iussu Editum a Benedicto XIV et Leone XIII Pontificibus Maximis Recognitum et Castigatum* (Mechliniae: H. Dessain, 1958), *"De Clerico Faciendo"* (12–16).

206. "Preserve me, O Lord, for I have put my trust in thee. I have said to the Lord, thou art my God, for thou hast no need of my goods. To the saints, who are in his land, he hath made wonderful all my desires in them. Their infirmities were multiplied: afterwards they made haste. I will not gather together their meetings for blood offerings: nor will I be mindful of their names by my lips. The Lord is the portion of my inheritance and of my cup: it is thou that wilt restore my inheritance to me. The lines are fallen unto me in goodly places: for my inheritance is goodly to me. I will bless the Lord, who hath given me understanding: moreover my reins also have corrected me even till night. I set the Lord always in my sight: for he is at my right hand, that I be not moved. Therefore my heart hath been glad, and my tongue hath rejoiced: moreover my flesh also shall rest in hope. Because thou wilt not leave my soul in hell; nor wilt thou give thy holy one to see corruption. Thou hast made known to me the ways of life, thou shalt fill me with joy with thy countenance: at thy right hand are delights even to the end."

clergy. Hence one may be a *secular* (state), a priest (order) and a pastor (office).

the religious state—the state of those bound by vows to the life of perfection, to the observance of the counsels and total renunciation of the world. Here too there may be diverse orders and offices. One may be in religion and yet not be a *monk*. Lay-brothers are religious, yet their name assimilates them to seculars; they do not have the *monachatus*—permanent obligation to divine praise in choir. One may also be a monk but not a priest (n.b. monastic and clerical tonsure are equivalent). One may be a religious (state), a priest (order) and an abbot (office).

The State of Perfection: the religious life is one in which the members *bind themselves* (this "binding" is what makes it a state) to tend always to perfection of charity and thus to union with God. This obligation is basic and common to all religious: they are all bound to follow the counsels and to seek to love Christ before and above all, with all their hearts, and secondarily to love their neighbor as themselves. Everything they do is ordered to this end, directly or indirectly. READ Matthew 19:11ff.:[207]

207. "Who said to them: all men take not this word, but they to whom it is given. For there are eunuchs, who were born so from their mother's womb: and there are eunuchs, who were made so by men: and there are eunuchs, who have made themselves eunuchs for the kingdom of heaven. He that can take, let him take it. Then were little children presented to him, that he should impose hands upon them and pray. And the disciples rebuked them. But Jesus said to them: Suffer the little children, and forbid them not to come to me: for the kingdom of heaven is for such. And when he had imposed hands upon them, he departed from thence. And behold one came and said to him: Good master, what good shall I do that I may have life everlasting? Who said to him: Why askest thou me concerning good? One is good, God. But if thou wilt enter into life, keep the commandments. He said to him: Which? And Jesus said: Thou shalt do no murder, Thou shalt not commit adultery, Thou shalt not steal, Thou shalt not bear false witness. Honour thy father and thy mother; and, Thou shalt love thy neighbour as thyself. The young man saith to him: All these have I kept from my youth, what is yet wanting to me? Jesus saith to him: If thou wilt be perfect, go sell what thou hast, and give to the poor, and thou shalt have treasure in heaven: and come follow me. And when the young man had heard this word, he went away sad: for he had great possessions. Then Jesus said to his disciples: Amen,

a) The life of consecrated virginity—those who are "eunuchs for the Kingdom of Heaven": this is a special call, not the vocation of all (11-12).

b) 13-14: the little children—the Kingdom of Heaven is of such. Authors do not usually place this in its context, but we may see in it an indication of the simplicity and humility essential to the religious life, and perhaps even a hint of the life of obedience.

c) 16ff.: the rich young man: here we see a clear distinction made between the commandments (by which perfection is attainable—they lead to union with God) and the counsels. Note the life of the counsels is *truly perfect* ("If thou wilt be perfect . . ."). It fulfills something that is *lacking* in the ordinary Christian life (v. 20). It means *renunciation of worldly possessions*. {Here is} a clear statement of the ideal of evangelical poverty (v. 21): it means giving up all, in favor of the poor, and following Christ.

d) The importance of poverty—possessions are *hindrances to union with God* (vv. 23-25). The disciples are shocked and "wonder who can be saved." Jesus stresses the necessity of God's grace. This whole passage has *a note of extraordinary urgency*. We know indeed from the context that it is possible to be saved without the following of the counsels, but here Jesus also stresses the fact that it is *difficult*. In our day, while we ought to do everything to remind the faithful of the fact that they are called to be saints "in the world," nevertheless we must also not forget that the counsels

---

I say to you, that a rich man shall hardly enter into the kingdom of heaven. And again I say to you: It is easier for a camel to pass through the eye of a needle, than for a rich man to enter into the kingdom of heaven. And when they had heard this, the disciples wondered very much, saying: Who then can be saved? And Jesus beholding, said to them: With men this is impossible: but with God all things are possible. Then Peter answering, said to him: Behold we have left all things, and have followed thee: what therefore shall we have? And Jesus said to them: Amen, I say to you, that you, who have followed me, in the regeneration, when the Son of man shall sit on the seat of his majesty, you also shall sit on twelve seats judging the twelve tribes of Israel. And every one that hath left house or brethren, or sisters, or father, or mother, or wife, or children, or lands for my name's sake, shall receive an hundredfold, and shall possess life everlasting. And many that are first, shall be last: and the last shall be first."

are of very great importance, and without them salvation is difficult. With them it is easy—by the grace of God.

e) Finally Jesus tells them the *reward of following Him* (vv. 27-30). The last line ("the last shall be first") again brings back our attention to the state of humility and renunciation which is necessary for the monk. In short, one must truly leave the world and all its attractions and pleasures and advantages and follow Christ in all sincerity, with a contrite and humble heart, detached from the things of the world and constantly remembering that we are pilgrims and strangers in this world and that we *cannot afford to rest* and seek our end, even implicitly, in anything here below. Our goal is heaven and the next life, and we must strive with all our power to keep our hearts in heaven.

The state of perfection is then the life of those who have taken the Gospel with full seriousness and who have realized, with deep compunction, the nothingness of earthly things, of human ambition and pleasure, etc., and the vital importance of listening to the voice of God calling us to Himself by a sure way, which is the following of Christ in poverty and obedience and renunciation of ourselves.

{Note also} *some other passages on the call to follow Jesus by the counsels of perfection.* READ Matthew 10:29-33:[208] {the} necessity of blind abandonment to {the} Providence of God, and confessing Christ before men, even at the cost of life itself; 34-39:[209] {the}

208. "Are not two sparrows sold for a farthing? and not one of them shall fall on the ground without your Father. But the very hairs of your head are all numbered. Fear not therefore: better are you than many sparrows. Every one therefore that shall confess me before men, I will also confess him before my Father who is in heaven. But he that shall deny me before men, I will also deny him before my Father who is in heaven."

209. "Do not think that I came to send peace upon earth: I came not to send peace, but the sword. For I came to set a man at variance against his father, and the daughter against her mother, and the daughter in law against her mother in law. And a man's enemies shall be they of his own household. He that loveth father or mother more than me, is not worthy of me; and he that loveth son or

urgency of uncompromising renunciation of one's family—the danger arising from the resistance of the family ("enemies of man are those of his own household"). {We} MUST TAKE UP THE CROSS. READ Luke 9:57-58:[210] foxes have holes . . . {but the} Son of Man {has} nowhere to lay His head; 59-62:[211] No man putting his hand to the plough and turning back is fit for the Kingdom of God. We must constantly study these texts and meditate on them. For if we confine our thoughts to abstract notions like "the perfection of charity," our religious life can easily degenerate into mere theory without practice.

There is nothing more lamentable than the state of one who, having vowed to leave the world and follow Christ, settles down in the cloister to lead a safe and worldly life, which belies the entire ideal to which he has dedicated his life. To live in such a state of contradiction means misery on earth and a long purgatory afterwards. Nothing is more important in the religious life than the sincerity of our renunciation and the totality of our dedication to Jesus Christ. *Amori Christi omnino nihil praeponere* (St. Benedict[212]).

From these Gospel texts it is clear above all that the perfection of charity means constantly seeking Christ, following Him

---

daughter more than me, is not worthy of me. And he that taketh not up his cross, and followeth me, is not worthy of me. He that findeth his life, shall lose it: and he that shall lose his life for me, shall find it."

210. "And it came to pass, as they walked in the way, that a certain man said to him: I will follow thee whithersoever thou goest. Jesus said to him: The foxes have holes, and the birds of the air nests; but the Son of man hath not where to lay his head."

211. "But he said to another: Follow me. And he said: Lord, suffer me first to go, and to bury my father. And Jesus said to him: Let the dead bury their dead: but go thou, and preach the kingdom of God. And another said: I will follow thee, Lord; but let me first take my leave of them that are at my house. Jesus said to him: No man putting his hand to the plough, and looking back, is fit for the kingdom of God."

212. "to prefer nothing at all to the love of Christ": this is a conflation of *Rule*, c. 4 ("*Nihil amori Christi praeponere*") (McCann, 26), and *Rule*, c. 72 ("*Christo omnino nihil praeponant*") (McCann, 160).

with all our heart, leaving behind the condition in which He is not to be found (that of riches and comfort and worldly security), sharing the *risks* and *insecurity*, the *misfortunes* and *sufferings* which He Himself embraced on earth and which are still, as always, the lot of the poor. We cannot be true monks if our monastic vows are nothing but a renunciation of responsibility and of risk. To come to the monastery merely to find security and comfort and a pleasant life (which is entirely possible) is the very reverse of the monastic ideal. Not that the life of the monk is meant to be miserable—but it is nevertheless a life of hardship and deprivation in which one must find his peace in *doing without* certain luxuries which are deemed to be necessities by the world, and even certain necessities, under particular circumstances.

It is true that our monastic consecration to Jesus is above all a matter of renouncing our own will by obedience. But obedience is not the entire essence of the religious life, and a life of comfort and ease and security, a life without hardship, but sanctioned by "obedience," can in fact be a travesty of the religious ideal. We must be careful of this also. But the responsibility here rests on the shoulders of the superiors and not of the subjects, because obviously the monks must not dictate the policy of the monastery to their abbot—this too would be a travesty of the Gospel ideal.

St. Thomas on the State of Perfection and the Religious Life: our vows guarantee that we will seek Christ with sincerity and live wholeheartedly the life of Gospel renunciation. This means not only observing the bare minimum of the letter of the vows, but living fully in their spirit of renunciation. St. Thomas first tells us what is the state of perfection (IIa-IIae, q. 184).[213] First, he reminds us that perfection is that charity which unites us to God, and this is man's last end. "Every being is said to be perfect in so far as it attains to its proper end. It is charity which unites us to God, Who is the ultimate end of the human soul, because he

---

213. Aquinas, *Opera Omnia*, 3.615–22.

who remains in charity remains in God and God in him" (a. 1).[214] In another place he distinguishes the charity of the perfect from that of beginners and progressives (II-II, q. 24, a. 9).[215] Beginners {are} those who break off from sin and renounce evil. Progressives {are} those who grow in virtue and in the knowledge of God. The Perfect {are} those who *rest in God* and are enabled to do so because they are possessed of all the virtues in a high degree and suffer no impediment from sin or passion. This view is strictly traditional and monastic—it goes back to Cassian and the desert fathers (*apatheia*,[216] etc.) and to St. Bernard's idea of pure love[217]—a love so purified of all self-seeking that it is sufficient to itself and rests in God as God rests in Himself—by virtue of its very purity. In I-II, q. 61, a. 5 (*read*),[218] {Aquinas says that} the *virtues* of beginners have a political cast: {they} are ordered to human living. In progressives, the virtues are proper to those who tend to divine union. In the perfect, the virtues are proper

214. "*Unumquodque dicitur esse perfectum, inquantum attingit proprium finem . . . . Charitas autem est quae unit nos Deo, qui est ultimus finis humanae mentis, quia qui manet in charitate, in Deo manet, et Deus in eo*" (Aquinas, *Opera Omnia*, 3.615, quoting 1 Jn. 4:16).

215. Aquinas, *Opera Omnia*, 3.92.

216. "freedom from passion": see "*The Question of Apatheia*," in Thomas Merton, *An Introduction to Christian Mysticism: Initiation into the Monastic Tradition* 3, ed. Patrick F. O'Connell, MW 13 (Kalamazoo, MI: Cistercian Publications, 2008), 102–106; see also *Cassian and the Fathers*, 93–94; Thomas Merton, *The Rule of Saint Benedict: Initiation into the Monastic Tradition* 4, ed. Patrick F. O'Connell, MW 19 (Collegeville, MN: Cistercian Publications, 2009), 24–26.

217. See Gilson's discussion of "pure love" in *Mystical Theology of St. Bernard*, 140–49, an analysis particularly of Sermon 83 on the Songs of Songs.

218. "*Et quia homo secundum suam naturam est animal politicum, virtutes hujusmodi, prout in homine existunt secundum conditionem suae naturae, politicae vocantur, prout scilicet homo secundum has virtutes recte se habet in rebus humanis gerendis; secundum quem modum hactenus de his virtutibus locuti sumus*" ("And because man according to his nature is a political animal, virtues of this sort, in so far as they are present in man according to the condition of his nature, are called political, in as much as man through these virtues conducts himself rightly in dealing with human affairs; it is according to this sense that we have been speaking of these virtues thus far") (Aquinas, *Opera Omnia*, 2.214).

to those who have *reached the divine likeness*—everything in them is a manifestation of union.

The ascent to perfect charity is proportionate to detachment from all that is not God. *Est perfectio caritatis ubi nulla est cupiditas. Quanto magis quis ascendit in Deum, tanto magis contemnit temporalia.*[219] That is, not that one loves *nothing* but that one loves all things in God and for God, and nothing outside of God. Perfect charity in the will is normally accompanied by contemplation, which is a perfection of the intellect illumined by divine love to know the secrets of God. But above all, never forget that perfection is summed up above all in following Christ: *sequela Christi*.[220]

What is the state St. Thomas talks about in the term "state of perfection"? {See} II-II, q. 183, a. 4: in the spiritual life, state refers to a *condition of servitude* (to grace or to sin).[221] The state of perfection is a state of spiritual liberty—freedom from sin and servitude to grace. This is a state of true freedom, he says, because when we serve justice we tend to what is proper to us, and hence to happiness in our last end, and to fulfillment and joy. *Read* Romans 6:11-23:[222] see this in context of the whole chapter. Buried together

219. *In Epistolam ad Hebraeos*, 5.2: "Where there is no cupidity, there is the perfection of charity. To the degree that one ascends closer to God, one scorns temporal things more" (Aquinas, *Opera Omnia*, 13.713, which reads: "*Est autem perfectio charitatis, ut dicit Augustinus, ubi nulla est cupiditas. Quanto enim quis magis ascendit in Deum, tanto plus contemnit temporalia*").

220. q. 188, a. 7: "the following of Christ" (Aquinas, *Opera Omnia*, 3.654, which reads: "*Christi sequela*"); see also St. Bernard, *Sermo de Diversis*, 62: *De Varia et Vera Sequela Christi* (*PL* 183, cols. 685D–686B).

221. Aquinas, *Opera Omnia*, 3.614–15.

222. "So do you also reckon, that you are dead to sin, but alive unto God, in Christ Jesus our Lord. Let not sin therefore reign in your mortal body, so as to obey the lusts thereof. Neither yield ye your members as instruments of iniquity unto sin; but present yourselves to God, as those that are alive from the dead, and your members as instruments of justice unto God. For sin shall not have dominion over you; for you are not under the law, but under grace. What then? Shall we sin, because we are not under the law, but under grace? God forbid. Know you not, that to whom you yield yourselves servants to obey, his servants you are whom you obey, whether it be of sin unto death, or of obedience unto justice. But thanks be to God, that you were the servants of sin, but have obeyed from the

with Christ by baptism, we lead a risen life. Our consecration to Christ by vow prolongs our baptismal consecration and perfects it, establishing us in a condition in which we "yield our members to serve justice unto sanctification." The wages of sin is death; but the grace of God life everlasting. {This is} a beautiful text for the religious life! (see especially verses 11-19). This text incites us to zeal born of compunction and gratitude. It is not enough for us to vegetate idly in the cloister. We are to bring forth much fruit and make use of all God's gifts to love and serve Him. We must be eager to perform every kind of good work in a spirit of love and reparation. We must welcome all the occasions of good offered by the *Rule* and not refuse opportunities of sacrifice.

What is a religious? He is one who has *bound himself in servitude to God. Religiosi dicuntur qui totaliter se mancipant servitio Dei, quasi holocaustum Deo offerentes* (II-II, q. 186, a. 1).[223] *Religiosi praecipue et propter se debent intendere ad hoc quod Deo vacent.*[224] St. Gregory (quoted by St. Thomas here) {says}: "There are some who reserve nothing for themselves, but they immolate their mind, tongue, life, and all their property to God."[225] Now this is

---

heart, unto that form of doctrine, into which you have been delivered. Being then freed from sin, we have been made servants of justice. I speak an human thing, because of the infirmity of your flesh. For as you have yielded your members to serve uncleanness and iniquity unto iniquity; so now yield your members to serve justice, unto sanctification. For when you were the servants of sin, you were free men to justice. What fruit therefore had you then in those things, of which you are now ashamed? For the end of them is death. But now being made free from sin, and become servants to God, you have your fruit unto sanctification, and the end life everlasting. For the wages of sin is death. But the grace of God, life everlasting, in Christ Jesus our Lord."

223. "They are called religious who devote themselves completely to the service of God, as though offering a holocaust to God" (Aquinas, *Opera Omnia*, 3.631, which reads: ". . . *dicuntur illi qui se totaliter . . . divino servitio, . . .*")

224. q. 187, a. 2: "What religious ought to intend for themselves above all is to devote themselves to God" (Aquinas, *Opera Omnia*, 3.642, which reads: "*Et ideo religiosi . . .*").

225. q. 186, a. 1, quoting Gregory, *Super Ezechiel*, 20: "*Sunt quidam qui nihil sibimetipsis reservant: sed sensum, linguam, vitam atque substantiam, quam perceperunt, omnipotenti Deo immolant*" (Aquinas, *Opera Omnia*, 3.631).

precisely what "perfection" means: *In hoc perfectio hominis consistit quod totaliter Deo inhaereat.*[226]

How does a religious bind himself to God? first by his profession, then by keeping his vows and the rule. *Ut ab affectu hominis excludatur* {. . .} *omne quod impedit ne affectus mentis totaliter dirigatur in Deum* (II-II, q. 184, a. 2).[227] Hence it is not enough to be juridically or sacramentally consecrated and joined to God. One must devote one's entire life *to certain actions and works which have as their effect the removal of impediments to perfect love*—the removal of distraction, the mortification of self-love, the performance of good works of charity and worship. This *immolation* of our being is not just a matter of formula, or an interior "affection," but also of works which carry out our promise and make us bit by bit grow in divine union and detachment from the things of the world. Religious profession does not make us perfect in one fell swoop. It is a solemn engagement to strive with all our power and by all our actions to tend to perfection, to remove from our lives what impedes the perfection of charity, and to get rid of all that stands between us and God.

Hence it can be seen how foolish and perilous is the life of a religious who, having vowed to give himself entirely to God, sits back and rests content with worldly and temporal things, seeks only his own comfort and advantage and is not really interested in the things of God except in a superficial and shallow way. Do not make vows unless you really intend to work at this great task of detaching yourself from created things and uniting yourself to God by doing His will in religion out of love for Him.

By what means does the religious live for God alone and detach himself from creatures? by making good use of the observances of his religious life, keeping his rule in letter and spirit, faithfully

226. "Human perfection consists in this, to adhere completely to God" (Aquinas, *Opera Omnia*, 3.631, which reads: "*In hoc autem perfectio . . .*").

227. "That everything which hinders the affections of the mind from being totally directed toward God be excluded from human affection" (Aquinas, *Opera Omnia*, 3.616, which reads: ". . . *inquantum ab affectu hominis excluditur . . . omne illud . . . ad Deum*") (emphasis added).

carrying out the works enjoined upon him, loving the common life and all its opportunities for sacrifice and self-dedication—in a word, by his life of *prayer and penance*, obedience and charity. St. Thomas regards the religious life as made up of exercises specifically designed to make the religious grow in charity by the removal of impediments and the creating of many opportunities to show God our love. *Religiosus status est principaliter institutus ad perfectionem adipiscendam* PER QUAEDAM EXERCITIA, QUIBUS TOLLUNTUR IMPEDIMENTA PERFECTAE CHARITATIS (II-II, q. 186, a. 1, ad. 4[228] [text 2[229]]); and he adds that for this reason, *Status religionis est* CONVENIENTISSI-MUS POENITENTIAE LOCUS.[230] (Cf. the first Cistercian Fathers regarded the Cistercian common life as the *formula perfectae paenitentiae*[231] in so far as by its poverty and community of goods and efforts, it most perfectly reproduced the life of the early Christians and thus represented a total conversion of the soul to Jesus Christ.)

Most particularly, the term "exercises of the religious life" as here used by St. Thomas designates the practice of the evangelical counsels. The "*quaedam exercitia*" referred to above does not mean primarily little things in the usages, customs, and what not, although these too have their proper place and must never be neglected. However, St. Thomas is talking of the big essentials: the practice of the counsels of poverty, chastity and obedience (under obedience we come to the details of the rule and usages).

But while all religious observe the three great counsels, not all observe other counsels which are accidental to religious perfection and therefore binding only on some, not on others. Why are the three main counsels binding on all religious? because they

---

228. "The religious state was instituted principally to lead to perfection through certain exercises by which obstacles to perfect charity might be removed" (Aquinas, *Opera Omnia*, 3.631, which reads: "*Religionis status principaliter est . . .*") (emphasis added).

229. The reference is to the collection of texts from Aquinas excerpted below (127–30).

230. "The religious state is the most suitable place for penance" (Aquinas, *Opera Omnia*, 3.631) (emphasis added).

231. "the rule of perfect penitence" (*Exordium Magnum*, 1.1 [*PL* 185, col. 997B]).

are essential to remove the great, universal impediments to love of God. Without these three, "the whole life of man becomes involved in worldly business" (II-II, q. 186, a. 2, ad. 3 [text 3]).[232] He distinguishes: perfection *essentially* consists in the *perfect observance of the commandment of charity* (text 7). *Dispositively*, it consists in the practice of the counsels of poverty, chastity and obedience in so far as these remove obstacles to charity and enable us to love more freely and more perfectly.

Other counsels, practiced by various different orders, also have this purpose: preaching, for instance; contemplation; works of mercy; care of the sick; education of the young; withdrawal and solitude (as a special aid to chastity and prayer). All these are valuable in so far as they remove obstacles and permit growth of charity.

What must every religious do, then, to make sure that he is living up to his obligations?

1) He must *tend to* perfect charity (he is by no means obliged to possess it).

2) He must have as his intention even the possession of the fruits of perfect charity—love of enemies for instance (cf. Fruits of the Holy Ghost,[233] contemplative prayer, etc., etc.).

3) He must make use of *specified means* to attain perfect charity:

　　a) the vows of poverty, chastity and obedience—common to all;

　　b) other means prescribed by his own particular rule—for instance, with us, stability, enclosure, silence, manual labor, *lectio divina*, etc., all of which, with poverty and chastity, come more or less closely under the obligation of conversion of manners.

What are some special works and observances which are appropriate to (some) religious?

---

232. "*tota vita hominis implicaretur negotiis saecularibus*" (Aquinas, *Opera Omnia*, 3.632).

233. See Gal. 5:22-23.

1) *Religious may seek perfection by preaching and teaching* (II-II, q. 187, a. 1).[234] But the mere fact that they are religious does not qualify them for this. It is a work to which they must be deputed by the Church. In our time this does not cause any surprise. In St. Thomas's time only the bishop ordinarily preached—until the coming of the mendicant orders.

2) *Business, on the other hand, is not proper either for monks or for clerics*, merely to make money. The aim of the religious life is not prosperity or ambition. But *causa charitatis*[235]—to earn money to feed the poor, religious may engage in business, but under supervision and with strict limitations (*id.*, a. 2).

3) *Manual labor*: what does St. Thomas mean by manual labor? "All human works by which men licitly make their living."[236] This is very broad. One must assume that he means purely *productive* work, not unproductive or parasitical "work," which has no real social value. The *obligation* to work is the same for religious as for all Christians! *All* are commanded to work for a living unless they have same other source of income. Work may be necessary also *to combat sloth*. But there are other means. It may be necessary to overcome temptations of the flesh. It may be necessary also to enable one to give alms. For Benedictines, manual labor is a strict obligation. We are normally not suffered to rely on "other sources of income." Cistercians, by their *Constitutions*, are bound to make their living *by the work of their hands* (*id.*, a. 3).

4) *Begging*: St. Thomas argues that begging is licit for religious from the fact that St. Benedict, at Subiaco, "though sound of mind and body,"[237] received his sustenance from the monk Romanus.[238] Alms may be due to religious who engage in spiritual duties which prevent them from working full-time for their

234. Aquinas, *Opera Omnia*, 3.640–41.

235. "for the sake of charity" (Aquinas, *Opera Omnia*, 3.642).

236. q. 187, a. 3: "*Omnia humana officia, ex quibus homines licite victum lucrantur*" (Aquinas, *Opera Omnia*, 3.643).

237. q. 187, a. 4: "*validus corpore existens*" (Aquinas, *Opera Omnia*, 3.645, which mentions body but not mind).

238. St. Gregory the Great, *Dialogues*, 2.1 (*PL* 66, cols. 128CD, 130A).

own living. But religious have *no right* to take alms that belong more truly to the poor. In time of necessity they *are obliged* to give what they can to the destitute and not accept alms that would otherwise go to the poor (*id.*, aa. 4–5).[239]

5) Religious should wear poorer clothing than others as a sign of contempt for worldly glory (*id.*, a. 6).[240]

6) *Military orders* (II-II, q. 188, a. 3):[241] it would appear that religious should not fight or shed human blood. Jesus said: "Resist not evil—turn the other cheek."[242] Religious are forbidden to be lawyers, and *a fortiori* they should not be soldiers. St. Thomas replies that David and the Macchabees were saints and soldiers. His principle {is that} it is licit to fight "*non propter aliquid mundanum,* sed propter defensionem divini cultus et publicae salutis,"[243] or to protect the poor and the oppressed. This is substantially the same argument used by St. Bernard {in} *De Laude Novae Militiae.*[244] As to resisting evil, St. Thomas caustically remarks {that} it is virtuous not to resist evil done to ourselves, but there is no virtue in "patiently suffering evil which is done to others."[245] This reminds us that we *cannot be indifferent* to the sufferings of others. We have to do something about it if we can. Remember the parable of the Good Samaritan.[246]

239. Aquinas, *Opera Omnia,* 3.644–47.

240. Aquinas, *Opera Omnia,* 3.647–48.

241. Aquinas, *Opera Omnia,* 3.650–51.

242. Mt. 5:39, quoted in Aquinas, *Opera Omnia,* 3.650.

243. "not for the sake of anything worldly but for the defense of divine worship and public safety" (Aquinas, *Opera Omnia,* 3.650, which reads: "*non quidem propter . . .*") (emphasis added).

244. *PL* 182, cols. 921–40; ET: Bernard of Clairvaux, *In Praise of the New Knighthood,* trans. M. Conrad Greenia, ocso, CF 19B (Kalamazoo, MI: Cistercian Publications, 2000).

245. ad. 1: "*tolerando patienter iniurias aliorum*" (Aquinas, *Opera Omnia,* 3.650).

246. Lk. 10:29-37.

7) *Study* (II-II, q. 188, a. 5):[247] *study is not only licit but necessary for all religious. Discamus in terris, quorum scientia nobis perseveret in coelis* (St. Jerome).[248]

a) for contemplatives, study is necessary for the contemplative life:

(1) *directly*—it illumines the mind as to divine things.

(2) *indirectly*—removing obstacles, errors, illusions to which contemplatives are sometimes more prone than others. {There is a} danger of attachment to false spirituality, to bogus mysticism, to heresy masking as a "purer" kind of doctrine. The devil seeks to delude those who travel alone in dangerous territory.

b) *for other religious*: all religious are helped by study.

(1) It is *a form of mortification and self-discipline: Ama Scripturarum scientiam, et carnis vitia non amabis.*[249]

(2) It helps combat avarice and love of earthly goods—spiritual goods are higher.

(3) It helps obedience—for we must put into practice what we study. Note that in these three reasons St. Thomas is clearly showing how *study fits in exactly with the program of the religious vows.*

8) *Active and Contemplative Lives*: {note} the distinction between "state" and "life": state implies a stable obligation—here, the obligation to tend to the perfection of charity; life {is} what one actually does—that to which one applies his energies and interests, that which is the center of all his strivings. *Unumquodque ostenditur vivere ex operatione sibi maxime propria, ad quam maxime*

247. Aquinas, *Opera Omnia*, 3.652–53.
248. "Let us learn on earth knowledge which will remain with us in heaven" (Letter to Paulinus, quoted in Aquinas, *Opera Omnia*, 3.652).
249. "Love the knowledge of scripture, and you will not love the vices of the flesh" (Jerome, Letter to Rusticus, quoted in Aquinas, *Opera Omnia*, 3.652).

inclinatur (II-II, q. 179, a. 1).[250] A bird is seen to be fully alive when it flies around. If it never flies, there is something wrong with it. It is not sufficient that we consecrate ourselves to God in the religious *state*. It is not sufficient for man just to find himself in a state. He must also live and act. It is not enough for a bird to be free; it must fly. So in the religious state, under vows of poverty, chastity, obedience, etc., there is something we must do to *live for God*. There must be something which engages our interests, something that occupies us precisely as men, as spiritual beings—some spiritual striving that unites and elevates all our being and gives it to God in charity, so our "life" is something which absorbs all our interests and gives them orientation to our goal.

Our love must take one of two forms: it must be principally *contemplative*, in which case we are concerned primarily and directly with interior striving to union with God by contemplation of His truth, by abandoning ourselves to His love; or else it must be principally *active*, concerned exteriorly with good works, reaching God in and through our neighbor. Note—the so-called mixed life does not constitute a third category. Why? St. Thomas answers: whenever there is a mixture, there is a superabundance of one of the elements. So in the mixed life there is sometimes a superabundance of contemplation, sometimes a superabundance of action (II-II, q. 179, a. 2, ad. 2).[251] Hence a mixed life that superabounds in contemplation is really a contemplative life. That is why a life in which the contemplative shares with others the fruits of his contemplation is higher than one in which he merely contemplates. It is a *higher form of contemplative life*.

The Contemplative Life: St. Thomas's teaching here on the contemplative life needs to be completed from texts outside the *Summa* and from other sources. Otherwise we might think he was speaking of a merely intellectual life. But when we see the

250. "Every being is shown to live through the operation most proper to itself, to which it is most inclined" (Aquinas, *Opera Omnia*, 3.598, which reads: "*unumquodque vivens ostenditur vivere . . .*").

251. Aquinas, *Opera Omnia*, 3.599.

background of St. Thomas (St. Gregory, Cassian, etc.) it is clear that he is talking of the contemplative life that is ordered to a loving knowledge of God.

1. The active life (in Cassian's sense—practice of all the virtues[252]) is a necessary preparation for contemplation. Above all, chastity is necessary.

2. The contemplative life centers in the *act of contemplation,* which is essential to it. And this act is a *simplex intuitus veritatis.*[253] The truth of God is here grasped by the intellect moved and inspired by love. Rather, it is an intuition of God beyond concepts and beyond "knowledge" in which God is known in the darkness of infused love. Note that both in the active life and in the contemplative life there is *work* to be done. This work is essentially the same in both—the *formation of Christ in the religious himself and in the souls of others.* In the active life this is done mainly *exteriorly* by outward and visible works such as were done by Jesus Himself when on earth. In the contemplative life this is done *interiorly* (chiefly) by participation in the prayer and sufferings and interior states of Jesus.

3. Contemplation is a beginning of beatitude—*quaedam inchoatio beatitudinis, quae hic incipit, ut in futuro continuetur.*[254] The monastic life is essentially contemplative, not merely because monks are within an enclosure, do not engage in active works, etc., and not merely because our days are taken up with the "exercises of the contemplative life," but because the whole point of our retirement is to *seek God* always and in everything. {For} a good example of this, READ William of St. Thierry: *Golden Epistle,*

---

252. See *Conference* 1, c. 8 (*PL* 49, cols. 490–91), and *Conference* 14, cc. 2–7 (*PL* 49, cols. 955–69); see also *Cassian and the Fathers*, 210–12, and Thomas Merton, *Pre-Benedictine Monasticism: Initiation into the Monastic Tradition* 2, ed. Patrick F. O'Connell, MW 9 (Kalamazoo, MI: Cistercian Publications, 2006), 45–51.

253. q. 180, a. 3, ad. 1: "the simple intuition of truth" (Aquinas, *Opera Omnia*, 3.601, which reads: "*simplicem intuitum veritatis*").

254. q. 180, a. 4: "a certain beginning of beatitude, which starts here so that it might continue in the future life" (Aquinas, *Opera Omnia*, 3.602).

c. ii.5: "To others it is given to believe in God . . . to you to savor of God, to understand Him, to apprehend Him, to enjoy Him" (Eng. trans. p. 14).[255]

Comparison of Active and Contemplative Lives:

1) We must always remember that the contemplative life is much *more of a mystery* than the active life. It is much more interior and more spiritual, and therefore harder to see and understand. That is why glib and easy justifications of the contemplative life do not satisfy the mind. There is always something much more to it than that. Souls called to such a life know this obscurely. Respect the *mystery* of your vocation.

2) It is much more difficult to lead the contemplative life *well* than the active life. Real success is much more rare in the contemplative life. The trials of the contemplative life are much more difficult to cope with than those of the active life. The ground simply gives way beneath your feet, and you no longer know where you are. But these trials are much more efficacious. They subject us to the *direct action of God*. Hence there is always a temptation to draw back from these trials and seek refuge in action, in which we are our own masters. Note: both in the active and contemplative lives, sanctity is essentially the same—it consists in a love which abandons itself entirely to the Holy Spirit and is moved entirely by Him.

3) *Vita contemplativa convenit homini secundum illud quod est optimum in ipso.*[256] Interpret this rightly! {It refers to} not just the intelligence, not just the faculty that *learns* and treasures up

---

255. *PL* 184, col. 511C; *The Golden Epistle of Abbot William of St. Thierry to the Carthusians of Mont Dieu*, trans. Walter Shewring, ed. Dom Justin McCann (London: Sheed and Ward, 1930), which reads: "It belongeth . . . to others to believe in God, to know, love and fear him; to you to savour of Him, to understand Him, to apprehend Him, to enjoy Him."

256. q. 182, a. 1: "The contemplative life is suited to man with regard to that which is best in him [i.e., the intellect]" (Aquinas, *Opera Omnia*, 3.609, citing Aristotle, *Ethics*, 10.7).

knowledge (*scientia inflat*[257])—but the *spirit*—that which is deepest, most hidden, most pure, most personal, most secret, most accessible to God. It is the thirst for this fulfillment of our *deepest and most intimate capacities for the gift of self* that calls us to the contemplative life. We must sacrifice the activities of lower faculties and mortify them, if this highest capacity is to regain its proper place in our lives—hence {the need for} solitude, silence, fasting, etc.; also prayer, reading. Hence {there is} *greater joy in contemplative life (major est delectatio contemplativae vitae*[258]*), greater rest (consistit in quadam vacatione et quiete*[259]*), greater continuity, greater independence (in vita contemplativa est homo magis sibi sufficiens*[260]*).*

Conclusion: the contemplative life is more divine, more truly spiritual, more according to man's inmost needs. But it requires greater courage, more complete self-sacrifice, more perfect humility. It is easier to fail as a contemplative. *Vita contemplativa simpliciter est melior quam activa.*[261] In itself {it is} more perfect. Active life can be more perfect—*secundum quid*[262]—in certain circumstances.

TEXTS FROM ST. THOMAS ON THE STATE OF PERFECTION AND CONTEMPLATION:

1. *Relgiosi dicuntur illi qui se totaliter mancipant servitio Dei, quasi holocaustum Deo offerentes* (II-II, q. 186, a. 1).[263]

2. *Status religionis est quoddam spirituale exercitium ad {consequendam} charitatis perfectionem, quod fit {inquantum} per religionis {observantias} auferuntur impedimenta charitatis . . . et etiam tolluntur*

---

257. "Knowledge puffeth up" (1 Cor. 8:1).

258. "The enjoyment of the contemplative life is greater [than of the active]" (Aquinas, *Opera Omnia*, 3.609, which reads: ". . . *vitae contemplativae*").

259. "consists in a certain leisure and rest" (Aquinas, *Opera Omnia*, 3.609).

260. "In the contemplative life man is more self-sufficient" (Aquinas, *Opera Omnia*, 3.609).

261. "The contemplative life is simply better than the active" (Aquinas, *Opera Omnia*, 3.609, which reads: ". . . *melior est* . . .").

262. "depending on circumstances" (Aquinas, *Opera Omnia*, 3.609).

263. See n. 223.

occasiones peccandi (II-II, q. 189, a. 1).[264] *Religionis status principaliter est institutus ad perfectionem adipiscendam* PER QUAEDAM EXERCITIA QUIBUS TOLLUNTUR IMPEDIMENTA PERFECTAE CHARITATIS (II-II, q. 186, a. 1, ad. 4).[265]

3. (In particular, he means the practice of poverty, chastity and obedience. Why?) *Quaedam consilia sunt, quae si praetermitterentur, tota vita hominis implicaretur in negotiis saecularibus* (II-II, q. 186, a. 2, ad. 3).[266]

4. *Ad perfectionem charitatis adquirendam primum fundamentum est voluntaria paupertas, ut aliquis absque proprio vivat* (II-II, q. 186, a. 3).[267]

5. (Value of obedience) NIHIL MAJUS POTEST HOMO DARE DEO QUAM PROPRIAM VOLUNTATEM (II-II, q. 186, a. 5, ad. 5).[268]

6. *Vita socialis necessaria est ad exercitium perfectionis* (II-II, q. {188}, a. 8).[269]

7. *Perfectio {non} consistit essentialiter in paupertate, sed in Christi sequela* (II-II, q. {188}, a. 7).[270]

---

264. "The state of religion is a certain spiritual practice leading to the perfection of charity, which happens mainly through obstacles to charity being removed by means of religious observances . . . and also through occasions of sin being taken away" (Aquinas, *Opera Omnia*, 3.658, which reads: ". . . *spirituale* . . . *quod quidem fit* . . . *impedimenta perfectae charitatis* . . . *ita etiam tollunt* . . ."; typescript erroneously reads: ". . . *consequendum* . . . *in quantum* . . . *observantiae* . . .").

265. See n. 228.

266. "If certain counsels were overlooked, the whole life of man would be involved in worldly affairs" (Aquinas, *Opera Omnia*, 3.632, which reads: ". . . *implicaretur negotiis* . . .").

267. "To acquire the perfection of charity, the first foundation is voluntary poverty, so that one lives without personal possessions" (Aquinas, *Opera Omnia*, 3.633, which reads: ". . . *acquirendam* . . .").

268. "Man can give nothing greater to God than his own will" (Aquinas, *Opera Omnia*, 3.636, which reads: ". . . *potest Deo dare* . . . *quam quod propriam voluntatem propter ipsum voluntati alterius subjiciat* [than that one subjects one's own will to the will of another for God's sake]"; emphasis added).

269. "Social life is necessary for the practice of perfection" (Aquinas, *Opera Omnia*, 3.657; typescript erroneously reads: "q. 186").

270. "Perfection essentially consists not in poverty but in following Christ" (Aquinas, *Opera Omnia*, 3.654; typescript erroneously omits "*non*" and reads: "q. 186").

8. *Facilius convertuntur ad religionem peccatores quam illi qui de sua innocentia praesumunt* (II-II, q. 189, a. 1, ad. 1).[271]

9. *Vita activa et contemplativa distinguuntur secundum diversa studia hominum intendentium ad diversos fines: quorum unum est {consideratio} veritatis, quae est finis contemplativae vitae; aliud autem est exterior operatio ad quam ordinatur vita activa. . . . Virtutes morales pertinent essentialiter ad vitam activam* (II-II, q. 181, a. 1).[272]

10. *Vita contemplativa simpliciter melior est quam activa* (II-II, q. 182, a. 1).[273] *Vita contemplativa convenit homini secundum illud quod est optimum in ipso. . . . Vita contemplativa potest esse magis continua. . . . Major est delectatio vitae contemplativae quam activae. . . . In vita contemplativa est homo magis sibi sufficiens, quia paucioribus ad eam indiget. . . . Vita contemplativa magis propter se diligitur, vita autem activa ad aliud ordinatur. . . . Vita contemplativa est secundum divina, vita activa est secundum humana. Vita contemplativa consistit in quadam vacatione et quiete* (all from II-II, q. 182, a. 1).[274]

271. "Sinners are more easily converted to religious life than those who presume their own innocence" (Aquinas, *Opera Omnia*, 3.658).

272. "The active and the contemplative lives are distinguished according to different occupations of men, who are focused on different ends, one of which is the consideration of truth, which is the goal of the contemplative life; another is external work, to which the active life is directed. . . . Moral virtues pertain essentially to the active life" (Aquinas, *Opera Omnia*, 3.606, which reads: ". . . *vitae contemplativae* . . ."; typescript erroneously reads: "*consideration*").

273. See n. 261.

274. "The contemplative life is suited to man as that which is best in itself. . . . The contemplative life can be more continuous. . . . There is more enjoyment in the contemplative life than in the active. . . . In the contemplative life man is more self-sufficient, because for that life he needs fewer things. . . . The contemplative life is valued more for itself, while the active is aimed at something else. . . . The contemplative life is oriented to the divine, the active life to the human. . . . The contemplative life consists in a certain leisure and rest" (Aquinas, *Opera Omnia*, 3.609, which reads: ". . . *vita autem activa secundum humana*"; the final sentence precedes the penultimate in the text).

11. *Secundum quid autem et in casu magis est eligenda {vita activa} propter necessitatem hujus vitae . . . non tamen hoc modo quod cogatur quis totaliter contemplationem deserere (ibid., ad. 3).*[275]

Contemplative Life in Our Time—Some special problems

1. {There is a} modern prejudice against contemplative life. Naturally, the materialism of the modern world does not dispose men of our time to appreciate the contemplative life. Enough has been said about this problem. Pope Pius XI has been quoted over and over again in his defense of the contemplative life in *Umbratilem.*[276] Note, however, {that} Pope Pius XI made several statements about the value of the contemplative life in this bull. One is more quoted than the others:

(1) He said that those who lead a contemplative life *do more* by their prayers to save souls than those in the active ministry.[277] This is the text that is so often quoted (by contemplatives especially!).

(2) He also said {of} contemplatives: "By their close union with God and their interior sanctity, those who live a solitary life in the silence of the cloister abundantly contribute to the sanctity which

---

275. "In a particular situation the active life should be preferred due to the needs of this life. . . . Nevertheless, not in this way should someone be forced to abandon contemplation completely" (Aquinas, *Opera Omnia*, 3.609–10, which reads: "*Secundum quid tamen . . . est magis . . . praesentis vitae . . . cogatur aliquis . . .*"; only the final clause is part of ad. 3; typescript erroneously reads: "*vitam activam*").

276. *Acta Apostolica Sedis*, 16.10 (Oct. 15, 1924), 385–90; ET: *The Church and the Carthusians: The Teaching of Pope Pius XI as Contained in the Apostolic Constitution "UMBRATILEM"* (Sky Farm, Whitingham, VT: Carthusian Foundation, 1951) (not used by Merton).

277. "*Facile, ceteroqui, intellegitur, multo plus ad Ecclesiae incrementa et humani generis salutem conferre eos, qui assiduo precum macerationumque officio funguntur, quam qui dominicum agrum laborando excolunt*" ("Otherwise, it is easily understood that those who continually fulfill the duty of prayers and penances contribute much more to the growth of the Church and the salvation of the human race than those who toil by working in the field of the Lord") (*Umbratilem*, 389).

the Immaculate Spouse of Jesus Christ presents for the admiration and imitation of all."[278] This, which is in itself a stronger and more important statement, is hardly quoted at all, even by contemplatives.

(3) He added: contemplatives "have certainly chosen the best part, like Mary of Bethany. One cannot propose to men a more perfect mode of life to embrace, a more perfect rule to follow—provided of course that they have been called by God."[279]

Remarks: there has been so much loose talk about action and contemplation, and the bull *Umbratilem* and other documents have been quoted right and left without understanding. We must weigh these words.

a) The Holy Father is talking only of those who are indeed *leading a truly contemplative life*, primarily in the juridical sense of the word; he is speaking only for such contemplative orders as have flourishing rules and are in good condition and are recognized as such by the Church. He is not speaking of contemplative houses where the rule is not kept, where the contemplative life is not lived, and where the monks are far below the level of their vocation. Pius XII in *Sponsa Christi*[280] takes up the problems of communities which are *contemplative in name only*.

b) The function of contemplatives in the Church is to *be* holy and to love God much; their contribution to the life of the Church is *not to be sought in any exterior work*, but in *interior sanctity*. It is this interior sanctity which gives their prayers value. Their

278. "*Arctissima autem cum Deo coniunctione atque interiore sanctitate eorum, qui solitariam vitam in claustris silentio degunt, ea copiose laus sanctitatis* [praise of sanctity] *alitur, quam immaculata Christi Iesu Sponsa conspiciendam omnibus praebet atque imitandam*" (*Umbratilem*, 385).

279. "*optimam partem, ut Maria e Bethania, elegisse. Nulla enim alia perfectior possit condicio ac lex vivendi hominibus proponi, quam, vocante utique Domino, capiant atque amplectantur*" (*Umbratilem*, 385; this material immediately precedes the previous quotation).

280. "If the canonical contemplative life under strict regular discipline cannot be habitually observed, the monastic character is not to be conferred, nor, if it is already conferred, to be retained" (Pope Pius XII, *Apostolic Constitution "Sponsa Christi"* [Derby, NY: Daughters of St. Paul, Apostolate of the Press, 1955], 41).

sanctity is generally to be associated with great purity of love, and this in turn might normally suggest high graces of prayer and union with God in mystical contemplation—not of course for everyone in the monastery, but for some at least. Where this love exists, the prayers of the contemplatives are truly powerful. But to imagine that we are supposed to contribute a great *quantity* of prayers, or to "turn out" the office as a mechanically finished and perfect product each time, would be to endanger the true interior spirit of prayer and greatly lessen the apostolic value of our life. Care for the externals is necessary, but only as a means to an end—interior purity of love. The office is not an end in itself. It is valuable in so far as it helps monks to become more truly men of prayer and more truly contemplatives.

c) The contemplative monk is *not called to be a shining light admired by men*; he is called to contribute to that light of sanctity by which the Church herself shines in the eyes of men. The contemplative is in the background. It is to the Church that the glory belongs of right. The contemplative orders have tended in our day to draw a little too much attention to themselves, *to seek to shine by publicity*. This is a serious error, especially if it leads to contemplatives taking themselves too seriously and elevating themselves above other orders. By the very fact that they do so, they *lose their right* to the superiority which Pius XI granted to them: for this superiority depends on the purity, humility and hiddenness of their life of prayer directed to God alone. Let us remember the words of Jesus (Matthew 6:5ff.): When ye pray you shall not be as the hypocrites that love to stand and pray in the synagogues. . . . Enter into thy chamber and having shut the door, pray to thy Father in secret. When our prayer is pure, we can truly apply to it the words of St. John of the Cross: "A VERY LITTLE OF THIS PURE LOVE IS MORE PRECIOUS . . . AND OF GREATER PROFIT TO THE CHURCH, THAN ARE ALL [OUTWARD] WORKS TOGETHER, EVEN THOUGH THE SOUL APPEAR TO BE DOING NOTHING AT ALL" (*Spiritual Canticle*, 28).[281]

---

281. Peers, *Complete Works of Saint John of the Cross*, 2.346, which reads: ". . . to the Church, even though the soul appear to be doing nothing, than are all these works together" (emphasis added).

Modern tendencies which militate against the purity of the contemplative life {include}:

a) {The} modern view that sanctity consists in active works of fraternal charity and apostolic self-sacrifice above all. So much is said about this that contemplatives tend to get an inferiority complex about it and to reply by an activism of their own. It is understandable that in the active life works should breed a certain unavoidable agitation—but to introduce such {a} fever of activity into our cloisters is utterly without justification. To fight this, we must remember that our first duty is to love God above all, and that there must be some in the Church who *put everything else aside purely in order to love God.* In doing so they love their neighbor also in Him, and there is always the community life with its exacting demands on our self-sacrifice.

b) In contemplative orders there is danger that too much agitation and anxiety creeps into the *quest for material support*—monks going overboard in business and farming in order to make more money, {having} excessive contacts with the world, certain ones constantly out of the monastery, others bringing salesmen, workmen, etc., into the monastery and thus creating a worldly atmosphere in the cloister. This can bring with it very serious dangers to the true contemplative life. The superiors are the ones who remain responsible, and we have to guard against abuses in our own departments: that is our responsibility.

This problem was discussed at the Congress of States of Perfection in Rome (1950). One reported as follows: "It is necessary to aim at a *very contemplative life* if in fact contemplation is to occupy, in our lives, a sufficient place at all."[282]

---

282. "Il faut viser à une vie très contemplative pourqu'en fait la contemplation occupe dans notre vie une place à peu près suffisante" (Aemilius Jombart, sj, in Sacra Congregatio de Religiosis, *Acta et Documenta Congressus Generalis de Statibus Perfectionis: Romae 1950*, 4 vols. [Rome: Pia Società San Paolo, 1952], 2.117; emphasis added).

Particular problems:

1) *Excessive work*: this has just been discussed. But there must be *manual labor*—this has been neglected in many orders—it is necessary for the contemplative life.

2) *Too little study and intellectual formation*. Pope Pius XI in *Unigenitus Dei Filius*[283] called attention of contemplative orders to the fact that solid grounding in theology is most necessary for contemplatives *above all*.[284] How are we really going to be contemplatives if we know nothing of divine revelation, if we do not understand the Scriptures, if we cannot find the mystery of Christ in the Psalms, if we do not understand the theology of grace on which the interior life depends? {Note the} danger of contemplatives who are nourished on illusions and fables and do not have a solid foundation in theology. Dom O. Lottin, at {the} Congress of States of Perfection, warned against illusion in contemplative life: "In some, fervor which affects the senses above all easily leads to exaltation of the imagination and to an illuminism full

283. Pope Pius XI, *Unigenitus Dei Filius*, *Acta Apostolica Sedis*, 16.4 (March 14, 1924), 133–48; ET: *Review for Religious*, 11 (1952), 183–98.

284. *"Cum enim iis, qui se Deo consecraverint, aut unum aut certe praecipuum propositum sit orare Deum et divina contemplari aut meditari, qui igitur gravissimo eiusmodi fungantur officio nisi fidei doctrinam plane cognitam habeant atque perspectam? Quod velimus eos in primis attendere, qui umbratilem in caelestium rerum contemplatione vitam degunt; errant enim, si putant, theologicis studiis aut ante neglectis aut postea depositis, posse se, copiosa illa destitutos, quae e doctrinis sacris hauritur, Dei mysteriorumque fidei cognitione, facile in excelsis versari atque ad interiorem cum Deo coniunctionem efferri atque evehi"* (137) ("For those who have consecrated themselves to God the one, or certainly the chief, obligation is that of prayer and the contemplation or meditation on divine things. How can they rightly fulfil this solemn duty without a profound and intimate comprehension of the doctrine of faith? The necessity of such study We urge on those particularly who devote their lives to divine contemplation in the cloister. Such souls err indeed if they believe that after having previously neglected or later discontinued their theological studies, they can, though deprived of that copious knowledge of God and the mysteries of faith which is derived from the sacred sciences, readily move in a high spiritual plane and be lifted up and borne aloft to interior union with God" [187]).

of illusion which has nothing in common with the peaceful and humble contemplative life."[285] Solid theological formation and guidance by a good theologian protect souls against this danger.

3) *Danger of strain*: one of the great problems of enclosed monastic life in our day is the problem of tension generated above all in those who perhaps lack aptitude for the life. But even those who have true vocations suffer more from this in our day when constitutions are somehow weaker and less able to bear an enclosed life.

4) *Problem of selecting vocations*: {it is} better to have one novice who belongs than twenty who don't belong here. At {the} Congress of States of Perfection it was stressed that souls are more fitted for active life in our time, and truly contemplative vocations are rarer. Vocations must be selected with strictness and care. *Non sufficit pietas juvenalis*,[286] says O. Lottin. Above all, a well-balanced mind must be present in the candidate, with common sense and the ability to avoid extremes.

5) *Problem of perseverence* in the contemplative life is even greater than heretofore. Many leave after profession. There must be true *fervor and generosity*, true love of solitude and prayer; the office must always be the expression of a deep interior life of prayer; there must be a taste for private contemplative prayer, love of silence and mortification, and detachment in regard to human affections. One who cultivates these things will normally persevere.

SELECTION OF VOCATIONS (cf. *Acta* of Religious Congress of 1950 [vol. ii, p. 625f. etc.][287])

Wrong theories of vocation {include}:

285. "*In quibusdam enim fervor, praesertim si in sensus diffunditur, facile in exaltationem imaginationibus vergit, in aliquem 'illuminismum,' illusionibus plenum, qui cum humili et placida oratione veri contemplativi nil commune habet*" (Odo Lottin, OSB, *Acta et Documenta*, 2.121).

286. "An adolescent piety is not sufficient" (*Acta et Documenta*, 2.121).

287. Ladislaus ab Immaculata, CP, "*De Vocationum Selectione*" (*Acta et Documenta*, 2.625–36).

a) Vocation has a material and formal element—matter: the dispositions, etc. of the candidate; formal: the admission into religion. The formal without the material can constitute a vocation—the mere fact of entering = vocation.

b) Others teach that there is no vocation where both the formal and material elements are not present. This would mean that one who in fact did not enter religion would never have a vocation.

c) Some hold vocation consists of the qualities required by Canon 538.

d) Others demand that the candidate *feel* a strong attraction from {the} Holy Spirit.

All these are wrong and dangerously misleading. {A} true notion {recognizes that}:

a) Religious vocation is an invitation on the part of the Holy Spirit, an inspiration or drive leading a man to desire to embrace the evangelical counsels. One is properly "called" to religious life when moved to embrace it by a divine grace.

b) Vocation is something antecedent to and distinct from the admission of the candidate. Canon 538 merely gives the *signs of vocation*, not the vocation itself. (Canon 538: *IN RELIGIONEM ADMITTI POTEST QUILIBET CATHOLICUS QUI NULLO LEGITIMO DETINEATUR IMPEDIMENTO RECTAQUE INTENTIONE MOVEATUR ET AD RELIGIONIS ONERA FERENDA SIT IDONEUS.*[288])

c) Vocation does not necessarily imply extraordinary and sensible movements in the soul. Vocation can coexist with repugnance.

d) Vocation must be evident in the external forum—i.e., by signs inducing moral certitude. {This is} to be gained by {the} declaration of the candidate himself, statements of those who

---

288. *Codex Iuris Canonici*, ed. Petrus Cardinal Gaspari (Westminster, MD: Newman Press, 1949), 181 ("Any Catholic may be admitted into religious life who is not prevented by any legal impediment and is moved by a right intention and suited for bearing the burdens of religious life").

know him, signs of vocation, reducible to three: right intention, fitness, absence of impediments. Vocation {is an} *afflatus divinus per signa manifestatus.*[289]

{The proper} way of procedure {includes}:

1) Not to be too easy in admitting candidates. *Facilis candidatorum admissio est pessima vocationum selectio.*[290] {The} source of all evils in religious communities {is} admitting vocations without sufficient care. Quality {must be stressed} rather than quantity. {It is} better to have an empty novitiate than one full of bad subjects (*Declaratio Sacrae Congregationis pro Religiosis*, 21 Dec. 1909[291]). Above all, {it is essential} not to accept them through human utility. NEVER ADMIT DOUBTFUL CANDIDATES—*DE QUIBUS IN INCERTO SIT AFFLATUNE DIVINO ISTAM VITAE RATIONEM DELIGANT.*[292]

2) Fitness: when God calls to a state of life, He gives what is needed to live it. *Absolute* fitness {is} not required, but {fitness} relative to this particular order:

a) *physical and psychological* {fitness includes} health, balance, right judgement, {the} ability to live community life without many dispensations.

b) *moral* {fitness includes} not sanctity, or heroic virtues, but qualities which indicate the candidate may persevere in virtue and make progress—especially willingness and ability to overcome his natural inclinations, especially obedience, humility, chastity, etc.

---

289. "divine inspiration, shown through signs."

290. "Easy admission of candidates is the worst selection process for vocations" (Ladislaus, *Acta et Documenta*, 2.628).

291. *Acta Apostolicae Sedis*, 2 (1910), 36, cited in Ladislaus, *Acta et Documenta*, 2.629.

292. "With regard to those for whom the divine inspiration is uncertain, let them set aside this way of life" (*Epistola Apostolica Cum Primum*, c. 1 [August 4, 1913], *Acta Apostolica Sedis*, 5 [1913], 388 [which reads: ". . . *divino sanctissimam istam* . . ."], quoted in Ladislaus, *Acta et Documenta*, 2.630) (emphasis added).

3) Who selects vocations?

a) *priests* are to "spot" and prepare them (Canon 1353)[293]—
not *discourage* them!

b) superiors, confessors, novice masters have {a} special
part to play—and {the} grace of state to fulfill their functions.
They must be loyal in their responsibility to {the} Church and to
souls, {and must} reject those not called.

{There are} other important factors in the selection of vocations. Parents should give an education and formation in piety
which will make vocations possible and likely in some of their
children. Preaching and writing should remind the faithful of
the beauty and nobility of religious vocations. Priests, by their
holiness and fervor, should give an "existential" lesson on the
beauty of vocation. The youth of our day will be much more
attracted to religious life by examples of zeal, holiness, fervor
in poverty, virginity, etc., than by ballyhoo and modern "techniques" unsupported by interior holiness. *Avoid indiscreet and
natural zeal, "pressure,"* etc.

4) *Signs of vocation* {include}: (negative) absence of impediment; (positive) *aptitude, right intention.* For further details, see
Notes on *Constitutions.*[294]

---

293. *"Dent operam sacerdotes, praesertim parochi, ut pueros, qui indicia praebeant
ecclesiasticae vocationis, peculiaribus curis a saeculi contagiis arceant, ad pietatem infor-
ment, primis littterarum studiis imbuant divinaeque in eis vocationis germen foveant"*
(*Codex Iuris Canonici*, 462) ("Let priests, especially parish priests, make an effort,
with particular care, to keep boys who display signs of a vocation to the Church
from the contagions of secular life, forming them in piety, training them in their
first studies of religious literature, and fostering in them the seed of their divine
vocation").

294. *"Constitutions* of the Cistercians," a set of conference notes for a course
given by Merton as master of novices and found in volume 15 of *Collected Essays*,
the 24-volume bound set of published and unpublished materials assembled at
the Abbey of Gethsemani and available both there and at the Thomas Merton
Center, Bellarmine University, Louisville, KY, 48–50.

5) Vocations must be *tested, formed, cultivated*—in postulancy and {in the} novitiate. *Time* is absolutely necessary to penetrate the inner depths of the candidate's motives, intentions, etc.— proved by constant fidelity in the regular life each day, true zeal for prayer, seeking God, accepting humiliations, labor and trial with truly supernatural dispositions—i.e., faith, not just equanimity of temperament. A vocation is proved when aptitudes are seen to be solid, when *intention* is seen to develop into a fixed *will to persevere* for the right (supernatural) reasons.

The Spirit of Our Order: the real test of a "vocation" {depends on the answer to the question}: is he capable of being "informed" by the spirit of the Order? You do not come here merely to be "good religious" or "contemplatives," but monks of St. Benedict and of Cîteaux. Of course the "spirit" of the Order is not something rigid and set, admitting no variations. The spirit of our Order (or any order) is a set of *attitudes and motives*—a *spiritual outlook*, an *ideal* which moves and guides all that we do to our common end. Our *communities* and all the religious in them should be filled with this spirit. It is simply the *way* the Holy Spirit Himself acts in Cistercians and sanctifies them. In our life, the Holy Spirit will normally sanctify us in ways that would not be normal for a Jesuit, a Franciscan, a Little Sister of the Poor. But it is *the same Holy Spirit*—"there are diversities of gifts but one Spirit."[295]

What then are the virtues and tendencies which characterize our spirit?

1) St. Benedict's signs: *si revera Deum quaerit*[296]—fervor at *office*, in *obedience*, in *humiliations*.

2) What does it mean for *us* to truly seek God? {It means} to *love silence*, in order to think more constantly of God, and be with Him rather than with men. *One who does not have {a} spirit of silence* does not have a vocation to our life. Many signs may indicate that one *does not want* to seek God or else that one is *unable to* seek Him

295. 1 Cor. 12:4.
296. "if he truly seeks God" (*Rule*, c. 58 [McCann, 130]).

in silence. {It means} *to love poverty* and *labor* (*pauperes cum paupere Christo*[297]). One who seeks many conveniences and comforts and little possessions shows he is attached more to material things, {that he} depends on them, needs them, cannot be satisfied with poverty and prayer alone. Love of poverty for us means *love of manual labor* and love of the "poor" prayer which is often all we can offer at work. {It means} *to love solitude* but in community, {with} a true family spirit, a love of all the brethren—with interior solitude for Christ. *This requires a very difficult and rather universal balance*. {It means} *to love reading and meditation*—these too are very necessary for our contemplative life, though perhaps less necessary in a laybrother. All should be able to develop this tendency somehow. If it is lacking, there is no vocation. {It means} *to love penance*—ours is a penitential life. If we truly seek God, we fly from sin, and hence one who has no *spirit of compunction*, who is hard and proud and self-sufficient and worldly, has no vocation to our life. Penance {is} manifested in a spirit of dependence. {It means} *to love humility*—but *true* humility, not the sham. One who has a contempt for "passive virtues" like humility and obedience has no vocation, unless he is able to change. {It means} *to love {the} divine office*—not for aesthetic reasons, but to praise and love God with all gratitude and adoration. A sense of the greatness and goodness of God our Father, and a simple need to praise Him at all times and give oneself to Him, is a good sign of {a} vocation to our life. {It means} *to love our nothingness and depend entirely on the grace of God*. One who depends too much on his own strength and virtues lacks the Christian and religious spirit. More particularly, he lacks the spirit of St. Benedict, which is one of *total dependence on prayer and on grace*—an instinct *to ask God* and expect all from Him before all else, rather than on our own efforts and techniques first (asking Him only after our own strength has failed).

---

297. "poor with the poor Christ" (*Exordium Cisterciense*, 15: "*Instituta Monachorum Cisterciensium de Molismo Venientium*" [*PL* 166, col. 1507D, which reads: "*cum paupere Christo pauperes*"]).

N.B. the above signs are *essential*. It is *not essential* to have a desire for contemplative or mystical prayer. A strong desire for contemplative prayer and a relative weakness in the above signs would indicate that one had no true vocation to our life.

States of Life: *Appendix—Contempt for the World*

Vos qui reliquistis omnia et secuti estis me, centuplum accipietis et vitam aeternam possidebitis;[298] *a saeculi actibus se facere alienum (Rule of St. Benedict).*[299]

1. {The} monk {is} essentially one who has left all to follow Christ. {See} the vocation of St. Anthony.[300] {The} spirit of the world {is} essentially opposed to {the} monastic spirit. {A} true monastic vocation implies a *total conversion* from the world to Christ. We must be convinced of the necessity of this—otherwise we will be monks in appearance only. If a monk is not what he is supposed to be, he gives grave scandal, and those who see him are confirmed in their evil ways.

2. What is the world? {the realm of} triple concupiscence ({cf.} 1 John[301]).

a) {In} Scripture, {a worldly spirit} cannot receive {the} Holy Spirit (John 15); cannot be subject to {the} law of God (Romans 8); {shows} undue solicitude for material things (Matt. 5). {This is the realm of} Babylon {in the} Apocalypse.

---

298. "You who have left everything and followed me will receive a hundredfold, and will possess eternal life" (communion prayer: Mass of a confessor not a bishop, from Mt. 19:27, 29 [*Missale Romanum*, (27); *Missale Cisterciense*, 22*]).

299. "to make oneself a stranger to the ways of the world" (*Rule*, c. 4 [Mc-Cann, 26]).

300. See *Life of St. Anthony*, trans. Sr. Mary Emily Keenan, scn, in *Early Christian Biographies*, ed. Roy J. Deferrari, trans. Roy J. Deferrari *et al.*, The Fathers of the Church, vol. 15 (New York: Fathers of the Church, 1952), c. 2 (135), and *Cassian and the Fathers*, 32.

301. "For all that is in the world, is the concupiscence of the flesh, and the concupiscence of the eyes, and the pride of life, which is not of the Father, but is of the world" (1 Jn. 2:16).

b) Characteristics of {a} worldly spirit {include}: (1) a temporal end, sought with all the power of the soul, (2) by temporal means. Temporal ends {include} comfort, pleasure, recreation, "divertissement," power, fame, influence, success. Both lead to exaltation of self; examples {are seen in} advertising, worldly conversations (analyze!), the other-directed mentality. Temporal means {include} money, publicity, {success} "by being smarter than the other fellow," techniques, "conforming," revenge (the world exercises threats and sanctions and severely punishes infidelity).

3. The world attacks the monastery. It will not leave you in peace; it will undermine your vocation—perhaps even through those dear to you ("A man's enemies are those of his own household"[302]).

a) It solicits and tempts: "Why so strict? So 'antisocial'?" "Aren't you being selfish?" "Why this waste?" {There may be} temptations to "action" under {the} guise of good. {There can be} daydreams, fears for the future—of self, of family, etc. {There may be a} *worldly spirit in the monastery itself.*
b) It threatens disaster.

4. How to resist:

a) understand what the world is and what it means; see {the} *vanity* of the world;
b) understand your weakness—fear sin;
c) appreciate your vocation—love silence, enclosure, solitude, etc., especially *holy reading*;
d) *respice finem:*[303] look to the last end—eternal life.

5. We are called not just to leave the world but above all to *follow Christ*. Stress this positive side—*nihil amori Christi praepo-*

302. Mt. 10:36.
303. "look to the result" (proverbial).

nere[304]—and frequently offer Him the full resolve of our hearts to leave all and follow Him!

ABNEGATION

Proem: the monastic life is a life in which we leave all to follow Christ. It is a life of abnegation. Without abnegation, our life in the monastery is a sham. On the other hand, abnegation improperly understood and badly practiced, even with the greatest good will, frustrates the spiritual life and to a great extent extinguishes the Holy Spirit in souls. {Here lies the} importance of knowing the *true* Christian teaching on abnegation and practicing it wholeheartedly. {There is a crucial} difference between accidentals and essentials: very often, misguided asceticism is a question of intransigeant emphasis on accidentals and neglect of essentials. True asceticism puts everything in the right place and is supremely generous in these essentials, admitting *no compromise*. In the accidentals, we need discretion to see what is willed by God and what is not. *Our principle* will then be *no Christian perfection without self-abnegation*. This is absolutely essential. If we think we can serve Jesus and not deny ourselves, we are in illusion. No man can serve two masters. {That is} utterly incompatible with the spirit and teaching of the Gospel. The wisdom of Christ is the wisdom of the Cross. The way of the Cross is the way divine love has planned for our salvation and for His glorification, and we cannot glorify Him by substituting some other way and wisdom of our own.

At the same time, we must have the right idea of abnegation—the idea Jesus came to teach—His own way of abnegation—the Church's way: *via media*.[305] We must not be misled by the extremism of this or that school of spirituality and press certain exaggerations beyond the point where they make sense. This would lead not to self-denial but to a subtle and inverted form of

304. "to prefer nothing to the love of Christ" (*Rule*, c. 4 [McCann, 26]).
305. "the middle way."

self-assertion. All pseudo-asceticism is nothing but a disguised self-assertion masking as self-denial.

Let us then be truly Catholic in our idea of abnegation. Cassian and St. Thomas give us our basic principles:

1. The value of exercises, observances, mortifications, etc. lies in their appropriateness and efficacy as *means to an end*—purity of heart—perfection of charity. Perfection does not consist in fasting, vigils, study, prayer, etc. in themselves—but these are *means to perfection*. When properly used, they promote perfection. When improperly used, they impede perfection. To cling to these things for their own sake against the will of God, or against charity or obedience, would be to turn them against oneself and one's perfection (cf. Cassian, *Conf.* 1[306]).

2. The value of exercises and observances is not proportionate to their hardness and difficulty, but to their efficacy as means to an end. *Arctitudo observantiarum non est illud quod praecipue in religione commmendatur* (II-II, q. 188, a. 6, ad. 3).[307] He continues: "A religious order is not superior by the fact that it has more strict observances, but by the fact that its observances are ordered with greater discretion toward achieving the end of the Order" (*id.*).[308]

3. *To leave certain sensible goods and then cling to other created goods of a slightly higher order is not abnegation.* To leave material things and become attached to moral good is not abnegation— only a higher and more spiritual form of attachment. True abnegation renounces even certain accidentally good moral values when they are opposed to what is essential—God's will in our regard. For instance, though contemplation is higher in itself than

---

306. *Collatio* 1, c. 7 (*PL* 49, cols. 489A–490B) focuses on monastic practices as means to the end of purity of heart, not ends in themselves; see *Cassian and the Fathers*, 206–10.

307. "Strictness of observances is not what should be particularly valued in religious life" (Aquinas, *Opera Omnia*, 3.653).

308. "*Et ideo non est potior religio ex hoc quod habet arctiores observantias, sed ex hoc quod ex majori discretione sunt ejus observantiae ordinatae ad finem religionis*" (Aquinas, *Opera Omnia*, 3.654).

action, it shows greater abnegation to leave contemplation for action under the requisite conditions, in order to serve God. (Note: there can never be question of abandoning the life of prayer and divine union, which is essential to Christian perfection—but of sacrificing certain helps, certain advantages, leisure, time, silence, etc., which would be valuable for our life of prayer. God will reward the sacrifice and make it good.)

Gospel text on abnegation—Matthew 16:24-26 and context: IF ANY MAN WILL COME AFTER ME, LET HIM DENY HIMSELF AND TAKE UP HIS CROSS AND COME FOLLOW ME—and the explanation, in l. 25: He that will save his life shall lose it, and he that shall lose his life for my sake shall find it.

1. *Si quis VULT*:[309] it is a question of free choice. One must embrace abnegation, but not for its own sake—rather, for the sake of Christ. If any man will come after me—if any man *wants to*. If you don't want to, then don't pretend—don't just go through the motions. The basis of our abnegation is not an ethical theory, not a mere desire for moral perfection. It is love of Jesus Christ—and His will and the mystery of the Father's providential design. The whole spiritual life is in the following of Christ *wherever* He goes {and} submission to the Holy Spirit *wherever* He may lead. It does not mean attachment to a system but to the Person of God, to Jesus, to the Holy Spirit. {It} does not mean an agreement to follow Jesus as long as He Himself follows an approved system. One cannot even hear the voice of the Spirit if he is attached to self and to the world—hence the reason for abnegation. On the other hand, the Spirit does not merely come to teach us abnegation for its own sake. He comes to unite us to Jesus, and He inspires in us the renunciation that is necessary for this. Hence the free choice to leave all and follow Christ—this is what dictates our abnegation.

2. *ABNEGET SEMETIPSUM*:[310] the Greek word used here (*aparneisthai*) is the very same used in Peter's denial of Jesus—striking!

309. "If anyone wishes."
310. "Let him deny himself."

It is a question of loyalties and rejections. If we are attached to self, we will deny Jesus. If we are His followers, we must then deny ourselves in the same way. Read the passage on Peter's denial (Mark 14:66-72[311]). {Note} the vehemence with which Peter denies that he "knows the man" or had anything to do with him. {Here it means} wanting no part with our false self! How far we are from this; how far even pious and ascetic men are from this (!)—how attached to themselves, to their own ideas, their own plans, projects, theories, opinions, all for the "glory of God," of course! Note {the} difference between abnegation and mortification. Mortification is a systematic self-discipline by *denying our faculties* and even our *very self* some basic satisfactions. But abnegation means more: mortification is like *pruning* a plant, abnegation like *transplanting* it. Luke adds, in this connection, that we must *hate our own soul*.[312] What does this mean? There is a self-hatred which is morbid and pathological, but it is really a self-love that is completely attached to self and immersed in self, but resents being imprisoned in itself—still, it cannot escape. Self-love means attachment *to our own excellence* and *to our own advantage*, irrespective of the excellence and advantage of others. Self-hatred means letting these go. We cannot totally discard all care for our own advantage: we are bound by the law of God (a) to preserve life and to go on working for Him; (b) above all to save our immortal soul and to become saints. Hence we have to

---

311. "Now when Peter was in the court below, there cometh one of the maidservants of the high priest. And when she had seen Peter warming himself, looking on him she saith: Thou also wast with Jesus of Nazareth. But he denied, saying: I neither know nor understand what thou sayest. And he went forth before the court; and the cock crew. And again a maidservant seeing him, began to say to the standers by: This is one of them. But he denied again. And after a while they that stood by said again to Peter: Surely thou art one of them; for thou art also a Galilean. But he began to curse and to swear, saying; I know not this man of whom you speak. And immediately the cock crew again. And Peter remembered the word that Jesus had said unto him: Before the cock crow twice, thou shalt thrice deny me. And he began to weep."

312. Lk. 14:26.

preserve our life as long as God wills us to do so, and we must make every effort to become saints and be perfectly united to His holy will by all the means He places at our disposal. BUT we must renounce all solicitude for ourselves and all agitated self-preservation. We must become detached from all inordinate concern with our own interests and our own advantage, *even in spiritual things*, as long as these are only accidental. In a word, we must always sacrifice the accidental to the essential when it is required—v.g., give up our own necessities and comforts in order to help others, give up convenience and spiritual advantage in accidentals in order to serve others and carry out the will of God. In a word, we must strive to become *totally unselfish* in all things, both material and spiritual. This means as far as possible forgetting our own interests and advantages in order to give preference to the interests and advantages of others and above all to the will of God, remembering always that what God wants of us above all is union with Him in love and submission to the Holy Spirit (hence we can *never* renounce what is essential for this growth in union with God). It means renouncing our inordinate anxiety to plan and direct our own lives and make everything "come out" the way we think it ought to. The true purpose of abnegation is to place us directly and entirely in the hands of God Who loves us and let our lives be formed and guided entirely by His love.

3. ET TOLLAT CRUCEM SUAM:[313] here we have to examine the context. {The} scene is on the road outside of Caesarea Philippi—Peter has made his confession of faith, and Jesus has begun to tell of His Passion. Peter reproves Him, and Jesus in turn tells Peter that he does not know what he is saying: it is *necessary* to take up the Cross. Peter has been elevated to the highest dignity in the Church and to a place in which he must cooperate most closely with Jesus—it is all the more necessary that he understand the wisdom of the Cross. Those who are to be closest to Jesus and to cooperate with Him in His work for the redemption of the world are also to be called to the most complete self-denial. The very

313. "and take up his cross."

nature of their vocation demands this and will take care of it if they are faithful. In any case, Peter rejecting the Cross is a disciple of Satan rather than of Christ and "savours not the things that are of God but the things that are of men" (16:23). Then follows Jesus' explanation—the words we are commenting {on}. The *Cross* meant ignominy and disgrace, total rejection by human society, as well as the greatest suffering and degradation and poverty. We must never forget that the Cross was not yet the sign of glory! Those whose asceticism is a matter of prowess and spiritual ambition, and who use it to elevate themselves in their own estimation and in the estimation of men, should remember this.

{4}. ET SEQUATUR ME:[314] *the main thing is the following of Christ.* This means, in the words of St. Augustine, giving up our own will and our own way in order that He may live and act in us: *Noli tu ipse vivere in te . . . noli facere voluntatem tuam, sed ejus qui habitat in te.*[315] {It means} total self-surrender to the will of Jesus, through obedience, acceptance of reality and of our duties of state, loving our brethren, and accepting providential indications of His will—even suffering evil that He permits in our lives—all this in the spirit of total abnegation. *Abnegation is not a particular virtue,* but it implies the exercise of all the Christian virtues with a particular slant—humility with the slant of self-forgetfulness and hiddenness, charity with the slant on putting others before self, etc. {It entails} *not seeking to please ourselves, to be pleased with ourselves.* Real abnegation means giving up the *search for* that inner glow of self-satisfaction and contentment with self (but accepting it gladly when it comes of itself, from the hands of God), especially giving up the self-satisfaction that is the reflection of what seems to be the approval of others. How can you believe who seek glory one from another?

---

314. "and follow me."
315. "Do not live in yourself. . . . Do not do your own will, but that of Him who dwells in you" (*Sermo* 330, *In Natali Martyrum* [PL 38, col. 1459]).

Abnegation is not self-destruction but true fulfillment. How is it that the Cross leads us to true fulfillment and true peace? because of the very constitution of man made in the image of God. Mankind itself is one divine image. The person does not have peace and rest in himself alone. He has peace in his place in the Mystical Body of Christ, when he is united to others in charity, when he feels himself completed by them and when he himself contributes to their own happiness. True abnegation cannot be understood outside the doctrine of the Mystical Body of Christ. It is when we realize that our true function as persons is to *fulfill our part* in a well-integrated spiritual whole, that we can begin to see how abnegation of our false, limited "self" is essential before we can function as parts of a whole. Attachment to self is precisely an attachment to the illusion that *we are the whole*. Each individual of a fallen race tends to regard himself as the whole cheese and {to} try to subordinate all the others to himself. He is the center, and everything else is seen in relation to his own interests and advantage—his sanctity even. But this is a false slant. The perfection of each person is found in charity—and charity is precisely what incorporates and integrates him in the whole Christ. Each one has in himself the "whole" in so far as each is the image of God—but the image is not fully realized until, united to all by charity, we receive all and receive God Himself into our own souls with the Holy Spirit. Abnegation means the renunciation of all that prevents this perfect integration in the whole Christ. This is the true Benedictine outlook.

The Practice of Abnegation:

1. Only love for Jesus can move us to true abnegation. The positive motive of love must overbalance everything else.

2. But we *must not wait until this love is felt*. To wait for a strong, sensible love that will carry us away and make us oblivious to all difficulty is an illusion. This love indeed will come when God wills, but for our part we must be prepared to renounce ourselves IN DRYNESS, WITH REPUGNANCE, WITH DIFFICULTY AND EVEN WITH GREAT IMPERFECTION, struggling as best

we can to give up self, and perhaps not succeeding. Here again, the principle of risk comes in again. We must be willing to take risks, to run the risk even of a certain amount of error, in order to follow what seems to be a genuine indication of God's will for us.

3. Above all, we must be faithful to *follow the Holy Spirit and not precede Him*. It is utterly useless to agitate ourselves in offering to God sacrifices which He does not ask, or to push ourselves forward in a spirit of pride and try to do things which He does not want from us *yet*. Many ruin their spiritual lives by trying to do at the beginning what they might have been capable of offering after long years. They are moved by pride rather than by submission to the will of God. It is useless to imagine great sacrifices and to overheat our imaginations in thinking about how we would like to do these things, while perhaps neglecting the ordinary simple sacrifices which God really asks of us here and now.

4. We must go forward in interior peace and tranquility based on confidence in God. *Non in commotione Dominus.*[316] The Spirit of the Lord is not in agitation and unrest—and if the way ahead leads to that, then we should stay where we are and wait for God to give further indications. The unrest may proceed from lack of generosity, but even then we will not make ourselves more generous by pushing ourselves forward by main force. We must beg God for grace and take it when it comes.

5. We must be faithful to graces received and truly cooperate with them.

6. We must not waste time *lamenting our mistakes* or blaming ourselves for errors of judgement or even for lack of generosity. Just be humble and promise the Holy Spirit to be more faithful in the future—and then be faithful!

Fr. de Guibert says:

Abnegation is the *strategic point* in the spiritual life—the gain or loss of which decides the battle for sanctity. Experience is there to prove it—study the lives of those who were not quite saints,

---

316. "The Lord is not in the earthquake" (3 Kings [1 Kings] 19:11).

priests, religious, simple faithful, excellent, fervent, zealous, pious, and devout and who nevertheless were not "saints" pure and simple, one will notice that what they lacked was not a deep interior life, nor a sincere and living love for God and for souls, but a certain *plenitude of renunciation*, a certain depth of abnegation and totality in self-forgetfulness which would have delivered them up to God's work in their souls and which strikes us in the true saints. They will love God and serve Him and even kill themselves with work for Him—but most of them draw back from the secret holocaust of dying totally to self, obscurely, in the silence of the soul, letting themselves be detached from all that is not God.[317]

Part III:

THE VOWS

1. *Vows in General*: THE THEOLOGICAL FOUNDATION OF RELIGIOUS PROFESSION. The consecration of our life to God by vow is *one* of the essential elements of religious profession. That is to say, the mere making of vows of obedience, poverty and chastity does not of itself exhaust the meaning of religious profession. Religious profession is *the act by which we formally embrace the religious state*. In ancient monasticism, emphasis was placed not so much on the juridical act of profession as on the *conversio*: the leaving of the world and the embracing of the monastic life— *renuntiatio—poenitentia*. Our modern emphasis on the juridical vows should not make us forget that monastic profession, before it can have juridical value, presupposes this *interior conversion*— that is to say, a real intent to leave the world and to follow Christ in the religious life, a real purpose to give one's life entirely to

317. Joseph de Guibert, "Abnégation: III. Notion Précise et Doctrine de l'Abnégation," *Dictionnaire de Spiritualité Ascétique et Mystique* [*DS*], ed. F. Cavallera *et al.*, 17 vols. (Paris: Beauchesne, 1932–95), vol. 1, cols. 105–106; Merton refers to the same passage in *Introduction to Christian Mysticism*, 20.

God. Hence religious profession is an act which includes the following essential elements: (1) renunciation of our former life and imitation of Christ; (2) incorporation in a society of love, the religious family; (3) consecration to God by vow.

1) *Renunciation of our former way of life and the putting on of Christ.* We have seen above what this involves, and we have examined the Gospel texts on poverty, etc. To make religious profession is to *put on Christ.* Nowadays, when the taking of the religious habit is separated by two years from profession itself, this is not as clear as it used to be. It is at the beginning of the novitiate that we focus our attention on the act of "putting on Christ."[318] Here we as it were anticipate one of the essential elements of profession. Obviously, the novitiate would be of little value if the novice did not resolve to imitate Christ with all his power, to put on Christ in spirit and in truth and to die to his old life, even during the novitiate. But the fact of this anticipation should not obscure the fact that the putting on of Christ is an essential element of our religious profession itself. The *habit* itself symbolizes Christ. The black scapular, it is said, symbolizes penance and the Cross; the cincture the perpetuity of our ascetic obligation; the robe and cowl, which are white, symbolize the joy and purity of the angelic life which we lead by the grace of Christ. The cowl particularly reminds us of the life of glory in heaven, which we shall live "in Christ"—all about our habit speaks of our new life and of our "conversation in heaven."[319] Hence at the taking of the habit, the abbot says, *"Exuat te Dominus veterem hominem cum actibus suis. . . . Induat te Dominus novum hominem, qui secundum Deum creatus est, in justitia et sanctitate veritatis."*[320]

318. Rom. 13:14; Gal. 3:27.
319. Phil. 3:20.
320. "May the Lord strip off from you the old man and his acts. . . . May the Lord put on you the new man, who was created according to God, in justice and holiness of life" (*Rituale Cisterciense ex Libro Usuum Definitionibus Ordinis et Caeremoniali Episcoporum Collectum* [Westmalle, Belgium: Ex Typographia Ordinis, 1948], 235–36 [VI.i.5–6]).

The *unchanging* *character* of the habit symbolizes the eternity of our life of contemplation. We do not seek novelties and new fashions like the children of the world. We are content with what is plain, constant, even uninteresting in the eyes of man. (We wear {the} same cowl as St. Bernard!) We have already seen that we put on Christ by a life of the theological virtues, a life especially of *faith*, in which faith enables us to see and judge all things with the mind of Christ and of His Church. The counsels enable us to have in our minds that which was in the mind of Jesus Himself, our Redeemer, when He descended to earth, emptied Himself to take the form of a slave, and was made obedient unto the death of the Cross.[321] READ *De Imitatione Christi*, Book {1}, c. 1.[322] The

---

321. Phil. 2:6-8.

322. "He who follows Me, says Christ our Saviour, walks not in darkness, for he will have the light of life. These are the words of our Lord Jesus Christ, and by them we are admonished to follow His teachings and His manner of living, if we would truly be enlightened and delivered from all blindness of heart.

"Let all the study of our heart be from now on to have our meditation fixed wholly on the life of Christ, for His holy teachings are of more virtue and strength than the words of all the angels and saints. And he who through grace has the inner eye of his soul opened to the true beholding of the Gospels of Christ will find in them hidden manna.

"It is often seen that those who hear the Gospels find little sweetness in them; the reason is that they do not have the spirit of Christ. So, if we desire to have a true understanding of His Gospels, we must study to conform our life as nearly as we can to His.

"What avail is it to a man to reason about the high, secret mysteries of the Trinity if he lack humility and so displeases the Holy Trinity? Truly, it avails nothing. Deeply inquisitive reasoning does not make a man holy or righteous, but a good life makes him beloved by God. I would rather feel compunction of heart for my sins than merely know the definition of compunction. If you know all the books of the Bible merely by rote and all the sayings of the philosophers by heart, what will it profit you without grace and charity? All that is in the world is vanity except to love God and to serve Him only. This is the most noble and the most excellent wisdom that can be in any creature: by despising the world to draw daily nearer and nearer to the kingdom of heaven" (Thomas à Kempis, *The Imitation of Christ*, trans. Richard Whitford, ed. Harold C. Gardiner, SJ [Garden City, NY: Doubleday Image, 1955], 31–32; typescript reads "Book 2," but in his January 14, 1963 conference Merton corrects the reference and reads this passage from Book 1).

monk is one who wants to imitate Christ in all things, to seek and find Jesus in all things. He not only imitates but follows Jesus. Hence the religious life is before all else a *sequela Christi*.[323] How do we follow Christ? By love, by self-denial, by sharing His poverty, His obedience, His mortification, His Cross—also His joys and His contemplation. We must see everything in our monastic life as a participation in the life of Jesus. We live on earth as He lived, in poverty, obedience, obscurity, self-sacrifice, labor. In all that we do we seek Him, for we know by faith that if we live as He lived and do His will, then He will live in us and His Father and the Holy Spirit will manifest themselves in us, and we will know Him secretly and intimately, by union of love with Him. The whole religious life is orientated to this intimate union with Christ Jesus. Without this union of love, the religious life is relatively sterile and meaningless. Unless our life is centered on the love of the Divine Person of Jesus, it will be relatively empty and fruitless. Let us not try to practice poverty, obedience, etc. merely for their own sakes, or for the sake of virtue or of perfection, but realize that the religious state is above all considered by the Church *the ideal way of living the Christ life and sharing in the mystery of Christ*. It is clear in our solemn profession, when we lay the schedule of profession on the altar, that we thus *publically profess* to unite our whole lives in sacrifice with the sacrifice of the Cross—renewed each day on the altar. Our religious life is a perfect participation in the sacrifice of Christ; it enables us to live each day our Mass most perfectly, for in the Mass we renew our offering to Jesus. (Emphasize the fact that in the Mass we offer ourselves daily as victims to God with Christ—giving our whole lives for His glory.) Hence the importance of the virtue of *devotion* with which we make our vows and live our entire lives.

   Devotio {is} defined by St. Thomas {as} *voluntas quaedam prompte se tradendi ad ea quae pertinent ad Dei famulatum* (II-II, q.

---

323. See above, n. 220.

{82}, a. 1).[324] It is an *act of will* by which man offers himself to the service of God and offers the acts of his other faculties to God, or directs them to God's service. Devotion, though an act of religion, is intimately related to charity, for love inspires more fervent devotion and devotion in turn leads to a deeper and purer love. Devotion governs our exterior acts of worship, and love is more concerned with the interior and immediate and secret union of our soul with God. But since religious profession is an exterior act, and since our religious life contains and includes so many exterior acts, the greater our devotion in performing these acts, the greater will be our interior love. The mainspring of all is our interior love for the Person of Jesus. Devotion springing from this love is pure, fervent, and strong. St. Thomas points out[325] that *meditation on the humanity of Christ* is a most perfect means of increasing our devotion. This is simply another way of saying what we have consistently repeated above—that fervor in our religious life and our *sequela Christi* depends on the strength of the love for the Person of Christ which prompts us to follow Him and seek Him.

2) *Incorporation in a community* is the second essential element of religious profession, after the imitation of Christ. This must not be regarded purely from a juridical point of view. Too often the incorporation of the religious into the community is studied purely and solely as a contract, involving mutual obligations. We will speak of this later.[326] At present, it is more important to realize the *theological* implications of incorporation in the monastic family.

324. "the will to give oneself promptly to what pertains to the service of God" (Aquinas, *Opera Omnia*, 3.293, which reads: ". . . *tradendi se* . . ."; typescript erroneously reads "182").

325. q. 82, a. 3, ad. 2: "*Et ideo ea quae pertinent ad Christi humanitatem, per modum cujusdam manuductionis, maxime devotionem excitant*" ("And so what is related to the humanity of Christ arouses devotion most strongly, in the manner of leading one by the hand") (Aquinas, *Opera Omnia*, 3.294).

326. See below, pages 163–65.

a) The religious family is a *society of love*, a supernatural society, bound together by the *charity of Christ*. The members of the family do not merely unite together to attain a common end in the natural order. They are brothers helping one another to attain to eternal life in Christ—not just natural peace and quiet, but supernatural security in faith; not just natural support, sharing of material goods, but sharing in supernatural goods and benefits, in the Holy Spirit. Unless the religious community is seen as a *supernatural family*, our vows do not fully make sense. There is no real justification for a vow of obedience outside of this perspective, because *love* is the only justification for the abandonment of our own will into the hands of another. Why? It would not be right to abandon our will and do the will of a superior unless there were a distinctly higher good involved. The sacrifice of love, by which we unite ourselves more closely to our brethren in bonds of charity, seeking their supernatural good rather than our own convenience—this justifies the abandonment of our liberty by obedience and confers a higher liberty. This point is important because in practice many act as if the renunciation of one's own will were a good in itself, justified by itself. This leads to the frustration of vocations and to the wrong practice of obedience.

b) The religious family, living and bound together by love, manifests in the world the love of the Father for the Son and the union of the Three Divine Persons by mutual circumincession. READ from John 17.[327]

327. "That they all may be one, as thou, Father, in me, and I in thee; that they also may be one in us; that the world may believe that thou hast sent me. And the glory which thou hast given me, I have given to them; that they may be one, as we also are one: I in them, and thou in me; that they may be made perfect in one: and the world may know that thou hast sent me, and hast loved them, as thou hast also loved me. Father, I will that where I am, they also whom thou hast given me may be with me; that they may see my glory which thou hast given me, because thou hast loved me before the creation of the world. Just Father, the world hath not known thee; but I have known thee: and these have known that thou hast sent me. And I have made known thy name to them, and

c) In this society of love, what matters is not the assertion of rights and the enforcement of obligations, but *mutual trust and love*. If our vowed life does not do something to further true and sincere fraternal union, then it is being lived wrongly, and the vows are being frustrated of their purpose. {It is} altogether insufficient to think that the vows simply nail us to the "cross of community life" and make us bear the intolerable deficiencies of "the others." The basis of this mutual trust and love and true union is self-forgetfulness. This is the *true renunciation* to which community life should eventually lead. Here again, some in practice pretend to act on the principle that renunciation *in itself* is good. They claim to renounce all, even their highest ideals, because the sacrifice is the most costly, therefore the most worthy. But in truth, what we renounce is balanced by a higher good: *the common patrimony of charity*—{a} realization that I find *my own* higher good in a good that is not mine only but can be shared by my brother. Hence if I have to sacrifice some high spiritual aim that is personal and mine alone, it must be in order to recover it in a still higher level in what in itself may be lower. But the recovery comes on a higher level because {it is} more spiritual, more common, more rooted in the charity of Christ—{for} example, renouncing an opportunity for contemplative prayer in order to help a brother in the kitchen.

d) The life-stream of love which flows through the truly supernatural family of the religious community united by true charity is what *vivifies the rules, observances*, etc. Without this vivifying effect of *charity and mutual understanding*, the rules are a dead letter, and "the letter killeth"[328]—i.e., {it} can prevent the growth of true family spirit and truly life-giving charity.

e) This sense of "family" spirit should extend to the whole Church and *to other orders*—{a} realization that we belong to one great family in Christ. {There should} not {be a} competitive and

---

will make it known; that the love wherewith thou hast loved me, may be in them, and I in them" (Jn. 17:21-26).

328. 2 Cor. 3:6.

belittling spirit towards other orders. We understand better the importance of this family spirit in the religious life if we remember that the religious orders are the *glory of the Church*. In what sense are they the glory of the Church? in the sense that the life of the Church is seen in them *in all its purity and perfection*. But the life of the Church is the life of Christ—the life of the Holy Trinity, of the Holy Spirit manifested in the world in the charity of Christians for one another. A religious family, animated by a true spirit of sacrifice and issuing in a *perfect communion* in the spiritual goods gained for us by the death and Resurrection of Jesus, is a perfectly *Eucharistic life*. This life truly praises God, truly adores Him. {It is} useless to spend our days in choir if we have not the unity and peace which testifies to God's love for man living in man and transforming man. {It is} useless to approach the altar and receive communion with distrust and hatred of our brother in our heart. A religious community that lives tied up in a complex of formalities and conflicts, involved in a tangle of observances cultivated for their own sake, engaged in ritual and exterior worship, with nothing of true family spirit, nothing of fraternal peace and union, but only petty jealousies and envies—such a community is not living the religious life. It is organized hypocrisy. Let us remember then: (a) our vows strip us of self not in order to decorate us with our own brand of "perfection" but in order to make us forget ourselves and lose ourselves in the common charity of our religious family; (b) the more we lose ourselves in this society of love, the more we *find* our true selves, and the more God manifests Himself in our lives, the more we "live the Mass," the more we are truly living and fruitful members of Christ's Mystical Body, the more we give glory to God and bring peace to men.

3) *Consecration to God by Vow*: this is but the *third* in importance of the three essential elements of religious profession. Remember always {that} profession means *first* taking up the Cross to follow Christ, *second* becoming a member of a family which is a supernatural society bound together by ties of love,

and then third—consecration to God by vow. In other words, charity comes first, even in religious profession—charity towards Christ—leaving all to follow Him; charity towards our brothers; and then *third*—the supreme act of *religion* ({a} moral, not theological virtue).

a) Love for God *seeks to determine itself* by definite obligations. The vows do not by their very nature beget love, but they are means by which love seeks to define and perpetuate itself.

b) Love for God seeks to *manifest itself publically* and to declare before the whole Church that God is above all—this for the glory of God, not for the glory of the one making profession. (N.B. how much vanity {there can be} in the religious life, in some souls.)

c) Love seeks *to respond perfectly* and completely to God's call and to give Him everything. By vows, we place *our whole life* on the altar.

d) Love seeks to unite itself to the supreme act of love and of worship by which Jesus gave glory to the Father and sacrificed Himself for men. Hence the sacrifice of our vows is united as closely as possible with the Holy Sacrifice of the Mass. Our whole life becomes a Mass, a sharing in the sacrifice of Jesus.

e) As a result of this, love can more easily find ways to express itself in all the rules, observances, etc. of the monastic life. These opportunities make themselves more clear, specific and definite as a result of the vows. The religious vows are a great expedient by which love enables itself to give itself more perfectly and completely to God.

Some particular points about religious profession:

1. *Why are vows necessary to make a religious?* One can be incorporated in a community and live a life of charity in imitation of Christ, but *vows* are considered necessary to make a religious, to place one in a stable state of perfection, by putting one under a *permanent threefold obligation* aimed against the triple concupiscence: the vow of poverty against the desire of riches (concupiscence of the eyes); the vow of chastity against the passions of the

flesh (concupiscence of the flesh); the vow of obedience against
the inordinate love of our own will and freedom (pride of life).
In this connection, it would be well to review what has been said
above[329] about the *passions*. Passions are given us by God to help
our sensible nature to serve Him. The purpose of the vows is not
to crush and exterminate the passions, to kill all man's normal
desires, but to bring them under the guidance of the Holy Spirit
so that we are able to love God with our whole *heart* as well as
with all our mind and all our strength.

2. It is necessary that we *consecrate our lives to God by vow*,
in order to enter a stable *state* of perfection. No human authority can demand the observance of such counsels as these. God
Himself does not demand it. He only invites us to embrace the
counsels. Hence *we must oblige ourselves*. We must freely embrace
the counsels and determine to keep them all our life, depending
entirely on the grace of God to help us do this. Then we enter into
a permanent "state." We cannot make such a promise to a human
authority; it must be made to God, through His representative.

3. *History of Religious Vows* (*in outline*): we have discussed
the origin of the vows, instituted by Jesus Christ (p. {110} etc.).
Review what was said there. In the beginning, *monastic vows were
general* and *implicit*. One embraced the monastic state by putting
himself under the direction of an ascete or hermit and taking the
monastic habit. This implied the *propositum monachi*[330]—*conversio
morum* (conversion of manners)—the intention to spend the rest
of his life in monastic renunciation. In those days nobody bothered too much about what was to be taught later on the state of
perfection, with its juridical implications. One simply "became a
monk." In *Cassian's* time things are already more systematic (see
Notes on Cassian[331]). *St. Benedict*[332] makes the obligations and the

329. See pages 18–34.
330. "the profession of a monk" (Jerome, *Epistola* 58, to Paulinus [*PL* 22, col.
582]; see also *Pre-Benedictine Monasticism*, 163).
331. See *Cassian and the Fathers*, 122–23, 145–56.
332. *Rule*, c. 58 (McCann, 128, 130, 132).

form of profession precise and explicit: obedience—*conversatio morum*—stability. One *signs a schedule* of profession which one has previously read aloud in the presence of all. This is placed on the altar. Then the community embraces the newly professed and receives him into its bosom. This form held sway until {the} Middle Ages. *Profession of the three vows*, which is common law today, first appears in 1148 at the convent of St. Genevieve {in} Paris (Abelard's house of studies).[333] The origin of the three vows {is} tied up with decadence of clerical life and the organization of clerics into regular communities of canons. Emphasis on poverty and chastity was particularly necessary. This was preparing the way for the Friars Minor and Preachers. Later, it was understood that the monks also had "five vows." Whether or not we really have five vows or three is disputable, but it brings home to us that like all religious we are bound to poverty and chastity—these are essential in fact to our *conversio morum*. N.B. a formula used by the canons of St. Victor promises *dilectio fraterna, communis substantia, communis obedientia*.[334] {This is} interesting in light of the fact that

333. See the first letter of Odo, former prior of St. Victor, who was appointed first abbot of Ste.-Geneviève in 1147–48: "*In professione igitur nostra quam fecimus, tria . . . promisimus, castitatem, communionem, obedientiam*" ("Therefore in our profession which we make, we promise three things . . . chastity, common life, obedience") (*Odonis Epistolae de Observantia Canonicae Professionis Recte Praestanda*, 1 [*PL* 196, col. 1399AB]); Odo goes on to relate the common life to poverty (cols. 1401D–1402B).

334. Merton's source for this information has not been located; the standard profession formula at St. Victor is actually quite close to the Benedictine formula: "*Ego, frater N., clericus (uel, si alterius fuerit ordinis, similiter dicet) stabilitatem corporis mei ecclesiae Beati Victoris promitto coram Deo et sanctis reliquiis eiusdem ecclesiae, in praesentia domni N. praelati et ceterorum fratrum, et emendationem morum meorum, praecipue in castitate, in communione, in oboedientia, secundum gratiam michi collatam a Deo et facultatem uirium meorum*" ("I, Brother N., cleric [or, if he were of another rank, let him speak similarly] promise the stability of my body to the Church of Blessed Victor before God and the holy relics of this same church, in the presence of Dom N., superior, and the other brothers, and the reformation of my manners, especially in chastity, in community, in obedience, in accordance with the grace given me by God and the extent of my abilities") (*Liber Ordinis S. Victoris Parisiensis*, ed. Lucas Jocqué and Ludovicus Milis, *Corpus Christianorum*,

the passions of the flesh are understood as being sublimated in the charity of community life. {It is} a very positive expression of the obligation! Benedictine commentators are divided on the point whether poverty and chastity for us are implicit in the vow of *conversatio morum* or in the vow of *obedience*. It does not make much difference. In {1202} a decretal of Innocent III to Subiaco declared that the vows of poverty and chastity were so essential to the monastic state that even the Holy See could not dispense a monk from one of them and leave him still a monk.[335] *Sed de mona-cho potest facere non monachum.*[336] It is possible to lift all the obligations of a monk and let him become once again a layman, but one cannot *at the same time* be a monk and be free from the obligations of poverty or chastity. This is interesting in view of the fact that St. Hedwig, while living the life of a Cistercian nun at Trebnitz, could not take vows because she wanted to retain the administration of her wealth in order to give it constantly to the poor.

4. *Are the vows a gift to God?* They are certainly a gift in the broad sense of the word. Theologians argue whether or not they constitute a gift in the strict sense of a *transfer of dominion*. Passerini[337] holds that by vows we do not give God anything over which He does not already have dominion. Rather, he says, vows are a gift of God to us.

Continuatio Mediaevalis, vol. 61 [Turnholt: Brepols, 1984], 282–83 [#76. *Forma Professionis Sollempniter Profitenda*]).

335. "*Nec aestimet abbas quod super habenda proprietate possit cum aliquo mona-cho dispensare, quoniam abdicatio proprietatis, sicut et custodia castitatis, adeo est annexa regulae monachi, ut contra eam nec summus pontifex possit licentiam indulgere*" ("An abbot should not think that he can dispense any monk with respect to the possession of property, since the renunciation of property, as well as the observance of chastity, are so much a part of the monastic rule that not even the supreme pontiff is able to give permission to the contrary") (Innocent III, *Epistolae*, 5.82, "*Abbati et Conventui Sublacensi: De Quibusdam Vitiis Emendandis Quae inter Mona-chos Irrepserant*" [PL 214, col. 1066BC], which later was included in the *Decretals, Liber extra*, III.35.6; text erroneously reads: "1252").

336. "But he can make a non-monk of a monk" (*Casus ad Comp*. III, 3.27.2).

337. The reference is evidently to Petrus Passerinus de Sextula, OP, *De Hominum Statibus et Officiis Inspectiones Morales*, 3 vols. (Rome, 1663).

This is in fact a rather trifling point, a question of haggling over the use of words. All will agree that in truth and in the strict sense, the *vows are a sacrifice and a holocaust to God*; and a sacrifice is something we offer or give to God. This fact is symbolized by the fact that the professed lays his schedule of profession on the altar during Holy Mass, uniting himself with the divine Victim of the Adorable Sacrifice. The monk, having renounced his own will, having given up the running of his own life and the free use of his body and even of his soul in some matters, unites himself to the monastic community and is placed *in a permanent state of victimhood*. Every religious act for the rest of his life will enable him to give in fact what he has already promised. To refuse to give in fact what he has given by his vow would be to take back his sacrifice and make his vows an empty form of words. In practice, we should remember that in giving to God, we receive from God. For it is love that makes us give, love that we give, and love that we receive.

5. *Is Religious Profession a Contract?*

a) Public religious vows cannot be made to God alone and be valid. They must be made into the hands of a religious superior, who is the representative of God. One makes a *promise to the superior*: "*Pater promitto tibi . . .*" [338]—and this promise to the superior is the matter of the vow which is made to God. To keep one's vow to God, one must keep one's promise to the superior. Hence *the vow of obedience is not a vow to obey God*. It is a vow to God that we will keep our promise of obedience to our superior and to our religious rule.

b) Do religious vows constitute an onerous contract with a bilateral obligation in commutative justice? This would mean in practice that there would be an obligation of restitution for any violation of the contract. The point is again more or less theoretical, but it has a certain importance in so far as it affects *our attitude towards religious profession*. The question whether religious

---

338. "Father, I promise to you . . ." (*Rituale*, 239 [VI.II.2]).

profession is a strict contract obliging in commutative justice is debated. Some theologians hold that it is, others that it is not. We believe that to regard profession as a contract in this sense is to misunderstand its nature and to get a wrong attitude toward the religious life. Religious profession is not a business deal. If it becomes a business deal, then it savors of simony. What is the actual "reciprocal obligation"?

(1) The professed renounces the free disposition of his own actions, his body, his property, and gives the Order the right to use him for its work, etc., within the limit of the *Rule*. Above all, he obliges himself to keep the *Rule* and to obey, etc. He will in all things carry out the functions proper to the Order.

(2) The Order obliges itself to give the monk food, clothing, lodging, care, as to a son of the family, to give him spiritual help and direction, to retain him in the Order as long as his presence is not harmful to the Order, to give him a fair share in the goods of the community, etc., to give him a fair opportunity to participate in all the activities, privileges, etc. of the community life (v.g., education, formation). But if we regard this as an obligation in commutative justice, we completely miss the point. Here we have a relationship between a *community and one of its members*: hence a matter of *legal justice,* which is something more than a business deal. That is to say, it *is not just a contract for the mutual advantage of the two parties considered as standing on equal ground.* The monk does not join the Order to get three meals a day, lodging, spiritual direction, education and what not; and the Order does not enlist the monk *in order to use* his talents, abilities, property, etc. Both the Order and the monk aim at something higher. Religious profession is aimed at the perfection of charity both of the monk and of the Order, both of the individual and of the society. The obligations contracted in religious profession are aimed *beyond the mere contract itself*: they are means to a higher end. Since it is not a *do ut des*[339] contract—a business deal by which the Order and the monk mutu-

339. "I give so that you will give."

ally agree to furnish one another with certain benefits—hence it follows: (a) a professed cannot take legal action against the superior for "violation of the contract"—sue him for damages (of course an abuse can be reported to Rome, but this is not a "lawsuit"); (b) neither can the community hold the professed bound to restitution for violation of the vows (except in the case of poverty; but this is beyond the contract itself—a matter of commutative justice *in se*). N.B. in religious profession, there is contracted a bond between the religious and his community, but this is of secondary importance compared with the *supernatural bond between the religious and God*. This supernatural bond rests on the mutual obligations contracted between the community and the professed as on a material basis. *It is the supernatural bond that is the real object of religious profession.*

6. *The Validity of Profession*: it is of the greatest importance to ensure that vows be made *validly* and licitly. Carelessness in these matters would show a lack of love and respect for God Himself. It would show that one had little appreciation of the meaning and seriousness of the vow. In preparing ourselves for vows, we should take care to study what we intend to do: to make ourselves thoroughly acquainted not only with the obligations assumed but with the manner of assuming them. We should do all that we can to make sure we know fully what we are doing and intend to do it with perfect love and self-abandonment. Vows should never be taken merely as a matter of routine. Conditions for the validity of religious profession follow:

a) Legitimate age: in our Order, seventeen years for temporary vows, twenty-one for solemn vows.

b) A valid and uninterrupted novitiate (for details, see Notes on *Constitutions*[340]).

c) Admission by {a} legitimate superior.

d) Profession must be *explicit and unconditional*: (a) explicit: a public, external act, normally, following the prescribed rite;

---

340. "*Constitutions* of the Cistercians," 65–66.

mere putting on of {the} habit, etc. is no longer sufficient; (b) un-conditional: a condition affecting the essence of the vows would invalidate them—v.g., "on condition that I receive permission to take a trip any time I feel like it" (against stability).

e) The professed must make his vows with KNOWLEDGE, LIBERTY, AND FULL CONSENT:

(1) He must have the use of reason, obviously.

(2) He must have sufficient knowledge of what he is doing: *substantial error* as to nature of the vow invalidates it; *accidental error*, if accompanied by fraud, invalidates the vow—if not proceeding from fraud, does not invalidate {it} (n.b. error affects the judgement, and hence the will, of the one making the vow, so that he cannot be said to will what he is promising; error invalidates the vow whether it proceeds from ignorance or from carelessness, from a chance mistake, from thoughtlessness or neglect).

(3) The professed must *freely will* to oblige himself. Grave fear (even relatively grave) unjustly inspired by an external agent would invalidate the vow. Fear justly inspired (v.g., fear of hell) would not invalidate {it}. The fear must come from outside the professed—v.g., from another person (fear inspired by an earthquake, a war, etc., probably does not invalidate vows). The professed must be free from all serious compulsion and fraud.

Logically, we should turn here at once to {the} *effects* of profession and to discussion of temporary and solemn profession. However, the question of the *will to obligate oneself* is of so great importance that we will take time here to go into it in a little more detail. How does one go about making a decision to obligate oneself for life? What are the different aspects of prudence entering into this act? How should we prepare ourselves properly to make such an act?

Theological Foundation of Religious Profession—a special aspect: THE WILL TO OBLIGATE ONESELF. Assuming that one has a genuine vocation, that one is called by divine grace, that one has received the normal aids of grace, there remains *the response of our own freedom* in the decision to embrace our divine call definitively, *to give ourselves completely and irrevocably to God by making our vows*. It is necessary to look into the workings of this great and sublime act of love. If we concentrate a little on the psychology of our human decision here, this does not mean that we exclude the work of grace or of the Holy Spirit. By far the greater part of this great act belongs to God. The ability to make vows is a gift of His grace, and we should reflect always that the mere desire to consecrate our lives to Him is a great gift. If we have made vows, the glory belongs not to us but to God, and we owe Him the love and trust of our hearts, believing that He will not fail to finish and perfect the work He has begun, if only we will follow the indications of His holy will as they present themselves to us from day to day.

Taking for granted the immense love of God working in our hearts, and realizing that these incomparable graces were purchased for us by an infinite price, the Precious Blood of Jesus Christ, let us consider the way in which our will responds. The main thing we must do in receiving this grace is to *respond with full and generous freedom*. A less total and generous response would tend to frustrate the work of grace. The grace of our vocation is a talent for which we will be held responsible. Love will naturally seek to respond with the most complete fervor and knowledge of the importance of its action. We do not respond to God's call by a kind of blind and passive "drifting" into the religious state. Some seem to think the most virtuous thing is to let another make the decision for him. This is false. Unless we decide ourselves, our vows will risk being invalid. By all means we should prudently consider the advice of others, and if a superior believes that we have a very good vocation, then we should beware of disregarding his opinion or taking it lightly. But the fact remains that *we must make the decision*. If we do not say "yes" with full consciousness of the gravity and import of our decision, we will not be giving God what He really seeks of us—for it is only by a free decision that we can surrender to Him our hearts.

What are the steps in such a decision?

1. The *intelligence*, enlightened by grace and faith, has shown us that the religious life is indeed good in itself, and we have reason to believe that it will be good for us. We have been further enlightened by *experience, advice,* etc., during the two years' novitiate. Through all these graces, the end in view, union with God by religious life, is seen to be a *very definite good.*

2. The *senses* and *emotions* may play their part in helping the will to embrace the life of the vows, in so far as they may contribute to our love of our monastic community in the concrete, its setting, etc. The feelings are not excluded from a supernatural vocation; one may have a very definite feeling of love for one's monastic community. This adds strength to our persuasion that it is *a good thing* to live here. However, senses and emotions may also rebel, may pull the will in the other direction. So too may the reason, for that matter. The will may approach the question of vows with a certain amount of conflict, or indeed with a very great struggle. All this implies that for us to make a decision with our will, our senses have to be mortified and disciplined.

3. The will *remains mistress of her own acts. Habet potestatem movendi seipsam ad volendum* (I-II, q. 9, a. 3).[341] The will is not moved by anything outside itself except God (and God's movement is no interference in the act of the will; God acts at one with {the} will). The intelligence does not move the will. The senses do not move the will. Passion does not move the will. However, when we talk about the will acting, we must remember that we are not dealing with a disembodied will, acting by itself. It is the *person* who acts freely, and into this free act of the person enter all the human resources of the personality—intelligence, passion (controlled or otherwise), and so forth. But above all, in a spiritual and supernatural act, the Holy Spirit acts in the will that acts freely; and this harmonious cooperation between the will and the Holy Spirit is

341. "It has the power to move itself to will" (Aquinas, *Opera Omnia*, 2.41, which reads: "*Movet seipsam ad volendum ea quae sunt ad finem*" ["It moves itself to will those things that are for the end"]).

an actual grace, a gift of God, not hampering the freedom of the person but enhancing and perfecting it, not interfering with the autonomy of the person but elevating and completing it.

4. How does the will then move? It *elicits* diverse acts within itself. These acts are discussed by St. Thomas in I-II, qq. 11–16.[342] He takes *fruition* first—we will leave it until last, for fruition is the will's rest in its ultimate attainment of the true good. Here are the elicited acts of the will.

a) INTENTION is the act by which a rational, free being looks to the end, directs his will to that end, and in the same act embraces the means to that end. I see that I am adapted to the religious life, that I can live it with the help of God's grace. I see that I can reach heaven by life in the cloister, and it seems that God is calling me to do so. I then *intend* to give my life to God in religion. I look forward to the life of the vows; I see what it involves; I direct my will to the end and the means. Generally speaking, this act is already present at the beginning of the novitiate. One would not take the religious habit if he did not *intend* to go on, finish the novitiate, make vows, etc. The precise purport of intention is then *ad finem, per aliquid aliud pervenire* (I-II, q. 12, a. 1, ad. 4).[343] It is an act of the will, not merely of the intellect surveying the whole prospect of things to be done. The person "intends," proposes, to start. But the act is distinct from actual *choice*, which commits him more definitely and directly to particular means to that end.

b) CHOICE (*electio*) is the selection of a *possible* and *free* human act as a means to an end. One may "intend" to become a religious in a vague or general way without actually choosing to do something special about it. But with choice, the die is cast to the extent that we commit ourselves to do this rather than that. We have *made our choice* of religious order and community. We have come here intending to be not only religious but Cistercians.

---

342. Aquinas, *Opera Omnia*, 2.46–62.

343. "to arrive at the end through another means" (Aquinas, *Opera Omnia*, 2.49, which reads: "*ad eam, per . . .*").

But now in the novitiate it is up to us to *choose for ourselves* to use the particular means at our disposal. We have to *"elect"* to be obedient, and to be humble, and to work, and to pray, etc., etc., and not merely *intend* all these things: cf. the Gospel parable of the man with two sons, one of whom said he would go to work and didn't, the other said he would not and did. One merely intended; the other also made the choice (and went beyond that also to the end of the process). Read Matthew 21:28-32.[344] {Note} an important psychological point: *choice means preference.* To prefer something is to will it in such a way that *alternatives are excluded* or sacrificed. To make choices, one must be mature. One must be able to take responsibility for his choice, to abide by the results of his choice. A child does not have sufficient security[345] to make choices in the full sense of the word; he cannot fully *commit himself* to one thing rather than another. An immature person in religion can to some extent rest on his superiors in matters of choice. But make no mistake about it; the life of the vows is not for immature minds. Never can the responsibility for really crucial choices be shoved off onto another, superior or otherwise. We have to make our choices ourselves and abide by them. For instance:

(a) When I keep my vow of obedience, I must do more than "intend" to obey—*I choose* to do the will of the superior rather than my own. Every time I obey, I renew this choice in new and different circumstances. By no means does my act of obedience entail simply that the superior makes a choice and I

---

344. "But what think you? A certain man had two sons; and coming to the first, he said: Son, go work today in my vineyard. And he answering, said: I will not. But afterwards, being moved with repentance, he went. And coming to the other, he said in like manner. And he answering, said: I go, Sir; and he went not. Which of the two did the father's will? They say to him: The first. Jesus saith to them: Amen I say to you, that the publicans and the harlots shall go into the kingdom of God before you. For John came to you in the way of justice, and you did not believe him. But the publicans and the harlots believed him: but you, seeing it, did not even afterwards repent, that you might believe him."

345. Reading of typescript; mimeo reads: "maturity."

follow automatically. I choose what he chooses, rather than what my own natural impulses or even my own reason alone would prompt me to choose. *To choose to do the will of the other and to try at the same time to cling to my own will produces an interior contradiction.* It is characteristic of the immature mind in the monastery that instead of fully and freely committing himself to a course of true obedience, he tries to renounce the responsibility for his own choices and shift the responsibility to the superior. In practice, this means that obedience for such a soul consists in trying to "do his own will with permission." With apparent docility he may consult the superior about everything, but in point of fact he is getting the superior to permit everything he himself wants and deluding himself that he is obeying. This leads to *very serious problems* in the religious life. Our decision to live lives of obedience must be a *real choice.* We must really *prefer* to live "*sub regula vel abbate*" [346] (*abbatem sibi praesse* desiderant[347]); this means that we *exclude* the preference dictated by our own impulses and impressions. To choose, then, is to make a real gift of our will to God, provided our choice is ratified by *consent* (see below).

(b) In making a vow of stability, I *choose one monastery* to the exclusion of all others. Henceforth, I have freely renounced the liberty to move about from place to place. I cannot serve two masters in this regard. Either a vow of stability is an *effective* preference for one monastery, or it is a contradiction in terms. (Note: one may naturally retain an *affective* tendency to long for change, but one has chosen not to follow these impulses.) Here too I must fully realize the meaning of my choice {and recognize the} difference between *affective* and *effective* inclinations of the appetite.

(c) In making vows of poverty and chastity, I must logically *choose* to be without comforts, possessions, affections and satisfactions of a certain kind. One cannot simply make a "vow

---

346. "under a rule and an abbot" (*Rule*, c. 1 [McCann, 14]).
347. "They desire an abbot to be over them" (*Rule*, c. 5 [McCann, 34]; emphasis added).

of poverty" and then continue to seek what is best in everything, to enjoy all kinds of privileges and luxuries. A vow of poverty without an effective choice of what is poor and less good, without effectively "doing without," is only a sham. So too with chastity— it is not enough to avoid formal sins against the sixth commandment. Chastity is a choice, a preference. One places *spiritual love* above all else, and *one dedicates his heart and body entirely to God.* One chooses to belong to God in spiritual love. One decides to face the sacrifices this involves on the physical and psychological plane, and to face them generously. In a word, one chooses to accept the necessary struggles, combats and renunciations. Making the vow of chastity in an immature way, one obscures and frustrates the element of choice. One simply evades the responsibility of married life and all it entails. But one continues to seek human affection "innocently"; one cultivates sentimental attachments, etc. In effect, there has not been a full and complete preference here. There has *not been a fully mature choice.* One has not really preferred the love of Jesus alone. One continues to seek and to enjoy human affections and attachments for their own sake. Further points on *electio* {include}:

(1) It is formally an act of will, *not an intellectual judgement that one good is to be preferred* over another (I-II, q. 13, a. 1, ad. 1).[348] Note the importance of this for religious vows. We do not vow merely to have a *theoretical respect* for obedience, chastity, etc., but to actually practice them.

(2) *Electio* does not apply to the end, but to the means. The final end is not a matter of choice. *Ultimus finis nullo modo sub electione cadit* (I-II, q. 13, a. 3).[349] The ultimate end is one only. There is no choice; there is only one beatitude. This has profound implications. One can say, and we have said it above,[350] that no matter what man loves, he is always loving his ultimate end.

348. Aquinas, *Opera Omnia*, 2.51.
349. "The ultimate end in no way comes under choice" (Aquinas, *Opera Omnia*, 2.53).
350. See above, pages 11–12.

But where he loves wrongly, he makes a wrong choice of means to that end. He always seeks happiness, but he chooses things which make happiness impossible.

(3) Choice only concerns (a) human acts—acts that are *contingent and free*; (b) acts that are *possible*. It determines the will to do something that is evidently a good to be done. If it cannot be done by us, then certainly there is no obligation to do it. If the thing chosen is in itself impossible, it must at least appear possible to us, somehow or other, before we can really choose it. *Quidquid ratio potest apprehendere ut bonum, in hoc voluntas tendere potest* (I-II, q. 13, a. 6).[351] In order to make a vow, one must choose a good that is *possible* and better than its opposite.

c) COUNSEL: an act of choice cannot be made rationally without *previous counsel*. *Consilium* has the following elements:

(1) It is an act in which the will works together with the intelligence. *Inquisitio rationis ante judicium de eligendis* (I-II, q. 14, a. 1).[352] *Pertinet ad voluntatem, circa quam et ex qua fit inquisitio (ibid., ad. 1).[353] Consilium* is a *search* for reasons and motives. One cannot act normally without motives. To seek to do so is a deordination. Failure to take counsel before acting in a serious matter is a sin against prudence.

(2) It concerns our operations, again the choice of means to the end ({the} same object as *electio*).

(3) It concerns *only operations and motives that are not clear in themselves*. Hence we do not take counsel in matters that are trivial; we do not take counsel in matters where a skill has become, as it were, instinctive (v.g., when one is proficient in an

---

351. "Whatever the reason can apprehend as good, toward this the will can aim" (Aquinas, *Opera Omnia*, 2.54, which reads: "*Quidquid enim ratio . . .*").

352. "An inquiry of reason before a decision about choices" (Aquinas, *Opera Omnia*, 2.55).

353. "It [counsel] belongs to the will, for which and by which the inquiry is made" (Aquinas, *Opera Omnia*, 2.55, which reads: "*Pertinere ostendat et ad voluntatem . . .*").

art). In certain cases, to judge spontaneously without counsel, as though by instinct, shows a higher perfection, for instance, when moved by the gift of counsel. This does not *exclude* counsel; rather, it is a higher form of counsel, more perfect than the rational and human mode of the act. Hence in making the vows one may be moved by a supernatural inspiration, and light may be given all at once to embrace the state of perfection. But even then the Church requires that a long period of probation elapse, so that there is *plenty of time* to take counsel within ourselves and with others and to weigh the consequences of our choice. READ LUKE 14:26-33.[354]

(4) This example (especially v. 30) shows that counsel *looks to the future* and examines future possibilities and judges what is to be done here and now in the light of consequences. Note that counsel when wise does not lose itself in an infinite series of possibilities. Such counsel is not rational.

d) CONSENT: *"finalis sententia in rebus agendis."*[355] Consent is the final act of the will in its practical decision to do something. Note that the "decision" is already inchoatively present from the moment we *intend* something. But it is only by consent that we finally and completely commit ourselves. Intention, counsel and

---

354. "If any man come to me, and hate not his father, and mother, and wife, and children, and brethren, and sisters, yea and his own life also, he cannot be my disciple. And whosoever doth not carry his cross and come after me, cannot be my disciple. For which of you having a mind to build a tower, doth not first sit down, and reckon the charges that are necessary, whether he have wherewithal to finish it: Lest, after he hath laid the foundation, and is not able to finish it, all that see it begin to mock him, Saying: This man began to build, and was not able to finish. Or what king, about to go to make war against another king, doth not first sit down, and think whether he be able, with ten thousand, to meet him that, with twenty thousand, cometh against him? Or else, whilst the other is yet afar off, sending an embassy, he desireth conditions of peace. So likewise every one of you that doth not renounce all that he possesseth, cannot be my disciple."

355. q. 15, a. 4: "the final decision about what is to be done" (Aquinas, *Opera Omnia*, 2.59; the phrase *"rebus agendis,"* used earlier about decision-making [q. 13, a. 6, ad. 2; q. 14, a. 1 (Aquinas, *Opera Omnia*, 2.54, 55)] is not repeated here).

choice all imply a partial self-commitment, but they also imply the ability to turn back; the will has not yet fully given itself, yielded its inmost stronghold. A comparison with marriage {is instructive}. One *intends* to marry. He takes counsel: whom to marry, how, etc. He makes his *choice* of a partner—let us say in becoming engaged. Then finally, when in the presence of the priest they both say "I do," the final consent is given. Then the marriage is sealed. (N.B. in the case of marriage, consummation is the fulfillment and ratification of the consent, and a consummated marriage that is valid in every other way cannot be dissolved. A valid but not consummated marriage can be dissolved. This throws light on the supreme importance of a consent that goes to the point of giving ourselves—*traditio sui*.[356]) In the religious life, intention is already present when one enters the novitiate. But experience shows how often one changes his intention. During the period of formation, one takes counsel, one studies the life and continues to advance toward a definite decision to make vows. This decision, ratified in our periodical petitions in chapter, is a publically expressed *choice* of one Order. Finally, it is when we make our vows that we totally commit our wills by a complete *consent*, a "yes" which in the case of simple vows is still revocable (cf. a marriage that is not consummated) and in the case of solemn vows is forever. ({A} difference from consummated marriage {is that} one can obtain a dispensation from solemn vows, but the reason must be extremely grave.) Consent is the final act upon which we must focus our attention. When we make our vows, we are not just expressing an intention, or taking counsel, or making a decision (choice); we are uttering our *final consent*. Very often the failure of vows is due to the fact that immature souls do not know how to enter deeply enough into themselves to make a true consent. Their vow is nothing more than the expression of a velleity which they hope will be bolstered up by the influence of others. It is an act of will that binds juridically, yet is morally unsatisfactory and psychologically inadequate. It is not a full

356. "handing over oneself" (see above, n. 324).

and irrevocable *choice*, in the integral sense of a *complete self-commitment*, a ratification of choice by *traditio sui*—the gift of self. {There is a} further difference between the act of consent and the other acts of the will. This is the *purest and noblest* of the acts we have seen so far. In the others there may be a greater admixture of passion, of feeling, of unconscious motivations, etc. In a true choice, the highest part of the soul, the rational will, is completely involved. Brute animals can in some sense seem to "intend" and to "choose," guided by their instincts. But they never truly *consent*. (Because of this absence of consent, their choices are not really choices. A choice without consent is incomplete and immature, even in a human being.) St. Thomas says the brute animal *desires* the sensible good but does not freely *apply himself* to desire it—he is led by instinct. We control our passions and guide *them*; they do not guide us. We *choose*. However, consent *marshals the passions and other faculties* of the soul and applies them to its object (I-II, q. 15, a. 1).[357] CONSENTIRE EST APPLICARE MOTUM APPETITIVUM AD ALIQUID APPETENDUM (I-II, q. 16, a. 2).[358] It is an act of the will; therefore, it *unites* one with the object. The intellect "assents" to the good as from a distance, but consent by the will apprehends the good in its own being.

e) USE (*usus*) (I-II, q. 16):[359] before the will can apply the other faculties to act, it must first of all put itself into constant action. Having consented to do a thing, then the will must apply itself to carry out the decision. The decision is complete with consent. But it is meaningless if it is not translated into action by *usus*. The action of the will applying itself to carry out the choice it has made involves the use of other faculties by the will, applying them and using them in its service. The difference between *usus* and *consent* {is that} by consent the will applies itself formally to desire the thing chosen. By *usus* it applies itself to action in car-

---

357. Aquinas, *Opera Omnia*, 2.58.

358. "To consent is to apply appetitive motion to that which is sought" (Aquinas, *Opera Omnia*, 2.61).

359. Aquinas, *Opera Omnia*, 2.60–62.

rying out the choice. Use is a specifically human and voluntary act. Animals do not "use" their faculties. *Solum animal rationale et consentit et utitur* (I-II, q. 16, a. 2).[360] The animal does not have free control over his faculties. Use implies freedom, choice, self-determination. It implies above all *conscious awareness* of the order of faculties to action—we do what we do, aware of the reason why, foreseeing and willing the results of our action. This is "use" in the technical sense. A trained pig who can spell out words with letters on blocks does not "use" the blocks for anything. Mechanical action is not "use." (This suggests what has been said above[361] about *habitus* and mere mechanical routine. It is by *use* that we develop a *habitus*.) St. Augustine discussed the difference between *uti* and *frui* and pointed out that all moral deordination could be referred in some way to the confusion {of} these two.[362] Use refers to means, fruition to the end. To "make use" of means to the end is right. To "make use" of the end—God, divine things—in order to attain a temporal end is a great deordination. This applies, of

360. "Only a rational animal both consents and uses" (Aquinas, *Opera Omnia*, 2.61).

361. See pages 35–36.

362. *De Doctrina Christiana*, 1.3: "*Res ergo aliae sunt quibus fruendum est, aliae quibus utendum, aliae quae fruuntur et utuntur. Ille quibus fruendum est, beatos nos faciunt. Istis quibus utendum est, tendentes ad beatitudinem adjuvamur, et quasi adminiculamur, ut ad illas quae nos beatus faciunt, pervenire, atque his inhaerere possimus. Nos vero qui fruimur et utimur, inter utrasque constituti, si eis quibus utendum est frui voluerimus, impeditur cursus noster, et aliquando etiam deflectitur, ut ab his rebus quibus fruendum est obtinendis vel retardemur, vel etiam revocemur, inferiorum amore praepediti*" (PL 34, col. 20). ET: "There are some things which are to be enjoyed, some which are to be used, and some whose function is both to enjoy and use. Those which are to be enjoyed make us happy; those which are to be used assist us and give us a boost, so to speak, as we press on towards our happiness, so that we may reach and hold fast to the things which make us happy. And we, placed as we are among things of both kinds, both enjoy and use them; but if we choose to enjoy things that are to be used, our advance is impeded and sometimes even diverted, and we are held back, or even put off, from attaining things which are to be enjoyed, because we are hamstrung by our love of lower things" (Augustine, *On Christian Teaching*, trans. R. P. H. Green, Oxford World's Classics [New York: Oxford University Press, 1997], 9).

course, to what actually goes on in the will attempting to "use" and exploit God for its own temporal ends. God really cannot be exploited objectively, but as far as the will is concerned, this deordinate "*usus*" is possible. ({A} common example {is} the use of prayer and love in order to make oneself appear more respectable in the eyes of men, in order to shine before men instead of just to please God.)

f) FRUITION (I-II, q. 11):[363] fruition is the act of the will *resting with delight and love* in the end which it has achieved. Here the action of the will is inseparably linked with the action of the intellect, which perceives the rightness and propriety of resting in the end achieved. The will in its turn takes intense joy and pleasure in this rest, as seen and perceived by the intelligence. The fruition of man is distinct from the pleasure and satisfaction of animals in this precisely—that it is the joy of resting in an end that has been attained by our own action and our own freedom, as a result of our self-determination. The animal takes pleasure in the end to which he has been led by his nature, but our fruition is attained *per modum imperantis*[364]—by the will *movens totam naturam per imperium.*[365] This implies knowledge of the end—the choice of what we knew and desired to attain. Fruition takes place *in the end which the will has proposed to itself* as ultimate. When St. Thomas says (I-II, q. 11, a. 3) *Fruitio est tantum ultimi finis,*[366] he does not mean that the act of fruition is only possible in God, the true ultimate end. This is precisely the reason why man can sin: he *can* seek and find fruition in an "ultimate" end that is not God. But the fact remains that this "fruition" is never perfect. Man cannot really rest anywhere except in God. But he can make created things his gods by trying to rest in them as in his last end.

363. Aquinas, *Opera Omnia*, 2.46–48.

364. a. 2: "a power of command" (Aquinas, *Opera Omnia*, 2.47).

365. a. 2: "moving all nature by command" (Aquinas, *Opera Omnia*, 2.47, which reads: "*quae sic movet totam . . .*").

366. "Enjoyment belongs to the final end" (Aquinas, *Opera Omnia*, 2.47; this is actually an objection ["*Non ergo fruitio est tantum ultimi finis*"] to which Aquinas responds in ad. 2).

Is it possible to find *"fruitio"* in the love of our brethren? That is, does fraternal charity constitute a valid and supernatural *fruitio*? Yes, says St. Thomas, if we love our brethren *"in Domino."*[367] The love which we have for them, when it is pure, when it is centered in God, terminates in God and not just in the brother for his own sake. Hence there is a kind of *fruitio* and rest in fraternal charity for the sake of God which participates in the *fruitio* of the soul in God (q. 11, a. 3, ad. 1).[368] *Is fruition possible in the present life?* Here he speaks of true *fruitio*, of God as our last end. Yes, imperfect fruition of God can be had in this life. Perfect *fruitio* is in the possession of God, union with Him by perfect love, as our last end, the final rest and satiation of all our strivings and all our love. But God can be possessed imperfectly yet truly as our last end even in this life, in hope. This explains how there can be joy in suffering. What the saints rejoice in when suffering is not suffering itself. To seek *fruitio* in suffering would be the greatest abuse. But it is the inchoate possession of God by loving hope that enables them to rise above their sufferings in perfect peace and union with the will of God. By union with God's will we can begin to taste the *fruitio* that will be ours in heaven. *Frui est amore alicui inhaerere propter se* (St. Augustine).[369] To love God's will and cling to it because it is His will, and in order to please Him, and to seek all our joy, rest and peace in this love is *fruitio* such as we can know it on earth. This is known even more perfectly when the union of our wills with God's will is raised to a mystical level, and God grants us the greater purity of His own freedom. Why is mystical *fruitio* more perfect than the ordinary union of wills with God? because of the greater freedom and purity, the greater "mastery" of the act of love which is achieved in the will delivered from its own natural limitations and motivated by the

367. "in the Lord."

368. Aquinas, *Opera Omnia*, 2.48.

369. "To enjoy is to adhere in love to something for its own sake" (*De Doctrina Christiana*, 1.4 [PL 34, col. 20, which reads: *"Frui enim . . . alicui rei . . . propter seipsam"*], quoted in Aquinas, *Opera Omnia*, 2.46, which reads: ". . . *inhaerere alicui rei propter seipsam"*).

Spirit of God Himself. This higher *fruitio* comes then not from the sense of the exaltation of our own natural powers, but from a share in the freedom and love which belong to God alone and which have been given to us as a free gift, beyond any merit of our own. This *fruitio* is then the result of the consent to abandon ourselves and all that we have and all that we are into the hands of God, giving Him mastery over our lives. In this abandonment of ourselves to Him, we recover our own autonomy in a higher and more mystical way, no longer in ourselves but in God.

DOUBTFUL OR INVALID PROFESSION: we have seen above[370] what are the conditions for valid profession. We have stressed particularly the *free will to obligate* oneself. As a digression, we have examined at some length the acts of will which go into the choice and consent by which we make our vows. Note that if one has the *will to assume the obligation of vows*, the vows are valid even though at the time one may explicitly *intend not to fulfill* the vows. Now supposing after profession it is discovered that *the vows are doubtful or invalid*. What is to be done?

Nullity of the vows: vows that are invalid have no juridical effect and therefore have no binding force whatever. The obligation does not exist. In the case that one's profession is invalid, one may either: (a) freely return to the world or go anywhere else; (b) CONVALIDATE his profession. The convalidation of profession is of two kinds, depending on whether the impediment to validity of the vows was *external or internal*.

1. {An} *external impediment* {is} one which can be proved in {the} external forum—for instance, a defective novitiate, lack of the proper age, etc. Where the impediment was external, vows *cannot be convalidated by a simple renewal*, but there is also required the *removal of the impediment*, and the matter must be *known both to the professed and to the legitimate superior*. These conditions being fulfilled, then profession is convalidated not by a confirmation

370. See above, pages 165–66.

of the previously invalid profession but *by a totally new profession* (not {a} new public ceremony, of course).

2. If there is an external impediment which cannot be made known without grave consequences, and if it is not otherwise possible to remove this impediment, then with the knowledge of both parties (professed and superiors), a *sanatio in radice*[371] can be sought from Rome. The impediment is thus removed by a juridical act of the Sacred Congregation.

3. In the case of an internal impediment (lack of consent, mental reservation, lack of desire to obligate oneself), then the vows are convalidated as *soon as the person interiorly makes the act of consent* or withdraws his mental reservation. (If the lack of consent can be proved externally—v.g., is in writing or was manifested somehow—then the profession must be convalidated externally.) (N.B. a difficult case: if a simple professed has made invalid vows internally because of lack of consent and convalidates his vows six months after profession, is the time for his solemn vows to be counted from the time of public profession or from the time of secret convalidation? probably from the time of public profession [Goyeneche,[372] Schaefer[373]]).

Where profession is *culpably invalid*:

a) Culpably invalid (i.e., deliberately invalid) profession is a grave sacrilege.

b) In one who has culpably made an invalid solemn vow and is afterwards ordained to minor orders, he is automatically reduced to the lay state; to major orders, he is suspended automatically. (He may be validly ordained, but is not licitly so and has no right to exercise his orders.)

---

371. "healing at the root": a papal dispensation that does not require the repetition of one's profession (see Timotheus Schaefer, OFM cap., *De Religiosis ad Normam Codicis Juris Canonici*, 4th ed. [Rome: Typis Polyglottis Vaticanis, 1947], 909 [#1527]).

372. Servo Goyeneche, CMF, *Quæstiones Canonicæ de Iure Religiosorum*, 2 vols. (Neapoli: M. d'Aurea, 1954–55), 1.477–79.

373. Schaefer, 586 [#1000].

c) Some authors hold that in certain cases of culpably invalid profession, the professed may be obliged to make restitution to the order, to convalidate his profession and to become a true religious (a Cervia[374]) (i.e., in case of grave scandal; cf. Canon 2387[375]).

Doubtful profession: if there is *positive doubt* as to the validity of profession:

a) the religious may convalidate his vows *ad cautelam* ("just in case");

b) he may seek a *sanatio in radice* to make sure;

c) if he refuses to take one of the above steps, then *the case must be referred to the Holy See* (Canon {569}, n. 3[376]).

"The Church does not permit a doubtful profession to continue, either in the case of the professed, or in the case of his Institute" (Schaefer[377]). The professed and the order are equally obliged to take steps to remove the doubt. If a person knows for certain that his profession is invalid yet cannot prove it in the external

---

374. Eugenio a Cervia, *De Professione Religiosa: Tractatus Iuridico-Canonicus, Dissertatio ad Lauream in Iuris Canonici Facultate Pontificiae Universitatis Gregorianae* (Bologna: 1938).

375. "*Religiosus clericus cuius professio ob admissum ab ipso dolum nulla fuerit declarata, si sit in minoribus ordinibus constitutus, e statu clericali abiiciatur; si in maioribus, ipso facto suspensus manet, donec Sedi Apostolicae aliter visum fuerit*" ("A cleric in religious life whose profession should have been declared null because of fraud admitted by himself should be expelled from the clerical state if he is in minor orders; if in major orders, he remains *ipso facto* suspended until the Apostolic See should have decided otherwise") (*Codex Iuris Canonici*, 755).

376. "*Si contra validitatem professionis religiosae gravia sint argumenta et religiosus renuat ad cautelam sive professionem renovare sive eiusdem sanationem petere, res ad Sedem Apostolicam deferatur*" ("If there are serious arguments against the validity of a religious profession, and the religious declines, out of caution, either to renew his profession or to seek a *sanatio* for it, the matter should be referred to the Apostolic See") (*Codex Iuris Canonici*, 198) (typescript erroneously reads: "568").

377. "*Ecclesia non permittit neque Religioso neque Religioni in professione dubia perseverare*" (587 [#1001]).

forum, he is by no means obliged to convalidate his profession (unless there may be some special reason: cf. above).

THE NATURE OF RELIGIOUS VOWS

What Is a Vow? We have seen that religious profession is the act by which a Christian formally embraces the religious state, renouncing his former way of life to follow Christ, uniting himself with a particular religious community, and finally *consecrating his life to God by public vows*. We have dwelt at some length upon the acts by which he makes profession. Now let us look specifically *at the vows*, and first of all, at the vow as such.

Vows in General: a vow is an act by which we give our will to God by predetermining it to certain good actions which we promise to perform, in such a way that we will thereby become better and more pleasing in God's sight.

1. A vow is a *gift*. It is a religious act by which we are enabled to give and consecrate to God our inmost liberty by promising to use this liberty in a way that is good, and indeed *better* than we would perhaps normally use it. It is understandable that the highest and most effective *motive* behind religious vows is this *desire to give ourselves* completely to God. Motivation that does not take into account this aspect of giving is usually not quite sufficient. The more clear and mature is our desire to make of our vows a perfect gift to God, the better will be our religious life. A vow is *more than a resolution*. Both vow and resolution have in common the *propositum faciendi*—the decision to do something. But the vow adds to a resolution the note of a *special gift* of the proposed act and of our will in carrying out that act. It accomplishes this by a *formal promise* which *obligates our will* to carry out the proposed act. If I violate a resolution, there is normally no sin in the mere violation itself (perhaps a sin of imprudence in some cases); the act I perform in defiance of my resolution may of course be in itself sinful or not. If I violate a vow, there is a definite fault, an injustice, a violation of religion, and in

sufficiently serious cases a sin and a sacrilege. In making a vow, the divine truth is called to witness that *I intend to fulfill my vow*, and if I then fail to do so, the truth of God is mocked and we are guilty of a special added infidelity. A *resolution* is primarily an ethical or ascetical act. It concerns the virtue of prudence and the right order of our own lives. It is more or less a personal matter, affecting our own progress in virtue, our own development. But a *vow* goes much deeper. The matter of the vow may indeed concern our own moral progress, etc., but the vow puts our action on an entirely new plane, the plane of *religion and worship*. God is brought into the picture in a very special way, and the *sanctity of God* is now emphasized, rather than our own perfection and progress. Hence in violating a vow, I am not merely concerned with something that goes against my own interests, but *God's glory*. When I promise a virtuous act by vow, then *that act belongs to God* and is due to Him as an act of worship. To withdraw this act of worship without a valid excuse is then a sacrilege, an insult to the holiness of God. It is very important to understand this distinction between a vow and a resolution. Too many religious look at the religious life purely from the point of view of ethics and asceticism, divorced from religion, and see it almost entirely in terms of their own spiritual interests. They consider the vow as a "very strong" resolution, something that God has somehow ratified and approved. But they fail to consider the element of religion and fail to see that the act promised by vow *now acquires an objectively religious quality* and is an act of worship which *must* be carried out for the honor and glory of God and not just for their own "perfection."

How do we explain this character of the vow? The vow acquires this special objective character of an act of worship *not* from a kind of superstitious and magical attitude one may have towards God. (This too would be a sin against religion. A vow is not something we bind ourselves to carry out as a result of some kind of superstitious compulsion.) It acquires its character from the fact of our *total dependence on God as our Creator and Savior*. For a true understanding of the vows, we must have a right understanding of God. As long as we implicitly regard God as another limited being, greater than ourselves but still on the contingent and finite plane, a *vow remains incomprehensible*. As long as our concept of God is the concept of someone who *needs* sacrifices, and who can profit by bargains with men, who is "interested" in getting something out of men, then our vows will have a superstitious and magical character. A vow as a religious act is primarily *a witness to the supreme transcendency of God*, which is another way of saying *His supreme holiness*. The holiness of God is, among other things, His "otherness," His being totally above and beyond all His creatures, so that He is utterly unlike any of them. *Only to such a One can we give our liberty without debasing it. Only to such a One can we give our liberty and become yet more free by doing so* (cf. II-II, q. 88, a. 4, esp. ad. 1).[378] Hence the inadequacy of a religious mentality which regards vows above all as a renunciation of freedom, a negation of a fundamental good which God has placed in our nature. Study the question of our *greater freedom* as a result of giving ourselves to God. Why? greater love, greater union with the Holy Spirit. *Ubi Spiritus Domini, ibi libertas.*[379] {The} basis of true freedom {is} *liberty from sin*. Because a vow consecrates our liberty to the infinite holiness of God:

a) It follows that the fulfillment of our vow unites us more perfectly with His will and His liberty and thereby takes us further beyond the sphere of the limited and the contingent. It takes us into the sanctuary of His infinite love.

b) And it follows that a violation of a vow makes us fall back into the realm of darkness and confusion and captivity, in separation from God (if the sin is mortal).

c) To *renounce* human and natural goods by vow is to place oneself in closer and more supernatural dependence on the Providence of God, and thereby to bear witness to His supreme goodness and love by preferring to abandon ourselves to Him in

---

378. Aquinas, *Opera Omnia*, 3.320–21.
379. "Where the Spirit of the Lord is, there is liberty" (2 Cor. 3:17).

mystery rather than rely on human expedients to satisfy special needs. To take back this gift of ourselves is an implicit declaration that we do not trust His Providence and His love.

2. *Votum est de meliori bono.*[380] A vow is always and necessarily {a} promise of a *bonum majus*, a greater good, and the exclusion of a lesser good, which would otherwise be licit. Naturally, if a vow is a promise of a greater good, it is necessarily a promise of a *good* act. Only virtuous acts can be promised to God by vow. (Note: the vow is a promise of a greater good, but *not necessarily of a more difficult act.* We must distinguish between "better" and "more difficult." St. Thomas points out [II-II, q. 88, a. 2, ad. 3][381] that inflicting punishment on our bodies can be acceptable to God, as matter of vow, only in so far as it is an act of virtue, and it is only virtuous in so far as it is done with due discretion. He adds, "Such vows are to be kept or set aside more properly according to the judgment of a superior,"[382] which concords perfectly with St. Benedict.[383] In that event it is a *better good* to accept something less arduous on the advice of a superior, even though one may intend to vow something *per se* more difficult.)

3. *Works done as a result of a vow are more meritorious than before.* To carry out a vow is an act of *latria*—adoration—the highest of all the moral virtues. All other virtues, when their acts are

---

380. q. 88, a. 2: "A vow is about a greater good" (Aquinas, *Opera Omnia*, 3.319, which reads: "*Votum dicitur esse de meliori bono*").

381. Aquinas, *Opera Omnia*, 3.319.

382. "*Talia vota congruentius secundum arbitrium superioris sunt vel servanda vel praetermittenda*" (Aquinas, *Opera Omnia*, 3.319).

383. See the discussion in chapter 49 of Lenten observances: "*Hoc ipsud tamen quod unusquisque offert, abbati suo suggerat, et cum ejus fiat oratione et voluntate; quia quod sine permissione patris spiritalis fit, praesumptioni deputabitur et vanae gloriae, non mercedi. Ergo cum voluntate abbatis omnia agenda sunt*" (McCann, 114) ("Let each one make known to his abbot that which he is offering, and let it be done according to his word and will; for what is done without the permission of one's spiritual father will be considered as coming from presumptuousness and vainglory, not from merit. Therefore everything should be done in accord with the will of the abbot").

performed in fulfillment of a vow, acquire the value and merit of *latria*. (In the case of the religious vows, all the good acts of a religious become acts of adoration towards God.) The virtues performed as {the} result of {a} vow are also more meritorious from an ethical viewpoint because they establish our will firmly in a good course, from which we are no longer free to withdraw (II-II, q. 88, a. 6).[384]

4. *Vows are for our own greater advantage*, even though formally made with a view primarily to God's glory rather than our own good. We have seen above[385] that the proper motive in making a vow is the desire to give ourselves with all honor and glory to God. Nevertheless, the vow is not so much for His good as for our own. This paradox must always be remembered in our dealings with God. When we seek ourselves, we gain less than when we seek Him alone. In seeking Him alone, we gain everything. "Seek ye first the Kingdom of God and all the rest will be added to you."[386] If we forget everything else and seek only to give ourselves to Him, then all our needs will be taken care of by Him, and above all our spiritual welfare will be left entirely to Him. St. Thomas {writes}: "*Promissionem Deo facimus, non propter ejus utilitatem, sed propter nostram*" (II-II, q. 88, a. 4).[387] He then quotes St. Augustine: *Benignus exactor est [Deus], et non egenus, ut qui non crescat ex redditis, sed in se faciat crescere redditores.*[388] St. Thomas explains {that} this advantage consists for one thing in the fact that we determine our will to the best course and hence confirm ourselves, by God's grace, in that which is for our good. *Vovendo voluntatem nostram firmamus immobiliter ad*

384. Aquinas, *Opera Omnia*, 3.321–22.

385. See above, pages 159, 184.

386. Mt. 6:33.

387. "We make a promise to God, not for His advantage, but for our own" (Aquinas, *Opera Omnia*, 3.320).

388. "He [God] is a kind and not a needy creditor, who does not increase his wealth from what is paid, but makes those paying become more wealthy themselves" (Aquinas, *Opera Omnia*, 3.320, which reads: ". . . *crescere faciat* . . ." [quoting from a letter of Augustine to Armentarius and Paulinus]).

id quod expedit facere.[389] Another dictum: *Felix necessitas quae ad meliora compellit.*[390] It is clear enough that by fidelity to our vows we advance in the way of sanctity and perfection. The *risk of sin* is no objection. God gives us special graces with which to resist sin against our vows. The very trials and temptations we must undergo are also for our advantage. This presupposes, of course, that one has made vows with sufficient aptitude and preparation. To make a vow which one is not able to keep is to make a vow which God has not willed for us and is not to our advantage or for His glory either; yet once such a vow has been made validly, even though it was made *imprudently, one must make every effort to keep it* and not immediately seek a dispensation. Dispensation should not be sought until it is clear that one is faced with a moral impossibility in trying to keep his vow, or when other very grave reasons are present. St. Thomas says, in reference to *dispensations*, when one makes a vow, it is presupposed that he makes for himself a "law" binding himself to a course of action which is generally speaking *better* and *higher* not only for others but also for *himself.* "But it can happen that in an individual case the vow may be simply an evil or else useless, or else it may stand in the way of a greater good, and this is against the underlying reason for the vow itself."[391] St. Bonaventure says[392] that this is

389. "By vowing we fix our will immoveably on that which it is expedient to do" (Aquinas, *Opera Omnia*, 3.320, which reads: ". . . *immobiliter firmamus* . . .").

390. "It is a happy necessity that compels us to what is better" (Aquinas, *Opera Omnia*, 3.320, which reads: ". . . *necessitas est quae in meliora* . . ." [quoted from the same letter of Augustine]).

391. q. 88, a. 10: "*Potest tamen contingere quod in aliquo casu sit vel simpliciter malum, vel inutile, vel majoris boni impeditivum; quod est contra rationem ejus quod cadit sub voto*" (Aquinas, *Opera Omnia*, 3.325).

392. *Commentaria in Quatuor Libros Sententiarum*, IV, Dist. 38, art. 1, q. 2: "*Ad illud vero quod quaeritur, utrum sit de minori bono; dicendum, quod minus bonum est dupliciter considerare: uno modo, prout dicit statum quendam licitum; alio modo, prout dicit privationem maioris boni. Primo modo licitum est vovere illud respectu mali, quia respectu illius est quodam modo maius bonum. Secundo modo, prout privatorium maioris boni, licitum non est, nec obligatur quis ad servandum, sed ad poenitendum; ut si quis voveat, quod Deo serviet caste in statu saeculari, et nunquam ingredietur religionem:*

the reason why one cannot make a vow to do some *lesser* good,
because thus one would be binding himself *not to go any higher*.
A vow should never be of such a kind that it prevents one from
doing better or from attaining to greater spiritual freedom and
fruitfulness. It is clear that we do not keep vows just for the sake
of keeping them. *The vows are not ends in themselves.* The Sabbath
was not made for man, but man for the Sabbath.[393] In such cases
the vow should be dispensed. St. Thomas is speaking of vows in
general, not of vows of religion in particular. In vows of religion,
in view of the long preparation and deliberation preceding them,
dispensations should only be sought for really serious causes

---

*primum bonum est et licitum, sed in quantum privat statum altiorem, illicitum est, quia
gratiam Dei duro corde repellit; et hoc est in praeiudicium salutis et in derogationem
abundantis iustitiae.—Et si tu obiicias: licitum est sic esse, ergo et vovere; dicendum,
quod sicut laudari non est malum, tamen appetere laudem est malum; sic in tali statu
esse non est malum, sed obligare se, ut non possit ad melius pervenire, obligatione, quae
fiat Deo, Deo iniuriam facit. Nec est simile de matrimonio, quia est obligatio facta alii
personae, quae contenta est illa et non quaerit perfectionem; Deus autem vult semper
quod melius est."* ("In response to the question whether a vow can be made for a
lesser good, it should be said that 'lesser good' can be regarded in two ways: in
one way it refers to a certain permissible state; in the other way it refers to the
exclusion of a greater good. As to the first way, it is permissible to vow such a
thing in comparison to some evil, because in such a context it is, in a certain sense,
a greater good. As for the second way, with regard to the exclusion of a greater
good, it is not permissible and no one is obligated to keep such a vow, but rather
to repent of it—for example, if someone should vow to serve God chastely in the
secular state and never to enter religious life; the first part is good and permissible, but inasmuch as it excludes a higher state it is not permissible, because it
drives away the grace of God with a hard heart; and this is prejudicial to salvation and undermines full justice. And if you should object that it is permissible
to be in such a state, and therefore to vow to be in it, it must be said that just as
it is not evil to be praised, but to seek praise is nonetheless evil, so to be in such
a state is not evil, but to obligate oneself so that one cannot advance to a better
one, by an obligation which is made to God, does God an injury. For it is not like
marriage, which is an obligation made to another person, who is satisfied with
that and is not seeking perfection; but God always desires what is better") (*Sancti
Bonaventurae Opera Omnia*, 4.817).

393. Mk. 2:27; Merton either inadvertently or ironically reverses the meaning here.

and those too must be carefully studied and weighed. The fact remains that vows, in general, are for the advantage, spiritual and perhaps even temporal, of the one making the vow. *If the vow is to his spiritual disadvantage* by reason of some circumstance or other, then it should be dispensed; it is no longer a "greater good." The individual religious should not delude himself by willfully thinking up reasons why his vows are to his spiritual disadvantage. There is great opportunity for deception here. But if a wise director sees the vow to be an obstacle to greater good, and especially if superiors also agree, then one can safely take it to be God's will and seek a dispensation.

5. *The Special Efficacy of Religious Vows*: religious vows normally have a very special efficacy in consecrating a man's whole life to God and in helping him to remove all the main obstacles to his moral and spiritual perfection.

a) The vows of poverty, chastity and obedience (in our case, conversion of manners and obedience) form a well-integrated system by which the whole life of the monk *is purified and tranquilized* by detaching it from the main roots of sin—the triple concupiscence: poverty from love of goods and money—avarice is in a sense the source of all evils (*radix malorum est cupiditas*[394]) {and the} source of greed, envy, hatreds, aggressiveness, hostilities, dishonesty, injustice; chastity from love of the flesh, its pleasures, and all the attendant comforts and luxuries of the flesh, which soften a man morally and weaken and blind him to the good, making him negligent and tepid in good works and in the love of God; obedience detaches a man from his own will and his own pride, enabling him to become meek, peaceable, tranquil, gentle, and thus disposing him perfectly for a life of prayer and sacrifice—it does the great work of *tearing a man away from himself*, pacifying his heart by no longer allowing him to be centered on self, but making his whole life revolve around the will of God; stability, for us (other special vows for other indi-

---

394. "For the desire of money is the root of all evils" (1 Tim. 6:10).

vidual orders), calms our natural restlessness and eagerness for change, makes us firm and quiet in our possession of the good, protects us against whims and useless fancies—again, a special guarantee of the purity of our contemplative life.

b) The vows are, in the language of our Cistercian Fathers, a *formula perfectae poenitentiae*.[395] They form the most efficacious and complete holocaust in reparation for sin, not only our own but those of the whole world. Because of the above reasons, they involve a complete turning of our whole being, permanently and definitively, from self to God (cf. St. Thomas: II-II, q. 189, a. 3, ad. 3[396]). St. Thomas holds that entrance into religion (by profession) is a second baptism, bringing with it the remission of sin and of temporal punishment due to sin: *"excedit omne genus satisfactionis, etiam publicae poenitentiae."*[397]

c) Hence the *vows offer us the most perfect way to sanctity* by bringing us entirely under the sway of the Holy Spirit, if we are faithful to them, and thus enabling us to live lives of perfect charity.

d) Also the religious vows are *a most perfect consecration of our whole life* to God, a perfect fulfillment of the program contained implicitly in our baptismal vows, making our whole life a complete and total act of adoration, perfect worship of God in union with the sacrifice offered to Him by His divine Son.

e) One of the reasons for the special efficacy of public religious vows is that they place the religious in a state of *very special submission to the Holy Spirit speaking and acting in the Church*. The religious is, more than anyone else, except the priest, a *vir ecclesiae*.[398] More fully than anyone else, he lives the life of the Church,

---

395. See above, n. 231.

396. Aquinas, *Opera Omnia*, 3.660–61.

397. "It surpasses all kinds of satisfaction, even public penance" (Aquinas, *Opera Omnia*, 3.660, which reads: *"Precedit . . ."*).

398. "man of the Church"; see Thomas Merton, *The Silent Life* (New York: Farrar, Straus & Cudahy, 1957), 76: "The monk of Solesmes is before all and above all a 'man of the Church' a *vir ecclesiae*, who contemplates Christ in the mystery of the Church."

and in our case, our vows plunge us into the very heart of the *praying Church*, the Church adoring and sacrificing, the Church as she praises God. We are in all truth the lips and the voice of the Church; we are in her heart as she prays. The thoughts, the love, the adoration which make up her prayer are in a very special way *ours*, for more than anyone else, we (the monks—Cistercians, Benedictines, Carthusians, etc.) live by and are nourished by these thoughts more exclusively than anyone else.

f) *Profession itself is a public and liturgical act of worship*, forming part of the great body of sacrifice and praise which is the Church's adoration of God. Our vows not only offer our actions to God as worship, but they also offer us to God as *members of a consecrated class* of men who, as a society, are set apart and deputed for worship. Our vows particularly make the religious life supremely *Eucharistic*. By our vows, our whole life is a prolongation of the Mass, an incorporation of ourselves and all that we do into the mystery of the Eucharist in a very close and special way. Hence the value of daily renewing our vows at Holy Mass or after it, during our communion. Novices at that time should, as fervently as possible, pray for the grace of being able to make their vows in the monastery.

THE OBLIGATIONS OF RELIGIOUS

Having explained the nature of profession and of vows, let us now look at the *obligations* which a professed religious contracts by making his vows, and which are consequent upon his vows. It is by fulfilling these obligations that the religious, in concrete fact, makes his life a holocaust of praise to God; or rather, it is by fulfilling these obligations that the religious places himself in a position in which his heart can respond to grace in the way God wishes, and thus he offers himself interiorly to God. The fulfillment of exterior obligations is not the whole essence and objective of the religious life; it is the framework of the life of love and of worship which the religious has promised to God in making vows. We must keep within this framework, normally, in order to give ourselves to God by love. What are these obligations?

1. OBLIGATIONS WHICH RELIGIOUS SHARE WITH CLERICS: there are certain obligations which are common to all who lead lives consecrated to the worship of God, whether they be religious or clerics.

a) *Obligation to sanctity of life*: besides the obligation to keep their vows and to be more perfect than the laity in the special matters of counsel covered by the vows, the religious must live a life that is, overall and in general, holier and on a more spiritual and supernatural level than that of laypersons. This does not mean that each individual religious is bound to be *de facto* more saintly than even the holiest layperson; such an idea would be nonsense. But it does mean that religious *as such* tend to, and strive to live, a holier life, in general, than the laity. They aim at a higher level and are obliged to keep this aim higher. If a religious in practice, while keeping his vows, thinks that in all else he is bound to no greater perfection and no more faithful worship of God than anybody else, he has misunderstood his vocation. N.B. that while this obligation is common to religious and clerics, it is greater for religious than for clerics. Religious are bound to aim at a higher level of life in general than the clergy. They are bound to tend to perfection by the practice of the counsels. *How are we to understand this obligation to sanctity of life?*

(a) Materially, in the eyes of the canonists, this obligation implies at least fidelity to the use of certain special means suggested or prescribed in the Code—daily mental prayer, examen of conscience, weekly confession, visits to {the} Most Blessed Sacrament, etc.

(b) Formally, going behind the surface of these exterior means, we can see that the religious and cleric, but especially the religious, are bound to a greater love of *prayer* and the means necessary for a life of prayer—that is, silence, solitude, spiritual reading, etc.; a greater love of *penance* and mortification—not only the mortification consequent upon the vows, but also living in a spirit of self-denial and abnegation in everything; a greater *fidelity to grace*, a more careful attention to the inspirations of the Holy Spirit within, to the directives of the Church and of superiors, etc.; a greater *spirit of charity* and of self-devotion for the cause of the Church, for the glory of God and for the good of souls. It is easy enough to fulfill this obligation materially by simply keeping our rule. But the spirit of the obligation is something more, and is implied in our vow of conversion of manners—a constant fidelity to God's call to live in Christ, to live in the Spirit and not according to the flesh, to be spiritual men, not animal men.

b) Obligation to study and to priestly work (i.e., for religious who are clerics). When a religious has been ordained he is obliged (1) to continue and keep alive his study of theology; (2) to remain at the disposal of his superiors and, in some cases, of the ordinary, for priestly work. This is not too great a problem with us.

c) Obligation to recite the canonical office: this is common to clerics in major orders and to religious with solemn vows. With us, this also includes the obligation of *the choir* (cf. Notes on *Constitutions*[399]). Fundamentally, the life of the religious and cleric, and especially of the monk, is a life of praise.

d) Obligation to wear a distinctive religious habit, and in some cases tonsure. But this varies according to local custom where there is a matter of wearing the habit in public. In practice, in America, when one is out of the monastery wearing a black suit and roman collar, or even just a simple black suit, one is easily marked out as a priest or religious. By our religious habit we confess Christ in the eyes of the world. This is a simple and silent testimony to our faith. It is not necessary to be aggressive about it, and it would probably be unwise to defy the present custom in America and attract more attention than necessary to our habit by appearing with it on the street of a big city. It is sufficient that we be identified, plainly and simply and modestly,

---

399. "*Constitutions* of the Cistercians," 11–12.

as men dedicated to God. "He who shall confess me before men, I will confess him before my Father in heaven."[400]

e) Obligation *to abstain from unbecoming activities*: these activities may be good in themselves, and perfectly all right for laymen, but they have nothing to do with the religious state, and to abstain from them is an important aspect of our worship of God. What are some of these activities? gambling (for money); hunting; frequenting taverns (without a special just cause) or certain types of theater; running for political office; practicing medicine (without special reason and with permission—this does not apply to first aid or to ordinary infirmary care); administering goods for seculars; bearing arms or volunteering for military service (in countries where religious and clerics can be drafted, this is tolerated by the Church but with an implied mute protest); engaging in business. {There are} two senses of business, broad and strict—business in the *strict* sense is discouraged: (a) selling for profit things which have been bought cheaper and/or processed—this is business in the strict sense ("making money"); (b) selling the fruits of our own soil and labor—this is business in the broad sense. Business in the broad sense is not frowned upon, but in the strict sense it is regarded as an unfitting activity for religious; however, the mind of the Church is changing on this point, in view of the special difficulties of religious at the present time, and in our Order there is a frank tendency to disregard completely any thought that it might be unbecoming, as long as it is kept within reasonable limits. Though we do have to make a living, one might still ask where the line is to be drawn in the *manner in which* we do business, the way we go about it, the methods used, etc. It would certainly seem to be the mind of the Church that religious engaging in business legitimately should nevertheless exercise a very definite restraint and discretion in the use of worldly and secular means—v.g., blatant advertising and the use of somewhat unscrupulous methods which are common among seculars. The business of religious should be marked in

400. Mt. 10:32; cf. Lk. 12:8.

all things by taste, restraint, scrupulous honesty, and absence of an unseemly thirst for gain. One can make money without falling all over himself in order to grab everything in sight and to push everyone else out of the way. In other words, business conducted by religious should be free of every taint of GREED AND AVARICE.

2. OBLIGATIONS PROPER TO THE RELIGIOUS STATE AS SUCH: *every religious*, by the very fact that he is a religious, is bound by certain very definite obligations peculiar to his state:

a) He is bound to a holy life, not only in a general way, as are clerics (as we have seen above), but by the use of very well-defined means: HIS VOWS. Hence the religious is obliged first of all to KEEP HIS VOWS. We shall later treat the obligation of the vows in detail.[401]

b) He is bound to keep his rule and constitutions—we shall touch upon this obligation and the controversy which surrounds it later on.[402]

c) He is bound to keep the laws of the Church regarding religious life. These Church laws affect above all: (1) COMMON LIFE; (2) ENCLOSURE—including regulations regarding correspondence; (3) RELIGIOUS HABIT (we have touched on this sufficiently above); {(4)} CHOIR AND DIVINE OFFICE (we treat it here only as an *obligation*—for details, see Notes on Observances[403]); {(5)} OTHER SPIRITUAL EXERCISES prescribed for all religious.

Let us begin here with the COMMON LIFE. The obligation to lead the common life *flows from the vow of poverty*. It binds all religious, even those who live as hermits or those who live as missionaries far from a monastery. In what sense, then, are all bound by the common life? Canon 487 defines the religious life

401. See below, pages 263–65, 287–89, 340–45, 386–88, 461–63.
402. See below, pages 225–34.
403. *Monastic Observances*, 45–103, 189–206.

as *STABILIS IN {COMMUNI} VIVENDI MODUS*[404] and explains that in this common life all alike strive for perfection by keeping the three vows of religion. Schaefer explains[405] that the common life, in its essence, is the *holding of all property in common* by the members of the religious family. Hence we see that in its essential canonical definition, the common life refers to the *common ownership and administration of material goods,* and other aspects simply flow from this. The main elements of common life, in this sense, are then: (a) common ownership; (b) the goods of the order are to be administered, as they are owned, by the order and not by outsiders (controlled by the order at least); (c) each member of the order is entitled to his fair share of the common goods of the order; (d) all are to be treated equally in the same situation, and with the same needs; (e) deviations from this community of goods are a matter of injustice, as well as a sin against religion (in important matters).

The NEW TESTAMENT gives us the source of the common life—it was the life led by the first Christians, surrounding the apostles, and is therefore a life that is most intimately bound up with the "presence" of Jesus in His Church—a Eucharistic life. Indeed, the first Christian community of charity was an eloquent witness to the *presence of Jesus in His faithful.* Hence the common life is necessary as a continued witness to this presence—and this explains why it is essential to the religious state (follow {with} comment {on} texts: John 13, esp. 35; Acts 2:44, etc.—the texts sung at our mandatum and their significance[406]).

404. "a stable way of living in common" (*Codex Iuris Canonici*, 162) ("*COMMUNI*" altered to "*COMMUNE*" in typescript).

405. Schaefer, 672 [#1135]).

406. Cf. *Regulations of the Order of Cistercians of the Strict Observance Published by the General Chapter of 1926* (Dublin: M. H. Gill & Sons, [1927]), 185: "393. . . . Every Saturday of the year, before the lecture before Compline, the **Mandatum** takes place. This ceremony is performed by the servant of the refectory who has finished his week, and the religious appointed to succeed him on the following day. It is announced by five tolls of the great bell, some time before the lecture, earlier or later, according to the number of the religious. 394. All the community

Canon 594[407] {is} an important canon dealing with poverty and the common life. It states (#2) that all goods which are acquired by the religious are acquired for his community and are to be kept with the goods of the community. This is explicitly meant to forbid the practice of keeping back small sums for oneself which one has "saved" or received "for personal use"—but which one has not submitted to control of the superiors; also that the furniture and things given to religious for their use must be in accordance with the poverty which they have professed (#3; i.e., as understood in {#3}[408]). The first paragraph of this canon, the most important (the other two paragraphs are clarifications of it), states: *IN QUAVIS RELIGIONE VITA COMMUNIS ACCURATE AB OMNIBUS SERVETUR ETIAM IN IIS QUAE AD VICTUM, AD VESTITUM ET AD SUPELLECTILEM PERTINENT.*[409] This applies to *all religious orders* and is fundamental to the religious state as such. It shows us clearly that though the essence of the common life lies in common ownership, nevertheless the real meaning of common life in practice is that this common ownership should lead to a *common and similar use* of what is used. The canon singles out especially the basic factors of our daily life—food, clothing, lodging and furniture. The uniformity here prescribed is not to be considered absolute. It is a uniformity in which all those *in the same circumstances* receive the

---

assist at it, although the feet of the choir religious only are washed. At the sound of the bell all repair to the cloister, and take their places in the same order as for the lecture before Compline. The Reverend Father Abbot uncovers his feet, as also do all the religious. Both feet are uncovered. . . . When the servants enter, the Abbot, or in his absence the Cantor, intones the antiphon **Postquam surrexit**, etc., without rising. The community continues the antiphon, which is repeated. The other antiphons are always intoned by the Cantor. Each religious, when his feet have been washed, makes a moderate bow to the servants. When the ceremony is nearly ended, the Cantor intones the antiphon **Benedicat nos Deus**. This antiphon, as also the first, should never be omitted. As soon as the **Mandatum** is finished, the lecture is begun, no bell being rung."

407. *Codex Iuris Canonici*, 201.

408. Number not repeated in text.

409. "In every religious order the common life must be precisely observed by all, even in what relates to food, to clothing and to furnishings."

same treatment and the same benefits. That is to say, not that the sick must eat exactly the same food as the healthy religious or be lodged exactly as they are, but that all may receive the same treatment and the same privileges when they are afflicted with a sickness of the same degree of seriousness. Also officers of the monastery, in view of the fact that they contribute something special to the life of the community and sacrifice themselves for their brethren, are entitled *not to rewards* or to special favors, but to those benefits which will enable them to *carry out their work effectively*. Also, anyone with a special job in the community naturally needs the equipment necessary for his job. If the carpenter needs certain tools, that does not mean that everyone has to have the same tools. A professor will naturally have more books for his use than one who has no such task. *Accurate servetur*—an excellent commentator (Vermeersch[410]) points out here that the purpose of the Code is to favor fervor and discipline and peace in the religious life. The force of these words is (besides the fact that each religious himself should be generous on this point) that the superiors should prudently and discreetly see that the canon is observed—not that every religious should constitute himself a censor and monitor of everyone else and that the tranquility of the community should be destroyed.

Canon 2389[411] {decrees that} religious who violate the constitutions in the matter of common life in a *grave and notable* matter are to be warned, and if they persist, are to be deprived of active and passive voice, and if they are superiors, shall be deprived of their office. Note: common life and poverty apply also to *travel-*

---

410. *"Secundum mentem Codicis, qui ita consulere vult fervori et disciplinae religiosae ut nullam violentam perturbationem adducat, verba 'accurate servetur' . . . hanc viam nobis habere videntur"* ("According to the mind of the Code, which wishes to foster the fervor and discipline of the religious so that it does not lead to any violent disturbance, the words 'accurate servetur' . . . seem to us to lead in this direction") (Arthur Vermeersch, sj and Louis Creusen, sj, *Epitome Iuris Canonici cum Commentariis ad Scholas et ad Usum Privatum*, 7th ed., 3 vols. [Mechlin: H. Dessain, 1949], 1.565).

411. *Codex Iuris Canonici*, 755.

ling—to be judged in the light of modern conveniences and the customs of the country ({a} sleeping car {or} aeroplane {is} not *per se* against religious poverty—at least in {the} USA.—{but there is} *no harm in preferring the cheaper way*!!). {How does this relate to} *common life in our Order*? The canon obliges us not only to practice common life in a general way, but as it is understood in our Order: (a) *common prayer in the church*—including mental prayer *in choir* (note: with sufficient reason and permission, one may be absent, but one must not get {into the} habit of absenting himself from common exercises without reason and above all without permission); (b) *common dormitory* (see *Constitutions*, n. 122[412]); (c) *common table* (see *Constitutions*, nn. 117–21[413]); (d) *common work.*

Some abuses: the *Constitutions* clearly show that where there is a *sufficient reason*, the superior may dispense a religious, for reasons of health, employment, or some other serious cause, from certain obligations of the common life. However, abuses must be guarded against, and we should be *especially careful not to seek pretexts*, for one reason or another, to evade the obligations of the common life, and hence it will be well to examine some of the points at which the common life tends to be weakened by the incursions of *a spirit of privacy and privilege*:

1. Useless permissions *to receive special articles from family or friends*: it is best to avoid as a temptation the habit of frequently receiving (and asking for) articles better than those used by the community and getting them from friends or relatives for one's own use—v.g., toilet articles, special shaving cream, etc., extra good writing materials, other such things—as for instance a special leather cover for {a} breviary or missal. (These may be used with permission, and there is no harm in one or two such objects, especially if they have not been deliberately sought or asked for.

---

412. *Constitutiones Ordinis Cisterciensium Strictioris Observantiae a Sancta Sede Approbatae et Confirmatae* (Westmalle, Belgium: Ex Typographia Ordinis, 1925), 23; *Constitutions of the Order of Cistercians of the Strict Observance* (Dublin: M. H. Gill & Sons, [1925]), 29.

413. *Constitutiones*, 23; *Constitutions*, 29.

But what is wrong is the *consistent tendency to seek and to acquire such things*, even though with permission. We should resist this inclination and school ourselves to put things to *the common use* when they are given us, though this is not always obligatory.) *Grave and notable matter* might be, for instance, to receive special clothing and furniture and bedding to the extent of a whole outfit and furnishings for a room of one's own—n.b. even with "permission" of {the} superior, a violation of the *Constitutions* would be a sin if the superior in fact had no real right to grant the permission.

2. *Useless dispensations and privileges*—in the refectory, in care of health, in clothing, etc. A fervent religious will guard against the tendency to *seek* special privileges in matters of diet, personal care, clothing. It is a good principle to seek, as far as possible, to be just like everybody else in these matters, to have what is issued to everyone and nothing more. However, one must use discretion. Here are some norms:

a) One should *always make known* a real need to the superior. It is good to do this in a spirit of trust and leave him to suggest or prescribe any exception he deems necessary. If one has only exceptions which have been suggested or commanded by {the} superior, then he can feel sure that he is not outside the spirit of the common life.

b) There are some variations in clothing which are rather normal and which do not amount to much more than a question of a routine permission—for example, sleeping without socks, sleeping without a scapular, a night cowl, etc. If there is a reason, there is no need for one to hesitate in asking these small permissions (but one *must ask permission*—not dispense oneself). Also, to have an extra pair of socks, or two extra pairs, to have an extra shirt—these are small matters. It is enough to *ask* and to have a reason. When one begins to *accumulate* extra articles of clothing, especially useless articles, then the matter is different.

c) There are some articles of food which are to certain individuals indigestible or harmful. We should not be too quick to judge in these matters, either in our own case or in that of another. Some may tend to decide without reason that they need a *special replacement*. First let them see if they cannot simply do without part of their food—enough is usually given for all to be able to nourish themselves somehow. If there is a *real need* for a replacement, it would be best and safest to let a doctor, or a superior, make the decision and prescribe. Note that if a novice cannot get along on the common diet and needs special food all the time, it may well indicate that he lacks a vocation. THE REFECTORY SHOULD NOT BECOME A PLACE IN WHICH EVERYONE HAS SOMETHING SPECIAL OR SOMETHING DIFFERENT. Normally, there should be a *regular method* of providing a uniform supplement to those who need it (regular relief and special food for those underage). One should avoid *very special* dietary requests in {the} common refectory (n.b. a normal permission {is} to ask for only one kind of bread, white or brown, {or} to ask for something instead of coffee). One could sin gravely by getting permission *groundlessly* for a six-months' stay in a health resort, for example—especially where this is rarely if ever given, as in our Order.

3. *The Private Room*: for certain officers in the community a private room is *prescribed*; it goes with their office and is necessary for it (cf. *Usages*: 543, 535, 526, 532[414]). It is also obvious that even those who are not granted a room by the *Usages* may nevertheless need one and legitimately be given one by the superior for their work—for instance *secretaries* especially, who need office space. Abuses creep in when one begins to use the private room in a way that violates the spirit of the common life—that is to say when the room becomes a private sanctuary, a "home." The first step {is taken} when the religious begins to extend the work time unnecessarily so as to remain apart from the others—working in the time of *lectio divina* without necessity or permission. {The} second step {is} accumulating useless personal objects in the place

---

414. *Regulations*, 256–57 (novice master); 252 (prior); 248 (rooms of officers not to be locked without permission of the superior); 250–51 (resigned abbot).

of work; {this} begins harmlessly perhaps with an electric razor (this might be understandable in the case of a guest master or prior, for instance), a few favorite pictures (this in itself is also perfectly legitimate), some special books (all right as long as they are necessary for the work), some special furniture (equally legitimate as long as necessary for the work)—but abuses creep in with useless articles tending to luxury: comfortable armchairs, carpets, drapes, a specially good typewriter. It is easy to see how real abuses could easily follow—a personal supply of food, an outside telephone without necessity ({this} *is* necessary for {the} cellarer, for instance), receiving many seculars in one's office more or less "socially"—finally, living there practically all the time! {A} grave matter {would be} needlessly having one's own "apartment" in the guest house.

4. *Particular friendships*: violating the common life from another aspect {would be} the need to surround oneself with special friends, to form a clique. This will be dealt with later[415] but may be pointed out here. One should live in the community as a member of a family, with equal respect for all and an affection that excludes none. Obviously, it is not possible to feel equally close to every other member of the community, and there may be estrangements and so forth. But one *must not cultivate* special friendships and surround *himself with others to whom one gives special attention and affection and with whom one shares more intimate experiences which are denied to the community at large*. {This can lead to} having "confidants," {or} worse still, getting together to complain about things in community and to deride or criticize other members or groups. This is very harmful, and if it leads to criticism of superiors and murmuring, then it is *a serious abuse*. A novice who shows a marked inclination to form cliques and special friendships should be advised to leave as probably unfit for the common life.

5. *Avoiding others*: the *instinct to shun individuals or the community as a whole*, to regard them as a bore or as a penance to

415. See below, pages 346–50.

be avoided at any cost, as something to "get away from" in order to "have a little peace"—this is not to be confused with the legitimate love of solitude and prayer, which is natural to contemplative souls. To cultivate this tendency to shun others, *to be antisocial and gloomy*, to be ostensibly cold and indifferent towards others, to treat them with disdain and disrespect, overtly or implicitly—all this is to sin against charity and the spirit of the common life. Ultimately, the one who is most harmed is the very one who does these things. He suffers more than anyone else. However, it is perfectly legitimate to have a taste for quiet parts of the garden and to go for walks in the woods, where these are permitted. It would be an exaggeration and an abuse to say that the common life demands that one should always be in the scriptorium or the church and nowhere else. The common life does not demand that the religious becomes a cramped and rigid eccentric. On the contrary, a good spirit, which is germane to the common life itself, presupposes a certain freedom in going about the places where the monks can go. One must be able to relax and seek a little fresh air and sunshine on a feast day afternoon, if one wishes, and this is precisely a part of the common life: a family life presupposes a garden and does not exclude a certain love for nature, but rather presupposes it.

6. *Lack of Cooperation in Work*: since one of our main obligations is to make our own living by our manual labor, the common life with us necessarily implies *cooperation in a common effort* to support the monastic community. Each individual member of the community is therefore obliged to two things: (a) to keep his *time* and his *abilities* free for the service of the community; (b) to spend his time and to make use of his abilities *in the way desired by his superiors*. This twofold obligation must be well understood. *The monk is first of all obliged to help support the community*. This is the outstanding *active* duty of the common life in our Order. This means that each one owes to the community a certain amount of work each day. Basically, this obligation is measured by the work time prescribed in the *Constitutions*. Unless assigned to something else, each one is obliged to present himself at the distribution of

work and to carry out the job given to him at that time. When he has finished the assigned job, if he does so before the end of work, then he should present himself at the common work and continue with the rest of the community. The *minimum* in regard to this obligation is satisfied when each one spends the regular work time, or its equivalent, in carrying out some task for the good of the community in some useful work, manual, clerical, spiritual, or etc. Only those who are *dispensed from* this obligation by reason of sickness or some other cause should absent themselves from work. Deliberate avoidance of work would certainly be sinful. *Every religious should be prepared to accept any job or charge the superior sees fit to give him,* even though it may be arduous and demand sacrifice that seems almost beyond our power. It is always legitimate to make known special difficulties to our superiors, as well as special tastes and talents. It is for this reason that the superior should know his subjects through and through. When he does in fact know them in this way, the religious can normally assume that the superior makes a wise choice in appointing him for a certain job, and can embrace that job in a spirit of faith.

{(1)}[416] The monk should *strive to detach himself* in the matter of employments. From the very beginning, the novice should school himself in generously accepting jobs which are not to his taste and not seeking, by devious ways, to be appointed to jobs which he especially likes. One can make known his special talents, with simplicity, to the superior. One should be indifferent and plastic in all things, ready to accept anything, whether pleasant or not, seeing only the common will, the good of the community, the will of God. In this way one will be able to work in a manner befitting a monk, calmly, with detachment, in a spirit of peace and prayer, and also profitably for the rest of the community. When one allows attachments to form, one's job can become a refuge and an escape, and this in turn can lead to loss of vocation.

---

416. Enumeration denoted by asterisks in text.

{(2)} The monk should be ready on occasion to sacrifice his time of *lectio divina* where his help is needed for the good of the community. Here again one should school himself, in the beginning, to be generous and to give his time unstintingly—also for special projects thought up by the superior, even though they may not be to our personal taste or may seem to us useless. We must be careful not to cherish too fondly our opinion that the project of the superior is a "waste of time" just because we would rather do something else. We must remember that our time does not really belong to us, and that we are completely at the disposal of the community in all things the superiors feel to be necessary or useful. Naturally our *lectio divina* is also a serious obligation, and one cannot allow oneself to be deprived of it consistently without making the matter known. The superior also is obliged to see that his monks get sufficient time for reading and prayer.

{(3)} The monk should school himself to remember that these humble and often boring services rendered to the community have a *special grace and a special merit*. They form part of the organism designed for God to sanctify us in a wholesome and simple manner, detaching us from ourselves and teaching us how to give ourselves in a way that is sane, moderate and healthy. Often those who resent these humble and unspectacular sacrifices are ones who have a strong attachment to things which seem to them more glamorous and which are more satisfying to their own self-esteem. These are just the ones who most need the humble sacrifices of the common life more than all the others.

{(4)} When a monk is told by his superiors to begin a course of studies to prepare for ordination, he should apply himself to really learn thoroughly all the things a priest needs to know. This is an obligation of justice which he owes to his community and to God Himself. One is bound, in a general way, *to prepare himself and to acquire knowledge* sufficient to carry out special tasks which may be given to him. This does not mean that one has to prepare himself long in advance for some job which the superior has, as yet, no thought of giving him; but we often may need to study and learn in order to carry out a work which the superior tells us he intends to give us shortly—v.g., retreat master in {the} guest house, cantor, professor, etc. The monk owes it to the community and to God to try to carry out any work competently and efficiently.

It goes without saying that when the monk is at the common work, he should apply himself generously to the work and not waste his own time and the time of others in useless dissipation or futile pursuits. All should cultivate a great *respect for the common work*, which is the "most monastic" occupation one can possibly have, and in a certain sense carries with it special merit and special grace. It has a very special formative efficacy and lacks many of the dangers which go along with more exclusive offices. It would be a bad sign for someone to assume too readily that the common work is usually a "waste of time," even though it may happen at times to be badly managed, or even though there is not much to be accomplished by it. One should not unconsciously give preference to other jobs in which one "accomplishes more"—except in so far as it is necessary to do what the superior wants of us. One should not manipulate work in order to evade the common work, even though on the theory that one thus "accomplishes more for the monastery." A good monk is one who knows how to achieve the delicate balance between the efforts necessary for his special job and devotion to the common work. He sincerely makes the necessary efforts to get to the common work when it is possible and does not make his special job an excuse for seldom or never joining the others. This matter has been stressed in recent visitation cards, and it is something to which we ought to give special attention. It is not always easy to strike the proper balance when one has onerous duties. But in the beginning of the religious life it should not be so hard, and certainly novices and scholastics ought to train themselves to fidelity in this matter.

Other points {include}:

a) fidelity to giving the *full time* to work when one is not under strict observation—not cultivating the habit of breaking off early for showers, shaves, etc., at the slightest pretext.

b) *paying attention to instructions* and really taking an active interest in the task to be done, not just going off and whiling away the time somehow or other. One should train himself not to be a clock watcher, and to avoid other ways of loafing on the job.

c) not regarding the manual work as a mere recreation; it should be taken seriously.

d) *care of tools and equipment*—accusations for breakage, etc. should not be just a pious routine without meaning. If you don't know how to use a tool, get the proper instruction. Don't attempt to drive horses, etc., if you don't know how.

e) patience and courtesy, attention to the needs and convenience of one's fellow workers.

f) one should be careful not to exploit the work, the manpower and the equipment of the monastery for one's own personal ends. We are supposed to work for the community, not get the community to work for us. This situation can arise where someone develops a private project beyond measure, to the extent of giving it not only his own time, but demanding the time and help of others and using the equipment of the community when it is required elsewhere. This also could be quite serious. What is meant by a "private project"? certain departments and crafts which may be very good and legitimate, may be the outcome of the fact that one monk with a particular talent gets permission to exercise this talent in a way that directly or indirectly profits the community: for instance, an artist or sculptor. It is conceivable that such a one might exist even in a Cistercian monastery. His work is not absolutely necessary for the community and remains more or less peripheral, depending entirely on the will of the superior. If a project of this nature begins to occupy more time and manpower than it deserves, and if it encroaches on the necessary work of the community, it would obviously constitute an abuse against the common life. Even in common projects which are necessary, the one in charge must take care not to demand more helpers or more machines than he really needs, for in this way he is an obstacle to other necessary work and offends against the principle of the common life.

7. *Lack of cooperation in the silence and prayer of the community*: naturally, each one owes the monastery above all his participation in the *opus Dei*.[417] This does not usually constitute a problem—except that those who have jobs must take care to see that their jobs do not encroach upon their choral service without real necessity. The common contemplative life of the Cistercian monk depends on silence in community. To disturb that silence by operating machines unnecessarily, by carelessness in noise and talking, etc., around the community, is a fault against the common life. Those who have come to the monastery to pray have a right to the silence which is one of the characteristic features of this life. To deprive them of it without a serious reason is an injustice to the individuals and to the community.

8. *A General Spirit of Singularity*: a monk may be very regular, bear his burden in the common work, and enjoy no special privileges, and yet *may offend much more against the spirit of the common life by singularity* than others who are excused, by legitimate exceptions, from keeping the whole rule. It is possible to be regular and at the same time singular, though singularity naturally leads to irregularity. The singular person is one who has a habit of always doing things in such a way as to attract attention to himself by being *notably different and queer*. He may not be conscious of this and should not necessarily be accused of hypocrisy. (We should never judge our brethren, especially those who are singular in some way or other, but we should not condone or imitate their peculiarities.) Singularity in choir is more serious than elsewhere, because it disturbs the dignity and recollection of the community at prayer. However, it is in choir that nervous strain inclines some people most to singularity. Singularity can become a deep-rooted sickness: it may spring from a subconscious resentment of the community and rebellion against the common life. In some persons it can constitute a very delicate problem. Proclamations made rightly and charitable advice in the beginning of one's religious life

417. "work of God," i.e., the divine office (see *Rule*, cc. 7, 22, 43, 44, 47, 50, 52, 58, 67 [McCann, 46, 70, 102, 104, 106, 108, 116, 118, 130, 152, 154]).

can remedy this distortion, but when habits become deep-rooted there is no longer any remedy. Thus in every community there are people who stand out as being a little queer. It is very important to avoid becoming like this if we can help it, and in the beginning all we need is the humility to take advice and correct ourselves, and the ability to see ourselves through the eyes of others.

The Spirit and Meaning of the Common Life: so far we have discussed the *material side* of the common life—the discipline and the obligations which it entails. But we must be careful not to take too exterior a view of the common life and to see in it *nothing but* these obligations. The obligations are for a purpose. One may carry out quite faithfully, materially, the obligations of the common life and still not really *live* the common life. For the common life is more than just the sum total of all the obligations which it implies. Mere observance of obligations and rules, without the attainment of the inner purpose for which they are instituted, is like a body without a soul. *The purpose of the common life* is greater charity, of the individual and of all the members of the community as a whole: it is the glory of God attained by common effort; {it} is the sharing of the life of perfection, with its benefits and privileges; {it} is the sharing of the divine praises offered by the monastic community. Our efforts to live a real, deep, yet simple life of charity as members one of another gives the most perfect glory to the Holy Trinity because it is by our fraternal union that the inner life of the Holy Trinity manifests itself outwardly on this earth. (Read John 17[418]—the pertinent verses on this subject.)

The liturgy is the greatest expression of our unity in Christ and our praise of Him. It is the festive overflow of communal charity, as well as the support of common charity. Common life {is} centered in the mystery of the Eucharist—common life means Eucharistic life. *Res hujus sacramenti est unitas corporis Christi* (St. Thomas).[419] The Church, in its unity, is the great "sign" of God on

---

418. See above, n. 327.

419. *Pars Tertia*, q. 73, a. 3: "The reality of this sacrament is the unity of the body of Christ" (Aquinas, *Opera Omnia*, 4.334, which reads: ". . . *corporis mystici*").

earth, the great "motive of credibility." Woe to those who by their narrowness and selfishness of life destroy the effectiveness of this motive of credibility. *The purpose of the common life is greater union with God* for each individual member, because the community itself is the Mystical Body of Christ. The way of the common life is the most effective, the safest, the most characteristically Christian way to sanctity. But the common life fails to a great extent to achieve this purpose if it is not understood. To LIVE THE COMMON LIFE FULLY AND INTELLIGENTLY MEANS TO STOP LIVING FOR ONESELF AND TO LIVE FOR ANOTHER—GOD AND OUR BRETHREN.

Wrong Ideas of the Common Life—harmful distortions: all the distortions of the true notion of common life generally involve more or less failure to live for others instead of self:

1. *Wrong idea of living for others*: {cf. the} exaggeration that living for others implies the sacrifice of all one's own interests, even one's highest spiritual interests. This is impossible. What doth it profit a man to gain the whole world and suffer the loss of his own soul?[420] Our prayer and solitude are valuable for the community, not only for ourselves. The needs of our own soul, the basic primary obligation to save our own soul and give ourselves completely to God, cannot be renounced in favor of the "totality"—common life must never be interpreted in such a way that one might renounce the spiritual life as such in order to plunge into work, community projects, helping others, etc. In Christianity, the *individual soul, the person*, comes first; the community is for the persons who compose it and not vice versa. The work of divine love and union which takes place in the intimate depths of each individual soul *comes first*. The common life exists for this and cannot be taken as more important than this. Hence there is in reality no contradiction between community life and interior or even exterior solitude. The two are closely interrelated, supplement one another. It is normal for the community life to lead souls, some more than others, to a more intimate solitude

420. Mt. 16:26; Mk. 8:36; cf. Lk. 9:25.

with God in prayer. Devotion to the common life should never interfere with aspirations for more intimate personal union with God. *Apparent contradictions* between community and solitude lead to much misunderstanding, to argument and to conflict, but mostly among souls not yet mature in the monastic life. The true monastic ideal does not stop short at the external, material element of community life. It is a wrong interpretation of St. Benedict to hold that when he calls the cenobites the *fortissimum genus*[421] that it is always and everywhere more perfect to be physically in close proximity with other monks, and that one *must necessarily* be more united with God when physically engaged in some group activity and *must necessarily* be less united with God when on his own. This is a perversion and oversimplification of Benedictine doctrine. Benedict's real meaning {is} that the common life is the royal road for all men to arrive at perfect charity, each one according to his needs and capacities. Membership in a monastic family leaves each monk with the grace and the chance to become most perfectly the person God wants him to be—and he does this by fulfilling his own particular part in the life of the group—whether this part may be centered in the midst of the group or remote from that center. The monk isolated at the gate is just as much a member of the community as any other. The monk working alone in the forest is living the "common life" by doing so.

2. *Wrong idea of the interior life*: on the other hand, one must not go to the other extreme and argue that all interior life is essentially inward and solitary and that therefore in order to be more united with God one *must necessarily* be permitted to withdraw from common life to a great extent and be left alone to one's own prayers. This error is just as materialistic and external as the other. Interior life does not depend on exterior conditions alone. It depends on interior charity, and the common life, with the sacrifices it demands and the graces it brings, purifies us and unites us to God not only by providing for us moments of silence

---

421. "the strongest kind" (*Rule*, c. 1 [McCann, 16]).

and solitary prayer, but also by the work, common prayer, etc. Common life rightly lived enables me to become more intimately united with God in the solitude of my own heart because it draws me into a union of deeper charity and peace with my brethren. The two go together.

3. *Parasitism*: a very common perversion of the common life {involves} souls who evade responsibility, *take all but give nothing*. The monastery is for them a refuge: all their needs are taken care of. They are satisfied with the relative simplicity, etc. of the life—this is the only price they pay for the satisfaction of being left without responsibility and allowed to evade obligations. The monastery becomes a pious boardinghouse—with a religious front. Behind this front, these souls do nothing. BUT THEIR LIFE IS EXTREMELY EMPTY AND UNHAPPY—they accomplish nothing; they do not have a real interior life; they remain children; their life becomes more and more unreal. They become involved in petty anxieties and conflicts in order to seek some kind of "meaning" for their life—actually they waste their days in futility and sterility. They do not really pray; they do not work; they do not really make any sacrifices; they just vegetate. THIS IS ACTUALLY THE FRUSTRATION OF THE COMMON LIFE, even though in all things these souls are exteriorly keeping the rule. They *give nothing*.

4. *Institutionalism and Regimentation*: a spirit of worldly institutionalism must not contaminate the monastery. Everything {is} efficient—efficiency {is seen as} an end in itself—but everything is also impersonal and mechanical—once the red tape is taken care of, anything can be obtained in the end; but it is all the result of a bureaucratic process. This is a real danger in proportion as the monastery is infected by {the} ideals of *technology and collectivism*, which are more and more characteristic of the modern world. The institution {becomes} an end in itself. Technology and {the} machine {become} the greatest support of the institution. Men exist rather for the sake of technology and the institution than for their own souls. Persons become *subordinate to* social process and to technology. Charity is no longer the spiritual force which unites and moves the community. Utilitarianism {and}

pragmatism have replaced charity in this sad situation. This out-look seriously corrupts the monk's sense of values, and nothing could be more inimical to the true Christian monastic spirit. It is a deadly poison to the monastic spirit. Why? because persons are no longer treated as valuable in themselves; they are treated as *objects, things,* which are more or less useful, according to the part they may be made to play in the running of an institution and in taking care of the mechanical operations which bring profit. {Such a situation} develops a class of egg-head monks, another class of mechanic monks, and a third class who are more or less on the fringe because they have no special productive value in the process.

4a. *Herd Mentality*: correlative to the above in a large "tech-nological" community, it is inevitable that most of the monks will live like sheep. Not being treated as persons, they will not bother to live up to their responsibility as persons. They will *live mechanically*—lives of routine—perhaps escaping from time to time in a dreamy kind of spirituality that is individualistic and impoverished, or "conforming" mechanically to the attitudes of the community at worship. Mere exterior conformity is taken as "monastic life," {bringing} danger to souls who merely conform and have *nothing inside* except confusion and disgust, which is not perhaps entirely felt or admitted, but which produces only a kind of dead, dissatisfied resignation. {This is the} danger of the pas-sive, inert resignation which comes over "sheep souls" and which they may be encouraged to look upon as true abandonment. These two ({4 and 4a}[422]) are the great corrosive forces of modern materialistic society, and therefore they are the things the monk is called above all *to react against*. It is a matter of the greatest importance for directors, and those who form souls, those who instruct, those who preach, those who administer the material affairs of the monastery, to be *very keenly aware* of this danger and to see that in all things the monks are formed rightly, so that they live as mature and responsible human persons capable of giving

422. Typescript reads: "3 and 3a."

themselves freely in love to God and to their community, which should always and above all be a *religious family* bound together in the bonds of a free and spontaneous and happy charity, to which everything else is subservient, because it is on this happiness that depends the fruitful life of prayer which is the greatest contribution offered to the Church both by the community and by the individuals in it. {It is an} *error* to think that by efficiency and technology one can produce ideal material conditions in which the life of prayer will then spontaneously flourish just because everything is running smoothly in the "institution." Conditions for a true contemplative life are produced not by technology but by charity and true peace. Efficiency has its place, and so do machines, but it is a place in the background.

5. *False or Deficient Charity*: since charity is the true force and genuine life that makes community a family, {it is} important to distinguish true from false:

a) Purely natural love, or largely natural, {prompts} the attempt to hold the community together by natural good manners, good humor, expansiveness, natural enthusiasm; the monastery thus becomes a club rather than a religious community. N.B. however, we must not overlook the fact that the supernatural life is the perfection of what is basically natural to man, and the natural social virtues have an important part to play, in their proper place.

b) {A} "totalitarian" spirit {operates by} forcing everyone into a unique mold, demanding that everyone conform to a definite pattern, doing violence to individual needs and capacities, and preventing the true spontaneous development of individual differences which contribute very much to the wholeness of the community as a well-rounded organism. It is *not charity* to demand that what is good for us be forced down everybody else's throat. True charity has discretion and understanding, by which it knows and attends to the differences of personality, talent and destiny in different persons.

c) {A} false democratic spirit {involves} letting everyone go to the other extreme, {exercising} no control, assuming that they all "know what they are doing," letting them drift or go to seed, on the ground that it is their lookout. The community owes it to the person to guide and form him. *Liturgy* {is} a good example of how the Church does this—the universal and the personal meet in truly Catholic worship of the liturgy. THE LITURGY GIVES US THE RIGHT UNDERSTANDING OF COMMUNITY LIFE, OF TRUE CHARITY, OR TRUE UNION IN PRAYER AND WORSHIP OF GOD.

Promoting Community Life {takes place}:

1. {through} understanding of the liturgy, sanely and broad-mindedly living the liturgy in the true Catholic spirit.

2. above all {through} understanding and living the mystery of the Eucharist. These two are the source of all true, deep interior life. The interior life of the individual member must develop in its own way, but it grows in this common soil. Guard against transplanting the interior life of the individual *outside* this one "garden." But in the garden itself there must be all kinds of plant and all kinds of growth.

3. {by} *giving each person a part to play*, not leaving them to drift or vegetate alone or to be merely cogs in a machine. The person, no matter how little talented, etc., must be allowed to make *a living and personal contribution* to the life of the community. This implies, in all simplicity, *a certain human recognition*, a certain appreciation and encouragement, not false and condescending but true and sincere. All must appreciate and value the contributions of the others and even their own. *False and rigid ideas of humility* have done a great deal to ruin true community spirit by surrounding each one's personal contribution with limitations of fear and shame. Where there is real simplicity in the community, pride will not be nourished. Hypocrisy grows where men go through all kinds of convolutions every time they feel a little natural pleasure in their works.

4. {by} *simplicity and sincere friendship among the brethren*. This implies the humility to see that we all need one another and that we all can use encouragement and appreciation at times. We should not always be criticizing and correcting, always fault-

finding. This too does great harm to community life. It is better not to be too rigid and perfectionistic—this creates a spirit of constraint and hostility which is inimical to true perfection. Perfect charity tends to flower easily and spontaneously under the influence of grace where true and simple charity exists and is freely expressed, with due reserve. READ ST. BENEDICT, chapter 72:[423] good zeal {is} the Benedictine formula for perfection of the common life.

5. {by a} *spirit of sacrifice oriented to common aims*: the community life will flourish when sacrifices are understood not so much as a means to "make oneself more perfect"—not as a means to "self-beautification." The monastery is not a spiritual beauty parlor where one has to undergo a certain amount of suffering to have one's face lifted and be more pleasing to God and man thereby. Rather, we should learn to look on sacrifice as our contribution to the common good: to value more highly those sacrifices which enable us to give something to another or to the community (for instance, to see that it is much better to chip in and work during an interval than to spend hours on one's knees—the former sacrifice is more healthy, more fruitful, because more communal; under-

---

423. "*Sicut est zelus amaritudinis malus qui separat a Deo et ducit ad infernum, ita est zelus bonus qui separat a vitio, et ducit ad Deum et ad vitam aeternam. Hunc ergo zelum ferventissimo amore exerceant monachi, id est, ut honore se invicem praeveniant. Infirmitates suas sive corporum sive morum patientissime tolerent; obedientiam sibi certatim impendant; nullus quod sibi utile judicat sequatur, sed quod magis alio; caritatem fraternitatis casto impendant amore; Deum timeant; abbatem suum sincera et humili caritate diligant; Christo omnino nihil praeponant, qui nos pariter ad vitam aeternam perducat*" (McCann, 158, 160) ("Just as there is an evil zeal of bitterness that separates from God and leads to hell, so there is a good zeal that separates from vice and leads to God and to eternal life. Therefore monks should practice this zeal with the most fervent love, that is, outdo one another in showing honor. Let them most patiently endure their weaknesses, whether of body or of behavior; let them emulate one another in obedience; let no one follow what he considers useful for himself, but what is more helpful for someone else; let them be committed to fraternal charity with pure love; let them fear God; let them love their abbot with sincere and humble love; let them prefer nothing at all to Christ, who leads us all alike to eternal life").

stand of course that work during intervals is always *exceptional* {and} must not become normal); to value those sacrifices which are humbler and less spectacular, which even make us less noteworthy and more hidden by sinking us more completely into the community.

ENCLOSURE AND SILENCE: having dealt summarily with the common life as an obligation common to all religious, let us turn to another common obligation. All religious are by their very state obliged to a certain amount of *separation from the world*. {The} purpose {is} to enable them more freely and effectively to cultivate their new life in Christ, undisturbed by alien influences and temptations. *For contemplatives* the obligation to enclosure, silence and solitude is even more strict than for other orders. It is an obligation characteristic of all contemplatives. The importance of our enclosure is to be judged by the fact that it is to be preferred by us even to the active ministry which is nevertheless so important. Let us weigh this well. Pope Pius XII has pointed out (*Sponsa Christi*[424]) that contemplatives who are not making a good use of their enclosure and solitude, and are not living lives of prayer, are obliged in conscience to devote themselves to active works and {are} no longer entitled to the advantages implied by this obligation. Cultivate a mentality which sees our enclosure as a privilege and a blessing which brings with it great gifts and advantages utterly unknown in the active life. We should love the opportunities for prayer which are given us—one who does not appreciate enclosure can seriously doubt his contemplative vocation.

Papal Enclosure: Canon 597[425] prescribes papal enclosure for all "regulars," that is to say, members of orders who take solemn vows and are exempt from jurisdiction of {the} local bishop, depending directly on {the} Holy See. This papal enclosure is protected by sanction of *excommunication* reserved to {the} Holy See.

424. See above, n. 280.
425. *Codex Iuris Canonici*, 202.

Papal enclosure affects the monastery itself, where the religious dwell, {as well as} the gardens and woods reserved for the use of the religious alone. The papal enclosure of nuns is far more strict even than that of men. Nuns need permission of {the} Holy See to leave {the} enclosure, unless in danger of death or other equally grave cause, and then must make known {the} cause in writing to {their} bishop (Canon 601[426]). Note {the} strictness of Carmelite enclosure, where the nuns are not even seen by anyone but their relatives or prelates, and must get out of sight when a workman or other comes into the enclosure, with special permission and *accompanied*. *Common enclosure* is prescribed for congregations (having simple vows) and *may* be supported by an episcopal censure.

Enclosure is active in so far as religious are prohibited *from going out* without permission (in our Order, {a} grave obligation at night, light during {the} day). Enclosure is passive in so far as others are prohibited from entering (see Notes on *Constitutions*[427] for all this). Canon 597 prescribes enclosure for monasteries of men even in the case where it is a *domus non formata*[428] (in our Order, a *domus formata* would be a community of six in which at least four were priests[429]). The most informal establishment of monks, as long as it is canonically erected, must keep enclosure.

Some consequences of legislation of enclosure:

1. Religious are not allowed to stay or live outside their monastery without a proportionately serious cause. To be outside the monastery for six months or over, except for studies, requires special permission of {the} Holy See. In our Order, since the only place where we are normally allowed to go to study is Rome

---

426. *Codex Iuris Canonici*, 205.

427. "*Constitutions* of the Cistercians," 41, 44–45.

428. "a house not formally established."

429. According to the 1924 *Constitutions* (#71), at least twelve persons, four of them priests, are required for a new foundation (*Constitutiones*, 15; *Constitutions*, 21).

(where the students live in a house of the Order), this case does not arise.

2. Our constitutions and rules are especially strict about contacts with seculars, admitting them to the monastery, visits, etc.

a) There should not be unlocked doors that admit seculars to the monastery without supervision.

b) Care should be taken that workmen and others here on business do not wander around in places where they should not be. If possible, work in the monastery itself should be done by monks in preference to seculars, to avoid talking and {a} secular atmosphere.

c) Everything possible is done to prevent useless contacts with the world. The monastery is to be built in a remote place—the ideal is to be in a place where it is *not especially easy or convenient* for seculars to come. Radios, newspapers, etc. are forbidden. Publicity is discouraged—the monk should remain hidden and forgotten. The monk concerns himself very little with worldly happenings.

3. *Letter Writing*: as a matter of principle in all religious orders, contacts with outsiders, whether by speech, phone, visits or writing, *should be subject to control*. The manner and extent of the control varies from order to order. In ours, naturally, it is strict. The only *exceptions* to control are letters to the Holy See, papal legate, cardinal protector, our own major superiors (abbot general and father immediate, but not the definitors), to our own abbot when he is absent or when we are in another house. Note that {the} General Chapter in our Order (1906, n. {15}[430]) reminds us

---

430. "The Gen. Ch. asks the Frs. Immediate to be watchful and see that the liberty of corresponding with major superiors be secured for religious of both sexes. He or she wishing to write to a higher authority has not to ask permission to do so. However, these religious are reminded that they should have just and grave reasons for writing. Otherwise they would render themselves liable to punishment by the Gen. Ch." (*Decisions and Definitions of the General Chapters of the Order of Cistercians of the Strict Observance, 1895–1950*, translated at St. Joseph's Abbey, Spencer, Mass [mimeograph] (Dubuque, Iowa: Our Lady of New Melleray, 1951) (typescript reads: "16").

that this freedom to write to superiors presupposes a *just and serious cause*, and those who abuse the privilege are liable to punishment by the General Chapter (for further details, see our Notes on *Constitutions*[431]). The freedom of correspondence *in these cases* is freedom both to write {and} to send and to receive letters. No permission is required. The letters can be handed in sealed, and the fact of writing need not be made known to superiors. Letters must be handed to the subject unopened when they come from one of the above sources. N.B. in our Order we do *not have freedom of correspondence with the local bishop*. ({There is} one exception: all the faithful are bound, in causes of beatification, to make known facts which militate against the beatification of the one concerned; in this event, a religious may and should write direct to the bishop, sending the letter sealed and exempt from control—{the} best way would be to handle the affair through one's confessor.)

Varieties of control depend on {the} constitutions of various orders. In some orders it is merely a matter of handing the letter in to the superiors. In others, the superiors have the right to read the mail of the junior religious. In our Order:

a) *all mail* except that specified above is subject to control.

b) This means that permission must be received in order to write the letter. {It is} not sufficient to write it and hand it opened to {the} superior.

c) All mail (except those mentioned in {the} previous paragraph) must be handed open to {the} superior, and he has the right to read it, and send it or not, at his discretion. {The} same {holds} with incoming mail: {he} has {the} right to not give letters or packages (cf. *Rule*, c. {54}[432]). (This right goes along with {the} *ius inspectionis*.[433]) By our vow of obedience we renounce the natural right to private correspondence. In our Order, sending letters or making {a} phone call without permission is grave

---

431. "*Constitutions* of the Cistercians," 26b–27.
432. McCann, 122 (chapter number left blank in typescript).
433. "the right of inspection."

SIN. This, however, admits parvity of matter. (In a case where the material of the letter or the phone call was in itself trivial, there would not be a mortal sin, unless there were formal contempt of authority involved.)

Conscience-Matter Letters: as a general principle, if nothing is said in the constitutions about conscience-matter letters, the following principles are given by authorities (Schaefer, n. 1196[434]):

a) What is meant by conscience matter (*res conscientiae*)? It means in general a revelation of the state of one's soul, in order to obtain help and counsel. It refers to *interior* and secret matters which are not manifest—and which one has a strict right to keep secret even from superiors. Superiors are forbidden to extract from their subjects a manifestation of conscience.

b) Since the subject has a strict right to keep this matter secret, and since at the same time the mind of the Church is that souls should have free access to spiritual help and counsel even outside their enclosure, there should be a means for the subject to exercise this right in special cases.

c) *The normal exercise of this right is in the confessional itself.* Every religious has a right to go to confession to any confessor with faculties, if he so desires, and for this he does not need the permission of his superior. However, one does not have the right to violate the enclosure in order to gain access to a confessor of one's choice (cf. Canon 519[435]). If one is outside, or if a confessor one prefers comes to the monastery, no further permission is needed in order to go to him.

---

434. Schaefer, 711–12.

435. The canon itself (*Codex Iuris Canonici*, 174) does not bring up the matter of leaving the enclosure, but cf. John A. Abbo and Jerome D. Hannan, *The Sacred Canons: A Concise Presentation of the Current Disciplinary Norms of the Church*, 2 vols. (St. Louis: Herder, 1952), 1.531: "Though the permission of the superior is not needed for the choice of a non-designated confessor, this permission is needed for departure from the religious house for the purpose of approaching the latter. It would, however, seem desirable that the permission should not be refused when the request for it is reasonably made."

d) It is presupposed that the right to go to any confessor is left sacred. Hence the subject *cannot presume a strict right to write a conscience-matter letter and send it out against the will of the superior.* If such a letter is written and handed in, sealed, the superior may do one of the following things: (a) send it, and let the matter go; (b) return it to the subject *unopened;* (c) in a very special case, if he has serious reasons for believing that the note *"res conscientiae"* is merely *an attempt at deception,* he is allowed to open the letter and verify his suspicions, but is in any case obliged to secrecy. Great prudence should be observed here.

e) *The regular procedure* among normal mature religious would be for one with serious reasons for writing a letter *res conscientiae* to ask permission of the superior to do this and for the superior to grant him permission. In such an event there need be no further complications. Naturally, one should not abuse this privilege. The reason why some superiors make things difficult for religious with serious reasons for certain exceptions is that other religious have made an irresponsible and abusive use of such permissions.

4. *Visits:* these also come under the heading of enclosure. *In general,* for *all orders,* contacts with outsiders are regulated by the constitutions and superiors in various orders. *Where there is strict enclosure,*

a) generally, the religious never leave the monastery merely for the sake of a visit, at home or elsewhere; visitors are received *at the monastery* at specified times;

b) the place for receiving visitors is more or less strictly limited: a parlor, a garden, the guest house, etc.;

c) the frequency of visits is controlled by the constitutions or by the superiors.

In our Order, what are our rules about visits? One of the main sacrifices in our life is the sacrifice of contact with our parents and friends. This sacrifice is exacted with special strictness in our own monastery.

a) *Rules of the Order* (*Usages* #327[436]): "The religious ordinarily receive visits *only from their near relatives*":[437] father, mother, brother and sister, grandparents—these are considered near relatives. In cases where one has been brought up by an aunt and uncle, these would be considered near relatives. Aunts and uncles come on visits with {the} rest of {the} family sometimes. This is not unusual. More distant relatives, and intimate friends, might normally be included in a visit at time of profession or ordination. (The superior is left free to determine whether in a particular case a friend or a distant relative rates a "visit.") "Visits should not be too frequent."[438] The *Usages* again leave the matter more or less vague; the local superior is the one to decide whether, in the case of his religious, or in the case of a particular one, visits should be frequent—*frequency is relative*. One assumes that over four visits a year would be "very frequent" (especially if all {the} same group). "And {visits} should not habitually be prolonged for more than three days."[439] The three-day limit is set as a norm. The superior may judge in special cases whether the norm may be exceeded. The superior is not normally free to demand that the religious cut down his visit to less than three days; this was brought out in one of our visitation cards at Gethsemani. "The religious should ascertain from the Superior the times when they remain with their visitors."[440] The general legislation is then broad, leaving everything rather fluid and relative and passing on to the local superior the job of deciding what special norms are to be used in his own community.

b) *Rules of our monastery*: (a) frequency: normally, *one visit a year* from the family {is permitted}; (b) time and place: visitors may come at any season. We speak to our visitors only during the day hours and should regularly be present at the divine of-

436. *Regulations*, 158–59.
437. *Regulations*, 159 (emphasis added).
438. *Regulations*, 159.
439. *Regulations*, 159.
440. *Regulations*, 159, which reads: ". . . they may remain . . ."

fice, meals, chapter. Time of work and of *lectio divina* is left free for our visit. Normally, we receive visitors in one of the rooms at the gatehouse. It is not permitted to go to the gatehouse normally after supper, but one may visit with the men of the family in their guest house room at that hour. One may drive anywhere on our own property. Picnics are not allowed. Eating, etc. is allowed in the gatehouse rooms. Norms to be followed: one should not be artificial or austere with visitors, but should be oneself, enjoy the visit, always remembering to observe the conduct of a good religious. A good religious is not formal, artificial or stiff with other people, but he is not rude or boisterous or unmortified either. Be careful about how you talk and what you say about the monastery! Be considerate of your guests and think of *their* pleasure rather than your own.

THE OBLIGATION TO KEEP THE RULE: Canon 593 declares that all religious, superiors and others must faithfully keep their vows and "order their lives according to the rules and constitutions of their own religious institute, and thus tend to the perfection of their state."[441] It is very important that we understand correctly our obligation to keep the rule. Let us return to our principles:

1. We have been created to love God. We reach union with God by *our actions*, under the guidance of His Holy Spirit.
2. We have entered the monastery, guided by grace, seeking to love God, seeking to give our lives to God *by vows* and by living according to a certain pattern of life, the life of the monk, of the monastic community.
3. Our life in the monastery will be a life of love for God in so far as we regulate our actions according to what, by the light of faith, we know to be God's will for the monk. God's will for the monk is manifested by the *Rule*.

441. *"secundum regulas et constitutiones propriae religionis vitam componere atque ita ad perfectionem sui status contendere"* (*Codex Iuris Canonici*, 200–201).

Hence in general it is obvious that to live a life of love in the monastery is not simply to tend to perfection in a general, haphazard way according to the fantasies of the moment, but *according to the Rule*. Hence, in making monastic profession, we have bound ourselves to live the life of the vows, to live the life of our monastic community—but the life of the community is the life set forth in the *Rule* of St. Benedict. It is clear then that as a monk I have an obligation to live according to the *Rule of St. Benedict* and the *Constitutions of the Order*. THE RULE: the question of the obligation to keep the *Rule* refers to the RULE OF ST. BENEDICT—not to the *Usages*, not to the *Consuetudines* of the twelfth century, not to the interpretations of the *Rule* given by writers of the Order, etc., although all these must guide me as a Cistercian in my interpretation of the *Rule*. THE *CONSTITUTIONS*: however, the only legal interpretation of the *Rule* that is officially binding in conscience is the *CONSTITUTIONS OF THE OCSO*. This document applies the *Rule* to our time and to our own situation in the present life of the Church. WE ARE CONCERNED THEN WITH AN OBLIGATION IN CONSCIENCE TO KEEP THE *RULE* OF ST. BENEDICT AS IT IS APPLIED AND UNDERSTOOD IN THE *CONSTITUTIONS OF THE OCSO*. This is an obligation *in conscience*. It is generally held that to fail in this obligation is to *run the risk* of sin. Here is where the problem of understanding comes in. One of the great problems of religious life in the twentieth century has been to adapt the ancient conception of "obligation" to the mentality of modern man. It is generally recognized that the strict obligations and sanctions which exercised such a powerful effect in sanctifying souls in the old days tend to disconcert and confuse souls today. This conception has been made clear in the life and autobiography of St. Thérèse,[442] and in

---

442. "It seems to me that if all creatures had received the same graces I received, God would be feared by none but would be loved to the point of folly; and through *love*, not through fear, no one would ever consent to cause Him any pain. I understand, however, that all souls cannot be the same, that it is necessary there be different types in order to honor each of God's perfections in a particular way. To me He has granted His *infinite Mercy*, and *through it* I contemplate and adore the other divine perfections! All of these perfections appear to be resplen-

her letters.[443] She confessed that to live under a rule of "fear" and harsh sanctions, constant threat of punishment for failure, etc., simply froze up in her the springs of action, but that on the contrary when moved *by love*, she was able to do much and attain to heroic fidelity. It is necessary that we see the *Rule* as a document leading us to God by love, and not just a code harshly dominating us by commands and punishments. *The mind of the Church* in the question of whether rules ought to oblige under pain of sin is now clear. Whereas ancient rules, like that of St. Benedict, have always been thought to oblige, in certain points, under sin, and the Church has changed nothing in this regard, nevertheless the

dent *with love*; even His Justice (and perhaps this even more so than the others) seems to me clothed in *love*. What a sweet joy it is to think that God is *Just*, i.e., that He takes into account our weakness, that He is perfectly aware of our fragile nature. What should I fear then? Ah! must not the infinitely just God, who deigns to pardon the faults of the prodigal son with so much kindness, be just also towards me who 'am with Him always'?" (*Story of a Soul: The Autobiography of St. Thérèse of Lisieux*, trans. John Clarke, ocd [Washington, DC: Institute of Carmelite Studies, 1976], 180). But see also her comments on her work with the novices: "I have heard the following on more than one occasion: 'If you want to get anything out of me, you will have to win me with sweetness; force will get you nothing.' I myself know that nobody is a good judge in his own case, and that a child, whom a doctor wants to perform a painful operation upon, will not fail to utter loud cries and to say that the remedy is worse than the sickness; however, when he is cured a few days later, he is very happy at being able to play and run. It is exactly the same for souls; soon they recognize that a little bit of bitterness is at times preferable to sugar and they don't fear to admit it" (240).

443. See the September 17, 1896 letter to Sr. Marie of the Sacred Heart: "It is trust, and nothing but trust, that must bring us to Love. . . . Fear brings us only to Justice"; and the May 9, 1897 letter to Père Roulland: "I don't understand souls who are afraid of so loving a Friend. Sometimes, when I read spiritual treatises, in which perfection is shown with a thousand obstacles in the way and a host of illusions round about it, my poor little mind grows very soon weary, I close the learned book, which leaves my head splitting and my heart parched, and I take the Holy Scripture. Then all seems luminous, a single word opens up infinite horizons to my soul, perfection seems easy; I see that it is enough to realize one's nothingness, and give ourself wholly, like a child, into the arms of the good God" (*Collected Letters of Saint Thérèse of Lisieux*, ed. Abbé Combes, trans. F. J. Sheed [New York: Sheed & Ward, 1949], 290, 332).

Dominicans, in the thirteenth century, specified that their rule *did not oblige under pain of sin*. And the Holy See in 1901, in article 320 of norms handed down for formulation of constitutions for new religious institutes,[444] decreed that religious rules should *no longer be made binding under pain of sin*. Thus, although the traditional interpretation of our obligation to obey the *Rule* of St. Benedict under sin still stands, it is clearly the mind of the Church that this should not be too strongly emphasized to the detriment of a more positive and more constructive understanding of the *Rule* as a body of counsels designed to lead us to a life of love and dependence on the mercy of God.

APPROACHES TO THE RULE: we can now discuss various approaches to the problem of the obligation of our rules:

a) Ultrastrict: *de Rancé*, following *St. Bernard*, distinguishes in the *Rule*:

1) precepts of charity, humility, obedience, etc., without which there cannot be an interior life or a Christian life. These of course bind under pain of sin—they are not only matters of rule, but in general matters of divine or natural law in any case.

2) exterior precepts, like fasting, silence, labor, etc. These admit of dispensation, in which case their nonobservance is no sin. They may also be violated through mistakes, deficient advertence, etc.—this can happen in the life of the best of religious: but it would constitute a venial sin against the *Rule*. BUT, says de Rancé, "For those who with full attention and determination and with an affected negligence [i.e., deliberate], with contempt and by reason of the fact that they hold the rules in small esteem and take them lightly, those who thus transgress these rules SIN MORTALLY WITHOUT A DOUBT, and the God Whom they have mocked will certainly cast them out forever from His presence, unless they repair their faults by a genuine repentance and a sincere conver-

444. *Normae, secundum Quas S. Congregatio Episcoporum et Regularium Procedere Solet in Approbandis Novis Institutis Votorum Simplicium* (Rome: Typis S. C. de Propaganda Fidei, 1901).

sion" (*Explication de la Règle*, c. iii [vol. I, p. 224][445]). This extremely
severe opinion is based on St. Bernard, who, in *De Praecepto et
Dispensatione*, c. 12, says that if one violates silence *ex contemptu
sciens et deliberans*, he sins *criminaliter . . . damnabiliter.*[446] This
extreme view does not accord with the mind of the Church at the
present day, or rather it leads to a misconception of the real view of
the Church, since it can very easily be misinterpreted and misap-
plied. One can say that the use of the term *contempt* here is open
to serious misunderstanding: (a) in the case of *formal contempt of
authority as such*, then there would certainly be a mortal sin; (b) but
if, as appears to be the case, the "contempt" is merely a matter of
treating this or that rule as trifling and secondary, while retaining
a fundamental respect for the *Rule* and its authority, there would
be venial sin only, and in the case of a prescription that was objectively of lesser moment, no sin at all (v.g., sleeping minus part
of the habit) (on this point see Schaefer, n. 1130[447]).

b) Relative Adaptation (*The Spiritual Directory*[448]): the *Directory*, c. 5,[449] strives to adapt and interpret the doctrine of St.
Bernard in the light of modern theology, taking *a moderately strict
view*. While quoting and following both St. Bernard and de Rancé,
the *Directory* nowhere states that the simple violation of a precept
of the *Rule* will be a mortal sin.

1) For there to be mortal sin, one would have to violate
something in the *Rule* that is *already forbidden* by divine, Church

---

445. Armand de Rancé, *Règle de Saint Benoist: Nouvellement Traduite, & Ex-
pliquée selon Son Véritable Esprit*, 2 vols. (Paris: Chez François Muguet, 1689).

446. "knowingly and deliberately, out of contempt . . . criminally . . .
damnably" (*PL* 182, col. 878B).

447. Schaefer, 669.

448. [Vital Lehodey, OCSO,] *A Spiritual Directory for Religious*, translated
from the original French text, "*Directoire Spirituel à l'Usage des Cisterciens de la
Stricte Observance*" by a priest of New Melleray Abbey, Peosta, Iowa (Trappist,
KY: Abbey of Our Lady of Gethsemani, 1946).

449. *Spiritual Directory*, part III: "The Vows," chapter V: "The Vow of Obedience (Continued): The Obligation of our Rules" (206–12).

or natural law; or something *contrary to the vows,* in a grave matter; or violate the *Rule* in such a way as to give *grave scandal;* or violate the *Rule* out of *formal contempt for authority.*

2) There can be *venial sin* when we deliberately and with full responsibility and without a reasonable excuse violate those precepts which are characteristic of the life of the Order, on which that life depends for its true character, such as silence, manual labor, choir, *lectio divina,* abstinence, vigils, enclosure (about this there is no doubt: cf. {the} statute—even mortal sin).

3) There is venial sin whenever we violate a rule out of some sinful motive: gluttony, laziness, pride, anger, etc.

4) The *Usages* are considered obliging only in the sense of *penal laws*—that we are bound in conscience to *carry out a penance* imposed for their violation. Violation of a point of {the} *Usages* only is not matter of sin.

c) St. Thomas (*Quodlibet,* i, art. xx[450]) supports this interpretation:

1) We violate our vow of obedience if we disobey the *precepts of the Rule.* These precepts bind *sub gravi*[451] (matters of charity, obedience, etc.).

2) We cannot violate the vow of obedience gravely in disobeying the rule on a point where dispensation is allowed in case of necessity. In necessity a sick monk can have meat. Ergo, even a healthy monk who eats meat without permission will not sin *mortally* merely by this violation of the rule ({but} would do so if there were formal contempt, etc.).

3) We cannot violate the vow gravely in disobeying what is merely a "statute" of the rule (i.e., a matter of observance, like silence). N.B. the superior can make any matter of observance a grave obligation by the power of his *precept.*

---

450. q. 9, a. 20: "*Utrum monachus peccet mortaliter, comedendo carnes*" (Aquinas, *Opera Omnia,* 9.470–71).

451. "under grave weight," i.e., under pain of serious sin.

d) *Modern Authors*: in order that moderns may not go to the opposite extreme, {it is necessary to} guard against *laxity*. The lax view would be that in the case of modern rules, which do not bind under sin, there is in *no sense any obligation to keep the rule*. No—even where the rule does not *per se* bind under pain of sin, we are obliged to keep it as a *duty of state*. (This is where our usages and customs come in.) It is always at least a positive imperfection to violate our rules and usages without sufficient reason. Wrong motives can make the violation sinful. *Habitual transgression* of a rule even when that rule is not binding in conscience becomes sinful—a departure from our obligation to live as religious and tend to perfection by keeping our rule. This is sinful (a) because of the harm done to common life; (b) because of the fact that the habit implies a permanent *lack of love* on this point.

Discussion and Practical Conclusions: in discussing the question of the obligation of the *Rule*, we must bear in mind the *end in view*—greater depth and spontaneity in our love for God. Hence we must not multiply obligations in such a way that souls are cramped and confused. We must not bind consciences in such a way that their true freedom to love God is hindered and frustrated. Obligations under pain of sin are necessary only where there is question of *preventing a real departure from the love of God*:

a) First of all, remember {the} difference between *sin* and *imperfection*. Sin {is} definitely a departure from love, a refusal of love. It is a rejection of the good and, to some extent, of God Himself. It is an act which displeases and offends God and should *be avoided at any cost* no matter what the good that might appear to come from it. One could not commit a deliberate venial sin even in order to prevent the destruction of a city. Hence, to make something binding under pain of sin, that thing must be relatively serious. It is not the mind of the Church that for any and every trivial reason souls should be placed in danger of *sin*. Imperfection is simply the choice of a lesser good. But it *is* the choice of a *good*. AN IMPERFECTION IS NOT DISPLEASING TO GOD.

IT DOES NOT OFFEND HIM IN ANY WAY. We should not be too ready to regard imperfections as rejections of grace or as refusals. True, a positive imperfection implies less fervent love for God. But on the other hand it is not always too clear just when and how there exists a choice that implies positive refusal to give God greater love. Very often those who see positive imperfections everywhere are in fact judging subjectively and according to feelings, not according to objective reality. However in the case of religious rules and observances, there is not much difficulty in saying that since one has engaged oneself, out of love, to keep his rule, a needless violation of the rule implies less perfect love. The fact remains that this less perfect choice *does not necessarily offend God.* He leaves us free to make these choices between two goods, and indeed quite often it happens that He wills us to choose what is in itself the less perfect (objectively) of two things (hence there is a margin for freedom in all these matters).

b) The fact remains that the *tradition of our Order* indicates that it is possible to sin against the *Rule* in certain matters. The fact that the tradition has been at times *overstrict* (saying, for instance, a violation of silence might be mortal sin) does not permit us to reject it wholesale. It should be held that it is *possible* to sin venially merely by violating the *Rule.*

c) There is no question that a violation of the *Usages* (not aggravated by some sinful motive) will never by itself constitute a venial sin and will never be more than an imperfection (n.b. contempt—distinguish). The *Usages* are a *penal* law, binding in conscience only in so far as one is obliged to do the penance imposed for violations.

d) Most single acts in violation of the *Rule*, even in the event that they are violations of *important precepts* which play a key role in regular observance, are not venial sins. {For} example, to smoke a cigarette (nothing is formally commanded on this point), to eat between meals, to read a newspaper, to eat meat (without permission and without sufficient reason, but also without sinful motive)—these would *not necessarily* be venial sins, in isolated cases. They could be. To develop *a habit* of such acts would however mean a practical abandonment of the *Rule* on important points and would probably be sinful.

e) One case of an important rule where a single notable violation might constitute venial sin {is} the rule of silence, since this rule is held to be so vitally important to our regular life. Note: this means a real violation of silence, a surreptitious conversation not justified by any real need, but merely to satisfy a personal desire for communication.

f) Once all this has been made clear, we must be careful not to draw a *false conclusion*. It may be true that in practice isolated violations of the *Rule* are seldom, in themselves, venial sin. But:

1) they can be imperfections, and most probably are, especially where there is a question of important observances.

2) an imperfection is not an offence against God, but it is a "missed chance" for greater love, for growth in freedom, for increasing one's potentiality to love, for growth in grace. When one commits imperfections he does not go backward, but he does not grow either—he develops a passive and inert mentality which should be resisted.

3) habitual violations of the rule come easily when one is not careful. But habitual violations of important rules can easily become venial sins.

Hence *regularity is very important*. One should not underestimate the value of fidelity to {the} rule, even to small rules and seemingly unimportant observances—without of course a *slavish* observance. Especially in the novitiate, it is important for the novice to *acquire habits of discipline* and to make use of the *Rule*, as he should, for his formation. *A novice who habitually disregards rules is not qualified to make profession in the Order*. Even though those violations may not be sinful (and in any case are certainly not sinful, *per se*, in a novice who does not have vows), yet they indicate a lack of adaptation to the monastic life. It is a matter obvious to common sense that no one should oblige himself to live by rules which he considers to be stupid and without meaning.

If a novice has not learned to respect the rules and observances, or to respect regularity in the right sense of the word, then he has no business to make vows and would be very unreasonable in doing so. The important thing then is to keep the rules out of love, not in a spirit of "conformity," not trying to show off one's regularity and please others by this external display, but because of their important place in the life which one has embraced out of love for God, and because they are a means of showing our love to God, uniting ourselves to His will, and thus giving Him pleasure.

Part III (b):

2. *The Vows in Particular*: The Benedictine Vows

At the beginning of this third part we studied the obligations of religious profession from the theological point of view, and then we went into the psychology of the act of will by which one obligates himself for life. Then we studied the nature of a religious vow, and after that the general obligations which flow from religious profession—the obligations which, apart from the vows themselves, are essential to the religious state. We saw that some of the obligations, like that of a holy life, of wearing a distinctive garment, of avoiding certain secular activities, were binding on clerics as well as on religious. We also saw that there were particular obligations, like the *common life* and *enclosure*, which were proper to the religious state and characteristic of it.

Now we come to the most important part of our study: the Benedictine Vows. It is by our vows above all that we seek to imitate Christ, that we seek to unite the sacrifice of our lives with His offering of Himself to the Father. It is by our vows above all that we seek to give ourselves entirely to God. *It is our vows above all that make us religious*. Therefore, we must study them carefully and know precisely what they mean, because they are our most professional concern. Just as a doctor has to know medicine, and a lawyer has to know law, so a religious has to know the meaning of his vows and live according to them fully.

WHAT VOWS DO WE TAKE? First of all, unlike other religious orders of more modern origin, we do not explicitly vow poverty, chastity and obedience, in so many words. These three are certainly contained in the formula of our vows, but two are implicit in the vow of conversion of manners, while we have one other special vow, stability, which is not common to all orders. Stability is a properly monastic vow, as we shall see.

The Benedictine formula of profession, in our Cistercian rite, reads: *Ego Frater N. (laicus,* or *sacerdos,* or etc.) PROMITTO STABILITATEM MEAM, CONVERSIONEM MORUM MEORUM ET OBEDIENTIAM SECUNDUM REGULAM SANCTI BENEDICTI ABBATIS USQUE AD MORTEM [in the case of simple vows: *ad normam juris canonici*] *coram Deo et omnibus sanctis quorum reliquiae hic habentur, in hoc loco qui vocatur . . .* [etc.] *in praesentia Reverendi Domini N.* etc.[452] The vows then are *stability, conversion of manners* and *obedience.* Note especially that the formula explicitly says: *I promise my stability,* etc. The statement is perfectly concrete, not abstract. It means I promise to live and die in this monastery (unless sent elsewhere by obedience), I promise to change my life and stop living like a worldling and to live as a monk, and I promise to obey the superiors in everything. God and the saints are called in to witness the act—concretely, the saints who, by virtue of their holy relics, are present in the abbey in a very special manner. (What are some of the saints whose relics are here and before whom we make our solemn vows?) The promise is made *"in hoc loco"*—this particular monastery, dedicated to the Blessed Virgin ({cf.} the special importance of Our Lady in our life of vows). It is made *in the presence* of the abbot, mentioned by name. Note that in simple profession and solemn profession there is a formal promise of obedience made *to* the superior, and "in his

452. "I, Brother N. (layman, or priest, etc.), promise my stability, conversion of my manners, and obedience, under the *Rule* of Saint Benedict the Abbot until death [in the case of simple vows: according to the norm of canon law] before God and all the saints whose relics are here present, in this place which is called . . . in the presence of Reverend Father N., etc." (*Rituale,* 239–40 [VI.II.4], which reads: ". . . *Sanctis ejus quorum . . .*" and which does not include here the phrase *"usque ad mortem"*; emphasis added).

hands." The professed places his joined hands between the hands of the superior and says: PATER, PROMITTO TIBI ET SUCCESSORIBUS TUIS LEGITIMIS OBEDIENTIAM SECUNDUM REGULAM SANCTI BENEDICTI USQUE AD MORTEM (*ad normam juris canonici* in simple profession).[453] We take our vows by solemnly and publically promising three things: stability, conversion of manners and obedience. It is when we read and sign our formula of profession (and lay it on the altar) that we actually make the vows. Both in the case of solemn and simple profession, the promise of obedience is not the actual making of our vows; it is simply an explicit and special promise of obedience *to the superior*. It drives home the meaning of the vow. The vow is made to God; obedience is promised to the superior as a result of the vow.

Note that in the old days (cf. Cistercian *Ritual*[454]), the promise of obedience was made in chapter about ten days before the end of the novitiate, and at the same time the one making profession *explicitly renounced his possessions* before all the others. Neither the renunciation of possessions nor the promise of obedience formally constituted his vows, which were only pronounced on the day of profession itself at the reading of the formula and the signing and delivery of the same. (See *Usages* #34 for when {the} solemnly professed renounces his property.[455]) N.B. also, before simple profession:

a) the novice makes a *"will"* for three years, ceding *administration* of property {and} disposing of use and usufruct during this period;

---

453. "Father, I promise to you and to your lawful successors obedience according to the *Rule* of Saint Benedict until death (according to the norm of canon law in simple profession)" (*Rituale*, 239 [VI.II.2]).

454. *Rituale*, 239 [VI.II.1].

455. "A religious professed under temporary vows cannot validly renounce his property until the sixtieth day before his solemn profession; but, before his profession retreat, he must renounce, in favour of whomsoever he wishes, all the property which he actually possesses, on condition of his future profession, and after the profession, he must immediately take all necessary measures to ensure that the renunciation be effective according to civil law" (*Regulations*, 17–18).

b) writes out and signs {the} formula of petition in accordance with {the} Decrees of {the} Holy See, guaranteeing that he goes on to the priesthood of his own free will, if ordained.

This is a formal and public act of choice, and one should reflect on the meaning of what one signs. Today, in the case of solemn profession, the promise of obedience is made on the morning when the one making profession begins his eight-day retreat (see Notes on *Constitutions*[456]). It is not a vow but an explicit recognition of his understanding that he will obey *this* superior and his successors and not just the abstract authority of the Church or the *Rule* alone. In the case of simple profession, the promise of obedience is made at the same time when one makes profession, just before the vows are formally taken by the reading of the formula and the signing and delivery of the same. The promise of obedience is not the formal taking of vows.

THE VOW OF OBEDIENCE

I. *The Primacy of Obedience*: let us now begin with the vow of obedience. It is the first of the Benedictine vows, and for all religious it is the *most important of the vows*. Hence it is *most important for our sanctification*. Why is obedience the most important of the vows? Remember the reason why we consecrate ourselves to God in the religious life: we seek to embrace a *special state* of life, a *stable condition* in which we are constantly following Christ and making use of chosen means to perfect our love for Him and to get rid of self-love. It is obedience which establishes us in a stable condition in the religious state. (One might argue that stability does this for us Benedictines. No, *stabilitas loci*[457] is a particular

---

456. "*Constitutions* of the Cistercians," 72–73.

457. "stability of the place": cf. the early form of profession recorded by Edmond Martène in his *Commentary on the Benedictine Rule*, c. 58: "*Promitto stabilitatem huius loci secundum Regulam S. Benedicti*" ("I promise stability of this place according to the *Rule* of St. Benedict") (*PL* 66, col. 820). The phrase is found as early as the mid-ninth century in the work of Paschasius Radbertus (*PL* 120,

means among others chosen to purify our hearts. But while it establishes us in the monastery of our profession, this does not fix us in any particular *state*. One may remain in his monastery and still be a disobedient monk, violate all the rules, etc. It is the vow of obedience that establishes our *will* in constant subjection to the will of God in all its expressions. The vow of stability establishes our *bodies* in the monastery—cf. {the} marriage vow which establishes in {the} married state.)

Obedience is the "professional virtue of the religious"—it is what makes him a religious more than anything else. Hence perfection in obedience is more vital and more important than perfection in the other religious virtues. Everything in the religious life hangs on our obedience: our charity follows upon our religious obedience, our spirit of prayer, our mortification, etc. If we are obedient, then we get grace for practicing the other virtues more perfectly. We obtain, through the merit of obedience, *specific graces necessary to us as religious*, graces to do things in a monastic way, to see them from a monastic viewpoint, to attain to the kind of spiritual life and inner perfection which is characteristic of a true monk. Obedience takes precedence over all the other religious virtues because by it we renounce what is more perfectly and intimately *our own*. St. Thomas says, *Inter virtutes morales tanto aliqua est potior quanto aliquis magis contemnit, ut Deo inhaereat.*[458] The sacrifice of our own will is far greater than that of our possessions or of our bodies or of our power to travel around. *Only an obedient monk* will have the charity towards his brethren that is proper to a monastic family. Where obedience is lacking, one's efforts at charity will be restless, disturbed and disturbing; they will not have the peace and efficacy that true mo-

---

col. 1059): see Cuthbert Butler, osb, *Benedictine Monachism* (London: Longmans, Green, 1919), 130.

458. *Secunda Secundae*, q. 104, a. 3: "Among the moral virtues, one is as much greater as is that which one scorns in order to adhere to God" (Aquinas, *Opera Omnia*, 3.378, which reads: ". . . *virtutes autem morales . . . potior est . . . aliquis majus aliquid . . .*").

nastic charity has; they will not establish peace in the community; in the long run they will lead to divisions and dissensions, and perhaps to the loss of vocations. By their fruits you shall know them.[459] Only an obedient monk will be mortified and penitential in the way in which a monk should be so. St. Benedict says[460] that penances undertaken outside of obedience and without the spirit of obedience are worthless in the sight of God. Obedience is *inseparably united with the humility* which is the very essence of {the} monastic spirit. St. Benedict says: PRIMUS HUMILITATIS GRADUS EST OBEDIENTIA SINE MORA. HAEC CONVENIT HIS QUI NIHIL SIBI A CHRISTO CARIUS EXISTIMANT.[461] Obedience is at once the test of our humility and of our love. It is the "beginning" of humility because it is the essential foundation without which no humility is possible. All humility that does not rest on a spirit of obedience is fake humility—at least in a monk. (Note that in other forms of the Christian life obedience does not play such a central part.)

OBEDIENCE IS THE SIGN AND TEST OF THE MONASTIC VOCATION. It is one of the most essential things to look for in a true vocation. One who seeks God, who is zealous for obedience, for the work of God, and for spiritual hardships (*opprobria*) has a true vocation, according to St. Benedict (c. 58).[462] If there is any one thing that is crucial in the making of a monk, it is obedience. This is in practice the most important factor in the monastic life. *Obedience is the key to all success in our struggle for sanctity and union with God in the monastic life.* Sanctity is essentially a matter of God living and loving and acting in us. He must be able to act freely in our will, our mind, our spirit. The chief obstacle to His

---

459. Mt. 7:20.

460. *Rule*, c. 49: "*Quod sine permissione patris spiritalis fit, praesumptioni deputabitur et vanae gloriae, non mercedi*" (McCann, 114) ("Because what is done without the permission of one's spiritual father will be reckoned as due to presumption and vainglory, not to merit").

461. *Rule*, c. 5 (McCann, 32, which reads: ". . . *carius aliquid existimant*") ("The first degree of humility is obedience without delay. This is proper for those who consider nothing dearer to them than Christ"; emphasis added).

462. McCann, 130.

action within us is our "self-love," our "own will." We shall see
that these notions must be properly understood. But in practice,
as long as a monk, who has embraced the life of obedience, refuses to obey, he is making it morally impossible for the grace of
God to gain perfect control over his soul; he is refusing to yield
himself to the action of the Holy Spirit. He is clinging to self-love.
The disobedient monk is not moved and guided by God, but by
himself. The disobedient monk wants to be his own Providence
and his own Lord. *The root of this error is lack of faith*—failure to
believe that in giving up his own will and his own way, he is
putting himself in God's hands in order to do what God wants,
failure to believe that God really will guide him. (N.B. we must of
course always remember that false ideas of obedience and a false
kind of passivity have evil effects and do not promote holiness of
life. Some souls draw back from obedience when they have been
confused by these false notions, and some have an *exaggerated
fear* of false obedience. In the long run the important thing is *faith*,
faith that God will take care of us if we have good will and trust
Him and take the *Rule* as it is given to us in simplicity.) A monk
who does not live by obedience does not live by faith either. It is
clear that obedience is in practice of such central importance in
the monastic life that it is intimately, inseparably bound up with
the practice of true charity and with faith and with humility and
with hope—on which our whole Christian life is built. But this
is only true of genuine obedience, and not of false or infantile or
superficial substitutes for real obedience.

II. *Why obedience?*

a) Submission to authority in God's name: we usually regard
Protestants as people who have thrown off the yoke of obedi-
ence to Church authority in order to go to God in their own way.
Hence a statement by a Protestant theologian on the importance
of authority should carry extra weight. Paul Tillich says: "HE
WHO TRIES TO BE WITHOUT AUTHORITY TRIES TO BE LIKE GOD, WHO
ALONE IS BY HIMSELF. AND EVERYONE WHO TRIES TO BE LIKE GOD IS

THROWN DOWN TO SELF-DESTRUCTION."[463] If a Protestant believes this, then *a fortiori* we Catholics should be convinced of it. The basic reason for obedience in general, the obedience necessary for *all*, is the fact that man is a contingent and dependent being, and that which is dependent *needs* the support and help of that upon which it depends. We depend on other men, on society, on God. Hence we have to live and act in accord with that dependence. Only in that way will we be happy, will we fulfill our destiny. But it is in man's blood and bones to rebel and to try to assert himself as if he alone were autonomous—as if he were God. Note: here there is a delicate distinction to be made. Man IS a person. Therefore, he IS AUTONOMOUS. He IS the master of his fate and of his life. God has put this mastery and this responsibility into his hands. Furthermore, man being a person is SUPERIOR to the state and the community. The value of a single person, an immortal soul, is superior to the *value of a human group or institution* considered in the abstract. The state exists for me, not I for the state. The monastery exists for me, not I for the monastery. Yet the superior value conferred on me by my freedom and personality does not alter the fact that I am *dependent on the state*, etc. I *must make use of the* laws, of my religious rule, of orders of superiors, etc. in order to exercise my freedom rightly and save my immortal soul. Where the error comes in is in thinking that because I am superior to the state, therefore I do not even need the state at all and can dispense with it entirely. I am superior also to food, but I cannot dispense with it. I have to eat. Eating is no hindrance to my freedom and to my personal dignity as a free man, provided that I use it—so with rules, etc. Hence obedience *is not* simply a blind abdication of our freedom by submission to another man. This would not be perfection, but great imperfection—an evasion, a lowering of our spiritual state. BY OBEDIENCE WE DO NOT RENOUNCE OUR FREEDOM; WE DEDICATE IT TO GOD; WE PROMISE TO USE IT IN THE SERVICE OF GOD ALONE AND FOR HIS

---

463. Paul Tillich, *The New Being* (New York: Scribner, 1955), 85, which reads: ". . . And like everyone . . . like God, he is thrown . . ." (emphasis added).

HONOR AND GLORY, with the explicit understanding that *servire Deo regnare est*,[464] that to obey God with freedom is man's highest dignity; it enables him to grow and mature spiritually. Hence the obedient man is not one who no longer acts freely. His freedom, on the contrary, must be exercised all the more; it is dedicated to God. He continually makes choices, but he chooses what is determined, in many cases, by another, in order thereby to consecrate his freedom to God. Note: the thing determined by the other is always something good in itself. It is never an evil. If the command of the superior bears on something less perfect than I myself would have chosen, this difference is so small {as} to be negligible. Obedience bears on exterior things which, compared to inner and spiritual goods, are of small moment. Hence the choice between choosing some exterior good that I want and choosing an exterior good that the superior wants (for instance, choosing to work under obedience rather than to pray or study) *is a matter of relatively small importance*. But the choice to dedicate my will to God interiorly by obeying is of very great importance: it is a recognition of the transcendence of God precisely by admission of the relative triviality of human choices and the human use of liberty in external things. Hence it is an act of worship; it is a gift of myself; it is a protestation of love and of desire for union. And it does, in fact, realize union of wills with God. To fail to obey, even when disobedience is not sinful, is to *miss an opportunity* to prove our love.

b) *St. Benedict gives a special reason of a deep theological character*: UT AD EUM PER OBEDIENTIAE LABOREM REDEAS, A QUO PER INOBEDI-ENTIAE DESIDIAM RECESSERAS.[465] These words are taken from the opening sentence of the Prologue and are the foundation stone on which the whole *Rule* is built. The very heart of original sin

464. "to serve God is to reign"; cf. *Sermo* 64 (attributed to St. Augustine): "*Jugum enim ejus obedientiae merito est suave, cui servire est regnare*" (PL 39, col. 1867) ("Rightly pleasant is the yoke of obedience to Him, to serve whom is to reign").

465. "that through the work of obedience you might return to Him from whom you have withdrawn through the idleness of disobedience" (*Rule*, Prologue [McCann, 6]; emphasis added).

is the *proclivity to do our own will* in opposition to the will of God, the inclination to follow our own whims even though they lead to the greatest evil—and the parallel inclination to see as good whatever attracts our own self-love at the moment. But the way to sanctity is the way of self-renunciation in order to love God more than ourselves, *in order to love not just the little selfish good that comes to us from self-satisfaction, but the great, universal, perfect good that is willed by God* and in which we find not just momentary self-satisfaction but eternal peace and happiness, because we are united to the perfect good, which is God's love. Hence the *Rule* is addressed to those who, "renouncing their own will to fight for the true King, Christ, take up the strong and glorious weapons of obedience" (Prologue).[466] And St. Benedict makes it quite clear that there is no charity, no love of Christ, that is not built on a foundation of obedience by which we renounce our selfishness and attachment to our own whims in order *to collaborate with others.* "Obedience without delay . . . is proper to those who hold nothing dearer to them than Christ" (c. 5).[467] What St. Benedict says here is simply an echo of the New Testament. St. Paul says it was by the sin of Adam—a sin of disobedience—that sin and death came into the world; man was separated from God and from his fellow man; there followed all other evils. But from the *obedience of Jesus Christ* comes all good. We are restored to friendship and union with God, we are united to God in Christ, and we are also united to one another, so that in the obedience of Christ is all our peace with God and with man. *Ipse est pax nostra.*[468] READ ROMANS 5:17-21:[469] the empire of death established by Adam's

<hr>

466. "*abrenuntians propriis voluntatibus, Domino Christo vero Regi militaturus, obedientiae fortissima atque praeclara arma sumis*" (McCann, 6/7, which reads: "renouncing thine . . . dost take up . . .").

467. "*Obedientia sine mora . . . . convenit his qui nihil sibi a Christo carius aliquid existimant*" (McCann, 32/33, which reads: ". . . becometh those who . . .").

468. "He is our peace" (Eph. 2:14).

469. "For if by one man's offence death reigned through one; much more they who receive abundance of grace, and of the gift, and of justice, shall reign in life through one, Jesus Christ. Therefore, as by the offence of one, unto all men

sin; the reign of life established by the obedience of Christ. As a consequence, in order to be like Christ, we must seek to become obedient as He was: READ PHILIPPIANS 2:1-15.[470] The nucleus of this passage is the famous pericope (vv. 5-11) used in the Holy Week liturgy:[471] Christ Jesus made obedient unto death, even the death of the Cross, wherefore the Father has exalted Him. But it is good to see this in its context: vv. 1-4: the perfection of the common life, which is absolutely essential to Christianity—all having one mind and one heart, "having the same charity, being of one accord, agreeing in sentiment." This is IMPOSSIBLE unless

---

to condemnation; so also by the justice of one, unto all men to justification of life. For as by the disobedience of one man, many were made sinners; so also by the obedience of one, many shall be made just. Now the law entered in, that sin might abound. And where sin abounded, grace did more abound. That as sin hath reigned to death; so also grace might reign by justice unto life everlasting, through Jesus Christ our Lord."

470. "If there be therefore any consolation in Christ, if any comfort of charity, if any society of the spirit, if any bowels of commiseration: Fulfil ye my joy, that you be of one mind, having the same charity, being of one accord, agreeing in sentiment. Let nothing be done through contention, neither by vain glory: but in humility, let each esteem others better than themselves: Each one not considering the things that are his own, but those that are other men's. For let this mind be in you, which was also in Christ Jesus: Who being in the form of God, thought it not robbery to be equal with God: But emptied himself, taking the form of a servant, being made in the likeness of men, and in habit found as a man. He humbled himself, becoming obedient unto death, even to the death of the cross. For which cause God also hath exalted him, and hath given him a name which is above all names: That in the name of Jesus every knee should bow, of those that are in heaven, on earth, and under the earth: And that every tongue should confess that the Lord Jesus Christ is in the glory of God the Father. Wherefore, my dearly beloved (as you have always obeyed, not as in my presence only, but much more now in my absence,) with fear and trembling work out your salvation. For it is God who worketh in you, both to will and to accomplish, according to his good will. And do ye all things without murmurings and hesitations; That you may be blameless, and sincere children of God, without reproof, in the midst of a crooked and perverse generation; among whom you shine as lights in the world."

471. Epistle for Palm Sunday; introit for Wednesday of Holy Week (vv. 10, 8, 11); gradual for Holy Thursday (vv. 8-9) (*Missale Romanum*, 146, 159, 167; *Missale Cisterciense*, 129, 140, 148).

the individual members of the group are willing to give in to one another, even in difficult things, and at the cost of sacrifice. Hence it necessarily implies that they obey one another; and for the sake of order, there must be some whom all obey, and hence there must be obedience. Without this obedience in the spirit of love and freedom, there can be no Christian life, none of that beautiful Christian charity which is characteristic of our faith and without which Christ cannot be seen in His Church and God cannot manifest Himself openly among men. {According to} vv. 12-15, hence they must obey with deep, supernatural motives and not complain, etc. This obedience that is necessary to the life of the Church is also necessary even in civil society to some extent. READ ROMANS 13:1-14[472]—it is essential to read this whole chapter to get the context. Even civil authority is from God (and

472. "Let every soul be subject to higher powers: for there is no power but from God: and those that are, are ordained of God. Therefore he that resisteth the power, resisteth the ordinance of God. And they that resist, purchase to themselves damnation. For princes are not a terror to the good work, but to the evil. Wilt thou then not be afraid of the power? Do that which is good: and thou shalt have praise from the same. For he is God's minister to thee, for good. But if thou do that which is evil, fear: for he beareth not the sword in vain. For he is God's minister: an avenger to execute wrath upon him that doth evil. Wherefore be subject of necessity, not only for wrath, but also for conscience' sake. For therefore also you pay tribute. For they are the ministers of God, serving unto this purpose. Render therefore to all men their dues. Tribute, to whom tribute is due: custom, to whom custom: fear, to whom fear: honour, to whom honour. Owe no man any thing, but to love one another. For he that loveth his neighbour, hath fulfilled the law. For Thou shalt not commit adultery: Thou shalt not kill: Thou shalt not steal, Thou shalt not bear false witness: Thou shalt not covet: and if there be any other commandment, it is comprised in this word, Thou shalt love thy neighbour as thyself. The love of our neighbour worketh no evil. Love therefore is the fulfilling of the law. And that knowing the season; that it is now the hour for us to rise from sleep. For now our salvation is nearer than when we believed. The night is passed, and the day is at hand. Let us therefore cast off the works of darkness, and put on the armour of light. Let us walk honestly, as in the day: not in rioting and drunkenness, not in chambering, and impurities, not in contention and envy: But put ye on the Lord Jesus Christ, and make not provision for the flesh in its concupiscences."

he meant the Roman Empire!), and the prince (even Nero) can be "the minister of God" for our good (v. 6). Hence they must be obeyed peacefully in all good (not of course in anything sinful). But the rest of the chapter gives us Paul's mind: obedience *does not make us servile instruments of civil authority*; obedience exacts from us small and exterior things which are of relative unimportance: tribute, custom, honor, etc. These things are accidentals. We *owe* them to the state, but when we acquit ourselves of this debt, *then we are free* for better things. St. Paul gives us here a very important principle. The Christian does not grovel before any man. He calmly and honestly gives every man his due, *and then he is free* for higher things. According to St. Paul, obedience is simply a necessary adjustment to social reality, and at the price of this trifling adjustment, we are free to function as persons in the spiritual realm where human princes cannot reach.

c) *Obedience leads to spiritual freedom*: this is a special and delicate point. To appreciate it, we must get rid of wrong ideas about obedience. What obedience of a religious *is not*:

(a) It is NOT the obedience of a SLAVE. A slave is a totally *alienated* person. His person and his actions are completely at the disposition of another in such a *way that his own personal good no longer is of any importance, but is subordinated entirely to the wishes and desires of another*. A slave is a person who has been reduced to an object, a thing, for the use of another—either of another person or of an organization (the state). {Note the} treatment of human beings as objects in concentration camps—made use of for scientific experiments purely as objects, discarded as things without worth—{likewise} the destruction of a human person merely for amusement, as a result of his reduction to a "worthless" status ({cf.} the classic example of the Roman millionaire who throws his slave to the man-eating fish in his pool for diversion; {there are} worse examples from concentration camps). Religious obedience *can never* legitimately be approximated to such violation of the natural law. Obedience is not the abdication of our personality and personal rights in their inmost, spiritual reality. Obedience is meant to *perfect and sanctify* our liberty and to elevate us above the sphere of mere rights and duties to the sphere of loving freedom. (Renunciation of rights {is}[473] to be seen in this light.). The religious does not exist simply for the sake of the work he does or the projects of his community and cannot be "used" merely for a finality outside his own sanctification. If his work or if obedience demands difficult and even costly sacrifices, which may involve the loss of certain values (health, etc.), this does not mean that he has become alienated and that his own spiritual benefit is no longer of any account. His acceptance of difficulty is a free gift of love. The important thing is that religious should learn the right attitude toward obedience. If one learns that obedience is a servile thing, then even in simple and comparatively easy things obedience will make one servile and alienated. If one learns that obedience is a gift of love, and is formed to make such gifts, then even the hardest and most onerous assignments can make a man more free, because he is able to rise above them in the giving of himself. Do not get a slavish notion of obedience. Do not obey slavishly, but with love. N.B. the case of those who are slaves of their own passions and who try to get superiors to command them in a way that suits their own passion—{a} complete inversion of obedience.

(b) It is NOT the obedience of a CHILD. The child is not alienated. His obedience is for his own benefit. But he does not have responsibility for the running of his own life. He is not guided by his own prudence but by the prudence of another. Everybody to some extent requires guidance from others; no one is self-sufficient, but this belongs to the sphere of docility and personal spiritual direction, not to obedience. The obedient monk obeys *as a fully autonomous and responsible person,* who is in full command of his own will, *and gives his will in response to the call of obedience.* The child has no alternative to the prudence of his parent except the motivation of his own whim. The monk is not a "child" divided between obedience to another who is prudent and following his

473. Typescript reads: "are."

own whim. *He obeys in the light of his own prudence.* He obeys not because he is "told" but because *he wants to obey.* Thus the motivation of religious obedience comes from within one's own self, from freedom and from love. Only thus can it be a real gift.

(c) It is NOT the obedience of a CITIZEN or of an EMPLOYEE. The citizen is not alienated, not subject to the prudence of another. He is fully responsible; he guides himself in obeying. But his obedience is an act of justice, *a fulfillment of external duty*— what is precisely *owed* to authority. The obedience of the citizen (or of the employee) is limited by the explicit or implicit contract which defines his obligation—so far and no further. The obedience of the citizen may indeed reach heroic proportions (giving one's life for one's country in time of war), but still, in itself, without any other added element, it does not have the quality of a gift to God. (It can become a gift by vow.) The obedience of the citizen is focused on the external act, the duty to be done. The interior dispositions are, in themselves, relatively unimportant. One can be an obedient citizen and obey the traffic lights yet still interiorly care nothing for the laws one way or another. Note the danger of overemphasizing {a} democratic spirit and {the} development of personality in religious houses of {the} USA. This is by no means the "freedom" to which obedience of {the} monk is supposed to lead. Religious communities are never run on a purely democratic pattern, in the sense of being run according to the *desires of the majority.* This is explicitly refuted in the *Rule* of St. Benedict.[474] Many (European) theologians see a "great danger" in this and exaggerate in the other direction. {A} monastery is not a democracy, but *neither should it be an autocracy.* God is the one we obey—God speaking through {the} superior and rules.

What religious obedience is: supernatural obedience is completely different from mere natural subjection. IT IS THE ACT OF A CHILD OF GOD UNITING HIMSELF TO CHRIST IN THE FREE AND

---

474. See chapter 3, in which the abbot consults with the community but has the ultimate responsibility to make the final decision (McCann, 24).

LOVING SACRIFICE OF HIS OWN WILL TO GIVE GLORY TO THE FATHER. It is a response to the call of grace which comes from beyond the visible world and the world of mere human feelings and desires, as well as the world of human or ethical duties. It is the response to a call *to unite ourselves with the liberty of Christ.* Obedience is based on faith. Because it is based on faith, it sees the true meaning of the Cross, the self-emptying of Christ. It sees supreme truth in the Cross of Christ. The Cross is the truth that makes us free. {The} paradox of the Cross {is that} Christ was free to die on the Cross or not to die on it. He had no obligation to die on the Cross. He chose this in an act of supreme freedom out of love for us. The fact that he chose this in obedience to the Father's will rather than out of an impulse of His own will makes it even "more free," more gratuitous. It was a pure gift of love. Obedience is also based on faith in a *special providence of God*, His promises to those who leave all things to seek Him alone above all else, apart from all merely human plans and motives.

Our obedience is a union of our will with the will of Christ dying on the Cross for love. By obeying we unite ourselves with the great act of freedom and truth, the supreme manifestation of love in the world, a love that is above and beyond the contradictions, the rights and wrongs of life in the world and in time. Just as Jesus made Himself indifferent to the wrongs that were done to Him and the violation of His rights, so in religious obedience we renounce our attachment to our own idea of what is best, most prudent, most wise, most expedient, and accept the judgement of another. (This judgement is necessarily bound by one essential limitation: it must always be *morally right.*)

How does this liberate us?

1. It liberates us from undue concern with choices and judgement between things which are of themselves relatively unimportant. It gives us a detached and supernatural perspective with which to judge events and things.

2. It liberates us from unconscious influence of our own self-will and egoism even in things which appear to be good in themselves.

3. It liberates us from the effects of sin, which blind and defile the soul. (We can never cleanse ourselves from these defilements—grace is necessary, and obedience is a most effective means of grace.)

4. It liberates us from the influence and deceits of the devil and from slavery to his wiles.

5. It liberates us from the forces of death and corruption which sin has placed in our souls. It liberates us also from the undue influence of human respect and worldly pressures.

III. *Wrong Approaches to Obedience*: avoid mistaken ideas— they vitiate our obedience.

a) Avoid the notion that Christian morality is a morality of duty first and foremost. No, it is a *morality of love*. This of course *includes* and transcends duty. We do not obey just because we "have to" but because we "want to." It is more perfect in the eyes of God to do a small thing out of love than to do a great thing by constraint and only half-willingly. What God wants of us is our hearts, our love, not our works. Hence in preparing for a life of obedience we should learn that obedience is not the whole of life. It is a means to an end—*love*. Perfection does not consist in obedience, but in love—but obedience is the greatest help to attaining perfection in love, since it enables us to give our will entirely to the beloved. We give our will not by "crushing" or "exterminating" it but by putting it at the disposal of another. Our obedience should not be soulless—it should be enlivened if possible with conscious desire. Avoid a dead, stoical kind of obedience. *Hilarem datorem diligit Deus.*[475] Keep *love* in mind before all else.

b) *Avoid an inordinate emphasis on "blind" obedience.* What is "blind obedience"? obedience which obliges us *without explanation*. It is true that sometimes a religious may be required to obey without having any idea why he is being commanded and without seeing the full meaning or implications of the command. But

---

475. "God loveth a cheerful giver" (2 Cor. 9:7).

blind obedience in the strict sense is rare. Ordinarily, obedience demands that *we apply our mind to understand what the superior wants of us*. Ordinary obedience has to be "clear-sighted" and not "blind." Understanding a command *means putting aside our own judgement in so far as it may interfere with our grasping the ideas of the superior*. But we turn away from our own ideas in order to *see* his ideas. Many fail to make any effort to see what the superior actually wants. Their obedience is too negative and passive. They obey more or less like machines and justify themselves by thinking that "blind" obedience is required of them. This lack of thought really frustrates obedience.

    c) *Avoid an inordinate emphasis on the "liberty and spontaneity" of the subject*. In our country where independence is the national ideal, many may fail to really obey at all. They may, without realizing it, make a mere formality out of obedience, a perfunctory gesture. They may have too great an inclination to force their own ideas on {the} superior or simply do things entirely their own way with no concern for his desires. Note the vice of *manipulating superiors*. Some think, naively, that if they can get a superior to tell them what they want, they are "obeying" him. This is not obedience at all—it is a pure illusion, hypocrisy. To do this, even in "good faith," is actually very harmful to the subject and to the discipline of the community. Manipulating superiors is an infantile trait and can be associated with neurotic trends. It is more common than we think. One who takes the monastic life seriously will be on his guard against this. One should learn when it is reasonable to offer suggestions, when one ought to make known a special difficulty or problem, and when not to do so. A difficulty should always be made known if it is clear that the superior does not see it and if it is clear that it would make a big difference to his command. Do not assume too readily that the superior is a fool who has not been able to see obvious difficulties. Obedience must be fully genuine, not just a pretense. Obedience must consist in something more than "doing your own will with permission."

IV. *The Right Approach*: Dom Olivier Rousseau, OSB points out:[476]

1. that we must *sharply distinguish supernatural obedience from natural subjection;*

2. {that} supernatural obedience does not just consist in natural obedience "offered up" to God: it is *a response* to a supernatural grace, *a call from God to return to His mercy;*

3. {that} this element of personal response is what makes obedience *an act of reparation for sin by which we have departed from God.*[477]

Hence religious obedience is not merely a question of obeying the superior because he is in authority. *It is a restoration of the order violated by sin;* it is a loving return to God our merciful Father. Our obedience gives great scope for His mercy in our lives. Our lack of obedience implies coldness towards His merciful love. This is a thoroughly Benedictine concept of religious obedience—*obedience to please and glorify God.* Love is the great motive. We obey not just in order to "be perfect" but to show our love for God in a real and concrete manner. *Everything that is done according to true obedience is certainly pleasing to God* (a) because it proceeds from God; (b) because it is ordered to God through superiors; (c) because obedience implies the greatest renunciation of self. One who wishes to please God will seek more and more ways of obeying His will more perfectly.

OBEDIENCE: DEFINITION—THE VOW AND AUTHORITY: having now cleared the way, we can study the vow of obedience in detail. In making our promise of obedience, we say: *Pater, promitto tibi obedientiam secundum Regulam Sancti Benedicti . . .*[478] {In saying} *PATER*, we are speaking to a living authority who represents Christ. This promise of obedience to our living abbot and, in him, to his successors, is what we have vowed to God. Our vow of obedience made to God implies this promise of obedience to the superior; we have vowed to God that we will obey our superior.

476. "Introduction: The Vocation of Obedience," *Obedience*, 5–19.
477. Rousseau, 6.
478. See above, n. 453.

Obedientiam: OBEDIENCE IS THAT VIRTUE BY WHICH WE PLACE OUR WILLS AT THE DISPOSITION OF OUR SUPERIOR IN ORDER TO CARRY OUT HIS WILL IN ACCORDANCE WITH OUR RULE, THUS BEARING WITNESS TO THE WILL OF GOD MANIFESTED IN THE HIERARCHICAL ORDER OF HIS CREATION. This definition is designed to emphasize the fact that religious obedience is an act of worship. It is designed to highlight the contemplative aspect of religious obedience ({a} recognition of divine wisdom and divine order). The essential thing about obedience is, however, not the abstract recognition of the superior's authority, not the act of faith by which we connect the will of the superior with the will of God, but the PROMPTITUDE WITH WHICH OUR WILL CARRIES OUT THE WILL OF THE SUPERIOR. *Obedientia reddit hominis voluntatem promptam ad implendam voluntatem alterius* (St. Thomas: II-II, q. 104, a. 2, ad. 3).[479] We must not confuse obedience with mere respect for the superior, or benevolent feelings toward the superior, or patience in allowing oneself to be commanded by a superior. For many religious, obedience in practice seems to resolve itself into the virtue of remaining patient and not being angry when a superior corrects or commands you. This is a caricature of true obedience, and is concerned with the accidentals of obedience. It comes from a subjective attitude towards obedience, stressing the fact that it purifies our own souls. One must on the contrary stress the *objective* element of obedience, the duty to carry out the superior's command. {For} example, take a case of two religious who receive a command. A. receives the command with feelings of impatience and repugnance, but carries it out to the letter and really fulfills perfectly what the superior has asked of him, even though he is tempted to think it foolish, etc. B. receives the command sweetly, agreeing with the superior. He loves the superior with his whole heart; he is crazy about the superior. He thinks the command is marvelous. He admires it and goes into ecstasy

---

479. "Obedience makes the will of a man prompt in fulfilling the will of another" (Aquinas, *Opera Omnia*, 3.377, which reads: ". . . *promptam hominis voluntatem* . . .").

over it. However, he does not really carry it out; he just makes a pass at it and is content with his lovely interior dispositions toward the superior. In this case, the obedient religious is not B. but A. It is true that the obedience of A. would be more perfect accidentally if he were able to receive such commands with no interior repugnance, but this is purely accidental. The important thing is the *essence*, carrying out the will of the superior. This is too often forgotten. Some people think that perfection consists in never feeling repugnances, irrespective of what you actually *do*.

Let us be a little more objective. We owe our superiors *respect*, both for their person and for their judgement. We owe them *docility* in so far as they are also our guides. Docility is a part of prudence which enables us to accept and profit by the guidance given by another. We owe them *reverence* as representatives of God. We owe them *gratitude and love* in so far as they sacrifice themselves for us and work hard to make our lives easier and more fruitful. We owe them the cooperation of our *prayers* and good will. We should make *sacrifices* for our superiors also. These are all virtues, but different from obedience. However, not one of the above is directly vowed by us. But we do vow obedience. The above accompany obedience usually.

The precise object of obedience is the PRECEPT OF THE SUPERIOR. To obey, then, implies first of all the alertness and willingness to *know and apprehend* the precept of the superior. An obedient monk *listens to his superior*. One can salve his conscience, but wrongly, by habitually *not paying attention* to the superior. This means that we do not apprehend his desires and his precepts and therefore are not able to obey them. This is part of our vow. If we vow to obey, we implicitly vow to "listen to" our superior and to "pay attention" to his commands. One who evades this duty is in danger of sinning against his vow by culpable neglect. *St. Thomas* (II-II, q. 104, a. 2) has some important points on this: *Obedientiae speciale objectum est praeceptum tacitum vel expressum; voluntas superioris* quocumque modo innotescat, est quoddam tacitum praeceptum.[480] In paying attention to our superior, we come to

---

480. "The particular object of obedience is an implicit or expressed command; the will of the superior, by whatever means it may become known, is an

know his will by signs other than express words. The obedient religious will seek to carry out the will of his superior even when that will is not made known to him formally and expressly in so many words. As soon as we know what our superior would like, we seek to carry out his will. It is not obedience to force the superior to express his will and to withhold obedience until he does so. (Of course, however, our interpretations may be wrong, and we should not obey if, in good faith, we sincerely doubt the will of the superior; this would involve the risk of doing what he *does not want*—i.e., of disobedience.) St. Thomas adds: "Obedience seems to be all the more prompt in proportion as it anticipates the express command, *once the will of the superior has been understood."*[481] The important phrase {is} *voluntate superioris intellecta*. Note, however, that in ad. 2[482] St. Thomas points out that there is indiscreet obedience which obeys a person whom one ought not to obey (one who has no authority), or a superior in things which are beyond his authority. It is therefore not perfect obedience to strive to conform to trivial whims of the superior in matters that are outside the *Rule* and have really nothing to do with the monastic life—personal idiosyncrasies and the like. It is presumed that the superior does not expect his subject to conform to him in every personal trifle, but only in his *will* with regard to *the observance of the Rule and what is related to it*. Obedience tends to be more perfect when the precept of the superior is contrary to our own will (says St. Thomas: *id.*, ad. 3),[483] because in that case our will is directed purely to the fulfillment of the precept and not to the attainment of what we ourselves desire. This, however, must not be exaggerated. There is also merit in obeying commands that conform to our own desires, and such obedience can lead to perfection. One must prepare himself more

---

implicit command" (Aquinas, *Opera Omnia*, 3.377, which reads: *"ejus speciale . . . voluntas enim superioris . . ."*; emphasis added).

481. *"Et tanto videtur obedientia promptior, quanto expressum praeceptum obediendo praevenit, voluntate superioris intellecta"* (Aquinas, *Opera Omnia*, 3.377).

482. Aquinas, *Opera Omnia*, 3.377.

483. Aquinas, *Opera Omnia*, 3.377–78.

particularly for the other kind, however (cf. St. Benedict: fourth degree {of} humility[484]).

OBEDIENCE AND AUTHORITY: the subject obeys because right order demands it; and his faith shows him the beauty of the divine order. Obedience manifests his particular place in the hierarchy established by God. In subjection, justly and freely, to those above him, he is able also to command, justly and prudently, those below him. We must understand that for each one, obedience is a question of taking his proper place as *a link in a chain* which binds all to God. Obedience enables us to participate in the goods which God distributes externally through a hierarchical community, and also to share those goods with others. God guides all to their end not only *interiorly* but also *exteriorly*. Both are important. In fact both are essential. We must not imagine that the divinely established order is merely external and juridical, merely a matter of laws and obedience. But we must not imagine either that it is merely a matter of personal inspiration and interior freedom. The true Christian notion is one of *freedom and dependence* working together; we are freely dependent, and because of our dependence we can grow in freedom, because we have only a limited autonomy and are not gods in our own right.

To understand this we must realize that the ideas of *authority* and of the *common good* are correlative. Authority exists to safeguard and promote the common good, and because the good of all is also the good of each individual, authority exists to safeguard our own good. In obeying, we do what is best for ourselves and work also for the common good of all. *Authority* rightly conceived, in a religious community, exists only *to dispose and order means to the common end.* Authority is not an end in itself. The community does not exist for the superiors. The superiors are

484. "*Quartus humilitatis gradus est, si in ipsa obedientia, duris et contrariis rebus vel etiam quibuslibet irrogatis injuriis, tacita conscientia patientiam amplectatur, et sustinens non lassescat vel discedat*" (*Rule*, c. 7 [McCann, 42]). ("The fourth degree of humility is that if one meets with difficult and contrary matters, or even some injustices, in this obedience, he should embrace patience with a quiet conscience, and while putting up with the situation neither become worn out nor withdraw").

the servants of the community. {For} example, if a religious were
to become dissatisfied with the food in the refectory and decide
to throw out the cook and do the cooking himself, he would take
on a great burden for the sake of a small gain and turn his religious life upside down. But that is exactly the case of one who
throws off the authority of the superior and takes upon himself
the superior's responsibilities to judge and dispose all things in
the community. He takes upon himself a burden which he has
not the strength or the grace to bear, and he simply ruins his own
life (cf. {also a} bus driver {or a} pilot of a ship). We should get
this attitude toward authority. The superior bears burdens for
us, makes decisions which we are not competent to make, *and
disposes all things for the greater freedom and efficacy of our own religious life*. To desire to be independent and to become one's own
boss, to be one's own authority and live life according to one's
own whims, is a contradiction in terms for a religious. It is to
throw the religious life itself overboard in order to take back the
burden and the tedium of secular life. To desire "independence"
in this sense is to relinquish true spiritual freedom. It is a return
to the slavery of our own will.

   The Source of Authority: {it is} VERY IMPORTANT {to ask}: what
gives the superior authority over us? the fact that he is wiser,
greater, holier? more powerful? NO. the fact that he is in a hierarchical position? NO. None of these things of themselves confer
upon a man the right to direct and control the life of another. THE
AUTHORITY OF THE SUPERIOR TO CONTROL MY LIFE IS GIVEN TO HIM
BY MY OWN FREE ACT IN MAKING A VOW OF OBEDIENCE. This is what
I do in making the vow: I give the abbot this power to demand
the acquiescence of my own will, by promising to acquiesce and
to submit to him. This must always be remembered. The superior
does not command me because *he* wants to, but rather because I
want him to. His exercise of dominion is not just a show of personal power for the sake of his own interest and gratification. It is
for my interest and for the common good. When I am disobedient,
I should not look at my disobedience primarily as an *infidelity to
the superior*. Rather, it is an *infidelity to my higher self*, an *infidelity*

to my own immortal soul, and *ultimately an infidelity to divine grace.*
Naturally, the hierarchical position of the superior is important.
I am not allowed to make a vow to one who is not in a position
to receive the vow. Hence I can only make a vow to a properly
constituted superior. Nevertheless, it is not merely the fact that he
is superior that gives him power over me, but primarily and above
all the fact that I have freely vowed to obey him and to submit to
his commands. The same applies to the RULE. The *Rule* does not
bind me because it is intrinsically wise, prudent, holy, etc. It does
not bind me because it is approved by the Church. IT BINDS ME
BECAUSE I HAVE FREELY BOUND MYSELF TO OBSERVE IT. I have by
a free act given my will to God by obligating myself to observe
this *Rule.* Such a binding of myself would not be reasonable or
permissible unless the *Rule* were itself good and holy, and unless it
were approved by the Church for communities with public vows.

The twofold aspect of dominion: when I make a vow of obedience I give the superior *dominion* over my exterior and even interior life, within certain limits (see below[485]). The vow of obedience
gives the superior *dominative power* over my life (*potestas dominativa*[486]). *Dominion (potestas dominativa)* {is} "mastery"—power to
command *with a command that obligates in conscience, even gravely.*
Dominative power gives the superior {a} right to command the
person of the religious and to enter into the interior of his soul,
for instance by annulling a vow made privately by the religious.
When one has a vow of obedience, he has no right to oppose the
superior and refuse obedience in any matter according to the rule
and constitutions, and disobedience in such matters becomes a
sin when there is a *formal precept* given by the superior.

Before vows, novices and oblates, etc. are equally with the
professed under the *domestic power* of the superior. This is not

485. See below, pages 259–63.
486. See Canon 501.1: "*Superiores et Capitula, ad normam constitutionum et
iuris communis potestatem habent dominativam in subditos*" ("Superiors and chapters,
according to the norm of constitutions and common law, have dominative power
over their subjects") (*Codex Iuris Canonici,* 168).

based on any vow; it is a natural right flowing from the fact that the superior is head of the community and has the obligation of directing it. Domestic power is the power to order things for the good of the community. Obedience is due to {the} superior by virtue of domestic power even from those who have no vows. The novice master has domestic power in the novitiate, and obedience is due to him by virtue of this power. The "right" of the novice master over the members of the novitiate is conferred upon him by them *when they enter the novitiate and place themselves under his guidance.*

The Exercise of the Superior's Power:

1. The superior has *domestic power* over everyone in the community and even in a certain limited way over guests in the guest house (he has {the} right to ask a guest to leave, or to demand that certain rules be kept in {the} guest house). This *domestic power* belongs also to subordinate officers in various fields.

2. The professed are subject to the *dominative power* of the superior by virtue of their vows. This includes also his *domestic power.* (Thus, when the superior commands a professed to carry out some order necessary for the good functioning of the community, the professed would be obliged to obey *even if he had no vow.* He cannot therefore say that just because the superior does not command him *vi voti,*[487] there is no sin. There is a sin, *at least against the virtue of obedience and perhaps also against the vow.*)

3. The *minimum* requirement is *material and external obedience.* The religious must carry out the act commanded by the superior. Interior and formal obedience {means} willing what the superior wills; {a} formal intention to carry out the precept is not *strictly* required, but a good religious *will always strive to obey formally.* Without this, obedience would be a mere formality and have little value for the interior life.

4. The superior is *limited* in the exercise of his power by the *Rule* and the *Constitutions:*

487. "by the power of the vow."

a) The superior cannot command anything that is against the natural or moral law or against Church law.

b) To say that the superior must command according to the *Rule*, etc. does not mean that he can never command anything forbidden in the *Rule*. For instance, the *Rule* normally forbids the monk to eat meat. The superior can command a monk to eat meat, and the monk is bound to obey, provided there is a just cause, because the superior has power to dispense from the *Rule* and to apply the *Rule* differently in certain particular cases. If in such a case there is doubt as to whether there is a just cause, the subject is *bound to give the benefit of the doubt to the superior*. In other words, the superior can command a monk to do something that is contrary to the ordinary prescriptions of the *Rule* if he sincerely believes there to be a good cause and if he has the power to apply or modify the application of the *Rule* on this point (examples {include} work, diet, sleep, choir, journeys, etc.).

c) Dominative power is brought to bear on {the} subject *only by a formal command.*

5. The superior "can command according to the *Rule*"[488] (i.e., can bring to bear his *potestas dominativa* on the subject) in the following cases:

a) Whenever something is *explicitly* contained in the *Rule*.

b) Whenever something is implicit in the *Rule*—v.g., anything *without which* the *Rule* and *Constitutions* cannot be observed: for instance, the work to be done, how it is to be done, etc.; the choral office; employments in the community, and offices; matters affecting the health of the community; studies of members of the community; penances; silence (v.g., {the} rule after compline in this house); fraternal charity (he can command a public apology to an injured brother).

c) *In the Rule of St. Benedict*, it is explicitly stated that the superior can exact heroic obedience from the monk—i.e., he can

---

488. See *Spiritual Directory*, 102: "The Abbot himself obeys by commanding according to the Rule."

even command him to attempt something which seems impossible (*Rule*, c. 68—Read[489]). It is doubtful whether such commands would necessarily be binding under pain of sin. The subject has the right to make representations. *Note* in the fourth degree of humility the monk is *counseled* to submit even to injurious and unjust commands.[490] N.B. the subject has the right to *refuse or accept* an election against the will of his superior (Canons 175–76;[491] cf. 507, #1[492]).

6. To say the superior can command according to the rule does not merely mean that he has *authority to enforce the rule*. In

489. "*Si cui fratri aliqua forte gravia aut impossibilia injunguntur, suscipiat quidem jubentis imperium cum omni mansuetudine et obedientia. Quod si omnino virium suarum mensuram viderit pondus oneris excedere, impossibilitatis suae causas ei qui sibi praeest patienter et opportune suggerat, non superbiendo aut resistendo vel contradicendo. Quod si post suggestionem suam in sua sententia prioris imperium perduraverit, sciat junior ita sibi expedire, et ex caritate confidens de adjutorio Dei obediat*" (McCann, 154) ("If anything difficult or impossible is enjoined upon any brother, let him accept the command of the one ordering with complete docility and obedience. But if he should see that the weight of the burden goes completely beyond the extent of his power, let him patiently and at the proper time explain the reasons for his inability to the one who is over him, without being arrogant or resisting or contradicting. If, after his explanation, the superior's command remain unaltered in his determination, let the subordinate know that it is best for him and obey out of love, confident in the assistance of God").

490. McCann, 42; see above, n. 484.

491. Canon 175 specifies that the one elected has eight days to decide whether to accept the election, after which time he forfeits the rights of the office (*Codex Iuris Canonici*, 49); Canon 176 decrees that by refusing the election a candidate loses any right associated with it, even if he should change his mind; that he may be chosen again at a subsequent election, which must be held within a month of the time of refusal; that by accepting the election the candidate receives full rights of office, unless the election requires confirmation by higher authority; that prior to such confirmation the one elected is not to interfere in temporal or spiritual administration, and any acts he performs in that regard have no validity (*Codex Iuris Canonici*, 49).

492. This canon decrees that in elections by chapters, general rules of canon law (nn. 160–82) are to be observed, along with the constitutions of the order (*Codex Iuris Canonici*, 179).

the *Rule* of St. Benedict, particularly, this would fall far short of his full powers; he can do much more than this. *Every decision that is not already made in the letter of the Rule is to be made by the superior*, and in numerous cases the *Rule* gives the superior power to modify and dispense and apply the letter differently in particular cases, as we have seen above. Hence the *Rule* not only does not form the limit of the superior's activity, but on the contrary it is only the beginning. It *points out the lines on which his activity goes on to carry out* what is not specifically indicated in the *Rule*. Not only does the superior have the *right* to impose his will in what is not clearly indicated by the letter of the *Rule*, but he has the *obligation to do so* wherever it is necessary for attaining the end proposed by the *Rule*—the sanctification of the monks and the spiritual and temporal good of the community. Our *Rule* puts the abbot in full charge of attaining its end, and he is *obliged to impose his will* in every case where he deems it necessary to attain this end. The fact that the subject may not clearly see how the superior's will tends to attain the end of the *Rule* in a given case *has nothing to do with the obligation to obey*. The subject has no business to sit in judgement on the superior's interpretation and application of the *Rule*. However, there are times—v.g., at regular visitations—when the subject can raise questions about the way the *Rule* is interpreted and applied by the local superior. Other ways exist for bringing such matters before higher superiors, but they should only be applied in very rare cases when there is clear evidence of abuse.

7. The superior can command exterior acts, and he can annul certain interior acts of the subject (v.g., vows), but *he cannot directly command interior acts of the will. In his quae pertinent ad interiorem motum voluntatis, non tenetur homo homini obedire, sed solum Deo* (St. Thomas: II-II, q. 104, a. 5).[493]

---

493. "In those things that pertain to the interior movement of the will, a man is not required to obey a man, but only God" (Aquinas, *Opera Omnia*, 3.380, which reads: ". . . *homo non tenetur* . . .").

8. Note, however, that we should not always be scrutinizing the *limits of obedience*. The limits define only the *minimum obligation*. But if one wishes to be perfect in obedience, he will not confine himself merely to keeping the strict minimum to which he is obliged under pain of sin. On the contrary, it is a matter of perfection *to seek to carry out the will of the superior even when one is not strictly obliged to do so*:

a) when the will of the superior is only tacitly expressed;

b) when the superior wishes us to dispose ourselves interiorly for some end or other, it is a good thing to seek to conform to his views interiorly, and to see things as he sees them, and accept his dispositions as our own;

c) one should not, however, try to obey the superior in things which are illicit, sinful, etc.

9. One should see in *a spirit of faith* all the counsels and tacit desires of the superior as ways of *pleasing God more*. One should be eager for these opportunities to practice obedience.

N.B. distinct from domestic and dominative power, our abbots also have *power of jurisdiction*, by which, for instance, he appoints confessors, reserves sins, etc.

When do we sin against obedience?

A. *Sins against the Vow*: when we sin against the vow, there is not only a sin of disobedience but a sin against religion—{a} sacrilege—a double sin. In general, remember that by the vow of obedience the religious obliges himself to carry out all rightful orders of his legitimate superiors in everything that has to do with the religious life and the Christian life. Who are the superiors who have the authority to command us under pain of sin? the Holy Father, the Sacred Congregation of Religious, the General Chapter and the abbot general (when the Chapter is not in session), the local abbot (the father immediate, during visitation, or in matters relative to the visitation, or when the local superiorship is vacant).

1) *Formal disobedience*: formal disobedience against an express command of the superior, in which he intends to bind us according to the vow, *is always a sin. In grave matter, it is a mortal sin.* Here we are speaking of *a sin against the vow*, hence not only disobedience but sacrilege. The formal command of the superior, by which he expresses the intention to bind us under pain of sinning against the vow, *is always explicitly expressed in easily recognizable formulas*: "I command you under holy obedience"; "I command you by reason of your vow"; "I command you in the name of God"—or "in the name of Our Lord Jesus Christ." In such formulas, and others like them, the superior makes quite evident that he intends the full exercise of his dominative power and that he is definitely speaking in the name of God and with all the authority vested in him by his office. Thus in disobeying him we are deliberately disobeying God Himself in the authority constituted by Him. This has to be clearly understood. By making our vow of obedience, we have removed all chance for quibbling on this point. We have agreed that when the superior commands us by his dominative power, we are bound under pain even of mortal sin to obey him. Exterior obedience is sufficient to avoid sin against the vow. (Interior obedience is necessary to avoid sinning against the virtue of obedience.)

2) *Flight*: a religious sins against the vow of obedience when he leaves the monastery in order to get away from the authority of the superior. In our Order, this illicit departure from the monastery explicitly involves mortal or venial sin against the law of enclosure. Flight and apostasy involve excommunication.

3) *Scandal*: there can be grave or light sin against the vow of obedience when one knowingly disobeys in such a way as to give scandal or to cause a definite harm to the community, whether the harm be spiritual or temporal—or even grave spiritual and temporal harm to the religious himself who disobeys.

4) *Contempt*: there is sin against the vow when disobedience, even though the command is not given with a special formula, *proceeds from formal contempt of authority*—that is to say, from contempt of authority as such, not from antipathy to the

personality and characteristics of the superior or from an idea that the command is unwise.

As the superior will rarely command under pain of sin, and as formal contempt and grave scandal are not common, it is seen that the religious will rarely have occasion to sin gravely against the vow of obedience. This must not lull him into false security. The fact remains that there are many occasions of sinning against the *virtue* of obedience.

B. *Sins against the Virtue*:

1. Disobedience of the ordinary commands of the superior is always a sin against the virtue of obedience when the commands are of sufficient consequence. Such sins are normally venial. (Distinguish *commands* and *counsels* of {the} superior, especially as regards {the} interior life.)

2. Negligence and habitual failure to carry out rules or commands of superiors through thoughtlessness, neglect, laziness, etc. {is sinful}. This habitual lack of regularity and obedience wounds the virtue of obedience, *and one who makes no attempt to correct himself sins*. Any willful neglect of {a} command of {the} superior is a sin if the command is sufficiently important. Note: indirect voluntary enters here! That is to say, if through attachment to something else I allow myself to become blinded to the will of the superior, I am guilty of disobedience even though at the moment I do not advert to the fact that I am failing to carry out his will. It is sufficient that I advert beforehand to the fact that my immersion in my own will tends to make me ignore the will of the superior. Hence, to say "I didn't realize that was what you wanted" is not a valid excuse.

3. Habitual disobedience is also a sin in so far as it tends to make us completely lose the spirit of our vows and thus prepares the way for grave defections and loss of vocation. Thus, one should not underestimate the importance of "little things." Many of our acts may not be sins of disobedience in themselves, but the cumulative effect of them all and the *habitual neglect of*

many little things tends to undermine one's whole religious life. *When one has a chance to realize this* and does not correspond with grace, *one's neglect becomes sinful.* Here is one of the cases where examen of conscience can become highly important for a religious—also days of recollection and annual retreats. Times of grace must never be neglected.

{4}.[494] Avoiding obedience: deliberately substracting oneself, being off the scene when unpleasant commands are given, "not knowing" what has been decreed or commanded {is sinful}: for instance, not coming to distribution of work, or avoiding common work, or creating situations in which one is withdrawn from common tasks where one is really needed.

{5}. {One may sin} by carelessness, sloppiness, lack of punctuality, ill will in carrying out orders of the superior, in one's work, in choir, etc.

{6}. {One may sin} by interior murmuring, {a} spirit of criticism, rebellion, resistance. Even interiorly these are offences against the virtue of obedience; exteriorly expressed, they risk becoming sins against the vow by reason of scandal, at least in serious matters, if there is sufficient deliberation. Usually griping and complaints are not fully deliberate and are only faults against the virtue, but the risk of scandal remains. One should make very serious efforts to overcome this fault by taking the right means: accusing himself, doing penances, {showing} fidelity in obeying further commands by way of reparation, etc., etc.

{7}. One may lose the merit of obedience through wrong motives—human respect, seeking to curry favor with or to flatter superiors, self-seeking, nest-feathering, ambition, monastery politics—or merely obeying out of the desire to look good, and not obeying when one thinks it will not be noticed.

C. *Defects in the Spirit of Obedience* {include} cultivating antipathies, disrespect for {the} superior, distaste for {the} rule and regular life, distaste for common life, disregard of common du-

---

494. Typescript reads "5" . . . "8."

ties and functions, the desire to "get out of" unpleasant duties as much as possible, manipulating the superior, extorting permissions by flattery and cajoling, apple polishing, repeated excuses, pretexts and alibis, malingering (playing sick to get out of hard work), bullying the superior by one's moods, constantly threatening him with reprisals (implicitly: "I will not be nice to you if you correct me again"; "You won't be able to handle me at all unless you treat me the way I like"—which eventually becomes: "If you do not give me what I want, I will leave the monastery"). This is all more or less serious, even though definite sin may be hard to identify in a particular case. {There is an} obligation to correct and resist these bad dispositions.

Toward Perfect Obedience: in what has been said so far, we have given many indications of the perfection of obedience and have described imperfect obedience. It is now sufficient to resume in brief, succinct points, the various aids to growth in the spirit of obedience.

1. *Per obedientiae laborem*:[495] first of all, we have to embrace the practice of obedience as a hard and lifelong task. It is *work*. It does not necessarily get easier as one goes on. It is a life-work. It is always likely to be hard, to demand sacrifice. Those who do not progress in obedience are often the ones who take it for granted that they are obedient, who are more or less passive and nonchalant about the routine of religious life and never really face the issue. We can never take obedience for granted. We always have to renew our decision to work hard at perfecting our obedience. In what does this work consist? It is important to have clearly defined objectives and to aim at them decisively.

2. *Cultivate convictions of faith*: our obedience cannot develop and become perfect without supernatural motives. As our spirit of faith grows, then obedience grows with it, and *vice versa*. One who is not generous in obedience will risk a gradual loss of faith.

---

495. "through the work of obedience" (*Rule*, Prologue [McCann, 6]).

a) St. Benedict proposes the basic motives for growth in obedience: *Convenit his qui* nihil sibi a Christo carius *aliquid existimant.*[496] When we obey, we prove that we love Christ above all else. {There is a} conviction that by obedience we are united to Christ: we share His sufferings; we give Him joy; we enable Him to love us and be merciful to us. Other motives {include} the dignity of our religious consecration (*servitium sanctum*[497]), the fear of hell (*metum gehennae*[498]), love of heaven.

b) *Qui vos audit, me audit:*[499] the conviction that what is willed by the superior is willed by God—this is the foundation stone of Benedictine obedience.

c) One cannot cultivate these convictions without some *intellectual* effort and preparation. READ classical sources on the subject (v.g., Marmion[500]); MEDITATE on the obedience of Jesus; PRAY ardently for the grace to grow in obedience; have an intense desire to be perfect in this virtue. READ St. John of the Cross: *Cautions* 1 and 2 against the devil (vol. iii, p. 223[501]). Reflect on the

496. "It is proper for those who consider nothing dearer to them than Christ" (c. 5 [McCann, 32]; emphasis added).

497. "holy service" (McCann, 32).

498. McCann, 32.

499. "He who hears you, hears me" (Lk. 10:16, quoted in c. 5 [McCann, 32]).

500. Columba Marmion, OSB, *Christ, the Ideal of the Monk: Spiritual Conferences on the Monastic and Religious Life*, trans. a nun of Tyburn Convent, 8th ed. (London: Herder, 1926); *Christ, the Ideal of the Priest: Spiritual Conferences*, trans. Matthew Dillon (St. Louis: Herder, 1952); *Christ, the Life of the Soul: Spiritual Conferences*, trans. a nun of Tyburn Convent (St. Louis: Herder, 1922).

501. "Let the first caution, then, be that, save when thou art so commanded by obligation, thou be moved to nothing, however good and full of charity it may seem, whether it be for thyself or for anyone within or without the house, without being ordered by obedience. In observing this thou gainest merit and security. Avoid attachment and thou shalt flee from the devil and from evils of which thou knowest not, but whereof God shall call for an account of thee in His time. And if thou observe not this caution, both in little things and in great, however successful thou seem to be, thou canst not fail, either to a small or to a great degree, to be deceived by the devil. And, although thou do no worse than fail to be ruled in all things by obedience, thou strayest and art therefore to be blamed; for God prefers obedience to sacrifice, and the actions of a religious are

fact that God desires our obedience, that He is pleased by it, that through our obedience He makes our lives fruitful for ourselves and for the whole Church, and that He desires to reward our obedience with an eternal reward, but that if we do not obey, our disobedience will meet with punishment and may even lead to the eternal loss of our soul. These *basic ideas* should sometimes be gone over in meditation or examen, especially at {the} time of {the} annual retreat, etc.

3. *Cultivate humility*: recognize the fact that disobedience is inseparable from pride, and pride is the sin of Satan: *non serviam;*[502] better to rule in hell than serve in heaven![503] ({a} complete misunderstanding of freedom and of love! Hell is the ultimate in servitude and degradation.) Fear the spirit of contradiction and criticism. In order to cultivate the humility that will enable us to be obedient:

---

not his own but belong to obedience, and if thou withdraw them from obedience, thou wilt have to account them as lost. . . . Let the second caution be that thou never consider thy superior as less than if he were God, be the superior who he may, for to thee he stands in the place of God. And observe that the devil, the enemy of humility, meddles herein greatly. If thou consider thy superior as has been said, thou gainest and profitest greatly, but otherwise thy loss and harm are great. Keep thyself, therefore, with great vigilance from considering his character, his ways or his habits or any of his other characteristics, for, if thou do this, thou wilt do thyself the harm of exchanging Divine obedience for human, by being moved, or not being moved, only by the visible characteristics of thy superior, instead of by the invisible God Whom thou servest in his person. And thy obedience will be vain, or will be the more unfruitful, if thou take offence at any unpleasing characteristic in thy superior, or rejoice when thou findest him good and pleasant. For I tell thee that the devil has ruined the perfection of a great multitude of religious by causing them to consider these characteristics, and their obedience is of very little worth in the eyes of God, because they have considered these things and not paid sole respect to obedience. If you strive not until thou come to regard no one superior as of more importance than another, in so far as thine own feelings are concerned, thou canst in no wise become a spiritual person nor keep thy vows well" (Peers, *Complete Works of Saint John of the Cross*, 3.223–24).

502. "I shall not serve" (Jer. 2:20).

503. John Milton, *Paradise Lost*, 1.263, which reads: "Better to reign . . ."

a) learn to do *everything* under obedience—*submit all projects* and undertakings, whether spiritual or material, to the judgement of {one's} superior, father master or director, until one knows more or less what the score is;

b) be specially attentive to instructions and wishes of the superior; try to enter into the full meaning of his orders and counsels; train yourself to *understand* properly; train yourself in putting aside your own opinion to see it in his way;

c) cultivate distrust of your own judgement and of your own desires. You might not be as wise as you think. The fact that something looks good to you at the moment does not mean that it is right. Learn to submit your ideas and decisions to the judgement and appraisal of others, and follow their advice. *Docility* in all things helps us to be obedient. It makes us open-minded and plastic. Disobedient monks are often stupid.

4. *Universality of Obedience*: do not pick and choose in your obedience, obeying only the higher superiors, or only certain commands, or only what refers to the important things in community life. Obey *every* superior down to the one who has been put in charge of the afternoon work, even though he is not an officer of the monastery. Obey *even brethren* (READ {the} *Rule* of St. Benedict, c. 71 [p. 158][504]). Obey *every command*, even {about} small

504. "*Obedientiae bonum non solum abbati exhibendum est ab omnibus, sed etiam sibi invicem ita obediant fratres, scientes per hanc obedientiae viam se ituros ad Deum. Praemisso ergo abbatis aut praepositorum qui ab eo constituuntur imperio, cui non permittimus privata imperia praeponi, de cetero omnes juniores prioribus suis omni caritate et sollicitudine obediant. Quod si quis contentiosus reperitur, corripiatur. Si quis autem frater pro quavis minima causa, ab abbate vel a quocumque priore suo corripitur quolibet modo, vel si leviter senserit animos prioris cujuscumque contra se iratos vel commotos quamvis modice, mox sine mora tamdiu prostratus in terra ante pedes ejus jaceat satisfaciens, usque dum benedictione sanetur illa commotio. Quod qui contempserit facere, aut corporali vindictae subjaceat, aut, si contumax fuerit, de monasterio expellatur*" ("Not only shall the virtue of obedience be practised by all towards the abbot, but the brethren shall also obey one another, knowing that by this road of obedience will they go to God. The commands of the abbot or of the superiors appointed by him must rank first, and no unofficial commands take precedence

matters. Regard nothing as lightly to be omitted. Take even the smallest rules seriously, unless there is a proportionately grave motive for passing them by. A novice should never take upon himself to bypass the smallest rule, even if he thinks he has a good motive. He should submit the case to the father master or someone, to get the right slant and to put it under obedience, or at least obtain the requisite permission. This does not mean one must cultivate *servility*. *Servility* is not real obedience. A really obedient monk will also be able to learn where the nature of things demands that he make decisions for himself. If the novice ought to get permission for everything, this is primarily so that he may *learn* when permission is and is not necessary. A servile monk is not obedient; he is just a pest and a nuisance to the superior. He gets in the superior's way and often frustrates true obedience. His obedience in any case is almost entirely exterior. One should not make a fetish of small exterior points of observance, and certainly one should not take vanity in these little things or imagine that perfection consists in doing them. But one should desire every opportunity to obey and to give one's will to God by regularity. One should even obey *tacit* and *implicit* commands, or the unexpressed will of the superior, if we know what that will is. One should *anticipate* the commands and the will of the superior or the good of {the} brethren. A perfect religious does not have to be asked to do certain special jobs or to volunteer for burdensome tasks. However, do not presume to do things that are beyond your sphere, and don't butt into somebody else's business.

---

of them; but, for the rest, let all the juniors obey their seniors with all love and diligence. If anyone be found quarrelsome, let him be corrected. And if any brother, for however trifling a reason, be corrected in any way by the abbot, or any of his seniors, or if he perceive that any senior, in however small a degree, is displeased or angry with him, let him at once without delay cast himself on the ground at his feet, and lie there making reparation, until that displeasure is appeased and he bless him. But if anyone should disdain to do this, let him either undergo corporal punishment, or, if he be stubborn, let him be expelled from the monastery") (McCann, 158/159).

5. *Cultivate promptitude and zeal in obedience*: try to do everything promptly, cheerfully and well (READ {the} *Rule* of St. Benedict, c. 5, l. 9ff. [p. 32][505]).

6. Realize that one should obey even when the task is extremely displeasing or when the command is given in an unpleasant or even brutal manner. *Cultivate obedience under difficulties.*

505. "*Et veluti uno momento praedicta magistri jussio et perfecta discipuli opera, in velocitate timoris Dei, ambae res communiter citius explicantur, quibus ad vitam aeternam gradiendi amor incumbit. Ideo angustam viam arripiunt, unde Dominus dicit:* Angusta via est quae ducit ad vitam; *ut non suo arbitrio viventes vel desideriis suis et voluptatibus obedientes, sed ambulantes alieno judicio et imperio in coenobiis degentes abbatem sibi praeesse desiderant. Sine dubio hi tales illam Domini imitantur sententiam qua dicit:* Non veni facere voluntatem meam, sed ejus qui misit me. *Sed haec ipsa obedientia tunc acceptabilis erit Deo et dulcis hominibus, si quod jubetur non trepide, non tarde, non tepide, aut cum murmurio, vel cum responso nolentis efficiatur. Quia obedientia quae majoribus praebetur Deo exhibetur; ipse enim dixit:* Qui vos audit, me audit. *Et cum bono animo a discipulis praeberi oportet, quia* hilarem datorem diligit Deus. *Nam cum malo animo si obedit discipulus, et non solum ore sed etiam in corde si murmuraverit, etiamsi impleat jussionem, tamen acceptum jam non erit Deo, qui cor ejus respicit murmurantem, et pro tali facto nullam consequitur gratiam; immo poenam murmurantium incurrit, si non cum satisfactione emendaverit*" ("And almost in the same moment of time that the master's order is issued, is the disciple's work completed, in the swiftness of the fear of the Lord; the two things being rapidly accomplished together by those who are impelled by the desire of attaining life everlasting. Therefore they choose the narrow way, according to the Lord's words: *Narrow is the way which leadeth unto life;* so that not living by their own will, and obeying their own desires and passions, but walking by another's judgement and orders, they dwell in monasteries, and desire to have an abbot over them. Assuredly such as these imitate that saying of the Lord wherein he saith: *I came not to do my own will, but the will of him who sent me.* But this obedience itself will then be acceptable to God and pleasing to men, if what is commanded be not done timorously, or tardily, or tepidly, nor with murmuring or the raising of objections. For the obedience which is given to superiors is given to God, since he himself said: *He who listens to you, listens to me.* And disciples should give their obedience with a good will, because *God loveth a cheerful giver.* For if the disciple obey with an ill will, and murmur not only in words but even in his heart, then even though he fulfil the command, his work will not be acceptable to God, who sees that his heart is murmuring. For work such as this he will gain no reward; nay, rather, he will incur the punishment due to murmurers, unless he amend and make reparation") (McCann, 32, 34/33, 35).

This is most important because otherwise one will not be prepared for trial and hardship that must inevitably come later on in the religious life, and may indeed come most unexpectedly (READ the fourth degree of humility: *Rule*, c. 7 [p. 42][506]). Finally, one should *cultivate obedience out of love for Christ* and in close union with the dispositions with which He obeyed (read Philippians 2:5-15[507]).

506. "*Quartus humilitatis gradus est, si in ipsa obedientia, duris et contrariis rebus vel etiam quibuslibet irrogatis injuriis, tacita conscientia patientiam amplectatur, et sustinens non lassescat vel discedat, dicente Scriptura:* Qui perseveraverit usque in finem, hic salvus erit; *item:* Confortetur cor tuum, et sustine Dominum. *Et ostendens fidelem pro Domino universa etiam contraria sustinere debere, dicit ex persona sufferentium:* Propter te morte afficimur tota die; aestimati sumus ut oves occisionis. *Et securi de spe retributionis divinae subsequuntur gaudentes et dicentes:* Sed in his omnibus superamus propter eum qui dilexit nos. *Et item alio loco Scriptura:* Probasti nos, Deus, igne nos examinasti, sicut igne examinatur argentum: induxisti nos in laqueo; posuisti tribulationes in dorso nostro. *Et ut ostendat sub priore debere nos esse, subsequitur dicens:* Imposuisti homines super capita nostra. *Sed et praeceptum Domini in adversis et injuriis per patientiam adimplentes, qui percussi in maxillam praebent et aliam, auferenti tunicam dimittunt et pallium, angariati miliario vadunt duo, cum Paulo Apostolo falsos fratres sustinent, et maledicentes se benedicent*" ("The fourth degree of humility is that, meeting in this obedience with difficulties and contradictions and even injustice, he should with a quiet mind hold fast to patience, and enduring neither tire nor run away; for the Scripture saith: *He that shall persevere to the end shall be saved*; and again: *Let thy heart take courage, and wait thou for the Lord.* And showing how the true disciple ought to endure all things, however contrary, for the Lord, it saith in the person of sufferers: *For thy sake we face death at every moment. We are reckoned no better than sheep marked down for slaughter.* Then, confident in their hope of the divine reward, they go on with joy to declare: *But in all these things we overcome, through him that hath loved us.* And again in another place the Scripture saith: *Thou, O God, hast put us to the proof: thou hast tested us as men test silver in the fire. Thou hast led us into a snare: thou hast bowed our backs with trouble.* And to show that we ought to be under a superior, it goeth on to say: *Thou hast set men over our heads.* Moreover, in adversities and injuries they patiently fulfil the Lord's commands: when struck on one cheek they offer the other, when robbed of their tunic they surrender also their cloak, when forced to go a mile they go two, with the apostle Paul they bear with false brethren, and they bless those that curse them") (McCann, 42, 44/43, 45).

507. See above, n. 470.

Conclusion: Hildemar, in his commentary on the *Rule*, says: *Obedientia est gladius, scutum, cassis et caetera arma: et sicut perit ille, qui sine armis pugnat in proelio, ita et monachus perit, qui obedientiam respuit.*[508]

CONVERSION OF MANNERS

The second of the Benedictine vows is *conversio morum*, or more correctly *conversatio morum*: PROMITTO STABILITATEM MEAM, CONVERSIONEM MORUM MEORUM ET OBEDIENTIAM.[509] The vow of "conversion of manners" is perhaps the most difficult to understand according to the modern way of looking at it. It seems to us rather vague, and religious seldom get a clear idea of the precise obligation of the vow of conversion of manners. First, let us look at the familiar, though rather inadequate, treatment of the vow in the *Spiritual Directory*[510] (reading *not* advised):

1. By this vow "one engages himself to advance without intermission from evil to good, from good to better, and from better to perfection" (*SD*, p. 186[511]).

2. "To tend to perfection all one's life according to our Rules" (*idem*). (Whereas #1 above is confusing and misleading, #2 is an adequate and correct summary. Can one engage oneself *to advance without intermission*? In that event, not to advance, for one reason or another, would apparently be sufficient to constitute a sin against the vow of conversion of manners [?]. However, to "tend to perfection" means clearly the normal generous and faithful use of the means at our disposal for becoming perfect monks—taking account of inevitable human frailties.)

---

508. "Obedience is the sword, the shield, the helmet and the rest of the armor; and as he perishes who fights in a battle without armor, so also the monk perishes who rejects obedience" (*Vita et Regula SS. P. Benedicti: Una cum Expositione Regulae a Hildemaro Tradita* [Ratisbon: F. Pustet, 1880], 542).

509. See above, n. 452.

510. *Spiritual Directory*, Part III, chapter 3 (186–96).

511. Text reads: ". . . engages oneself to advance . . ."

3. {The} description of conversion of manners (p. 186) is good: transforming one's habits of thought and one's general behavior from those of a worldling to those of a monk, imitating Christ.

4. {It is} misleading when it says (p. 187) "tending to perfection by the purgative, illuminative, and unitive ways." In the *Rule* of St. Benedict there is nothing whatever to justify this idea, except in a vague and general way. It surely has nothing definite to do with the real obligation of the vow.

5. "All should purpose to go forward without ever believing that they have arrived at the bourne. . . . The most advanced should become yet more perfect" (187).[512] This may indeed be part of the *spirit* of the vow, but it is hardly an exact definition of its obligation: cf. "We must never deliberately say It is enough" (188).[513]

6. A good qualification is made on page 187: "The vow does not require that each of our actions be a step forward: this would be requiring the impossible."[514]

7. {It is} confusing on page 188 when it says that conversion of manners means using the *five vows and the Rule* to attain to perfection. This means that conversion of manners overlaps all the other vows. This requires clarification. It is true that poverty and chastity probably come under the vow of *conversio morum* itself. But a sin against obedience is a sin against obedience, and not against *conversio morum*. Would habitual disobedience become a sin against *conversio morum*? Again, this leads to further confusion.

8. "Conversion according to our Rules signifies the observance of the essential prescriptions without overlooking those of lesser importance" (189).[515] Again, this is the spirit of *conversio morum*, no doubt. But the essential obligation of the vow does not seem to be such that the infraction of the slightest rule, or the habitual neglect of small rules, constitutes a *sin against the vow*. It is

---

512. The second sentence quoted precedes the first in the text.
513. Text reads: ". . . never say . . ."
514. Text reads: ". . . forward in the way of perfection: . . ."
515. Text reads: ". . . less importance."

not clear whether or not this is what the writer intends. Probably he does not mean it to be taken in this way. But it is confusing.

9. Grave sins against the vow, according to the *Directory* (p. 189ff.):

a) Deliberate disposition to make no effort to tend to perfection; habitual neglect of means of perfection which are recognized as essential, "such as the serious duties of the christian life, the vows, and at least some observance of the Rules." Does this mean that if one habitually neglects the other vows, or habitually breaks a commandment, it is a sin against *conversio morum*? It would seem obvious that this is so: but the way it is put here is not clear or convincing. Here again, while speaking of grave sins against the vow, the writer says, "As soon as one says, *It is enough*, one is undone" (189). This would seem to indicate that to say one has gone far enough in the spiritual life and one is content to stay at the point reached {means} he commits *a grave sin*!!! This is surely fantastic, though of course it is quite true that one should always desire to advance and that in practice not to advance is to fall back. But we are now discussing what constitutes a *sin, not just a lack of the true spirit of the vow.*

b) One sins gravely against the vow of conversion of manners by "remaining in a state of sin [this makes sense], habitually transgressing in a serious degree the duties of the christian life, the vows of religion . . . etc." (189).[516] Again, {there is} overlapping and confusion.

10. Page 190 gives a good description of tepidity, obviously contrary to the spirit of the vow. One can easily agree that one main purpose of the vow is to prevent and to combat tepidity. The danger of tepidity in the monastic life is very great, and we may return to this subject later (READ p. 190 and top of 191[517]).

516. Text reads: ". . . remains . . . transgresses . . ."
517. "As the habit of committing serious faults is most prejudicial to this vow, so *tepidity is also very dangerous*, the more so because it is less feared. Tepidity is not the same as aridity since generosity of soul can coexist with spiritual

However, the trouble with this passage is that here he seems to imply that to remain in a state of tepidity constitutes a grave sin against the vow of conversion of manners, or at any rate a sin against the vow. But the matter is not made clear, and the reasons are not given in a convincing and definite manner. It is not quite clear what is being argued. But we certainly accept in principle that tepidity is a great evil and that the vow of conversion of manners is the monk's chief weapon against it.

11. The "spirit of the vow" according to the *Directory* {is} "to foster an ardent desire of perfection."[518] This is evident. Then {it} goes on with advice on humility, love of the *Rule* and of the

---

dryness. Neither are light faults promptly repaired a mark of tepidity. Habitual tepidity consists in *a state of indifference regarding venial sin*, attachment to such sin and committing it without disquietude. A tepid person commits such sins quite indifferently and feels no remorse; he lives in that wretched state without any qualm of conscience. This state is brought about by *habitual* resistance to grace, or by neglect of the recognized duty in light matters, or by absolutely refusing to God something that he demands; or rather by *habitual* negligence which does not amount to a determined refusal but which recoils in the presence of sacrifice. Tepidity is manifested by an unchecked habit of venial sin, a practical contempt of little things, constant infractions of Rule, dissipation, attachments, prayer said without fervor, the careless reception of the sacraments, and other negligences which one does not take sufficient care to correct. Tepidity obstructs the channels of grace, dims the light of faith, makes the conscience less delicate, makes nature rebel and holds the will in bondage. This is a dangerous state for a religious whose vocation requires him to strive after perfection; it is especially perilous in an Order such as ours which furnishes abundant means necessary to acquire and maintain fervor and leaves no excuse to the tepid. Its weakening effect becomes disastrous with time and the evil is all the more difficult to remedy inasmuch as grace and the ordinary means of amendment have been abused in a deplorable manner. The religious who has in his heart rashly disposed to descend in a career of negligence is according to St. Alphonsus 'in grave peril of being lost.' The Order is austere and renowned; but this is of no avail if one leads in it a lax life. Let those, therefore, who have fallen from their first fervor and who, after passing years in our contemplative and penitential life, would need to re-enter the noviciate—let these renounce evil, and reform their life by vigilance, prayer and the spiritual combat. They have, indeed, covered much ground, but alas! in a downward course."

518. *Spiritual Directory*, 192.

monastic state, etc.—all good things, and they should be attended to. The remainder of the chapter is spiritual counsel on the life of fervor, with some good observations in it; for instance: "It costs much less to the fervent religious to sanctify himself than it does to the tepid to drag along the heavy weight of his imperfections."[519] On page 195 there is good advice against discouragement and on the right attitude towards our inevitable faults.

We have discussed this chapter of the *Directory* in detail in view of the fact that it is practically the only source thus far available to our monks and novices on the most important subject of one of the main vows which they take. It is easy to see that this treatment is all right up to a point; it contains good advice, and it urges the monk to persevere fervently in his desire to be a saint. But due to *lack of sufficient knowledge of monastic tradition*, this chapter is inadequate and gives *a misleading notion of the obligation of the vow*. The attitude taken by the *Directory* is that the vow bears on *the subjective desire to advance from one degree to another in the interior life*. This is not the mind of St. Benedict. For St. Benedict the vow of conversion of manners is the vow to *persevere in the monastic state* and *to live and die as a monk*, having left the world, faithful to all the practices that distinguish a monk from the worldling, and especially poverty, chastity, enclosure, austerity, etc.

1. Conversion of Manners: THE TRADITIONAL IDEA

a) *Conversatio morum*: first of all in our discussion of the traditional meaning of *conversio morum*, we run up against the fact that the earliest manuscripts speak of *conversatio morum*. *Conversatio* is the original and authentic reading. What does it mean? Does it mean anything different from *conversio*? (N.B. the term *conversio morum*, which is on the whole easier to understand, came in very early and became universally accepted. It is used by the early commentators; in practice it was used throughout monastic tradition from early days.)

---

519. *Spiritual Directory*, 194.

(a) *Conversatio* is a familiar word in the *Rule*: *Processu vero conversationis et fidei*[520] (Prologue); *honestatem morum vel initium conversationis*[521] (last chapter). It signifies generally "manner of life" and especially monastic manner of life. Observance might take in part of its meaning. It is practically equivalent to *conversio*—a new or changed life. What does the monastic life mean to St. Benedict, Cassian, etc. {Philibert} Schmitz, OSB in {his} *Dictionnaire {de} Spiritualité* article *"Conversatio Morum"*[522] sums it up: "The monastic life for St. Benedict and Cassian consists in a life of constant struggle against the habits of the world, the vices, the passions and everything that can draw us away from God, and a life of continual effort to acquire virtues—it is the *vita actualis* or *activa* of Cassian."[523] *Conversatio morum* or *conversio morum* is simply the monastic life in its active aspect of struggle against vice and growth in virtue, the "spiritual combat" which is essential to make a monk: the *militia Christi*.[524]

(b) Some modern renderings {include}[525] "monastic life"[526] (Dom Butler), "monasticity of behaviour"[527] (Dom Chapman), "self-discipline"[528] (Dom McCann). Some ancient explanations {are as

---

520. McCann, 12 ("by progress in monastic commitment and in faith").

521. "authenticity of behavior and the beginning of monastic transformation" (c. 73 [McCann, 160, which reads: ". . . *morum aut initium* . . ."]).

522. *DS* 2, cols. 2206–12.

523. "La vie monastique pour l'un et pour l'autre [i.e., Cassian and Benedict] consiste dans une vie constante de lutte contre les habitudes du siècle, les vices, les passions, contre tout ce qui peut éloigner de Dieu, et dans une vie d'effort continu pour l'acquisition des vertus, en un mot elle est la *vita actualis, activa* de Cassien" (Schmitz, col. 2207).

524. Schmitz, col. 2208.

525. Cited in Schmitz, col. 2208.

526. "In three places in which 'conversio' is found in inferior MSS, 'conversatio' means simply the monastic life." He goes on to say, "'Conversatio morum suorum' . . . may perhaps best be rendered into English 'the conduct of one's life'" (Butler, 137).

527. Dom John Chapman, *Saint Benedict and the Sixth Century* (New York: Longmans, Green, 1929), 162; see his entire discussion of the question (207–31).

528. Justin McCann, OSB, *Saint Benedict* (New York: Sheed and Ward, 1937), c. 10, "The Second Vow" (147–67), which concludes: "How, then, at the last, must

follows} ({n.b. when} studying traditional texts, get {the} exact meaning—{this is the} scientific procedure): *Paul the Deacon* (taken up by Hildemar): *Conversio morum est* eradicatio vitiorum et plantatio virtutum . . . *si enim non eradicaveris vitia et quasi plantaveris virtutes non est conversio morum;*[529] *Bernard of Monte Cassino: Per conversionem morum obligatur monachus ut non saeculariter vivat, sed mores per conversionem a saecularibus habeat distinctos et diversos*[530] (a complete turning away from the ways of the world, and sin, and all that incites to sin, and a complete turning—"*conversio*"—to God; it means putting on Christ); *Boherius: In hoc renuntiat sibi frater, id est primae consuetudini vel vitae suae. Renuntiat autem et* moribus et delectationibus hujus saeculi, *sed* et sanguinitati corporali, *maxime ei quae impedire ejus propositum potest.* . . . CONVERSIO MORUM IDEM EST QUOD ABRENUNTIATIO MUNDANORUM;[531] *Turrecremata: Conversio morum per quam monachus obligat se ut non saeculariter vivat* . . . UT VERACITER MUTETUR IN VIRUM ALTERUM *UT POSSIT DICERE VIVO EGO JAM NON EGO VIVIT*

---

we translate St. Benedict's three vows? With full realization of the inadequacy of the words to convey the whole meaning of his pregnant language, and yet seeking to convey at least some part of that meaning in concise and simple English, I offer the brief form: Stability, Self-discipline, Obedience" (167). McCann never uses this term to translate "*conversatio*" in his edition of the *Rule;* see n. 107 (202–208) for an extensive discussion of the term.

529. "Conversion of manners is the eradication of vices and the planting of virtues . . . for if you have not eradicated vices and, as it were, planted virtues, there is no conversion of manners" (*PL* 102, col. 723, quoted in Schmitz, col. 2208).

530. "Through conversion of manners a monk is obligated not to live in a worldly way but through conversion to have ways of behaving distinctly different from those of the world" (*Bernardi I Abbatis Casinensis in Regulam S. Benedicti Expositio* [Monte Cassino: Ex Typographia Montis Casini, 1894], 364, which reads ". . . *obligatur ut non . . . distinctos habeat . . .*," quoted in Schmitz, col. 2209).

531. "In this a brother renounces himself, that is, his first manner of behavior and his life. He renounces both the patterns and the pleasures of this age, as well as blood relationships, and especially whatever can interfere with his profession. . . . Conversion of manners is the same as renunciation of worldly matters" (*Petri Boherii in Regulam S. Benedicti Commentarium,* ed. L. Allodi [Subiaco: 1908], 670, which reads: ". . . *conversio morum in hoc casu idem est . . .*," quoted in Schmitz, col. 2210; emphasis added).

VERO IN ME CHRISTUS;[532] *Haeften*: by *conversio morum* the monk promises to observe *quae* vitae monasticae sunt substantialia *et . . . illas
corporales observantias quae secundum Regulam observabantur eo
tempore quo professio facta est*[533] (Haeften sums up the obligation of the
vow—to which we return later—under three headings: (1) *omnimoda
saeculi renuntiatio;* (2) *exacta regulae observatio;* (3) *bonae consuetudines
loci*[534]); *Martène: Conversio morum est duplex: a malo ad bonum [eradi-
catio vitiorum]; de bono ad melius [plantatio virtutum];*[535] *Delatte:* C'est
l'adieu à la vie de péché, à la vie mondaine, avec direction de notre
activité vers les choses surnaturelles;[536] *Herwegen:* [D]ie Auswirkung
des Mönch-Seins im Leben der Tugend, im Streben nach Heiligkeit
und steht so im Gegensatz zu den Werken des Bösen, stellt positiv
die Nachfolge Jesu Christi dar.[537] *Philibert Schmitz,* summing up, says

532. "Conversion of manners, through which a monk obligates himself not
to live in a worldly manner . . . so that he may be truly changed into another
man and be able to say, It is no longer I who live but Christ lives in me" (*Regula
S. Benedicti, cum doctiss[imis] et piiss[imis] Commentariis Ioannis de Turre Cremata,
S.R.E. Cardinalis, et Smaragdi Abbatis. Item de viris illustribus ordinis S. Benedicti, Libri
IIII. Ioannis Trithemij, Abbatis Spanheimen[sis]* (Coloniae Agrippinae: Geruinum
Calenium & Hæredes Quentelios, 1575), 262–63, which reads: "*Morum conversa-
tio . . . vivit autem in me . . . ,*" quoted in Schmitz, col. 2210; emphasis added).

533. "the essential elements of the monastic life and those bodily observances which were observed according to the rule from that time at which profession was made" (*Disquisitionum Monasticarum Libri Duodecim* [Anvers, 1644],
421–23, which reads: "*. . . observationes quae . . . ,*" quoted in Schmitz, col. 2210;
emphasis added).

534. "complete renunciation of secular life; precise observance of the rule;
the good customs of the place," quoted by Martène (*PL* 66, col. 823C, which reads:
"*1. ad omnimodam renuntiationem saeculi; 2. ad exactam regulae observantiam; 3. ad
bonas consuetudines loci*").

535. "Conversion of manners is twofold: from evil to good [eradication of
vices]; from good to better [planting of virtues]" (*PL* 66, col. 822C).

536. "It is a farewell to the life of sin, to a worldly life, with the direction of
our activity toward supernatural things" (Paul Delatte, OSB, *Commentaire sur la
Règle de Saint Benoît,* 2nd ed. [Paris: Plon-Nourrit/G. Oudin, 1913], 444, quoted
by Schmitz, col. 2211).

537. "The practice of monastic life in a life of virtue, in striving for holiness,
stands in opposition to the works of evil and represents positively the following

the following:[538] (a) that if poverty and chastity are not mentioned specifically among our vows, it is because they are so essential to the monastic state that they belong obviously to that *conversio morum* which we have promised; he says that the opinion of those who think poverty and chastity come under obedience is "hardly probable"—it does not seem to concord with monastic tradition; (b) the vow of conversion of manners obliges us to the daily struggle to correct our vices and grow in virtue, to tend constantly to perfection in the monastic life, and to persevere in it to the end.

Conclusions: these texts give us the main traditional sources of monastic teaching on the vow of conversion of manners. Now let us sum this teaching up and make it our own so that we can see precisely what is meant by conversion of manners and what we promise by it.

1. We can endorse fully the basic definition given by our *Directory*:[539] TO TEND TO PERFECTION ALL ONE'S LIFE ACCORDING TO OUR RULES. This is a satisfactory definition of the obligation of our vow—but the explanations given later tend to confuse and obscure this plain definition by introducing subjective factors.

2. *Conversio* means a turning *away from the world* and a *turning to God*. Under the obligation of *conversio morum* comes the instrument of good works: *A SAECULI ACTIBUS SE FACERE ALIENUM*[540] (we shall look into this further in a moment).

3. *Conversio* means *fidelity in the use of certain well-defined means*: poverty and chastity; monastic virtues; our rules and observances; and all the monastic customs, etc., in the concrete milieu where we make this vow (n.b. {one should} not take {this} too rigidly). The novice who prepares to make this vow learns in what way the life

---

of Jesus Christ" (Ildefons Herwegen, OSB, *Sinn und Geist der Benediktinerregel* [Einsiedeln: Benziger, 1944], 336, quoted in Schmitz, col. 2211).

538. Col. 2211.

539. *Spiritual Directory*, 186.

540. "to make himself a stranger to the ways of the world" (*Rule*, c. 4 [McCann, 26, which reads: "*Saeculi . . .*"]).

led in his monastery constitutes a real separation from the world and a life with God; then he decides to live this life as it is lived in his community. This is worthy of special attention. By the vow of *conversio morum* we do not promise to live the monastic life in some *ideal* form, but according to the concrete observances of an established and fervent monastery of our choice. In all monasteries there may be deficiencies. Where there exist deficiencies, our vow of *conversio morum* demands not that we reform the monastery or stir up confusion by our criticisms, but that we strive to be good monks ourselves and do our own part to keep up the fervor and observance of the house. But a superior is obliged by his own vow and by his office to see that observance is kept on a high level, that is, on a level high enough to guarantee that the monks are really living "converted" and unworldly lives.

4. *A supine acceptance of any habit of sin is obviously against the vow* of conversion of manners. To have a habit of sin and not struggle against it would be a sin against the vow of *conversio morum*. Such an eventuality would be very unlikely, of course. The vow demands *concrete efforts to eradicate all our vices*. These efforts normally accord with the rules, observances and practices of our monastery, which are designed for this purpose. But rules {are} not {an} end in themselves—*use* rules when they are to be used.

5. The essence of the vow of conversion of manners {lies in} putting off the world—renouncing one's old ways; putting on Christ—acquiring new ways:

a) *Putting off the world*: *Ut non saeculariter vivat* (Bernard of Monte Cassino[541]): *abrenuntiatio mundanorum* (Boherius[542]); *omnimoda saeculi renuntiatio* (Haeften[543]). *What does this mean?*

---

541. "Let him not live in a worldly way" (Bernard, 364, quoted in Schmitz, col. 2209).

542. "The renunciation of worldly affairs" (Boherius, 670, quoted in Schmitz, col. 2210).

543. "The complete renunciation of the world" (Haeften, quoted in Martène [*PL* 66, col. 823C]).

(1) Obviously, it includes first of all everything that the common law of the Church forbids as unbecoming to religious (see p. {195} above): gambling, hunting, engaging in worldly business, etc.

(2) It also means, especially for us, keeping within our enclosure or on the monastic property, not leaving these without permission and a valid reason; cultivating a spirit of solitude and unworldliness; not seeking excuses to go back to the world and engage in its distractions. This also includes the serious practice of monastic silence and the avoidance of worldly amusement and conversations, radio, TV, etc. Not that these are evil in themselves, but to be immersed in them means to have a *worldly attitude*, which is entirely foreign to the monastic state.

(3) It means in general avoiding *everything which creates in the mind a worldly attitude* and keeps *alive a worldly sense of values*. The vow of conversion of manners would have us avoid, within reason and without scrupulosity, inordinate involvement in anything which fosters the spirit of ambition, vanity, the cult of success, pleasure, popularity. There is no problem whatever in this respect for anyone who stays in his monastery and lives the monastic life in its simplicity. The problem of attachment to worldly ways and worldly things begins when through one's *job* or for other reasons (*sickness*, etc.) one is taken out of the monastery or brought into a more direct contact with worldly people and affairs. Reasonable care and detachment from one's job and from business in general will protect the religious against these dangers. Danger exists for someone who, lacking the monastic spirit, lets himself be fascinated by worldly things, cheap music, advertising, TV, newspapers and magazines, drinks, conversations, smoking, etc. A monk who indulges freely in all these things and really forms an appetite for them is endangering his vow of conversion of manners because he is endangering his vocation. When a monk *knows* that indulging in these things out of the monastery (or in it) is a threat to his monastic life and to his interior spirit, he must not indulge in them. To indulge in them, knowing their danger, is putting oneself in an occasion of

sin against the vow of conversion of manners. To indulge them habitually, knowing the danger, *is a sin against the vow*. When a monk has a job which leads him into occasions of serious sin in the world, he is *obliged by virtue of his vow of conversion of manners* to discuss this problem either with his superior or at least with his confessor, and to take the steps which they advise. He is not strictly obliged to ask to be relieved of his job unless it is clear that it is a direct threat to his vocation. But in such a case, for him to conceal the facts and try to hold on to his job against the judgement of conscience or the advice of a confessor, he would sin, perhaps mortally, against his vow. If the superior does not agree to the existence of a danger and orders the monk to continue with his work, then the occasions of sin which he meets are to be regarded as necessary and not culpable. But the monk is still obliged to take all possible precautions. In practice, we should take a balanced and common-sense attitude. The monastic formation we receive should normally make us relatively impervious to the cheap and obvious temptations of the world. A monk should be able, if necessary, to move about in the world discreetly and with the poise of a mature and self-possessed person, a son of God, and a worthy priest (if he is a priest). For a mature religious, there is no harm in a discreet, ordinate use of certain things which belong more to the world than the monastery (v.g., looking at {a} magazine or newspaper, listening to {the} radio in the hospital, etc.), as long as he is able to leave these without regret on his return to the monastery. A craving for these things is to be regarded as highly undesirable. The reading of good literature, though not specifically religious, and enjoyment of good art, music, etc., which may not necessarily be religious, are not to be considered "worldly" and "evil" if they contribute to the monk's formation and education in the humanities. It is to be remembered that a solid and deep cultural formation contributes much to the spiritual life. For the young monk, the simple and obvious thing to do is to follow the guidance of superiors and instructors in this matter and to be docile about it. An excessive and unbalanced interest in secular art and literature can, of course, undermine one's vocation. Normally, a monastic vocation means leaving this behind, at least in a general way. There is so little time in {the} monastic life for the reading and prayer that we really need: it is not easy to see how much reading of secular literature can be fitted into our life. Such reading is not to be regarded as sinful, except in special circumstances.

b) *Putting on Christ*: as far as the vow of conversion of manners is concerned, the "putting on of Christ" means the sincere and generous use of those means which the monastic life provides for our reformation and transformation in Christ:

(1) *Penance*: one keeps his vow of conversion of manners by accepting and carrying out the penances which are an integral part of the *Rule* and observances of the monastery. This includes also everything which goes with one's monastic situation: the climate, the diet, the characteristic forms of work by which each community makes its living. To seek many unnecessary dispensations, to avoid all hard work and to get around many rules and difficulties *so that one's life is without any exterior bodily penance at all* would probably be against the vow of conversion of manners. One would have to go pretty far to commit a serious sin in this regard. Living in *luxury* with all the comforts of a rich man and without any labor at all would probably be a mortal sin against the vow of conversion of manners.

(2) *Prayer*: one keeps his vow of conversion of manners by devoting himself generously to the monastic life of prayer and cultivating a spirit of prayer, first of all by fidelity to the divine office, the *opus Dei*; by a Eucharistic life—Mass, communion, visits; by *lectio divina*; by silence, meditation, etc. Obligations of the vow in this regard {require one} to follow the monastic observances faithfully, in so far as one can. *The following would be violations of the vow*: (a) to be *always* absent from choir without sufficient reason would probably be a sin against the vow; (b) to *neglect lectio divina* continually and habitually without excuse might become a sin; (c) to neglect silence in a flagrant and habitual way could be a sin against this vow. (It should be obvious that occasional

absences from choir or breaches of silence or missing *lectio divina* do not constitute sins against the vow of conversion of manners. It is the *habitual neglect* of these means of prayer that is against the vow. Probably it takes a *formal contempt* and *deliberate abandonment* of these means of prayer to make a sin against the vow. Certainly, there could not be a mortal sin against the vow without formal contempt of prayer and its deliberate abandonment, with full understanding of the consequences and implications of this act. (This is hardly likely to happen to a monk in our time, though it may have happened in the past in decadent monasteries).

6. *When does the vow of conversion of manners oblige under sin?* The practical formulation of this question would be: to what extent is "secular life" sinful for a monk, and at what point does failure to strive after perfect imitation of Christ become a matter of sin?

a) *Poverty and Chastity*: these two great and characteristic obligations of the monk fall under the vow of conversion of manners. We shall treat them in detail shortly. For the moment it will suffice to say that ANY MORTAL OR VENIAL SIN AGAINST POVERTY AND CHASTITY IS A MORTAL OR VENIAL SIN AGAINST THE VOW OF CONVERSION OF MANNERS.

(1) against poverty: (a) when there is sufficient matter for a sin against justice, then there are *two* sins—one a sin against commutative justice (for instance, theft), and one against the vow of conversion of manners; or when there is a sin against another virtue—v.g., a sin of avarice—then there are also two sins—one against a virtue, one against the vow; (b) when the matter is *quite small in itself* but sufficient to constitute a sin in a monk, it is a sin only against the vow of conversion of manners—one sin only, not two.

(2) against chastity: every sin against chastity is a double sin for a monk with a vow—a sin against the sixth commandment and a violation of the vow, i.e. a sacrilege.

In confessing sins against the vows to a confessor in the monastery who knows one, it is sufficient to mention the sin itself. To a confessor outside, a stranger, one should make known the fact of one's religious vow but should say, "I sinned against my vow of poverty . . . or chastity." Outsiders haven't heard of the vow of conversion of manners.

b) *Characteristic and Essential Observances of the Monastic Life*: we are bound by our vow of conversion of manners to tend to perfection of self-renunciation and love for Christ by the use of certain well-defined means:

(1) *Enclosure and silence*: the General Chapter (Statutes: 1927, n. 1[544]) defines when violation of enclosure by egress constitutes a sin. {For} enclosure, (a) stealthy going out at night {is} always mortal; (b) going out during {the} day without permission {is} venial, {but} can be mortal in some monasteries where {the} superior decrees that {the} situation is dangerous. {For} silence, (a) {with regard to} letters, it is a mortal sin to send a letter against the will of the abbot and without his permission. This applies also to telephone calls and telegrams, but admits parvity

544. "For the purpose of more fully securing the maintenance of enclosure, the General Chapter made the following enactments: 1. Any religious who, taking advantage of the darkness, steals out of the enclosure at night without the permission (at least legitimately presumed) of his superior, commits a mortal sin, no matter what his intention or how brief his absence may be. 2. Permission given by the superiors to go out during the day time automatically expires at nightfall. Consequently a religious who, without a legitimate reason, is not back in the monastery at nightfall is considered as being out at night without permission and commits a mortal sin. 3. A religious who secretly leaves the enclosure during the day time without the permission, either explicit or legitimately presumed of the superiors, commits at least a venial sin. Furthermore, since the obligation of observing enclosure is a grave one for the religious of our Order, the General Chapter reminds Superiors of their equally grave responsibility of securing, by their utmost vigilance, the perfect maintenance of enclosure in their monasteries. It places on them the responsibility of deciding, after taking into consideration the requirements and circumstances of each house, whether or not a religious who leaves the enclosure secretly during the day time commits a mortal sin. This will depend on the duration of his absence, his reason for going out, and the location and lay-out of the monastery" (*Decisions and Definitions*, n.p.).

of matter (General Chapter[545]); (b) the superior can declare when and how violations of silence in his community are forbidden under pain of sin.

Besides these clearly defined cases, *which are probably to be considered as sins against the vow of conversion of manners rather than sins against obedience* (the question is open for debate), there are other cases of *habitual neglect* of silence or enclosure which could become sinful: (a) in the case where a religious can normally get permissions to go out or to talk *but habitually abuses the confidence of his superior* to go out more than necessary, to speak when not necessary, to indulge in worldly things when he is out, etc., etc.; habitual abuse in this matter is a sin against the vow; (b) isolated instances could also be sins: for instance, a monk gets permission to go out on a legal-seeming pretext, but in order to attend a party of a worldly character, which might be a danger to his morals; (c) habitual carelessness about silence, with frequent violations of silence, constitute a sin against the vow of conversion of manners; (d) in an isolated instance, a deliberate, long conversation, against {the} will of superiors and without even presumed permission, can be sinful (venial); reasons {include} the importance of silence in the monastic life and the fact that for any legitimate and useful speaking, permission can be obtained; violations of silence on a large scale would then be presumed to be accompanied by bad will and sinful dispositions; in a case of good faith, there would not be sin; in any case, these things should be confessed, not because they would be necessary matter, but because one with a vow of conversion of manners should make such things known and follow the judgement of a competent guide (sacramental confession {is} not necessary).

---

545. "The General Chapter declares that the term letters in Const. n 98 includes any communication by writing with the outside. Telephone communications are classed with letters. . . . Such correspondence without the knowledge of the Superior is of its nature a grievous sin admitting however lightness of matter" (quoted in "*Constitutions* of the Cistercians," 26a).

(2) *Fasting, Austerity*: eating between meals is probably not sinful, unless on a really inordinate scale (of course, we speak here only of eating between meals without permission or necessity). Failure to keep the monastic fasts may be sinful if there is no reason for the evasion and no real need for it. Failure to fast can easily become sinful in a healthy person who can fast and who needs to fast in order to control the flesh and prevent occasions of serious sin against the sixth commandment. *Habitual seeking of inordinate pleasures of taste* and comforts that are far beyond the common rule can easily be sins when there is no need for them. Our life is no longer physically hard, and normally every healthy person can get along with the common rule. No one should *exempt himself* from the common fasts and austerities, and {everyone} *should be slow to seek* legitimate exceptions in order to keep the spirit of the vow. The safest thing is to accept exceptions when imposed or prescribed and not to ask for them. One may, however, ask when there is very real need, especially if one is advised to do so by {one's} spiritual director.

(3) *Prayer and Lectio*: we have spoken of this above. Here we only repeat in summary form: *habitual and continual* absence from choir without sufficient reason could be a sin against the vow (venial); habitual neglect of *lectio divina* and meditative prayer could be a sin against the vow. We say *lectio and* meditative prayer—one can substitute for the other. *Contempt for all prayer and all interior life* and the deliberate abandonment of all prayer and interior life, except perhaps for an occasional purely external gesture, could be a mortal sin against the vow. In our opinion it would be a mortal sin because the life of prayer is so essential to the monastic state. (N.B. of course in certain circumstances, for instance in a case of severe mental strain, scruples or something like that, such a step might be necessary and would obviously not be sinful and would not imply contempt.) In practice, the case of "contempt" for all prayer is theoretical, because before one reached such a point he would already have abandoned his vocation in any case, thereby sinning mortally.

(4) *Manual Labor, Common Life*: it is essential to the monastic state that a monk contribute to the support of his monastic community in whatever way he can, and that he bear his fair share in the burdens of community life. We have discussed above (see p. {266}) cases of refusal to work or evasion of work which would be sins against the vow of obedience. The vow of conversion of manners could be violated by a *habitual neglect of all work* or of all sharing in the burdens of the common life. A monk who *out of contempt, pride, laziness, etc. would refuse all work* and do absolutely nothing to help support his community, when able to do so, would probably sin gravely against his vow of conversion of manners. Note, however, for this sin to be grave, it would have to imply not only the refusal to work and the *fact of not doing any* work whatsoever, but also at the same time continuing to live well, and perhaps very well, at the community's expense. A note of definite *worldliness* must be included for mortal sin. The *evasion of manual work*, habitually and constantly, in an order like ours where it is of great importance, without any excusing cause and without compensating for it by a proportionately more important contribution in some other form of work, might be a sin (venial). The above thoughts are mere suggestions and opinions, *salvo meliori judicio.*[546]

c) *The Monastic State as such*: we have offered some tentative opinions as to what might constitute sins against the vow of conversion of manners in various important observances of the monastic life. On these points there might be considerable difference of opinion. Perhaps the norms laid down above could be admitted as probable. It is of little use to split hairs about most of these points. In practice, it is important for the monk to cultivate a *fervent spirit of regularity* in order to preserve his monastic vocation. We can now come to definite and clear-cut violations of the vow about which there is no doubt. THE CHIEF SIN AGAINST THE VOW OF CONVERSION OF MANNERS, BESIDES

546. "unless there is a better conclusion."

VIOLATIONS OF POVERTY AND CHASTITY MENTIONED ABOVE, WOULD
BE TO ABANDON THE MONASTIC STATE AND THE PURSUIT OF PERFEC-
TION without any valid reason and return to the world and its
ways. *Conversio morum* means living as a monk and leaving the
world altogether in order to seek God. To give this up, by *flight
or apostasy*, would be a *clear mortal sin against the vow of conversion of manners*. In our Order, both these sins bring with them the
censure of excommunication:

APOSTASY: what is an apostate? Canon 644, n. 1, defines
apostasy as follows: an apostate is "one who has made *profession of perpetual* vows whether solemn or simple, who unlawfully
leaves his religious house *with the intention of not returning*, [or
who] with the intention of withdrawing himself from religious
obedience does not return to his house though he has lawfully
left it."[547] The apostasy referred to here is *desertion of the religious
life*, as distinct from apostasy from holy orders (Canon 2379[548])
and apostasy from the faith (Canon 1325, n. 2[549]). Note: only a
solemnly professed monk in our Order can be an apostate; simple
profession with us is always temporary—a simple professed
can be guilty of *flight* in the eyes of the law, but not of apostasy.

Distinctions and questions: the *crime* of apostasy, the exterior
act of apostatizing or formal and material desertion of the religious state, comes under excommunication. The *sin* of apostasy
can be purely interior—the *formal intention* of apostatizing. This
does not merit excommunication, but it remains a mortal sin
against the vow of conversion of manners. In the sight of the law,
a simple professed who leaves with no intention of returning is
not considered an apostate. But in view of our vow of conversion
of manners, if he deserts the monastic life altogether, and without
reason, it is probable, if not certain, that he commits a mortal sin

---

547. "*Apostata a religione dicitur professus a votis perpetuis sive sollemnibus
sive simplicibus qui e domo religiosa illegitime egreditur cum animo non redeundi, vel
qui, etsi legitime egressus, non redit eo animo ut religiosae obedientiae sese subtrahat*"
(*Codex Iuris Canonici*, 218).

548. *Codex Iuris Canonici*, 752.

549. *Codex Iuris Canonici*, 452.

against the vow. The reason why this is less certain than the case of a solemnly professed religious is because of the difference in their juridical condition—a simple professed is not bound for life. Does a simple or solemn professed who is guilty of *flight* commit a mortal sin against the vow of conversion of manners? The answer would seem to be YES, because in our Order this sin is punished by excommunication *ipso facto*, and this would not be possible if it were not mortal. It can be disputed whether this is a sin against conversion of manners or obedience. It can be one or the other, in our opinion. {The} difference {lies in} the motive. If one flies to get away from the authority of the superior, it is a sin against obedience. If one flies to get away from monastic observance, then it is against conversion of manners, especially if there is danger of sins against chastity, etc. NOTE: *a religious who flies from religion with a member of the opposite sex is ipso facto excommunicated and dismissed from the Order* (cf. Canon 646, n. 1[550]). This applies also to those who attempt matrimony, even though not flying from religion. HERE WE HAVE THE MOST OBVIOUS AND INDISPUTABLE CASE OF A GRAVE SIN AGAINST THE VOW OF CONVERSION OF MANNERS. With this clear case in mind, so evident and so obvious, we can easily see how confused and inadequate is the presentation of the matter in the *Directory* (see above, p. {274ff.}).

SUMMARY: for the sake of clarity, we can resume this section on the obligations of the vow and the violations which involve sin.

MORTAL SINS:

1. There is grave sin against the vow of conversion of manners whenever there is a *grave violation of poverty or chastity*.

2. There is a most grave sin against the vow of conversion of manners and also a crime punishable by excommunication when a religious *abandons the monastic state* permanently by apostasy or temporarily by flight (even {an} interior intention {to do so constitutes} grave sin).

550. *Codex Iuris Canonici*, 219.

3. There is a most grave sin against the vow and a crime punishable by excommunication and automatic dismissal from the Order when a member of the Order *takes flight from it with a member of the opposite sex.*

These are all clear-cut cases of mortal sin against the vow of conversion of manners. There is no dispute about the seriousness of the obligation in these cases.

4. There may be mortal sin against the vow of conversion of manners when out of contempt a monk formally gives up *all use* of certain essential means to monastic perfection, such as prayer, enclosure, etc., or when he shows *complete contempt for all observance.* (Individual violations of enclosure are punished by the law of the Order and are sins.)

5. There may be mortal sin against the vow of conversion of manners when a monk refuses to take any steps to overcome a habit of serious sin, or when he does *nothing* to prevent total loss of vocation.

The above cases are more hypothetical, and the opinions offered are only probable at best.

VENIAL SINS:

1. Venial sins against the vow of conversion of manners can be committed by varying degrees of contempt, etc. in neglect of monastic observance, lack of regularity, voluntary tepidity in {the} interior life, etc.

2. The chief venial sins against the vow would probably consist in *habitual attachment* to worldly pleasures and occupations which militate against the monastic life: v.g., drinking, smoking, going about in the world, consorting with seculars without necessity, TV, worldly reading, movies, etc. Toleration in ourselves of definitely worldly habits, even though not in themselves sinful, can be venial sin against {the} vow. But the attachment must be notable—{an} occasional drink or cigarette would not necessarily be a sin. Everything would depend on the person and the circumstances.

3. Note that habitually worldly conduct on the part of a monk could be a mortal sin by reason of grave *scandal* or by reason of the *occasion* of serious sin for the monk himself.
Caution: even voluntary neglect of certain small rules is *not* necessarily sinful, but it ought to be avoided, and regularity ought to be cultivated in order to preserve the spirit of the vow. Carelessness in keeping the usages, even though voluntary, is not necessarily a sin against the vow of conversion of manners, but we must avoid negligence and scandal.

The SPIRIT OF THE VOW OF CONVERSION OF MANNERS: we have now examined in some detail the nature of the *obligation* which is assumed by the monk who makes a vow of conversion of manners. We have tried to determine what might be a sin against the vow. This is something that one has to know. But to know only this is to have a false idea of the vow and of its purpose. Such a view would be merely one-sided and exterior. In no other vow is the *spirit* more important than in this one. We may say that the vow of obedience is the most important of the vows from the point of view of *discipline*. But a monk may be perfect in obedience and still lack the true monastic spirit. It is false and misleading, therefore, to treat obedience as being the "whole" of the monastic life and regard everything else as subsidiary to it. In reality, the vow of conversion of manners, particularly in its spirit, *is what really makes the monk*. To observe the letter of the vow of conversion of manners would be even more insufficient than the mere literal observance of obedience. If a monk has the letter of obedience yet lacks the spirit, he nevertheless obeys and carries out his duties externally. And this is very important. But if a monk merely refrains from apostatizing and merely keeps his monastic obligations externally without the spirit of conversion of manners, his monastic life will be more or less of a sham; it will be empty and sterile; it will not enable him really to grow as he should; it will not be a spiritual life of transformation in Christ. This is all the more important in view of the fact that recent popes have insisted so strongly on *renovation of the religious spirit* in all orders, as part of a universal campaign for *Christian renewal* in everything. "Religious must by a continual struggle overcome the concupiscence of the flesh, the concupiscence of the eyes and the pride of life, becoming ever more holy and more tireless collaborators with God in obtaining the salvation of the human race" (Pius XII).[551]

What is meant by the *spirit* of the vow? The literal exterior observance of the obligations is something *material*; it does not of itself contribute anything special to the monk's interior perfection if the spirit is lacking. Staying within the enclosure, renouncing possessions, keeping silence would all be worthless if one did not know why he was doing these things, and had no appreciation of their meaning, and did not know how to use them in order to love God more. The *spirit* of the vow implies two things: (a) *understanding* (appreciation) of the motives for renouncing the world; (b) *love* for the monastic life and the renunciations it involves. One must know the meaning of the monastic life and freely embrace it for personal and spiritual motives. The spirit of the vow of conversion of manners *is a deep love of the monastic life of renunciation and prayer*, based on an appreciation of the fact that by this life *we can come to find God, Whom we seek with all our heart*.

I. SEEKING GOD: St. Benedict believes that the most reliable indication that a novice has a true vocation is the fact that he "truly seeks God."[552] If one does not seek God in the monastery, then his life of conversion of manners has no deep inner meaning; it is without soul; it does not imply a real "change of heart." The soul and spirit of the vow is then to "prefer absolutely nothing to Christ,"[553] as St. Benedict says. This means in fact a life of love for

---

551. ". . . *ut adsiduo bello concupiscentiam carnis, concupiscentiam oculorum et superbiam vitae edometis atque inde sanctiores usque evadatis et in procuranda humanae subolis salute alacres Dei administri sitis*" (Pius XII, *Annus Sacer* [December 8, 1950], allocution to the International Congress of Religious [*Acta Apostolica Sedis*, 43.1 (1951), 35], citing 1 Jn. 2:16).

552. "*revera Deum quaerit*" (*Rule*, c. 58 [McCann, 130/131]).

553. "*Christo omnino nihil praeponant*" (*Rule*, c. 72 [McCann, 160]).

another, in which we place the beloved before all else and forget ourselves for the beloved. The first basic element of the spirit of conversion of manners is the motive of love by which we seek God and prefer Him to ourselves, renouncing all seeking of self.

II. LOVE OF RENUNCIATION: just as in our baptismal vows we renounce Satan in order to give ourselves to God, so in our monastic vows we are keenly conscious of the fact that fallen man in this world leads *a divided life*. On the one hand, we are attracted to false goods, to inordinate pleasures, to self-satisfaction, to self-love. Behind the false front offered by the "world" and so attractive to the flesh, we realize the hidden presence of "the enemy"—that mysterious fallen spirit, a creature of great power, who is opposed with all his being to God and out of hatred for God wishes to see the divine image defiled in our own souls. Hence we realize that we are in reality caught in a *spiritual battle*. READ 1 JOHN 2:15-18:[554] the world, concupiscence, and Antichrist; *idem* 3:2-14:[555] we are the sons of God; the sons of God do not sin.

554. "Love not the world, nor the things which are in the world. If any man love the world, the charity of the Father is not in him. For all that is in the world, is the concupiscence of the flesh, and the concupiscence of the eyes, and the pride of life, which is not of the Father, but is of the world. And the world passeth away, and the concupiscence thereof: but he that doth the will of God, abideth for ever. Little children, it is the last hour; and as you have heard that Antichrist cometh, even now there are become many Antichrists: whereby we know that it is the last hour."

555. "Dearly beloved, we are now the sons of God; and it hath not yet appeared what we shall be. We know, that, when he shall appear, we shall be like to him: because we shall see him as he is. And every one that hath this hope in him, sanctifieth himself, as he also is holy. Whosoever committeth sin committeth also iniquity; and sin is iniquity. And you know that he appeared to take away our sins, and in him there is no sin. Whosoever abideth in him, sinneth not; and whosoever sinneth, hath not seen him, nor known him. Little children, let no man deceive you. He that doth justice is just, even as he is just. He that committeth sin is of the devil: for the devil sinneth from the beginning. For this purpose, the Son of God appeared, that he might destroy the works of the devil. Whosoever is born of God, committeth not sin: for his seed abideth in him, and he can not sin, because he is born of God. In this the children of God are manifest, and the children of the devil. Whosoever is not just, is not of God, nor he that loveth not

Sin is the mark of those who give themselves to the devil, love of the brethren the mark of those who belong to God. These two passages give us a deep insight into the spirit of monastic renunciation. It is born of a holy fear of offending God by sin and of a realization that it is very easy to fall into sin unless one takes steps to renounce the world and deny oneself. Not that a man cannot be saved outside the cloister or become a saint outside the cloister, but there is always danger in "the world." Hence St. Benedict insists on *a saeculi actibus se facere alienum*: to be a stranger to the ways and principles of the world; not to know how to "get along" in the world; to be utterly out of place, helpless, stupid in worldly things; to be a fool for the sake of Christ—foolish and ridiculous in worldly things but wise in the things of God. What is worldly wisdom? Knowing how to get one's own way, how to manipulate others, how to "use" others and take advantage of them, how to get ahead by trickery, graft, gall, push, etc., how to have a good time, how to make a good bargain, etc., etc.

a) *Hence the monk renounces "the world"* and takes special care to leave all that savors of the world far behind him. For the devil is in "the world." READ Apocalypse 12 *in toto*:[556] a revealing

his brother. For this is the declaration, which you have heard from the beginning, that you should love one another. Not as Cain, who was of the wicked one, and killed his brother. And wherefore did he kill him? Because his own works were wicked: and his brother's just. Wonder not, brethren, if the world hate you. We know that we have passed from death to life, because we love the brethren. He that loveth not, abideth in death."

556. "And a great sign appeared in heaven: A woman clothed with the sun, and the moon under her feet, and on her head a crown of twelve stars: And being with child, she cried travailing in birth, and was in pain to be delivered. And there was seen another sign in heaven: and behold a great red dragon, having seven heads, and ten horns: and on his heads seven diadems: And his tail drew the third part of the stars of heaven, and cast them to the earth: and the dragon stood before the woman who was ready to be delivered; that, when she should be delivered, he might devour her son. And she brought forth a man child, who was to rule all nations with an iron rod: and her son was taken up to God, and to his throne. And the woman fled into the wilderness, where she had a place prepared by God, that there they should feed her a thousand two hundred sixty

chapter which must have been very much present to the primitive Fathers of monasticism. The Church, the woman clothed with the sun, the great dragon, the battle in heaven, and especially line 12: "Woe to the earth, for the devil has come down to you . . . knowing that he has but a short time" etc. READ also Apocalypse 13:1-9:[557] the world adores the dragon, who wars on the saints.

---

days. And there was a great battle in heaven, Michael and his angels fought with the dragon, and the dragon fought and his angels: And they prevailed not, neither was their place found any more in heaven. And that great dragon was cast out, that old serpent, who is called the devil and Satan, who seduceth the whole world; and he was cast unto the earth, and his angels were thrown down with him. And I heard a loud voice in heaven, saying: Now is come salvation, and strength, and the kingdom of our God, and the power of his Christ: because the accuser of our brethren is cast forth, who accused them before our God day and night. And they overcame him by the blood of the Lamb, and by the word of the testimony, and they loved not their lives unto death. Therefore rejoice, O heavens, and you that dwell therein. Woe to the earth, and to the sea, because the devil is come down unto you, having great wrath, knowing that he hath but a short time. And when the dragon saw that he was cast unto the earth, he persecuted the woman, who brought forth the man child: And there were given to the woman two wings of a great eagle, that she might fly into the desert unto her place, where she is nourished for a time and times, and half a time, from the face of the serpent. And the serpent cast out of his mouth after the woman, water as it were a river; that he might cause her to be carried away by the river. And the earth helped the woman, and the earth opened her mouth, and swallowed up the river, which the dragon cast out of his mouth. And the dragon was angry against the woman: and went to make war with the rest of her seed, who keep the commandments of God, and have the testimony of Jesus Christ. And he stood upon the sand of the sea."

557. "And I saw a beast coming up out of the sea, having seven heads and ten horns, and upon his horns ten diadems, and upon his heads names of blasphemy. And the beast, which I saw, was like to a leopard, and his feet were as the feet of a bear, and his mouth as the mouth of a lion. And the dragon gave him his own strength, and great power. And I saw one of his heads as it were slain to death: and his death's wound was healed. And all the earth was in admiration after the beast. And they adored the dragon, which gave power to the beast: and they adored the beast, saying: Who is like to the beast? and who shall be able to fight with him? And there was given to him a mouth speaking great things, and blasphemies: and power was given to him to do two and forty months. And he opened his mouth unto blasphemies against God, to blaspheme

b) *Furthermore, the world is passing away and is marked for destruction.* READ Apocalypse 17:1-6:[558] the scarlet woman, drunk with the blood of the saints; 18:1ff.:[559] the fall of Babylon—especially {verse} 4: Go out from her, my people, etc.; 20-24:[560] the

---

his name, and his tabernacle, and them that dwell in heaven. And it was given unto him to make war with the saints, and to overcome them. And power was given him over every tribe, and people, and tongue, and nation. And all that dwell upon the earth adored him, whose names are not written in the book of life of the Lamb, which was slain from the beginning of the world. If any man have an ear, let him hear."

558. "And there came one of the seven angels, who had the seven vials, and spoke with me, saying: Come, I will shew thee the condemnation of the great harlot, who sitteth upon many waters, With whom the kings of the earth have committed fornication; and they who inhabit the earth, have been made drunk with the wine of her whoredom. And he took me away in spirit into the desert. And I saw a woman sitting upon a scarlet coloured beast, full of names of blasphemy, having seven heads and ten horns. And the woman was clothed round about with purple and scarlet, and gilt with gold, and precious stones and pearls, having a golden cup in her hand, full of the abomination and filthiness of her fornication. And on her forehead a name was written: A mystery; Babylon the great, the mother of the fornications, and the abominations of the earth. And I saw the woman drunk with the blood of the saints, and with the blood of the martyrs of Jesus. And I wondered, when I had seen her, with great admiration."

559. "And after these things, I saw another angel come down from heaven, having great power: and the earth was enlightened with his glory. And he cried out with a strong voice, saying: Babylon the great is fallen, is fallen; and is become the habitation of devils, and the hold of every unclean spirit, and the hold of every unclean and hateful bird: Because all nations have drunk of the wine of the wrath of her fornication; and the kings of the earth have committed fornication with her; and the merchants of the earth have been made rich by the power of her delicacies. And I heard another voice from heaven, saying: Go out from her, my people; that you be not partakers of her sins, and that you receive not of her plagues" (vv. 1-4).

560. "Rejoice over her, thou heaven, and ye holy apostles and prophets; for God hath judged your judgment on her. And a mighty angel took up a stone, as it were a great millstone, and cast it into the sea, saying: With such violence as this shall Babylon, that great city, be thrown down, and shall be found no more at all. And the voice of harpers, and of musicians, and of them that play on the pipe, and on the trumpet, shall no more be heard at all in thee; and no craftsman of any art whatsoever shall be found any more at all in thee; and the sound of the

destruction of Babylon. In the limited time that remains before the destruction of Babylon, the servants of God must be "signed" by the angel: READ Apocalypse 7:1-4.[561] The perspectives of monastic renunciation and conversion of manners are therefore by no means merely moral or ethical or psychological. They are *supernatural and apocalyptic*. The *vow of conversion of manners has an entirely eschatological spirit*. We renounce the world, put off the old man and put on the new, in order that when the Judgement comes we may be found in Christ, and signed with His Cross, and washed in His Precious Blood, and not marked with the sign of the beast and numbered among the followers of Antichrist. Hence conversion of manners is something much more fundamental than mere "good behavior" or even asceticism. It is renunciation of everything that belongs to this world in order to "pass over" to the Kingdom of God. This must not be taken in the sense that the world is considered "evil"—far from it. But God's creation is unable to help or to sanctify anyone unless the Spirit of God has taken possession of him. Then created things are restored to their original function as means to unite us to God and to awaken love in our hearts at all times. Otherwise, creatures become a snare. The difference lies not in the creatures themselves but in our hearts. If we are full of self-love, then creatures contribute to our ruin. But if we are purified by grace, then creatures help us to love God.

---

mill shall be heard no more at all in thee; And the light of the lamp shall shine no more at all in thee; and the voice of the bridegroom and the bride shall be heard no more at all in thee: for thy merchants were the great men of the earth, for all nations have been deceived by thy enchantments. And in her was found the blood of prophets and of saints, and of all that were slain upon the earth."

561. "After these things, I saw four angels standing on the four corners of the earth, holding the four winds of the earth, that they should not blow upon the earth, nor upon the sea, nor on any tree. And I saw another angel ascending from the rising of the sun, having the sign of the living God; and he cried with a loud voice to the four angels, to whom it was given to hurt the earth and the sea, Saying: Hurt not the earth, nor the sea, nor the trees, till we sign the servants of our God in their foreheads. And I heard the number of them that were signed, an hundred forty-four thousand were signed, of every tribe of the children of Israel."

c) *Hence the most important thing is the renunciation of self.* A man who has renounced himself can use the things of the world in peace and impunity; they will bear a fruitful part in his life. But a man who has renounced the things of the world yet still not renounced himself is in an even worse position than before, for his asceticism entrenches him in the most dangerous form of pride. The most fundamental thing in the spirit of the vow of conversion of manners is the *renunciation of self* and its correlative, *the love of Christ.* ABNEGARE SEMETIPSUM SIBI, UT SEQUATUR CHRISTUM (*Rule*: Instruments of Good Works).[562]

d) *The monk embraces the monastic life as the formula perfectae poenitentiae:*[563] How are we going to renounce the world and ourselves? Can such an important undertaking be left to chance? Can we take the risk of error by trying to find our own way in the darkness of the present life? The monastic way is the way of the first disciples of Christ, preserved faithfully by the Church. It is the "form of perfect penance," as our *Exordium Magnum* describes it. In the monastic life there is the safe, universal and perfect way of renouncing self, not by mere ascetic fortitude and feats of penance, but by the way of *poverty and the common life, which was the way of the first apostles.* {See} ACTS 4:32-35: Christian renunciation is not the mere rejection of created things and the goods of this world. It is the *sharing* of these goods with others who do not have them. Thus created things are at the same time sacrificed and redeemed. They are offered to God when we give them up. They are given to Christ in our brother. They are respected and ennobled by their use by the brethren. They remain a consolation and a joy to us, spiritually, when they are used by Christ in the brethren. Thus we possess them without possessing them, and possessing nothing become masters of all things.

---

562. "to deny oneself in order to follow Christ" (c. 4 [McCann, 26]; emphasis added).

563. See above, n. 231.

III. Love of Good Works: it is not sufficient for us to be "the sons of God"; we must also live and act as sons of God. We have to do the good things that are willed for us by our heavenly Father, that we may manifest His love in the world and give Him glory. Read St. Matthew 5:14-16:[564] "You are the light of the world . . . so let your light shine before men that they may see your good works," etc. Read St. John 8:28-51,[565] a complex and

564. "You are the light of the world. A city seated on a mountain cannot be hid. Neither do men light a candle and put it under a bushel, but upon a candlestick, that it may shine to all that are in the house. So let your light shine before men, that they may see your good works, and glorify your Father who is in heaven."

565. "Jesus therefore said to them: When you shall have lifted up the Son of man, then shall you know, that I am he, and that I do nothing of myself, but as the Father hath taught me, these things I speak: And he that sent me, is with me, and he hath not left me alone: for I do always the things that please him. When he spoke these things, many believed in him. Then Jesus said to those Jews, who believed him: If you continue in my word, you shall be my disciples indeed. And you shall know the truth, and the truth shall make you free. They answered him: We are the seed of Abraham, and we have never been slaves to any man: how sayest thou: you shall be free? Jesus answered them: Amen, amen I say unto you: that whosoever committeth sin, is the servant of sin. Now the servant abideth not in the house for ever; but the son abideth for ever. If therefore the son shall make you free, you shall be free indeed. I know that you are the children of Abraham: but you seek to kill me, because my word hath no place in you. I speak that which I have seen with my Father: and you do the things that you have seen with your father. They answered, and said to him: Abraham is our father. Jesus saith to them: If you be the children of Abraham, do the works of Abraham. But now you seek to kill me, a man who have spoken the truth to you, which I have heard of God. This Abraham did not. You do the works of your father. They said therefore to him: We are not born of fornication: we have one Father, even God. Jesus therefore said to them: If God were your Father, you would indeed love me. For from God I proceeded, and came; for I came not of myself, but he sent me: Why do you not know my speech? Because you cannot hear my word. You are of your father the devil, and the desires of your father you will do. He was a murderer from the beginning, and he stood not in the truth; because truth is not in him. When he speaketh a lie, he speaketh of his own: for he is a liar, and the father thereof. But if I say the truth, you believe me not. Which of you shall convince me of sin? If I say the truth to you, why do you not believe me? He that is of God, heareth the words of God. Therefore you hear them not, because

important pericope: Christ does always those things which please the Father (vv. 28-29). To be His disciples, we must "continue in His word," and the truth shall make us free. If we do not do this, we shall instead be the servants of sin (34). If the Jews are the sons of Abraham, let them do the works of Abraham (39). Instead, they do the works of their father the devil and seek to kill Him (44). If we hear His word and keep it, we shall not taste death forever (51). We will desire to bear much fruit, therefore, and to give glory to the Father. READ St. John 15:1-8:[566] but what are these good works? They are all summed up in LOVE. Faith is the root of their goodness (this is the work of God, that you believe in Him whom He hath sent[567]).

St. Benedict lists many typical works that are good and belong to a son of God. Chapter 4 of the *Rule*—The Instruments of Good Works—gives us many indications of the true spirit of conversion of manners in this regard: first, to love God with one's whole heart, one's whole mind and all one's strength, and to love one's brother as oneself. This contains all the rest. This is the perfect spirit of conversion of manners, and everything

---

you are not of God. The Jews therefore answered, and said to him: Do not we say well that thou art a Samaritan, and hast a devil? Jesus answered: I have not a devil: but I honour my Father, and you have dishonoured me. But I seek not my own glory: there is one that seeketh and judgeth. Amen, amen I say to you: If any man keep my word, he shall not see death for ever."

566. "I am the true vine; and my Father is the husbandman. Every branch in me, that beareth not fruit, he will take away: and every one that beareth fruit, he will purge it, that it may bring forth more fruit. Now you are clean by reason of the word, which I have spoken to you. Abide in me, and I in you. As the branch cannot bear fruit of itself, unless it abide in the vine, so neither can you, unless you abide in me. I am the vine; you the branches: he that abideth in me, and I in him, the same beareth much fruit: for without me you can do nothing. If any one abide not in me, he shall be cast forth as a branch, and shall wither, and they shall gather him up, and cast him into the fire, and he burneth. If you abide in me, and my words abide in you, you shall ask whatever you will, and it shall be done unto you. In this is my Father glorified; that you bring forth very much fruit, and become my disciples."

567. Jn. 6:29.

in the monastic life should be seen as a means of putting this into practice. Otherwise, if we just carry out a lot of prescriptions for their own sake, we will not have the spirit of conversion of manners at all, but a mere spirit of literalism without life and without purpose. What are some characteristic groups of good works St. Benedict adds to this one? (a) works of abnegation: *corpus castigare, jejunium amare, voluntatem propriam odire;*[568] (b) works of mercy: *pauperes recreare, infirmum visitare, dolentem consolari;*[569] (c) works of meekness: *iram non perficere, injuriam non facere, sed factas patienter sufferre, maledicentes se non remaledicere, persecutionem sustinere;*[570] (d) works of truth: *veritatem ex corde et ore proferre, non jurare, pacem falsam non dare;*[571] (e) works of love: *caritatem non derelinquere, inimicos diligere, nullum odire, invidiam non exercere, contentionem non amare, in Christi amore pro inimicis orare, cum discordante ante solis occasum in pacem redire, nihil amori Christi praeponere;*[572] (f) works of prayer: *diem judicii timere, orationi frequenter incumbere, mala sua . . . in oratione Deo confiteri;*[573] (g) works of humility: *non velle dici sanctum antequam sit, elationem fugere, multum loqui non amare,*[574] etc. All these works and others

568. McCann, 26, 30 ("to discipline the body"; "to love fasting"; "to hate one's own will").

569. McCann, 26 ("to refresh the poor"; "to visit the sick"; "to console the sorrowing").

570. McCann, 26, 28, which reads: *"sed et factus. . ."; "Persecutionem pro justitia* [for the sake of justice] *sustinere"* ("not to give in to anger"; "to do no injury, and patiently to bear with those done to oneself"; "not to curse those who curse oneself"; "to endure persecution").

571. McCann, 28, 26 ("to declare the truth from the heart and from the mouth"; "not to swear"; "not to extend a false peace").

572. McCann, 28, 30, 26 ("not to abandon charity"; "to love one's enemies"; "to hate no one"; "not to engage in envy"; "not to love discord"; "to pray for one's enemies in the love of Christ"; "to restore peace with an adversary before the sun sets"; "to prefer nothing to the love of Christ").

573. McCann, 28, 30 ("to fear the day of judgement"; "to attend frequently to prayer"; "to confess one's bad deeds to God in prayer").

574. McCann, 30, 28 ("not to wish to be called holy before one is so"; "to flee exaltation"; "not to love to speak much").

like them are to be practiced UNCEASINGLY DAY AND NIGHT. The spirit of conversion of manners is one of *zealous application to all forms of good*. It would be vain and futile simply to have a theoretical love of the monastic life and not to strive earnestly to put into practice the things that make a true monk. It can be said with truth that the chapter on the instruments of good works is sealed and closed to many modern monks, especially the younger ones. It is one they do not properly understand. The series of counsels confuses and mystifies them. They do not see that they ought to apply themselves to *doing* such things and that it is worthwhile to do them. This applies above all to works of *abnegation*, of *meekness* and of *love*. It is strange that the works of mercy are sometimes forgotten not only by individuals but also even by whole communities. This is a scandal. We should visit our sick brethren. We should realize that the fruits of our labor help the monastery to give alms to the poor. We should always be ready in whatever way possible to give sympathy and understanding and help to our brother when he is in difficulty. Other passages in the *Rule* give indications of St. Benedict's idea of the spirit of conversion of manners. In the chapter on novices, besides seeking God, he mentions zeal for the work of God, love for obedience, love for humiliations.[575] Finally, chapter 72 on good zeal[576] is another perfect summary of the whole spirit of conversion of manners according to the monastic tradition.

IV. TRANSFORMATION IN CHRIST: the final and perhaps most important note of the spirit of the vow of conversion of manners is *ardent desire for transformation in Christ*. If we renounce the old man and take on the new man, what does this mean but that we desire to die completely to our old life and to our old self, and become new men in Christ, to be made perfectly Christlike, to have the thoughts, desires, aspirations of Christ, and

---

575. "*si sollicitus est ad opus Dei, ad obedientiam, ad opprobria*" (c. 58 [McCann, 130]).

576. McCann, 158, 160; see above, n. 423.

in a word to "become Christ." READ Galatians 2:19-21:[577] With
Christ I am nailed to the Cross. I live, now not I, but Christ lives
in me. This means that Christ Himself must be the principle of
my supernatural acts. How? by His Holy Spirit. Hence I must,
after mortifying my selfishness, be guided by the Holy Spirit. It
is not enough to cast away sinful things. I must also renounce
myself, not in order to remain in a void but in order that the
Holy Spirit may take the place of my own spirit and that I may
be "one Spirit" with the Lord. READ Romans 8:1{ff.}:[578] wisdom
of the flesh and of the Spirit; those that are "in Christ" must live

577. "For I, through the law, am dead to the law, that I may live to God:
with Christ I am nailed to the cross. And I live, now not I; but Christ liveth in me.
And that I live now in the flesh: I live in the faith of the Son of God, who loved
me, and delivered himself for me. I cast not away the grace of God. For if justice
be by the law, then Christ died in vain."

578. "There is now therefore no condemnation to them that are in Christ
Jesus, who walk not according to the flesh. For the law of the spirit of life, in
Christ Jesus, hath delivered me from the law of sin and of death. For what the
law could not do, in that it was weak through the flesh; God sending his own
Son, in the likeness of sinful flesh and of sin, hath condemned sin in the flesh;
That the justification of the law might be fulfilled in us, who walk not according
to the flesh, but according to the spirit. For they that are according to the flesh,
mind the things that are of the flesh; but they that are according to the spirit,
mind the things that are of the spirit. For the wisdom of the flesh is death; but
the wisdom of the spirit is life and peace. Because the wisdom of the flesh is an
enemy to God; for it is not subject to the law of God, neither can it be. And they
who are in the flesh, cannot please God. But you are not in the flesh, but in the
spirit, if so be that the Spirit of God dwell in you. Now if any man have not the
Spirit of Christ, he is none of his. And if Christ be in you, the body indeed is
dead, because of sin; but the spirit liveth because of justification. And if the Spirit
of him that raised up Jesus from the dead, dwell in you; he that raised up Jesus
Christ from the dead, shall quicken also your mortal bodies, because of his Spirit
that dwelleth in you. Therefore, brethren, we are debtors, not to the flesh, to live
according to the flesh. For if you live according to the flesh, you shall die: but if
by the Spirit you mortify the deeds of the flesh, you shall live. For whosoever
are led by the Spirit of God, they are the sons of God. For you have not received
the spirit of bondage again in fear; but you have received the spirit of adoption
of sons, whereby we cry: Abba (Father). For the Spirit himself giveth testimony
to our spirit, that we are the sons of God. And if sons, heirs also; heirs indeed of

by the Spirit (see especially v. 11 {with its} eschatological slant);
united with the Spirit of the Risen Christ, we are living a risen
life in union with Christ, in preparation for the life of glory with
Him in eternity—our monastic life must be seen in this perspective; v. 14: those who are led by the Spirit of God are the sons
of God—the Spirit of liberty, of sonship; vv. 18-23:[579] toward the
redemption and transformation of the whole cosmos—another
essential perspective of the vow of conversion of manners; vv.
24-39:[580] the problem of suffering and weakness and trial—the

---

God, and joint heirs with Christ: yet so, if we suffer with him, that we may be
also glorified with him" (vv. 1-17).

579. "For I reckon that the sufferings of this time are not worthy to be compared with the glory to come, that shall be revealed in us. For the expectation of
the creature waiteth for the revelation of the sons of God. For the creature was
made subject to vanity, not willingly, but by reason of him that made it subject,
in hope: Because the creature also itself shall be delivered from the servitude of
corruption, into the liberty of the glory of the children of God. For we know that
every creature groaneth and travaileth in pain, even till now. And not only it,
but ourselves also, who have the firstfruits of the Spirit, even we ourselves groan
within ourselves, waiting for the adoption of the sons of God, the redemption
of our body."

580. "For we are saved by hope. But hope that is seen, is not hope. For what
a man seeth, why doth he hope for? But if we hope for that which we see not, we
wait for it with patience. Likewise the Spirit also helpeth our infirmity. For we
know not what we should pray for as we ought; but the Spirit himself asketh for
us with unspeakable groanings. And he that searcheth the hearts, knoweth what
the Spirit desireth; because he asketh for the saints according to God. And we
know that to them that love God, all things work together unto good, to such as,
according to his purpose, are called to be saints. For whom he foreknew, he also
predestinated to be made conformable to the image of his Son; that he might be
the firstborn amongst many brethren. And whom he predestinated, them he also
called. And whom he called, them he also justified. And whom he justified, them
he also glorified. What shall we then say to these things? If God be for us, who
is against us? He that spared not even his own Son, but delivered him up for us
all, how hath he not also, with him, given us all things? Who shall accuse against
the elect of God? God that justifieth. Who is he that shall condemn? Christ Jesus
that died, yea that is risen also again; who is at the right hand of God, who also
maketh intercession for us. Who then shall separate us from the love of Christ?
Shall tribulation? or distress? or famine? or nakedness? or danger? or persecution?

Spirit is in those who hope in spite of their darkness and tribulation; nothing can harm us then; all things are for our good; who can separate us from the charity of Christ? The eighth chapter of Romans is a complete exposition of the meaning of our vow, so let us frequently read it and meditate on it. Our life is built on this. It is one of the most important chapters in Scripture for the theological basis of the monastic life. READ 2 Corinthians 3:17-18:[581] "We all beholding the glory of the Lord with face unveiled are transformed into the same image from glory to glory as by the Spirit of the Lord." What is meant by this transformation, then? Is it *mystical*? Yes, the spirit of our vow of conversion of manners is *to aspire to a mystical transformation in Christ*—not in order to outshine other men, not in order to bask in the light of our own sanctity, but because this is pleasing to God, because it is His good pleasure to call to Himself men in whose poverty He can freely manifest the glory of His grace and His immense mercy to those that are in Christ Jesus. *We owe it to the all-merciful God to allow Him to transform our nothingness in the light of His grace.* This is not pride; it is plain gratitude for the grace of our vocation, nothing more. READ Ephesians 1:3-23:[582] called to the praise

---

or the sword? (As it is written: For thy sake we are put to death all the day long. We are accounted as sheep for the slaughter.) But in all these things we overcome, because of him that hath loved us. For I am sure that neither death, nor life, nor angels, nor principalities, nor powers, nor things present, nor things to come, nor might, Nor height, nor depth, nor any other creature, shall be able to separate us from the love of God, which is in Christ Jesus our Lord."

581. "Now the Lord is a Spirit. And where the Spirit of the Lord is, there is liberty. But we all beholding the glory of the Lord with open face, are transformed into the same image from glory to glory, as by the Spirit of the Lord."

582. "Blessed be the God and Father of our Lord Jesus Christ, who hath blessed us with spiritual blessings in heavenly places, in Christ: As he chose us in him before the foundation of the world, that we should be holy and unspotted in his sight in charity. Who hath predestinated us unto the adoption of children through Jesus Christ unto himself: according to the purpose of his will: Unto the praise of the glory of his grace, in which he hath graced us in his beloved son. In whom we have redemption through his blood, the remission of sins, according to the riches of his grace, Which hath superabounded in us in all wisdom and

of the glory of God's grace. We are simply called to generously give ourselves to God's love for us in order that He may fulfill in us what He intends for all men. READ {the} papal statement on this: *Doctor Mellifluus*:

> In our day this sublime teaching of the Doctor of Clair-vaux on the mystical life, which exceeds and can satisfy all human desires, seems sometimes to be neglected and relegated to a secondary place, or even forgotten by many who, completely taken up with the worries and business of daily life, seek and desire only what is useful and profitable for this mortal life, almost never lift their eyes and minds to heaven, and almost never aspire after heavenly things and values that cannot perish.
>
> Yet, although not all can attain the summit of that exalted contemplation of which Bernard speaks with sublime words

---

prudence, That he might make known unto us the mystery of his will, according to his good pleasure, which he hath purposed in him, In the dispensation of the fulness of times, to re-establish all things in Christ, that are in heaven and on earth, in him. In whom we also are called by lot, being predestinated according to the purpose of him who worketh all things according to the counsel of his will. That we may be unto the praise of his glory, we who before hoped in Christ: In whom you also, after you had heard the word of truth, (the gospel of your salvation;) in whom also believing, you were signed with the holy Spirit of promise, Who is the pledge of our inheritance, unto the redemption of acquisition, unto the praise of his glory. Wherefore I also, hearing of your faith that is in the Lord Jesus and of your love towards all the saints, Cease not to give thanks for you, making commemoration of you in my prayers, That the God of our Lord Jesus Christ, the Father of glory, may give unto you the spirit of wisdom and of revelation, in the knowledge of him: The eyes of your heart enlightened, that you may know what the hope is of his calling, and what are the riches of the glory of his inheritance in the saints. And what is the exceeding greatness of his power towards us, who believe according to the operation of the might of his power, Which he wrought in Christ, raising him up from the dead, and setting him on his right hand in the heavenly places. Above all principality, and power, and virtue, and dominion, and every name that is named, not only in this world, but also in that which is to come. And he hath subjected all things under his feet, and hath made him head over all the church. Which is his body, and the fulness of him who is filled all in all."

and sentences, and although not all can unite themselves so closely with God as to feel themselves linked in a mysterious manner with the Supreme Good through the bonds of heavenly marriage; nevertheless, all can and must from time to time lift their hearts from the earthly things around them to those of heaven, and most earnestly love the Supreme Giver of all good things. . . .

Hence, that divine love which burned so mightily in the Doctor of Clairvaux must be re-enkindled in the hearts of all men, if we desire the restoration of Christian morality, if the Catholic religion is to carry out its mission successfully, and if, through the calming of dissension and the restoration of order in justice and equity, serene peace is to shine forth for a worn and anguished humanity.

May those who have embraced the Order of the Mellifluous Doctor, and all the members of the clergy, whose special task it is to exhort and urge others to the fervor of divine love, be most ardently inflamed with that love which ought always to unite us most perfectly with God. In our own day, more than at any other time—as we have said—men need this divine love; family life needs it; the whole of human society needs it. Where it burns and urges souls on to God, Who is the supreme goal of all mortals, all other virtues wax strong; when, on the contrary, it is absent or has died out, then tranquillity, peace, joy, and all other genuine good things gradually disappear or are completely destroyed, since they flow from Him who "is love."[583]

CHASTITY and VIRGINITY

a) *Introduction*: having considered the obligations and the spirit of the vow of conversion of manners, we now turn to two of the principal aspects of this vow—*chastity* and *poverty*. We take

583. *Doctor Mellifluus: Encyclical Letter of His Holiness Pope Pius XII on the Occasion of the Eighth Centenary of the Death of Saint Bernard* (1953), quoted from Merton's own translation in Thomas Merton, *The Last of the Fathers: Saint Bernard of Clairvaux and the Encyclical Letter Doctor Mellifluus* (New York: Harcourt, Brace, 1954), 101–103.

chastity first because in its primitive conception, this will follow most logically and appropriately upon what has just been said about the spirit of the vow of conversion of manners and especially about *transformation in Christ*. In point of fact, the original monastic conception of chastity and virginity is so closely tied up with the spirit of conversion of manners that it is absolutely essential to that vow as it was understood in the early days of the Church. If sometimes it is possible for modern writers to regard chastity as an aspect of obedience, it is because they consider it negatively and in a very restricted way, namely as an obligation to abstain from sex pleasure. It is true, obviously, that this obligation is essential to monastic chastity, but to make chastity consist *only* in this, or *primarily* in this, is to fail completely to understand its purport. In actual fact, chastity means above all a renunciation of partial and limited forms of love to *embrace the perfection of love in a nuptial union with Christ*. This renunciation of earthly love *in order to surrender one's whole being, body and soul, to Christ*, leads in turn *to transformation in Christ*. It is easy to see that the whole concept of conversion of manners and the pure spirit of the vow is implicit in this notion. Chastity is, in fact, the most eloquent and obvious witness to the fact that one has left the world to follow Christ, to seek perfect union with Him, to be united to Him in spiritual marriage. In reality, a vow of *conversatio morum* that would not include this renunciation of earthly love and cleaving to Christ in spiritual union would be unthinkable to the early Fathers. Hence chastity is not primarily a negative renunciation of earthly love, and still more crudely a mere renunciation of sex pleasure—it is primarily and above all a liberation from the bonds of earthly love in order to be free to unite oneself to Christ in spiritual love. The renunciation of sex pleasure is the most obvious *sine qua non*—without it one cannot even begin to think of such a union with Christ. But to say that the mere renunciation of sex pleasure constitutes chastity in this deeply spiritual sense is to fail to have any concept of the meaning of chastity in the life of a monk. Furthermore, those who have only a very crude and insufficient notion of chastity will inevitably find it harder to practice even this elementary kind of chastity. They will not have the deep spiritual motives of love for Christ, the hope of union with Him, which gives strength to our ascetic strivings and helps us to overcome the temptations of the flesh, which can sometimes be very strong even in the cloister—or perhaps in some cases, *especially* in the cloister. Those who are called to prove their love for Christ by overcoming a richly endowed natural temperament with strong passions can only do so if they have very powerful spiritual motives, *motives of the highest kind of love*, motives of personal and "nuptial" love for Jesus Christ, the Spouse of Souls. Otherwise there will always be danger of, if not sinning, at least being deluded by apparently harmless human substitutes for divine love, compromises between the spiritual love of Christ and carnal love of human beings.

Historical Note: it can be said that the "vow of chastity" is the most ancient of the vows because in fact the first evidence of a life of vows in the Church comes with the *consecration of virgins*, which goes back at least as far as the fourth century. But if formal public and liturgical consecration of virgins is dated only from the fourth century, the virgins formed a special group, a kind of "order," from the very earliest days. We shall see that St. Paul speaks of their status and obligations. From the very first, the Church clearly considered the virgins as *brides of Christ*: *Virgo sponsa Christi* (Tertullian[584]). They were Christian women who for love of Christ had renounced matrimony and consecrated themselves to lives of prayer, not by a public and solemn vow but by an act of self-dedication which was certainly a private vow in everything but its juridical form. Hence even before public and formal consecration of virgins existed, if a virgin dedicated to Christ left her virginal life, it was regarded as a scandal and severe punishments were inflicted by the bishops and by councils

---

584. "The virgin is a spouse of Christ" (*Adversus Marcionem*, 2.4 [*PL* 2, col. 289A]), quoted in *Chastity, Being the English Version of "La Chasteté" in "Problèmes de la Religieuse d'Aujourd'hui,"* trans. Lancelot C. Sheppard (Westminster, MD: Newman Press, 1955), 6.

of the Church. The virgin who thus made light of her promise was excommunicated and only admitted back into the Church with difficulty. There was even considerable discussion as to the validity of marriage contracted by these virgins, even before the time when there was a public and solemn consecration of virgins. From the fourth century on, the consecration of virgins was public and liturgical. The ritual still exists and is one of the most beautiful rites in the Roman liturgy. Only the bishop could consecrate a virgin to Christ. When solemn and public vows of religion became universal, the special consecration of virgins was abandoned, except in rare cases. However, consecration of virgins outside religion was still theoretically possible. In modern times, those who have sought to reintroduce the solemn consecration of virgins for those embracing a life of virginity outside religion have so far had no success. Nowadays one takes a private vow of chastity, for which the Code provides certain legislation. (Canon 1309:[585] {a} private vow of perfect and perpetual chastity is one of the two *reserved to the Holy See*. Dispensation can only be obtained from the Holy See—Sacred Penitentiary. The other vow is the vow to enter a religious order having solemn vows. Other private vows are reserved to the bishop, to {the} superior of an exempt religious house [for those in the house] or to those having special faculties. N.B. one with dominative power over the subject can annul his private vows.) Hence the *vow of virginity* is, historically speaking, the earliest and most solemn example of religious consecration to God by vow in the Church, another reason why monastic tradition would tend to associate chastity with conversion of manners.

Scriptural Background (see {the} interesting article by Sœur Jeanne d'Arc in *Chastity*):[586] in the *Old Testament*, salvation is asso-

585. *Codex Iuris Canonici*, 446.
586. Sister Jeanne d'Arc, OP, "Chastity and Consecrated Virginity in the Old and New Testaments," *Chastity*, 3–27; Merton mentions reading this article in preparation for his novitiate conferences in a journal entry from February 14, 1959 (Thomas Merton, *A Search for Solitude: Pursuing the Monk's True Life. Journals, vol. 3: 1952–1960*, ed. Lawrence S. Cunningham [San Francisco: HarperCollins, 1996], 261).

ciated with the idea of *fecundity*. Sex is nowhere regarded simply as an evil in the Bible. On the contrary, both before and after the fall it is clear that the mission of Adam and Eve was to "increase and multiply" and bring forth the family of man in which God was to be glorified. (READ Genesis 1:27-28; 2:24; and 3:15;[587] cf. St. Paul: even after sin, etc., woman is saved "by being a mother" [1 Tim. 2:15].) {Note} the aprons of fig leaves—meaning what? Shame at sex comes *after the fall*. The Old Testament is nowhere especially preoccupied with the angle of pleasure connected with sex. Sex is a good *because children are a blessing from God*. However, the Torah does surround the exercise of the sex faculty with ritual purifications (cf. Leviticus 12), *a fortiori* sexual "accidents" (cf. Leviticus 15; Deuteronomy 23:10-11). In Job 14:4, man is impure because he is conceived with impure seed, {the} germ of the doctrine of original sin. But this is a carryover from the idea of ritual uncleanness. It is not so much the idea of moral evil as the idea of indecency that leads to the purifications described above. Nowhere in the Bible is there any indication that *sex pleasure as such* is morally evil or vile. It is evil and vile only in its misuse. *The chief misuse of sex* castigated by the Old Testament is in religion. Sex played an important part in pagan fertility cults and idolatry (cf. the golden calf). {There was a} prohibition of Jewish girls and boys becoming sacred prostitutes and {a} prohibition of frequenting these, with the "offering" being given religiously (Deut. 23:17-18; cf. Baruch 6:42-43: temple prostitution {as a} sign that these gods are false). Sexual worship was regarded as characteristic of the pagan cults that were supposed to be wiped out by the children of Israel and which were constantly

---

587. "And God created man to his own image: to the image of God he created him: male and female he created them. And God blessed them, saying: Increase and multiply, and fill the earth, and subdue it, and rule over the fishes of the sea, and the fowls of the air, and all living creatures that move upon the earth." "Wherefore a man shall leave father and mother and shall cleave to his wife: and they shall be two in one flesh." "I will put enmities between thee and the woman, and thy seed and her seed: she shall crush thy head, and thou shalt lie in wait for her heel."

being reintroduced by the kings of Israel. The reason that God desired to prepare the people of Israel for a truly spiritual worship {was} to understand the Incarnation that was to come and the life of man in Christ. *To return to the idea of fecundity*—it was for the glory of God, and the women of Israel longed to have many children (READ Genesis 30[588]—Rachel: "Give me children, or I die"). *Sterility* in general is regarded as accursed, but there are special cases when it is allowed in order that God may show His special power in a miracle: v.g., Sara; Anna the mother of Samuel (READ 1 Kings 1 [Anna];[589] cf. Isaias 54). But since this is

---

588. "And Rachel, seeing herself without children, envied her sister, and said to her husband: Give me children, otherwise I shall die. And Jacob being angry with her, answered: Am I as God, who hath deprived thee of the fruit of thy womb? But she said: I have here my servant Bala: go in unto her, that she may bear upon my knees, and I may have children by her. And she gave him Bala in marriage: who, When her husband had gone in unto her, conceived and bore a son. And Rachel said: The Lord hath judged for me, and hath heard my voice, giving me a son, and therefore she called his name Dan. And again Bala conceived and bore another, For whom Rachel said: God hath compared me with my sister, and I have prevailed: and she called him Nephtali. . . . The Lord also remembering Rachel, heard her, and opened her womb. And she conceived, and bore a son, saying: God hath taken away my reproach. And she called his name Joseph, saying: The Lord give me also another son" (vv. 1-8, 22-24).

589. "There was a man of Ramathaimsophim, of mount Ephraim, and his name was Elcana, the son of Jeroham, the son of Eliu, the son of Thohu, the son of Suph, an Ephraimite: And he had two wives, the name of one was Anna, and the name of the other Phenenna. Phenenna had children: but Anna had no children. And this man went up out of his city upon the appointed days, to adore and to offer sacrifice to the Lord of hosts in Silo. And the two sons of Heli, Ophni and Phinees, were there priests of the Lord. Now the day came, and Elcana offered sacrifice, and gave to Phenenna his wife, and to all her sons and daughters, portions: But to Anna he gave one portion with sorrow, because he loved Anna. And the Lord had shut up her womb. Her rival also afflicted her, and troubled her exceedingly, insomuch that she upbraided her, that the Lord had shut up her womb: And thus she did every year, when the time returned that they went up to the temple of the Lord: and thus she provoked her: but Anna wept, and did not eat. Then Elcana her husband said to her: Anna, why weepest thou? and why dost thou not eat? And why dost thou afflict thy heart? Am not I better to thee than ten children? So Anna arose after she had eaten and drunk in Silo: And Heli

in fact a hard faculty to control, much prayer and self-denial are required over and above the ordinary level of the "minimum" in order to live continently. Hence Ecclesiasticus 9:1-13 prescribes modesty and caution in dealing with women. In summary, the

---

the priest sitting upon a stool before the door of the temple of the Lord: As Anna had her heart full of grief, she prayed to the Lord, shedding many tears. And she made a vow, saying: O Lord of hosts, if thou wilt look down on the affliction of thy servant, and wilt be mindful of me, and not forget thy handmaid, and wilt give to thy servant a man child: I will give him to the Lord all the days of his life, and no razor shall come upon his head. And it came to pass, as she multiplied prayers before the Lord, that Heli observed her mouth. Now Anna spoke in her heart, and only her lips moved, but her voice was not heard at all. Heli therefore thought her to be drunk, And said to her: How long wilt thou be drunk? digest a little the wine, of which thou hast taken too much. Anna answering, said: Not so, my lord: for I am an exceeding unhappy woman, and have drunk neither wine nor any strong drink, but I have poured out my soul before the Lord. Count not thy handmaid for one of the daughters of Belial: for out of the abundance of my sorrow and grief have I spoken till now. Then Heli said to her: Go in peace: and the God of Israel grant thee thy petition, which thou hast asked of him. And she said: Would to God thy handmaid may find grace in thy eyes. So the woman went on her way, and ate, and her countenance was no more changed. And they rose in the morning, and worshipped before the Lord: and they returned, and came into their house at Ramatha. And Elcana knew Anna his wife: and the Lord remembered her. And it came to pass when the time was come about, Anna conceived, and bore a son, and called his name Samuel: because she had asked him of the Lord. And Elcana her husband went up, and all his house, to offer to the Lord the solemn sacrifice, and his vow. But Anna went not up: for she said to her husband: I will not go till the child be weaned, and till I may carry him, that he may appear before the Lord, and may abide always there. And Elcana her husband said to her: Do what seemeth good to thee, and stay till thou wean him: and I pray that the Lord may fulfil his word. So the woman stayed at home, and gave her son suck, till she weaned him. And after she had weaned him, she carried him with her, with three calves, and three bushels of flour, and a bottle of wine, and she brought him to the house of the Lord in Silo. Now the child was as yet very young: And they immolated a calf, and offered the child to Heli. And Anna said: I beseech thee, my lord, as thy soul liveth, my lord: I am that woman who stood before thee here praying to the Lord. For this child did I pray, and the Lord hath granted me my petition, which I asked of him. Therefore I also have lent him to the Lord all the days of his life, he shall be lent to the Lord. And they adored the Lord there."

Old Testament contains essential elements for a theology of chastity. The New Testament will develop these bare essentials into a much greater and deeper mystery: chastity is connected with the union of Christ and His Church just as marriage is; they are two aspects of the same mystery in fact.

New Testament texts: the classic text on chastity in the New Testament is Matthew 19, in which Our Lord Himself reveals to us the existence of the chaste life and its value before God. The whole chapter deals with matters most vital to the life of the vows, so we take it in its entirety, leaving however a detailed discussion of the matter on *poverty* until later. READ Matthew 19:3-12:[590] the question of divorce. This provides the occasion and the setting. The Pharisees, tempting Him, raise a debated question which divided two schools, that of divorce. From this Jesus will go on to speak of chastity—but first the question of marriage and divorce:

a) {This was a} subject of debate between the schools of Shammai and Hillel[591]—*Deuteronomy 24:1* permitting divorce if {a} hus-

---

590. "And there came to him the Pharisees tempting him, and saying: Is it lawful for a man to put away his wife for every cause? Who answering, said to them: Have ye not read, that he who made man from the beginning, Made them male and female? And he said: For this cause shall a man leave father and mother, and shall cleave to his wife, and they two shall be in one flesh. Therefore now they are not two, but one flesh. What therefore God hath joined together, let no man put asunder. They say to him: Why then did Moses command to give a bill of divorce, and to put away? He saith to them: Because Moses by reason of the hardness of your heart permitted you to put away your wives: but from the beginning it was not so. And I say to you, that whosoever shall put away his wife, except it be for fornication, and shall marry another, committeth adultery: and he that shall marry her that is put away, committeth adultery. His disciples say unto him: If the case of a man with his wife be so, it is not expedient to marry. Who said to them: All men take not this word, but they to whom it is given. For there are eunuchs, who were born so from their mother's womb: and there are eunuchs, who were made so by men: and there are eunuchs, who have made themselves eunuchs for the kingdom of heaven. He that can take, let him take it."

591. The two leading Jewish rabbis at the beginning of the first century of the common era; the interpretations of Shammai and his disciples were gener-

band finds in {his} wife some "uncleanness"—meaning what? {In the} strict view it means adultery; {in the} broad view {it} means any defect.

b) {The} purpose of the question {was} to trap Christ into committing Himself to the opinion of one or the other school, a partial view. Note the meaning of these tests—a deep meaning, and the meaning of Jesus' refusal to participate in the debates of rabbinical schools. Christ and the Christian are both above and beyond these divergent opinions, which are human and stupid, which prove nothing but only lead to involvement in error and confusion (cf. St. Paul: Eph. 4:14; Col. 2:16-23; 1 Tim. 1:1-7; 2 Tim. 3). Note how Christ cuts through the difficulty and comes right to the truth.

c) In this case He goes back to what is certain and clearly revealed—the word of God (Gen. 1:27 and 2:24). In order to do this He had to run the risk of being accused, as He was, of being against Moses. In reply He gives an authoritative answer, that Moses permitted divorce because of their "hardness of heart"—i.e., spiritual immaturity.

From this part of the discourse we conclude:

1. The absolute, clear, and uncompromising statement about the inviolability of the marriage bond: they are henceforth *two in one flesh*, and this cannot be dissolved by man.

2. The exceptive clause—"except for fornication"—presents a difficulty:

a) {it} is missing in Mark and Luke, but Matthew is probably genuine: he could hardly have inserted it against the meaning of Christ.

b) {it} is interpreted variously: *either* it means that a man is entitled to *separate* from an adulterous wife, or *vice versa* (*not* to remarry); or fornication means here concubinage; as in the case

---

ally stricter than those of Hillel and his followers; for the dispute on divorce, see the *Babylonian Talmud*, tractate Gittin, 90a, in which the school of Hillel allows a man to divorce his wife much more easily than does the school of Shammai.

of an invalid marriage (due to consanguinity), or no marriage at all, this union can and should be dissolved.

READ Matthew 19:10-12: the disciples protest. The doctrine of Christ seems to them exceedingly strict. He reaffirms His teaching, thus showing that He means business and is to be taken quite literally. But then He proposes another alternative: the LIFE OF PERFECT CHASTITY.

a) This life is a *special vocation*, not given to all; and to those who have it, it is a gift from God, hence proposed only to a few.

b) This is a life of chastity freely and deliberately embraced, not of course literally by castration, but by self-denial; a life of sacrifice for the Kingdom of Heaven: *Qui potest capere capiat*[592]— this includes an *invitation*.

The *blessing of the little children* (13-15) implies blessing of a life of purity and also humility and docility. The *rich young man* {passage} (READ 16-24[593]) {describes} the difficulties of a life of poverty {and} its necessity. The disciples are again shocked. Jesus concludes (25-30) on the rewards of a life of sacrifice for the love of God. This {is} commonly accepted as applying to religious life ({it is used as the} gospel in {the} Common of Abbots[594]).

Eschatological Character of Christian Virginity: according to the New Testament texts, the purpose of virginity and union with Christ is not simply ascetic. The life of virginity is a preparation and a prefiguring of the blessed life in heaven, not because it implies liberation from certain responsibilities but because it implies a greater and more universal capacity for love. Love that is spiritualized reaches out to the whole world. {It is the} *bios angelikos*—the life of chastity is like the life of the angels in heaven. READ Matthew 22:23-33:[595] Christ {is} tempted by the

---

592. "He that can take, let him take it" (Mt. 19:12).

593. See above, n. 207.

594. Mt. 19:27-29 (*Missale Romanum*, (28); *Missale Cisterciense*, 23*).

595. "That day there came to him the Sadducees, who say there is no resurrection: and asked him, Saying: Master, Moses said: If a man die having no son,

Sadducees, "who say there is no resurrection"; {they raise} the problem of the wife married to seven brothers who all die. Whose wife will she be "in the resurrection"? Christ's reply (30) {is that} "in the resurrection they shall neither marry nor be married; but shall be as the angels of God in heaven." Then note his statement about the resurrection itself: God is the God of the living. Hence we must live before His face even in our bodies. Comment: the context is important. It is not a question of what will happen "in heaven" but "in the resurrection," when we dwell in spiritualized and risen bodies. The term of Christian hope is this risen life, not just a purely mental "heaven." The life of virgins on earth is a prefiguring of this angelic life in risen bodies. READ Apocalypse 14:1-5:[596] the virgins follow the Lamb everywhere.

The Wise and Foolish Virgins (Matthew 25:1-13): {in} the parable of the wise and foolish virgins, the life of virginity is {presented as} a life of eschatological expectation, waiting for the advent of Christ, the "return of the Bridegroom." But there is

---

his brother shall marry his wife, and raise up issue to his brother. Now there were with us seven brethren: and the first having married a wife, died; and not having issue, left his wife to his brother. In like manner the second, and the third, and so on to the seventh. And last of all the woman died also. At the resurrection therefore whose wife of the seven shall she be? for they all had her. And Jesus answering, said to them: You err, not knowing the Scriptures, nor the power of God. For in the resurrection they shall neither marry nor be married; but shall be as the angels of God in heaven. And concerning the resurrection of the dead, have you not read that which was spoken by God, saying to you: I am the God of Abraham, and the God of Isaac, and the God of Jacob? He is not the God of the dead, but of the living. And the multitudes hearing it, were in admiration at his doctrine."

596. "And I beheld, and lo a lamb stood upon mount Sion, and with him an hundred forty-four thousand, having his name, and the name of his Father, written on their foreheads. And I heard a voice from heaven, as the noise of many waters, and as the voice of great thunder; and the voice which I heard, was as the voice of harpers, harping on their harps. And they sung as it were a new canticle, before the throne, and before the four living creatures, and the ancients; and no man could say the canticle, but those hundred forty-four thousand, who were purchased from the earth. These are they who were not defiled with women: for they are virgins. These follow the Lamb whithersoever he goeth. These were purchased from among men, the firstfruits to God and to the Lamb: And in their mouth there was found no lie; for they are without spot before the throne of God."

a difference between the virgins who are "awake" and have in their lamps the oil of good works, and those who sleep, content simply with being virgins. St. Chrysostom {writes that the} oil in the lamp refers to poverty and almsgiving, or charity in short.[597] Tradition has made it clear that the mere fact of being physically intact is of no value in itself. What matters is the sacrifice of one's whole being by love. This love is proved by the existence of other virtues and good works besides virginity, especially poverty and almsgiving (in the sense of sharing with others the goods of which we deprive ourselves).

Virginity in St. Paul: READ 1 Corinthians 7:7-10[598] ({the} doctrine on marriage: better to marry than to burn—*qui potest capere capiat;*[599] virginal life is better *in se*); 25-28:[600] it is no sin to marry; if

---

597. See St. John Chrysostom, *Homily 78 on Matthew* (*PG* 58, cols. 710–11), in Philip Schaff, ed., *Nicene and Post-Nicene Fathers*, 1st series, trans. George Prevost (1888; reprint: Grand Rapids, MI: Eerdmans, 1969), 10:470–71: "He putteth forth this parable sufficient to persuade them, that virginity, though it should have everything else, if destitute of the good things arising out of almsgiving, is cast out with the harlots, and He sets the inhuman and merciless with them. And most reasonably, for the one was overcome by the love of carnal pleasure, but these of money. . . . Therefore also He calls them foolish, for that having undergone the greater labor, they have betrayed all for want of the less. But by lamps here, He meaneth the gift itself of virginity, the purity of holiness; and by oil, humanity, almsgiving, succor to them that are in need. . . . For nothing is more sullied than virginity not having mercy; so that even the multitude are wont to call the unmerciful dark."

598. "For I would that all men were even as myself: but every one hath his proper gift from God: one after this manner, and another after that. But I say to the unmarried, and to the widows: It is good for them if they so continue, even as I. But if they do not contain themselves, let them marry. For it is better to marry than to be burnt. But to them that are married, not I but the Lord commandeth, that the wife depart not from her husband."

599. "He that can take, let him take it" (Mt. 19:12).

600. "Now concerning virgins, I have no commandment of the Lord; but I give counsel, as having obtained mercy of the Lord, to be faithful. I think therefore that this is good for the present necessity, that it is good for a man so to be. Art thou bound to a wife? seek not to be loosed. Art thou loosed from a wife? seek not a wife. But if thou take a wife, thou hast not sinned. And if a virgin marry,

one has a wife, let him stay with her and not embrace a continent life, but if one is not married and feels called to virginity, that is to be regarded as a good thing—why? 29-38:[601] the "time is short" ({the} eschatological reason); all have to be detached, the married included. It is easier to be detached and carefree when one is free of cares about wife or husband. One who is thus free is at liberty to occupy himself entirely with the things of the Lord: "how he may please God." Married people are divided; {they} have also to please one another. The great thing {is the} "power to attend upon the Lord without impediment": to marry is good; to be a virgin is better. READ 2 Corinthians 11:1-3:[602] spiritual virginity {means} purity of faith, purity in the spirit of the Church, the one Bride of Christ. This also is an important aspect of the question. {A}

she hath not sinned: nevertheless, such shall have tribulation of the flesh. But I spare you."

601. "This therefore I say, brethren; the time is short; it remaineth, that they also who have wives, be as if they had none; And they that weep, as though they wept not; and they that rejoice, as if they rejoiced not; and they that buy, as though they possessed not; And they that use this world, as if they used it not: for the fashion of this world passeth away. But I would have you to be without solicitude. He that is without a wife, is solicitous for the things that belong to the Lord, how he may please God. But he that is with a wife, is solicitous for the things of the world, how he may please his wife: and he is divided. And the unmarried woman and the virgin thinketh on the things of the Lord, that she may be holy both in body and in spirit. But she that is married thinketh on the things of the world, how she may please her husband. And this I speak for your profit: not to cast a snare upon you; but for that which is decent, and which may give you power to attend upon the Lord, without impediment. But if any man think that he seemeth dishonoured, with regard to his virgin, for that she is above the age, and it must so be: let him do what he will; he sinneth not, if she marry. For he that hath determined being steadfast in his heart, having no necessity, but having power of his own will; and hath judged this in his heart, to keep his virgin, doth well. Therefore, both he that giveth his virgin in marriage, doth well; and he that giveth her not, doth better."

602. "Would to God you could bear with some little of my folly: but do bear with me. For I am jealous of you with the jealousy of God. For I have espoused you to one husband that I may present you as a chaste virgin to Christ. But I fear lest, as the serpent seduced Eve by his subtilty, so your minds should be corrupted, and fall from the simplicity that is in Christ."

virginal heart is better able to *understand* divine truths (*beati mundi corde*[603]); hence, {the} virginal life is adapted to contemplation.

Chastity (II): *the Virtue of Temperance*: we have seen that Our Lord demands that we control the passions of the flesh and that He calls certain ones to a life of perfect sacrifice by renunciation of all use, even legitimate, of the reproductive faculties. If human love is to be consecrated to Christ, how then is this done? by *virtue*. Chastity is part of the virtue of *temperance*. It is important to understand that the control of the flesh and its consecration to God is something *eminently reasonable*. It is an *ordering* of our being to God in accordance with reason and with grace. Our consecration is not a matter of *exalted feeling* only. (Feelings of fervor are good, in accompaniment to genuine virtue.) The virtue of chastity is something that can and should be properly understood. One who makes a vow of chastity must know what he is doing, must be morally certain that he is able to do it. He must have understanding, not merely theoretical and abstract, but connatural and practical, of the virtue of chastity. He must know how chastity "works." He must understand the nature of the virtue, have a reasonable idea of temperance above all. He must understand the *problems* that confront the chaste man and the special means which virtue offers him in order to solve these problems. He must understand *how to use these means*.

It will be useful here to *review what has been said about the passions*. Read what has been given in these notes (pp. {18–27}: passion; and pp. {35–40}: virtue). *Passion* {refers to} acts which are in themselves instinctive and involuntary and which are to be brought under the control and guidance of reason in order to become fully human and virtuous. The passions are acts of man's animal nature. They are not to be regarded as evil or immoral. They are not to be merely *suppressed*. They are forces to be harnessed and used in conjunction with the reason, to give our human activity a fullness and tone and richness which it needs in order to be fully and integrally human, and even for it to be

---

603. "Blessed are the clean of heart" (Mt. 5:8).

spiritual in a full and human way. There is very grave danger of warping and even serious harm to man's nature where passion is *violently excluded* from his moral life by arbitrary efforts of will. In such cases, passion, being pushed beyond the area where it naturally collaborates with the will, tends to take on an irresponsible and uncontrollable activity of its own. This can lead to serious harm. For example, in the case of the passion of sexual desire, this is not merely something that has to be crushed in man and violently suppressed so that it is no longer felt. The "power" of this passion can and should be "used" and converted to higher moral purposes. It should be harnessed by rational and virtuous family love, in the case of married persons. It should contribute to a high spiritual joy and fervor in the sacrifice made by consecrated souls. The animal element in lust is converted by transformation into love—first a higher human love, then into charity. Sexual love does not become charity all by itself, simply by being "sublimated." But the power of this love can be used and adapted to the higher power of spiritual charity. Then our spiritual love takes on an emotional tone and warmth and coloring which come from the incorporation of our bodily nature, spiritualized, in the action of charity. This passion then lends a note of warmth and affectivity to our life of prayer and charity. But we must be sure that the affective "color" of our fervor is truly spiritual. Otherwise the passion can easily drag down and convert charity into thinly disguised sensuality under a religious mask. Passions, more precisely, are *acts of the soul in so far as it informs a body*. Control of the passions is what spiritualizes the life of our body. Notice the operation of passion in the human nature of Jesus Christ: His love for His disciples (with desire have I desired to eat this Pasch[604]); His tears at the tomb of Lazarus and over Jerusalem; His anger with the money changers and Pharisees; His indignation with pettiness and selfishness in the disciples, etc. We know that Our Lord *felt* strongly these human emotions, and especially in the Garden of Gethsemani. Note that

604. Lk. 22:15.

a traditional way of approaching the problem of the sanctification of our passions is affective meditation on the expression of feeling shown by Our Lord, with the desire to identify ourselves with Him and to share by grace in His way of feeling things and reacting to them. This cannot be done merely by human efforts and ingenuity. It requires the grace of the Holy Spirit and His action. It requires love.

Reason governs passion by governing the instinctive judgements made by the *vis cogitativa*.[605] (This *vis cogitativa* sums things up at a glance on the basis of emotional data and "feels" that something is good or evil. Reason corrects this judgement by objective data and shows how to coordinate subjective and objective factors in a concrete judgement here and now.) Instinctual drives are then spiritualized by participation in the freedom proper to the will. {For} example:

1) The *vis cogitativa*, in conjunction with passions of fear, anger, etc., sizes up the conduct of another man as *hostile* to me. Reason comes along and points out, on the basis of past experience, that I am inclined to see hostility where there is little or none, that I am sensitive and suspicious. Yet there may also be a little objective basis for my feeling. Instead of withdrawing and showing resentment, I resolve to overcome the incipient bad relations by an expression of cordiality and good will. The force of passion that would have turned into {an} expression of anger and hate is instead used for friendship and love.

2) The *vis cogitativa* diagnoses a condition of sadness I feel as the result of having "committed a fault." The *vis cogitativa* is not conscience. It simply registers emotional discomfort and applies the more or less arbitrary label of *guilt*. Reason comes along and shows there is no real objective basis for this. I have not done anything wrong. I discover that what has happened is that someone seems to have expressed disapproval of something I did. This was what started the trouble. Reason judges the case:

605. See above, n. 23.

the disapproval was called forth by an unconscious and involuntary action of mine for which I was not responsible, but now that I see it I will make sure to avoid the same thing in the future.

Note situations where {the} *vis cogitativa*, pinch-hitting for conscience, causes trouble by registering diffuse guilt practically all the time. This is a disorder, a state of anxiety. It requires correction with the help of an experienced person.

Passion and bodily change: the passions affect the circulation, glandular secretions, respiration, nervous reactions, etc. To some extent reason can modify the intensity of passion by acting on these bodily manifestations—control of respiration, relaxation of muscular tension, etc. This can form an important part of ascetic practice and should be remembered. Note that {with regard to} intense acts of will, efforts to generate a "right feeling" or to evoke "good images" to replace bad feelings and undescribable images, *this generally does not work well*. It should be avoided, especially in the case of sexual passion. *Indirect* control is better. (Turn to some peaceful good action in some other field. Take the mind entirely away from the difficulty.)

Virtues (*virtus—habitus*) {are} not just a mechanical "habit." Mechanical habit degrades man's actions, making them routine and unconscious. *Habitus* perfects man's freedom and awareness of good action. *Habitus* {is} a principle *quo quis utitur quando vult*;[606] {it} makes our actions more stable, sure, efficient, peaceful, joyful, etc. A virtue is an *elective habit*, a habit of good choice, enlightened by prudence and perfected by connatural affinity for the good which is its object. It makes choices that are right, that are called for by the circumstances, that further the moral life of the individual and the group. These choices are ordered to the medium between extremes. (See {on} page {38} what is said about the growth of good habits.)

Temperance is one of the four moral virtues:

606. See above, n. 62.

a) It is the *last* of the four moral virtues. Prudence is the first: it regulates all the other moral virtues; justice is next: {it} considers the common good; fortitude {is} next.

b) Yet temperance is also the *most beautiful* of the moral virtues (St. Thomas: *Summa*, II-II, q. 141, a. 8, ad. 1)[607] because it eradicates all that is most ugly and malformed in the soul due to disorder of the sense appetites. Gluttony, lust—these are the *most debasing* of the sins, the ones that strike most powerfully at the *spirituality* of our nature, degrading and darkening the reason, weakening the will, perverting love. Also, they *work the fastest and most effectively* in polluting the soul. And finally they *gain the most powerful grip on the soul* and keep it under their tyranny.

c) In some ways temperance is *one of the most difficult* of the moral virtues. It is certainly the most difficult for the beginner, and it is the one the beginner has to face with the greatest patience and courage. But fortitude is more difficult than temperance when we look at the main object of fortitude—control over the fear of death.

The full meaning of temperance: Pieper[608] (*Fortitude and Temperance*, p. 47) warns against just taking temperance to mean restraint in eating and drinking, especially restraint in quantity. The temperate man would then be merely one who ate and drank sparingly. This is a degradation of the true idea. Temperance orders and harmonizes the parts of man's being in a whole. From this inner order flows serenity of spirit. "Temperance is selfless self-preservation. Intemperance is self-destruction through the selfish degradation of the powers that aim at self-preservation" (Pieper, p. 49).[609] Notice that while temperance controls above all the instincts for food and drink and sex, it also has to do with other aspects of our urge for self-preservation. Humility is a branch of temperance in St. Thomas—it orders our self-

---

607. Aquinas, *Opera Omnia*, 3.476.
608. Josef Pieper, *Fortitude and Temperance* (New York: Pantheon Books, 1954).
609. Text reads: ". . . powers which aim . . ."

assertiveness; study is a branch of temperance—it orders our appetite for knowledge correctly. (Curiosity, intemperate desire for knowledge, is something we should know about.)

St. Thomas on Temperance: the teaching of St. Thomas on temperance is clear, balanced and sane. It should be studied by all who wish to have a correct idea of Christian self-control and self-denial. In speaking of temperance, St. Thomas is talking of a virtue which orders man's acts *according to reason*, that is to say, according to his true nature. Now of course this is not yet supernatural heroism. Temperance needs to be perfected by the gifts of fear, which leads us to supernatural acts of self-denial and raises us above ourselves to heroic levels in Christian virginity, fasting, etc. Nevertheless, these will not be understood properly unless we see them in the light of the reasonable virtue of temperance. And note that the temperance St. Thomas talks about is not merely natural. It is a supernatural, infused virtue. But it orders us according to the standards of our nature, which standards, of course, are willed by God. Once these requirements are met, then grace also *builds on* nature.

1. Temperance is a virtue which inclines a man to *moderation* in the use of certain bodily goods which tend to the preservation of life. This moderation regulates *pleasures*, but only inhibits those pleasures which are against reason and against nature. *Temperantia retrahit ab his quae contra rationem appetitum alliciunt* (II-II, q. 141, art. 2).[610] Hence, temperance *per se* does not prohibit licit and good natural pleasures. It uses and directs them rightly, making use of them as means to bring us to our last end. The temperate man uses the pleasures of eating, drinking, learning, etc., and of sex also, in order to become a saint and to be united with God. *Temperantia non contrariatur inclinationi naturae humanae, sed convenit cum ea* (II-II, q. 141, art. 1, ad. 1).[611]

610. "Temperance draws back from those things which attract the appetite contrary to reason" (Aquinas, *Opera Omnia*, 3.472).

611. "Temperance does not run contrary to the inclination of human nature, but accords with it" (Aquinas, *Opera Omnia*, 3.471).

2. Temperance is not merely a *temperamental inclination* to sparing use of pleasures. It is willed freely and directed by prudence. It is a *choice* of moderation (*idem*, ad. 2).

3. Special effects of temperance are *peace* and *beauty of soul*, as we have already said (II-II, q. 141, a. 2, ad. 2–3).[612] He who is moderate in his desires for bodily pleasure and comfort is also not too troubled by the absence of pleasure and comfort, and is not inclined to seek them inordinately or to hope for them—in a word, to be distracted by them (*idem*, art. 3, ad. 1).[613]

4. Temperance is essentially the regulator of the *most vehement bodily pleasures* which are strong precisely because they are necessary for conservation of life and of the species (*idem*, art. 4).[614]

5. *What is the standard of temperance?* This is important. Once we know what temperance is, what it regulates, we need to know *how much* it regulates bodily pleasure. When does bodily pleasure cease to be rational and become intemperate? When do you draw the line? How do you know? This is determined by *necessity. Necessitas hujus vitae est regula temperantiae.*[615] {An} act is temperate when man makes use of bodily goods and the attendant pleasure *as far as the necessity of his earthly life requires* (*idem*, art. 6).[616] If you eat the food that you need to live a normal healthy life and do your work, the satisfaction connected with this act *is virtuous*. It gives glory to God. St. Thomas makes clear that the necessity he means is not only what we need to subsist, to keep on living, but to *live a fully human life* ("*convenienter*") (*idem*, ad. 2).[617] And this also takes into account a person's *station in life* (ad. 3).[618]

---

612. Aquinas, *Opera Omnia*, 3.472.

613. Aquinas, *Opera Omnia*, 3.473.

614. Aquinas, *Opera Omnia*, 3.473–74.

615. a. 6: "The necessity of this life is the rule of temperance" (Aquinas, *Opera Omnia*, 3.475, which reads: "*Regula temperantiae secundum praesentis vitae necessitatem sumenda est*" ["The rule of temperance is assumed to be the necessity of the present life"]).

616. Aquinas, *Opera Omnia*, 3.475.

617. Aquinas, *Opera Omnia*, 3.475.

618. Aquinas, *Opera Omnia*, 3.475.

The Vices Opposed to Temperance: the two vices opposed to temperance are *intemperance and insensibility*. Those who have not properly understood the Christian ascetic tradition or who have been affected unduly by the heritage of the Stoics with their *"apatheia"* (immunity to passion) may be tempted to act in practice as if insensibility were a virtue. Actually it is a vice. A clear understanding of this will make us appreciate the thought of St. Thomas.

Insensibility (II-II, q. 142, a. 1)[619] is a violation of that natural order which demands that man make use of certain pleasures in order to live humanly. However, this violation would be sinful only when one became insensible to pleasure to such an extent that he would cease to exercise such functions as eating, etc., which are necessary to life. This sometimes happens, however, among those who are ascetically inclined; they sometimes so violently suppress their appetite that they lose it altogether, and lose the ability to enjoy food, {and} almost stop eating. This is not virtuous if it reaches the point where their health is harmed. *However*, to abstain from pleasures of sense for a good end, such as to do penance or to dispose oneself for contemplation, is virtuous and good and is indeed a higher good than mere rational temperance. But due measure must always be observed. St. Thomas says, "Those men who have taken upon themselves the office of contemplation and who transmit to others, as by a kind of spiritual propagation, this spiritual good, are praiseworthy in that they abstain from many pleasures; and from these same pleasures others, engaged in bodily works and bodily generation, are praiseworthy in that they do not abstain" (a. 1, ad. 2).[620]

Intemperance (II-II, q. 142, a. 2–4):[621]

---

619. Aquinas, *Opera Omnia*, 3.476–77.

620. "*Et ideo homines, qui hoc officium assumpserunt ut contemplationi vacent, et bonum spirituale quasi quadam spirituali propagatione in alios transmittant, a multis delectabilibus laudabiliter abstinent, a quibus illi quibus ex officio competit operibus corporalibus et generationi carnali vacare, laudabiliter non abstinent*" (Aquinas, *Opera Omnia*, 3.477).

621. Aquinas, *Opera Omnia*, 3.477–79.

1. Intemperance is a *"puerile peccatum"*[622]—an infantile sin. This is a very interesting point, which puts St. Thomas on the plane of modern psychological thought. In what sense is intemperance "infantile"?

a) It goes for the superficial and obvious goods, not for the real and deep values according to reason.

b) It evades discipline and quickly grows beyond all bounds, avoiding rational limits. Excess quickly becomes "necessity" which one "must have" at any cost.

c) In order to control intemperate desires, we must resist and curb them with reason and not simply let them run wild.

(This does not mean that passions are to be controlled by violence. In asceticism, as in education, we must follow reason and not violence. Avoid both extremes. The theory of education that would let children do everything they feel like is fatal, but so is that which thinks that the child is to be frequently and heartily spanked and that will solve everything. The child must be *shown* the right thing and led to do it reasonably but firmly, in such a way that he learns not only how to do what he does, but acquires reasonable motives for doing it; so also in asceticism.) St. Thomas quotes Aristotle on this point: "As the child must live according to the precept of his teacher, so the desires must live according to reason."[623] Another good point on education {is found} in ad. 3: St. Thomas replies to {the} objection {that} children are to be cherished and brought up with care, but desires are to be extirpated. His reply {is} "That which pertains to nature in children is to be cherished and encouraged, and that which is contrary to reason in them is to be not favored but corrected."[624] Hence temperance, control of desires, {is} essential for maturity.

---

622. a. 2: "a childish sin" (Aquinas, *Opera Omnia*, 3.477).

623. *"Quemadmodum puerum oportet secundum praeceptum paedagogi vivere, sic et concupiscibile consonare rationi"* (Aquinas, *Opera Omnia*, 3.478).

624. *"Id quod ad naturam pertinet, in pueris est augmentandum et fovendum; quod autem pertinet ad defectum rationis in eis, non est fovendum, sed emendandum"* (Aquinas, *Opera Omnia*, 3.478).

2. St. Thomas emphasizes the fact that intemperance is a *notable disgrace* in man who is a spiritual being. It is a "servile" vice, repugnant to the "light of reason in which is the clarity and beauty of virtue" (art. 4).[625]

The Division of Temperance (II-II, q. 143, a. 1):[626] this division may seem unnecessarily abstract and schematic, and indeed we must not attach too much importance to this kind of analysis. However, it does throw light on the subject of temperance and its various aspects. *Integral parts* (required for the full and integral exercise of the virtue) {include} *verecundia* (shame)[627]—avoidance of the filth and disgrace of intemperance—{and} *honestas*[628]— love of the beauty of temperance. (Note: besides being virtues, *verecundia* and *honestas* are also passions, and they work to some extent automatically. Avoid an excessive emphasis on *verecundia*: it produces scrupulosity and {an} exaggerated sense of guilt over very small things or things which in themselves have nothing disgraceful about them. Some people think that all temperance and chastity consists in *verecundia*. These are not rightly balanced.) *Subjective parts* (species of temperance according to various objects) {include} *abstinentia*:[629] temperance in food (also fasting[630]); *sobrietas*:[631] temperance in drink; *castitas*:[632] temperance in pleasures of sex; *pudicitia*:[633] temperance in secondary pleasures of sex. (Note: for some people, temperance has become synonymous with sobriety; this again is a distortion.) Important for our study of chastity is the distinction between *castitas* and *pudicitia*. It is the formal and deliberate sins against chastity which are always by

625. "*de lumine rationis, ex qua est tota claritas et pulchritudo virtutis*" (Aquinas, *Opera Omnia*, 3.479).

626. Aquinas, *Opera Omnia*, 3.479–80.

627. *Secunda Secundae*, q. 144 (Aquinas, *Opera Omnia*, 3.480–83).

628. *Secunda Secundae*, q. 145 (Aquinas, *Opera Omnia*, 3.484–86).

629. *Secunda Secundae*, q. 146 (Aquinas, *Opera Omnia*, 3.486–87).

630. *Secunda Secundae*, q. 147 (Aquinas, *Opera Omnia*, 3.487–93).

631. *Secunda Secundae*, q. 149 (Aquinas, *Opera Omnia*, 3.497–99).

632. *Secunda Secundae*, q. 151 (Aquinas, *Opera Omnia*, 3.501–503).

633. *Secunda Secundae*, q. 151, a. 4 (Aquinas, *Opera Omnia*, 3.503).

their nature mortal. Chastity regards the pleasure of the complete sexual act or pleasures leading to this complete act and willed for that reason (*ad delectationem principalem ipsius coitus*[634]). *Pudicitia* regards the secondary pleasures in *tactibus, osculis et amplexibus.*[635] Here, kisses and embraces may or may not be sinful, depending on their nature and their orientation. We should remember the difference between a sin of impurity (against chastity) and a sin of sensuality (against *pudicitia*). The latter are generally venial, or more likely to be venial; the former, when deliberate, are mortal. *Potential parts* (accessory virtues, controlling body and soul in accord with temperance) {include} *continency*, {which} moderates {the} passion of lust in the will; *humility*, {which} moderates hope and audacity in {the} will seeking goods for {the} self; *meekness and clemency*, {which} moderates anger seeking revenge; *modesty*, {which consists in} good order, decency (simplicity) {and} austerity (restraint in showing natural affection to friends).

Chastity (according to St. Thomas):

1. What is the function of chastity? *to control the use of the reproductive faculty: ut secundum judicium rationis et electionem voluntatis aliquis moderate utatur corporalibus membris* (II-II, q. 151, a. 1, ad. 1).[636]

secundum judicium rationis: it implies then a judgement. Judgement is impeded by passion and by bad habit, so that he who is carried away by passion or is a slave to habit *cannot* practice the virtue of chastity because he *cannot* follow the light of reason in this matter. On the other hand, the fact that reason is blinded may diminish culpability in some respects. But the point is *not merely to avoid formal sin* but to *practice chastity as a virtue.* Sometimes *material* sin occurs in sexual matters, but one cannot

---

634. q. 143: "for the principal pleasure of the act of intercourse itself" (Aquinas, *Opera Omnia*, 3.480).

635. q. 143: "touches, kisses and embraces" (Aquinas, *Opera Omnia*, 3.480, which reads: "*osculis, tactibus et amplexibus*").

636. "that one use one's bodily members in moderation, in accordance with the judgement of reason and the choice of the will" (Aquinas, *Opera Omnia*, 3.502).

be passively content with a state of affairs in which this might happen frequently. One should take every means to be perfectly chaste in every way. There can be no compromise in a virtue so difficult. The passion of sexual desire is the one which one must treat most firmly and uncompromisingly; otherwise control is impossible. He says: the judgement of *reason*. Misuse of sex is forbidden by the natural law, but also our faith teaches us that our bodies belong to God and must be used according to His will only. Chastity must be practiced according to faith as well as reason, supernatural standards as well as natural. We have seen above what these are. The norm of chastity, as for all temperance, is *necessitas naturae*.[637] Chastity is the virtue of those who use sexual faculties only within the bounds proper to maintain the family, that is to say, in wedlock and with a certain moderation and spirituality proper to Christian spouses. This virtuous use of sex naturally allows of passion and pleasure (ordained by God as part of the use of this faculty), but the Christian virtue of chastity implies that this pleasure is subordinate to something higher. What is this something higher? duty?—no; it is subordinated to sincere and deep and mature *human love*. The pleasure of sex is virtuous when it is *subordinated to true love in the married state*. True love means a love that is *oblative*, that implies a gift of self to the partner, regard for and respect for the partner as a person, and respect for the holiness of their union. Where love is immature, the marriage union is imperfect (though perfectly legitimate and valid according to legal standards)—the partners treat each other as *objects* from which satisfaction is to be derived for oneself. Such love is *narcissistic*. Each partner wishes merely to enjoy his own pleasure and reflect on his self-enjoyment.

   et electionem voluntatis (not just a yielding to instinct): the use of sex pleasure is virtuous when it represents a free choice of the will, according to the norms of reason (true human love) and of God's revealed will.

---

637. "the necessity of nature" (see above, n. 615).

moderate utatur: the use of sex pleasure is a *use* (a means to an end), not a fruition (sought as an end in itself)—and it must be moderate. The moderate use of sex pleasure among married persons does not exclude embraces and touches ordained to their natural purpose.

corporalibus membris: the bodily members are *used or kept unused*; respect for the body {is} implied.

Hence it is clear that chastity is a virtue which can and must be practiced by *every Christian*, whether in the married state or out of it. But those who are not married are obliged to *perfect chastity*, that is to say, to complete abstention from all use of the generative faculty. Religious make perfect chastity the object of a vow.

Sins of Impurity: first of all, here, for the sake of clarity, we will follow in brief outline what is said by the moral theologians (especially Génicot[638]).

1. Sins of impurity properly so-called are sins *circa venerea*, that is to say, sins in the realm of strictly sexual pleasure. This means in the performance of acts which are *for the sake of generation*. This means the deliberate excitation of the generative powers, outside of the limits set by reason and by the matrimonial state.

2. The *physiological* manifestations of sexual activity are known. A few remarks may be to the point:

a) Purely bodily manifestations of sex are automatic, instinctive, and may take place with no cooperation of the will, or indeed without advertence at all. *Such manifestations are not sinful*; they are indifferent. The mere fact that the members undergo some change is of no moral significance. *The emission of semen during sleep* is purely natural and normal and is in no way to be considered sinful, unless there was definitely some series of acts or thoughts during waking hours which may have caused

---

638. Édouard Génicot, sj, *Theologiae Moralis Institutiones*, 5th ed., 2 vols. (Louvain: Polleunis et Ceuterick, 1905), 1:366–89: "6.6. *De Sexto et Nono Praeceptis*."

it. Temptation resolutely resisted is no sin and no cause of moral evil in a mechanical act that follows during sleep.

b) *Distillatio*, the emission of moisture from {the} prostate gland and from pituitary glands of the urethra, has no connection with semination. In practice it is of no importance and does not produce any pleasure or become the object of evil desire. If it accompanies vehement excitation of the desires, or improper actions, what is to be determined is the voluntariness of *these actions*, not the voluntariness of the *distillatio*. *Distillatio* in no way indicates "completeness" of a sex act.

3. *Sentimentality, sensibility, sensuality, sexuality*—a definition of terms: it is important to distinguish between these various forms of pleasure. Remember that sin is not in feeling or in pleasure but *in the will*. In what does venereal pleasure consist? Let us distinguish various forms of pleasure.

Sentimentality is not venereal and not sinful and generally does not lead directly to sin. It is an immature emotional affection which exists largely in the imagination and feelings and is concerned not so much with a desire for sexual union as with the desire for affection and emotional consolation. Feelings of sentimental love for a person of the same sex are not necessarily to be regarded as indicative of sexual perversion. However, sentimentality is to be cautioned against and avoided on the *ascetic* plane. Sentimental affection is *remotely connected* with impurity and should be controlled by a virile austerity which *elevates* affection to a higher and more manly level. We should not be ashamed to love others, particularly our parents and relatives. We should have a warm and virile affection for our friends and brethren in the monastery. Such affections are not usually sentimental. Soft, sentimental affections with a feminine cast to them are very harmful in the spiritual life, and persons who are very much inclined to these affections should realize that this may indicate that they lack a monastic vocation.

Sensibility: some people have strongly emotional natures or are acutely sensitive in some way or other, perhaps especially as regards the sense of touch. Thus their emotions, feelings and members are often very easily aroused by causes that may have little or nothing to do with sex. For such people, any sense pleasure, or even a spiritual pleasure, may overflow into the sex faculties without any desire or even advertence on their part. Sometimes also they are aroused by anxiety or fear and undergo sexual reactions without foreseeing them. Such reactions, if they are not willed and sought, are not sinful. They are purely neutral. One should take care *to withhold consent* and turn the will to God. The physical reactions need not be prevented; nor is it wise to try to prevent them *directly*. Indirect resistance, prayer, etc., is necessary. Note that persons with a sensible nature easily conceive images, and perhaps they may spontaneously and without premeditation have vivid impure thoughts. If they remain at peace and quietly take the usual precautions, by prayer, etc., they can keep their minds at rest. They should not worry about these things and not lose their heads trying to resist with indiscreet violence.

Sensuality: when we speak of *sensibility*, we refer rather to a natural and temperamental inclination of character. When we speak of *sensuality*, we imply willful indulgence of the senses in matters *bordering on impurity*. Whereas sensibility has nothing wrong in it, *sensuality* is dangerous and should be mortified in anyone who wishes to practice perfect chastity. Sensuality, in the context of the sixth and ninth commandments, involves pleasures of sense, especially of touch, which, though not directly venereal, are closely connected with venereal pleasure.

a) *Sensual curiosity* {is} a love of looking at (clothed) bodily beauty for the sake of the purely sense pleasure which it arouses, habitually taking delight in looking at women, their faces, figures, movements, etc., for the sake of the sense pleasure aroused—{the} same with pictures or with any object pleasing to the senses in this particular way. Where there is indulgence in *sensual* pleasure in admiring a person of the same sex, the pleasure is to be reproved and mortified. (Merely *adverting* to beauty and feeling pleasure at it is sensibility rather than sensuality, and there is nothing wrong with it. Sensuality in looking at beauty is a matter of *conscious and willful seeking of sense pleasure by dwelling with the eyes on an attractive object*. When one looks at attractive objects not only to enjoy sense pleasure but to feel oneself aroused sexually, then it goes beyond sensuality and becomes mortally sinful because it is venereal pleasure not permitted outside matrimony. It must of course be fully deliberate, sought or accepted with full knowledge.) Sensual curiosity is usually a venial sin, when fully consented {to}. Men of habitually good conscience should not be troubled if by chance and inadvertence they happen to look at some sensual object. There may be carelessness present. It should be regretted, and one should, with sincere sorrow, resolve to be more careful in the future. However, accidents should not be given an exaggerated importance. Special care should be taken in reading secular magazines, etc. when one is outside the monastery.

b) *Sensual contacts* {consist in} pleasure sought or accepted in bodily contacts with others for the sake of the sense stimulation it offers—caresses, kissing, embraces, brushing up against people, sitting close to them, etc. NOTE: where this is simply an expression of normal affection and not a search for sense pleasure for its own sake, there is nothing wrong with it in legitimate cases. Such affection should be expressed in this manner. Coldness is not Christianity. But where there is no reason for these contacts, and where they lead rather to sensuality or even to venereal pleasure, they are to be avoided as sinful—venial or even mortal (if sex is involved). Note the special danger of *scandal* in sensual contacts, touching others, etc. It may seem like nothing to you, but to another person it may come as a great shock, especially if it is the sensuality of a *religious*. In the monastery, particular care should be taken to avoid all such contacts, however innocent. Monks do not express their affection, however legitimate, in this manner. This is a necessary point of monastic regularity and asceticism.

c) *Sensual love of comfort*, an inordinate love of relaxed and easy postures, verging on softness and sought for the sake of pleasure in ease, though not in itself sinful, can lead to a state of mind which easily accepts sinful forms of pleasure. We should be relaxed and free as children of God and not prudish or tense. We should not be afraid to take care of our bodies in an ordinate way. There is nothing wrong with touching any part of the body provided there is a reasonable cause for it. But sensuality can easily come in when, under pretext of taking care of normal needs, we prolong attentions uselessly or go about them in too gratifying a manner, more for the sake of indulgence than for necessity. Such sensuality is quite dangerous and must be firmly resisted. *In this point, one who has a vow of chastity cannot afford any compromise.* One has to be very definite and not hesitate to draw the line. Develop a straight and tender conscience and follow it, and for the rest, don't worry.

d) *Other forms of sensuality* {may include} inordinate love of perfume, amorous or sensual music, etc. In general, one should learn to avoid all the softness and amorousness that is seen everywhere in "the world."

Sexuality: sensuality is not yet, in itself, venereal. Hence it is not directly forbidden by the sixth commandment. Venereal pleasure strictly so-called is that pleasure which is inseparable from the excitation of the sex organs and the emission of seed. {The} *principle* {is that} *all deliberately willed, or sought, or accepted venereal pleasure is a mortal sin* outside of wedlock. Here is the real matter of the vow of chastity. No Christian is allowed to indulge in venereal pleasure outside of holy matrimony. By our vow we take on a more strict obligation, and we offer to God our renunciation of these pleasures, whether in matrimony or out of it. Perfect chastity is the obligation *to refuse all venereal pleasure whatever*, at least as far as the will is concerned. When such pleasure occurs unavoidably and without our consent, there is no fault.

Venereal acts:

1. Any act which of its nature leads to the excitation of the sexual organs and eventually to the emission of seed is a venereal

act. Such acts may be *external*, such as fornication {and} masturbation, or they may be *internal*, willful desires for the above acts or for pleasures connected with them. Here we refer to acts that are clearly and definitely sexual *by nature*, not to acts which may become venereal *by accident*.

2. Any act which, though it is *not venereal by nature*, is nevertheless *willed and sought for the sake of venereal pleasure* {becomes venereal}: for instance, kissing when it is passionate and directed to venereal pleasure; reading when it is a question of reading immoral material for the deliberate purpose of obtaining sexual pleasure (most "dangerous" reading is sensual rather than venereal, but books that are openly pornographic seek to arouse venereal pleasure); talking when it is a question of deliberately speaking of matters that actually arouse venereal pleasure; dancing when it is of a highly sensual nature and deliberately sought for venereal pleasure; thoughts of sensual things, for the sake of venereal pleasure.

Sins against the Sixth Commandment (sexual or sensual): without going into all the different species (incest, rape, etc.), we will content ourselves with what is most obvious and practical for our understanding of the vow of chastity.

1. *Mortal sins* {include the following}:

a) to willfully, deliberately carry out an action which is clearly and by its nature venereal, that clearly and by its nature leads to a complete sexual act, with the emission of seed; this is a mortal sin even if the pleasure is not desired or consented to (note: it is not the *pleasure* that is sinful, but the deliberate act);

b) to consent willfully and deliberately to fully venereal pleasure even in an action which is not by itself venereal, but which accidentally arouses the sexual instinct. The sin is mortal when the venereal act is *complete* either *physically* (emission of seed) or *mentally and internally* (the complete act is willed and accepted even though it is not carried out externally). If the venereal act is *externally incomplete*, and if interiorly one has not fully given in to the desire of consummated pleasure but has resisted it all along, then there may or may not be mortal sin, but it *is doubtful*.

2. *Venial sins* {include the following}:

a) an act which is materially venereal and complete may be formally a venial sin by reason of lack of consent or lack of sufficient knowledge or awareness; such an act may be no sin at all if all consent is totally lacking (v.g., in a case of rape);

b) acts of sensuality, semi-deliberate carelessness with venereal pleasure, etc.;

c) failure to prevent unpredicted sexual motions which arise without our action and could easily be prevented—v.g., in a case of accidental pollution (if *consent* is given, the act becomes a mortal sin);

d) filthy talk, for the sake of "humor," etc., {is} generally venial.

3. {There is} *no sin at all* {when}:

a) {there is a} *double effect*: for instance, a student has to study material in moral theology, {and} this material causes him to be sexually aroused and feel venereal pleasure. There is no sin here *if the following conditions are observed*: (1) there exists a serious reason for reading this material; it could not be avoided without notable difficulty and detriment; (2) consent {is} withheld from all venereal pleasure; (3) the venereal pleasure is merely accidental and is not sought as a means to some other end. These principles may apply to many other possible cases, but one should not be too easy to assume that there is always sufficient reason for exposing himself to danger.

b) *There is no sin* in the mere fact of thinking about a venereal act; for instance, the *thought* of fornication or the *thought* of a naked person is not in itself a sin at all; there is nothing wrong with the human body, and there is no sin in thinking about it. But sin would come in if one were to deliberately accept and exploit these thoughts for the sake of arousing venereal pleasure, or if one were to consent to sensual pleasure arising from the thoughts and indulge it willfully. One should be on his guard not to indulge these thoughts uselessly, even without pleasure. One should have a rational motive in accepting thoughts like these and avoid danger following from them, but there is no sense in being fearful and scrupulous and trying to exclude the very thought of sex from one's mind at all times and under all circumstances—sometimes it is unavoidable.

c) There is no sin in taking *satisfaction in the relief* following the accidental emission of seed and relaxation of tension, provided one does not dwell on the pleasure that accompanied this for its own sake. {For} example, if one were to have a nocturnal pollution, one would not sin in being glad to get up with a relief of tension and with greater bodily comfort in the morning. But note: one must not consent to an inordinate pleasure of a past sexual act, whether voluntary or involuntary.

d) There is no sin in seeing or looking at (with reason) parts of the body, one's own or others', or in seeing animals perform a sexual act. What must be avoided here is useless or unhealthy curiosity about these things and a desire to indulge sensual desires in this way, which would not ordinarily exceed venial sin. *Warning*: in the above cases where generally there would be "no sin," we must take care to remember that in our own case there may be circumstances that alter the morality of the act entirely. For instance, a person who knows he is weak should never uselessly expose himself to temptation even in matters which are slight *for others* or slight in themselves. In general, though we should be careful at all times and avoid scruples *post factum*, we should cultivate a delicate conscience along with common sense and seek to avoid anything that is out of harmony with our life of chastity. The above principles are merely *minimum* standards. Remember that for a religious with vows, there is a high ideal to be maintained. This will be discussed later.

Chastity and the Religious: we have now got a clear notion of what is strictly "venereal pleasure" and what is sensuality.

Venereal pleasure is what is formally renounced, under grave obligation, by the vow of chastity. But the virtue of chastity in a religious demands also the avoidance of sensuality.

The Obligation of Religious Chastity: it is not sufficient to define the obligation of the vow of chastity as a renunciation of all venereal pleasure. This is too narrow a definition. The full extent of the obligation is as follows:

a) The renunciation of all thought or desire of marriage: there is normally no sin against chastity for a person without vows in thinking about marriage or planning to marry; on the contrary, it would be a good and virtuous thing in a Christian eligible to marry. But for a religious to seriously and deliberately plan to enter into a marriage contract, even without dwelling on the thought of venereal pleasure, would be a sin against the vow. *A fortiori*, the fact of attempting matrimony would be a sin against the vow, even if the act were not followed by sexual union.

b) The practice of chastity on a higher level and with the aim of definitive consecration of one's body and soul to Christ: this means, fundamentally, the renunciation *sub gravi*[639] of every venereal act whatever. But it also means, though not *sub gravi*, the obligation to *cultivate chastity* by the avoidance of sensuality and of occasions of unchastity and by positive means such as prayer, penance and the frequentation of the sacraments.

Hence a religious who simply avoids mortal sin against the sixth commandment and does not entertain any desire of getting married is not fully living up to his vow of chastity, though at the same time he is not necessarily violating it mortally. He must also avoid all compromise and trifling with sensuality and with acts that foster weakness and predispose one to venereal indulgence. However, not every act of sensuality is necessarily a sin against the vow of chastity. But a person who is *habitually sensual* and realizes the danger for himself in this habitual sensuality is sin-

639. "under pain of serious sin."

ning at least venially against his vow of chastity if he permits the state of affairs to continue and makes no effort to cultivate positive chastity. Hence the vow of chastity implies a *positive duty* to live a life of prayer and self-denial, of discipline and of consecration. The religious vowed to chastity must strive to cultivate that love of Christ which will elevate and consecrate his affections to God. It is morally and psychologically unhealthy for a person to make a merely negative vow of chastity, promising merely "not to indulge in venereal acts." He must dedicate to God the love he has removed from physical objects. To neglect prayer and love, and to become merely hardened against the flesh, is to produce insensibility, and this is a vice. It is not true Christian chastity, which demands interior and spiritual love for Christ, overflowing in a dedicated love for other men and works of mercy. *Hence it follows* that every sin committed by a religious against the sixth or ninth commandment is a violation of his vow and is a twofold sin—one of intemperance and one of *sacrilege*. Both sins must be made known in confession.

Special Problems:

a) *Impure Thoughts*: some religious are bothered more than necessary with "impure thoughts." This may be due to the fact of the tension under which they live. Memories and images come back to haunt them. The following counsels are offered:

1) The protection offered by the monastery generally keeps us far from occasions of sin. The thoughts that come to us are inevitable and should not be feared. *Fear and scrupulosity* often aggravate "impure thoughts" and make the trial much more serious than it ought to be.

2) Are the thoughts really "impure"? We have seen above[640] {that} the mere image of a body, even unclothed, or the mere thought of sex is not necessarily sinful or evil. To have an image in one's mind is no sin. There is even nothing wrong with the

640. See page 342.

image in itself. It is dangerous and can lead us to sinful desire. But if we are really distressed by the presence of the image and really wish it were not there, then it is hardly likely that we are consenting to pleasure arising from it. *There is no obligation to force the image* out of the mind. If it won't go, let it stay, as long as you do not desire it there or seek to exploit it for sensual pleasure.

3) Even if the thought is *sensual* and you feel attraction to it, do not be too quick to imagine either that the object is seriously evil or above all that you "have consented" to it.

4) In all matters of interior temptation regarding the sixth or ninth commandment, what is required is *positive resistance only, not direct resistance. Positive resistance* {entails} definite acts contrary to the attraction—for instance, prayer, acts of love for God, renewal of our vow, etc. *Direct resistance* {involves} efforts to make the thought or feeling go away. This is not only not obligatory, but it is also not advisable. It may even be much *less perfect*.

5) Humility and manifestation of conscience are often the best way of dealing with this problem.

6) Confident, loving prayer, love of {the} Blessed Sacrament and of Our Lady {are effective responses}.

Note {that} in certain stages of the interior life, where there is great dryness in prayer and interior suffering, impure obsessions may add themselves to the torment of the soul. At such times, follow the advice of a wise director. This is part of a purifying trial, very good for the soul, though very difficult to handle with peace. It may even be a sign of a certain progress in the life of prayer, paradoxical though this may seem. The counsels offered above regarding impure thoughts may be taken as generally valid for all problems of chastity confronting pure souls.

b) *Particular Friendships*: are particular friendships a really serious problem in the monastic life? We may begin the discussion with this question. If it is faced frankly, it will be more easily understood. {There are} various opinions:

(a) There are some who *exaggerate* the danger of particular friendships in two ways: (1) they tend to consider *all* friendship and all affection as "particular" and therefore obnoxious; (2) they tend to regard real particular friendship as something disastrous, as an irreparable error. The result of this exaggerated opinion is to produce fear and scrupulosity and to obscure the real issue. Exaggerated fear of particular friendship tends in some cases to *foster* particular friendships.

(b) There are some who *minimize* the danger of particular friendships. They say all friendship is a good thing, affection is good, and therefore one should have friends, and show them affection, even special affection. There is truth in all these statements, but those who err in applying them do not distinguish between a *healthy and normal* friendship and an *unhealthy* one.

What is meant by particular friendship? It is an exaggerated, immature, *sentimental or even sensual attachment* between persons who are usually members of special enclosed groups, living cut off from normal society. The term particular friendship is not applied to a normal, mature friendship, even though that friendship may be very intimate and affectionate. Mature friendships can exist anywhere and should exist even in monasteries, provided they do not become "attachments."

How does one distinguish between particular friendship and genuine friendship? It is clear that a "particular" friendship is somehow not a real friendship. Why? A particular friendship is *exclusive, possessive* and *compulsive.* {It is} *exclusive*: it is an exaggerated and inordinate attachment. The friend looks upon his friend as someone utterly unique among all the others, as a "beloved" in the sentimental sense. His reaction to the beloved is unique in its intensity. The presence of the beloved is appreciated and sought, often with great pains. Others in turn are regarded at times with indifference or even revulsion. {A} very evident contrast {is perceived} between them and the "beloved." Secrets, cliques, etc. arise. (In a genuine friendship, one may have a high esteem of the special qualities of his friend and prefer his company to that of others, but there is none of this exclusiveness, particularly in the emotional realm. Presence and absence of the friend entail no especially marked emotional reaction.) {It is} *possessive*: the "beloved" is regarded as a possession, to be enjoyed by the friend and denied to others. Hence *jealousy* is a mark of particular friendship, {as well as} rivalry, {the} desire to cut others out, to have for oneself all the company, conversation, etc. of the beloved. (In a genuine friendship, one enjoys the company and conversation of a friend, and enjoys privacy to converse more intimately, but there is no emotional need to exclude others or to prevent them from occupying the attention of the friend.) {It is} *compulsive*: the particular friend is *driven* by his emotions to seek out his friend, to look at him, to talk with him, to seek assurances of affection, loyalty, etc. Where friends are always being put to the test there is this emotional need for reassurance, hence compulsivity. The demands become more and more exacting. The friend is obsessed with the "beloved," sometimes thinks of him almost all the time. Where one is habitually distracted in prayer, meditation, etc. by the thought of another monk, then there is present an inclination to particular friendship. (A genuine friendship is natural and spontaneous. One is very glad to be with his friend and seeks his company, but without the domination of a heavy emotional need. And when one is not with his friend, the mind is free to think about anything else—the friend does not come between us and God or between us and our work, etc. There is no sentimentality or obsessiveness present.) One further note: where there is particular friendship there is also usually an *obscure sense of guilt*. The one involved may use up much effort to justify the friendship and to argue that it is not false, but he struggles to suppress his guilt, and this complicates matters. However, the sense of guilt may be the result of a malformed conscience. It is not decisive. In practice, however, it is usually present, whether suppressed or felt, in particular friendships.

Particular Friendships and the Spiritual Life: the question of the danger of particular friendships needs to be treated with more subtlety than it usually receives. It is not enough to say that particular friendships are silly, or dangerous, or to be avoided. That should be quite obvious. Anyone who is sufficiently mature will be able to see this at a glance, and it will not cause any problem to him. Unfortunately, the *immaturity* which always goes with particular friendships is generally not taken into account. Immaturity is the real problem.

(a) Particular friendships tend to spring up among those who enter religion at an early age, who are not yet emotionally developed, who are not yet able to judge and to control their affections, and who still live in great measure according to their senses.

(b) It is unfortunate that in some (indeed very many) religious houses, especially among enclosed orders, immaturity is prevalent and encouraged, and extends beyond the years of youth all through the religious life. The enclosed life has many great advantages, but at the same time those who profit by these advantages may remain too passive and simply drift along in a state of irresponsibility. They then remain children in the bad sense of the word. They do not grow up; they remain the victim of their whims and fantasies and the prey of every emotion. Hence, even though mature in years, they can give themselves to petty emotional friendships and displays of sentimental affection.

(c) This in turn makes it difficult for the younger ones to grow up; and indeed it may affect and warp the development of good vocations. Many vocations have been ruined by stupid and sentimental relationships which interfered with the proper formation of a novice and prevented him from growing spiritually strong and mature.

In general, then, the effect of sentimental friendship is to stunt the *spiritual growth* of individuals and of communities. It keeps the soul weak, naturally and supernaturally. It kills the spirit of detachment and prayer. It prevents one from giving himself to God. It blocks the channels of much needed grace, and exposes the soul to great danger. These are the effects of a sentimental friendship which remains more or less undeveloped and does not lead to anything else.

But there are *further developments* which we need only touch on, without giving them undue emphasis. Sentimental friendship leads to sensuality and even to impure temptations. When there is any open or physical expression of special affection, it becomes an evil to be combated and strict measures must be taken. One who receives such marks of attention should always express an objection and manifest his distaste for such things. If such manifestations are repeated, the matter must be made known to a superior.

Practical advice: in addition to the general advice on chastity (below[641]), avoid all manifestation of special affection, even under the guise of piety or "charity"— i.e., *special* favors for certain ones and not for others, etc. Do not seek out the company of those for whom you have a special liking, and do not go out of your way to make signs to them or to see them. As soon as a particular affection seriously interferes with your life of prayer, discuss it in spiritual direction and follow the advice given.

True Friendship and the Spiritual Life: we do not come to the monastery merely to seek friends. However, we do *find* them. But a true and supernatural friendship is always spiritual and detached. It is not so much the human accidents of the friend that are loved: God is loved in him. There is no attachment to physical or spiritual qualities. They may be seen and appreciated. But the presence of a friend is an aid in loving God, not a means of self-gratification. True friendship in the monastery must be almost entirely devoid of self-seeking and self-gratification. It then does not constitute a distraction or an obstacle. One loves one's companions not so much because they are naturally pleasing as because they are the brethren chosen for us by God, and with whom we are closely united in the mystery of our salvation. This implies a deep affection, which can certainly even be "felt," but it is not in any sense sentimental. Such friendship expresses itself in sacrifice: not so much a matter of putting oneself out for this or that "friend," but one expresses his love for his brother

641. See below, pages 353–60.

by sacrificing himself for the community, for *all* the brethren without distinction, by the wholehearted giving of oneself. Monastic friendship is always mingled with a spirit of solitude. One loves one's brothers but does not "need" consolation from them. Indeed, one is glad of their company, yet one is also glad to be alone. True friendship in the cloister is self-effacing. It seeks God, not human consolation. It desires one's friend to enjoy peace in solitude with God, and does not seek to disturb him in order to gain a little personal consolation for oneself. We must learn to live alone in community, closely united to our brothers without any need for special recognition or expressions of friendship other than the ordinary smile and courteous behavior which constitutes a recognition of one by another.

c) *Other Escapes from Chastity*: besides manifest impurity and sensuality, or sentimentality, there are other evasions by which we tend unconsciously to react against the difficulties of solitude of heart. Much of the ordinary restlessness and inability to settle down to pray and meditate is due to sensuality, insufficient control of our emotions and of our flesh. These are very subtle problems and cannot be solved without the guidance of a good director. We need only mention them in passing.

Excessive activism, masking as "zeal," can be merely an escape from the solitude of heart imposed by our vow of chastity. The religious tries to forget his anxieties in hectic work. (Generous work and self-sacrificing zeal are indeed a necessity; they help us to consecrate to God the energies which are not devoted to the generation and raising of children. But the work must be calm, fruitful and mature. It must be really productive. Mere hectic activism, even though materially it may produce "results," is no solution to the problem of solitude of heart and chastity: in the long run it only aggravates the problem.)

Excessive preoccupation with the spiritual needs of others: sometimes under the guise of good, spiritual direction, etc., a religious can interfere too much in the lives of his brothers, try to direct them unduly, tell them what to do, or even impose on them his own ideas and lead them into paths they do not seek.

Those who have no official mission to take care of souls are very wrong to mix in such things, and it may happen that they do so because they are restless and not fully able to cope with their own solitude and need for consolation. Even those who have a mission to take care of souls must be careful that it does not become a substitute for family life and an inordinate source of self-gratification. All this is simply an evasion, an escape from true chastity of heart.

Bitterness, aggressivity: one of the worst and most unpleasant "escapes" from the difficulties of a chaste life occurs when the energy that would normally be released through human love becomes channeled instead into bitterness and hostility. The monk is impatient of everyone and everything and takes it out on his brothers and superiors. This may have no obvious or conscious connection with sex, and still be an unconscious escape. At other times the person may recognize that bursts of bitterness and hostility coincide with the times when he suffers impure temptation. This can be a great trial: one should do his best to accept it with meekness and patience and not turn his resentments onto everyone else. Prayer is the only solution, and the generous effort to overcome our bitterness in order to be nice to others in spite of everything.

Curiosity, involvement in things outside our vocation: while intellectual activity is good and should be encouraged, since it does help one to get his mind off sensual things and attach them to the things of God, we must be careful of an "escape" into mere curiosity—reading that is so light that it is purely and simply an anodyne (pain-killer). This is not so much of a problem where our libraries are kept full of books on a high level of quality. But bad and low-grade reading, even supposedly "spiritual" reading, can be used as a mere distraction. Such reading can become a vice, especially when it has nothing whatever to do with anything serious or worthwhile. (Note: the reading of a monk need not be confined necessarily to exclusively spiritual topics. History, science, art, etc. have their place. But these things must not become an "escape." The matter should be settled in spiritual direction.)

Sentimentality and sensuality in devotion: a very obvious escape from chastity of heart is to seek a thinly disguised substitute in emotional and sentimental ways of prayer—sugary attachments to consolation, to sweetness, and the inordinate use of pictures, of female saints especially, to produce an emotional kick in prayer. This may seem to be legitimate, but in the long run it has bad effects, especially when (as soon must happen) the sentimentality becomes allied with "dolorism"—a sentimental cult of pain for the sake of the stimulation and self-pity which it arouses. This is extremely harmful and poisons the spiritual life.

Aids in practicing chastity: knowledge is one of the most important helps. We have discussed at length the difficulties and problems that may arise, in order to lay down a good foundation of knowledge on the subject. Ignorance is one of the great sources of trouble in this matter. When one knows what the situation really is, it is not too hard for him to conclude what ought to be done. However, practical hints are of great help. In controlling the flesh, we must remember that self-discipline is all-important and that without a spirit of ascetic self-denial we will not get anywhere. However, in addition to the traditional ascetic means of cultivating chastity and purity of heart, we must take note of the ordinary, common-sense, natural facts of hygiene. Finally, it is most important to go beyond asceticism in the other direction and to have a high ideal, indeed a mystical ideal, of consecrated virginity. We shall discuss first of all the point of hygiene, then go on to ascetic means, and finally touch once more on the ideal of virginity which was discussed in the beginning.

Hygiene: we practice chastity *with* our body, not in spite of our body. Taking into account the intimate union of body and soul, the balance and integration that should exist between them, we will realize that bodily and psychological health has a great deal to do with the practice of chastity. This does not mean that chastity is something that can be attained merely by hygiene. But the sane practice of hygiene, united with asceticism, will make the success of ascetic means more assured and more lasting.

Health: sometimes ascetics have thought in the past that it was good to have an unhealthy body and that this made the practice of holiness easier. A distinction must be made: putting up with bad health certainly gives opportunities to practice virtue and detachment from one's self. One must not be attached to health or worry about it. There is definitely a tendency among moderns to worry too much about the body. This is an extreme that must be avoided; it is more dangerous today than the other extreme. However, in a healthy body it is easier and simpler to live a balanced ascetic life. No one is permitted to deliberately ruin his health or allow it to be ruined merely for ascetic purposes. This would be very harmful and could lead to the wreck of a vocation in some cases. *Conclusion*: we should appreciate health of body as a gift of God which can aid in our sanctification and life of virtue. We should be grateful and preserve it without undue solicitude. *Note*: it is a fact that sometimes decline of health and loss of strength, especially nervous strength, may lead to a decline in resistance to temptation. This is generally true of beginners, but can happen to anyone.

Diet: there is a close relationship between diet and sexuality, hence the fact that traditional asceticism uses *fasting* as one of the chief means to control the flesh. Fasting as an ascetic means will not be useful if it is not practiced prudently, in relation to a sane diet. In our Order, the food is purposely simple and abundant. It is not stimulating or highly spiced. There is no meat. The ordinary food in the refectory is suited to a life of chastity and is sufficiently healthy. One should be careful to take plenty of milk and cheese, a necessary source of protein, also eggs if you are "on relief." These will not hurt. When candy and cake and other sweets are given, they might perhaps be used with discretion, especially at night. But one should not be scrupulous on these points. Individuals differ. Some are affected by candy or strong coffee, and in that case they should be reserved in their use of these things. Otherwise, one should eat without scruple what comes in the refectory, with perhaps a little care not to take too great a quantity of food or drink in the evening. To go soon to bed with a full stomach and to have to get up many times in the night might interfere with normal sleep and lead to difficulties. Where there is no special difficulty, one can disregard the above recommendations. *Note*: outside the monastic life, or in special situations, the use of *alcohol* is either sexually stimulating or releases inhibitions and makes it easier to give in to sexual urges. St. Benedict would have the monk use wine only sparingly.[642] *Lack of appetite* is not a healthy sign. In our life one should eat well in the refectory. Normal health usually depends on this. One should not fear food or become obsessed with the idea that eating will cause temptations. This would lead to an obsessive condition which is mentally unhealthy and might cause more trouble still in the realm of purity.

Cleanliness: personal cleanliness is of the greatest importance. The *Rule* says that the young should not take baths too frequently.[643] But remember what St. Benedict had in mind: the Roman baths, places of luxury and sensuality. Nowadays a daily shower is normal, though crowding sometimes makes it difficult. There is nothing wrong with wanting to have a daily shower. It is not obligatory: one can compromise and take showers less frequently than that in order not to lose too much reading time. Whatever the frequency of one's showers, the important thing for chastity is to keep the genital organs clean. Infections (fungus) and other irritations in this area are very common, especially in summer. *Underclothing* should be loose, cool, and comfortable, {and} should not be of a type to irritate. One should not sleep in sweaty clothes or too heavily clad.

Exercise: it is important to have a normal and healthy amount of hard work. This is one of the benefits connected with our manual labor. Regular physical exercise provides the necessary balance for our nervous system, releases energy and makes temptation less likely (ordinarily). When one has a job that deprives him of real exercise, then exercise should be taken during free

642. *Rule*, c. 40 (McCann, 96).
643. *Rule*, c. 36 (McCann, 90).

time. One should go for walks, or read outside, or perhaps get some manual labor on feast days. It is however an illusion to imagine that when one is undergoing temptation one can shake it off by feverish exercise. This only makes things worse. The function of manual labor is to keep our condition balanced and healthy so that in the long run we will be not inordinately sub-jected to movements of the flesh. But when these movements arise, labor is of little or no avail to combat them *per se*. {As to} "exercises," in some cases, health will require the performance of some physical exercises, deep breathing, etc. But this is a personal matter and should be settled in private, in the individual case. For most religious, manual labor is sufficient.

Rest: a normal amount of sleep which guarantees the proper balance of the physique will, like work, etc., aid in living a chaste life. Though vigils are a traditional form of asceticism, one should not attempt to combat temptations by deliberately staying awake and out of bed praying for a long time. On the contrary, the best {thing} is to relax and try to go to sleep. Brief prayers are sufficient to indicate that our will is fixed on the love of God and that we reject everything contrary to His will. When one is rested and alert, temptations during the daytime will be less frequent. One will be able to pray better in choir and thus obtain the graces necessary to live a holy life. We need seven hours sleep.

"Change of phantasm": though there is no recreation in our Order, it is logical that each monk on his own should provide for himself a recreative type of reading or some other activity that will provide a change of the images passing through the mind. Our imagination needs a normal and healthy activity; otherwise it can become fixed on morbid and obsessional thoughts, which may or may not be concerned with impurity. If we provide for ourselves (under the guidance of a wise director) a suitable form of mental relaxation, this will be obviated. The mind and imagi-nation will be rested. Examples {include} a prudent variety in reading matter, devotions, ways of prayer, work, etc.

Pathological conditions: it sometimes happens that trouble with impurity is to be traced to some nervous or glandular disorder, or to a neurotic condition. In that event, a physician should be consulted. In order that the matter may receive the proper attention, the one concerned should have the sense and humility to be perfectly open about it with his director or father master and with the doctor. It may happen that a person is, for some reason beyond his control, physically or morally incapable of leading a chaste life: such a one should never make a vow of chastity.

The Ascetic Way: it is all very well to use common sense and make use of the natural means, hygiene, etc., which help to control the desires of the flesh. However, these alone will never suffice to keep a man chaste. They are important *aids*, but for Christian chastity the grace of God is absolutely necessary, since we have seen it is a gift of God. Hence a supernatural practice of asceticism, based above all on faith and love of Christ Jesus, is necessary if we are to live chastely for the glory of God. First, {we note} some general dispositions for ascetic self-control:

Determination: as a basis for the ascetic life of chastity, one must have a firm and total determination to give himself to God in this manner. No half-measures will suffice. One must be clearly convinced of the necessity of chastity for a life of contemplation, of the necessity of *interior purity*, and firmly resolved to allow no compromises. A spirit of *absolute generosity* is required in this matter, even in matters of sensuality or sentimentality that are not of themselves sinful. One must be fully determined *to take every means* and *to make any sacrifice* which God may require. The price He may ask us to {pay} for the conquest of our passions may be very high. But we must be humbly prepared to pay it, even at the cost of a few falls in the beginning. READ Luke 14:27-35,[644] on

---

644. "And whosoever doth not carry his cross and come after me, cannot be my disciple. For which of you having a mind to build a tower, doth not first sit down, and reckon the charges that are necessary, whether he have wherewithal to finish it: Lest, after he hath laid the foundation, and is not able to finish it, all that see it begin to mock him, Saying: This man began to build, and was not able to finish. Or what king, about to go to make war against another king, doth not first sit down, and think whether he be able, with ten thousand, to meet him that, with twenty thousand, cometh against him? Or else, whilst the other is yet afar

the necessity of renunciation to be a disciple of Christ {and the} clear-sighted embracing of consequences; {and} Matthew 5:27-30,[645] on the necessity of renouncing even thoughts and minor gratifications ("If thy right eye offend thee . . ."). We must be firm in avoiding everything that is an avoidable occasion of sin. When occasions are unavoidable, then face them peacefully with our heart set on the will of God, armed with prayer and seeking only to please Him.

Confidence: our asceticism must also be based on supernatural confidence in God. We shall emphasize this later in speaking of the importance of the *theological* virtues in overcoming the flesh. If our hope is fixed on God, He will give us grace no matter how bad things may look. It is His will for all to lead chaste lives in some way; hence there is no man who cannot hope that God will give him grace to keep the commandments. When one has embraced the religious life or answered the call to religion, and the aptitude for religious life is present, God will certainly give grace to overcome temptation. READ 1 Corinthians 10:12-13[646] ("God will not suffer you to be tempted above that which you are able . . ."). We must then unite determination to do all in

---

off, sending an embassy, he desireth conditions of peace. So likewise every one of you that doth not renounce all that he possesseth, cannot be my disciple. Salt is good. But if the salt shall lose its savour, wherewith shall it be seasoned? It is neither profitable for the land nor for the dunghill, but shall be cast out. He that hath ears to hear, let him hear."

645. "You have heard that it was said to them of old: Thou shalt not commit adultery. But I say to you, that whosoever shall look on a woman to lust after her, hath already committed adultery with her in his heart. And if thy right eye scandalize thee, pluck it out and cast it from thee. For it is expedient for thee that one of thy members should perish, rather than that thy whole body be cast into hell. And if thy right hand scandalize thee, cut it off, and cast it from thee: for it is expedient for thee that one of thy members should perish, rather than that thy whole body go into hell."

646. "Wherefore he that thinketh himself to stand, let him take heed lest he fall. Let no temptation take hold on you, but such as is human. And God is faithful, who will not suffer you to be tempted above that which you are able: but will make also with temptation issue, that you may be able to bear it."

our power, with confidence in the love and grace of God. This is the beginning. Without these two things, all ascetic practices are more or less vain. With these, asceticism is useful and helpful. The most helpful forms of asceticism are those which strengthen our determination and our hope in God, deepen our peace and spirit of prayer, and unite us more closely to Him. All forms of asceticism which cause agitation or which disturb the soul with frantic ups and downs of elation and despair *should be avoided*. Perhaps in such cases asceticism is not properly understood. Enlightenment should be sought in spiritual direction.

Balance: our practice of asceticism must be balanced, sane, realistic and humble. That means that it must be based on a truly Christian and realistic idea of man. We are beings of body and soul, and the practice of chastity, the angelic virtue, is not going to turn us quickly into pure spirits. On the contrary, we must remember that we are men and not angels. Hence we must fully and humbly accept our condition, with the difficulties it entails. A balanced, common-sense, realistic view of our passions and temptations will enable us to fight them more calmly and sanely. We will not expect the impossible—we will not expect to be without temptations and sensual reactions. But we will face these calmly and realistically, with generosity and patience, not becoming discouraged or dejected at the necessity to struggle in the "purgative way" when, according to our own idea of ourselves, we should already be far above all such things in the realms of mysticism. Remember that the saints were tried in this way, and the purification means not that one becomes a pure spirit but that he is able to remain pure and spiritual in the fallen condition of man's flesh.

Gradual: our conquest of the flesh is a long and gradual process, requiring patience. One should begin at the beginning and keep on working. Some embrace an unwise and sporadic asceticism, by fits and starts. They start off with something extreme, and seek to perform extraordinary penances, when they are not able to walk the ordinary ascetic way. Discipline is important, but so are obedience, humility, subjection to the common rule, etc. It is an illusion of beginners to want to start with extreme measures. Generosity is good and indeed necessary, but it should be united with a realistic view of the spiritual life, which takes things by steps and *perseveres* until the end. The *gradual* ascetic conquest of self implies at the same time *perseverance and patience*. As St. John of the Cross says, "God moves all things according to their nature. For God to move the soul and raise it up from the extreme depth of its lowliness to the extreme height of His loftiness, in Divine union with Him, He must do it with order and sweetness and according to the nature of the soul itself" (*Ascent*, ii, 17).[647]

The above are broad, *general dispositions* of soul with which we must approach the ascesis of chastity. Let us now turn to the *more practical matters*, the *things that are to be done and avoided*. There are two important levels: one the exterior and immediate need *to control and mortify the senses*, and then the more interior and fundamental need of *faith, hope and love* which *supernaturalize* our chastity, uniting us with Christ, consecrating our chastity to God in union with His sacrifice.

The Mortification of the Senses: the great task of chastity is the preservation of inner purity and tranquility of soul, so that our soul is not defiled by any consent to movements of the flesh, at least where there is venereal pleasure. But it is obvious to anyone that in order to prevent sin, and to keep our soul pure, it is not sufficient merely to train the will "not to consent" when pleasures arise. It is also vitally important to gain control of the senses to prevent those movements from arising unnecessarily or inordinately. One who does not guard his senses will be quickly drawn into occasions of sin in which perhaps he will not be able to resist. Hence to neglect the guard over our senses willfully is to make oneself responsible for the consequences—hence the necessity for *mortification*. Mortification means "putting to death"—not that one destroys the sense faculties themselves, but one "puts

---

647. Peers, *Complete Works of Saint John of the Cross*, 1.138–39, which reads: ". . . nature. It is clear, then, from these fundamental points, that for God . . . and to raise . . ."

to death" the movements that gratify the senses. One denies the senses various pleasures, *even legitimate* pleasures. *Read* St. John of the Cross, *Ascent*, Bk. I, c. XI, nn. 5–6 (pp. 54–55).[648] Mortification is twofold: first, there is a necessary mortification which can in no sense be neglected—the denial of sinful pleasures, or plea-

648. "5. It is greatly to be lamented that, when God has granted them strength to break the other and stouter cords of affections for sins and vanities, they should fail to attain to such blessing because they have not shaken off some childish thing which God has bidden them conquer for love of Him, and which is nothing more than a thread or a hair. And what is worse, not only do they make no progress, but because of this attachment they fall back, lose that which they have gained, and retrace that part of the road along which they have travelled at the cost of so much time and labour; for we know that, on this road, not to go forward is to turn back, and not to be gaining is to be losing. This Our Lord desired to teach us when He said: He that is not with Me is against Me; and he that gathereth not with Me scattereth. He that takes not the trouble to repair the vessel, however slight be the crack in it, is likely to spill all the liquid that is within it. The Preacher taught us this clearly when he said: he that contemneth small things shall fall little by little. For, as he himself says, the fire is increased by a single spark. And thus one imperfection is sufficient to lead to another; and these lead to yet more; wherefore you will hardly ever see a soul that is negligent in conquering one desire, and that has not many more arising from the same weakness and imperfection that this desire causes. In this way they are continually falling; we have seen many persons to whom God has been granting the favour of leading them a long way, into a state of great detachment and liberty, yet who, merely through beginning to indulge some small attachment, under the pretext of being good, or in the guise of conversation and friendship, often lose their spirituality and desire for God and holy solitude, fall from the joy and whole-hearted devotion which they had in their spiritual exercises, and cease not until they have lost everything; and this because they broke not with that beginning of sensual desire and pleasure and kept not themselves in solitude for God. 6. Upon this road we must ever journey in order to attain our goal; which means that we must ever be mortifying our desires and not indulging them; and if they are not all completely mortified we shall not completely attain. For even as a log of wood may fail to be transformed in the fire because a single degree of heat is wanting to it, even so the soul will not be transformed in God if it have but one imperfection, although it be something less than voluntary desire; for as we shall say hereafter concerning the night of faith, the soul has only one will, and that will, if it be embarrassed by aught and set upon aught, is not free, solitary and pure, as is necessary for Divine transformation."

sures which lead directly to sin; second, there is a mortification of innocent pleasures which are good in themselves but which we reject for the sake of self-discipline.

Sight: it is first of all important for a chaste person to know how to mortify his curiosity. It is impossible to lead a really chaste life if one allows himself to be passively affected by all the appeals to sensuality that are seen on all sides in "the world." True, an experienced and well-balanced person may perhaps not be affected by pictures, advertisements, or the way women dress. But one does not acquire this balance without discipline. Pope Pius XII in *Sacra Virginitas* condemns {the} error of those who hold that young clerics should be "prepared for life" by seeing and reading everything. He quotes St. Augustine: "Do not say that you have a chaste mind if your eyes are unchaste, because an unchaste eye betrays an unchaste heart."[649] Hence it is *necessary* to mortify our eyes outside the monastery or when we come across periodicals or books that offer occasions for unchaste thoughts. But we should also *voluntarily* mortify our eyes in the monastery at times—denying ourselves the pleasure of looking at things out of mere curiosity or for the sake of the satisfaction we derive from looking even at something good and harmless, to be *free* from the *need* to take in everything that appeals to us. In the monastery, this means mortification of one's eyes and curiosity in community exercises, not merely for the sake of this one virtue, but as a point of monastic discipline. But *ne quid nimis*[650]—avoid self-conscious scrupulosity or a strained attitude. Train yourself to deny yourself any gratification of sight that you know to be somehow connected with sentimentality or even sensuality.

Hearing: one should mortify the desire to hear flattering or entertaining talk, first of all the kind that leads to sensual and sentimental attachments, but also things which gratify our self-love

---

649. *On Holy Virginity: Encyclical Letter of His Holiness Pope Pius XII, Issued March 25, 1954* (Washington: National Catholic Welfare Conference, [1954]), 19 (#55), quoting St. Augustine, *Ep.* 211.10 (*PL* 33, col. 961).

650. "nothing in excess."

in some way or other. Many young people entering religion are not on their guard against this and do not know how to restrain their desire to be loved, flattered, praised, verbally petted, or at least entertained, "appreciated." They are not on their guard because in America flattery and praise are oblique, not direct. Everything is said half-seriously. There is a way of kidding a person which is, in effect, flattery and verbal gratification. Such speech can be called in a broad and relatively superficial sense "seductive." There are many young people in monasteries who are helpless to resist their need for this kind of entertainment and self-gratification. It is a great weakness and a point on which mortification can be very helpful. *A fortiori*[651] when we are outside, we should not be too quick to have long entertaining conversations with women or to hear about things which exercise too much attraction on our heart.

Taste and Smell: it is one of the most elementary facts of the monastic life that a monk ought to be in control of his desires for food and drink and other allied pleasures. We should occasionally mortify our desires in the refectory to keep "in training," and this can be done not only by leaving something that we like (n.b. cold drinks), but equally well by eating something that we dislike, especially where obedience comes in. We should be alert to opportunities to deny ourselves in this matter. It is not necessary to systematically deprive ourselves of necessary food. Note however that we should be sufficiently mortified to be free from *all care* and anxiety about our diet, whether we are getting enough, etc.

Touch: in the practice of chastity, mortification of the sense of touch is above all important because it is with this sense that the virtue is most concerned. The *necessary mortification* in this regard is obvious from all that has been said about the obligation of the vow. All pleasures of touch that can be classed as venereal are to be avoided under pain of mortal sin. Those that are sensual and closely connected with venereal pleasures are also to be avoided, often under pain of mortal sin, by a religious. In

---

651. "all the more so."

this regard, *necessary* mortification aims especially at cutting off all desire for or tendency to seek pleasure in embraces, caresses, kisses and other signs of intimate affection for others, even when there is apparently no immediate harm. Such things do not fit in with a life of chastity, and mortification in them is a matter of elementary common sense and prudence. This is not something "optional." (N.B. the formal "kiss of peace" in its liturgical context, or in social situations where it is more or less expected—v.g., in monastic greetings of a more solemn type—does not count as sensuality. It is understood that this is simply a social custom.) Necessary mortification also includes the control of all inordinate attentions to self when one is washing, applying medicines, etc. But in this one should be natural and not scrupulous.

The *voluntary* mortification of the sense of touch, as an aid to chastity, can take a more or less large part in our life. It includes things which have nothing to do with sex. The acceptance and even the seeking of mortifications that diminish our comfort and ease in any way is part of the monastic outlook. The monk is an austere man whose sense of touch is mortified—for instance:

in the matter of bearing heat and cold: not seeking too quickly to cool off when it is hot or to warm up when it is cold; staying in the cold or in the heat; not bundling up too fully in cold weather.

in clothing: {wearing} rough garments next to the skin ({this} may or may not be a good mortification—{it} depends on the person); not always wearing the lightest underwear in summer.

at work: here there is a wide field for mortification and self-discipline: when one is bending over, not straightening up too soon or too often; accepting hard or uncomfortable work without seeking frequent letups; letting oneself get tired, letting muscles ache, etc.; at the same time working hard and perseveringly—this is very good discipline; a mortified man can be seen by the way he acts at manual labor.

posture: sitting up straight or not adopting easy and comfort-loving positions; not sitting down immediately when tired; kneeling a little longer than usual on occasions, etc.

discipline: take a good discipline on Friday mornings!

controlling restlessness: this is important and can be classed as a mortification of the sense of touch: one should be able to sit down and read a book, remaining in one place for a while, not always wandering around from place to place or seeking different positions, etc.—this is a discipline of the whole being, not just of {the} sense of touch. It is very valuable. {It} trains one in patience and emotional stability. Impatience and emotional instability are two of the things which most weaken resistance to temptation.

Special instruments of penance? The use of hair shirts, chains, and other instruments to mortify the flesh is not normally encouraged in our Order. Such things ought not to be necessary for us when we work hard at manual labor. Manual labor is a more effective and healthy way of mortifying the flesh. Sometimes special instruments have been used or permitted here, and there has been no indication, in the writer's experience, that they have contributed anything to the perfection of the ones using them. Yet the fact remains that in special cases, with humility and the blessing of obedience, these things might play a part in the struggle against the flesh. But one must not be attached to his own will in this regard, for thus he would lose more than he gained.

The Interior Senses: the control of two interior senses is particularly important in the cultivation of chastity—the *imagination* and the *memory*. It is often hard to say where a temptation arises: whether it starts in the flesh and then enlists the aid of the interior senses, or whether it starts in the interior senses and excites the flesh. Both are common, but perhaps it is more common for evil to come into our hearts through the imagination and memory. The flesh would not be as active if it were not incited to action by the senses, exterior or interior. When a person is restless and unstable, his imagination works overtime, and this keeps him in a state of vulnerability to temptations. Hence the imagination must be controlled, along with general restlessness of the whole person.

How to control the imagination and memory: control of these two interior senses is very difficult, and sometimes it becomes more difficult as time goes on. It is especially hard in certain periods of spiritual dryness and trial. *Direct control* is very often useless. In general it should not be attempted, except in rare circumstances when it is likely to work, notably when one is in a period of sensible fervor. {By} *indirect control*, instead of waiting for the imagination to go into action and then trying to control it, we must approach the problem from a long-range standpoint. We must educate and nourish the imagination and memory with good things that drive out the bad. Here is where *reading and meditation* are most important. The imagination and memory are going to work almost automatically whether we like it or not. Hence they must be given something good to work on. If they do not have good material at hand and are left to themselves, they will sooner or later dig up something of doubtful worth, or positively evil. Remember that our sense faculties cannot just be left to themselves. St. Teresa compares them to children which must be humored and educated.[652] They will run wild and make

---

652. See the contrast Teresa makes in chapter 29 of her *Life* between the movements of mystical love and those prompted by devotional feelings rooted in the senses and emotions: "No one who has not experienced these vehement impulses can possibly understand this: it is no question of physical restlessness within the breast, or of uncontrollable devotional feelings which occur frequently and seem to stifle the spirit. That is prayer of a much lower kind, and we should check such quickenings of emotion by endeavouring gently to turn them into inward recollection and to keep the soul hushed and still. Such prayer is like the violent sobbing of children: they seem as if they are going to choke, but if they are given something to drink their superabundant emotion is checked immediately. So it is here: reason must step in and take the reins, for it may be that this is partly accountable for by the temperament. On reflection comes a fear that there is some imperfection, which may in great part be due to the senses. So this child must be hushed with a loving caress which will move it to a gentle kind of love; it must not, as they say, be driven at the point of the fist. Its love must find an outlet in interior recollection and not be allowed to boil right over like a pot to which fuel has been applied indiscriminately. The fire must be controlled at its source and an endeavour must be made to quench the flame with gentle tears, not with tears caused by affliction, for these proceed from the emotions already referred to and do a great deal of harm. I used at first to shed tears of this kind, which left my brain so distracted and my spirit so wearied that for a day

some noise on occasions, but they must be patiently brought along to a quiet absorption in the good.

Good reading is the traditional aid to control of the imagination and memory. Our reading should be *interesting* so that it will occupy our minds and imaginations. It should be *varied* so that the interest is sustained. It should be *substantial* so that when we put the book down the thoughts *stay with us*. Traditionally, the *Scriptures* are the best way to drive out evil images and substitute good ones in their place. The Scriptures are the word of God and they have a supernatural efficacy, besides their natural interest. Hence they have a privileged place in our ascetic life.

Meditation: the imagination and memory work mechanically, but if we train our minds in meditation, we can harness the energy of imagination and direct it to good ends. A mind that is unable to meditate also has no control over imagination, and the faculty goes where it wills. Note: in periods of dryness this is normal; even one who knows how to meditate is sometimes unable to, and then the imagination goes off on its own. But it must not be allowed simply to run riot at its own desires. Good reading and thoughtful consideration of what we read will keep this process in check. *We should never simply sit down and indulge our memory or imagination* or give them a free rein, whether in community exercises or out of them, even if the images are "not bad."

Mortification of the Intellect and Will: the mortification of the spiritual faculties of the soul is of indirect importance for the control of the flesh. Obviously, mortification of the senses is the main thing. However, in the practice of all virtues, it is important to *overcome self-will*. The man who gratifies his own will is easily vulnerable in other things. If we seek self spiritually, we will seek ourselves also in the flesh.

---

or more I was not fit to return to prayer. Great discretion, then, is necessary at first so that everything may proceed gently and the operations of the spirit may express themselves interiorly; great care should be taken to prevent operations of an exterior kind" (*The Complete Works of Saint Teresa of Jesus*, trans. and ed. E. Allison Peers, 3 vols. [New York: Sheed & Ward, 1946], 1.190–91).

It is most important *to be humble*. Humility and chastity go together. A proud man may keep chaste, but his chastity is always in danger. Indeed, often sins against chastity are due in the long run to pride. This may be true especially in the case of a proud religious. The Lord sometimes permits that those who seemed to be very virtuous and who despised others fall into serious sins and even apostatize from religion because of unchastity. Also, as the Desert Fathers point out, anger and unchastity are closely related. In the *Verba Seniorum* we read: "If you cannot control your anger, you will not be able to control your lust."[653] Humility and meekness, being types of temperance, are related to chastity and to all the other forms of temperance. If we want to be temperate in the flesh, we must also strive to be temperate in our intellectual life, in our spiritual life and in our will. The obedient and humble religious is the one who is in the best position for cultivating chastity and {the} spirit of virginity.

Compunction and Prayer: the spirit of deep interior compunction and of fervent prayer unites all the faculties of the soul, the whole being, sense and spirit, in adoration of God. This spirit of compunction is of the greatest value in cultivating chastity. *The gift of fear*, the first of the gifts of the Holy Ghost, produces in us this supernatural compunction. It reaches down deep into the soul, producing a sincere and heartfelt sorrow for sin and hatred for everything that is opposed to the love of God. When the soul is moved by this compunction, it easily resists sin and loves all virtues. The gift of fear is an *infused* and supernatural hatred for sin, which makes it easy to turn away from sin and to God. It produces a real experience of hatred for sin, not just a mental sense of duty to avoid sin. The gift of fear, when it is strong in the soul, affects even the senses and deadens the lust that is in

---

653. *Verba Seniorum*, V.4.49 (*PL* 73, col. 870D); the saying is included, in a somewhat different translation, in Thomas Merton, *The Wisdom of the Desert: Sayings from the Desert Fathers of the Fourth Century* (New York: New Directions, 1960), 79 (#cxlvii): "Abbot Hyperichius said: A monk who cannot hold his tongue when he is angry will not be able to control the passion of lust either."

them. Compunction and prayer are nourished by frequent communion and devotion to the Blessed Eucharist. One of the special graces of this sacrament is to spiritualize our flesh and to purify the heart so that we are less affected by temptation. It is not, however, a magic means for removing temptation. Graces are given; we must use them. The bread of angels is also the food of virgin souls. Devotion to the Blessed Mother is also essential in the practice of Christian virginity. When she is close to the soul, she refreshes it and protects it against concupiscence. But all these exterior means are not to be regarded as magic. They are means *which we ourselves must use*. They arouse love and strength of will, but we ourselves must will not to sin and resist at every cost. Otherwise these means will be of little use to us.

The Spirit of Purity: here we can consider some important points about the inner spirit and meaning of purity. They are taken mostly from an excellent book: *In Defence of Purity* by Dietrich von Hildebrand.[654] This should be read by all who want to understand the real meaning of Christian chastity. The basic theme that runs through the early chapters of this book is the important one of *respect for the mystery of sex*. This instinct is so deep and so fundamental in man that it plays a very important part in his spiritual life. Man's relation towards sex is indicative of his relations with God in many ways. Sex is a mystery implanted in human nature by the Creator. Respect for this mystery implies respect for the Creator. Neglect of this mystery means neglect of the Creator. Sex is intimately related to personality. One is a true, integral and mature person only when he fully knows how to use, or abstain from the use of, this instinct (cf. Freud), and this is intimately connected with the capacity to love. Sex without love is meaningless. With love, it plays an important part in the development of man and in his salvation. Those who abuse sex think they can do so without harm to themselves. In reality, *our deepest self is involved in the use of the sexual faculty*. In primitive

654. Dietrich von Hildebrand, *In Defence of Purity: An Analysis of the Catholic Ideals of Purity and Virginity* (New York: Sheed & Ward, 1935).

society, the mystery of sex enters frankly and intimately into religious worship. This is because of the depth of the instinct, which is rooted at the very heart of our being and is bound up with our inmost self. But if we are spiritually pure and elevated above sex, then our sex life is purified along with our spirit. If we are not spiritual, then our spiritual life becomes degraded to a sexual level. In much false mysticism, if not in all of it, there are clear elements of repressed or distorted sexuality.

The symbolic quality of sex: to appreciate the meaning and the mystery of sex, we must preserve some sense of its symbolic elements. The act of sexual union is not a mere animal act, for the sake of procreation. It is not something one can perform and forget. It has deep spiritual repercussions, and it is symbolic of spiritual activity that should, by rights, go with it. Materialists think that man is just a biological organism, that the mechanism of sex produces subjective feelings of love and idealism which are without moral significance; they are just psychological accompaniments of the biological act. On the contrary, a spiritual view of man shows that he is a being who wills and loves, who on a very deep level gives himself. The spiritual act is essential to him. Sexual union expresses outwardly this inward giving of himself. Man is made for *love*, not for sex and procreation. These latter are secondary and accidental. Our vow of chastity takes this attitude. Sexual love is then valid and good when the symbolic external act corresponds to something interior and spiritual. Sexual love {is} the yielding up of what is most secret and personal in myself to another—what is most vulnerable too. But this signifies the gift of what is most hidden, delicate, personal and intimate in myself, the secret of my inner self, my heart, my very being. This mystery of my inner personality cannot be given away lightly in "love." It is the most serious and tremendous of all gifts. So too with sex: the gift of myself should be correspondingly serious and sacred on the bodily level too. To give up one's "personal secret"[655] to another in sex is to fling oneself away, if there is no corresponding

655. Von Hildebrand, 35.

intention of interior surrender. This interior surrender must be a surrender of genuine love, which means *it must be final.* SELFISH AND CARELESS use of {the} sex faculty is a "squandering of self,"[656] a mutual betrayal, a mutual desecration. This is effected by *seduction*, which is pseudo-love. By seduction, by pretending to give, the partners simply enmesh and entrap one another mutually in their passion and degrade themselves and each other with what is really a lie. When this happens, "a mysterious apostasy from God takes place, unmatched for its peculiar enigmatic quality by any other sin" (p. 38); and in this apostasy the devil very easily mixes himself. There easily becomes a kind of *diabolical rebellion* in lust. This is seen in very impure people who have given themselves over completely to lust, who consciously defy God and purity in their lust, and exercise lust with a kind of fanaticism *against* God. They seem to glory in their shame and abandon themselves to lust with a kind of pride.

However, there is the problem of *unconscious sexuality*. This is the case when hidden sex instincts are gratified in a roundabout and seemingly innocent way. Dietrich von Hildebrand treats of this {on} p. 41ff. He takes the case of men who seem consciously to be disgusted with sex and turn away from it puritanically; they want nothing to do with it, they think. Yet they are not really pure and they do not enjoy the real interior freedom of the pure.

> All the while their nature is charged with an oppressive sexuality; they live in an atmosphere of sexual constraint, and the manner in which they move, speak, and meet particular situations betrays the presence of sex. . . . They are not genuinely pure, because they seek and find a certain sexual satisfaction in their love of excitement, their craving to make an impression, their sensibility, their self-importance, their carriage, the entire rhythm of their lives. . . . There is here, strictly speaking, no sin, but simply an imperfect general attitude. . . . But, on the other hand, such men miss the

656. Von Hildebrand, 36.

peculiar freedom of the pure: the unconfined spirituality, the radiance which is theirs alone. (pp. 41–42)[657]

The pure man is one who perceives the mystery of sex. He has deep reverence for the mystery. Some are this way temperamentally, others because they have had a sound upbringing or have received it from the Christian faith. Such people have no contempt for sex as such. They do not shrink from it. But they shrink from every abuse of sex—that is to say, they refuse to play with sex; they refuse the insincerity of seduction, of yielding to seduction. They will approach sex only when it manifests a real intention of interior surrender which is personal and true and which therefore gives glory to God (obviously, this implies obedience to the will of God and the acceptance of the matrimonial state). The pure man understands that "sex belongs in a special manner to God"[658] (p. 61). Hence he approaches sex with awe and a spirit of *reverent obedience to God*, not just a conformist desire to have everything OK with society, by a formal marriage, but an inner need to feel that his exercise of sex is sanctioned by God, is according to the will of God, that he has a divine permission to enter into a sacred mystery. Then in the exercise of sex, he surrenders to the beloved but does not surrender completely to the seduction of sex. "In a special sense the pure man walks with God. He never departs from the divine presence."[659] Hence even in the exercise of this faculty, he worships God.

The Spirit of Virginity: we must always remember the high ideal to which we have devoted our lives in the vow of chastity. It is not simply an engagement *not to sin*. It is something much more positive and more lofty. *Consecrated virginity is a marriage to*

---

657. In the text, the middle sentence quoted precedes the first and reads: ". . . but who nevertheless are not genuinely pure, for they . . ."; in the original, the first sentence reads: "all the while their entire nature . . . betrays the active presence . . ."; the third reads: "Indeed, there is here, . . ."; and the last reads: ". . . spirituality, the temperance, the radiance . . ."

658. "sex *belongs in a special manner to God*" in the original.

659. Von Hildebrand, 62.

the Word of God. Every soul in the state of grace is married to the Word, but in a broad sense. But the soul that has left all desires and pleasures and seeks Him alone, finds joy in Him alone, seeks creatures only in Him and for His sake—this is the virgin soul who is wedded to Him. The full spirit of virginity is not merely avoidance of sex but total positive consecration to God. Pius XII in *Sacra Virginitas* says: "This, then, is the primary purpose, this the central idea of Christian virginity: to aim only at the divine, to turn thereto the whole mind and soul, to want to please God in everything, to think of Him continually, to consecrate body and soul to Him" (#15).[660] The state of virginity is higher than that of marriage, and it is an error to exalt the married state above it. For virginity brings a special liberty of soul and the ability to consecrate oneself *without division* to Christ. *Read* 1 Corinthians 7:25ff. on virgins (which we have seen above[661]): the virgin state is "without solicitude," {a} complete detachment from passing things. Virginity leads more quickly and efficaciously to sanctity and helps to sanctify others too. The virginal life is a witness to the union of the Church with Christ: "Virgins make tangible, as it were, the perfect virginity of their mother the Church and the sanctity of her intimate union with Christ. . . . The greatest glory of virgins is undoubtedly to be the living images of the perfect integrity of the union between the Church and her divine Spouse" (*Sacra Virginitas*, 30–31).[662] Explanation: the theological basis of this is the hypostatic union, the Word united to human nature in the Person of Christ—a most intimate and perfect union of God and man. The Church is His Mystical Body. {She} prolongs this intimate union. Those who give themselves with undivided heart to God come closest in themselves to this perfect union between the Church and Christ; hence the profound truth {that} the virgins possess a reality of which marriage is only the symbol—deeper union with God.

660. *On Holy Virginity*, 4 (which reads: ". . . soul completely to Him").
661. See n. 600.
662. *On Holy Virginity*, 10–11.

In order to understand all this better, we can conclude these notes on chastity by considering the *liturgical rite* for the consecration of virgins from the *Roman Pontifical*.[663] *The rite of the consecration of virgins* takes place during solemn Mass and in many ways reminds us of the rites of ordination, marriage, and our own solemn profession (which is after all a similar consecration). The consecration of virgins takes place after the *Alleluia*. It is preceded by an interrogation, in which the bishop formally and publically inquires as to the fitness of the candidates: *Scis illas dignas esse?*[664] This reminds us that virginity, like ordination, is a lofty grace and one which is not to be sought lightly. But whereas in ordination there is a simple and laconic command for the *ordinandi* to step forward, here there is a very beautiful rite symbolizing the call of the virgins to follow Christ: the bishop sings, *Venite*; the virgins reply, *Et nunc sequimur*; the bishop repeats, *Venite*; virgins: *Et nunc sequimur in toto corde*; bishop: *Venite filiae, audite me, timorem Domini docebo vos*; virgins: *Timemus te, et quaerimus faciem tuam videre*, etc.[665] Notice the beauty of this rite, its simplicity, {its} depth. It corresponds to something that has already taken place in the depths of the soul. It corresponds to an interior and mystical reality. (READ—compare St. Teresa's words on the call to interior prayer: *Interior Castle*, IV, c. 3 [pp. 240–41]: the virgin soul is called to contemplation as well as to virginity, for purity of heart is the ordinary disposition for contemplation.[666]

663. *Pontificale*, 212–36.

664. "Do you know that they are worthy?" (*Pontificale*, 213).

665. "Come"; "And now we follow"; "Come"; "And now we follow with our whole heart"; "Come, daughters, listen to me; I will teach you the fear of the Lord"; "We fear You and seek to see Your face" (*Pontificale*, 214–15).

666. "It is a form of recollection which also seems to me supernatural, for it does not involve remaining in the dark, or closing the eyes, nor is it dependent upon anything exterior. A person involuntarily closes his eyes and desires solitude; and, without the display of any human skill there seems gradually to be built for him a temple in which he can make the prayer already described; the senses and all external things seem gradually to lose their hold on him, while the soul, on the other hand, regains its lost control. . . . The great King, Who dwells in the Mansion within this castle, perceives their good will, and in His

Beati mundo corde quoniam ipsi Deum videbunt.[667]) Notice that the virgins boldly and explicitly say: "We seek to see Thy face" (in the rite of consecration above). READ also—cf. Canticle of Canticles 2:8-14;[668] {according to} St. Bernard, the spouse (virgin soul) is the soul that seeks union with God: *Quaenam est sponsa*—anima sitiens Deum, etc. (*Sermo 7, In Cantica*).[669] After this beautiful dialogue, the virgins sing the *suscipe* as at our solemn profession: *Suscipe me, Domine, secundum eloquium tuum, et vivam, et non confundas me ab expectatione mea.*[670] {Note} the desire to be

---

great mercy desires to bring them back to Him. So, like a good Shepherd, with a call so gentle that even they can hardly recognize it, he teaches them to know His voice and not to go away and get lost but to return to their Mansion; and so powerful is this Shepherd's call that they give up the things outside the castle which had led them astray, and once again enter it. . . . [I]t is not a question of our will—it happens only when God is pleased to grant us this favour. For my own part, I believe that, when His Majesty grants it, He does so to people who are already leaving the things of the world. I do not mean that people who are married must actually leave the world—they can do so only in desire: his call to them is a special one and aims at making them intent upon interior things. I believe, however, that if we wish to give His Majesty free course, He will grant more than this to those whom He is beginning to call still higher" (Peers, *Complete Works of Saint Teresa of Jesus*, 2.240–41).

667. "Blessed are the clean of heart: for they shall see God" (Mt. 5:8).

668. "The voice of my beloved, behold he cometh leaping upon the mountains, skipping over the hills. My beloved is like a roe, or a young hart. Behold he standeth behind our wall, looking through the windows, looking through the lattices. Behold my beloved speaketh to me: Arise, make haste, my love, my dove, my beautiful one, and come. For winter is now past, the rain is over and gone. The flowers have appeared in our land, the time of pruning is come: the voice of the turtle is heard in our land: The fig tree hath put forth her green figs: the vines in flower yield their sweet smell. Arise, my love, my beautiful one, and come: My dove in the clefts of the rock, in the hollow places of the wall, shew me thy face, let thy voice sound in my ears: for thy voice is sweet, and thy face comely."

669. "Who is the spouse—the soul thirsting for God" (*In Cantica*, 7.2 [PL 183, col. 807A, which reads: "*Quis dicit? Sponsa. Quaenam ipsa? Anima sitiens Deum*" ["Who is speaking? The spouse. Who is she? The soul thirsting for God"]).

670. "Uphold me according to thy word, O Lord, and I shall live: and let me not be confounded in my expectation" (Ps. 118[119]:116; *Pontificale*, 215, which actually reads: ". . . *secundum eloquium tuum, ut non dominetur mei omnis*

received {into} union with God, not a mechanical conjunction of objects but a union of souls in *mutual giving*: again, a marriage, a rendering up to God of the inmost secret of our own being; and God in turn renders up to the spouse His own secret. {Note} how this is symbolized in the Canticle of Canticles: READ, for instance, chapter 5.[671] (Comment in the light of the contemplative vocation of the virgin soul.)

---

iniustitia" ["according to thy word: and let no iniquity have dominion over me" (Ps. 118[119]:133)]).

671. "Let my beloved come into his garden, and eat the fruit of his apple trees. I am come into my garden, O my sister, my spouse, I have gathered my myrrh, with my aromatical spices: I have eaten the honeycomb with my honey, I have drunk my wine with my milk: eat, O friends, and drink, and be inebriated, my dearly beloved. I sleep, and my heart watcheth: the voice of my beloved knocking: Open to me, my sister, my love, my dove, my undefiled: for my head is full of dew, and my locks of the drops of the nights. I have put off my garment, how shall I put it on? I have washed my feet, how shall I defile them? My beloved put his hand through the key hole, and my bowels were moved at his touch. I arose up to open to my beloved: my hands dropped with myrrh, and my fingers were full of the choicest myrrh. I opened the bolt of my door to my beloved: but he had turned aside, and was gone. My soul melted when he spoke: I sought him, and found him not: I called, and he did not answer me. The keepers that go about the city found me: they struck me: and wounded me: the keepers of the walls took away my veil from me. I adjure you, O daughters of Jerusalem, if you find my beloved, that you tell him that I languish with love. What manner of one is thy beloved of the beloved, O thou most beautiful among women? what manner of one is thy beloved of the beloved, that thou hast so adjured us? My beloved is white and ruddy, chosen out of thousands. His head is as the finest gold: his locks as branches of palm trees, black as a raven. His eyes as doves upon brooks of waters, which are washed with milk, and sit beside the plentiful streams. His cheeks are as beds of aromatical spices set by the perfumers. His lips are as lilies dropping choice myrrh. His hands are turned and as of gold, full of hyacinths. His belly as of ivory, set with sapphires. His legs as pillars of marble, that are set upon bases of gold. His form as of Libanus, excellent as the cedars. His throat most sweet, and he is all lovely: such is my beloved, and he is my friend, O ye daughters of Jerusalem. Whither is thy beloved gone, O thou most beautiful among women? whither is thy beloved turned aside, and we will seek him with thee?"

The rite of consecration continues with a *litany*, *Veni Creator*,[672] then *prayers* blessing the habit of the virgins: the robe—a pledge of immortality (Risen Christ) and a defense against temptations; {the} veil—sign of love for Jesus, sign of the "prudent virgins",[673] {the} crown (of flowers)—pledge of {an} eternal crown. The virgins then sing {the} responsory: *Regnum mundi, et omnem ornatum saeculi contempsi propter amorem Domini nostri Jesu Christi: Quem vidi, quem amavi, in quem credidi, quem dilexi*, etc.[674] Then follows the long preface, filled with the theology of the rite. {Note the following} points from the *preface*:

1. *Agnovit Auctorem suum beata virginitas*:[675] virginity and contemplation—the virgin soul knows the Creator in a secret and ineffable way; *aemula integritatis angelicae*:[676] the virgin seeks to be as pure as the angels (the perfect contemplative spirits), but this purity is a marriage with Him Who is the Spouse of virgins and of no other souls, because He is also the Son of a virgin (note the mystery of virginity in its close connection with the Incarnation).

2. The special virtues of virgins asked for in this preface: vigilance, lest the devil slip into their souls *per aliquam mentis incuriam*[677] ({cf.} the wise and foolish virgins). The life of a virgin soul is not one of static and automatic purity. It implies choices, selection. One does not remain pure passively and by habit. One has to consciously choose what is spiritual and according to God and exclude what is fleshly and according to the world. One must be attuned to the slightest harmful influence and reject it. The monk by self-custody avoids all *mentis incuria*. Other virtues of

---

672. "Come, Creator [Spirit]" (*Pontificale*, 216).

673. Cf. Mt. 25:1-13.

674. "I scorn the kingdom of the world and all the pomp of the age for the love of Our Lord Jesus Christ, Whom I have seen, Whom I have loved, in Whom I have believed, Whom I have cherished" (*Pontificale*, 219).

675. "Blessed virginity recognizes its Source" (*Pontificale*, 223).

676. "rivaling the angelic integrity" (*Pontificale*, 223).

677. "through some negligence of mind" (*Pontificale*, 224, which reads ". . . *mentis serpat* [he may creep] *incuriam*").

the virgin soul—all are gifts of the Holy Spirit—{include} *prudens modestia; sapiens benignitas*[678] ({this is} important: some "virgin" souls are hard and cruel—they are not truly virgin); *gravis lenitas; casta libertas.*[679]

In caritate ferveant, et nihil extra te diligant:[680] this {is} very important for {the} spirit of virginity. The virgin souls love all things in and for God and nothing outside of God. Hence anything that is loved for itself rather than for God is a distraction and a deviation from interior virginity—{thus} the importance of not becoming *preoccupied with the love* of anything other then God, even if it is something "for" God. That is to say, a truly virgin soul will not be so absorbed in work, or in offices, as to be seeking them first rather than God. {In the story of} Martha and Mary,[681] Mary {is} more truly a virgin soul.

Laudabiliter vivant, laudarique non appetant[682] (true humility). *Te in sanctitate corporis, te in animae suae puritate glorificant.*[683] {This is} another beautiful passage which shows the true spirit of virginity. God is all in all for the virgin soul: her food, her shelter, her protection, her consolation, etc.

Tu sis ei honor, tu gaudium, tu voluntas; tu in maerore solatium; tu in ambiguitate consilium; tu in iniuria defensio; in tribulatione patientia; in paupertate abundantia, in ieiunio cibus; in infirmitate medicina. In Te habeant omnia, quem diligere appetant super omnia.[684]

---

678. "prudent modesty; wise kindness" (*Pontificale*, 224).

679. "serious tenderness; chaste freedom" (*Pontificale*, 224–25).

680. "May they be fervent in charity, and love nothing outside of You" (*Pontificale*, 225).

681. Lk. 10:38-42.

682. "May they live in a praiseworthy manner, yet not seek to be praised" (*Pontificale*, 225).

683. "May they glorify You in the holiness of their bodies and in the purity of their souls" (*Pontificale*, 225).

684. "May You be for her honor, joy, good will; consolation in sorrow, counsel in uncertainty, defense against injuries, patience in tribulation, abundance in poverty, food in fasting, medicine in infirmity. May they have all things in You,

This is beautiful and deep. The soul that can learn this and live accordingly is truly a saint.

After the preface {comes the} imposition of the veil, at which the virgins sing: *Ancilla Christi sum, ideo me ostendo servilem personam.*[685] "Receive the holy veil by which thou mayest be known to have contemned the world, to have subjected thyself as a spouse to Christ Jesus truly, humbly, with all the strength of thy heart";[686] then the *ring*: "I espouse thee to Jesus Christ the Son of the Most High Father";[687] finally the *crown*, pledge of eternal glory; {then a} long blessing and a final anathema on anyone who withdraws the virgin from the service of God.

THE VOW OF POVERTY

Poverty, like chastity, comes under the vow of conversion of manners, and it is not for us a separate vow, strictly speaking.

INTRODUCTION: in our treatment of the other vows we have discussed the theological background and history first, in order to come eventually to the actual obligation of the vow. Here, in the case of poverty, for special reasons we will start right out with the actual obligation of the vow: what is matter of sin against the vow? What are the material acts which are contrary to the observance of religious poverty? It is necessary to dispose of these exterior obligations first, to make them *very clear*, because we intend to point out that real religious poverty is actually something much more than the minimum obligation binding under pain of sin.

Whom they seek to love above all things" (*Pontificale*, 225, which reads: "*Tu eis* [for them] *sis honor . . .*").

685. "I am the handmaid of Christ, and so I show myself a servant" (*Pontificale*, 228, which reads: ". . . *ostendo servilem habere personam* [to have a servant's role]").

686. "*Accipe velamen sacrum, quo cognoscaris mundum contempsisse, et te Christo Iesu veraciter humiliterque, toto cordis annisu, sponsam perpetualiter subdidisse*" (*Pontificale*, 228).

687. "*Desponso te Jesu Christo, Filio summi Patris*" (*Pontificale*, 229).

In no vow is the spirit more essential than in the vow of poverty. St. Thomas says poverty is *third* in importance,[688] after obedience and chastity, but this could be misleading. The whole religious life depends indeed on the actual observance of obedience and chastity, an observance in spirit and in truth. But the whole life must be impregnated and suffused with a spirit of poverty. Obedience and chastity themselves must be in a certain way an expression of poverty. St. Benedict makes this clear when he reminds the monk in the chapter on poverty (33)[689] that the reason why it is right that the monk have no property of his own is that he does not even have command any more over his body or over his own will—hence the intimate relation of obedience and poverty in the monastic life.

The importance of poverty is especially crucial today, in America. In actual practice, it is in the realm of poverty that we are weakest and here lies our greatest danger. If the monastic life is corrupted in America, it will be because of *the corruption of the spirit and practice of poverty*—hence the importance of understanding clearly what is involved and of seeing that one can actually keep all the strict obligations of poverty before the law and yet remain very deficient in religious poverty. Theologians distinguish between the vow and the virtue of poverty, and this distinction is to be found in the case of all the vows. But in the case of poverty it is *of crucial importance* because it would seem that the vow does not cover all that is really essential to religious poverty, and that if the vow is not supplemented by the virtue

688. *Secunda Secundae*, q. 186, a. 8: "*Votum obedientiae est praecipuum inter tria vota religionis. . . . Quia per votum obedientiae aliquid majus homo offert Deo, scilicet ipsam voluntatem; quae est potior, quam corpus proprium, quod offert homo Deo per continentiam, et quam res exteriores, quas offert homo Deo per votum paupertatis*" ("The vow of obedience is the most important of the three vows of religion . . . . Because through the vow of obedience man offers to God something greater, that is, his own will, which is of more importance than his own body, which man offers to God through continence, and than exterior things, which man offers to God through the vow of poverty") (Aquinas, *Opera Omnia*, 3.638).

689. McCann, 84, 86.

we can fall far short of what God expects of us in our vocation. Why is this? The vow can deprive us of *proprietorship* and of the independent exercise of ownership, use and disposition of material things. But a person without the spirit of poverty can easily cultivate a habit of obtaining formal permissions which make his use of things legal, but which do not absolve him from sinning against the virtue of poverty nevertheless. I may have permission to use and have at my disposal all sorts of useless or luxurious articles, which may perhaps be legitimate if we stretch a point, but they may involve a real violation of the virtue of poverty, which demands a Christ-like detachment from and independence of such things. If a person makes use of permissions in order to gratify attachments and acquisitive instincts, he is certainly not "poor" in the true sense of religious poverty. Then again there is the question of *collective* poverty, which has a great effect on the poverty of the individual. This is the responsibility of the superior, but everyone must understand that the spirit of poverty is of great importance *collectively* as well as individually. *The community as such must be poor*, in the sense in which poverty is necessary to attain the end of that particular form of religious life. As we shall see, in practice one of the great problems of poverty for us arises in connection with our work, with the department or shop which may be under our charge. A monk may be quite "poor" in his own personal life, in his clothing, cell, books, personal effects, etc. But in his job, his department, he may easily exceed the bounds of poverty, and even of justice perhaps, and utterly lose the spirit of monastic poverty, even in very grave matters, by heedless and useless ordering of expensive machines or tools, *by a wasteful and self-indulgent budget*, by demands on the resources and manpower of the monastery that are far beyond his rightful claims, etc. We must face the fact that here in our American monasteries poverty can go completely overboard in work, and in imagined needs and necessities connected with a job that mushrooms beyond all reason in the mind of the one in charge of it. A Trappist monk may in fact indulge his material attachments beyond all reason and become the victim of whims and childish needs, all under the pretext of "working for the common good of the community." He may completely lose not only the spirit of poverty by becoming a mere businessman, but even lose his vocation itself. Note that if these people became genuine businessmen, it would not be so bad. The tragedy is that monks "play at" being businessmen and engineers, etc., and often do so in an extremely wasteful and prodigal fashion. Dom Delatte, in his Commentary on the *Rule*, says: "It is a matter of experience that apostasy begins almost always with violations of poverty."[690] We must gain the conviction (which is very remote from Americans) that the love of material possessions and of gain is *fatal* to a monk because it gives him a basically worldly spirit. And Our Lord has said, "You cannot serve God and Mammon."[691] Have we forgotten the urgency of this warning? Though material things are not evil in themselves, though the right use of riches is certainly a virtuous thing for a man in some other state than ours, yet for a monk, who has left the world and seeks to live in perfect imitation of Jesus Christ, *worldly possessions are a subtle but fatal corrupting influence*. The love of *possessions and of gain* defiles our souls in a much subtler and less "felt" manner than the love of sexual pleasure, but the defilement is just as real and perhaps all the more dangerous in that it is not felt. Note too that it is *per se* easier to resist if we will only pay attention to it. But negligence in resisting the desire of possessions and of gain is all the more blameworthy, says St. Chrysostom, in that it is less difficult a temptation than the love of bodily pleasure.[692] It is very important to respond to every impulse of grace that would draw us to a better practice and spirit of poverty. These inspirations are of crucial importance in our religious life. Dom G. Morin says:

690. "Il est d'expérience que l'apostasie commence presque toujours par une lésion de la pauvreté" (Delatte, 279).

691. Mt. 6:24.

692. "But the love of carnal pleasure and of money are not equal, but that of carnal pleasure is far keener and more tyrannical. And the weaker the antagonist, the less excusable are these that are overcome thereby" (*Homily 78 on Matthew* [*PG* 58, col. 710], *Nicene and Post-Nicene Fathers*, 1st series, 10:470).

"Correspondence with grace in this matter is one of the clearest signs of the progress of the religious soul toward union with God and with Christ crucified" (*Ideal of {the} Monastic Life*, p. 145).[693] When monks are attached to material things, the monastery is for them not the house of God where they are guests and children of the heavenly Father; it is merely their own house, where they are masters and proprietors—hence the fatal loss of the simplicity and joy of the life of faith and its replacement by the agitation and strain of a worldly spirit.

Poverty as a means to an end: poverty is a necessary means to an end—religious perfection, charity in union with Christ. But also the perfection of poverty is *relative to the particular end of the Order*. This must always be borne in mind when considering the practical application of norms of poverty. Possession of goods is not in itself evil, and poverty is not good as such, but only in relation to love of Christ. St. Thomas says the poverty of each religious order is perfect in so far as it is better proportioned to the end of the order, so that the order that is most perfect in poverty is not the one where poverty is more strict in the absolute sense of the word, but the one where poverty conforms best to the purpose of the order. *Tanto erit unaquaeque religio secundum paupertatem {perfectior}, quanto habet paupertatem magis {proportionatam suo} fini* (II-II, q. 188, a. 7).[694] In the active life, material possessions are necessary. In the apostolic life, the most perfect poverty is necessary because the apostle must be absolutely detached from all possessions and all reliance on material support—hence the ideal of the mendicant and preaching orders. This is to be taken seriously because in proportion as the apostolic life is lived on a level of comfort, it is no longer proportioned to its end. *The contemplative life* requires

693. Germain Morin, osb, *The Ideal of the Monastic Life Found in the Apostolic Age*, trans. C. Gunning (1914; Westminster, MD: Newman Press, 1950) (which reads: "correspondence to grace . . . of the soul of the religious towards . . .").

694. "Each religious institute will be more perfect with respect to poverty to the degree that its poverty is better proportioned to its end" (Aquinas, *Opera Omnia*, 3.655; text erroneously reads: "*perfectio . . . proportionatum suue . . .*" [Merton corrects the first in his conference from late September 1962]).

moderate possessions, held communally, and poverty of the individual to the end that *temporal solicitude is reduced to the minimum.*

Evangelical poverty: we shall speak later[695] in more detail of the poverty of Christ Our Lord and of the poverty to which He has called us. It is sufficient here at the beginning to recall:

1. The ideal of the founders of Cîteaux: we should be *pauperes cum paupere Christo.*[696]

2. The absolute and firm declaration of Christ that poverty and detachment are *necessary* in anyone following His footsteps. READ Matthew 19:21-27:[697] the rich young man. We have already seen this, but we cannot return to it too often. It was this attachment to possessions that prevented the young man from becoming a disciple of Christ. Jesus explicitly says: *"A rich man shall hardly enter* into the Kingdom of Heaven." It has always been understood by the Church that even where a Christian possesses things, he must do so in a detached manner, that is, in a spirit of poverty. Otherwise he shall not enter into the Kingdom of Heaven. Much more does this apply to monks who have deliberately left all things and possess nothing. READ Luke 14:26-33:[698] *Every one of you that doth not renounce all that he possesses cannot be my disciple.*

3. In the *Rule* of St. Benedict it is quite clear that the monk must possess *nothing at all.* READ chapter 33,[699] {which} forbids

695. See below, pages 430–35.
696. See above, n. 297.
697. See above, n. 207.
698. See above, n. 354.
699. *"Praecipue hoc vitium radicitus amputandum est de monasterio. Ne quis praesumat aliquid dare aut accipere sine jussione abbatis, neque aliquid habere proprium, nullam omnino rem, neque codicem, neque tabulas, neque graphium, sed nihil omnino: quippe quibus nec corpora sua nec voluntates licet habere in propria voluntate; omnia vero necessaria a patre sperare monasterii. Nec quidquam liceat habere, quod abbas non dederit aut permiserit. Omniaque omnibus sint communia, ut scriptum est; nec quisquam suum aliquid dicat vel praesumat. Quod si quisquam huic nequissimo vitio deprehensus fuerit delectari, admoneatur semel et iterum; si non emendaverit correptioni subjaceat"* (McCann, 84, 86) ("This vice in particular must be cut off at its root from

independent use (giving {or} receiving) of everything, prescribes *absolute dependence* on {the} abbot for all material things, prescribes complete *community of goods* with punishment for proprietorship, and all to be done in a *spirit of detachment* (see c. 54—letters and small gifts;[700] see also c. 59 [READ[701]]—the sons of the rich to be protected against any temptation to desire property ever).

---

the monastery. No one should presume to give or to receive anything without the command of the abbot, and no one should have anything of his own, anything at all, not a book or tablets or a pen or anything else; for them it is not allowed even to have their bodies or their wills under their own will, but to trust to the father of the monastery for all that is needed. It should be permitted to have nothing that the abbot has not given or allowed. As it is written: Let all things be in common for all, and let no one call anything his own or presume it to be his. If anyone were to be found indulging in this most wicked vice, he should be warned once and then again; if he should fail to amend, let him be subjected to punishment").

700. McCann, 122.

701. "*Si quis forte de nobilibus offert filium suum Deo in monasterio, si ipse puer minori aetate est, parentes ejus faciant petitionem quam supra diximus; et cum oblatione ipsam petitionem et manum pueri involvant in palla altaris, et sic eum offerant. De rebus autem suis aut in praesenti petitione promittant sub jurejurando, quia numquam per se, numquam per suffectam personam, nec quolibet modo, ei aliquando aliquid dant aut tribuunt occasionem habendi; vel certe, si hoc facere noluerint et aliquid offere volunt in eleemosynam monasterio pro mercede sua, faciant ex rebus quas dare volunt monasterio donationem, reservato sibi, si ita voluerint, usu fructu. Atque ita omnia obstruantur, ut nulla suspicio remaneat puero, per quam deceptus perire posset (quid absit); quod experimento didicimus. Similiter autem et pauperiores faciant. Qui vero ex toto nihil habent, simpliciter petitionem faciant et cum oblatione offerant filium suum coram testibus*" (McCann 134) ("If someone of the nobility offers his son to God in the monastery, if the boy himself is still a minor, let his parents make the petition which we have spoken of above; and with the offering let them wrap the petition itself and the hand of the boy in the altar cloth, and thus offer him. Concerning his property, let them promise in the same petition under oath that they will never by themselves or through a substitute or in any way whatsoever give him anything nor provide him an opportunity to possess anything; if they are unwilling to do this and wish to offer anything to the monastery as alms for their own benefit, let them from their property which they want to give to the monastery make a donation, reserving for themselves, if they so desire, the income. And thus may everything be blocked, so that no suspicion remain for the boy through which he could be deceived and perish (far be it); we have learned this by experience. Poorer persons should act in a similar way. But those who

St. Benedict wants total detachment from possession, but supplies adequate clothes, food, etc. as {the} fruit of work and on {the} level of local farmers.

POVERTY—THE BASIC OBLIGATION: here we consider the canonical legislation at the present day, as the basic minimum which *everyone has to observe*. This is the obvious starting point for any discussion of the practice of religious poverty. This is the framework on which our religious poverty is built. But it is not in itself the whole story. The *canonical definition of religious poverty* (cf. Schaefer, n. 1110) {is as follows}: "The vow of religious poverty is a promise made to God in Religion, by which the professed takes on the obligation not to use or dispose of anything worth money for his own interest as his own, that is to say, independently of the superior."[702] This is important because it makes several things very clear *regarding the vow*. But we must not assume that these restrictions and limitations on the matter of the vow should be taken over into the virtue. This is the bare minimum which concerns us in the vow, but is not what constitutes the true spirit of poverty, which implies something a little more.

1. Canonists distinguish the matter of the vow into two classes. *Materia remota* {includes} all objects *worth money*, whether they belong to the community or to someone else. These must be *temporal and external* goods. NOT under the vow of poverty are the following: *internal goods*—health, honor, good name, freedom of conscience, science, art, talent, virtues, academic degrees, civil rights; we should deal with these things according to a spirit of detachment, but they have nothing to do with the vow; *external spiritual things* do not come under the vow—relics are a case in point; they have no money value, but poverty can come in when

---

have nothing at all may simply make the petition and present their son with the offering in the presence of witnesses").

702. "*Votum paupertatis religiosae est promissio Deo in Religione facta, qua profitens nulla re pretio aestimabili uti vult in suum commodum tanquam propria, id est independenter a competente Superiore*" (Schaefer, 656).

we consider the relic cases, etc. Some say religious articles, if we have them with permission, can be disposed of by us. This is not the custom in our Order, however—cf. {the} *Rule* of St. Benedict.[703] Some more "cases"—the *private* notes and manuscripts of a monk are not matter of {the} vow of poverty unless there is question of their sale and publication, or unless they have a money value and might be published sometime, or unless they were written at the command of the superior for the good of the community. The term manuscripts includes typed manuscripts and carbon copies as well as mimeographed material; manuscripts which {a} religious possessed before entering religion are disposed of with other possessions when one makes {one's} vow. The question of manuscripts concerns one's private notes which may be taken with one on leaving a house without special permission. But a religious who would destroy on his own initiative manuscripts that seem to be worthwhile, even though not intended for publication, may commit an injustice and sin against {one's} vow, though this is disputed by authors. It would be sinful to destroy a manuscript that one had been *appointed* to write under obedience. This applies only to extended works, like {the} manuscript of a whole book, for example; it *does not* apply to personal notes, especially spiritual and private notes, kept on one's own initiative. *Works of art* belong to the Order unless one has made them in {one's} own spare time for an outsider with materials provided by him. But in our Order this would require permission or one would sin against obedience.

Materia proxima[704] {refers to} the acts of proprietorship themselves, exercised on the above articles. These are independent acts,

---

703. See *Rule*, c. 33: "*Ne quis praesumat aliquid dare . . . sine jussione abbatis*" (McCann, 84) ("Let no one presume to give anything . . . without the command of the abbot"); c. 54: "*Nullatenus liceat monacho . . . eulogias, vel quaelibet munuscula . . . dare sine praecepto abbatis*" (McCann, 122) ("On no account may it be permitted to the monk to give religious articles or any small gifts without the permission of the abbot").

704. "proximate matter," i.e., that which is most immediately and directly involved.

in which the monk uses temporal goods according to his own views and for his own purposes, or even for others, without the necessary dependence on his religious superior. The thing aimed at is the *free and independent use and handling of temporal goods*.

Poverty and the Novice: Canon 568 reads: during the course of the novitiate, if the novice in any way shall have renounced his benefices or goods or shall have encumbered them in any way, the renunciation or encumbrance [*obligatio*?] is *not only illicit but is invalidated by the law*.[705] This canon does not affect (a) a *will* made during novitiate; (b) small gifts and expenses, v.g., Masses said—not more than one-third of novices' property; (c) renunciation of goods made during postulancy is not affected by it. {The} purpose {is} to make sure the novice is not withheld from returning to {the} world by fear of destitution. Canon 570[706] {stipulates that the} novice who leaves cannot be charged for board, etc. during novitiate and postulancy (!!!), but *can* be asked to replace extraordinary expenses (v.g., medical). *Hence the novice:*

1. retains full ownership of his property owned before entering. Novices are not bound by vow to observe monastic poverty, but they are bound by obedience and by the obligation to acquire monastic formation to conform to the rules of poverty enforced in the novitiate and to acquire a serious spirit of poverty. They do not sin by acts of proprietorship or acts against poverty, but if they do not have an ability to be poor in the monastic sense, they lose their right to be considered fit candidates for monastic profession.

2. If a novice dies intestate, his goods go to his natural heirs and not to the monastery.

3. Novices can acquire goods by gift, legacy, etc. What they acquire must not be spent but must be placed on their account

---

705. "*In novitiatus decursu, si suis beneficiis vel bonis quovis modo novitius renuntiaverit eademve obligaverit, renuntiatio vel obligatio non solum illicit, sed ipso iure irrita est*" (*Codex Iuris Canonici*, 192).

706. *Codex Iuris Canonici*, 192–93.

and kept for them until they either make profession or leave the monastery. However, they are perfectly free to refuse gifts, legacies, etc.

4. Novices may have *permission* to make use of gifts, and they need this permission from the novice master. Otherwise the money or objects must be kept for them. They cannot use money beyond insignificant amounts (in proportion to their total goods). They may be permitted to use a few dollars for Mass stipends or small expenses, but these expenditures must not add up to a notable part of what is on their account.

5. If a novice receives revenues from investment, he may add the revenues to his capital. He is also free to dispose of these revenues, as usufruct of goods is not prohibited by Canon 568.

6. When the canon forbids *encumbrance* of property, this means that a novice is not allowed to mortgage, lease or loan property. But he would be permitted encumbrance of interest on investment.

7. Regarding the Mass stipends received by priest novices, an agreement should be possible whereby the priest receives the stipends and says the Masses. The practice on this point is not very clear or satisfactory here at the moment.

8. The novice signs a document saying he will make no claim on the Order for "wages" for his services if he leaves.

9. Novices retain the administration of their property, but the novice master may demand that they cede this administration if he sees that it interferes with their novitiate duties and formation. This would be a matter of obedience to the novice master.

10. In asking for and giving gifts, even small ones, the novices should conform to the *Rule* of St. Benedict and not seek or give even small gifts without permission. READ {the} *Rule*, c. 54.[707]

---

707. "*Nullatenus liceat monacho neque a parentibus suis neque a quoquam hominum nec sibi invicem litteras, eulogias, vel quaelibet munuscula accipere aut dare sine praecepto abbatis. Quod si etiam a parentibus suis ei quidquam directum fuerit, non praesumat suscipere illud, nisi prius indicatum fuerit abbati. Quod si jusserit suscipi, in abbatis sit potestate cui illud jubeat dari; et non contristetur frater cui forte directum fuerat, ut non detur occasio diabolo. Qui autem aliter praesumpserit, disciplinae regulari*

11. A novice could, without special permission, ask for alms for another or for the monastery. But of course if this were to be done by letter, he would have to ask permission to write the letter.

12. A novice might conceivably receive a gift *intuitu religionis*[708] (offered obviously not for him personally but to the Order). He would then be obliged in justice to turn it in to the superior.

13. A novice would sin against justice by taking, retaining or hiding community property without permission, *a fortiori* by taking things with him if he left. This would be stealing. Of course it admits of small matter.

14. Novices should conform to the *Rule* (c. 54) in regard to lending and exchanging, giving, etc. of goods that are given for his use by the monastery. That is, he cannot dispose of these things freely and without permission.

15. In things given for one's use, the novice, like the professed, is bound to make use of these things in the way and during the time intended: for example, food, clothing, etc. Taking food from {the} refectory and storing it to be eaten at other times and places would be a fault; in the novice's case it would be a disciplinary fault against obedience. Keeping books from the common box would be another such fault. Permission is needed to eat and drink with outsiders.

16. Notable negligence and culpable loss of monastery goods would be faults in the novice.

17. *Sins*: the novice is not able to sin against poverty, but he can sin against justice. The sin is computed by the ordinary norms of justice, depending on the financial status of the physical or

subjaceat" (McCann, 122) ("On no account may it be permitted for a monk to receive from his parents nor from anyone else, nor to give, letters, religious articles, or any small gifts, without the permission of the abbot. If anything were sent to him by his parents, he should not presume to accept it unless it had already been disclosed to the abbot. If the abbot should order it to be accepted, let it be in his power to determine to whom it should be given; and let the brother to whom it happened to be sent not be upset, so that no opportunity is given to the devil. Let anyone who should presume otherwise be subject to the discipline of the rule").

708. "out of esteem for the order"; see below, n. 725, and pages 400–401.

moral person whose rights are violated. Ordinarily, there would not be mortal sin in the faults committed by novices in the misuse of monastery property or in taking common goods. {An} example of a mortal sin {would be} to steal a car belonging to the monastery and to leave (doubtfully mortal if the car is only "borrowed" and the monastery is informed where to get it back—v.g., at {the} airport).

18. Where there is violation of justice, there is also {the} obligation of restitution. A novice who culpably allows the loss or destruction of monastery property can legitimately be called upon to pay for it or to contribute in some way to recovery of the loss.

In general the novice should not only keep all the rules regarding poverty as if he were already professed, but he should strive to be *perfect* in poverty and to acquire from the start a real spirit of evangelical poverty in order that when he is professed he may continue throughout his whole life to observe poverty according to the rule and to *grow* in the spirit of poverty.

The Simple Vow of Poverty: we now come to the simple vow of poverty, which in our Order is temporary. In order to understand clearly the canonical concept of the simple vow of poverty and the obligations which flow from it, the following terms must be grasped clearly. *The concept of ownership (dominium)*: by the vow of poverty we renounce ownership and/or enjoyment of the things we own. Canonically, we are not occupied with the instinct for proprietorship or with the psychology of proprietorship, nor are we considering the ascetic principles involved. Here we study merely a canonical conception of *objective rights*. *Dominium*—ownership, or mastery—is the power to possess an object having a money value. It is the mastery over that object which flows from the fact of being its owner. One can do with it what he likes. However, a distinction is made between {two types of *dominium*}. *Dominium radicale* {is} direct or radical ownership. This means that one has possession of the thing itself, but only that—one does not have the right to dispose of it: {for} example, a heir who owns a property which, by the terms of the will, he cannot dispose of until he comes of age. It is his, but he does not become able to use and dispose of it until reaching {his} majority. {It is distinguished from} *dominium utile*: this is indirect or "useful" ownership, which gives one access to the benefits and fruits of the thing owned. For instance, if A. owns a property and leases it to B. for him to cultivate and exploit, B. has *dominium utile*, and can even sublet the property, but he cannot sell it; he does not have radical *dominium*. When a person has *both* radical dominion and useful dominion together at the same time, then he is said to have *perfect dominion*. When he has only radical dominion, or only useful dominion, but not both, then he is said to have *imperfect dominion.*

Under the concept of useful dominion, we must also distinguish the following ideas:

1. *Use (usus)* is defined as *simplex fruitio rei.*[709] This definition would be confusing for one who was thinking in terms of the theological distinction between *usus* and *fruitio*. {These are} two very different ideas for the theologian, but the canonist does not bother to make a distinction. To use an object is then to *make it serve our needs and desires.* Properly speaking, the *use* of a thing is its application to a purpose for which it is adapted by its nature. The right use of an apple pie is to eat it. An "extended" use {would be} to throw the pie at somebody. In either case, the pie is destroyed. It is "used up." There are objects which are not immediately destroyed by use. A car, if properly driven, is not used up and finished in the first hundred miles.

2. *Usufruct* is the right to *dominion over the fruits of a thing.* At times usufruct and use are the same thing, and at times they are different. Usufruct and use *can be the same whenever the* thing is not destroyed by use. Usufruct implies that the object *remains substantially intact*, and one simply disposes of or exploits its products—or fruits. If I eat an apple pie, then I have use, but there is no usufruct. If I sell the pie, there is (use and) usufruct. If I hire

709. "the simple enjoyment of a thing."

out a car, then there is usufruct and use in a certain sense. In the case of hiring a car, the hire is the "fruit" of my act of dominion, and at the same time I am "using" the car to make money. But really I am selling the use of it to another and thus getting the *usufruct*, the fruit of the use.

3. *Administration*: administration is the right *to conserve and provide for* property and to *carry out all the acts necessary to take care of this*. Thus if I own a piece of real estate, I have the right of administration over it. I can provide for the care of the property, see that bills are paid, taxes are up to date, that the property is protected against trespassers, etc. To administer property is an act of proprietorship and a violation of the vow. However, the professed can *receive reports* on the administration of his property, and should do so.

With these terms clear in our mind we can very simply and easily understand the position of the simple professed with regard to the vow of poverty. *Canon 580, n. 1,* reads: EVERY PRO-FESSED UNDER SIMPLE VOWS WHETHER PERPETUAL OR TEMPORARY, UNLESS OTHERWISE PROVIDED FOR IN THE CONSTITUTIONS, KEEPS THE OWNERSHIP OF HIS GOODS AND THE CAPACITY TO ACQUIRE OTHER GOODS, WITH DUE CONSIDERATION FOR THE PRESCRIPTIONS OF CANON 569.[710] Canon 569[711] declares that (1) before the profession of simple vows the novice must *cede the administration* of his goods to anyone he likes; (2) and *freely dispose of the use and usufruct* of his goods; (3) he must freely *make a will disposing of his goods* and of any that may come to him in the future, to any testator he pleases, in the event of his own death. ({The phrase} "unless otherwise provided for in the Constitutions" {refers}, for instance, {to} the laybrothers in the Jesuits, {who} renounce ownership although they have only simple perpetual vows.)

---

710. "*Quolibet professus a votis simplicibus, sive perpetuis sive temporariis, nisi aliud in constitutionibus cautum sit, conservat proprietatem bonorum suorum et capacitatem alia bona acquirendi, salvis quae in can. 569 praescripta sunt*" (*Codex Iuris Canonici*, 196; emphasis added).

711. *Codex Iuris Canonici*, 192.

Thus, in few words, he retains the *radical dominion* of his goods only and renounces the *useful dominion*.

Our *Constitutions* (n. 162) {read} as follows: "The professed under temporary vows shall retain the ownership of their property, but the administration of it, and the disposal and use of the revenues derived from it, are absolutely forbidden to them."[712] These provisions add nothing to those laid down in Canon 580. The *Constitutions* continue: "Before profession, therefore, they must cede, for the whole period during which they will be bound with temporary vows, the administration of their property to whomsoever they please, and dispose freely of its use and usufruct, even in favour of their monastery, if it seem good to them."[713] These words are repeated almost identically in *Usages*, n. 30.[714]

1. This is done in the "will" which the novice makes before his profession of simple vows. This document, which the novice usually signs *pro forma*, takes care of the use and usufruct and administration of property in a general way, providing for heirs in case of death and stating that one retains ownership as long as one is alive and only under simple vows. Note: all that one acquires during simple vows by way of legacy or personal gift is added to one's capital and disposed of in case of death, according to the will.

2. The *form* at present in use, signed more or less automatically by novices, without thought because they usually don't have any property, declares as follows: (1) the abbot of the monastery is appointed executor, administrator and trustee of "the entire income of my property both real and personal"[715]—in other

---

712. *Constitutions*, 38.

713. *Constitutions*, 38, which reads: ". . . bound by temporary . . ."

714. "Before the profession of temporary vows, the novice must cede, for the period during which he will be bound by his vows, the administration of his property to whomsoever he pleases, and dispose freely of its use and usufruct" (*Regulations*, 13).

715. See Merton's own will before making profession, dated February 17, 1944, which includes this phrase, in Thomas Merton, *The School of Charity: Letters*

words, administration is entrusted to the abbot, and it is assumed that usufruct of property will mean simply adding income to capital already in our possession; (2) the monastery is made the heir in case the testator dies during his simple vows.

Note: although most novices automatically sign this document, probably without paying much attention to what they are doing, the following points are to be carefully observed:

1. You are absolutely free to dispose of the usufruct of your property as you see fit before vows, and there is no obligation whatever to dispose of it in favor of the monastery. In point of fact the form used does *not* take the usufruct for the monastery, but adds it to the capital of the simple professed.

2. You do not have to make the abbot the administrator of your property. You can choose a friend or relative or anyone else you like. However, in practice, no one should hesitate on this point without a definite reason. If you have really little or no property to administer, the point makes no difference. If an outside administrator is appointed, the appointment should be *revocable* in case he proves incompetent. (N.B. it is not against poverty to administer the property of *another* hence the abbot can be administrator.)

3. You are absolutely free to leave your property to anyone you like. Sometimes it is argued that one has a kind of moral obligation to leave his property to the monastery in case of death, because of the expenses the monastery may incur in case of one's sickness, etc. But this obligation is not to be taken too seriously if the monastery in any case is prosperous, and if one has relatives or other heirs who might be in need. If there is any priority, one might expect that the *natural* heirs would have the preference, unless one's monastic community is quite poor.

4. *When* is the will made? In practice, the will is best made between the time one has been voted on for profession and the time

on *Religious Renewal and Spiritual Direction*, ed. Patrick Hart (New York: Farrar, Straus, Giroux, 1990), 7–8.

of retreat before vows. *De jure*[716] it can be made any time during the novitiate, but this is not usual. Before your profession retreat, you should consult your father master about making this will.

Obligation to make a formal "cession" of goods:

1. Every novice should make formal disposition of his goods before he pronounces his simple vow of poverty. The will is obligatory for simple professed in institutes having only simple vows. In our Order, where solemn vows are taken, the will is *not strictly obligatory* for the simple professed, but is made usually.

2. The cession of goods should be made by a novice who owns nothing, because during the time of his simple vows he may become the possessor of property.

3. If the disposition of goods for some reason was not made before profession, then it ought to be made after profession. Even though he has a vow, the professed still has the right and duty to make this, if he has not made it before. Our *Constitutions* read (#163): "This cession or disposition of goods, if it was omitted because of lack of possessions and these are later acquired, or it was made and other possessions were afterwards acquired by any title, should be made or repeated according to the norms laid down in n. 162, notwithstanding the fact that simple profession has been made."[717] This indicates that for us it is not absolutely obligatory to make the will if there are no possessions, but in practice it is better, and it is always done.

4. *Changing the will* after profession: according to Canon 580, n. 3,[718] the simple professed needs the permission of the head of the order to change his will after profession. However it seems

---

716. "according to law."

717. This translation does not correspond to that in *Constitutions* and apparently was made by Merton himself directly from the Latin original: "*Ea cessio ac dispositio, si praetermissa fuerit ob defectum bonorum et haec postea supervenerint, aut si facta fuerit et postea alia bona quovis titulo obvenerint, fiat aut iteretur secundum normas N. 162 statutas, non obstante temporaria professione emissa*" (*Constitutiones*, 31).

718. *Codex Iuris Canonici*, 197.

more likely that the permission of the local abbot is sufficient in our case. But the professed is not allowed to change his will on his own initiative, without permission. Nothing is said in the *Constitutions* about changing the will. If a simple professed changed his will without permission, the act would be a sin against the vow of poverty, but the will would be valid. If the beneficiary named in the will dies, then there is no need of a special permission to make a new disposition of goods, as the professed is in the position of one who has not made a will.

5. *Before solemn profession*: at solemn profession the simple professed will lose the right to own property. Consequently, before solemn profession he must make a juridical act renouncing such things as he still possesses. This act is *not valid* until within 60 days before solemn profession. It must be made within these 60 days (see *Constitutions*, 167[719] and Canon 581[720]).

6. *Can the simple professed, with permission, make gifts* taken from his capital while he is professed? (a) obviously, he cannot give away, even with permission, *all* his property; (b) nor can he give away, even with permission, a *notable part* of his property if it would mean that he would be in a state of want in case he left the Order; (c) if he would not be in need, in case of leaving the Order, it is probable that a simple professed *could* give away a notable part of his goods, say one-third, with permission; in practice it would be wise for the superior to refer the case to our General's House, at least; (d) if a simple professed wished to change his disposition of goods so as to give a *notable part of his property* to the Order or monastery, the matter would have to be referred to the Holy See (reply given by Pontifical Commission for Interpretation of the Code, May 15, 1936[721]); (e) This would also apply to a change in disposition of the *administration* of one's goods in favor of the Order or the monastery; the matter should

719. *Constitutiones*, 32; *Constitutions*, 39.
720. *Codex Iuris Canonici*, 197.
721. See Schaefer, 568 (#979).

be referred to the Holy See; (f) SMALL SUMS may be given away with permission of {the} abbot.

Effects of the Simple Vow of Poverty—this material is important; you should know it thoroughly:

1. First of all, the simple vow of poverty differs from the solemn in one very important respect. The simple professed retains radical ownership; the solemn professed does not: (a) acts of proprietorship carried out by a simple professed are *illicit* but remain valid in the eyes of Church law; (b) acts of proprietorship by a solemn professed are both *illicit and invalid*. ({For} example, {a} simple professed, without permission, using money of which he retains radical ownership, buys a car. He sins mortally against {his} vow, but the car remains his in the eyes of the law. {A} solemn professed has no money with which to buy {a} car, but supposing it is given to him. He cannot validly receive it. It is not "his" in any legal sense; he acquires no title to the gift, and of course he sins by receiving it, or trying to do so, for himself—n.b. he can and must receive the gift for the monastery.)

2. What the simple professed renounces is all right to dispose freely of the property he owns. He renounces all acts of proprietorship except what is included in *radical dominion*. Any act of proprietorship, whether use, usufruct or administration, of the property he owns, is a sin against the vow of poverty (n.b. simple professed laybrothers of the Society {of} Jesus are excepted from the rules above—they do not even retain radical dominion of property).

3. The simple professed can *acquire new property*. Gifts and interest, etc. may be added to the wealth he radically owns (patrimony), but he has no right to use it or dispose of it. To receive a gift, he requires permission of the superior. Once permission is granted, he retains possession. (He would validly retain possession even if he acquired the gift without permission: see example above.[722])

---

722. The reference is presumably to the car, though there it was a question of puchase rather than gift.

4. He is not able to dispose of his property licitly (see above[723]).

5. Concerning *personal effects* owned before profession—watch, books, clothes, etc.—are these objects still under his radical dominion? and if so, who is to use them? the religious, or are these goods tacitly handed over to common use? According to a response of {the} Sacred Congregation {of} Religious (27 January 1919),[724] we gather the following: (a) such goods remain in the radical possession of the professed; (b) but as to their *use*, they are supposed to be for the common use of the community *unless* the professed has explicitly stated that he wishes them to be set aside and kept; (c) the personal effects of the professed must be either given to common use or stored away—they are *not to be used by the professed himself*; however, he can obtain permission to keep for his own use such things as books if they are of a special nature ({for} example, your clothes: during your simple profession they may be used by anyone having to go out of the community and may be worn out before you reach time for solemn profession).

6. *The fruits of industry and gifts*: here the general principle given in Canon 580, n. 2 holds for both simple and solemn professed: *QUIDQUID AUTEM INDUSTRIA SUA VEL INTUITU RELIGIONIS ACQUIRIT, RELIGIONI ACQUIRIT*.[725] The simple professed has no right to the fruits of his labor. It does not enter into what he owns with radical dominion. It is all for the community, including its use, usufruct, etc. This arises out of the contract entered into at profession, in which the professed gives {the} fruits of industry to {the} community in exchange for temporal care. What is meant by industry? manual or mental work, in fact any form of work that brings in a wage or other increment. It includes stipends for Masses, preaching, etc. Hence:

a) A professed cannot *refuse* pay or stipends which come to him for work or ministry—these belong by right to the order.

723. See above, page 398, #2.
724. See Schaefer, 663–64 (#1121).
725. *Codex Iuris Canonici*, 196 ("But whatever a religious acquires through his own industry or through esteem for the order, he acquires for the order").

He sins against poverty in refusing them. But of course this is subject to circumstances. One does not have to extort a sum of money from a poor person, out of "poverty," in order to bring it home to the monastery. However, we are not permitted to say Mass for no stipend without permission.

b) When a professed leaves the order, on expiration of vows or with {an} indult of secularization, he has no right to claim the fruits of his labor. This is upheld by civil law (U.S. Supreme Court: Order of St. Benedict vs. Steinhauser[726]).

c) {Note the} case {of} a simple professed religious {who} is injured in a railway accident and receives compensation. This is not {the} fruit of labor and does not go to {the} institute. But equity demands, according to some authors, that he give it to {the} institute. For this he needs permission of the Holy See. In practice, here it would be better to add it to his capital and then transfer it to the order on making solemn profession.

d) If a religious is in {the} armed services in war and receives {a} pension or other grants, this money belongs to the order, and if he later leaves, anything of this kind that comes to him for service goes to {the} order as long as he was under vows when in the service (S. C. Relig., March 16, 1922[727]). In practice, a well-to-do house ought to arrange things so that in such a case the ex-religious would get his pension.

e) Gifts *intuitu religionis*: these include every gift given in view of the institute or the religious character of the receiver. Any gift that is directed to the receiver out of respect and esteem for the order, for the work of the order, for the function he performs as a member of the order, etc., is a gift *intuitu religionis*. Excluded from this are gifts based on the title of friendship, which is to be presumed in the case of an old friend or relative unless other-

726. "Order of St. Benedict of New Jersey v. Albert Steinhauser" (1914), *United States Reports*, vol. 234 (Washington, DC: Government Printing Office, 1914), 640–52; the major finding of the case was that the royalties of a deceased Benedictine author did indeed belong to the monastery of which he was a member at the time of his death.

727. See Schaefer, 664–65 (#1123).

wise stated. *Gifts given out of friendship may be received or refused.* Distinction must be made between *gifts for patrimony* (usually large) and *gifts for personal use. Gifts for patrimony* are received without special permission and added to patrimony. *Gifts for personal use* are presumed to be like any other use of common goods, and *permission is required* to receive and spend them. They may be added to patrimony without special permission. Here they are simply added to patrimony as a matter of course. {As to} *other gifts*, if someone gives me a gift "for the poor" or "to buy something for your folks," I can accept it and dispose of it without violating poverty, as I am acting as his agent. However, it should be made known to {the} superior in a notable case. *Gifts ex intuitu religionis* must be received {and} must be handed over to the superior; to keep or use these without permission is {a} sin against poverty; to refuse such gifts would be {a} violation of charity (to the order).

7. *Administration of property*: the simple professed retains {the} right to administer his property, but the administration itself is transferred to another during vows. Administration of property of another—v.g., another religious—would be licit. Administration of property of a secular—v.g., a relative—would not be contrary to poverty but against Canon 139, n. 3,[728] and the general obligation of religious not to engage in secular business; with a grave cause, permission could be granted by the abbot.

8. *Common obligations*: besides the above, which are peculiar to the religious with simple vows, we now come to common obligations of poverty which bind all religious whether of simple or solemn vows.

Independent acts of ownership with regard to community goods:

(1) *To take* any community property for oneself without permission is a violation of the vow of poverty, unless the object

---

728. *Codex Iuris Canonici*, 38–39: this canon forbids clerics from administering property of laypersons without the consent of their ordinary.

is of completely insignificant value. In that case, though the vow is not violated, the spirit certainly is if we exercise proprietorship. Hence one should not make easy distinctions and be free about taking and using "little things," because it is precisely here that we lose the spirit of poverty. Customs determine what objects for common use can be taken without permission: here, for example, scrap paper, pencils, razor blades, paper clips, rubber bands, and the things in the common medicine chest. These require no permission, but one should still use them in a spirit of restraint and poverty. {Instances} where poverty could be offended by appropriation {include} taking and keeping clothing issued for the use of another (charity and justice {would be} offended here also); taking and keeping books from {the} common library; taking food, tools, materials. It should be obvious that taking things belonging to outsiders is a worse fault, unless it is evident that they are willing for us to have these things. But actually to help oneself to the small things belonging to an outsider in the monastery—for instance, cigarettes—would certainly give much scandal, even though he might be perfectly willing to offer one some cigarettes if the occasion arose. Stealing is despicable in anyone, but especially so in a religious with a vow of poverty.

(2) *Retaining*: we can sin against poverty by retaining things for which we had permission *beyond the time when the permission expires*. In a large monastery there are likely to be many cases where this is not checked on. In practice, the individual should be very careful to return things once he has no further need of them, once a job is done, once an assignment has been completed. In many cases it is not so much a matter of formal sin against poverty as just plain thoughtlessness and laziness. We must train ourselves to get rid of things and return them promptly as soon as we have no further need of them. When the need ceases, we really have no right to have the things, even though *technically* we still have permission. In reality the permission is no longer justified. A bad habit {is} saving up even small things "for a rainy day"; {it is} against the spirit of poverty to be relying on things "I may need some day." *Hiding* things from {the} superior, so that he

no longer has control over them and they pass from his control to mine, is a sin against poverty. Hiding them from brethren, when we have permission, for safekeeping, is no sin.

(3) *Borrowing*: to borrow community goods without permission is a sin against poverty, presuming that the object has some value. To borrow without permission an expensive tool which the one in charge may reasonably be unwilling to lend, and with danger of harming the tool, is certainly a sin against poverty. There is a great deal of carelessness about this in some quarters. Other angles besides poverty enter in: justice and obedience, charity to those who may be inconvenienced by our thoughtless and illegal act, etc. *Minor superiors* often are unnecessarily free about their use of objects; they assume that because they have a position of slight authority, they are able to make use of everything as they please without consulting anyone. Hence great inconvenience is sometimes caused to others. Even where poverty may not be at stake, charity and good order require that these borrowings be made known at the proper time, to the proper person.

(4) *Lending*: to lend something without permission is a violation of poverty. To lend something valuable belonging to {the} monastery to an outsider, whom one cannot reasonably trust, is more serious. To lend it to another monk is less serious, because there is no sin against justice. The lending of small objects between monks (for instance, articles of clothing for temporary use—v.g., a work blouse for one work period) is implicitly permitted, especially in cases of necessity. But the spirit of poverty demands that one check with {the} superior, especially if he is easily available (v.g., at distribution of work). Books should never be lent without permission. They should pass through ordinary channels, that is, be handed on by the superior. This applies especially to books which are of an unusual nature and are not in common use: here it is a question not so much of poverty as of prudence or obedience. Such books may not be good for all. If {the} superior gives Fr. A. permission to lend to Fr. B., this implies B. has permission to borrow.

(5) *Exchanging* is equivalent to *disposing* of things, and cannot be done without permission. Gravity is lessened, however,

and generally absent among religious themselves. But one would have to be careful of an instinct to barter and trade which might creep in and ruin {the} spirit of poverty in some religious. (This is to be watched in some employments. Some religious become obsessed with ideas of trading in machines and making good deals with old trucks, tractors, etc. With permission there is no sin, but there can be {a} loss of {the} spirit of poverty.) We are not allowed to exchange items of food in the refectory. To do so is no sin, but {it is} a breach of discipline and lack of mortification ({an} imperfection).

(6) *Giving*: a simple professed who gives something that is his own without permission sins against poverty. A simple or solemn professed who gives what belongs to {the} community or to another sins against both poverty and justice. However, one must take into account certain *gifts to the poor* which would not come under this ban if the religious is justified by his position, etc. in giving them. The superior should normally be presumed to consent. It would be very bad to cultivate a spirit of avarice under the guise of poverty. We do have a certain obligation to the poor, but the individual should not irresponsibly take {it} upon himself to go out of his way to make certain gifts when this is not part of his function (gatekeepers, cellarers, etc. have this as part of their function, also guestmasters; traveling religious run into occasions of this kind). The lives of monastic saints frequently tell us of monks who gave lavishly to the poor from the goods of the monastery, even to the point of causing difficulty to the community. Discretion is required, but charity takes precedence over all else. But in general it must be said that {the} monastic spirit implies a certain generosity, and an avaricious monk would be very unchristian and give great scandal. Note that when a poor man is in *grave need*, he has a *right* to help. In such a case, no permission is necessary: it can be taken for granted.

(7) *Destroying* and culpable neglect: {there is a} distinction between destroying what is useful and what is useless. {It is} no sin to destroy what is simply in the way (discretion, please), no sin to destroy a manuscript, private or saleable even, unless com-

posed under obedience—this belongs to {the} house. To destroy, allow to deteriorate, or to lose culpably a valuable article, tool or anything serviceable, is a sin against poverty. It must be made good in some way—it *must be made known*. We must cultivate great care in this matter, for it is in careless destruction or misuse of monastery property that most religious in fact most frequently *violate poverty*, especially in {the} U.S., where respect for things is rare. Note: when you lose an object belonging to the monastery, this means that you are obliged to make *serious efforts* to find it again. Special care must be taken not to carelessly leave tools lying around at the place of work. This year, when we returned in the fall to work in the woods, no fewer than *eight* wedges were found, which had been left there since the previous winter. Axes are often found rusted and rendered useless in the woods where novices have been working. If you have slightly damaged something which you can reasonably repair yourself, with a little trouble, then you ought to take that trouble, even if you take it out of your own free time. It is not in accord with the spirit of poverty to leave other members of the community to clean up after you, to repair the breakage due to you, to tidy up the mess in which you have left implements, etc., etc. READ St. Benedict, chapter 32,[729] on the tools and property of the monastery, and also the

---

729. "*Substantia monasterii in ferramentis vel vestibus seu quibuslibet rebus, praevideat abbas fratres de quorum vita et moribus securus sit, et eis singula, ut judicaverit utile, consignet custodienda atque recolligenda. Ex quibus abbas brevem teneat, ut dum sibi in ipsa assignata fratres vicissim succedunt, sciat quid dat aut quid recipit. Si quis autem sordide aut negligenter res monasterii tractaverit, corripiatur; si non emendaverit, disciplinae regulari subjaceat*" (McCann, 84) ("As for the property of the monastery in tools, clothing and other objects, let the abbot appoint brothers of whose life and behavior he is assured, and let him assign to them as he judges proper the particular articles to be taken care of and gathered up. Let the abbot have a list of these, so that as the brothers take one another's place in assignments, he may know what he is giving and what he is receiving. If anyone should treat the possessions of the monastery shabbily or negligently, let him be corrected; if he does not mend his ways, let him undergo the discipline of the rule").

section of chapter 31[730] where it is said that the cellarer must look on the tools as if they were the sacred vessels of the altar. This must be understood—not that he treats them as sacred objects in themselves, but that he takes care of them, keeps track of them, looks after them with as much solicitude as if they were sacred. You would not leave a chalice lying in the woods overnight. If by mistake you left it in some out-of-the-way place, you would immediately go to look for it.

(8) *Use of things beyond reasonable permission*: another frequently violated point of poverty is the *extension of use* of objects given to us, beyond permission, implicit or explicit. {For} example, one has a watch for a certain job. He keeps the watch semi-permanently or permanently. This is the same as retaining—treated above. One has some money to buy lunch when going to town, saves on the money, and buys some small object without permission. This is not what the money was permitted for. It would be a sin against poverty, provided there were sufficient matter. *Food and drink*: in the use of food and drink, which is permitted to us at certain times and places, not at others, is it a sin against poverty to eat between meals? {A} distinction {should be made}: to eat here and there—for instance, at one's work, without reason or permission—would not be a violation of poverty but a slight breach of discipline and a lack of mortification. *Habitual extra meals*, yes—{this would be a} violation of poverty. To keep a supply of food, without permission, in one's place of work or elsewhere, could be a sin against poverty. To accept {the} invitation of seculars to eat and drink, without permission, would not be a sin against poverty. It might be a breach against discipline. It is better to get permission when visitors ask you to eat with them, though here it has tended to become customary to do this. There are certain restrictions as to place, etc. Keep within the limits set by obedience. Remember your obligation as a monk consecrated

---

730. "*Omnia vasa monasterii cunctamque substantiam ac si altaris vasa sacrata conspiciat*" (McCann, 82) ("Let him regard all the vessels of the monastery and the whole property as if they were the sacred vessels of the altar").

to a life of self-denial. The fact that there is a "custom" growing up does not make everything and anything perfectly legitimate.

(9) *Common life*: here we need only refer back to what has already been said about the obligation of the common life above (pp. {196, 210}, etc.), especially in what concerns *common ownership* and *equal participation* in the common goods—that is to say, the avoidance of useless or excessive privileges. In general, the common life obliges under the vow of poverty, and for one to have very notable exceptions, to have things that are notably better than what anyone else has, even with permission, could be a violation of poverty if there were absolutely no real need for it. But of course it would have to be a glaring case.

Note: Canon 2389[731] prescribes that those who violate the common life in a *notable degree* (relative in any order) are to be warned and then deprived of active and passive voice. If superiors, they are to be deprived of office. This implies a *judicial process*. *Peculium*[732]—a sum granted by {the} superior for spending without strings or conditions attached—is against common life and a violation of poverty. If one monastery were to live on a level notably higher and more comfortable than all the other houses of the order—what then?

Obligations of Poverty—Practical Summary—Sins against the Vow:

1. A religious sins against poverty *whenever he acts as a proprietor* and acquires or disposes of things independently, without any permission. For sin, there must be sufficient matter.

2. Interior sins against poverty are possible—fully deliberate, consented {to, with a} desire to violate the vow in a sufficiently serious matter.

3. Mortal sin against poverty is computed relatively; {it} depends on the country, the economic situation of the house, whether the money or goods are taken from the community or

---

731. *Codex Iuris Canonici*, 755.
732. See Schaefer, 673–75 (##1138–41).

from an outsider. {As a general} principle, authors agree that the same amount is required to constitute a sin against poverty as to constitute a sin against justice. This is computed as any sum that can reasonably be considered as causing serious damage to the victim—enough serious damage to justify indignant protest in a reasonable mature person. To take ten cents might cause indignation *ratione scandali*[733] in a monastery, but it is not sufficient matter for a sin against justice, because the average person is not regarded as unwilling to lose ten cents. To take the last ten cents from a beggar would be a mortal sin. It is all that he has. To take a fairly large proportion of a man's weekly wage would be a mortal sin. This is a *relative* norm. One can assume that there is an *absolutely* grave sum, but sins against poverty are not computed by this norm, but by the relative norm. To take from the monastery and give to an outsider without permission a brand new typewriter would be a mortal sin because the cost of the typewriter {would} be much more than a week's wage of a secular living on our own level. We must compute sin, in practice, according to the norm of what a farm worker or relatively comfortable farmer makes around here. Twenty or twenty-five dollars, or say thirty dollars, are relatively a serious sum for the people living around here. Therefore, to give away or freely dispose of something belonging to the monastery worth thirty dollars, without permission, could be a grave sin.

4. *Extenuating circumstances*: what is said above refers rather to outright alienation of property, without permission—taking things belonging to the community and removing them altogether from common use, either taking them for oneself alone, in a completely selfish way, or giving them, selling them to an outsider. When there is question of *borrowing* or *giving to another member of {the} community*—in other words, when the object or money remains in the community and serves the purposes of part of the community—then the gravity is lessened.

733. "by reason of scandal."

5. *Aggravating circumstances*: a relatively smaller amount, with *scandal*, or taken from a poorer person, could be a grave sin.

6. If a religious (under simple vows) were to dispose of *goods belonging to him*, obviously the norm would be different. Here it would be a matter of the proportion of his patrimony disposed of when the patrimony itself is a seriously large sum—over $50. Thus, if a person had a patrimony of $200 and disposed independently of $75, it could be a mortal sin; but if he had $50 and gave away $25, it would probably not be a serious sin. {It is} hard to estimate, but in general when the amount is a hundred dollars or over, it will very likely be grave matter.

{7}.[734] *Double sins*: some violations of poverty are at the same time *sins against* justice—when the rights of others are violated: v.g., taking from outsiders or from {the} community. In this case, {there would be} two sins, one against religion, one against justice. When one disposes of his own goods ({in} simple vows), then {there is} only {a} sin against poverty.

{8}. *Restitution*: where there is a sin against justice, there is {an} obligation of *restitution*. A religious with simple vows may be obliged to make restitution out of his patrimony. One with solemn vows can only make restitution by *extra work* or by *foregoing benefits*.

The Spirit and Practice of Evangelical Poverty

What we have considered so far is purely and simply the juridical obligation of poverty. A religious faithful to his vow will be careful to practice all the things set down there. He will live up to this obligation. But the fact remains that mere keeping of these rules does not suffice to make a man really "poor" as Christ would have him be. The externals without the inner spirit are a pure illusion, a self-deception all the more dangerous when we try to delude ourselves that in these externals perfection consists, and that we are really poor with the *charity* of Christ. It is fatal to

734. Typescript reads: "6. . . . 7."

embrace merely the external routine of poverty with no understanding of the inner meaning of the vow, the spirit of poverty.
Too few religious stop to consider what is meant by the *instinct
of possession*. Very few consider its subtle ramifications. But it is
this instinct which poverty attempts to mortify in order to unite
us to Christ. Poverty mortifies inordinate desires to possess material things or to use them. If we do not understand the way
this instinct works, we will keep the obligation without actually
mortifying ourselves. We can easily substitute other ways of ex-
ercising this instinct. It is possible to be regular and observant in
matters of poverty—i.e., getting the proper permissions—and
yet be sunk in avarice and possessiveness, in a word, completely
selfish and self-seeking in our use of material goods. Note also
the very important fact that there is a kind of group satisfaction
in the possession of things from which each individual is theoretically detached. We have to be filled with the spirit of poverty
not only as individuals but also as a group. It is in a certain sense
much easier for the group to offend than the individual. The individual has to be very careful about every step he takes. He is
more aware of his own responsibility, and this awareness is kept
alive by admonitions of others. But in the community the sense
of responsibility is less. It is more vague. Everyone may leave it to
the superior to judge and assume responsibility, and the superior
may at the same time be assuming that the judgements of inferiors
are made wisely in the spirit of poverty. Thus the community can
go to excess, in satisfying its "needs," without anyone being the
wiser, or one may think about it only when it is too late.

Furthermore, we must not consider our instinct of possession *in the abstract*. It is a strictly concrete and relative affair. It
is not only that each one is prohibited from being personally
attached, but also there is a basic obligation for every Christian
to use material things in a way that takes account of the *needs
and opportunities of others*. For instance, if I have a farm on high
ground in an area where my neighbors are flooded out by a
river, I owe them shelter and assistance. For me to selfishly keep
supplies that would normally be legitimate, and not share them

with those in need, would be a sin. Possessions that would be perfectly legitimate when all others have about the same, in the same situation, cease to be so legitimate when others are in grave need and I can assist them. This {is the case} for ordinary Christians. Religious not only vow to renounce property rights, but religious poverty assumes the obligation of charity, of sharing the lot and difficulties of the poor, and sharing in the work by which the poor take care of their needs, in one way or another. Hence when religious, even when strictly "regular" about permissions, etc., live as comfortable, well-to-do people among poor men who have only the bare necessities of life, poverty is not a reality any more for those religious. But the poor do not necessarily have to be at the doors of the monastery. The religious vowed to poverty takes upon himself a *standard*, *a measure*. Primarily this measure, relative in each case, is found in a certain class of "poor" person in the immediate society in which the religious community exists—chiefly where it *was founded*. But by extension, the level of existence of all poor people, everywhere in the world, can be relevant for religious. It must be taken into account. The Cistercians are a French, agricultural group. Basically, our standard is the level of living of the French peasant. In practice, it becomes the level of the farmer in the country where we are. As Cistercians in Kentucky, our instinct for possession must be regulated not only by canon law, etc., but also by the measure of the farmers of Kentucky. This means our neighbors, normally. They are not for the most part in dire poverty. Some of them are well-to-do; others get along. Some are in indigence—and these we must aid in whatever way we can. The norm for us, generally speaking, is to live on the level not of the *rich* farmer but of the *average* farmer in our area, and to *help* the indigent farmer. For us to cultivate the desires, the "needs," the standards of a big plantation owner in the Bluegrass region would of course be a prevarication. There is nothing wrong with running a *successful* farm, and naturally it will have to be a large one, for a large community. ({The} advantage of a small community {is that it can} get along with less.) But when one looks closely at the various aspects of the problems thus raised, he sees that they are *extremely delicate and require much attention and thought.*

To what extent can we invest in a larger and larger plant in order to make more money? When should we draw the line? It is always evident that expenditures will increase along with income, and there need never be a place where we draw the line because we have too big a surplus! The mere fact of not having a surplus is no excuse for constant growth and expansion. Details of all this kind of thing can only be settled by superiors, and it is not the business of the subject to make judgements without sufficient knowledge. But the novice of today may be the cellarer or even the abbot of tomorrow, and you must be thoroughly grounded in monastic tradition on the matter of poverty. Here are two fundamental principles: (1) it is not legitimate to run a monastery, from the material viewpoint, merely on the *same standards as any other business;* we are not in it merely to make money; (2) *what is permissible in ordinary business ethics may be highly questionable in a context of monastic poverty.* These are some of the questions that superiors have to wrestle with. Meanwhile, let us consider the basic problem of the *possessive instinct.*

The Instinct to Possess: {first of all, there is} the *right to possess.* Man has a natural right to make use of things, to have dominion over them, and the Church teaches that after original sin man not only has the right to own material things, even as a private individual, but that this ownership is *morally necessary* for mankind at large. But this right must be kept *within just limits.* It can be restricted by social authority for the common good, and those who possess must remember that they are administrators in the name of God of these goods, and that charity demands that they share their surplus with those who have not enough for themselves: *Possidere res privatim ut suas, jus est homini a natura datum* (Leo XIII).[735]

---

735. *Rerum Novarum* (*Acta Sanctae Sedis,* 23 [1890–91], 643); "For every man has by nature the right to possess property as his own" (*Rerum Novarum, Encyclical Letter of Pope Leo XIII on The Condition of Labor* [New York: Paulist Press, 1939], 5).

Valid possession: there are obviously certain normal, ordinate and reasonable ways of providing for our basic needs by possessions. Here the instinct for possession is used properly, for the service of life and for the glory of God:

1. As a *source of sustenance and support* in life, for ourselves and our dependents. Every human being normally has a right to the things he needs to preserve life and to live a healthy, full, integrated human life: {the} right to own *money* in order to purchase the things he needs; {the} right to own *land*, {a} house, etc., a car for transportation, clothes, etc.—all according to his station in life, within reason.

2. In *order to support others*, especially those depending directly on him—family, children.

3. In *order to carry on his work*. Every man has a right to own those things which are necessary for him to contribute productive work: land for the farmer; tools for the artisan; a workshop; a factory for the manufacturer. Note: it is fully Christian to have land, {a} factory, etc., *owned in common* on a cooperative basis by those who work there. This does not in any way contradict Christian morality—on the contrary. We see that in religious orders this kind of ownership is considered to be more in accordance with the Gospel ideal.

4. It is just and right for persons to own what serves them *for reasonable recreation* and enjoyment—a hi-fi set, sports goods, {a} cottage at the lake, etc.

So far, the ordinary rules of morality {apply}. This is reasonable and ordinate possession. If it were easy and common to keep to these rational norms, and if everybody could keep his possessive instincts within these limits, there would be no need for a vow of poverty. The vow is necessary because *it is easier and surer* to give up all possessions than to strive to strike the right balance in ordinary, legitimate forms of proprietorship. In actual practice, normal and licit proprietorship is rather uncommon. *Too much is possessed by too few*. We easily delude ourselves that inordinate needs are really necessities, or we love possessions inordinately and for inadequate reasons. As a result of our greed, others have to suffer. Because there is so much avarice, love of money and greed in the world, *the vow of poverty is especially necessary*, that the possessive instinct may be kept within the bounds set by Christ.

Abnormal expressions of the possessive instinct {occur} when we seek to possess things that *we do not need* for the above reasonable causes. {A} wrong instinct to possess is based on *inordinate needs*, or on no need at all. It becomes a desire to *possess for possessions' sake*, or for the *sake of inordinate pleasure*, or as *a result of inordinate fears*.

1. Possession as *power*: here we see a distortion of the personality—the man who imagines that the *self-affirmation* involved in {the} act of possession really proves him stronger, better, higher, greater. {This is} common in modern society. Everyone {is} more or less infected with this disease, imagining that a man with a better house, a better car, is himself better than others. This is not altogether without foundation, because such people are *treated better* than others, with greater obsequiousness, etc., because others think they will be rewarded for so doing. {For} example, a man drives up in a Cadillac, with a chauffeur, expensively dressed, steps out, pulls out a wallet stuffed with bills: watch everybody fall over themselves to be nice to him. {Take the} case of a rich woman who went into a fashionable store dressed in slacks and was told that "they did not have" whatever it was she wanted. {She} came back the next day all dressed up. . . . See the *Rule of St. Benedict*, c. 53:[736] special attention to be paid to the *reception of the poor and pilgrims*—{this is the} spirit of the *Rule* and of the Gospel. *In ipsis magis Christus suscipitur.*[737] We are not to let ourselves be too impressed by the power of the wealthy. Note a special angle—the *acquisitive instinct*. Here the act of *taking possession* is too highly valued, loved as an end in itself. {One takes} inordinate

---

736. McCann, 118, 120, 122.
737. McCann, 120 ("In them Christ is more especially received").

joy in the *smart bargain* or in the *brute force* by which one extorts the goods of another, or in the *manipulation* by which apparent weakness gets around the power of a possessor. Here we begin to see some of the subtle ramifications of the vice of proprietorship. Proprietorship when it becomes a vice is *pure egoism* even in its more subtle forms—especially in its more subtle forms.

2. *Conspicuous waste* {is} another manifestation of power—the enormous and useless expenditures of the very rich, just to show that they are so powerful that to them large sums of money are "nothing"—they still have plenty more: the Roman millionaire who threw his slaves to the lampreys; the American millionaires of the end of the nineteenth century who lit cigars with hundred-dollar bills. This is actually a very great sin of pride and crass selfishness, especially when one realizes the condition of millions of others starving. The sin becomes almost diabolical. Note: this same instinct flourishes, though within certain limitations, in communist states. The party bosses have the best of everything, and others are excluded by barbed wire fences, etc. {The} only difference {is that} the chauffeur is called comrade and is probably a secret police spy.

3. *Patronage—Paternalism*: this is a milder but sometimes much subtler and deeper form of the use of possession as a way to show power: having innumerable dependents; causing people to become dependent on you hand and foot so that to them you are, practically speaking, "Providence." This can be done even outside the sphere of economics—just emotionally. In this way, one comes to "own" even the souls of other men, in a certain sense. One dominates them completely and refashions them at will, running their whole life. It is easy to see that this inner, more spiritual aspect of possessiveness can be a subtle pitfall for priests and religious in office. It can be a great sin and do unutterable harm. Note the harm done by this kind of possessiveness on the part of parents—in a more overt form in the past; then parents almost "owned" their children as objects—disposed of them for their own interest, e.g., in marriage, practically "selling" them. Today it is more subtle and undercover.

4. *Other forms of self-assertion by possessing*: here we get into subtle and hidden manifestations of the vice. These do not and *cannot come under the vow of poverty* unless material things are somehow involved. But they really violate the spirit of poverty—and all the more so because they are *substitutes* for outward and material possessions. {They include} attachments to our *gifts, our talents*, using these in such a way as to show off and make ourselves seem superior because we "have" something that others do not have. {They include} attachment to *our own "style,"* our own way of doing things; it often happens that a dominant personality imposes on others his characteristic expressions of speech, his attitudes and opinions. He enjoys doing this. Others become a reflection of himself, a witness to his exceptional character. There is *nothing wrong with being individual*; we are certainly not expected to become mere cogs in a machine, mere passive conformists. But in being oneself, one must remain detached and humble, not seek to flaunt his individuality. {They include} attachment to our *experiences, friends*: some people "collect" different experiences. They go to special places and ever after they can say they have been there. They want to meet special people and ever after they can say that they "know" these people. They eat special foods, hear special music, etc. This can be pitifully trivial sometimes: a man can be proud that he was on the same train, the same boat, as a movie star, though he never even saw the famous person. It makes him imagine that he is somehow *special, singled out* and *set apart* from the rest of men. Note that this is an illusion in the first place, and becomes more so because of the tendency to *embellish the facts by lying*. Before long, the man on the train begins to say that he *did* see the star; he spoke to her; they had a long conversation; they became close friends, etc., etc.

5. *Possessions as a source of security—the fear of deprivation*: hitherto we have considered the possessive instinct as positive self-gratification and self-assertion. But now, turning it around—and this applies more to religious—we see the need to possess *generated by fear*, the sense of an *inordinate need*, the insecurity and anxiety that come from having to be without certain things. This

generally arises when there is real or proximately real poverty. It easily arises in religion when perhaps the vow begins to pinch.

a) We need things to sustain life, health, etc. We may begin to fear that unless certain special needs are taken care of, we will suffer in our health. Hence, {there arises a} desire for comforts, special privileges, etc. as an aid to preserve health. In America, there are religious who are deeply anxious when they do not have almost all the comforts they enjoyed at home before entering the cloister. In this country, things which are great luxuries in other parts of the world seem to be necessities.

b) A special aspect of this {is} *fear of boredom and interior emptiness*. One of the greatest sources of anxiety and need is this fear of being left to ourselves, alone, without support—hence the need for diversions, recreations, radio, TV, parties, etc., sports. It is easy to begin imagining that as a community we need many special helps of this kind. One example would be an inordinate interest in a wide variety of special, non-religious books. It is good to have broad cultural interests, but within the limits of our vocation. Another case {might be} records, hi-fi; or extra good foods on feast days. In a very small way, the need for news and information that merely satisfies curiosity is an escape from inner emptiness. *This inner poverty is actually very important in the contemplative life.*

c) The fear that we will *not be able to carry out our work properly* or that inordinate difficulties in work will become a distraction and upset our life of prayer. In our monasteries there is much willingness to spend money on labor-saving machinery, on the theory that if the work is smooth and successful, the interior life will thereby be aided. Is this true, or is it another illusion? Certainly it is true that machines can save time, and to that extent they are helpful. But the increase of pressure and tension, due to mechanization, may perhaps offset the advantage and neutralize it. In any case, it is for the individual monk to resist the temptation to think he "needs" more and better machines in order to work better and thus to pray better. This certainly can be in many cases a very grave illusion, fatal to the spirit and even the vow of poverty.

Effects of inordinate possession: it is very important for us to realize the harmful effects of indulging this instinct. It really destroys our capacity to progress in religious perfection, in prayer and in union with God, even though we may "sincerely" try to "purify our intention." It does no good to make "acts of purity of intention" if in fact we are enslaved to anxieties and needs that flow from the inordinate desire of possessions: (1) the need for possessions cramps and destroys my capacity to *give myself*, which is essential for religious perfection and true charity; (2) it *enslaves* me to things that are outside me and beneath me; I become dependent on them; I am *alienated* from myself and from God; (3) it makes me self-centered and binds me with the bonds of attachment; this paralyzes my whole interior life. Thus the person who thinks he is improving himself and bettering his lot by acquiring inordinate possessions and enjoying the satisfactions that flow from them is in actual fact *hurting himself* and paralyzing his true power to live happily and fruitfully. He is making his life selfish, sterile and inert. A genuine spirit of poverty is the only cure.

The Mystery of Poverty—in Scripture and in Life

We have seen something of man's instinct to possess—how it possesses *him*, how he becomes the slave of things by desiring to affirm himself through possession. This is not merely a problem for the individual, not merely a matter for personal realization, a personal problem to be negotiated. It is a social problem. Above all, we must realize that *it is a religious problem*. This is very clear in the revealed word of God. We seem to a great extent to have forgotten this. Today Catholics tend to regard poverty as a social question, indeed, and as a personal moral problem. But they do not see it as a religious question, a spiritual sign, a mystery. To say that poverty is a religious mystery is to say that it has something to do *with God's dealings with men*.

The Bible teaches us that the poor man, the suffering child of God, is placed in the world as a kind of sign and touchstone.

He represents God Himself. What the others do to him and fail to do to him is *in fact a clear test of their own religion*. The poor man in the world is: (a) an accusation against the unjust rich, against an unjust society, against the falsity and hypocrisy of a society that claims to be just and religious; (b) a vindication of the truly religious man who identifies himself with the poor, sharing everything possible with him, because he sees God in the poor man; (c) but there are few truly spiritual men in this sense; hence God reserves for Himself a special spiritual care of the poor and a special reward for them, and He pays very special attention to their prayers and their rights—He makes Himself *their avenger*. The theme of this section is, then, that the inordinate instinct to possess can be *a very terrible sign* in our life. One of the social sins most reproved in the Bible is the sin of the pseudo-religious, seemingly "just" man who leads a comfortable and respected life on the unjust spoils of the poor. Let us briefly consider some of the texts:

1. The seventh and ninth commandments: Thou shalt not steal; Thou shalt not covet thy neighbor's house . . . nor anything that is his (Exodus 20). Note that these commandments are seldom properly understood. "Steal": respectable people relegate stealing to the social underworld of burglars and crooks; {they} forget that cheating in business, extortion, oppression of {the} poor, etc. is also stealing—appropriating what belongs by right to others. Stealing does not just mean taking a material thing or a bill with your hand. It can be done very "cleanly" through a respectable business transaction in which apparently no one is soiled by anything sordid. *Covet*: most people just associate this with the desire of adultery which they conceive chiefly as impurity. In the commandment the angle of justice is paramount—and the wife is considered among the man's "goods."

2. The Year of Jubilee (Deuteronomy 15—read {vv.} 1-4[738]): to remit all debts in the seventh year. Why? {the} importance of

---

738. "In the seventh year thou shalt make a remission, Which shall be celebrated in this order. He to whom any thing is owing from his friend or neighbour

avoiding poverty in the Chosen People. "There shall be no poor or beggar among you." {This is} very important. The presence of {the} poor is {a} sign that God is not fully recognized in His people. The Chosen People is a *plebs sancta*[739] when poverty is abolished in it.

3. The special concept of property in the Promised Land: all the land belongs to the Lord, and it is portioned out to tribes and individuals. An individual or family should not be definitively deprived of his portion; hence if he has alienated it in some way, it should return to him in the Jubilee year (*read* Leviticus 25:23-34[740]).

4. No Israelite can become a slave of his fellow Jew, nor should Jews exact usury from one another (*read* Leviticus 25:35-44[741]). (However, note that slaves from the Gentiles are perfectly

---

or brother, cannot demand it again, because it is the year of remission of the Lord, Of the foreigner or stranger thou mayst exact it: of thy countryman and neighbour thou shalt not have power to demand it again. And there shall be no poor nor beggar among you: that the Lord thy God may bless thee in the land which he will give thee in possession."

739. "holy people."

740. "The land also shall not be sold for ever: because it is mine, and you are strangers and sojourners with me. For which cause all the country of your possession shall be under the condition of redemption. If thy brother being impoverished sell his little possession, and his kinsman will, he may redeem what he had sold. But if he have no kinsman, and he himself can find the price to redeem it: The value of the fruits shall be counted from that time when he sold it: and the overplus he shall restore to the buyer, and so shall receive his possession again. But if his hands find not the means to repay the price, the buyer shall have what he bought, until the year of the jubilee. For in that year all that is sold shall return to the owner, and to the ancient possessor. He that selleth a house within the walls of a city, shall have the liberty to redeem it, until one year be expired: If he redeem it not, and the whole year be fully out, the buyer shall possess it, and his posterity for ever, and it cannot be redeemed, not even in the jubilee. But if the house be in a village, that hath no walls, it shall be sold according to the same law as the fields: if it be not redeemed before, in the jubilee it shall return to the owner. The houses of Levites, which are in cities, may always be redeemed: If they be not redeemed, in the jubilee they shall all return to the owners, because the houses of the cities of the Levites are for their possessions among the children of Israel. But let not their suburbs be sold, because it is a perpetual possession."

741. "If thy brother be impoverished, and weak of hand, and thou receive him as a stranger and sojourner, and he live with thee, Take not usury of him

acceptable to the law.) Note the religious significance of freedom as a sign of redemption and of rescue from Egypt. One who belongs to the race God has redeemed should never be in want, should never be oppressed or enslaved. But note that this responsibility rests with the people itself. If the chosen ones forget their relationship to God, {if they} oppress, dispossess, enslave one another, then the people is no longer what it is meant to be. It loses its significance and becomes a religious lie.

5. Hence {there are} special rules of mercy and justice: great care {is taken} to protect {the} rights of the poor. *Read* Exodus 22:21-27:[742] note the stranger is here included; note how God expressly says He hears the cry of the poor. This "cry" is not necessarily a high and pure prayer; it is heard not so much because of the poor man's virtue but because of his *need*. God has taken upon Himself {the} special protection of the needy.

6. {There must be} no double-dealing and trickery to get around the law; one must honestly and frankly help the needy,

---

nor more than thou gavest: fear thy God, that thy brother may live with thee. Thou shalt not give him thy money upon usury, nor exact of him any increase of fruits. I am the Lord your God, who brought you out of the land of Egypt, that I might give you the land of Chanaan, and might be your God. If thy brother constrained by poverty, sell himself to thee, thou shalt not oppress him with the service of bondservants: But he shall be as a hireling, and a sojourner: he shall work with thee until the year of the jubilee, And afterwards he shall go out with his children, and shall return to his kindred and to the possession of his fathers, For they are my servants, and I brought them out of the land of Egypt: let them not be sold as bondmen: Afflict him not by might, but fear thy God. Let your bondmen, and your bondwomen, be of the nations that are round about you."

742. "Thou shalt not molest a stranger, nor afflict him: for yourselves also were strangers in the land of Egypt. You shall not hurt a widow or an orphan. If you hurt them they will cry out to me, and I will hear their cry: And my rage shall be enkindled, and I will strike you with the sword, and your wives shall be widows, and your children fatherless. If thou lend money to any of my people that is poor, that dwelleth with thee, thou shalt not be hard upon them as an extortioner, nor oppress them with usuries. If thou take of thy neighbour a garment in pledge, thou shalt give it him again before sunset. For that same is the only thing wherewith he is covered, the clothing of his body, neither hath he any other to sleep in: if he cry to me, I will hear him, because I am compassionate."

without evasions and without subterfuge. *Read* Deuteronomy 15:7-11:[743] note here the recognition that there will always be the poor. Though ideally no one should be poor at all, yet the law recognizes the reality and allows for it: it is sufficient that the poor be not left in need and that their more fortunate brethren take care of them. Sapiential literature takes up this theme of the law also: *read* Ecclesiasticus 34:17ff.[744] Note {the} implication of {verse} 17: he who fears the Lord is normally the poor man (we

743. "If one of thy brethren that dwelleth within the gates of thy city in the land which the Lord thy God will give thee, come to poverty: thou shalt not harden thy heart, nor close thy hand, But shalt open it to the poor man, thou shalt lend him, that which thou perceivest he hath need of. Beware lest perhaps a wicked thought steal in upon thee, and thou say in thy heart: The seventh year of remission draweth nigh; and thou turn away thy eyes from thy poor brother, denying to lend him that which he asketh: lest he cry against thee to the Lord, and it become a sin unto thee. But thou shalt give to him: neither shalt thou do any thing craftily in relieving his necessities: that the Lord thy God may bless thee at all times, and in all things to which thou shalt put thy hand. There will not be wanting poor in the land of thy habitation: therefore I command thee to open thy hand to thy needy and poor brother, that liveth in the land."

744. "The soul of him that feareth the Lord is blessed. To whom doth he look, and who in his strength? The eyes of the Lord are upon them that fear him, he is their powerful protector, and strong stay, a defence from the heat, and a cover from the sun at noon, A preservation from stumbling, and a help from falling; he raiseth up the soul, and enlighteneth the eyes, and giveth health, and life, and blessing. The offering of him that sacrificeth of a thing wrongfully gotten, is stained, and the mockeries of the unjust are not acceptable. The Lord is only for them that wait upon him in the way of truth and justice. The most High approveth not the gifts of the wicked: neither hath he respect to the oblations of the unjust, nor will he be pacified for sins by the multitude of their sacrifices. He that offereth sacrifice of the goods of the poor, is as one that sacrificeth the son in the presence of his father. The bread of the needy, is the life of the poor: he that defraudeth them thereof, is a man of blood. He that taketh away the bread gotten by sweat, is like him that killeth his neighbour. He that sheddeth blood, and he that defraudeth the labourer of his hire, are brothers. When one buildeth up, and another pulleth down: what profit have they but the labour? When one prayeth, and another curseth: whose voice will God hear? He that washeth himself after touching the dead, if he toucheth him again, what doth his washing avail? So a man that fasteth for his sins, and doth the same again, what doth his humbling himself profit him? who will hear his prayer?" (vv. 17–26).

shall see this in a moment); {verse} 21ff. reproves the offering of the rich extortioner (cf. especially 24); 25ff. makes clear that defrauding the poor is like murder.

7. The prophets, accordingly, inveighed against those who had forgotten the laws and who went about extorting gain from the poor, oppressing them, and failing to hear the cry of the widow and orphan. *Read* Amos 2:6 to {the} end[745] ({in verse} 6, selling the poor for a pair of shoes refers to bribery in law courts). Note the reproaches of Yaweh, {who} reminds His people how He had brought them up out of Egypt, destroyed the Amorrhite, etc. In connection with {the} corruption of justice, there is also the attempt to pervert the holy and to silence the prophets. The three things go together: avarice with injustice, unholiness, and efforts to silence the voice of truth. This is typical of the "great"—the rich and powerful. The prophets return to this theme again and again. *Read* Michaeas 3:[746] the rich compared to cannibals eating

---

745. "Thus saith the Lord: For three crimes of Israel, and for four I will not convert him: because he hath sold the just man for silver, and the poor man for a pair of shoes. They bruise the heads of the poor upon the dust of the earth, and turn aside the way of the humble: and the son and his father have gone to the same young woman, to profane my holy name. And they sat down upon garments laid to pledge by every altar: and drank the wine of the condemned in the house of their God. Yet I cast out the Amorrhite before their face: whose height was like the height of cedars, and who was strong as an oak: and I destroyed his fruit from above, and his roots beneath. It is I that brought you up out of the land of Egypt, and I led you forty years through the wilderness, that you might possess the land of the Amorrhite. And I raised up of your sons for prophets, and of your young men for Nazarites. Is it not so, O ye children of Israel, saith the Lord? And you will present wine to the Nazarites: and command the prophets, saying: Prophesy not. Behold, I will screak under you as a wain screaketh that is laden with hay. And flight shall perish from the swift, and the valiant shall not possess his strength, neither shall the strong save his life. And he that holdeth the bow shall not stand, and the swift of foot shall not escape, neither shall the rider of the horse save his life. And the stout of heart among the valiant shall flee away naked in that day, saith the Lord."

746. "And I said: Hear, O ye princes of Jacob, and ye chiefs of the house of Israel: Is it not your part to know judgment, You that hate good, and love evil: that violently pluck off their skins from them, and their flesh from their bones?

and butchering the poor. False prophets bring blindness upon the people: the result will be destruction. *Read* Isaias 1, especially 10-27:[747] the corruption of Israel, the great compared to princes of

---

Who have eaten the flesh of my people, and have flayed their skin from off them: and have broken, and chopped their bones as for the kettle, and as flesh in the midst of the pot. Then shall they cry to the Lord, and he will not hear them: and he will hide his face from them at that time, as they have behaved wickedly in their devices. Thus saith the Lord concerning the prophets that make my people err: that bite with their teeth, and preach peace: and if a man give not something into their mouth, they prepare war against him. Therefore night shall be to you instead of vision, and darkness to you instead of divination; and the sun shall go down upon the prophets, and the day shall be darkened over them. And they shall be confounded that see visions, and the diviners shall be confounded: and they shall all cover their faces, because there is no answer of God. But yet I am filled with the strength of the spirit of the Lord, with judgment, and power: to declare unto Jacob his wickedness, and to Israel his sin. Hear this, ye princes of the house of Jacob, and ye judges of the house of Israel: you that abhor judgment, and pervert all that is right. You that build up Sion with blood, and Jerusalem with iniquity. Her princes have judged for bribes, and her priests have taught for hire, and her prophets divined for money: and they leaned upon the Lord, saying: Is not the Lord in the midst of us? no evil shall come upon us. Therefore, because of you, Sion shall be ploughed as a field, and Jerusalem shall be as a heap of stones, and the mountain of the temple as the high places of the forests."

747. "Hear the word of the Lord, ye rulers of Sodom, give ear to the law of our God, ye people of Gomorrha. To what purpose do you offer me the multitude of your victims, saith the Lord? I am full, I desire not holocausts of rams, and fat of fatlings, and blood of calves, and lambs, and buck goats. When you came to appear before me, who required these things at your hands, that you should walk in my courts? Offer sacrifice no more in vain: incense is an abomination to me. The new moons, and the sabbaths, and other festivals I will not abide, your assemblies are wicked. My soul hateth your new moons, and your solemnities: they are become troublesome to me, I am weary of bearing them. And when you stretch forth your hands, I will turn away my eyes from you: and when you multiply prayer, I will not hear: for your hands are full of blood. Wash yourselves, be clean, take away the evil of your devices from my eyes: cease to do perversely, Learn to do well: seek judgment, relieve the oppressed, judge for the fatherless, defend the widow. And then come, and accuse me, saith the Lord: if your sins be as scarlet, they shall be made as white as snow: and if they be red as crimson, they shall be white as wool. If you be willing, and will hearken to me, you shall eat the good things of the land. But if you will not, and will provoke me to wrath:

Sodom. The sacrificial worship of the temple is not acceptable to Yaweh as long as the poor are oppressed, and especially as long as judges are corrupt and neglect their duty to defend the rights of the poor and helpless. Forgiveness of the sins of the people and {the} salvation of Juda depends on justice being done and mercy to the poor (16-20). But the Lord Himself will purify His people with suffering. This is standard "social teaching" of the Old Testament, and it applies equally in the New. This is a regular "pattern" in history which recurs over and over again, and we can apply the standards given by the prophets to every such situation: the corruption of a society—manifested in luxury, injustice, falsification of truth, hypocrisy in religion—calls for punishment, the destruction of that society, and the merciful purification of the society in question by "fire" (hence wars, exile, revolutions, etc.).

8. *The Anawim*: the poor then exist and are oppressed. Among these oppressed poor are found the remnant of Israel that is the apple of God's eye, the "just" whose justice does not consist in sacrifices and works of virtue so much as in *faith in God alone in the midst of oppression*. The Anawim form a very important group in Israel. It is the Anawim who speak in many of the psalms. It is the Anawim that God *prefers*, whose prayer He *hears*. He takes their cause upon Himself. He makes Himself responsible for them. The psalms of the Anawim echo the teaching of the prophets. *Read* Psalm 34: (a) begin with 9-14:[748] the humility,

---

the sword shall devour you because the mouth of the Lord hath spoken it. How is the faithful city, that was full of judgment, become a harlot? justice dwelt in it, but now murderers. Thy silver is turned into dross: thy wine is mingled with water. Thy princes are faithless, companions of thieves: they all love bribes, they run after rewards. They judge not for the fatherless, and the widows cometh not in to them. Therefore saith the Lord the God of hosts, the mighty one of Israel: Ah! I will comfort myself over my adversaries: and I will be revenged of my enemies. And I will turn my hand to thee, and I will clean purge away thy dross, and I will take away all thy tin. And I will restore thy judges as they were before, and thy counsellors as of old. After this thou shalt be called the city of the just, a faithful city. Sion shall be redeemed in judgment, and they shall bring her back in justice."

748. "But my soul shall rejoice in the Lord; and shall be delighted in his salvation. All my bones shall say: Lord, who is like to thee? Who deliverest the

trust and faith of the poor man; (b) 15-22[749]—the test of faith: the wicked not only triumph but are convinced of their own rightness; note that the Church has identified Christ in His Passion with the "poor man" of this and other psalms (cf. Passion week liturgy[750]); (c) hence the prayer of the poor man in these psalms is the prayer of Christ. Christ has made it His own. It is then infallibly heard. But what is this prayer? *Read* {verses} 1-8:[751] the

---

poor from the hand of them that are stronger than he; the needy and the poor from them that strip him. Unjust witnesses rising up have asked me things I knew not. They repaid me evil for good: to the depriving me of my soul. But as for me, when they were troublesome to me, I was clothed with haircloth. I humble my soul with fasting; and my prayer shall be turned into my bosom. As a neighbour and as an own brother, so did I please: as one mourning and sorrowful so was I humbled."

749. "But they rejoiced against me, and came together: scourges were gathered together upon me, and I knew not. They were separated, and repented not: they tempted me, they scoffed at me with scorn: they gnashed upon me with their teeth. Lord, when wilt thou look upon me? rescue thou my soul from their malice: my only one from the lions. I will give thanks to thee in a great church; I will praise thee in a strong people. Let not them that are my enemies wrongfully rejoice over me: who have hated me without cause, and wink with the eyes. For they spoke indeed peaceably to me: and speaking in the anger of the earth they devised guile. And they opened their mouth wide against me; they said: Well done, well done, our eyes have seen it. Thou hast seen, O Lord, be not thou silent: O Lord, depart not from me."

750. Ps. 34[35]:20-22 was used as the gradual in the Mass of Friday and Saturday of Passion Week (i.e., the fifth week of Lent) (*Missale Romanum*, 134, 136; *Missale Cisterciense*, 122, 124), as the introit (vv. 1-2) and gradual (vv. 23, 3) and communion (v. 26) for Monday in Holy Week (*Missale Romanum*, 153; *Missale Cisterciense*, 134, 135), and as the gradual for Tuesday in Holy Week (*Missale Romanum*, 154; *Missale Cisterciense*, 136).

751. "Judge thou, O Lord, them that wrong me: overthrow them that fight against me. Take hold of arms and shield: and rise up to help me. Bring out the sword, and shut up the way against them that persecute me: say to my soul: I am thy salvation. Let them be confounded and ashamed that seek after my soul. Let them be turned back and be confounded that devise evil against me. Let them become as dust before the wind: and let the angel of the Lord straiten them. Let their way become dark and slippery; and let the angel of the Lord pursue them. For without cause they have hidden their net for me unto destruction: without cause they have upbraided my soul. Let the snare which he knoweth not come

Lord will arise and judge them; He will destroy them like dust before a whirlwind; 23-28:[752] again {a} prayer for judgement, {a} prayer that the wicked may know shame and thus implicitly be converted to truth. Other examples {include} the *trials of the poor man*: read Psalm 36:12-18;[753] {Psalm} 40:6-14[754] (n.b. this psalm {is} chanted at the administration of {the} Last Sacraments); {Psalm} 41:10-12[755]—when we say these psalms we must take care to be

---

upon him: and let the net which he hath hidden catch him: and into that very snare let them fall."

752. "Arise, and be attentive to my judgment: to my cause, my God, and my Lord. Judge me, O Lord my God according to thy justice, and let them not rejoice over me. Let them not say in their hearts: It is well, it is well, to our mind: neither let them say: We have swallowed him up. Let them blush: and be ashamed together, who rejoice at my evils. Let them be clothed with confusion and shame, who speak great things against me. Let them rejoice and be glad, who are well pleased with my justice, and let them say always: The Lord be magnified, who delights in the peace of his servant. And my tongue shall meditate thy justice, thy praise all the day long."

753. "The sinner shall watch the just man: and shall gnash upon him with his teeth. But the Lord shall laugh at him: for he foreseeth that his day shall come. The wicked have drawn out the sword: they have bent their bow. To cast down the poor and needy, to kill the upright of heart. Let their sword enter into their own hearts, and let their bow be broken. Better is a little to the just, than the great riches of the wicked. For the arms of the wicked shall be broken in pieces; but the Lord strengtheneth the just. The Lord knoweth the days of the undefiled; and their inheritance shall be for ever."

754. "My enemies have spoken evils against me: when shall he die and his name perish? And if he came in to see me, he spoke vain things: his heart gathered together iniquity to itself. He went out and spoke to the same purpose. All my enemies whispered together against me: they devised evils to me. They determined against me an unjust word: shall he that sleepeth rise again no more? For even the man of my peace, in whom I trusted, who ate my bread, hath greatly supplanted me. But thou, O Lord, have mercy on me, and raise me up again: and I will requite them. By this I know, that thou hast had a good will for me: because my enemy shall not rejoice over me. But thou hast upheld me by reason of my innocence: and hast established me in thy sight for ever. Blessed be the Lord the God of Israel from eternity to eternity. So be it. So be it."

755. "I will say to God: Thou art my support. Why hast thou forgotten me? and why go I mourning, whilst my enemy afflicteth me? Whilst my bones are broken, my enemies who trouble me have reproached me; Whilst they say to me

true to what we are saying; otherwise we may be praying against ourselves! {For} the *consolations of the poor man's faith*, read Psalm 32:16-22[756] (hope in the Lord, source of salvation); 33:1-11[757] (cf. {the} Magnificat[758]—Mary {is} the crown of the Anawim); 35:6-13;[759] 39:1-10[760] (again, the obedience of Christ here).

---

day by day: Where is thy God? Why art thou cast down, O my soul? and why dost thou disquiet me? Hope thou in God, for I will still give praise to him: the salvation of my countenance, and my God."

756. "The king is not saved by a great army: nor shall the giant be saved by his own great strength. Vain is the horse for safety: neither shall he be saved by the abundance of his strength. Behold the eyes of the Lord are on them that fear him: and on them that hope in his mercy. To deliver their souls from death: and feed them in famine. Our soul waiteth for the Lord: for he is our helper and protector. For in him our heart shall rejoice: and in his holy name we have trusted. Let thy mercy, O Lord, be upon us, as we have hoped in thee."

757. "I will bless the Lord at all times, his praise shall be always in my mouth. In the Lord shall my soul be praised: let the meek hear and rejoice. O magnify the Lord with me; and let us extol his name together. I sought the Lord, and he heard me: and he delivered me from all my troubles. Come ye to him and be enlightened: and your faces shall not be confounded. This poor man cried, and the Lord heard him: and saved him out of all his troubles. The angel of the Lord shall encamp round about them that fear him: and shall deliver them. O taste, and see that the Lord is sweet: blessed is the man that hopeth in him. Fear the Lord, all ye his saints: for there is no want to them that fear him. The rich have wanted, and have suffered hunger: but they that seek the Lord shall not be deprived of any good."

758. Lk. 1:46-55.

759. "O Lord, thy mercy is in heaven, and thy truth reacheth even to the clouds. Thy justice is as the mountains of God, thy judgments are a great deep. Men and beasts thou wilt preserve, O Lord: O how hast thou multiplied thy mercy, O God! But the children of men shall put their trust under the covert of thy wings. They shall be inebriated with the plenty of thy house: and thou shalt make them drink of the torrent of thy pleasure. For with thee is the fountain of life: and in thy light we shall see light. Extend thy mercy to them that know thee, and thy justice to them that are right in heart. Let not the foot of pride come to me, and let not the hand of the sinner move me. There the workers of iniquity are fallen, they are cast out, and could not stand."

760. "With expectation I have waited for the Lord, and he was attentive to me. And he heard my prayers, and brought me out of the pit of misery and the mire of dregs. And he set my feet upon a rock, and directed my steps. And he put

Poverty in the New Testament: Christ came to preach the Gospel to the poor. This was not only part of His personal mission or the manifestation of a personal preference of His. It was a specific fulfillment of the prophecies of the Old Testament which pointed to the messianic time as the age when justice would be done to the poor and injustice rectified—a time of peace and new order. When John the Baptist sends for formal confirmation of Christ's messiaship, the Lord replies: "The blind see, the deaf hear, the poor have the Gospel preached to them." READ here Matthew 11:2-6:[761] preaching of {the} Gospel to the poor is equal to miracles as {a} sign of {the} messianic kingdom. Blessed is he that is not scandalized may implicitly refer to Christ's own poverty: cf. the people of Nazareth who did not believe because Jesus was a simple carpenter Whom they had known all their lives as poor and humble. READ the prophecy alluded to here—Isaias 61:1-3:[762] the Servant of Yaweh preaches to the meek (Anawim), heals the

a new canticle into my mouth, a song to our God. Many shall see, and shall fear: and they shall hope in the Lord. Blessed is the man whose trust is in the name of the Lord; and who hath not had regard to vanities, and lying follies. Thou hast multiplied thy wonderful works, O Lord my God: and in thy thoughts there is no one like to thee. I have declared and I have spoken: they are multiplied above number. Sacrifice and oblation thou didst not desire; but thou hast pierced ears for me. Burnt offering and sin offering thou didst not require: then said I, Behold I come. In the head of the book it is written of me that I should do thy will: O my God, I have desired it, and thy law in the midst of my heart. I have declared thy justice in a great church, lo I will not restrain my lips: O Lord, thou knowest it."

761. "Now when John had heard in prison the works of Christ: sending two of his disciples he said to him: Art thou he that art to come, or look we for another? And Jesus making answer said to them: Go and relate to John what you have heard and seen. The blind see, the lame walk, the lepers are cleansed, the deaf hear, the dead rise again, the poor have the gospel preached to them. And blessed is he that shall not be scandalized in me."

762. "The spirit of the Lord is upon me, because the Lord hath anointed me: he hath sent me to preach to the meek, to heal the contrite of heart, and to preach a release to the captives, and deliverance to them that are shut up. To proclaim the acceptable year of the Lord, and the day of vengeance of our God: to comfort all that mourn: To appoint to the mourners of Sion, and to give them a crown for ashes, the oil of joy for mourning, a garment of praise for the spirit

contrite of heart ({which} implies spiritual poverty), {proclaims} release to the captives (poverty of prisoners). The Lord loved the poor, was Himself poor, and wanted His disciples to be poor. In fact, the apostles remained poor men, working with their hands. The rich who became Christians distributed their goods to the poor, and the whole community lived a common life, not of destitution but of simplicity, proper to the poor.

The Poverty of Christ Himself: one or two texts are sufficient to remind us of this familiar and basic truth. {For the} poverty in His birth, READ Luke 2:1-12,[763] the Christmas Gospel: Mary and Joseph, like all the other poor people, obey the decree; {because there is} no room in the inn, the child is laid in the manger; the (poor) shepherds are summoned, and the sign given them is precisely the sign of the Lord's poverty. What do we need more than this to show us that poverty is of the essence of our vocation to follow Christ? How can we ever forget it! There is a special emphasis on *homelessness* in this Gospel, the *xeniteia*[764] which is

---

of grief: and they shall be called in it the mighty ones of justice, the planting of the Lord to glorify him."

763. "And it came to pass, that in those days there went out a decree from Caesar Augustus, that the whole world should be enrolled. This enrolling was first made by Cyrinus, the governor of Syria. And all went to be enrolled, every one into his own city. And Joseph also went up from Galilee, out of the city of Nazareth into Judea, to the city of David, which is called Bethlehem: because he was of the house and family of David, To be enrolled with Mary his espoused wife, who was with child. And it came to pass, that when they were there, her days were accomplished, that she should be delivered. And she brought forth her firstborn son, and wrapped him up in swaddling clothes, and laid him in a manger; because there was no room for them in the inn. And there were in the same country shepherds watching, and keeping the night watches over their flock. And behold an angel of the Lord stood by them, and the brightness of God shone round about them; and they feared with a great fear. And the angel said to them: Fear not; for, behold, I bring you good tidings of great joy, that shall be to all the people: For, this day, is born to you a Saviour, who is Christ the Lord, in the city of David. And this shall be a sign unto you. You shall find the infant wrapped in swaddling clothes, and laid in a manger."

764. "the quality of being a stranger or an exile, a man without any fixed abode or home, in the likeness of Christ who had nowhere to rest His head" (*Cassian and the Fathers*, 78).

characteristic of Christ's public life. READ Matthew 8:14-20:[765] first
Jesus heals Peter's mother-in-law, and many other poor and sick
and possessed are brought to Him. What is poorer than a possessed man, who belongs to his enemy the devil? Jesus heals them
all, and the Gospel refers to Isaias 53:4: "He took our infirmities;
He bore our diseases," which implies much more than just the
power to cure. It implies that the compassion which led Christ
to suffer with and among men was associated with this power.
Then He has to leave, flees the crowd, crosses {the} lake. A lawyer
wants to follow Him, and He answers: "Foxes have holes . . .
The Son of Man has nowhere to lay His head."

We can pass over all the examples of poverty in the life of
Christ and consider His *poverty in His Passion*. First, {we note} the
spiritual poverty in Gethsemani when He wills to be destitute
of spiritual power and fortitude, in order to feel the anguish of
suffering and the burden of sin, to such an extent that He sweats
blood. Here He takes upon Himself the poverty of the *sinner*, the
inner, moral destitution of the night of sin; and He takes upon
Himself the *punishment* due to sinners. He is in the position of the
poor man who cannot protest, who has to bear the burden that
rightfully belongs to others, who pays the price for the pleasures
and ambitions of others. {This is} the ultimate in poverty: you
pay the price for the gratifications of others! Then {we note} the
many forms of destitution: He loses all His friends—the poor
man is abandoned by all; they even betray Him, deny Him; He
loses all His honor—His dignity as King, as Messiah, is denied

---

765. "And when Jesus was come into Peter's house, he saw his wife's
mother lying, and sick of a fever: And he touched her hand, and the fever left
her, and she arose and ministered to them. And when evening was come, they
brought to him many that were possessed with devils: and he cast out the spirits
with his word: and all that were sick he healed: That it might be fulfilled, which
was spoken by the prophet Isaias, saying: He took our infirmities, and bore our
diseases. And Jesus seeing great multitudes about him, gave orders to pass over
the water. And a certain scribe came and said to him: Master, I will follow thee
whithersoever thou shalt go. And Jesus saith to him: The foxes have holes, and
the birds of the air nests: but the son of man hath not where to lay his head."

and derided, but not only that—His human dignity as man is reduced to nothing. *Ego sum vermis et non homo.*[766] He suffers in His body helplessly—complete subjection to torture, injustice, anguish. All His possessions are taken away and divided by His executioners. He dies in complete helplessness, among thieves, criminals. He is abandoned even by His heavenly Father—complete interior and spiritual destitution, humanly speaking. He is buried in another man's tomb. Note, however, it is a rich man's tomb, for the rich as such are not absolutely reprobated. They must use their riches for God and their fellow man.

This impoverishment of Christ is the whole key to Christian poverty. He Who emptied Himself in death thereby established His title to be the King and Lord of all, and for Him to be King meant not to dominate but to serve, to give. *Thus, His Kingship is a Kingship of giving and enriching.*

1. Read Philippians 2:6-11:[767] He emptied Himself, taking the form of a servant that in the name of Jesus every knee should bow. In the light of other texts we see that this lordship of Christ and this bowing of the knee implies acknowledgement of a power of life that saves and enriches, a power that transforms, in the likeness of Christ. We do not simply acknowledge His *domination*. (But those who do not accept His love must necessarily acknowledge Him as Lord of life and death. They do so from outside the orbit of His grace, since they do not accept it. But it is offered to them.)

2. READ Matthew 20:20-28:[768] the sons of Zebedee want places of honor. Jesus replies: Princes of the Gentiles lord it over them

766. "I am a worm, and no man" (Ps. 21[22]:7).

767. See above, n. 470.

768. "Then came to him the mother of the sons of Zebedee with her sons, adoring and asking something of him. Who said to her: What wilt thou? She saith to him: Say that these my two sons may sit, the one on thy right hand, and the other on thy left, in thy kingdom. And Jesus answering, said: You know not what you ask. Can you drink the chalice that I shall drink? They say to him: We can. He saith to them: My chalice indeed you shall drink; but to sit on my right

(worldly domination and power—{a} king uses it for himself, uses others for his own aggrandizement). Divine power (shared by disciples of Christ) {is} a lordship that serves. THE SON OF MAN DID NOT COME TO BE SERVED BUT TO SERVE AND GIVE HIS LIFE AS RANSOM FOR MANY.

3. READ 2 Corinthians 8:9,[769] and see {the} context: Christ was impoverished "THAT YOU MIGHT BECOME RICH THROUGH HIS POVERTY." This is a parenthesis in {Paul's} exhortation to {the} Corinthians to share their surplus with the church of Jerusalem, where there is much need. Hence, Christian poverty and charity {means} loving one another and serving one another as Christ has loved and served us: cf. Isaac of Stella, *Sermo* XLIV (Pentecost): *Interim {. . .} gustemus cum Christo quod pro nobis ipse gustavit, sedentes ad mensam divitis, qui pro nobis factus est pauper, praeparemus similia, ut ejus paupertate ditemur, et cum ipso fruamur divitiis cujus paupertatem non refugimus* (PL 194:1841).[770] Just as Christ emptied Himself in order to enrich us, then it is one of the first fundamentals of evangelical poverty that we empty ourselves to give to the poor and to follow Christ. We must get rid of the one-sided idea of Christian poverty in which all that matters is our own detachment. The full picture of Gospel poverty is the renunciation of our goods *in favor of others*, sharing with those who have not, in order to imitate Christ, and in order to create a

---

or left hand, is not mine to give to you, but to them for whom it is prepared by my Father. And the ten hearing it, were moved with indignation against the two brethren. But Jesus called them to him, and said: You know that the princes of the Gentiles lord it over them; and they that are the greater, exercise power upon them. It shall not be so among you: but whosoever will be the greater among you, let him be your minister: And he that will be first among you, shall be your servant. Even as the Son of man is not come to be ministered unto, but to minister, and to give his life a redemption for many."

769. "For you know the grace of our Lord Jesus Christ, that being rich he became poor, for your sakes; that through his poverty you might be rich."

770. "Meanwhile let us taste with Christ what he himself tasted for us; sitting at the table of the Rich Man Who became poor for us, let us prepare similar fare, so that through His poverty we might become rich, and we might enjoy riches with Him Whose poverty we did not flee."

new society in which all have what they need and no one is left in destitution. Just as in the Old Testament it was considered a great evil and a dishonor to God if there should be anyone destitute in the Chosen People, so in the New Testament the Church is a society of love in which by mutual giving the Christians sustain one another, no one is in need, and all live together praising God in charity and simplicity. Texts: in addition to the classical text, Matthew 19:21f., which need only be recalled here—"Give to the poor . . . {and} follow Me"—READ Matthew 10:9-20:[771] apostolic poverty. The poverty is here that of apostles on a special mission, a deep mystery of poverty, in relation to the word of God. The disciples go forth possessing *nothing*. They enter in wherever they are received. They are entitled to sustenance and they give what they have—the message of salvation. They have no way of preparing themselves against emergencies; their sole riches are the word of God. When they are persecuted they need not think in advance how to reply; the Spirit will reply in them and for them. The summit of evangelical and apostolic poverty is here. This is however a very special case. Returning to the poverty of the "ordinary Christian," READ Acts 2:42 to the end:[772] the fruits

---

771. "Do not possess gold, nor silver, nor money in your purses: Nor scrip for your journey, nor two coats, nor shoes, nor a staff; for the workman is worthy of his meat. And into whatsoever city or town you shall enter, inquire who in it is worthy, and there abide till you go thence. And when you come into the house, salute it, saying: Peace be to this house. And if that house be worthy, your peace shall come upon it; but if it be not worthy, your peace shall return to you. And whosoever shall not receive you, nor hear your words: going forth out of that house or city shake off the dust from your feet. Amen I say to you, it shall be more tolerable for the land of Sodom and Gomorrha in the day of judgment, than for that city. Behold I send you as sheep in the midst of wolves. Be ye therefore wise as serpents and simple as doves. But beware of men. For they will deliver you up in councils, and they will scourge you in their synagogues. And you shall be brought before governors, and before kings for my sake, for a testimony to them and to the Gentiles: But when they shall deliver you up, take no thought how or what to speak: for it shall be given you in that hour what to speak. For it is not you that speak, but the Spirit of your Father that speaketh in you."

772. "And they were persevering in the doctrine of the apostles, and in the communication of the breaking of bread, and in prayers. And fear came upon

of Pentecost—the nascent Church, {where} all pray together and
have all things in common together, dividing to each according as
he had need. This was a realization of {the} messianic prophecy
also—no needy in the Kingdom of God. READ also Acts 4:33-35:[773]
the same idea, taken up in greater detail. All who have superfluous property sell it and give the proceeds to the Church for distribution to the poor. {This text witnesses to the} common life of the
early Christians. This, then, is the basis of religious poverty—the
idea that in renouncing the world we renounce our possessions
and give them to the poor of the Christian community ({the} poor
outside the Church {are} not excluded, but the idea is that the
Church itself should be in a position to take care of all in need).
Then we enter into the common life.

But how is the community to be maintained after the original
donations have been spent?

a) WORK: see St. Paul's doctrine. The apostles work with their
hands; all Christians should work for a living. {See} Acts 20:33f.:
it is work that enables man to live justly, not coveting the possessions of others or imposing on others—not being a parasite.
This {is maintained} in spite of the doctrine of ideal apostolic
poverty above, which gives the apostle a right to support by the
people. St. Paul wishes to avoid all confusion and to give a thoroughly understandable example that cannot be mistaken. READ 2

---

every soul: many wonders also and signs were done by the apostles in Jerusalem,
and there was great fear in all. And all they that believed, were together, and had
all things common. Their possessions and goods they sold, and divided them to
all, according as every one had need. And continuing daily with one accord in
the temple, and breaking bread from house to house, they took their meat with
gladness and simplicity of heart; Praising God, and having favour with all the
people. And the Lord increased daily together such as should be saved."

773. "And with great power did the apostles give testimony of the resurrection of Jesus Christ our Lord; and great grace was in them all. For neither
was there any one needy among them. For as many as were owners of lands
or houses, sold them, and brought the price of the things they sold, And laid it
down before the feet of the apostles. And distribution was made to every one,
according as he had need."

Thessalonians 3:6ff.:[774] against the false mysticism and confusion of those who gave up work, expecting the last day at any
moment. Paul worked. If a Christian does not work, let him not
eat either.

b) Mutual Charity: *work and mutual charity among the churches*
go together. Where one community prospers in work, it shares
with other less fortunate ones. READ 1 Thessalonians 4:9-11,[775]
{which} unites the ideas of work and mutual sharing. READ 2
Corinthians 8, especially 9ff.[776] (we have already seen this principle above). This is a very important chapter.

774. "And we charge you, brethren, in the name of our Lord Jesus Christ,
that you withdraw yourselves from every brother walking disorderly, and not
according to the tradition which they have received of us. For yourselves know
how you ought to imitate us: for we were not disorderly among you; Neither
did we eat any man's bread for nothing, but in labour and in toil we worked
night and day, lest we should be chargeable to any of you. Not as if we had not
power: but that we might give ourselves a pattern unto you, to imitate us. For
also when we were with you, this we declared to you: that, if any man will not
work, neither let him eat. For we have heard there are some among you who walk
disorderly, working not at all, but curiously meddling. Now we charge them that
are such, and beseech them by the Lord Jesus Christ, that, working with silence,
they would eat their own bread. But you, brethren, be not weary in well doing.
And if any man obey not our word by this epistle, note that man, and do not
keep company with him, that he may be ashamed: Yet do not esteem him as an
enemy, but admonish him as a brother."

775. "But as touching the charity of brotherhood, we have no need to write
to you: for yourselves have learned of God to love one another. For indeed you
do it towards all the brethren in all Macedonia. But we entreat you, brethren,
that you abound more: And that you use your endeavour to be quiet, and that
you do your own business, and work with your own hands, as we commanded
you: and that you walk honestly towards them that are without; and that you
want nothing of any man's."

776. "For you know the grace of our Lord Jesus Christ, that being rich he
became poor, for your sakes; that through his poverty you might be rich. And
herein I give my advice; for this is profitable for you, who have begun not only
to do, but also to be willing, a year ago. Now therefore perform ye it also in deed;
that as your mind is forward to be willing, so it may be also to perform, out of
that which you have. For if the will be forward, it is accepted according to that
which a man hath, not according to that which he hath not. For I mean not that

The New Testament is full of texts like these. And today the charity of the Church remains a witness to the true meaning of Christianity. It is important that the generosity with which Christians give to good causes be not lowered to a kind of automatic and formal routine, a mere reaching into the pocket to shut up an importunate preacher. There is money given, but is there sufficient thought of the need of the poor? At the present time, it would seem that Christian charity ought to take on a somewhat different dimension. By giving money to an organization, we can fulfill in theory the obligations of Christian charity, but in actual fact we can remove ourselves and insulate ourselves against the problems and suffering of our fellow man. We turn over a few dollars to an organization that "takes care of the poor," and this sets our minds at rest. We have no further responsibility now. But today, with the immense resources of technology and the things that can be done to improve living conditions, Christian charity demands something more than just working to enrich myself and then sharing the surplus with others through the medium of an organization. Today we need to emphasize once again the importance of *work* in the context of Christian charity: work not just to make our living and have something to share, but work in order to *make a better world*, to *abolish poverty* or to make it less terrible. Christian work and charity demand today a deep and well thought-out cooperation in the striving *to better man's conditions everywhere*. This brings us necessarily into the realm of politics. And thus we confront many complex and terrible problems. But it would certainly seem that Christian charity today, necessarily presupposing Christian justice, brings Christian society face to face with the need for a *social movement*, and therefore a political movement, dedicated to the improvement of conditions for the masses of men, not only spiritually but first and foremost *ma-*

---

others should be eased, and you burthened, but by an equality. In this present time let your abundance supply their want, that their abundance also may supply your want, that there may be an equality, As it is written: He that had much, had nothing over; and he that had little, had no want" (vv. 9-15).

terially. There can be such a thing as emphasizing the spiritual in a way that avoids real obligations. A starving man cannot be moved by a spiritual message. He first needs to be fed, clothed, etc., and this is what Christ Himself said. The *society of Christians* will be judged, as much as the individual Christian, by the standards in Matthew 25 (In as much as you did it to one of these least, etc.). Let us now take account of the state of the world and of the poverty that is in it, and conclude by questioning ourselves on our Christian obligations.

THE PRACTICE OF CISTERCIAN POVERTY:

a) The *Cistercian Ideal*: in the *Exordium Parvum*, the following foundations are laid down for Cistercian poverty:

1. The norm is the *Rule of St. Benedict*. This Cistercian practices poverty by trying to keep as close as possible to the actual prescriptions of the *Rule* in regard to poverty. Besides the obvious principle of *no ownership*, which is absolutely essential to all Benedictine poverty, however the *Rule* may be interpreted (*Ne quis praesumat aliquid* dare *aut* accipere *neque* aliquid habere proprium, *nullam omnino rem . . .* [c. 33][777]), there is also the specifically Cistercian emphasis on *the use of common property*. The idea of the Cistercian Fathers was that the clothing, the food, the whole life of the monks should *conform exactly to the prescriptions of the Rule* (*Exordium Parvum*, XV [*Instituta* of St. Alberic]: REJICIENTES A SE QUIDQUID REGULAE REFRAGABATUR):[778]

(a) Clothing: the *Rule* permits clothing *secundum locorum qualitatem*.[779] {It} prescribes for temperate climates: two cowls,

---

777. McCann, 84, which reads: ". . . *accipere sine jussione abbatis*" (emphasis added) ("No one should presume to give or to receive anything [without the command of the abbot], and no one should have anything of his own, anything at all").

778. "casting away from himself whatever is opposed to the rule" (*PL* 166, col. 1507AB).

779. "according to local circumstances" (c. 55 [McCann, 124]).

one for winter, one for summer; two robes; a scapular for work; stockings and shoes (pants for those on a journey). The Cistercian Fathers rejected special garments, fur coats, flowing robes and specially good coats or cloaks, elaborate hoods.

(b) Bedding: "mattress, blanket, coverlet, pillow." {The} Cistercian Fathers rejected *stramina lectorum*[780] (quilts?). Sufficient bedclothes {were} allowed, but not excessive or of too fine {a} quality.

(c) Food (*Rule*, cc. 39, 40):[781] {the} *Rule* permits two portions daily (cooked) plus a third (uncooked?) of fruit and vegetables if available, fresh or special; one pound {of} bread for the whole day, divided if two meals {were taken} ({the} abbot can add to {the} amount or quality of food if {there is} extra work or {for} some other reason, avoiding gluttony); flesh of four-footed animals {is} forbidden; a hemine of wine a day, with more if extra work or heat warrants. The Cistercian Fathers rejected elaborate cooking with meat fat, special tasty dishes, and concern for the excellence and tastiness of food.

2. *The Income of the Monastic Community*: simplicity in the above matters is of course essential; however the real key to Cistercian poverty is in the *insistence on work*. THE ESSENCE OF CISTERCIAN POVERTY IS THAT THE MONK SHOULD TOIL TO SUPPORT HIMSELF. *Productive work*, under obedience to his superiors and for the common good of the community, is essential for every monk in good health. Furthermore, this productive work should normally be *manual labor*, either in the form of farm work or of craftsmanship, the exercise of a trade, for the good of the community. The monk of Cîteaux should *work with his hands*. From the beginning, the work of the scriptorium was included as manual labor—manuscript copying, etc.: the exercise of an art, but not of aestheticism. It was productive work, "making" things for the use of others. The Cistercian Fathers discouraged intellectual work,

---

780. *PL* 166, col. 1507B.
781. McCann, 94, 96, 98.

or at least arranged their lives so that there was little place for it. Only in very exceptional cases did certain monks contribute to the common life by the work of their minds. A case in point was William of St. Thierry, whose writings compensated for the fact that he could not work. But this was an exception. Writing was discouraged by the first Fathers of the Order.

Sources of income that were rejected: if the monk had to live by productive work, the work of his hands, then he could not live by alms or sources of income which involved the exploitation of *the labor of others*. It is essential to the Cistercian concept of poverty that the monk should have no source of income which makes him in fact dependent on the labor of others rather than on the work of his own hands. Mentioned specifically in the *Exordium* {are} parish churches or other chapels and oratories; altars, special endowments and benefices, especially in connection with the burial of benefactors in {the} monastery; tithes; manorial mills or bakeries (where a small fee was charged for services to local peasantry); tenant farmers; serfs (sharecroppers).[782] *What was permitted*, besides the labor of the monks themselves, {was the work of} laybrothers, {which} supplemented and even assumed most of the burden of the community work.[783] (This is important as showing how {the} Cistercian Fathers interpreted {the} *Rule*. They did not hesitate to make this *radical innovation* of which nothing was said in the *Rule*. Hence their "literalism" was not blind and narrow at all.) Family brothers and hired laborers were called upon to assist.

Secular Business: the monks were supposed as far as possible to dissociate themselves from the business of people in the world and from involvement in commercial and legal affairs. However, they did have to sell their products, and this involved journeys and necessary, unavoidable contacts with the outside. But an aspect of Cistercian poverty is the aspect of *remote solitude*, living apart from the world and diminishing contacts with the world.

782. *PL* 166, col. 1507BC.
783. *PL* 166, col. 1508A.

{In} summary, the *Exordium* interprets the *Rule* with emphasis on (a) simplicity of the monk's personal life; (b) work as the source of income; (c) rejection of alms, tithes, etc.; (d) remoteness from the world. To this St. Stephen added a special emphasis *on liturgical simplicity*,[784] poverty in the very prayer life of the monk. This involved a certain austerity, a deprivation of aids which might seem helpful or even necessary. The aim of this deprivation was (a) absence of *expensive or luxurious* objects of worship; (b) simplification of the monk's own prayer life. As a consequence of this, Cistercian poverty in practice reaches into the prayer life of the monk, his spiritual life, his intellectual life. All is marked with simplicity, poverty, the renunciation of complicated means.

Cistercian Poverty Today: applying these norms to present practice, we are not absolutely bound to carry out in every detail all the prescriptions and interpretations of our Fathers as understood in the twelfth century. A certain amount of adaptation to modern times is legitimate and even necessary, and we must take this into account. However, we are obliged to proceed on the same principles as our Fathers. We must keep closely to the spirit of St. Benedict, and even to the letter where this is possible. {It is} *essential* {that} *we must live by our own productive work*, which should be normally *manual work*. Hence the Cistercian monk is obliged by his vow of poverty to contribute zealously and effectively, in so far as he is able, to the support of his community. He has to do this by his own labor, not merely by begging. In doing this, he should be mindful that he helps his community share its products with the poor. The monk does not work {only} for his own poor brethren but also for the poor neighbors of the monastery, so that he may help them along also. The community as such takes care of this, however, not the individual monk.

We must accept the work conditions given to us by obedience, by providential circumstances, etc., in the spirit of poverty. The Cistercian monk practices poverty along with obedience in his humble, detached and submissive attitude toward the work of

784. *PL* 166, col. 1509AB.

the monastery. He does not seek specially good or interesting jobs for himself; he does not try to manipulate his life so as to have work conditions that are pleasing and comfortable for himself. He accepts the betterment of conditions in so far as this may make his work more productive and efficacious. The monk is not his own boss. This is an aspect of his poverty. For further details on this aspect of poverty, see all that was said above about the common life (pp. {196–218}). In our work, if we practice poverty as Cistercians, we must be content with difficult or trying conditions, inadequate tools, inefficient direction. It may be contrary to the purpose of Cistercian poverty if the work is not well organized, but as far as the individual is concerned, on occasions when this happens he must learn to accept it in a spirit of poverty, provided that there is no clear indication that there is something he can do about it. This is a corollary to the fact that the monk is not his own boss. The poor workman may have to work under an unreasonable boss, and so it is an aspect of monastic poverty to accept trying, inefficient conditions, even though *per se* it is desirable that the work be efficiently organized. And indeed a president of the work who through his own negligence allows the work time to be wasted, tools to be misused and things to be spoiled, is certainly offending against poverty. It is also a matter of poverty for the monk *to learn how to work* and apply himself to doing his job right, to *perfect himself in his work*. Mere good will is not enough in Cistercian manual labor. The monk who practices poverty in the spirit of his vocation becomes a *good workman*.

Another aspect of poverty {is that} we should *not seek to be dispensed from work for very slight causes*—an ordinary cold, a headache, a sore back (if not unusually painful) are not sufficient reason for being absent from work, at least where the weather conditions are not too bad. (One with a cold is entitled to ask not to go out in a storm of rain or snow, though we should remember that a poor laborer in the world would not perhaps be able to get away with this; and think of those in forced labor camps!) *The noise, dirt*, etc. that go with our work, particularly when there are machines—all this is to be taken in the spirit of poverty. The working conditions today involve noise, dirt, machines. That is what the poor man is subject to. His working conditions are sometimes boring, tedious, burdensome in the extreme. We must accept the same kind of conditions, though essentially we are farmers and not industrialists. (It would be wrong for the Cistercian in his monastery to become a proletarian-type laborer, working under factory conditions.)

Personal Poverty: THE PERSONAL POVERTY OF THE CISTERCIAN MONK SHOULD BE STRICT TODAY AS IN THE PAST. Poverty in clothing: we now permit special work clothes, but the regular clothes should be accepted according to the *Rule*—not extra garments without necessity, not {a} specially good habit. {There should be} simplicity and austerity in bedding. Food: the food should be abundant and simple; personal poverty can be practiced in {the} refectory occasionally {by} leaving things that are given more for the taste than for food value (eat what is nourishing—this is part of poverty; keep up the strength to work and participate in the life of the monastery fully). Those in charge of providing the food for the monastery must not go overboard in producing special delicacies more and more frequently, more and more extras for "feast days"—this is contrary to {the} Cistercian spirit. Poverty in monastic furnishings: furniture should be adequate, but comfort should not become a dominant concern, nor should we be too occupied with elegance, style. In building or decorating a monastery, modern synthetic materials lend themselves to economic use. Terrazzo tile, for instance, has points in its advantage. But we should not seek the best and latest in everything just because it is stylish or adds a minimal extra comfort or convenience for which we have no need. *Machines* should not be accumulated without real necessity. It is in furnishings, machines, etc. that the spirit of Cistercian poverty is *most threatened* in our American Cistercian monasteries. We must train ourselves to be on our guard in these matters, without however becoming cranks or eccentrics. We do not have to go back in all things to the twelfth century. Books, music, etc.: another place where we can practice poverty is in our use of books and other intellectual satisfactions. Here we have to be on our guard against relatively trivial or superficial interests, mere *amusements*, books and magazines that *divert* and recreate rather than really nourishing our intellectual and spiritual lives. This applies also to music, art, etc. TO MAINTAIN OUR CISTERCIAN SPIRIT OF POVERTY AND SIMPLICITY, WE HAVE TO BE ON OUR GUARD AGAINST EXCESSIVE ADDICTION TO INTELLECTUAL AND CULTURAL VALUES THAT ARE NOT GERMANE TO OUR VOCATION. But here discretion is to be practiced, and individual differences are to be taken into account. In general, radio, TV, hi-fi sets, secular magazines do not belong in our monasteries except for very special purposes (even then radio and TV {are to be} excluded, also movies).

Poverty as regards exceptions: it is the spirit of poverty that should regulate our exceptions from the *Rule*. Exceptions are sometimes necessary. When they are really necessary, then they are permitted and licit. In this case the superiors should always be the judges, and they should be the guardians of the poverty of the community. To *insist* on exceptions that are not deemed necessary by superiors is certainly a *lack of poverty*, even though the exceptions may be objectively necessary. A poor man has to sometimes do even without necessities. However, there is nothing wrong with humbly making known one's needs. A religious without the spirit of poverty seeks all kinds of exceptions and favors which would be permissible perhaps in a middle-class home in the world. But the standards of the monastery are not those of a middle-class home. This ought to be very clear. It must be learned in the novitiate. In the matter of exceptions, the spirit of poverty demands that we do as follows:

a) Learn the objective standards of simplicity proper to the Order. Get rid of the needs and desires of middle-class society outside the monastery. Be ready to do without things we may have hitherto regarded as necessary, if they are not considered so in the Order.

b) Be slow to decide that one has a need for an exception. Wait a little before making it known, unless it is *obviously* urgent. Be a little austere and patient, especially with minor afflictions.

c) Make known one's need humbly and factually, with simplicity, and then abide by the decision of the superior, infirmarian, etc.

Notes regarding exceptions: the *confessor* of a professed religious is not empowered to dispense from {a} point of the *Rule*, exactly. He may offer suggestions. Strictly speaking, the dispensation should be asked of the competent superior. In very special cases a confessor may perhaps take upon himself the responsibility for giving certain permissions, but in that event he himself ought to have this approved, in a general way, by the superior. When one superior has refused a permission, one should not then go and ask another one without making this refusal known. {It is} *very important for the spirit of poverty* {that we} do not get a habit of *manipulating*: i.e., once you find out that one superior is "easier" than another, you ask permissions habitually from him. In the novitiate, all significant dispensations, etc. should be asked of the father master, minor permissions from the undermaster. In the community, all significant dispensations should come from the abbot, or at least the prior ({for} minor matters, see {the} subprior). In cases like the above, there is not really a choice: one should go to the superior whose normal function it is to grant permissions and give dispensations. When a permission is given or refused, when a superior makes known his will, do not immediately dispute it or try to get him to change it. *Accept* his decision and abide by it until there is a very serious reason to make a new circumstance known to him.

Toward mature poverty: poverty is something we should develop. It is a "talent" given us by the Lord which we should strive to double or triple. We must grow in poverty, and the vow of conversion of manners obligates us to this *spirit of growth in poverty. Immature poverty*: many monks make their vow and keep it by asking permissions when necessary. But they never grow in poverty. They just "observe" it indifferently and get used to it as a routine. On the contrary, they unconsciously *relax their standards* as they go on, and more and more they permit themselves to ask for superfluous things. Worse still, they undermine the poverty of the community by introducing new customs and new needs, bringing others into the same condition as themselves and leading the community, by their example, to favor a more comfortable, less strict life, in which sacrifice is more and more discounted. Hence, though all are "asking permission," the poverty of the community is really undermined and finally ceases to exist except as a kind of formality. In such a state one never really feels poverty or *has to do without anything*. Growth in poverty means *restricting one's needs*. It means learning, if possible, *to get along with less and less* as time goes on—not of course that one cuts in on the real necessities of life, but one is able to realize more and more that *certain things are superfluous*. Where poverty is seriously kept, the monks begin to realize as they go on that *what once seemed necessary is not really so, and they are able to get along without it*. (Such was the attitude of our Cistercian Fathers when they went to Molesme.) There is growth in the desire for unostentatious sacrifice. One *wants to* do with less. One is *glad of* deprivation. One *seeks opportunities* to forego things, especially when the sacrifice can be of service to someone else. This can reach into many ramifications of the monk's life, not only his useful objects, but his time, his tastes, his work, etc. One should keep in view a *high ideal of poverty*, seeing it not only negatively but also positively, seeing the joy and freedom of heart that belongs *only* to the man who is *glad to be stripped of everything*. Dependence {deepens} trust.

Exterior poverty is essential before we can advance into the realm of real interior poverty. Do not kid yourself that you are practicing poverty of spirit if exteriorly you are accumulating useless objects and permissions, and protecting yourself against the hardships of life by all kinds of shock absorbers. This is not poverty or freedom; it is only weakness and evasion. Interior poverty, based on serious exterior poverty, is an emptying of self and an inner deprivation, a death of self, a disappearance of "I" and "mine." One ceases to be attached to one's desires, opinions, tastes, virtues, spirituality, progress—everything that makes the

"I" solid and evident, even in apparently good things. It is better for the "I" to disappear. One should desire to lose this "I," this "self," for the sake of Christ. Thus to lose oneself is to find oneself, and thus to die is to be saved, to live in Christ. This should be our ideal. Without such an ideal, our monastic life will not be solid and we cannot really be happy in the monastery.

THE VOW OF STABILITY

Finally we come to the concluding vow: stability. There is less to be said about this than about the others: the obligation is essentially simple and uncomplicated, and there are not many special aspects of the question, no special problems. By the vow of stability one obligates himself to live and die in the community of his profession. This requires little explanation and commentary—just a few words that make quite clear what the obligation means, as if it were not already obvious in the definition itself. The implications are not hard to see. The exceptions are few, and they too are what one would expect. However, the one thing that needs to be stressed is that *this vow is most characteristic of the Benedictine* spirit. It is one of St. Benedict's own characteristic contributions to monastic life, and it is very close to his spirit of sobriety, order, peace. Stability is essential to the full Benedictine ascesis. It is an integral part of the Benedictine concept of monastic *disciplina*.

STABILITY IN THE *RULE* OF ST. BENEDICT: first, let us see the text of the *Rule* itself:

1. Chapter one: St. Benedict's disapproval of sarabaites and gyrovagues. "There are four kinds of monks."[785] St. Benedict approves of two: the cenobites and hermits. The cenobites dwell in a monastery under a rule and an abbot. This life is a spiritual warfare, hence difficult, requiring perseverance and courage: *militans*

---

785. *"Monachorum quattuor esse genera manifestum est"* (McCann, 14).

sub regula.[786] As the Prologue tells us, in the cenobitic life there must be "some strictness of discipline";[787] the life is *paululum restrictius.*[788] And he foresees the temptation on the part of the weak to evade this discipline and this strictness. Fear and impatience may lead one to fly from the "way of salvation": *Non ilico pavore perterritus refugias viam salutis.*[789] This temptation afflicts especially beginners, as is implied in the context of this (he explains that the way of salvation *non est nisi angusto initio incipienda*[790]). Hence he makes it quite clear that the true monastic vocation demands perseverance to the end, and this perseverance is greatly helped by special graces from God if one will bear patiently with hardships and wait for grace to come. By means of this grace we persevere until the end; we share in the Passion of Christ by patience, and merit to become sharers in His glory. *Ab ipsius magisterio numquam discedentes. . . . In ejus doctrina usque ad mortem* in monasterio *perseverantes . . . . Passionibus Christi per patientiam participemur, ut et regni ejus mereamur esse consortes.*[791] In a word, stability is necessary for the grace of vocation to bear its full fruit. Instability, which may help a man to find relief temporarily and escape a painful burden, will also deprive him of grace and consolation—hence the importance of remaining in the "school of Christ."[792] Stability guarantees that we will not withdraw from the sweet yoke of Christ when the weakness of the flesh makes us feel that the yoke is hard. St. Benedict would have his monks guard against *acedia* and discouragement.

786. McCann, 14 ("serving under a rule").

787. McCann, 13.

788. McCann, 12 (the phrase just translated).

789. McCann, 12 ("May you not flee the way of salvation, terrified immediately by fear").

790. McCann, 12 ("cannot be undertaken except from a narrow entryway").

791. McCann, 12, which reads: " . . . *numquam magisterio* . . ." (the three phrases are actually continuous; emphasis added) ("Never withdrawing from his instruction, persevering in his teaching in the monastery up until death, let us share with patience in the sufferings of Christ, so that we may merit to be sharers in His kingdom").

792. St. Bernard, *Ep.* 320 (*PL* 182, col. 525C); *Ep.* 385 (*PL* 182, col. 588A); *In Nativitate S. Joannis Baptistae* (*PL* 183, col. 397D); *De Diversis,* 121 (*PL* 183, col. 743B).

Stability will prove a great help in this matter. If a man knows he is bound by vow to remain in the struggle, that he has closed the door behind him, he will not play with the idea of escape. Then he will concentrate manfully on the struggle, and give his best energies to the service of the Lord, instead of dissipating them in desires for "a better situation," and plans to improve his lot by seeking another monastery, or worse, life in the world. We must guard against a psychology of "escapism," especially prevalent in our day.

Sarabaites and Gyrovagues: one of the characteristics of these monks who have *failed in their vocation* is their instability. The sarabaites are weak and soft, without consistency. They have not faced trial; they have not let themselves be tested by hardship; they have found ways to escape every trial. Hence they have never really given up the world. They live by their own will rather than by a rule: *Non dominicis sed suis inclusi ovilibus*, pro lege est eis desideriorum voluptas;[793] they think that what they like is good, what they don't like is evil. Hence they are at the mercy of their own desires. The instability of the sarabaites is more interior than exterior. But they are at least potential wanderers.

Gyrovagues: these are essentially unstable in the full sense of the word. For St. Benedict the *worst kind of monk* is by his very definition an unstable and self-willed being. His physical instability is the sign and root of all the other vices which are in him. He is a tramp, in the bad sense of the word. (Note of course that there have been genuine wandering saints, beggars and pilgrims. Such things are possible, but St. Benedict regards the danger as too great, and he severely reproves gyrovagues or anything resembling gyrovagism.) *Tota vita sua per diversas provincias . . . SEMPER VAGI ET NUMQUAM STABILES.*[794] To be unable to live under a rule like the sarabaites is to fail as a monk. To be unable even to

---

793. McCann, 14, which reads: ". . . *eis est* . . ." (emphasis added) ("enclosed not in the Lord's sheepfolds but in their own; the pleasure of their own desires functions as the law for them").

794. McCann, 14, 16 (emphasis added) ("during their entire life always roaming through various provinces and never stable").

stay in one place is the complete fiasco of a monastic vocation; St. Benedict regards it almost as a sign of reprobation, though this would undoubtedly be extreme. But it is certainly in his eyes the complete shipwreck of monasticism. It is not just wandering about that is evil, but for St. Benedict this wandering is simply the root and expression of all the other vices, for the gyrovague is at the mercy of all his passions, cannot deny himself anything; or at least they cannot deny any desire of their will and they are the slaves of gluttony, he says. It is clear from this why St. Benedict thought the vow of stability was of the highest importance. Note however that there is *one exception*: the hermit is able to leave his community and fight alone in the desert—*fraterna ex acie ad singularem pugnam eremi*.[795] This does not imply loss of stability; on the contrary, it is the fulfillment of stability if the hermit is true to his call. He is one who will now have an even harder combat: the struggle to be faithful and stable in his lonely life, the struggle to overcome temptations that might make him fall into the condition of sarabaite or gyrovague. Only one who is already very strong in all the cenobitic virtues, *especially stability*, can permit himself to aspire to solitude. For there *perfect stability*, interior and exterior, is required.

2. Instruments of Good Works (n.b. comment on this chapter): at the end of the chapter, after listing in detail all the virtues and practices which are proper to the monastic life, St. Benedict sums up all he has said and makes *all these virtues depend in some measure upon stability*. With stability in the monastery, these virtues are possible. Without stability, they are not possible. Such is the implication of the last lines of chapter 4: *Officina vero, ubi haec omnia diligenter operemur, claustra sunt monasterii et stabilitas in congregatione*.[796] Here St. Benedict makes a distinction between

---

795. McCann, 14, which reads: ". . . *heremi*" ("out of the fraternal battle-line to the solitary combat of the desert").

796. McCann, 32 (emphasis added) ("Indeed the workshop where we diligently work at all these things is the cloister of the monastery and stability in the community").

enclosure and *stability*. In reality they go together: one is the extension of the other. {With respect to} *enclosure*, even though one might have the monastery as his domicile, he might spend a great deal of time outside it, and hence miss the opportunity to do the real work of the monk. To be frequently outside the monastery, while keeping it as one's home, is not strictly speaking a violation of *stability*. But it is a violation of the monastic spirit, of conversion of manners, which demands that one remain as much as possible isolated from the world and from its affairs, in the monastery, engaged in the things of God. {With regard to} *stability*, on the other hand, one might go from monastery to monastery, spending only a day or two en route, and for the rest remaining "enclosed" in the divers communities. But this would be instability. Both stability and enclosure are necessary for the work of the monk. They are essential to the *disciplina* of monastic life.

Chapter 58—*the actual vow of stability*: when the monk makes profession, stability is explicitly stated, first of all, together with conversion of manners and obedience. *PROMITTAT DE STABILITATE SUA ET CONVERSIONE MORUM SUORUM ET OBEDIENTIA coram Deo et Sanctis ejus.*[797] The solemnity of this obligation is stressed: it is assumed in the presence of the community, in the presence of God and His saints, and it is understood that to fail in these vows, in the sense of final and total infidelity to any one of them, would mean {the} loss of the monk's soul. In other words, it is a serious obligation. *Stability binds under pain of mortal sin.* This is what St. Benedict is telling us. Here in a few succinct phrases we have the mind of St. Benedict regarding the vow and spirit of stability. From his point of view it is of primary importance. It is an integral part {of} the monastic life, as he conceives it. Of course there have been saints who did not make the vow and did not remain in one

---

797. McCann, 130, which reads: ". . . *conversatione morum . . . obedientiam* . . ." (emphasis added) ("let him make a promise about stability, conversion of his manners and obedience, before God and his saints").

place. They were exceptions. St. Benedict believes it safer for the ordinary monk to make use of this as a very important means to preserve his vocation. He should *stay in one place*.

Interpretation of Benedictine Stability: St. Benedict says *promittat de stabilitate sua*, and we have seen that he means "staying in one place" as opposed to the gyrovagues who wander about and are *numquam stabiles*. But nevertheless this may still mean many things: what is the precise juridical obligation intended by St. Benedict? It might mean:

1. simple perseverance in the monastic *state*, in obedience to one definite abbot, but dwelling successively in several different monasteries under his jurisdiction. The Maurists interpreted stability in terms of a *province*. A monk who was in some house in the province was keeping his vow of stability. This is rather a large interpretation.

2. It might also mean remaining in one monastery and never under any circumstances going elsewhere. This would be an exceptionally strict interpretation.

3. It might mean remaining affiliated to one monastery for life but in practice actually travelling to various places and dwelling temporarily in other monasteries. This is rather frequent.

4. Or finally it might mean dwelling ordinarily in the monastery of one's profession until death, never leaving it except in very unusual cases, and never transferring to another monastery except with a very special reason and with permission (dispensation). This is the interpretation in our Order.

Is there a question of interpretation? Someone might be tempted to think that St. Benedict's meaning was "obvious": for instance, that it was almost self-evident that he meant the fourth instance above. But is it perfectly self-evident? There has been much discussion of the topic. *Dom Cuthbert Butler* says: "The determination of the meaning and force of Benedictine stability is, in my judgement, perhaps the most difficult point in the study of Benedictine life" (*Benedictine Monachism*, p. 123). *"All agree* that the vow of stability was St Benedict's most important and characteristic contribution to the course of Western monachism" (Butler, *loc. cit.*[798]). *Cardinal Gasquet* {writes}: "Stability may be regarded as the note of St Benedict's legislation for his monastic order; it is the key to the spirit of monasticism as interpreted by his Rule" (quoted in Butler, *l.c.*, note[799]). {According to} *Bishop Ullathorne*, "St Benedict's great reform is expressed in the single word stability" (*ibid.*[800]). However, it must be noted that St. Caesarius, though not expressly mentioning a vow, makes stability an explicit condition for the validity of vows: *In primis si quis ad conversionem venerit, ea {conditione} excipiatur, ut usque ad mortem ibi perseveret* (*Regula ad Monachos*, c. 1).[801] The word *ibi* in this text of St. Caesarius refers to the monastery of the monk's profession, and it seems clear that this is also St. Benedict's mind. In any case, the more common and reliable opinion, expressed by Butler, following Ullathorne, etc., is that stability means *local stability* and not just stability in the monastic state, or in regularity. *Ullathorne* {says}: "St Benedict binds his monks by the vow of stability to an irrevocable life in the community which has witnessed his profession" (in Butler, p. 125[802]). However, we disagree when Ullathorne declares that the vow of stability means a vow to an "irrevocable life in community." On the contrary, it is clear from the first chapter of St. Benedict that a monk can become a hermit, presumably without violating his vow of stability, since this course is presented as a very perfect and praiseworthy one for those who have the special vocation. Note, in chapter 61 of the

798. Text reads: "It is felt on all hands that the introduction of this vow was St Benedict's . . ."

799. Butler, 123, n. 4, which reads: ". . . for the monastic . . ."

800. Butler, 123, n. 4, which reads: ". . . expressed by the . . ."

801. "First of all if anyone comes to conversion, this condition is to be accepted, that he persevere there up until death" (*PL* 67, col. 1099B, which reads: "*Imprimis . . . mortem suam ibi . . .*"; quoted as cited in Butler, 123, n. 4; typescript reads "condition").

802. Text reads: ". . . community that has witnessed his training and profession."

Rule, where there is question of receiving a monk from another monastery (presumably one where he does not have a vow of stability), then he is to make his stability (*stabilitatem suam firmare*[803]) in the community of his adoption. St. Benedict uses the term *egredi de monasterio*[804] (c. 58) for leaving the monastic state. Hence for St. Benedict, stability means *stabilitas loci*, which means abiding in the monastery of one's profession until death, at least as one's habitual residence. And this means not just having it as a legal domicile, but living in it for the greater part of the time, except for special and unusual journeys.

CONCLUSION: THE CORRECT IDEA OF BENEDICTINE STABILITY IS THAT THE VOW OBLIGES THE MONK TO LIVE IN THE COMMUNITY OF HIS PROFESSION ALL HIS LIFE, EVEN UNTIL DEATH: *perseverantes in monasterio*[805] (Prologue). Normally, our vow obliges us to spend our whole life in the community of our profession, not to have a domicile there and live elsewhere, not to make the monastery the headquarters from which we range about on various activities. It is in the monastery that we are domiciled, that we live, that we work, that we save our souls. The monastery is the center of our whole life and of all our activities. This is the genuine Benedictine concept. It is clearly the Cistercian conception, for in our Order the monastery of one's profession is *explicitly named* in the schedule of profession. Note also the importance of referring to the "relics of the saints here present" as living stones on which the community is spiritually erected.

EXCEPTIONAL CASES: however, the vow of stability obviously admits of certain exceptions:

1. The case of a MONASTIC FOUNDATION: in making a vow of stability, a monk aggregates himself to a community and gives himself to the community in order to serve it in any capacity

803. McCann, 138 ("to confirm his stability").
804. McCann, 132, which reads: "*egrediatur . . .*" ("to go forth from the monastery").
805. McCann, 12, which reads: "*in monasterio perseverantes*" ("persevering in the monastery").

desired by his superiors. But if the community is to make a foundation, obviously it must send its own members. To go on a foundation is then not a matter of breaking off from one's community, so much as serving the community and helping it to form a new branch. This is then perfectly according to the spirit of the vow of stability. For the spirit of the vow is not merely that one stays in one place, but rather that one gives himself to a community in order to identify himself, for a whole lifetime, with the works, vicissitudes, etc. of that community. But making a foundation can be one of the most important and significant developments of the life of a community. A stabiliated religious who participates in this work actually fulfills his vow of stability by transcending it and passing to a higher level: it means in a sense the *sacrifice* of some of the benefits of his community life, its security and regularity, in order to carry on a work desired by that community. His sacrifice *benefits the community* in many ways. It also enables other monks in the community who do not leave for the foundation to preserve the benefits of security, etc. Finally, those who go on foundations are generally chosen for their spirit of regularity and *stability*. It takes a *more stable* monk to make a foundation. *Offering to help a small monastery or foundation:* when it is known that a small monastery needs men (for instance, when the superior of such a foundation explicitly or implicitly appeals for help, which often happens), then one can *offer himself as a volunteer* to go to the small monastery or foundation temporarily or even permanently. This act is in no way a violation of the vow of stability, provided that one remains entirely within the orbit of obedience—that is to say, as long as one does not insist and press the point against the obvious and express wishes of superiors. It is always permissible and even virtuous to offer oneself to help out when a small monastery needs men, but obedience comes first. *Note:* subtle temptations can arise here, in this connection. One must first be sure that the desire to go and "help out" on a small foundation does not proceed merely from instability and from the desire of change. It would *not be advisable* for a person to make this kind of offer if he is already having a very difficult time in his own monastery, especially if he is beset with *problems in work and in community relations*. Very often the people who most want to go and "help" the foundation are unsettled and poorly adapted in their actual position, and might only take their troubles with them to the foundation, and indeed make them worse there. It is always inadvisable to consider going to a small foundation merely to "get away from" a painful situation. At least the subject should be very slow to take the initiative in this matter. Superiors also should be careful of the temptation to "get rid of" troublesome subjects by unloading them on a foundation. {A} *practical procedure* {would be}:

a) If a monk wishes to volunteer to help in a small foundation somewhere, he should first take care that he is not merely yielding to temptation and justifying himself in his own eyes by making it look like a sacrifice.

b) Very positive approval of a spiritual director should be had, and it should be obtained without extortion and manipulation.

c) When the director is obviously and positively in favor of one volunteering to go on a foundation, then one can make the suggestion humbly to the superiors.

d) The superior remains the judge. One should not try to force the superior to consent, and if his decision is negative one should accept it cheerfully as the will of God, and forget about the whole thing.

In general it is best not to make such offers unless they are clearly *asked for*. However, in special cases one may spontaneously make the suggestion even when there is no explicit appeal for volunteers. But then the reasons must be all the more weighty.

2. SPECIAL OBEDIENCES: it can happen that a monk is appointed by superiors or by the General Chapter to carry out some task or to fill some office that requires his absence from the monastery or even a change of stability: for instance, he may be elected definitor; he may be sent to fill an office in some other

monastery (for instance, professor, novice master); he may be sent as a confessor of nuns of our Order; he may be sent to Rome to study. Here there is no violation either of the spirit or of the letter of stability. There is no problem. All is governed by *obedience* (such appointments should not be *sought*). Note: it can happen that a monk becomes a BISHOP. This too does not violate stability, even though he spends the rest of his life outside his monastery. However, it must be recognized that there are very strict limits to this obedience. Neither the Order nor the superiors of individual houses have the right to command a subject under obedience to absent himself from the monastery for a very long time in order to carry out some work that is contrary to the ideal and purpose of the Order. For instance a superior could not compel a subject in our Order, bound by the vow of stability, to go and take charge of a parish or to teach in a college, living outside a monastery of the Order. One so commanded would be bound to lay the matter before higher superiors. (However, the Holy See could in special cases overrule the vow of stability altogether and demand that monks give themselves to certain active works. It does not seem likely however that the Holy See will do this, because it appreciates the high apostolic value of the contemplative ideal.) In time of war, can a monk with a vow of stability volunteer as chaplain in the armed forces? Should he do so? Here again, it would require the permission of his superiors. Against the will of superiors, a monk could not in conscience leave to serve as chaplain in the armed forces. He would be violating his vow of stability. He would have to be dispensed from his vows and exclaustrated by the Holy See before it would be permissible. Should he desire to serve as chaplain? It would be more in accordance with his vocation to *stay in the monastery*, and this is what he should desire to do. His efforts will be more effective if he remains in the vocation where God has placed him. He will do more for souls and for the cause of peace if he is leading his life of prayer and sacrifice.

3. HEALTH: a temporary stay in a hospital does not bring into question the monk's vow of stability. The question arises when

there is a case of the monk leaving his monastery and going elsewhere for reasons of health. Is health sufficient reason to permit a change of stability? If it is clear that a change of stability to another monastery in a different climate would *notably improve and even reestablish a monk's health* which is affected by conditions in his own monastery, then a change of stability would be not only legitimate but perhaps even desirable (depending on other conditions, especially spiritual ones). However, it must be admitted that such cases would probably be quite rare in reality. All too frequently a kind of hypochondriac spirit tempts monks to think that they are very sick and that this sickness calls for a transfer to another climate; or even when there is a genuine complaint—for instance, an allergy—the "hopes" that it will be alleviated elsewhere may be largely imaginary. Such hopes should generally be discounted and dismissed. If one has made a vow of stability, he has assumed the risk of undergoing everything that goes with the monastery—the climate, the living conditions, etc. All this should be taken into account at the time of the vow. One should make the vow with the intention of living and dying in the monastery, and this implies also the intention *not to leave on account of sickness* (except of course for necessary hospitalization)—even to go to another monastery. Only in very special cases, when there are definite and positive indications given by the doctor, should one change stability for the sake of health. Once again, monks must be very careful not to let themselves be deluded in this regard, and they should learn to dismiss as temptations the obsession with such ideas until it is objectively certain that there is some real hope for betterment as a result of change.

4. GREATER SPIRITUAL GOOD: if it is licit to change one's stability for the health of the body, it is also theoretically licit to change for the good of one's soul—that is, to go to another monastery or to another order in which one might make greater progress and attain to a higher union with God. However, it must be remembered that one of the *main reasons for the vow* of stability is to guard *against the temptation to seek a greater good* by changing one's monastery or order. The vow of stability is based on the

fact that *under the guise of a greater good*, the monk may in reality
be led to give up the good which he already has and, in the end,
lose his vocation. The other vows are concerned with resisting
evils that are more or less evident: sinful pleasures, self-will, ac-
cumulation of possessions. Stability deals more than any other
with the problem of possible evil disguised as good. The vow
does not absolutely make it impossible to change, but the purpose of the vow is to remind the monk that *stability itself is a very
great good* and that it is probably in the majority of cases a much
greater good than could be achieved by changing to another
place, because if we cling to stability we will be enabled to make
the change that really matters, within our own selves. If we are
thinking of finding a greater good elsewhere, we will not work
to achieve the good that is possible here and now. Therefore the
*vow of stability by its very nature means a vow to renounce the thought
of seeking a greater good, even a greater spiritual good, in another monastery or order*. Therefore all thoughts of going to another place
are to be regarded with suspicion. They are temptations until it
is clear in the minds of superiors or directors that there may be
some truth in them (see below, texts of St. Bernard and William
of St. Thierry[806]). One can sin against the vow of stability by willfully entertaining thoughts of going to another monastery when
one has reason to believe that this is a temptation and must not
be entertained. However, if one is docile and resolves to manifest all such thoughts to a director, there will probably be no sin.

When is it licit to change stability for a greater spiritual good?

a) It may happen that another monastery might be more
propitious for the spiritual development of an individual. If the
director or superior agrees that it might be so, then it is certainly
licit to ask for a change of stability. However, the following conditions should be observed, and will be observed by prudent
superiors. The desire to change stability must not {be} a whim
of the moment; it must be tested by time. The one who wants

806. See pages 466–68.

to change must be a man of solid and mature character. It must not be mere self-will; it must be tested by obedience; the one concerned must show by obedience and by humble acceptance of decisions that his motives are supernatural. It must not be mere escape; the normal problems of community life should be *faced*, not evaded. However, it is sometimes better for certain types to be in a smaller or larger community than the one in which they find themselves. *Note*: those who are deeply shaken in their vocation and hope to save it by changing to another monastery rarely succeed in doing so. It is not to be recommended.

b) *Change to another order*: as a general rule, we should not seek to change orders except to a more perfect and higher kind of life. This is difficult to interpret even theoretically. For one thing, Cistercian superiors often admit with difficulty that any life can be "higher" than the Cistercian. Nowadays the Code does not state explicitly whether or not one should be concerned about the life in the other order being "higher." It just allows one to get a *transitus*. In practice, the Church does favor passing from an active life to a contemplative life, but does not favor passing from one contemplative order to another. In practice, a genuine desire to pass from the Cistercians to the Carthusians, though good in itself, might not be advisable for many reasons. The Carthusians themselves are not too eager to receive professed members from other orders, including the Cistercians. They discourage applications, but they will at times consider them. If it is clear in the mind of a director that a monk of our Order ought to live a more solitary life, then it is certainly licit for that monk to take steps to enter another order. However, even when monks have been permitted to leave to join other orders (for instance, at the end of temporary vows), it has very often happened that they have failed in the other order or not even got to enter it. Thus they have lost what they had and gained nothing at all. Maybe in some cases they have lost everything. It is certainly a grave danger!! *Under what conditions should a desire to enter another and more contemplative order be taken seriously?* if the desire is very long-standing—over a period of several years; if the religious

concerned is really a man of prayer, solid, well-balanced, obedient, and has lived virtuously the Cistercian life but {is} lacking
some important element in his prayer life there (the mere desire
for more prayer, for a deeper life of prayer, for some physical
solitude, is not enough to indicate that one has a vocation to a
more solitary manner of life—it may only indicate that one has to
work harder to be a man of prayer and interior solitude here in
our own monastery); if the religious is obedient and not merely
trying to assert his own will. There should be some indication that
this desire *does not* proceed from mere restlessness and natural
dissatisfaction. Often some *unusual indication* of a special vocation is to be sought.

c) *Can it be a greater spiritual good for a religious to pass from
our Order to the active ministry?* The orders that combine the contemplative and active lives are theoretically the "highest" in the
Church. In practice, the movement to a "higher life" is usually
made from the apostolic orders to the contemplative orders. It
would be very rare in fact for a monk who had made a good adjustment in the Cistercian life to find a "greater spiritual good"
for himself by a transfer, on his own initiative, to an apostolic
life. Only if the Lord Himself somehow indicated the transfer
was His Will, in an extraordinary manner, should this kind of
step be taken. In a particular case, one who was badly adjusted
in the Cistercian life and who had been ordained, might licitly
transfer to a more active order or (what commonly happens) to
the secular clergy. These last cases are not to be regarded as satisfactory. They do not generally solve problems. Very often they
create greater problems for the priest in question and even for
the souls he may deal with. One who undertakes the direction of
souls when he is really incompetent and unprepared is placing
himself in grave spiritual danger.

WHEN DOES ONE SIN AGAINST THE VOW OF STABILITY? *exteriorly*—by apostasy: the gravest sin for a monk is apostasy, in which
he sins gravely both against conversion of manners and stability; he leaves the monastic state and he leaves his monastery; he

incurs excommunication *ipso facto*; by flight: a monk could sin against stability by leaving his own monastery without permission, even if he intended to go to another monastery or to return to his own monastery; this would be a grave sin against the vow of stability; it incurs an excommunication *ipso facto*, reserved to the abbot. One might also sin against stability by illicitly staying out of the monastery, overstaying one's permission, refusing to return immediately when summoned to do so by the superior, or forcing the superior to permit (unwillingly) a long stay outside which he cannot prevent. All these would be serious sins, except perhaps the latter. But the latter case would be very dangerous. {He would also sin} by threatening to leave. It would be a serious sin against stability to utter seriously and in cold blood a determined threat to leave the monastery without permission, in order to influence the superior or members of the community. This applies only to {a} *fully deliberate* and well-understood intention to leave, not a passing remark made in a state of nervous excitement. There is no venial external sin against stability, objectively speaking, unless one includes violations of enclosure during the daytime, which are venial, but enclosure and stability are two different obligations. Subjectively, flight from the monastery might be venial through deficient understanding or lack of deliberation, especially if the person quickly changed his mind on realizing the seriousness of his act. (However, if one is out overnight, the fault is regarded as a mortal sin against the obligation of enclosure.) *Interiorly*—it should be realized that interior sins against stability are possible. Mortal sin is possible—the deliberate *intention to* apostatize or to take flight from the monastery. This would be a mortal sin against the vow, but would not involve excommunication. The determination to obtain an indult without sufficient reason would be sinful. However, where a director *permits* the step, even grudgingly, though there may be some sin and it may be spiritually dangerous, there is probably not mortal sin. What person would think sincerely that he did not have some reason to get an indult, if things got that far? He might be sinning against prudence and exposing his soul to grave danger. It would be hard to say he was formally sinning against his vow, except in some rare case. *Thoughts of changing to another place,* if deliberately entertained *against* one's conscience, are venial sins (if they are fully willed and accepted with an intention to take some action). One must avoid the habit of daydreaming about a "better place." It is at least an imperfection and is dangerous for the vow.

Texts on Stability: it is important here to study some of the traditional teaching on stability in the monastic life. The reasons for stability are deep and complex. We need to see what the Fathers of the Church thought about it, especially the monastic fathers. But before that, let us look at a pagan philosopher who attached importance to stability as a virtue.

Stoic texts on stability: *Seneca,* the Stoic writer, lays great emphasis on stability in the spiritual life. The Stoics believed that the spiritual man *rose above* the constantly changing conditions of earth and by his union with the universal plan of Providence became stable and fixed like the heavens in their unchanging order. Seneca certainly contributed something, at least indirectly, to St. Benedict's ideas on stability. In the *Epistulae Morales* of Seneca we read: "Restlessness reveals a disordered spirit. The first sign of a well-ordered mind is the ability to remain in one place and pass the time in one's own company" (II.1).[807] *Animum debes mutare, non caelum* (XXVIII.1).[808] "Where one lives means little for one's peace of soul; it is the mind that must render all things agreeable to itself" (LV.8).[809] "The soul cannot through retirement grow into unity until it has given over its casting about and its roaming" (LXIX.1).[810]

The *Desert Fathers* in some cases admitted a wandering life in the desert, as practiced by Abbot Bessarion. But in other cases they attached great importance to *remaining in the cell.* "Remain in

---

807. Quoted in A.-J. Festugière, OP, *Personal Religion among the Greeks* (Berkeley: University of California Press, 1954), 60 (which reads: "For such restlessness. . . . The first sign, to my thinking, of . . .").

808. "It's your soul you must change, not your environment" (Festugière, 60).

809. Festugière, 60.

810. Festugière, 60.

your cell and your cell will teach you all things" (*Apothegmata*).[811]
Also: "Just as a tree cannot bear fruit if it is often transplanted, so
neither can a monk bear fruit if he frequently changes his abode"
(*Verba Seniorum*; cf. our *What Ought I to Do?* n. 24[812]). However,
another important saying throws light indirectly on stability. "If
a man settles in a certain place and does not bring forth the fruit
of that place, the place itself casts him out, as one who has not
borne its fruit" (cf. *What Ought I {to Do?}* n. 47[813]). This is worth
meditating on. Perhaps the monk who is restless and believes
that he has to go elsewhere in order to become perfect is justifying his fruitlesssness in the monastery. He has not borne fruit
and thinks he will do better elsewhere, but the "place itself" is
working on him to "cast him out." But this is a very dangerous
situation. He might lose his vocation and his soul. The remedy
is not to go elsewhere but to make efforts to become fervent and
to really sacrifice himself in order to be a good monk here and
now, relinquishing vain hopes of being better "somewhere else."
In either case the idea of fruitfulness is linked up with stability
in one's chosen place. One of the Desert Fathers, Abbot Alonius,
gave as a "word of salvation" the following: "Humility is the
land in which the Lord wants us to go and offer sacrifice." It may
have been a reply to a question of a monk who wanted to change
his abode and was asking where, in what land, he might go and
please the Lord better (*What Ought I {to Do?}* n. 67[814]). Many of the

811. *Verba Seniorum*, V.2.9 (*PL* 73, col. 859C); *What Ought I to Do?: Sayings of
the Desert Fathers*, translated by Thomas Merton (Lexington, KY: Stamperia del
Santuccio, 1959), 9 (#10); *Wisdom of the Desert*, 30 (#xiii). *What Ought I to Do?*, a
limited edition of 100 sayings from the *Verba Seniorum*, was later published in an
expanded edition of 150 sayings as *The Wisdom of the Desert*. Merton's translation
of the saying in these volumes is "Go, sit in your cell, and your cell will teach
you everything."

812. *Verba Seniorum*, V.7.36 (*PL* 73, col. 902A); *What Ought I to Do?* 12 (#xxiv);
Wisdom of the Desert, 34 (#xxvii).

813. *Verba Seniorum*, V.10.79 (*PL* 73, col. 927C); *What Ought I to Do?* 20
(#xlvii); *Wisdom of the Desert*, 45 (#liv).

814. *Verba Seniorum*, V.15.37 (*PL* 73, col. 961A); *What Ought I to Do?* 24–25
(#lxvii); *Wisdom of the Desert*, 53 (#lxxxiii), which reads ". . . land where God . . ."

Desert Fathers insisted that the monks should not go out of their desert and work for the farmers in the Nile Valley in harvest time, because it would make them worldly and unstable. "Abbot Anthony said: Just as fish die if they remain on dry land so monks, remaining away from their cells or dwelling with men of the world, lose their determination to persevere in solitary prayer. Therefore, just as the fish should go back to the sea, so we must return to our cells, lest remaining outside we forget to watch over ourselves intently" (*What Ought I {to Do?}* n. 12[815]). Other Desert Fathers recommended that the hermit should remain in the same place *within his cell*, praying and reading and working steadily without wandering around even in his cell. This was the perfection of stability. We can sum up the doctrine of the Desert Fathers in one important saying: "Someone asked Abbot Anthony: 'What rules shall I keep to please God?' The old man replied: 'Keep my instructions, and they are these: Wherever you go, recollect God in your mind's eye. Whatever you do, do it after the example of Holy Scripture. And *wherever you stay, be in no hurry to move.* If you keep these three rules you will be safe.'"[816] In this text, moving to another place is not absolutely prohibited, but one should not move heedlessly and without serious reason. This is the spirit of monastic stability. To protect this spirit, we should take it *as a basic ascetic principle* that difficulties and trials should never induce us to think of changing our stability. On the contrary, when in time of trial we are tempted to think of moving elsewhere, we should always put the thought out of our mind. We must face the trial *here.* "The Fathers used to say: If some temptation arises in the place where you dwell in the desert, do not leave that place in time of temptation. For if you leave it then, no matter where you go, you will find the same temptation waiting for you. But

---

815. *Verba Seniorum*, V.2.1 (*PL* 73, col. 858A); *What Ought I to Do?* 10 (#xii); *Wisdom of the Desert*, 29 (#xi), which reads ". . . ourselves interiorly."

816. *Verba Seniorum*, V.1.1 (*PL* 73, col. 855A); ET: *Western Asceticism*, ed. and trans. Owen Chadwick, Library of Christian Classics, vol. 12 (Philadelphia: Westminster, 1958), 37; the same saying is also found in *Verba Seniorum*, III.108 (*PL* 73, col. 781A).

be patient until the temptation goes away, lest your departure scandalize the brethren who dwell in the same place, and bring tribulation upon them" (*What Ought I {to Do?}* n. 94[817]). This text brings out another important reason for stability: not only for the monk's own soul but also *for the good of other monks*, to avoid scandal and bad example (even though in an individual case the one might have good reason to change stability).

St. Bernard on Stability: the *locus classicus* of St. Bernard on stability is in the book *De Praecepto et Dispensatione*, c. 16 (Migne, *PL* 182, col. 885). He takes up the question of change of stability: is it LICIT? Is it EXPEDIENT (in the sense of worthwhile)? *Is it licit?* His basic principle is this: *A BONO QUOD SEMEL QUIS VOVERIT,* DESCENDERE NON LICET.[818] How is this principle applied to stability? We must never change our stability *for the worse*. He gives the following cases: (a) leaving the monastery or the religious state *out of weakness* or *in conflict with the brethren* (*remisso descensui, contentioso discessui*[819]); (b) any form of *inconstancy. However, if the change is for the better, it is perfectly licit.* Any change which is in line with one's monastic conversion (*conversio morum*)—tending to ever greater good—and according to obedience and the *Rule* (this would include foundations) is good. {With regard to} *conversio morum*, if one lives in a *relaxed* monastery in which one cannot live a fully regular life and the example of the brethren is tepid, then *DUCE SPIRITU LIBERTATIS TRANSIRE INDUBITANTER SUADEO ad locum alium, ubi non impediatur homo reddere Deo vota sua.*[820] *However, further precisions* {need to be made}: in the case of a well-ordered and regular monastery, he *would not counsel anyone* to change stability even in search of a greater good, *except with permission of his*

---

817. *Verba Seniorum*, V.7.32 (*PL* 73, col. 901A); *What Ought I to Do?* 34 (#xciv); *Wisdom of the Desert*, 73 (#cxxvii).

818. "From the good which someone has once vowed it is not permitted to back down" (text reads: ". . . *licere*").

819. "a descent through negligence; a departure through disagreement."

820. "I unquestionably recommend transferring to another place, led by the Spirit of liberty, where a person is not impeded from fulfilling his vows to God" (emphasis added).

abbot. (Hence, in St. Bernard's eyes *no permission* was necessary to leave a relaxed monastery.) He says this applies to Benedictines wanting to become Cistercians (886). Why should one not leave a good monastery for a higher good? (a) *propter scandalum*,[821] {the} danger of upsetting the spiritual life of those who belong in the monastery of one's profession and who would be unsettled; (b) *certa pro dubiis relinquere tutum non est*[822]—a solid principle—not to leave what is certainly and definitely good for a possible and uncertain good, even though the latter may be "better"; (c) *suspectam habeo levitatem*[823]—even in this theoretically good case, St. Bernard says there may well be danger of "levity" and instability, rather than real desire for higher virtue—just desire of change. *If one has changed stability for the better*, then one should not return to one's former monastery, since this would mean a descent. In summary, the principles of St. Bernard as given here are {as follows}. Change of stability is *illicit* when it proceeds from natural restlessness, or when it means a change to a less good monastery or state of life. Hence he would never permit anyone to return to the world, or to go from the Cistercians to a more relaxed rule, or from a fervent house to a less fervent one. Change of stability is *licit but rarely advisable* when one goes to a better monastery or to a really higher form of life from a *good monastery*; even in such a situation, even where a greater good exists, there are other reasons for still not making a change of stability. Change of stability (this is implicit) *would be advisable* where there is question of going from a really lax monastery to a really good one.

William of St. Thierry, in the *Golden Epistle*, gives excellent ascetic principles for stability (see Bk. 1, c. 9). It is impossible to lead a recollected life unless you live in one place and stay there. A man cannot settle his mind on one thing unless he settles his body in one place. The man who tries to escape his distractions by wandering to new places only takes his troubles with him,

---

821. "on account of scandal."
822. "It is not safe to leave certainties behind for the sake of what is doubtful."
823. "I am wary of lightmindedness."

in taking himself. *Locum mutat, non animum.*[824] The remedy for the soul's sickness is stability and quiet, solitude and obedience. He stresses the fact that stability *goes hand in hand with docility in direction.* It is important not merely to remain in one place but under the direction of one spiritual physician. This is a new and important aspect of the question, for it takes time for one man to get to know us thoroughly. The three guardians of our soul in solitude are God, our conscience and the spiritual father.

Blessed Guerric ("the need for roots"): in his first sermon for St. Benedict (*PL* vol. 185, col. 99f.), Blessed Guerric makes an interesting application of the parable of the sower to the topic of stability (cf. Luke 8:13). The word of God falls on stony ground: there is initial belief, but because of *lack of roots* the word does not grow. It takes time and courage for faith to develop "roots"; hence the need for stability, to allow the divine vocation to take root in our soul. This is especially true of the contemplative vocation, the vocation to wisdom, to experiential knowledge of God by love, which is what Blessed Guerric is discussing in the context (his text is: *Beatus vir qui in sapientia* morabitur . . .[825]). *Quomodo radicari poterunt* nisi morentur? *JUSTUS PLANTATUS IN DOMO DOMINI NEC RADICARI NEC FUNDARI IN CARITATE POTERIT NISI MORA ET STABILITATE LOCI.*[826] This is a strong statement. It might of course be discussed and disputed, but the fact remains that it is a witness to the belief and to the spirituality of the early Cistercians. For a Cistercian, the test of true charity is, among other things, patient and persevering stability. This shows how *concrete and objective* the monastic spirit really is. It is not enough for the monk to have right intentions and cultivate right attitudes, not enough for him

---

824. "He alters his location, not his mind" (*PL* 184, col. 324A).

825. "Blessed is the man that shall continue in wisdom" (Ecclesiasticus [Sirach] 14:22; col. 99A).

826. "How can they become rooted unless they stay put? The just man planted in the house of the Lord can be neither rooted nor founded except by staying put and by stability of place" (col. 99D–100A, which reads: "*Quomodo autem . . . morentur? . . . Justus . . .*"; emphasis added).

to be *disposed to* remain with the same brethren until death. Let his disposition be proved by the actuality. Let him *remain* stable in one monastic community. Then we will see that he is really disposed to do so, and not merely using fine words about his love for the brethren. *Fruitfulness in the spiritual life depends on roots.* A really deep and solid contemplative vocation is *not proved by mere initial fervor.* A good start is something to thank God for, but how many start out well and show much promise but get nowhere? How often {does it happen that} a spiritual life that begins with great fervor and sensible consolation actually wilts in a few years? It cannot stand up under the difficulty and the monotony of community life. It is eroded by the constant little trials of every day. It is perseverance that counts. Perseverance is the proof of real lasting generosity. {It is} much better to have a relatively colorless and ordinary spirituality that even seems ungenerous or less generous, but which in reality stays the course and perseveres until the end—better this than a brilliant beginning that quits before the halfway mark, or even at the very first lap of the race. To those who do not have deep roots Guerric applies a sentence of Isaias: *Ante messem totus floruit, et immatura perfectio germinavit* (Is. 18:5).[827] The fruit of such ones {is} like fruit of a tree plucked and eaten by every passerby along the road. St. Benedict makes everything depend on stability (Guerric quotes the end of {the} *Rule*, c. 4, which we have discussed above[828]). Another metaphor {he uses is} the bird leaving its nest before the eggs are hatched (taken from Prov. 27:8).[829] This theme already was familiar to {the} Desert Fathers (cf. *Verba Seniorum*: "St. Syncletica said: Do not wander from place to place; {. . .} it will harm you. If a hen stops sitting on the eggs she will hatch no chickens: and the monk or nun who moves from place to place

---

827. "For before the harvest it was all flourishing, and it shall bud without perfect ripeness" (col. 100A).

828. See pages 450–51 above.

829. Col. 100B.

grows cold and dead in faith."[830]). In explaining, Guerric says[831] that he would rarely counsel a man to change monasteries, since the hope of an uncertain good is less valuable than the certitude of a good in itself lesser. However he intimates that progress of some special souls may be helped by a change of scene. But in general he believes that what prompts most monks to want to change is only *impatience and restlessness*, and that in yielding to this natural fickleness under the guise of a great spiritual good, they yield to an illusion and let go of a very real good that was being offered them by God, in order to grasp at a figment of their own imagination.

CONCLUSION: THE SPIRIT OF STABILITY: we have seen the nature of the obligation; we have seen the wise words of the Fathers of our Order on stability, its meaning, its necessity. How then are we to remain true to our vow? Above all, how can we keep to the real *spirit* of the vow? A few practical remarks are called for:

1. *The need for a positive attitude*: just as chastity is something much more than "not sinning" against the sixth commandment, just as obedience is something much more than "not disobeying," so we have to realize that stability is something much more than "not leaving" one's monastery. It is not just a matter of "hanging on" and staying in one's community. This of course is the bare minimum. But negative motives are not good enough. A monastery full of people who really want to leave but are restrained from doing so merely because their vow makes it impossible is not going to be a true monastic family; it will be little more than a prison or a reform school. It will have the spirit of a prison, and the vow will not really be well kept. It will not be a truly contemplative monastery. It will certainly not be a "family." It is certain that a monk cannot really live as a monk and as a contemplative if he is simply held in place by force, and his frustrated,

---

830. *Verba Seniorum*, V.7.15 (*PL* 73, col. 895C); *Western Asceticism*, 85, which reads: "Syncletice."
831. Col. 100BC.

dour attitude will tend to communicate itself to his neighbors. It is for the wisdom and prudence of superiors to decide when, for the greater good of the community, it is better to let a restless and dissatisfied monk get dispensed from his vows, rather than permit the bad effect of his presence in the community. One must have real *positive motives* for staying in one's monastery. These must be something more than *fear of evil* in case one leaves, fear of displeasing superiors who frown on departures and inveigh against them day and night. This is not enough. One must have *motives of love*. One must be able to see that it is the *love of God* that keeps us in our monastery, and the *love of our community*, specifically of our brethren, the actual flesh-and-blood brothers around us, not just of the community in the abstract.

2. *Charity towards those who fail*: there are inevitably departures from the monastic life. Professed monks are sometimes dispensed from vows, or even violate their vows shamefully. This latter case is alas not unknown. These are sad truths. We must regret the fact that sins are committed against God. The sanctity of obligations is violated. But at the same time let us not be too self-righteous about these cases. Let us not be constantly holding up our hands in horror at the departure of a brother when his departure may in large measure be partly *our own fault*. Let us not automatically suppose that the individual is always wrong and the community is always right. It may well happen that the blame is to be distributed more evenly. God alone can judge. A little elementary humility ought to teach us that we ourselves may have been to blame. Seniors in the community, superiors, those who laid heavy burdens on the shoulder of the one who defected, those who gave him a bad example, those who encouraged him in the way of defection, all share the blame. Perhaps the tepidity of the community itself, its lack of charity, may be partly to blame. The defaulter lost patience with the community, but perhaps also the community long ago lost patience with him. If we condemn too easily those who leave, and *fail to understand* realistically the causes for their departure (assuming that it may be our business to understand), then we will create a situation in

which the *same misunderstandings may recur*, and recur frequently. The best way to prevent defections is not to condemn instability but to create an atmosphere of genuine fraternal understanding and love.

3. *Love for the Order*: one of the chief remedies for instability is love for the Order. Indeed, love for the Order is an essential element in the spirit of stability. It would be of little value to remain in the Order while interiorly hating it. The presence in the Order of members who do not love the Order is, as a matter of fact, a great danger to the stability and perseverance of many vocations. Why is this so? because those who come to our Order seeking a spiritual life, spiritual support, encouragement, a climate of contemplative love, are unconsciously affected, indeed infected, by the spirit of rebellion and opposition generated by those who, while bound by their vow, are nevertheless reacting *against* the Order. This can be a serious difficulty. Anyone who is planning to make a vow to remain until death in this Order had better be sure that he has a genuine love for the Order, and if he means to retain his spirit of stability, he must continue to cultivate this love for the Order all his life. Cultivating love for the Order all one's life does not mean desperately clinging to the same love for the Order one had as a novice. Still less does it mean retaining the idealistic love one cherished before entering. One's love for the Order changes and deepens, and it tends to become more realistic and less emotional as time goes on. One who is going to keep his vow of stability to the full must resolve to do everything he can to live peacefully and fruitfully in the spirit of his vocation. He must try to be a fruitful and productive member of the Order, leading a happy and worthwhile spiritual life in the Order. He must strive to be a healthy member of the organism, not a rebellious obstruction.

What is love for the Order? One of the difficulties is that a false or insufficient kind of "love for the Order" actually repels and disconcerts souls, and makes it difficult for them to fully appreciate the riches of their vocation. *Unreality* in love for the Order is very harmful. It leads to frustration and antagonizes members of the Order. By unreality we mean a *false idealization* of the Order, as if one had to be absolutely blind to any of its faults and shortcomings, as if one had to convince himself that his order is by far the best and most perfect order in the whole Church. The insistence that we contemplatives are always and everywhere "superior" to those leading the active life, {along with} easy generalizations and facile quotations of the Bull *Umbratilem* (written for the Carthusians), tends to create the impression that love of the Order implies a *belief in the absolute superiority of our Order* over all others. This is, as a matter of fact, both childish and absurd, {and} also very "human" in every sense, {a sign of a} lack of faith. To try to build genuine love of the Order on legends like this is to build on unreality. This is not a solid basis for true love of the Order. When the reality (which must inevitably be faced) is seen, one will come into conflict with those artificially manufactured ideal pictures. Frustration is the result. One reason why stability and love of the Order become difficult for some souls is that they are irritated and their patience is undermined by the *constant sales talks* in which we try to boost our spirit of stability and love for the Order. We are always telling ourselves how great we are, how sublime our vocation is, how terrible are those who fail to live up to its heights. We are delighted when visiting clergy and bishops tell us in chapter how marvelous we are, how much the Church depends on us, that we are the salt of the earth. As a consequence, we who are supposed to be one of humblest orders in the Church are in actual fact too often inordinately occupied with our own importance, with our dignity, our superiority, our achievements, etc. This creates an unhealthy climate of fixation upon ourselves, and in large measure the rebellion of some souls against it is a *healthy* one. But since this rebellion implies an overt conflict with the Order, it soon turns into instability and dissatisfaction and eventually to loss of vocation. *False love of the Order* is then based on a childish conviction of our superiority, and this conviction has to be bolstered up at all times by statements and sales talks. We strive to convince ourselves, and in our eagerness to do so we arouse misgivings and undermine the real love of the Order. In trying to produce security, we arouse insecurity and doubt. *True love for the Order* is based on reality. It accepts the Order *as it is*. This in itself means a kind of modest and humble revulsion from the spirit of self-advertisement which is sometimes too common. We do not love the Order because it is theoretically "superior," but because it is the sign and sacrament of the divine mercy in our lives. It is the order chosen by God for us. It offers us what our hearts have really sought and desired: seclusion from the world and from its dangers, a penitential life that will help us to atone for our sins, silence which will enable us to be with God, the liturgical life which will enrich our days with graces and with many spiritual joys, etc. In a word, this is an order which represents for us that interpretation of the Gospel best suited for us. It enables us to seek God, to live in the mysteries of Christ, to live "in Christ." In this sense, love for our Order is nothing more than love for Jesus Christ Himself, since our Order is our way to God, in Christ. This of course is only true in so far as we have *genuine vocations* to seek God as Cistercian monks. (Is it true that our vocation is genuine? Let us remember how we came here: the graces of our first days in the Order; the certitude which led us to make our vows; the fruitfulness with which God has blessed our profession and our priestly lives—all these are signs of a true vocation.) When vocations are not thoroughly tested during the time of probation, then it is clear that there will be men in the Order who are not fully capable of loving it because they do not have genuine vocations. In a case where one without a solid vocation has been admitted to solemn profession, it is for the director to help him make an adjustment. If he is there, perhaps he can learn to love the Order even though he does not really belong in it. If he cannot love the Order and if his whole attitude is destructive and negative, then it might perhaps be better for the superiors to help him get a dispensation. The important thing is not to allow those who do not have real vocations to make profession. A genuine and sincere love for the Order in the novitiate is one sign of a good vocation: a person who later turns against the Order when he has previously loved it and has been clearly adjusted to the life is probably being unfaithful to his vocation in one way or other. Note: true love of the Order does not mean love of the faults and shortcomings of some members of the Order. It means love of the genuine spirit of the Order, of the genuine Cistercian life, not of the life in a corrupt and degenerate form. Severe conflicts can be generated where there is a real love for the true spirit, and that love is frustrated by the lack of true spirit in the community. But the fact remains we must be practical. That means we must love the Order *as it is, not just as it ought to be*, and we must remember that there is a subtle form of hypocrisy which condemns the faults of others (of the Order) in order to whitewash our own lack of generosity and our own infidelity to grace. In practice, we must love the genuine Cistercian ideal and at the same time love the Order in the concrete form which may fall short of the ideal. We must accept an imperfect situation and strive loyally to work for the ideal that has been proposed to us by our Fathers, in the situation created by ourselves and our brethren. True love of the Order should not rest on what we *hope to get out of the Order*. Very often dissatisfied monks are peeved because they do not find in the Order the constant inspiration, love, encouragement and help which they demand of it, as if it were enough to be carried along passively by the *Rule* and the community life. This is not a realistic expectation. "If you seek love in your monastic life, put love into your monastic life."[832] Then you will get love out of it. But if you just expect the life to "do you good" and "make you happy," you will be disillusioned. True love of the Order demands, in the long run, generosity toward the Order.

4. *Love of One's Monastic Community*: all that has been said above about love for the Order applies even more strongly to the love of one's monastic community: *realism, generosity, self-forgetfulness*. The Order remains an abstract entity. The monastic

---

832. Merton adapts the saying of St. John of the Cross: "And where there is no love, put love and you will find love" (Letter 22, to M. María de la Encarnación [July 6, 1591] [Peers, *Complete Works of Saint John of the Cross*, 3.296]).

community is the concrete embodiment of the Order and of its spirit in our own lives. When you say "the Order," you mean in practice "the monastery" where you yourself live the *Rule* and life of the Order. However, there is something in the community which evades definition and abstract analysis—the particular situation; the particular character of the men who form the community; the character of the house; the superiors; our own relationship with brethren and superiors. All this is a spiritual mystery. We cannot understand it clearly. Everyone is called not only to the Order but to *his own monastery*. Each should see his own monastery as a sacrament of the divine mercy in his own life. The particular monks who are there have been called to the monastery in view of one another's sanctification. Each one of the monks is there for the good of the others as well as for his own. God has brought them all together that they may all help one another and be helped by one another. *Stability* depends in large measure upon our ability *to see and accept our insertion into the particular community* as a *grace and a mission* given us by God. As a *grace*—we need faith to see that our brethren are there to help us and that we need and ought to appreciate their help. It is a grace. It is something planned for us by the mercy of God. They complete us in the things we lack. As a *mission*—but they also depend on us. We have something to contribute to their life too. We aid in their salvation. The smallest thing we do for them is a work done for God and done in a very special way: it is part of the lifework which has been mapped out for us by God, part of His eternal plan and therefore it is something which is exceptionally pleasing to Him. {A} true spirit of stability depends, then, on a deep faith and understanding of the mystery of divine Providence. We will want to remain in our monastery because it is the place where we have been placed with work to do for God, for our brethren, for the Church and for the Kingdom of God. This is very important. We might be able to do another work somewhere else, but it is not precisely the work chosen for us by God. It has less spiritual value, less significance. It takes much humility and faith to accept one's actual situation, one's own monastery with its inevitable human imperfections. It takes charity and generosity to be faithful to the community and to carry out one's task loyally though others may seem to be unfaithful or ungenerous. We must learn not to criticize them, not to criticize the community, and to avoid comparisons. He who stands back and sets himself apart from others, in order to compare the generosity and the achievement of others with what he thinks to be his own generosity, will sooner or later be tempted against his vocation. He will want to leave, on the ground that the others are not faithful enough, generous enough, etc. This can be a very serious illusion and proceeds from pride. The cure is a genuine community spirit. Love of one's monastery means generous dedication to one's part in the life of the community. It is futile to say you love the monastery if all you love is the scenery. If you do not contribute to the life of the monastic community, you cannot love the community. (The contribution of an individual to the community is not necessarily measured by quantitative output. One who is on his back in the infirmary can contribute very much to his community, just by his sufferings, his prayer, his *being* there.) This is the very heart of stability. In order to have the spirit of stability, pray for a great and generous love of the monastic community. This is the very spirit of the Gospels. If one has this love, his stability and his vocation will never be in serious danger. If one does not have this love, even though he may remain sternly faithful to his vow and never go outside the monastic enclosure even for ten minutes, he can still lose his vocation. He can live in the monastery as one without a vocation, because he is without love. He has ceased to respond to God's love which calls him to love; hence he has "lost his vocation." Notes: love for one's monastery is certainly helped by many *accidentals*. One can and should love the *place* itself. The monastery and its surroundings become impregnated with memories and holy associations after years of prayer and sacrifice and work. One is rooted in the land of the monastery by one's sacrifices, the work one does in union with one's brethren year by year, the accidents, the trials, the challenges that called forth special effort. All these play an important part in creating spiritual bonds which tie one to one's monastery. They have much to do with monastic stability. Love for the monastic community means love for the brethren who are there, for the superiors, and for all who share in the communal effort. Stability helps us to share permanently in this love. After you have been for years in the monastery, a good meditation in the monastic cemetery, over the graves of those brethren you have known and at whose side you have worked, can be very meaningful in terms of monastic stability. (Those lying in the cemetery are those who have won the victory of stability. Their perseverance has been crowned, and their prayers help us to follow in their path.) We should be particularly grateful for and appreciative of this vow of stability which gives a very special value and richness to our whole life of the vows. Everything else—obedience, conversion of manners, monastic observance—all is made much more noble and solid by our monastic stability.

FINALE

To have been called to make these vows and to live them is a very great grace, a special gift of God. The life of the vows brings us very close to God, because it enables us to follow Christ most perfectly in the simplicity of the Gospel counsels. He who makes these vows and keeps them faithfully will without any doubt be closely united with God in Christ. He will be another Christ. He will save his soul and will bring many other souls to heaven with himself. He will be guided at all times by the Holy Spirit. It is a great thing to make profession, to pronounce one's vows in the sight of God and of the community. But then one must keep the vows. In making vows, let us remember that the important thing is not the "profession day" but the lifelong fulfillment of our promise to God. It is by carrying out what we have promised that we effectively give our lives to God. Let us remember that without a strictly objective and concrete sense of our obligations, we will not be pleasing to God in our monastic life. Let us remember that the vows, once made, become an obligation of justice. But love makes us glad to fulfill this obligation. Without the grace of God at every moment, we will be in danger of infidelity to our vows. Therefore let us be faithful above all to the obligation of prayer. For only by constant and humble prayer can we obtain the graces necessary to keep our vows. Let us never forget that grace is vitally necessary. The religious who forgets his dependence on the grace of God will slowly but surely work himself into a position where he will be unfaithful in small things or great. Yet his very infidelities will be permitted by God to awaken him to compunction and to the realization of his need for grace. Let the religious who has vowed his life to God pray especially for a keen sense of his own unworthiness. When one has kept the vows for a while, one begins to trust in himself, to lose the sense of respect for others who are seemingly less faithful. One tends to trust his own ideas and judgement and to become independent of the superiors and the brethren, as if one had no need of them. But the monk who trusts himself and is attached to his own will cannot be truly faithful to his vows. Hence let such a one always pray for the grace to keep his eyes open, to live in vigilance, lest he lose the delicacy of conscience that he needs to remain faithful. The monk should always regard infidelity to his vows in any shape or form as *the greatest of evils*. We can no longer be indifferent or detached in this matter of fidelity. Before we made our vows, we were free to carry out these counsels or not, according to our choice. But now the vows are made, and what was {a} matter of choice and counsel has become for us a matter of obligation. It is no longer a matter of choice. Let us not claim to love God and to love prayer if in fact our attitude is one of carelessness toward our vows. The life of the vows makes us very special people in the sight of God. We are in a very special way the sons of God, and we have a claim upon His special love and protection. Let us glory in our poverty and our infirmity and rest on Him alone, not trusting in ourselves. And let us rely at all times on the intercession of Our Blessed Lady whose life we imitate in our monastery. By her help, our vows will bring us deep into the mystery of the Cross and the Resurrection of the Lord Jesus. Amen.

Abbey of Gethsemani
Feast of {the} Exaltation of {the} Holy Cross 1960

Appendix to the Vows
The Statement of the American Bishops on the Need for Personal Responsibility[833]
(November 1960)

Prefatory Note:

We are mimeographing this forthright and authoritative statement of the American Bishops because it recommends itself for the special study and meditation of monks as well as laypeople. All such statements naturally have great importance for all Catholics and all citizens in the United States. But this one deals with a particularly dangerous tendency of our time which affects everybody, including those who enter monasteries.

The statement declares that the sense of personal responsibility, which is at once characteristically Christian and characteristically American, is rapidly declining. It stresses the special need to renew this sense of responsibility and to emphasize it in education.

What is meant by the "sense of personal responsibility"? Certainly it is not mere "rugged individualism." We must learn as Christians to distinguish carefully between the *person* and the *individual.* The main constituent of the difference is precisely that the person is able to accept his dignity and freedom as a son of

---

833. The statement has been published in *Pastoral Letters of the American Hierarchy, 1792–1970,* ed. Hugh J. Nolan (Huntington, IN: Our Sunday Visitor, 1971), 530–35, and *Pastoral Letters of the United States Catholic Bishops,* ed. Hugh J. Nolan, 4 vols. (Washington, DC: United States Catholic Conference / National Conference of Catholic Bishops, 1984), 2.234–40.

God and consecrate his life to the service of God. The individual is dominated by irresponsible fantasy and appetite, and seeks in the long run to abdicate his responsibility, to hand it over to the collectivity, in order to sink into what the Bishops call the *"moral laxity of the mass mind."* The great danger is that we will cease to live and act as persons and confuse Christian virtue with passivity, resting in the "uniformity of thought and supine loyalty to the organization" which more and more characterize the "organization man" of today.

Where this weakness is particularly felt in Cistercian life is in the sphere of vocations and vows, for here precisely the obligation to assume personal responsibility for one's life before God is inescapable. There are many who, without realizing it themselves, come to the monastery to escape responsibility, to let someone else do all their thinking for them, to passively abdicate the obligation for acting as free men before God and pushing it all off on to the community and the superiors. The true concept of vows and of obedience implies, on the contrary, not the *abdication* of freedom but its *consecration* to God. Vows are not the rejection of responsibility, but a full assumption of the highest religious obligations for one's entire life. The Bishops' statement refers to the repeated failures of Christian marriages, due to the fact that the parties concerned were not faithful to their mutual obligations. The same might be said for the numerous failures of religious vocations, for the same reasons.

This statement is therefore of great value to religious, particularly because it brings out the basic fact that the Christian (and religious) life is to *be accepted as a mission from God,* and thus lived in a creative and dynamic fashion. The present educational trend which seeks more and more (in secular schools) to bring about a passive adaptation to "the group" is here specifically censured by the Bishops. It is also to be noted that this statement simply amplifies what has been repeatedly taught in the social documents of the modern popes, and stresses the humanism and Christian personalism which are highlighted in the recent encyclical *Mater et Magistra* of Pope John XXIII.

Unreasonable fear that emphasis on the Christian person is somehow dangerous or "antisocial" might be an unconscious symptom of the mentality which the Bishops are criticizing here.

Choir Novitiate, Abbey of Gethsemani 1961

Text of the Bishops' Statement:

The history and achievements of America stand as a monument to the personal responsibility of free men. Our institutions and our industry, the fruit of the American sense of responsibility, have in the past inspired, guided, and helped many other nations of the world. If our future is to be worthy of our past, if the fruit of America's promise is not to wither before it has reached full maturity, our present pre-eminent need is to reaffirm the sense of individual obligation, to place clearly before ourselves the foundation on which personal responsibility rests, to determine the causes of its decay and to seek the means by which it can be revived.

The foremost signs of the decline of personal responsibility are to be found in the family. Marriage, a sacred and binding contract, all too often is considered merely as an arbitrary arrangement to satisfy the instinct of pleasure. The failure of parents to fulfill their responsibilities, as revealed in the frequency of divorce, desertion, and broken homes, is a national disgrace. Any delinquency of parents may well be reflected in the delinquency of youth, which is now commonly considered our greatest national domestic problem.

Equally conspicuous is the evidence of decline in the sense of responsibility within our industrial organization and in our general economic life. At a time when so much depends upon the soundness of our economy and upon our ability to produce to meet the needs of a rapidly developing world, we have been faced by a frequent lack of truly responsible leadership, both on the part of management and of labor. Among the evident instances of the breakdown of personal responsibility most deplorable has been the widespread cynical reaction to the recent revelation of dishonesty, waste, and malfeasance in industrial relations.

Although personal responsibility and initiative have been our national characteristics, explaining in large measure our country's progress in human welfare, yet pressures are growing for a constantly greater reliance on the collectivity rather than on the individual. An inordinate demand for benefits, most easily secured by the pressures of organization, has led an ever-growing number of our people to relinquish their rights and to abdicate their responsibilities. This concession creates a widening spiral of increasing demands and pressures with a further infringement on personal freedom and responsibility. The result is the condition recently noted by our Holy Father: "Modern man sees that the sphere in which he can think for himself, act on his own initiative, exercise his responsibilities and affirm and enrich his personality is in many cases restricted to an excessive degree" (Letter of July 12, 1960, to the "Semaine Sociale" in Grenoble). Intensive socialization can achieve mass benefits, but man and morality can be seriously hurt in the process.

This tendency to delegate excessive responsibility to an organization is discernible also in the realm of international affairs. Some manifest no sense of personal responsibility in the affairs of the international community. On the other hand, many citizens seem to feel that our mere adherence to the United Nations absolves us from further responsibility in the international order and that decisions made by the United Nations, regardless of their objective value, are always to be regarded as morally right. Admitting the undoubted value of a policy of supporting the United Nations and recognizing the genuine contribution it has made in many areas, we must understand clearly that the citizens of this country, and of all countries, have a responsibility to judge and to evaluate the United Nations' deliberations and decisions according to objective norms of morality universally binding. This involves also the duty of citizens to make proper representation of such judgment to their respective governments.

However varied the above-mentioned evils, ranging from the single act of wrongdoing to the moral laxity of the mass mind, the root cause is the same—the rejection of personal responsibility. This is a moral evil, as are all the major ills that beset the present world. As such their cure is largely within the power of individual persons. A godly society is the work of godly men. Even the most universal evil and the threatened mechanization of man can be made to yield before the just and determined wills of individual persons.

Our Holy Father has pointed out the capacity of the individual in the face of such problems.

> Does it follow that the process of socialization is impossible to control and that, increasing constantly in its breadth and depth, it will one day surely reduce men to the role of automatons? Certainly not. For socialization is not the result of forces of nature acting according to determinism that cannot be changed. It is the work of man, of a free being conscious of and responsible for his acts (Letter of July 12, 1960 to "Semaine Sociale" in Grenoble).

In our national life we have experienced the truth of this statement. Our progress has been achieved chiefly according to the measure of individual commitment to responsibility. The heroes of our history have not been blind forces but stout-hearted persons; our worthy national goals have been achieved not as a result of environment but by men who made their environment. A strong and responsible nation is fashioned by responsible persons, not group pressures. As Pope Pius XII stated: "The people live from the fullness of the life of the men who make it up; each of them in his place and in the manner proper to him is a person conscious of his own responsibilities and of his own convictions" (Christmas Message, 1944).

What is personal responsibility in the context of man's relation to the world? It presupposes the acceptance of one's dignity as a son of God in whatever environment he may be placed and the acknowledgement of binding moral law. It requires the free and deliberate acceptance of one's obligations in the position he occupies—in the family, in the church, in the corporation, in the labor union, in the community, in the nation, in the family of nations. It demands the rule of conscience, not self-satisfaction. It recognizes that every deliberate action of the human person has a relationship with his Creator and His purpose in creating the world. It affirms that every human action a man performs derives its significance from that relationship and makes him a cooperator with his Creator in forwarding the Kingdom of God. It is the solemn profession that consequently every product of his mind and his hand, every bounty wrung from the earth is to serve that high purpose. As man, bearing the image of his Creator, is the brother of every other human person, his noblest work is to bring to his fellow-man the blessings of the destiny intended for him by God.

It must be emphasized, especially in these times, that the freedom innate in man, as well as the social nature he enjoys, demands as a correlative the fullest personal responsibility. "Therefore every one of us will render an account for himself to God" (Rom. 14:12). The marvelous inventiveness of the human mind, conquering space and making each man a neighbor of every other human being on earth, gives urgency to this twofold need: to maintain one's freedom by using it according to the limits and norms of rightful authority; to use it also according to his social nature and the needs of his fellow man.

> For you have been called to liberty, brethren; only, do not use liberty as an occasion for sensuality but by charity serve one another. For the whole law is fulfilled in one word, "Thou shalt love thy neighbor as thyself" (Galatians 5:13, 14).

The social pressures of today's complex life do not excuse from, but rather create a demand for, a greater exercise of personal responsibility. No man can be neutral in a moral cause. By his creation he is born to be committed to the cause of God. The more difficult the situation the more imperative the need for such a commitment.

If we are to restore man to his sense of personal responsibility and to the acceptance of life as a mission, we must understand more clearly the moral causes which have undermined men's sense of responsibility.

First among these causes has been the marked decline in the force of religious convictions. Washington warned the American people that they should indulge with caution the supposition that national morality could exist without religion. In spite of the much discussed increase of church membership it cannot be doubted that for a long time religious influences have been losing their vigor among the American people, with a debilitating effect in consequence on both public and private life.

As a result of this decline of religious convictions the grasp on moral principles has been greatly weakened. Through a faulty concept of morality modern man has come to imagine that sudden and drastic changes in situations change principles; that principles no longer control situations, but rather that situations shape principles. Inevitably this type of "situational ethics" denies all unchanging principles and makes futile all moral judgments on which the sense of responsibility rests. The need which the world faces is the acceptance of an objective norm of morality, and hence of conduct.

This decline in religious belief and moral conviction leaves modern man blind to his immutable spiritual nature. Thus, wittingly or unwittingly, he aligns himself with the forces of materialism among whose tenets there is no room for the concept of personal responsibility.

Finally, the social ideals and purposes of modern man, due to the declining influence of religious and moral convictions and to the triumph of the material, tend in many subtle ways to efface the sense of responsibility. As a people we seem to be moving more deeply into a sensate culture. There is an excessive preoccupation with material security at the expense of spiritual well-being. Uniformity of thought and supine loyalty to the organization, whether it be the industrial corporation, the labor union, or the political party, are too often encouraged and rewarded. The organizational man, cloaked in a sort of anonymity, rather than the responsible individual, is favored and advanced. The preparation for this condition is found even in the field of education, where emphasis is placed on adapting oneself to the thinking of the group. This pattern is so prevalent that some psychologists consider juvenile delinquency as a revolt, just for the sake of rebellion, against a stifling uniformity that fails to challenge the individuality of the student.

The correction of these basically moral evils and the restoration of a vigorous sense of personal responsibility belong primarily to the field of religion. The development of a truly Christian character is primarily the task of religion, although its inculcation is of vital concern to the state. It is the function of religion to teach man his unique dignity as a son of God and brother of Christ. Pope Pius XII explicitly stated this in describing the function of the Church:

> Always and everywhere, by unceasingly adapting herself to the circumstances of time and place, she seeks to model persons, individuals and, as far as possible, all individuals according to the laws of Christ, thus attaining the moral basis for social life. The object of the Church is man, naturally good, imbued, ennobled and strengthened by the truth and grace of Christ (September 19, 1955).

Deepened religious convictions will bolster and reactivate the sense of personal responsibility. We must seek to enlarge the area of personal autonomy to protect the human personality from a greater encroachment on its freedom and responsibility. The individual person must assume as his proud right the accomplishment of whatever he can for himself and for others, especially those of his family, and herein lies the importance of the Christian home. The same principle of responsibility must be consistently applied to every level of action. Pope Pius XI explicitly emphasized this principle of subsidiarity in the *Quadragesimo Anno* published in 1931:

> Just as one cannot take away from individuals and transfer to the community the tasks they are capable of accomplishing by themselves, thus it would also be an injustice—and at the same time a harmful disturbance of the social order—if one were to remove from groups of lower rank functions

they can exercise themselves and entrust them to a wider collectivity of higher rank. The natural objective of any intervention in social matters is to assist the members of the social body and not to destroy or absorb them.

Even when man enters into associations, as he must to achieve the goals which lie beyond his individual capacity, he should remember their purpose is in relation to his freedom and responsibility. In this respect, the Holy Father stated:

> But this is to be done on the condition that each of these institutions remains within its own sphere of responsibility; that it be offered to, not imposed upon, the free choice of mankind. They must under no circumstances look upon themselves as an end making their members an instrument of their activity (Letter of July 12, 1960 to "Semaine Sociale" in Grenoble).

A fresh evocation of the principle and practice of personal responsibility can revivify our society and help to stem the seemingly inexorable march toward the automation of human beings and the steady loss of that freedom which is man's distinctive attribute. It will cure the mental lethargy and inertia which permit organizations to usurp, mainly by default, the rights of their members. It will stimulate a self-reliance which will automatically restore the balance between freedom and security. It will reject unwarranted pressure from groups that seek unjustly to aggrandize their power and will restrict them to their lawful ends. It will see in all business ventures of whatever size a means of serving others as well as self. It will have an immediate effect in every sphere of life—in the home, in the office, as well as in the workshop, in the factory, in our schools, in our cultural groups.

An effective response to a call for personal responsibility need not wait for a mass movement. The response belongs to the individual person, as our Holy Father indicated:

> Fully conscious of what is at stake, moved by his apostolic zeal, he then makes a personal engagement with these communities that surround him, the result of a free and justified

choice of careful thought about himself, his destiny and
the world (Letter of July 12, 1960 to "Semaine Sociale" in
Grenoble).

Such a response by a representative number, given only in the
silent sanctuary of the heart, will begin to have its leavening
effect. Our appeal for action is made directly to our Catholic
fellow-citizens, but it reaches out also to all Americans who face
the same problems as ourselves.

Before it is too late, we must revive in our midst and present
to the world the ideals that have been the real source of national
greatness. For America will fulfill its destiny when we have
achieved that spiritual maturity, described by Pope Pius XII, as
men,

> established in their inviolable integrity as images of God;
> men proud of their personal dignity and of their wholesome
> freedom; men justly jealous of their equality with their fel-
> low creatures in all that concerns the most intimate depths
> of human dignity; men solidly attached to their land and
> their tradition (Pope Pius XII, February 20, 1946).

APPENDIX A

Textual Notes

Additions and Alterations Found in Typescript and in Mimeograph

7   striving] *preceded by x'd out* actions
man's life] *preceded by x'd out* the
definite] *preceded by x'd out* conception
there exists] *interlined with a caret*

8   an enormous] *preceded by x'd out* an enormous
sake of humanity] *followed by x'd out* the common good
scientific techniques] *followed by x'd out* and
desirability of] *followed by x'd out* a type, of a

9   Hence the religious . . . do something.] *opposite page*
lives his vows] *preceded by x'd out* is
The vows are . . . present life.] *added on line*

10   *activity are*] *followed by x'd out both*
above himself,] *followed by x'd out* in
objective] *preceded by x'd out* reality

11   whole lives] *followed by x'd out* in the se
READ . . . 18:14-22] *added on line*
derives] *followed by x'd out* is determined

12   (subjectively)] *typed interlined with a caret*
aim for] *preceded by x'd out* place that
Further, . . . for himself.] *added in lower margin*
d) *The last end of man is*] *added in upper margin*
the good . . . by God] *interlined with a caret*
seeks] *followed by x'd out* consciously
e)] *added in left margin before cancelled* d)

13 f)] *added in left margin before cancelled* e)
 g)] *added in left margin before cancelled* f)
 h)] *added in left margin before cancelled* f)
14 i)] *added in left margin before cancelled* g)
 j)] *added in left margin before cancelled* h)
 i.e. . . . FOR US] *added on line*
 his own] *preceded by cancelled its own*
15 The person is . . . Savior.] *opposite page*
 using] *preceded by cancelled* lead
17 man's soul] *preceded by x'd out* man as a
 intelligence] *preceded by x'd out* will
 passions with] *preceded by x'd out* sense
18 They become . . . will.] *added on line*
 If we are to] *typed interlined above x'd out* To
 aid] *altered from* aiding
 in] *interlined below cancelled* to
 reaching] *altered from* reach
 But the passions . . . soul.] *interlined above cancelled*
  Before studying the will, and its activity, let us look
  at the passions. What are they?
19 Hence, to describe . . . Ghost.] *interlined*
21 An involuntary . . . indifferent.] *added in left margin*
 perfectionem] *followed by x'd out* boni moralis humani
  boni pertinet
22 most important] *preceded by x'd out* principal
25 fully] *preceded by x'd out* freely
 Altruistic] *interlined above cancelled* Other-directed
28 lifted up] *preceded by x'd out* sublimated
 good for] *preceded by x'd out* other
31 right ordering] *preceded by x'd out* ordering
 passion] *followed by x'd out* is a sensible
32 sharing] *preceded by x'd out* a sharing and
 grace] *followed by x'd out* and the Holy Spirit
 is raised] *preceded by x'd out* become
 one might read] *preceded by x'd out* thus showing both
  the

34   paragraph] *preceded by x'd out* speech
        know] *preceded by x'd out* commune dir
        principally] *preceded by x'd out* from
        personal fulfillment] *preceded by x'd out* fulfilment
35   automatically from] *followed by x'd out* an
        disposition] *followed by x'd out* required by
        urged] *preceded by x'd out* compelled to smoke
        degrades] *preceded by x'd out* Habitus *in left margin*
37   sensible appetite, intelligence or will] *typed interlined*
            above x'd out soul
        acquired] *followed by x'd out* and
38   abandon,] *followed by x'd out* deliberation
        acts.] *followed by x'd out* There are also
        offer] *preceded by x'd out* complete our intellectual
        intellectual {virtues] *preceded by x'd out Acquired*
40   vows aim . . . religion] *added in left margin*
        S$_{IN}$] *preceded by x'd out* The Infused
        to wisdom and] *followed by x'd out* truth
41   in some] *followed by x'd out* that i
        relative] *preceded by x'd out* culpability
        roots] *typed interlined above cancelled sources*
        This explains] *preceded by x'd out* The gr
        world of ours,] *preceded by x'd out* society
42   disfigurement] *preceded by x'd out* defilement
        unrepentant] *preceded by x'd out* formal sinners
43   economy] *preceded by x'd out* world and the
        fervent] *preceded by x'd out* of the
44   good action,] *preceded by x'd out* action
        management] *interlined below cancelled* government
        We must . . . Plan."] *opposite page*
        the divine] *interlined above cancelled* that
45   He is our . . . after this.] *added in right margin*
        children must] *preceded by x'd out* we
47   *Human Law*] *preceded by x'd out Divine Law* Because the
            natural law
        Relatively] *preceded by x'd out* A f

48   *accords with the natural law.*] *followed by x'd out* No
         human law binds when it is practically impossible
         or useless for attaining the end of the natural law
     respect for authority] *preceded by x'd out* sense an
         authority

49   *relation of*] *preceded by x'd out* evident
     Respect] *preceded by x'd out* This
     besides . . . (*observantia*)] *interlined with a caret*
     deep] *interlined with a caret* clear
     is necessary] *preceded by x'd out* was
     Jesus the Man-God] *interlined above cancelled* human
         legislators

50   *The divine law . . . phases:*] The divine law . . . phases:
     1.] *added in left margin*
     2.] *added in left margin*
     a higher] *preceded by x'd out* it
     spiritual] *interlined below and marked for insertion*
     This interior . . . clear.] *opposite page*
     interior character] *preceded by cancelled* concept of the
     makes us] *preceded by cancelled* prompts

51   for the brethren.] *preceded by x'd out* from
     perfectly on His own] *followed by cancelled perfect*

52   The life of . . . New Law] *added in left margin*
     fidelity] *interlined above cancelled* the
     virtue] *typed interlined above x'd out* study
     in the religious life] *added on line*
     emphasis] *preceded by x'd out* justice would reduce our
         re
     conduct] *followed by x'd out* conform in all
     reason] *followed by x'd out* and the
     exterior] *interlined with a caret*
     interior] *added in left margin and marked for insertion*
     supernatural] *preceded by x'd out* in
     More precisely . . . *world*] *added on line*

52–53   When we . . . crucified] *opposite page*

53   The infused] *preceded by cancelled* In a strict sense

(the Body of Christ)] *interlined below and marked for insertion*

starving] *altered from* starved

attain] *preceded by x'd out* freely and successfully accomplish

It is especially . . . 1957).] *opposite page*

wealth] *followed by cancelled* which is t

54   social context] *preceded by x'd out* structure of the socie

rights of men] men *typed interlined above cancelled* others

or to] *added in lower margin and marked for insertion*

keeping] *preceded by x'd out* doing it

keep the rule,] *preceded by x'd out* do

carry out] *preceded by x'd out* obs live up to your own little obligations

temperance] *preceded by x'd out* charity

important is] *preceded by x'd out* importance

55   hectic] *added in left margin and marked for insertion to replace cancelled* exaggerated

impurity] *followed by x'd out* In this "battle" (against windmills, usually) one must make a place the greatest importance on

man is] *preceded by x'd out* there

inordinate] *preceded by x'd out* passions

accept] *preceded by x'd out* take them up

upside down] *followed by x'd out* it fails to see that

matter of] *followed by x'd out* how one thinks and fee

and small] *typed after* narrow *and marked for insertion*

values.] *followed by x'd out* With In

56   so far as he is] *preceded by x'd out* the natur

outside] *preceded by x'd out* over

57   for sure] *preceded by x'd out* to sure

59   or even] *followed by x'd out* about

60   conversion] *preceded by x'd out* obedience)

neglecting] *preceded by x'd out* unfulfilment

The same . . . of another.] *opposite page*

61   reverence to God] *followed by x'd out* in whom
          a supreme] *preceded by x'd out* supremely iniquitous
          of persons] *followed by x'd out* and a
          This shows . . . dictate.] *interlined*
62   circumstances] *followed by x'd out* and th
          decides] followed by x'd out what means to use.
          a hard] *preceded by x'd out* some
          or make . . . keep.] *added in lower margin*
          goods.] *preceded by x'd out* things
65   conformity to] *preceded by x'd out* perfect
66   establishes] *preceded by x'd out* demands
          Strict] *preceded by x'd out* Hence
          and for] *preceded by x'd out* for what
          relations] *added in left margin to replace* dealings
          come to] *interlined with a caret*
67   takes us] *preceded by cancelled* really
          true prudence] *preceded by x'd out* reason
          Our worship . . . holiness of God.] *interlined*
          sacrifice] *preceded by x'd out* penance and
          To what . . . (Isaias 1:11-15)] insert—copy here Isaias
             I:11-15 *added in lower margin and marked for insertion*
68   and were . . . life.)] *added on line*
          the actual] *preceded by x'd out* our actual deal
          the Kingdom] *preceded by x'd out* eternal life
69   enter into] *preceded by x'd out* love
          His Passion] *preceded by x'd out* the Mass
          explains why] *preceded by x'd out* is
70   Thyself,] *preceded by x'd out* thee
          the glory] *preceded by x'd out* that
71   adversity] *preceded by x'd out* temporal
          wisdom,] *preceded by x'd out* his
72   Since] *preceded by x'd out* If
          faith and life,] *preceded by x'd out* life and fait
          human prince] *preceded by x'd out* man
73   *redeeming] preceded by x'd out* satisfying
          First of all, it was] *added on line before cancelled* As

in quo] *preceded by* x'd out et

corp.] *preceded by* x'd out ad

It is also] *added on line before cancelled* As

It is then, too] *added on line before cancelled* As

74 suffered an] *preceded by* x'd out died an intolerable

agony,] *preceded by* x'd out and inconceivable

acute] *preceded by* x'd out suffering in every

75 We can . . . of his soul.] *opposite page*

would be] *followed by* x'd out much less of

77 left Him completely] *preceded by* x'd out not preven

reached] *preceded by* x'd out at

for salvation] *followed by* x'd out was to

Priests] *preceded by* x'd out High

central thought] *preceded by* x'd out Epistle

78 provided . . . of it.] *added on line*

79 otherwise.] *followed by* x'd out It als

obvious.] *The following text is written on the verso of this page with an arrow that does not correspond to material on the facing recto page*: Like all other graces, the joy of paschal tide is not something which comes to us automatically + passively—without our having to do anything. The joy is all there in the liturgy + it is easy to get yet we must work to *deepen* it in ourselves—by digging deeper roots of faith into the mystery of the Resurrection Paschal tide is a "eucharistic" season par excellence. That is a season of praise + thanksgiving to God because *He* is good—not just because He is good *to us* but because he is infinitely good in Himself. *Confitemini Domino quoniam bonus.* How do we come to appreciate this better? By a deeper realization that the paschal mystery is the great revelation of His love + His *mercy—quoniam in aeternum misericordia ejus.*

81 all shall] *preceded by* x'd out every

83 This then . . . a message?] *added on line*

85   *cannot*] *followed by x'd out* mercy

86   it is not . . . orientation.] *added in upper margin and marked for insertion*

    abandon] *preceded by x'd out* unite ourselves

    But *what* . . . end?] *added on line*

    There are different] *preceded by cancelled* But

    our] *interlined above cancelled* this

    understanding.] *followed by x'd out* Later we

    John 6:] *followed by x'd out* 268

    a lasting] *preceded by x'd out* and

    "bring forth] *preceded by x'd out* and do His will as He does the will

87   It also . . . follow Him.] *added in left margin and marked for insertion*

    to see . . . Church.] *interlined*

    manifested in . . . Church.] *added on line*

88   understand] *preceded by x'd out* see and

    (explain)] *added in lower margin*

88–89   St. Maximus the . . . brotherhood.] *opposite page*

89   worship,] *preceded by x'd out* cult,

90   implies] *followed by x'd out* as we

    participation] *preceded by x'd out* life

91   diversity] *preceded by x'd out* unite

    as it were,] *preceded by x'd out* it

93   develop] *interlined above cancelled* cultivate

94   Word in us] *preceded by x'd out* Holy Spirit in us draws us to the

    three] *preceded by x'd out* two

    quotations] *preceded by x'd out* statements f

95   intimacy] *preceded by x'd out* love

96   Do not think] *preceded by x'd out* The

97   kept in mind] *typed in lower margin before x'd out* served

    come to you.] *followed by x'd out* If you "possess grace"

    cf. St. John of the Cross] *added in left margin*

98   *share His love*] *followed by x'd out* for us

This is . . . soul.] *added on line*
special vocation.] *followed by x'd out* Everyone, ev
99   is perfectly] *preceded by x'd out* is not
friendship for God] God *interlined below cancelled* Him
We pray . . . heart."] *added in lower margin*
taken] *preceded by x'd out* this
100   needs of others] *followed by x'd out* as well as with his
        own
and to . . . really are.] added on line
101   Note that . . . character.] *opposite page*
103   is full of] *preceded by cancelled* reflects ourselv
104   offers itself] *preceded by x'd out* is a
106   Note that . . . from God.] *opposite page*
Religious] *interlined above cancelled* They
pay for] *followed by x'd out* this
106–107 It is important . . . Gospels.] *interlined*
109   stability in] *followed by x'd out* a
111   possible to] *preceded by x'd out* good in
112   importance,] *preceded by x'd out* urgency and
nothingness] *preceded by x'd out* urgency of
of listening] *preceded by x'd out* the
calling us] us *interlined with a caret*
114   proper] *preceded by x'd out* last end
116   The ascent . . . *Christi.] opposite page*
117   see . . . 11-19] *added on line*
This text . . . sacrifice.] *opposite page*
mancipant] preceded by x'd out Deo
Religiosi praecipue . . . vacent.] opposite page
they immolate their mind] *typed interlined above x'd out*
        their senses
118   *How does . . . rule.] typed interlined above and below x'd
        out* First of all by baptism and by consecration, but
        also in his acts and faculties
the rule.] his rule.
and perilous] *typed interlined*
of the observances] *followed by x'd out* and

119   TOLLUNTUR] *followed by x'd out* PER
       term] *typed interlined*
       as here . . . Thomas] *typed interlined*
122   if we can] *interlined with a caret*
124   so our . . . goal.] *added on line*
       think he] *preceded by x'd out* he
125   chastity is] *followed by x'd out* the
       Rather] *followed by cancelled* other mystics would tell
         us,
       Note that . . . of Jesus.] *opposite page*
       mainly] *interlined with a caret*
130   sanctity] *followed by x'd out* of the Church
131   best] *preceded by x'd out* better
       more perfect] *preceded by cancelled* a better rule
       word] *preceded by cancelled* world
132   union] *preceded by cancelled* contemplative
133   breed] *followed by x'd out* and
       reported] *preceded by x'd out* writer
135   better . . . belong here.] *added on line*
       cf.] *interlined above and marked for insertion*
       etc.] *interlined above and marked for insertion*
136   the mere . . . vocation] *added on line*
       This would . . . have a vocation.] *added on line*
       All these . . . misleading.] *interlined*
137   Vocation . . . manifestatus.] *added in left margin*
       DELIGANT] *followed by x'd out* ([   ] primum)
       to live] *followed by x'd out* in
138   3) Who . . . functions.] *added in lower margin*
       They must . . . not called.] *added in left margin and
         marked for insertion*
       fervor, should give] give *interlined above cancelled* show
139   *unable to] followed by cancelled* find
140   *to love our nothingness . . . failed).] written below* N.B.
         . . . *our life. and marked for transposition*
141   If a monk . . . ways.] *added in left margin*
142   "by being . . . fellow,"] *interlined*

b) . . . disaster.] *interlined*
145 shows] *preceded by x'd out* is
COME AFTER] *typed interlined above x'd out* FOLLOW
If any man *wants to* . . . motions.] *added on line*
does not mean an agreement . . . system.] *added on line*
146 Note . . . *transplanting* it.] *opposite page*
Self-hatred . . . go.] *added on line*
147 of the world] *followed by x'd out* and
148 "savours] *followed by x'd out* the things that
{4}] 3 *in text*
149 feels himself] *preceded by x'd out* complete
This is . . . outlook.] *added on line*
150 faithful!] *followed by* close—quote from De Guibert *in lower margin*
150–51 Fr. De Guibert . . . not God.] *opposite page*
150 Abnegation] *preceded by cancelled* "Experience is there to prove it."
151 elements of religious] *followed by x'd out* life
chastity] *followed by x'd out* do not of themselves fully exha
152 *Dominus*] *typed interlined*
154 glory.] *followed by x'd out* Why? To be perfectly unit
156 a] *preceded by x'd out* 1
It would] *preceded by x'd out* Because
act as if] *preceded by x'd out* think
the union] *preceded by x'd out* of the
157 eventually lead.] *followed by x'd out* Not just the renunciation
the sacrifice] *followed by x'd out* as such is the most worthy.] *followed by x'd out* In pr
effect of] *followed by x'd out* true
158 if we remember] *preceded by x'd out* and
sacrifice and] *followed by x'd out* communion
organized] *preceded by x'd out* an
159 in religious profession] *followed by x'd out* which is an act of religion.

160　　what was . . . later] *interlined above cancelled* St Thomas's
　　　　　teaching
　　　　the state of] *preceded by x'd out* monastic
161　　until] *preceded by x'd out* during
162　　St. Hedwig,] *preceded by x'd out* three of our saints in
　　　　　Portugal at this time did not make vows, but lived
　　　　　in the community with
163　　*Contract?*] *? added on line*
　　　　Public religious] *typed interlined and marked for insertion*
　　　　To keep] *preceded by cancelled* Hence
164　　regard] *followed by x'd out* the vo
　　　　Above all, he] *preceded by x'd out* There
165　　it is of the greatest] *preceded by x'd out* In
166　　is promising] *preceded by x'd out* promises
　　　　Assuming that] *preceded by x'd out* Called and inspired
　　　　　by divine grace, aided by
167　　*freedom*] *preceded by x'd out* will
　　　　incomparable] *added in left margin to replace cancelled*
　　　　　precious
　　　　The main thing] *typed interlined above x'd out* One of
　　　　　the things
168　　end in view] *preceded by x'd out* the
　　　　This adds] *preceded by x'd out* On th
　　　　Holy Spirit acts] *preceded by x'd out* grace
169　　to that end.] *followed by x'd out* I have reached the end
　　　　　of my novitiate.
　　　　give my] *preceded by x'd out* take the necessa
　　　　done] *followed by x'd out* with approval
　　　　selection] *interlined above cancelled* state
170　　particular] *interlined with a caret*
　　　　Read . . . 28-32.] *added in lower margin*
　　　　keep my] *typed interlined above x'd out* make a
　　　　I must . . . obey] *interlined*
　　　　Every time] *preceded by x'd out* I cannot
171　　about] *added in left margin before cancelled* for
　　　　To choose, then, . . . below).] *added on line*

difference . . . appetite.] *interlined*

172   seek] *interlined above cancelled* choose

Further points on *electio*] *notes on opposite page without indication of insertion:* Mature + immature conscience Psychic *mechanism*—infantile (private) religion + moral code. undifferentiated drives child must learn to form himself but first be formed from without (introjected standard) interior merely under surface of rigid (external) code—*seeking approval guided by effect on* others apply this to vow—dependence hostility mere removal of code is no help Growth = conscience formed in terms of *objective love*—false objectivity of the adolescent Mature conscience—capacity for *evaluation responsibility judgement*

173   obligation] *preceded by x'd out* reason for our trying to

to make] *followed by x'd out* the choice required

rationally] *typed interlined*

One cannot . . . deordination.] *interlined*

Failure . . . prudence.] *opposite page*

174   done] *followed by x'd out* in

175   know] *preceded by x'd out* how

an act] *preceded by x'd out* a case

176   integral] *followed by x'd out* mature

sense of] *followed by x'd out* the word.

St. Thomas . . . choose.] *opposite page*

being] *interlined below cancelled* nature

service] *followed by x'd out* and

178   11] *preceded by x'd out* 13

179   union] *preceded by x'd out* love

180   not exist] *followed by x'd out* Examples: it is discovered that the one who made vows was not yet of the legitimate age: or there was something wrong with his novitiate, which was not complete. Or there was a substantial error as to the nature of the vows. Etc. In all these cases the "professed" may either

a) *convalidate his vows*—that is to say rectify the
error, make up what was lacking in the required
conditions and then renew his consent

proved in] *followed by x'd out* an

181   mental reservation,] *interlined with a caret*
or withdraws . . . reservation] *interlined below and
marked for insertion*
automatically] *preceded by x'd out* unfrocked

183   will thereby] *interlined below and marked for insertion*
by promising] *preceded by x'd out* the sanctuary of our
soul,
It is understandable . . . religious life.] *opposite page*
defiance] *preceded by x'd out* violating the resoluti
of religion,] *followed by x'd out* perhaps

184   something] *preceded by x'd out* my pun
glory] *interlined above cancelled interests*
to God] *followed by x'd out* as a
act] *preceded by x'd out* vow
for the honor . . . "perfection."] *added on line*
acquires] *preceded by x'd out* attains

185   another] *preceded by x'd out* somehow
"otherness,"] *preceded by x'd out* quality of bein
Hence . . . *from sin.*] *opposite page*

186   special] *interlined above cancelled* normal
promised] *followed by x'd out* by
All other virtues,] *preceded by x'd out* To do a thing
because it is vowed

187   firmly] *preceded by x'd out* in
6).] *preceded by x'd out* 4

188   yet once] *preceded by x'd out* provided it is
not be sought until] *interlined below cancelled* be sought
only when
clear] *preceded by x'd out* very
when] *interlined below and marked for insertion*

189   St. Bonaventure . . . for the Sabbath.] *opposite page*

be dispensed.] *preceded by x'd out* not be kept.

St. Thomas] *added in left margin to replace cancelled* He

190   the vow to be . . . greater good] *added in left margin and marked to replace cancelled* this to be the case

191   St. Thomas holds . . . poenitentiae.] *opposite page*

very special] *preceded by x'd out* direct and very special union with the

193   If a religious] *preceded by cancelled* Hence *preceded by* insert *added in left margin and cancelled referring to* The simple cleric is not bound, as is the religious, to tend to perfection (this in practice centers in the vows of religion) *added on opposite page and cancelled*

They are . . . counsels.] *added on line*

194   in everything] *added on line*

i.e.] *typed interlined*

Notes on] *preceded by x'd out* in

by appearing] *preceded by x'd out* and order

195   of theater] *of interlined*

political office] *followed by cancelled* Engaging in secular business

broad and strict . . . discouraged] *added on line*

as long . . . limits] *added on line*

196   In other . . . AVARICE] Read Rule ch. *added in left margin and cancelled*

to a holy life] *interlined above cancelled* the tend to perfection

198   to be kept] *followed by x'd out* in the common chest

This is explicitly . . . superiors] *opposite page*

use"] *followed by cancelled* (only

must be] *followed by x'd out* of *and uncancelled* the

199   Canon 2389 . . . office.] *opposite page*

200   per se] *interlined below and marked for insertion*

at least . . . way!!] *added on line*

(d) *common work] added in lower margin*

sufficient] *preceded by x'd out* reason

privacy] *preceded by x'd out* private

201   *Grave . . .* permission.] *opposite page*
             would be] *preceded by cancelled* is a sin
             It is good] *preceded by x'd out* and abide by
             outside the spirit] *preceded by x'd out* seriously
202   part of] *preceded by x'd out* the
             Note that . . . vocation.] *opposite page*
             One could . . . Order.] *added in lower margin*
             sanctuary] *added in left margin to replace cancelled* refuge
203   prior, for instance),] *followed by x'd out* and what goes
                with it
             a specially] a *added on line following x'd out* then
             grave matter . . . house.] *added on line*
204–205 the *instinct . . .* anyone else.] *preceded by cancelled*
             However *and following* presupposes it. *and marked for*
             transposition
204   However] *added on line*
             permitted.] *followed by x'd out* There is
             spend his] *preceded by x'd out* use
             This is . . . our Order.] *added on line*
             the outstanding] *preceded by cancelled* one of
205   and to carry] *preceded by x'd out* at
             Deliberate . . . sinful.] *added on line*
             {(1)}] * *in text*
             strive] *preceded by x'd out* detach
             One can . . . superior.] *added on line*
             {(2)}] ** *in text*
             on occasion] *interlined with a caret*
             his help] *preceded by x'd out* it
206   sufficient] *preceded by x'd out* a
             {(3)}] *** *in text*
             {(4)}] **** *in text*
             long in advance] *preceded by x'd out* before han
208   avoid other] *followed by x'd out* form
             use a tool,] *followed by x'd out* or driv
             one's fellow] *preceded by x'd out* others
             to the extent] *followed by x'd out* to

210   It is very . . . of others.] *added in lower margin*
211   destroy] *followed by x'd out* this
       involve] *preceded by x'd out* boil down to
       sacrifice of] *followed by x'd out* everything
       Our prayer . . . ourselves.] *interlined*
       normal for] *followed by x'd out* certain souls
212   *must necessarily*] *preceded by x'd out* can be more closely
          united with God
       The monk . . . doing so.] *added on line*
213   unreal.] *followed by x'd out* To
       4] *added in left margin before cancelled* 3
       mechanical] *followed by x'd out* a
214   4a] 4 *added in left margin before cancelled* 3
       ({4 and 4a})] (3 and 3a) *in text*
215   5] *added in left margin before cancelled* 4
216   *sincere*] *preceded by x'd out* a
217   "self-beautification."] *preceded by x'd out* beautify
218   Cultivate . . . vocation.] *opposite page*
219   keep enclosure.] *followed by x'd out* Particular law on
          enclosure, for us
220   Everything . . . happenings.] *opposite page to replace
       cancelled* c) Visits should be rare, on principle.
          When with visitors we should preserve the spirit
          of enclosure, without being stiff and unnatural. In
          the matter of visits, we leave the Superior to judge
          their frequency etc. Normally a visit does not ex-
          ceed three days, once a year. Rules about picnics
          etc.
220–21 Note that . . . *Constitutions*] *opposite page*
221   those . . . paragraph] *added in left margin to replace
       cancelled* as above
222   *Conscience-matter letters*] *preceded by cancelled* Question of
       extract from] *typed interlined before x'd out* impose on
       If one is . . . go to him.] *interlined*
223   abusive] *preceded by x'd out* inordinate
       4] *added in left margin*

In general, . . . various orders.] added on line
monastery] *typed interlined above cancelled* enclosure
at specified times] *added on line following cancelled* more
   or less frequently.
In our Order] added in upper margin
224   habitually] *preceded by x'd out* normally
225   with the men] *followed by x'd out* guests in the guest
       Be careful . . . your own.] *added in lower margin*
       been created] *interlined above cancelled* come *followed by*
         x'd out to the *followed by cancelled* into the world
226   life of love] *followed by x'd out* is to
       set forth] *preceded by x'd out* prescribed and
       of the Order.] followed by x'd out (The cons
228   by reason] *preceded by x'd out* with
       they hold the] *followed by x'd out* rooms
229   open to] *preceded by x'd out* liable to
       would certainly] *interlined with a caret above cancelled*
        could
       treating] *followed by x'd out* the Rule as trifling and
        secondary
       its authority] *followed by cancelled* Here
       sin only,] *followed by x'd out* or p
       b)] *followed by x'd out* Adaptation
230   can be] *interlined with a caret above cancelled* is
       gravely] *typed interlined*
       In necessity] *preceded by cancelled* Hence
       contempt, etc.] *followed by interlined and cancelled*
        (would sin venially)
231   in danger of] *followed by x'd out* separating t
232   implies] *followed by x'd out* this imperfection
       refusal] *followed by x'd out* of
       necessarily] interlined with a caret
       Usages] *followed by x'd out* that is
       n.b. contempt . . . violations.] *added on line*
       do the penance] the *interlined with a caret*
       (nothing . . . point)] *interlined above and marked for*
        insertion

They could be.] *added on line*

233 especially where] *followed by x'd out* the

2] *followed by x'd out* To

very] *interlined with a caret*

Especially in] *preceded by x'd out* of the exterior only.

use of the] *followed by x'd out* educational

adaptation to] *followed by x'd out* this

234 uniting] *preceded by cancelled* and

and thus . . . pleasure.] *added on line*

At the beginning] *preceded by x'd out The Benedictine Vows.*

obligates] *preceded by x'd out* decides to obl

after that] *interlined above cancelled* then

were binding] were *interlined above cancelled* was

235 origin] *interlined above cancelled* date

These three] *preceded by x'd out* Our

we have] *preceded by x'd out* there is

in everything] *followed by x'd out* N.B. The actual making of vows is

and solemn] *preceded by x'd out* the actual making

236 We take] *preceded by x'd out* When we vow obedien

promising] *followed by x'd out* to keep stabi

making of] *followed by x'd out* the vow of obedience

explicit] *altered from* explicitly *by x'ing out*

Ritual] *followed by x'd out* there was

See *Usages* #34 . . . property.] *added on line*

236–37 N.B. also, . . . one signs.] *opposite page*

236 novice makes] *preceded by cancelled* simple profes

237 a formal] *preceded by cancelled* an

Rule alone.] *preceded by x'd out* Laws

profession, just] *preceded by cancelled* the full

taking of vows.] *followed by x'd out* OBEDIENCE *followed by cancelled* (new page—obedience

I.] *typed in left margin before x'd out* a)

a stable] *preceded by x'd out* to embrace

238 Obedience takes . . . travel around.] *opposite page*

239 58] *altered from* 59

240   He is clinging to self-love.] *added on line*
        what God wants,] *preceded by x'd out* something
        a) Submission . . . name] *interlined*
241   If a Protestant . . . of it.] *interlined*
        our destiny.] *followed by x'd out* NOTE—a source of
             confusion arises from the fa
        AUTONOMOUS.] *followed by x'd out* But
        and the community.] *preceded by x'd out* to
        must make] *preceded by x'd out* am
        rightly and] *preceded by x'd out* and
242   not one] *preceded by x'd out* one
        chosen, this] *followed by x'd out* remains indifferent
        disobedience is] *interlined below and marked for insertion*
        to *miss*] *preceded by x'd out* a
243   proper to] *preceded by x'd out* fitting
246   *of another.*] *followed by x'd out* Thus In an extreme
        experiments] *followed by x'd out* with
        inmost,] *preceded by x'd out* reality
247   finality outside] *followed by x'd out* him
        thing, then] *followed by x'd out* in
249   mere human] *preceded by x'd out* our own
250   hearts, our] *followed by cancelled* If a person can love
             God in a
        enlivened] *interlined above cancelled* moved
251   One who] *preceded by x'd out* A
252   OBEDIENCE:] *preceded by x'd out* THE VOW OF OBEDIENCE
        promise of obedience] *typed interlined above x'd out* vow
253   WITNESS TO THE] *followed by x'd out* GLORY
        command.] *preceded by x'd out* will
        example,] *preceded by x'd out* The
254   These are . . . from obedience.] *interlined*
        One can salve] *preceded by x'd out* It is disobedience to
255   It is presumed] *preceded by x'd out* No Superior
        OBEDIENCE] *preceded by x'd out* Our
        right order . . . divine order] *typed interlined above x'd*
             out he is a subject.

257   powerful? NO] NO *added on line*
            position? NO] NO *added on line*

258   to his commands] *followed by x'd out* and counsels
            even gravely.] *followed by x'd out* Hence by dominative
            power, the Superior can reach into the interior, and
            demand *not only the external act but also internal*
            conformity to his will. He has the right to demand
            not only that we carry out his command, but also
            specifically that *we will to carry it out*, as a matter
            of obedience. He has a right to formal obedience,
            interior, spiritual, personal and free. This does not
            imply that he has a right to demand conformity of
            our intellect, and complete *speculative* agreement
            with him. The vow of obedience does not affect
            our own opinion, as a matter of justice, only our
            will.

259   for the good] *followed by cancelled* order
            (Thus, when] *preceded by x'd out* When
            necessary] *preceded by x'd out* in
            at least] *preceded by x'd out* even a sin *against the vow.*

260   forbidden] *preceded by x'd out* contrary
            If in such] *preceded by x'd out* in
            for instance, . . . brother)] *opposite page*

261   necessarily] *preceded by cancelled* always
            The subject] *preceded by cancelled* but in [   ] they might.
            N.B. the subject] *preceded by uncancelled* 6)

262   see how] *followed by x'd out* this

263   see things] *preceded by x'd out* will
            A] *added in left margin*
            when we sin . . . double sin.] *added on line*

264   1] *added in left margin*
            expresses] *preceded by x'd out* intends
            under holy] *preceded by x'd out* in virtue of
            your vow] *preceded by x'd out* of obedience"
            (Interior] *(added*
            obedience.)]) *added*

2) *Flight*] *interlined above cancelled* 3

involve] *preceded by x'd out* are

3] *added in left margin before cancelled* 4

4] *added in left margin before cancelled* 5

265   consequence.] *followed by x'd out* The sins are usual

(Distinguish . . . life.)] *added on line*

266   neglected.] *followed by x'd out* 4- attempts to

manipulate authority—"doing one's own will with

permission"

{4}] 5 *in text followed by x'd out* Staying out of the way

of commands

{5}] 6 *in text*

{6}] 7 *in text*

resistance.] *followed by x'd out* (as long as these are not

expressed.

{7}] 8 *in text*

One may lose . . . through] *interlined above cancelled*

From

267   particular case.] *followed by x'd out* Strict

various aids] *preceded by x'd out* most necessary [   ]

aids in

268   conviction . . . merciful to us.] *opposite page*

270   try to enter] *preceded by x'd out* pay

Learn to] *followed by x'd out* present

It makes . . . stupid.] *added on line*

271   or someone,] *followed by x'd out* later

get the right] *preceded by x'd out* learn whether he was

had sufficient reas

This does not . . . *servility.*] *added on line*

Servility is not . . . entirely exterior.] *opposite page*

consists in] *followed by x'd out* them

275   one's habits] *followed by x'd out* and thought

does not seem to be] *added in left margin and marked for

insertion to replace cancelled* cannot *and uncancelled* be

habitual neglect] *preceded by x'd out* neglect

277   matter is not] *preceded by x'd out* reason

evident.] *preceded by x'd out* accept

278 misleading] *interlined above cancelled completely wrong*

faithful to] *preceded by x'd out* making

281 under three] *preceded by x'd out* Delatte

à la vie] à *typed interlined*

282 but the explanations] *preceded by x'd out* his explanations
tend to confuse and obscu

poverty . . . virtues] *added on line*

n.b. . . . rigidly] *added in left margin*

in what way] *interlined above cancelled* whether

284 a more direct] *preceded by x'd out* intense

detachment from] *followed by x'd out* business

is putting] *preceded by x'd out* and to

285 serious] *typed interlined above and marked for insertion*

work, then] *followed by x'd out* he has no further
responsibility

worthy] *preceded by x'd out* priest

excessive] *followed by x'd out* at

286 much reading] *preceded by x'd out* a stud

To seek] *followed by x'd out* to

to avoid . . . work] *added in left margin and marked for
insertion*

all] *interlined with a caret*

probably] *added in left margin and marked for insertion to
replace cancelled* certainly

serious] *typed interlined below to replace x'd out* mortal

with all . . . rich man] *interlined with a caret*

without any] *followed by x'd out* manual

at all] *added in lower margin and marked for insertion*

manners.] *followed by cancelled* 2- *Common life and
Labor*—One keeps his vow of conversion of manners by taking his part generously in the common
life and in laboring to support the monastery—see
above, p 107 ff—this will be treated in detail under
the special heading of *poverty.*

2] *added in left margin before cancelled* 3

The following . . . vow:] added on line
(a)] *added in left margin*
choir without] *preceded by x'd out* the
(b)] *added in left margin*
without excuse] *interlined with a caret*
(c)] *added in left margin*
287   do not constitute] *preceded by x'd out* is not a
at what point] *preceded by x'd out* to what extent does
he sin by fail
matter of sin?] *followed by x'd out* The monk sins when he
OF MANNERS.] *followed by x'd out* In such a case there
are not two sins (one against poverty and one
against conversion of manners) for the vow is one.
The obligation to poverty comes under the vow of
conversion of manners, and this is what is violated.
There can however be a double sin, against poverty the vow of conversion of manners and against
a virtue or divine precept when one sins against
chastity (one sin against the 6th commandment, another sin of sacrilege, violation of the vow.)
sufficient matter] *preceded by x'd out* not
288   make known] *preceded by x'd out* say he
enclosure] *typed in left margin*
silence] *typed in left margin*
and without his] *preceded by x'd out* This applies also to
289   can declare] *followed by x'd out* that
violations of silence] *followed by x'd out* in order
290   we speak here only of] *interlined below and marked for
insertion*
inordinate] *added in left margin and marked for insertion*
far] *interlined with a caret*
especially if] *added in left margin and marked for insertion*
and continual] *interlined with a caret*
could] *interlined above cancelled* would
(venial).] *followed by* This is only an opinion *added on
line and cancelled*
would be] *followed by x'd out* so.

and would . . . contempt.] *added on line*
one reached] *followed by x'd out* some
291 discussed above] *followed by x'd out* when
could] *altered from* would
burdens] *followed by x'd out* in
The Monastic] *preceded by interlined and cancelled*
  Abandoning
considerable] *preceded by x'd out* some
We can . . . doubt.] *interlined*
292 bring with] *preceded by x'd out* are
unlawfully] *preceded by x'd out* leaves
with the intention] *preceded by x'd out* without the
  intention of
or formal] *followed by x'd out* desertion
293 bound for life.] *followed by cancelled* This question is left
  open—we do not attempt to decide whether a
  simple professed who leaves the monastery for
  good without authorization commits a mortal sin
  or only a venial sin. We think it more probably
  mortal.
or solemn] *preceded by x'd out* professed who take
in our opinion] *followed by x'd out* but not both
from religion.] *followed by cancelled* (Hard to imagine
  how such an act would not imply flight).
SUMMARY] *interlined above cancelled* RESUME
294 These are . . . cases.] *added on line to replace cancelled*
  The above are all certain, and there is no dispute
  about them. Clear cut cases of violation of the vow.
or when . . . observance.] *added on line*
or when . . . of vocation.] *added on line*
varying degrees] *preceded by cancelled* neglect
neglect] *interlined below cancelled* misuse
voluntary] *added in left margin*
295 3. Note . . . and scandal.] *added at bottom of page to*
  replace cancelled THE SPIRIT OF THE VOW OF
  CONVERSION OF MANNERS
habitually] *interlined with a caret*

in keeping] *preceded by cancelled* of the

necessarily] *interlined with a caret*

and scandal] *followed by cancelled* contempt for

be even] *preceded by x'd out* not

empty and sterile;] *preceded by x'd out* highly unstati

296   What is meant] *preceded by x'd out* without

297   element of the] *followed by x'd out* vow is then

creature] *interlined with a caret above cancelled* being

298   Hence St. Benedict . . . etc., etc.] *opposite page*

301   possession of him] him *added in left margin and marked*
        for insertion to replace cancelled them.

302   fundamental] *followed by x'd out* poit of

305   *nihil . . . praeponere*] *added on line*

confiteri] *followed by cancelled* non velle dici sanctum etc.

(g) works . . . etc.] *opposite page*

306   like them are] are *interlined above cancelled* and

309   23] *preceded by x'd out* 14

311   the principal] *followed by x'd out* fields

312   tied up with the] *followed by x'd out* vow of conversion
        of manners

sometimes it is] *preceded by x'd out* conceive chastity
        sometimes today

implicit in] *preceded by x'd out* contained

313   carnal love] *preceded by x'd out* love of

Virgo . . . (Tertullian)] *interlined above and marked for*
        insertion

314   annul his] *followed by x'd out* vows

315   mission of] *preceded by x'd out* des[t]iny of

319   meaning of] *preceded by x'd out* will

320   preparation and] *preceded by x'd out* prefiguring

321   "in the resurrection"?] *preceded by x'd out* in heaven?

324   virtuous] *followed by x'd out* acts

324–25   and even . . . human way] *added on line*

325   *informs*] *preceded by x'd out* is

326   instinctive] *preceded by x'd out* instinctual

I discover] *preceded by cancelled* Vis cog. applies its
        lights again and

328   Intemperance is] *followed by x'd out* selfish

329   perfected by] *followed by x'd out* Christian virginity
        rationem appetitum] *preceded by x'd out naturam*

330   2-3)] *preceded by x'd out* 3-4).
        art. 3] *preceded by x'd out* ad
        And this . . . *life* (ad. 3).] *added in lower margin*

331   a. 1] 1 *preceded by x'd out* 2
        (II-II, q. 142, a. 2–4)] *added on line*

332   replies to] *preceded by x'd out* says: "
        are to be cherished] *preceded by x'd out* and t
        Hence temperance, . . . for maturity.] *added on line*

333   formal and deliberate] *preceded by x'd out* sins

334   complete act] *followed by x'd out* directly
        151] *preceded by x'd out* 141

335   so difficult] *followed by x'd out* to control when
        passion and] *followed by cancelled* intense
        (not just . . . instinct)] *added on line*
        (true human love)] *interlined below*

336   *corporalibus* . . . implied] *interlined*
        deliberate] *added in right margin and marked for insertion*
        outside of the limits] *preceded by cancelled* whether
          properly used or not

337   a mechanical act] *preceded by x'd out* an act that
        not the . . . *distillatio*] *interlined below and marked for*
          insertion
        a definition of terms] *added on line*
        forms of pleasure.] *followed by cancelled* Especially since
          as religious we are involved generally in interior
          and mental temptations more than anything else.
        In what does . . . forms of pleasure] *added on line*
        venereal and not] *added on line*

338   nor is it . . . is necessary.] *added on line*
        and not lose . . . violence] *added on line*
        the sixth] *followed by x'd out* commandment
        (clothed)] *interlined with a caret*
        their faces,] *preceded by x'd out* figures, t

339   Men of habitually . . . importance.] *opposite page*

Such affection] *preceded by x'd out* It should be
venial or . . . involved)] *added on line*
manner. This] This *added in left margin before cancelled* It
340   in ease,] *preceded by x'd out* and
But sensuality] But *interlined with a caret*
definite and] *followed by x'd out* careful, and not go
     beyond strict necessity.
in "the world."] *followed by x'd out* Guard
Sexuality:] *followed by x'd out* The above
emission] *preceded by x'd out* production
of seed.] *followed by cancelled* Note there is a real
     distinction between the ordinary sense pleasure
     felt by these organs, as by all other parts of the
     body, as a result of pleasant sensations touching
     the skin. This is not venereal pleasure in itself,
     because it does not in itself involve the excitation
     of the members. *followed by x'd out* Only when ex-
     citation begins does the pleasure become venereal.
     followed by cancelled But of course it easily becomes
     venereal.
principle] *preceded by x'd out* Note 2
outside of] *preceded by x'd out* in a
When such . . . no fault.] *interlined*
Venereal acts:] *preceded by x'd out* when is there a
340–41   a venereal act] *followed by x'd out* whether
341   willful desires for] *added in left margin and marked for*
     insertion to replace cancelled thoughts of
or for] for *written over* of
nevertheless] *followed by x'd out* sensual,
deliberate] *added on line*
most "dangerous" . . . venereal pleasure] *opposite page*
deliberately] *typed interlined below*
actually] *interlined with a caret*
deliberately] *interlined with a caret*
(sexual or sensual)] *added on line*
this is a . . . deliberate act] *opposite page*
even] *added in left margin*

act] *interlined above to replace cancelled* pleasure

342 semi-deliberate] *added in left margin and marked for insertion*

pleasure, etc.] *followed by x'd out* Acts of sensuality which, const carried out with another, are a clear invitation to sexual union (touches, passionate kissing)

v.g., in a . . . sin)] *added in left margin to replace cancelled* (Note, where consent to the pleasure is withheld, there is venial sin. But if the pleasure is fully accepted and consented to, the sin would become mortal).

feel venereal pleasure] *added in left margin to replace cancelled* even to suffer an accidental pollution.

withheld] *preceded by x'd out* from

to danger.] *followed by cancelled* However, even is such a case, where there might be carelessness, the sin would not generally be more than venial, unless the danger were clearly foreseen and deliberately ignored without reason. In such a case the ven. pleasure would almost certainly be sought for its own sake.

sin at all] *followed by cancelled* To enjoy the beauty of

about it] it *altered from* its *followed by cancelled* beauty

accept and] *added in left margin and marked for insertion*

343 uselessly,] *preceded by cancelled* (even without

at all times . . . unavoidable.] *added on line*

accidental] *added in left margin and marked for insertion*

But note: . . . involuntary.] *interlined*

and a desire] *preceded by x'd out* But a health

in our own] *preceded by x'd out* the case

maintained] *followed by x'd out* and

344 indulgence.] *preceded by x'd out* acts

346 pleasure arising from] *added in left margin and marked for insertion*

thought is] *followed by x'd out* sexual and invol

pure souls.] *followed by cancelled* Since it is presupposed that one will not enter the monastery at all
without having first learned to avoid mortal sins
of unchastity, actual problems of sin will be for-
tunately rare in the monastery. But in such cases,
if they occur, the usual method of fighting temptation and sin are to be taken. especially prayer,
self-discipline, obedience, docility to a director,
humility and above all *love of Jesus in the Blessed
Sacrament and love of the Most Blessed Virgin Mary.*
will be more] *preceded by x'd out* must
in two] *preceded by x'd out* who

347   to regard] *followed by x'd out* in
even though] *preceded by x'd out* between
Why?] *followed by cancelled* a)
exclusive,] *followed by x'd out* and
emotional realm.] *followed by x'd out* One feels pretty
much the

348   to be enjoyed] *followed by x'd out* b)
(In a genuine] *preceded by x'd out* compulsive
sometimes] *preceded by x'd out* can
Particular Friendships and] *preceded by x'd out* The
Danger of part

350   even under . . . others, etc.] *added on line*
seek out] *preceded by x'd out* in
chosen for us] *preceded by x'd out* we have been

351   Much of . . . our flesh.] *opposite page*
not seek] *followed by x'd out* and

352   All this . . . of heart.] *added in lower margin*

353   the long run] *preceded by x'd out* effect
bad effects,] *preceded by cancelled* very
to lay] *followed by x'd out* and
hints] *preceded by x'd out* aids

354   temptation.] *followed by x'd out* Also
This is . . . anyone.] *added on line*
Fasting as an] *preceded by x'd out* The notion of fasting

When candy] *preceded by x'd out* Excessive

355 St. Benedict . . . sparingly.] *added on line*

The *Rule* says] *preceded by x'd out* Some

in summer] *followed by x'd out* and cause more
difficulty than

heavily clad.] *followed by x'd out* In general—one
should live in such a way as to be normally
unconscious of

356 undergoing temptation] *followed by x'd out* that

357 First . . . self-control] *interlined*

dispositions for] *followed by cancelled* the

{pay}] pray *in typescript*

358 and minor] *preceded by x'd out* are

359 going to turn] *preceded by x'd out* for all that

so are obedience] are *interlined above cancelled* is

360 exterior and] *followed by x'd out* practical one

at least where] *preceded by x'd out* in

361 that gratify] *preceded by x'd out* of gratif

Read St. John . . . 55).] *added in lower margin*

362 affected by] *followed by x'd out* the

in the monastery] *interlined with a caret*

something good] *followed by x'd out* in

harmless] *interlined above*

not merely] *preceded by x'd out* above all

things which] *preceded by x'd out* everything that ten

363 verbal gratification] *preceded by x'd out* verbal
seduction"

have long] *followed by x'd out* pleasant

364 attentions to self] *followed by x'd out* in washing,
medical care

365 two of the] *preceded by x'd out* one of the

keeps him in a] *followed by x'd out* constant state of

369 (cf. Freud)] *added on line*

371 SELFISH AND CARELESS . . . faculty] *interlined above
cancelled* This

372 The pure man] *added in left margin before cancelled* He

373   continually, to] *followed by x'd out* turn
375   *Cantica*] *followed by uncancelled* p
377   then sing] *preceded by cancelled* receiving all there,
378   *appetant*] *followed by x'd out* humility and other
379   holy veil] *preceded by x'd out* veil
380   St. Thomas . . . misleading.] *interlined*
381   department or] *followed by x'd out* change
382   Dom Delatte,] *preceded by x'd out* Dom G. Morin says,
            in the *Ideal of the Monastic* Life
        the love of] *preceded by x'd out* material
383   Possession . . . of Christ.] *interlined*
385   59] *preceded by x'd out* 29
386   wants total] *preceded by x'd out* presupposes
        or dispose of] *interlined above and marked for insertion*
        internal goods] *added on line*
        academic . . . rights] *added on line*
        Some say . . . St. Benedict.] *added in left margin and*
            marked for insertion
387   The term . . . vow.] *opposite page*
        though this . . . under obedience.] *opposite page*
        sinful] *added on line before cancelled* dangerous
        This applies . . . initiative.] *added on line*
388   encumbered] *interlined above and marked for insertion to*
            replace cancelled forfeited
        encumbrance] *interlined below cancelled* forfeit
        not more . . . property] *added on line*
        but *can* . . . medical)] *added in lower margin*
        entering. Novices] Novices *typed in left margin before*
            x'd out They
389   legacies, etc.] *followed by* Small sums may be spent for
            masses etc. *added on line and cancelled*
        or small] *preceded by x'd out* but
        his capital.] *followed by x'd out* Should not spent them,
            except a provided in 4 above.
        Canon 568] *added on line*
        on investment] *followed by cancelled* or other revenues.
        Rule, c. 54] 54 *added on line*

390 (c. 54)] 54 *added on line*
391 doubtfully] *added in left margin to replace cancelled* Not
      and/or] /or *interlined*
      occupied] *preceded by x'd out* concerned
392 definition] *preceded by x'd out* distinct
393 To administer . . . do so.] *opposite page*
      WITH DUE] *preceded by x'd out* EXCEPT IN SO FAR
      unless . . . perpetual vows.] *opposite page*
394 few] *interlined above cancelled* simple
      This is done] *preceded by x'd out* At what time does one
         make the
      Note: all . . . the will.] *added on line*
395 If an outside . . . incompetent.] *added on line*
      N.B. . . . administrator.] *opposite page*
      unless one's . . . poor.] *added on line*
396 *formal "cession" of goods*] *added on line after cancelled* will
      should] *interlined above cancelled* is obligated to
      formal . . . his goods] *interlined above cancelled* a will
      The will is . . . made usually.] *opposite page to replace*
         cancelled If he is under the age at which a will can
         be made legally according to civil law, the will
         must be drawn up anyway (it is valid according to
         Canon Law) and it must be *ratified* when he comes
         of age civilly. (Probable).
      institutes] *preceded by cancelled* orders
      cession of goods] *added in left margin to replace typed*
         interlined and cancelled will
      should be made by] *typed interlined above x'd out*
         obligation binds
      disposition of goods] *interlined above cancelled* will
      reason] *followed by x'd out* must
      not] *typed interlined*
      make this] *followed by cancelled* will
      "This cession] *preceded by x'd out* 4- But if the will is
         to be *changed*, after profession, the simple pro-
         fessed needs the permission of the Holy See.
397 *gifts* taken] *preceded by x'd out small*
      change his] *preceded by x'd out* give a

398 material] *preceded by x'd out* page
  simple vow] *preceded by x'd out* vow of pover
  the simple professed . . . does not] *added on line*
  without permission] *typed interlined*
  for himself] *interlined below and marked for insertion*
  and must] *interlined below and marked for insertion*
  new property] *followed by cancelled* but not by direct acts
   of proprietorship
  (patrimony)] *added in left margin and marked for insertion*
  (He would] *preceded by x'd out* 4-
399 *and gifts*] *added on line*
400 for no stipend] *added in left margin before cancelled* gratis
  simple professed] *interlined with a caret*
  his capital] *followed by x'd out* which
  and if he] *preceded by x'd out* if he was
  anything of] *preceded by x'd out* what
  kind] *preceded by x'd out* time
401 *of friendship*] *followed by x'd out* are to
  Distinction must . . . notable case.] *opposite page to*
   replace cancelled If received—at least presumed
   permission of Supr is required. And if received, the
   gift is added to the account of the professed unless
   he receives permission to spend it.
  receive and] *interlined above and marked for insertion*
  the general] *preceded by x'd out* would not in practice
   accord with the spirit of our Order unless there
   were a grave cause, and then permission of the
   Abbot would be required.
402 Customs determine] *preceded by x'd out* To appropriate
  an outsider] *preceded by x'd out* another
  Stealing is . . . of poverty.] *interlined*
  thoughtlessness] ness *interlined with a caret*
  In reality . . . justified.] *added on line*
  bad habit] *preceded by cancelled* very
402–403 *Hiding* things . . . no sin.] *opposite page*
403 borrowings] *interlined below cancelled* things
  to the proper person.] *added on line*

(4)] *added in left margin*
temporary] *preceded by x'd out* a
(5)] *added in left margin*
404   (6)] *added in left margin*
tell us of] *followed by x'd out* men
but charity . . . else] *added on line*
taken for granted.] *preceded by x'd out* assumed
(7)] *added in left margin*
or saleable] *preceded by x'd out* or even composed
    under obed. (with reaso
407   Note: Canon . . . violation of poverty.] *opposite page*
408   causing] *preceded by x'd out* doing se
be much more] *preceded by x'd out* would exceed a sum
    that would the amount of sum equal to
409   (under simple vows)] *typed interlined*
{7}] 6 *in typescript*
{8}] 7 *in typescript*
Restitution: . . . benefits.] *opposite page*
out of] *preceded by cancelled* of
410   It is] *preceded by cancelled* Note
in a certain sense] *interlined with a caret*
kept alive] *preceded by x'd out* point
poverty. Thus] *followed by x'd out* one
411   when religious] when *interlined with a caret above*
    cancelled for
big plantation] big *interlined with a caret*
for a large . . . less.)] *added on line*
412   cellarer] *preceded by x'd out* Superior
Here are . . . principles:] *interlined*
(1)] *added in left margin*
we are not . . . money] *added on line*
(2)] *added in left margin*
over them,] *followed by x'd out* the
teaches that] *followed by x'd out* even
413   Gospel ideal.] *followed by x'd out* There
413–14 If it were . . . set by Christ.] *opposite page*
414   is based] *preceded by x'd out* thrives

possessions' sake,] *preceded by x'd out* its own sake
will be rewarded] *preceded by x'd out* are rich
415   when it becomes] *preceded by x'd out* is a form
       2] *added in left margin*
       3] *added in left margin*
416   4] *added in left margin*
       begins to say that he] *added in left margin and marked for
          insertion*
       anxiety] *preceded by x'd out* fear
417   almost all] *preceded by x'd out* not onl
       In this country, . . . necessities.] *added on line*
       within the limits] *preceded by x'd out* when
418   acquiring inordinate] inordinate *interlined with a caret*
419   and He pays . . . avenger.] *added on line*
       social underworld] *preceded by x'd out* world
       impurity.] *followed by x'd out* Covet anything—not just
          wife.
       Deuteronomy] *interlined above cancelled* Leviticus
420   abolished in it.] *followed by cancelled* (cf early Church
          esp READ Acts 2:44-47.)
421   to the race] *followed by x'd out* whom
422   Deuteronomy 15:7-11] *preceded by x'd out* Exodus 15:
423   extortioner] *followed by cancelled* (Apply to monasteries
          that are inordinately wealthy)
427   Other examples] *followed by x'd out* The ju
       N.B. this . . . Sacraments] *added on line*
428   33:1] *followed by x'd out* 0
429   Matthew 11:] *followed by x'd out* 6-
431   He has to] *preceded by x'd out* a lawyer
432   life and death.] *followed by x'd out* but not for them.)
       grace, since] *preceded by x'd out* accepted
433   cf. Isaac . . . 1841).] *opposite page*
434   21] *interlined above cancelled* 29
       sustenance] *followed by x'd out* in
435   outside the Church] *preceded by x'd out* of other
439   quilts] *preceded by x'd out* especially
442   unusually painful] *preceded by x'd out* grave,

all this is] *preceded by x'd out* I Personal Poverty.

443 in his monastery] *typed interlined*

445 factually,] *preceded by x'd out* realist

one superior is] *preceded by x'd out* a Superior

habitually from him.] *followed by x'd out* Better and
more secure spiritually to ask permission of the
one whose authority is higher and whose ways are
more strict. Supposing these two don't coincide,
at least learn to face the one who is likely to refuse
you rather than habitually go to the one who you
think. In a word, go to the one who, in the situation, is most likely to represe clearly the representation of God.

minor permissions] *followed by x'd out* only

447 one of St. Benedict's] *preceded by x'd out* an innovation
and hermits.] *added on line*

The cenobites] *added in left margin before cancelled* who

449 We must . . . our day.] *added on line*

to fail as] *preceded by x'd out* the

450 this wandering] *preceded by x'd out* it is taken for granted

It is clear] *preceded by x'd out* We

aspire to] *preceded by x'd out* become a hermit

omnia] *typed interlined*

451 assumed in] *preceded by x'd out* taken

an integral part] *interlined above cancelled* essential to

as he conceives] *preceded by x'd out* Without it one
cannot be a true monk, or at least one seriously
risks his vocation (Saints who have been saints in
the monastic life without this vow nevertheless
possessed the virtue in some degr in their hearts,
without the vow

452 He should . . . place.] *added in lower margin*

but dwelling] *preceded by x'd out* or communi

except in] *preceded by x'd out* for

452–53 agree that] *followed by x'd out* stability is in the first place

453 Note,] *preceded by x'd out* It

61] *typed interlined above x'd out* 58

454   It is clearly . . . erected.] *opposite page*
           named in] *preceded by cancelled* stated
455   actually fulfills] *preceded by x'd out* thus
           subtle] *preceded by x'd out* in the
456   unsettled] *preceded by x'd out* actually
           and justifying] *preceded by x'd out* under the
           Very positive] *preceded by x'd out* Before making
           approval] *preceded by x'd out* of a
           forget about] *followed by x'd out* it
           whole thing] *followed by x'd out* as long
           clearly *asked*] *preceded by x'd out* more or less
           by superiors . . . Chapter] *interlined with a caret*
457   All is . . . *sought*)] *added on line*
           in our Order] *typed interlined*
           He would have] *preceded by x'd out* However, if he felt
458   of undergoing] *preceded by x'd out* and the
           real hope] *preceded by x'd out* basis
458–59   The vow of stability . . . as good.] *opposite page*
459   The other vows] *preceded by cancelled* Now
           clear] *altered from* clearly *followed by cancelled* proved,
               by a director
           in them] *followed by x'd out* only
           (see . . . Thierry)] *interlined*
           One can] *preceded by x'd out* When is it right to seek a
               change of
           has reason to believe] *interlined below cancelled* has
               been told definitely
           However, if one . . . no sin.] *added in left margin*
459–60   The one who . . . character.] *added in left margin and
               marked for insertion*
460   It is . . . recommended.] *added on line*
           than the Cistercian.] *followed by cancelled* But we have
               to accept the practical outlook of the Church,
               which regards the Carthusians as "higher". In the
               old legislation it was licit for *anyone* to go to the
               Carthusians as to a higher life.
           state explicitly] *followed by x'd out* what that one

should pass to a higher life in a

but does not . . . another.] *added on line before cancelled*
    And from a contemplative order to a more
    contemplative Order.

in the mind] *preceded by x'd out* that

another order] *added in left margin and marked for
    insertion to replace cancelled* an Order like the Car-
    thusians. It may be not only licit, but if the director
    is convinced that he has this other vocation, then
    the monk is bound to follow the director's advice.
    followed by x'd out If it is *followed by cancelled* He
    should make application, and then if the applica-
    tion is rejected he can be satisfied that he has not
    disobeyed the divine will.

However, even . . . danger!!] *opposite page*

461   lacking *some*] *preceded by x'd out* without

life there] *followed by cancelled* for instance, a genuinely
    needed element of solitude

Often some . . . sought.] *interlined*

combine the] *preceded by x'd out* are

Very often . . . danger.] *added in lower margin*

462   lack of] *preceded by x'd out* consent.

reason would] would *typed in left margin before x'd
    out might*

463   *against* one's conscience] *interlined with a caret above
        cancelled* and in cases where the director has indi-
        cated that such things are temptations

and is dangerous for the vow] *added on line*

as a virtue.] *followed by uncancelled* (Copy here Stoic
    texts on Stability see p. 208a)

Stoic writer,] *preceded by cancelled* great

casting about] about *interlined with a caret*

464   bring forth] *preceded by x'd out* bear fort

465   important] *interlined above cancelled* last

To protect] *preceded by x'd out* To protect this spirit and
    to protect the monk against his own restlessness,
    St Benedict introduces the vow.

466   takes up] up *interlined with a caret*
         worthwhile] *preceded by cancelled* is it
         (conversio morum)] *interlined with a caret*
         relaxed] *interlined with a caret*
467   (Hence in . . . monastery.)] *added on line*
         natural restlessness] *interlined with a caret above*
             cancelled instability
         monastery] *interlined below*
         St. Thierry] *followed by uncancelled* (quis?) *added on line*
         settle his] *preceded by x'd out* find
468   It takes . . . "roots"] *added on line*
         Domini nec] nec *interlined with a caret*
         cultivate] *interlined with a caret*
469   nowhere?] *altered from* nowhere.
         years?] *altered from* years.
         Perseverance . . . generosity.] *added on line*
         plucked and] *interlined with a caret*
         every] *interlined with a caret*
         passerby] *altered from* passers-by
         Rule] *interlined with a caret*
469–70   This theme . . . faith."] *opposite page*
470   of their own imagination.] *added in lower margin*
         Above all, . . . vow?] *added on line*
         It will . . . "family."] *added on line*
471   real *positive*] real *interlined with a caret*
         sometimes] *added on line*
         truths] *interlined above and marked for insertion to replace*
             cancelled things
         cases] *interlined above cancelled* things
         God alone] *preceded by x'd out* But
472   The best . . . and love.] *added in lower margin*
         chief] *interlined above cancelled* great
         all his life.] *added on line*
         Cultivating love . . . goes on.] *opposite page*
         strive to] *interlined below and marked for insertion*
         not a rebellious obstruction.] *added on line*

473   that we are . . . earth] *added on line*
474   In trying . . . doubt.] *added on line*
        too common.] *added on line following cancelled* rife.
        better for] *followed by x'd out* him
        help him] *preceded by x'd out* permit him to
475   in the situation . . . brethren.] *added on line*
        toward the Order.] *followed by interlined uncancelled*
              (leave big space—to show new section)
        4] *added in left margin*
476   our own . . . clearly.] *added on line*
        planned for] *preceded by x'd out* we badly need
477   sets . . . others,] *interlined above cancelled* separates
              himself,
478   help us] *preceded by cancelled* urgently
        particularly] *interlined above cancelled* especially
        He will be guided . . . Spirit.] *added on line*
479   seemingly] *added in left margin and marked for insertion*
        Before we] *preceded by x'd out* It was
480   deep] *added in right margin and marked for insertion*
        Abbey of Gethsemani] *added in lower margin and marked
              for insertion*

Additions and Alterations Taken from Mimeograph

1-6   **AN INTRODUCTION TO** . . . V. Finale] *added*
7   In modern] In more modern
8   Communist] communist
        sense, no!] sense, no.
        God] God
9   *kind of a job*] *kind of job*
        accidental in so far] accidental as far
        The religious may lose] He loses
        ourselves] our *selves*
        orientated] *oriented*
        as *to be*] as to *be*
10   This conception . . . on life.] *added*

what man is] *what he is*
orientated] oriented
or rather for] to be more exact for
intelligence] intelligence
free will] free will
his whole moral] his moral
"Everything . . . in view."] *added*
11   *not free*] not free
in turn is] is in turn
READ] Read
18:14-22] 15:14-22
in view of . . . choose,] in view of . . . choose,
only . . . for man,] *only . . . for man,*
simply the purposeless] simply purposeless
But . . . everyone] At the same time, everyone
11–12   or even . . . at all,] *added*
12   deviation of sin comes] deviation comes
the sinner *places*] he *places*
conceived . . . in itself] *added*
apart from . . . true good.] *added*
for him] for man
if . . . by God] if . . . by God
READ] Read
beatitude is *the*] beatitude *is the*
act of man,] act of man,
13   *Beatific Vision.*] *beatific vision.*
here is used] here used
the supereminent] a supereminent
whole Christ] Whole Christ
What has been . . . moment.] *added*
14   For the pragmatist, . . . senseless.] *added*
However, even in] However, in
This fact . . . "worthwhile."] *added*
but nevertheless, . . . grace,] but nevertheless, . . . grace,
What are . . . beatitude?] What are . . . beatitude?
THE THINGS . . . FOR US] the things . . . for us
by religious vows] by religious vows

15   of the Incarnate Word,] *added*
        depend] *depends*
        which inserts] inserting
        The life of the vows fixes] And it fixes
15–16   With our . . . until death.] *added*
16   a) First he studies *the will and how it acts*] a) The will
            and how it acts
        voluntary acts] *voluntary* acts
17   involuntary] involuntarily
        good—virtues] good or virtues
        bad—vices] bad or vices
        After this we] Here we
        reorientating] reorienting
        perverting the passions] the passions
        Laws] Laws
        Then last] and last
18   our *free*] *our free*
        other human acts] *other human acts*
        man's voluntary search] man's search
        A false view] False view
        they must] must
        But the passions] But passions
        To regard . . . heretical.] *added*
        The passions are human] They are human
        in so far . . . body] *in so far . . . body*
        Our nature is inclined] Our nature—inclined
        inclination is subconscious] inclination—subconscious
        yet a passion] yet passion
19   hence, the passions,] hence, of the passions,
        mind] "mind"
        dwells mystically, moves] mystically moves
        our faculties] the faculties
        in the state . . . by God] *added*
        Holy Ghost] Holy Spirit
        William] All men have these three, but William
        the *anima*)] *anima*)
        the *animus*)] *animus*)

spontaneous attraction] spontaneous natural attraction
20   fully a child] a child
        homo spiritualis] homo spiritualis
        thus they become] become
        eyes of man] eyes of men
        Read] Read
21   *Regulation*] (External influence of demons can be
            present) *Regulation*
        will be frustrated] frustrated
        should cooperate like] like
        the relation . . . slave] *added*
22   Hence, . . . for God.] *added*
        How . . . passion?] How . . . passion?
        by spiritualization] spiritualization
        drives through] drives by
        the morality . . . passion] the morality . . . passion
22–23   all the passions] all the other passions
23   and tend . . . Glory] and tend . . . Glory
        Love] *Love*
25   Love] Love
        as an end in itself] *added*
27   It is clear] Clear
        most sublime spiritual] most spiritual
        true spiritual tradition] true tradition
28   *amor* (love)] love
31   his liberty] liberty
        Love is the beginning] Love is the beginning
        the passion of love] passion
32   *volitional*] volitional
        rational love and] rational and
        which is . . . to the good] and in this sense *we
            transform ourselves in the presence of the good*
        transformating] transforming
        Augustine and Monica] They
33   Augustine recognizes] He recognizes
        this kind of knowledge] this knowledge
34   takes place] took place

in those . . . spiritual love] *added*

35   acts of charity] *acts of charity*
infused habit] *infused habit*
HABITUS—a habit. But *habitus*] HABITUS. *Habitus*
consider the habitual] the habitual
(He is responsible] (Responsible
of the will] of will
not sinful.] not evil.
Note the] Note the

36   To understand . . . routine.] *added*
The true notion of habitus] The true notion of *habitus*
a good *"habitus"* is] It is
freedom] *freedom*
It aids] which aids

37   we enjoy growth] growth
gain command] command

38   for the growth] for growth
of our acts.] of our acts.
by the cultivation . . . virtues.] by the cultivation . . .
    virtues.
science] science
art] art
prudence, which] prudence which

39   We will consider . . . of the vows.] *added*
choice] choice
the connatural] a connatural
on the basis] in the basis
it is utterly useless] useless
This alternation] The alternation
otherwise we . . . vocation.] *added*

40   the development] development
The vows] Vows
SIN] SIN
What is sinful habit?] *added*
remove all the great] remove the great
LOVE *is missing.*] Love is missing.
rejects love,] *rejects love,*

to the disordered] to disordered
It rebels . . . self-will.] *added*
has to be] *has to be*
41   "Judge not, . . . judged."] *added*
Who plants the seed?] *Who plants the seed?*
WILL.] will
Where . . . come from?] *Where . . . come from?*
What favors . . . seed?] *What favors . . . seed?*
malforms] *malforms*
This thought . . . consecrated life.] *added*
assume] *assume*
42   (1) the corruption] The corruption
(2) the disfigurement] The disfigurement
(3) the obligation] the obligation
In resumé,] *In resumé,*
gifts of the Holy Ghost] Gifts
43   and *Grace*] *and Grace*
We will first . . . All-Holy God.] *added*
and is a fervent] *and is a fervent*
44   *What is Law?*] What is Law?
God is LOVE.] God is love.
life, is LOVE.] life, is love.
46   ethic] ethics
in their place] in the place of another
people's spheres] people's sphere
48   evolves] *evolves*
49   Church law] *Church law*
promulgation of the] promulgation of
50   *Law speaks*] *law of grace speaks*
It is a law of grace.] *added*
52   orientated] oriented
54   *religious obedience*] religious obedience
come] comes
An immature] An *immature*
through suffering] by suffering
55   *What is wrong with this outlook?*] What is wrong with
          this outlook?

on self] on the self
56 body] *body*
57 these acts)] these evil acts)
We must take] We must *take*
59 *Pieper*] Pieper
61 destructive agency] *destructive agency*
63 any right] any *right*
66 an ordinary] any ordinary
67 sin.] sins.
excess] "excess"
based on the] based on a
68 *by which we*] by which we
72 had become] became
incapable] uncapable
73 It is then, too] Then too, it is
74 and a perversion] and perversion
75 have unfelt] have the unfelt
76 is beyond] was beyond
permitted] *permitted*
corp., ad. 3)] corp and ad 3
78 all other] all the other
only that men] only men
79 attain to] come to
80 torment men] torment man
84 law and justice.] law and of justice.
entirely in Christ] entirely *in Christ*
86 which is His will] which is *His will*
is the act of faith] is in the *act of faith*
87 I may *perfect*] I *may perfect*
fully and truly] truly
89 in *any* way] *in any way*
90 into a religious community] *into a religious community*
92 whole cosmic order] *whole cosmic order*
93 open our hearts] *open our hearts*
94 permanent] *permanent*
97 our own being] our being

100   EMBRACES THE RELIGIOUS] EMBRACES THIS RELIGIOUS
        seek God is in] seek Him is in

101   yet as we know] yet we know

103   esp. v. 11] esp. 11

103–104 Luke . . . Days] Gospel Mass of Rogation Days
           Luke 11:5-13

104   prayer is the greatest] prayer the greatest

107   given to man] given by man

115   perfect] *perfect*
        who rest] *who rest*

115–16 In I-II, . . . of union.] *following Christi.*

116   What is . . . about] *What is . . . about*
        Read] READ

118   of formula] of a formula
        stands] stand

120   *Dispositively*] *Dispositive*

121   of the religious life] of a religious
        be necessary also] also be necessary

124   intellectual] *intellectual*

126   the intelligence] his intelligence

127–30 TEXTS FROM . . . (*ibid.*, ad. 3).] added

130   several] *several*

295–96 This is all . . . (Pius XII).] *marked* insert *but not present*
           in typescript

310–11 In our day . . . "is love."] *not in typescript*

315–16 The Old Testament is nowhere . . . Isaias 54).]
           replacement for The Old Testament emphasizes
           God's blessing on fecundity. At the same time,
           the fruit of original sin is that woman brings forth
           children in suffering, while man toils to extract
           a living from the unfriendly soil. The women of
           the Old Testament crave children, as a blessing
           from God. Rachel cries to Jacob: da mihi liberos.
           (Gen: 30:1) Sterility is regarded as a curse. How-
           ever, there are many exceptional cases: sterility
           which is permitted by God as a preparation for

miraculous fruitfulness, in which His power and
fidelity to His promises will be most manifest for
instance—Sarah. (Genesis 18:9-15. 21:1-3) Anna
(I Kings 1:1-17) cases like these are often types of
the Bl Mother. Continency praised in the Old Testament—in connection with marriage. cf Tobias 6
Jeremias—embraces a life of virginity but as a prophetic act, with special significance for Jerusalem.
Jeremias 16:12. By the time of Our Lord the *Essenes*
had made the Jewish people familiar with the idea
of a life of ascetic chastity. Other texts of the OT regarding sex. In the Torah there are certain exterior
prescriptions regarding the sexual act as producing
ritual uncleanness For instance Leviticus 15. Here
what is impure is the simple fact of emission of
seed, regardless of voluntary disposition or other
circumstances, the idea being the sense of "fit-
tingness". This purely exterior consideration has
remained with us and is a deep source of shame at
the mere fact of sex, irrespective of any guilt or not.
In point of fact we must remember, as Our Lord
taught, what is evil is not the physiological fact of
the emission of seed, or the mere bodily pleasure
attached to this—what is wrong is the *selfish use* of
this faculty outside and beyond the will of God in
our regard.

368   for cultivating chastity] for cultivation of chastity
      in cultivating chastity.] in cultivation of chastity.
369   They are means] They are helps
      strength of will,] strength the will,
370   moral significance] real significance
      of the biological] to the biological
371   SELFISH AND CARELESS] Selfish and careless
      lust, who] lust, the
481–90   APPENDIX . . . 1946).] *added*

Additions and Alterations Found in Typescript Only

15   acts perfectly. . . . less a] *omitted in mimeo*

20   once more "animals,"] more "animals,"

       In order . . . of reason.] In order . . . of reason.

21   *reason governs . . . collaborator*] reason governs . . .
         collaborator

22   (cf. St. Benedict, c. 7)] *added in lower margin*

       breathing] *added on line*

24   guided by the Holy Spirit] *added in left margin and*
         marked for insertion

25   *The whole . . . point."*] The whole . . . point."

       Narcissistic love . . . fulfills itself.] *opposite page*

27   *Nature of love*] *added in left margin*

28   loves] love

       Cause of love] *added in left margin*

       proportion or likeness] proportion or likeness

       Effects of love] *added in left margin followed by* Insert here
         page 8a

28–31   *the effects of love, . . . true love.*] The effects of love are
         physical and moral union, a kind of mutual in-
         dwelling, an ecstasy in which we go out of our-
         selves (not necessarily mystically, but at least
         morally) zeal for the good of the beloved (or jeal-
         ousy for our own good in the case of amor concu-
         piscentiae). Finally, the immanent activity of love
         perfects the beloved within himself and lifts him to a
         higher level.

28   let us] *preceded by cancelled* We have already seen an
         example of the effects of love.

       analysis] *followed by cancelled* however

29   Note {the} connection . . . beloved.] *added in left margin*

30   goes] *interlined with a caret*

       injures us] us *interlined with a caret*

31   fitness of the good, of] fitness of the good, or

32   *it is a*] it is a

       transformation] transformation

34   ecstatic character of love] *added on line*
no need] not need

35   *merely automatic function*] merely automatic function

38–39   The intellectual . . . infused.] *omitted*

39   *good habits*] good *interlined with a caret*

53   and to his perfect justice.] *added*

56   *orient . . . the good.*] orient . . . the good.

58   *social being*] social being

59   *The values . . . change them.*] The values. . . change
them.

61   *is really . . . himself"*] is really . . . himself"

62   VOLUNTAS] *omitted*

67   *true . . . of God.*] true . . . of God.

84   It is the *life of the Church.*] *added on line*

85   *cannot be . . . love God.*] cannot be . . . love God.

87   whom He sends"] who He sends"

88   For St. Maximus] For Maximus

90   seeking His glory] seeing His glory

94   *in Him . . . His Spirit.*] in Him . . . His Spirit.

98   *Mediator Dei*] Mediator

99   of his deepest] to his deepest

115   (read)] *added in left margin*

117   perfects it] perfects
offerentes] *offerente*

119   text 2] *added in left margin*

120   text 3] *added in left margin*
text 7] *added in left margin*

122   (II-II, q. 188, a. 3)] *added on line*

124   *The contemplative life*] *omitted*

133   of the monastery,] *followed by cancelled* in contact with
the world,

152   (1) renunciation . . . by vow.] *added on line*

153   *unchanging*] unchanging
We wear . . . Bernard!] *added on line*

164   simony.] *followed by interlined and cancelled* (But it is not
simony even then.)

	is not just . . . ground.] is not just . . . ground.
166	*the response. . . freedom*] the response . . . freedom
168	All this . . . disciplined.] *added in lower margin*
205	When one . . . vocation.] *opposite page*
	one's job] *preceded by cancelled* such
243	*in order . . . willed by God,*] in order willed by God,
247	N.B. the case . . . of obedience.] *opposite page*
248	Note the danger . . . and rules.] *opposite page*
	God is] *followed by cancelled* our
	supernatural . . . subjection.] *interlined*
249	Obedience is also . . . and motives.] *opposite page*
	By obeying] *interlined with a caret above cancelled* In doing this
251	*manipulating superiors*] manipulating superiors
252	*The Right Approach*] The Right Approach
	sharply distinguish . . . subjection;] sharply distinguish . . . subjection;
	a response] a response
	a call . . . mercy;] a call . . . mercy;
	an act of . . . from God.] an act of . . . from God.
	It is a restoration . . . by sin;] It is a restoration . . . by sin;
	obedience to . . . glorify God.] obedience to . . . glorify God.
	Everything that . . . to God] Everything that . . . to God
257	cf. . . . ship] *interlined*
274	(reading *not* advised)] *added on line*
280	studying . . . procedure] *interlined*
	moribus . . . saeculi] *moribus . . . saeculi*
	et sanguinitati corporali], *et sanguinitati corporali,*
	VERACITER . . . ALTERUM] *VERACITER . . . ALTERUM*
281	vitae . . . substantialia] *vitae . . . substantialia*
	corporales . . . regulam] *corporales . . . regulam*
283	*A supine . . . vow*] A supine . . . vow
	concrete . . . vices.] concrete . . . vices.
	But rules . . . used] *added on line*
289	*which are . . . obedience*] which are . . . obedience

290   *Habitual . . . of taste*] Habitual . . . of taste
315   2:24] *interlined with a caret*
      the aprons . . . *fall.*] *added in lower margin*
332   an infantile sin] *interlined above cancelled* a sign of
         infantilism.
339   Special care . . . monastery.] *opposite page*
      Note the special . . . *religious.*] *opposite page followed by*
         cancelled It is a
      if it is] *preceded by cancelled* in a reli
347   provided . . . "attachments."] *added on line*
363   n.b. cold drinks] *added in left margin*
      especially . . . comes in] *added on line*
387   *Works of art . . .* obedience.] *opposite page*
440   This is important . . . narrow at all.] *opposite page*
446   Dependence . . . trust.] *added on line*
450   n.b. comment . . . chapter] *added in upper margin and*
         marked for insertion
      claustra . . . .congregatione] *claustra . . . congregatione*
455   from the desire] from *altered from* for
473   also . . . of faith] *added on line*

APPENDIX B

Table of Correspondences:

The Life of the Vows—Lectures and Taped Conferences

Date	Page #	Opening Words	TMC CD #	Published Tape Title & #
4/27/62	280	*Paul the Deacon*	1-1	
5/4/62	—		1-4	Quest for the Grail & Conversion of Manners (AA3403)
5/8/62	284	(3) In means in general	2-1	
5/14/62	283	4. *A supine acceptance*	2-4	
5/17/62	294	4. There may be	3-4	
5/21/62	295	THE SPIRIT OF	4-2	
[5/24/62]	—		4-4	
5/28/62	—		6-2	Religious Meaning of Chastity (AA2129)
6/1/62	312	If sometimes it is possible	6-4	
6/4/62	318	New Testament texts	7-2	
6/7/62	320	*The blessing of the little*	7-4	Uses of Chastity (AA2131)
6/15/62	326	*Reason* governs passion	8-4	
6/19/62	327	Virtues (*virtus—habitus*)	9-1	Virtue of Temperance (AA3401)
[6/26/62]	329	*St. Thomas on temperance*	9-4	Virtue of Temperance (AA3401)
[6/62]	331	*Insensibility*	10-1	Virtue of Temperance (AA3401)

Date	Page #	Opening Words	TMC CD #	Published Tape Title & #
7/4/62	334	*Chastity* (according to	10-3	
7/9/62	336	*Sins of impurity:*	11-2	
7/13/62	340	*Sexuality:*	11-4	
7/18/62	342	b) *There is no sin*	12-2	
7/26/62	346	b) *Particular Friendships:*	13-1	
7/30/62	348	{It is} possessive	14-1	
[8/4/62]	350	*True Friendship*	14-3	
[8/62]	351	c) *Other escapes*	15-2	
8/10/62	353	*Hygiene:*	15-3	
8/27/62	360	faith, hope, and love	20-1	
[9/3/62]	369	*The Spirit of Purity:*	21-3	Mystic Life (III.V.Ia)
[9/10/62]	373	Pius XII	22-3	
[9/62]	379	THE VOW OF POVERTY	25-3	Modern Cult of Efficiency (AA2101)
10/1/62	384	2. The absolute	26-2	Modern Cult of Efficiency (AA2101)
[10/8/62]	387	(Some more "cases"	27-2	
[10/15/62]	391	*The Simple Vow*	28-2	Vow of Poverty (AA2102)
[10/22/62]	394	Our *Constitutions*	29-2	
[10/29/62]	399	6. *The fruits*	30-2	Vow of Poverty (AA2102)
[11/5/62]	402	taking and keeping	31-1	Sins against Poverty (AA2103)
[11/12/62]	407	*Obligations of Poverty*	32-4	Sins against Poverty (AA2103)
[11/19/62]	409	*The Spirit and Practice*	33-4	Inner & Outer Poverty (AA2104)
[11/30/62]	438	THE PRACTICE	34-2	
[12/3/62]	411	The religious vowed	37-2	
[12/10/62]	412	*The Instinct to Possess*	34-3	Inner & Outer Poverty (AA2104)
[12/17/62]	414	1. Possession as *power:*	35-1	

Date	Page #	Opening Words	TMC CD #	Published Tape Title & #
1/7/63	—		38-1	
1/14/63	151	1. *Vows in General*	41-1	
1/29/63	155	2) *Incorporation*	41-3	
2/4/63	156	a) The religious family	43-2	
2/11/63	158	3) *Consecration*	44-1	Love Casts Out Fear (AA2134)
2/18/63	159	1. *Why are vows*	44-4	
[2/25/63]	160	2. It is necessary	46-3	
3/4/63	165	6. *The Validity*	47-1	
3/11/63	169	b) CHOICE	47-4	
4/1/63	174	d) CONSENT	50-4	
4/17/63	—		52-1	
5/8/63	384	3. In the *Rule*	54-2	
5/15/63	438	THE PRACTICE	56-1	
[5/22/63]	—		56-3	
5/29/63	441	(a) absence	58-1	
6/26/63	441	*We must accept*	59-1	Spirit of Poverty (AA2807)
7/10/63	443	*Personal Poverty*	59-2	Spirit of Poverty (AA2807)
7/24/63	443	Poverty in monastic	60-4	Poverty in Religious Experience (AA3019)
7/31/63	443	Books, music,	61-2	Poverty: Vocation to Work (AA2806)
8/14/63	—		63-2	
8/21/63	447	THE VOW OF STABILITY	63-4	
8/28/63	448	And he foresees	64-2	
9/4/63	449	*Sarabaites and*	64-4	
10/16/63	454	CONCLUSION	80-1	
10/23/63	456	a) If a monk	80-3	
11/6/63	456	2. SPECIAL OBEDIENCES	83-2	
11/27/63	457	3. HEALTH	86-2	
12/4/63	460	b) *Change*	86-3	
12/11/63	461	WHEN DOES ONE SIN	89-1	
2/5/64	237	THE VOW OF OBEDIENCE	94-4	Obedience: Means of Letting Go (AA2616)

Date	Page #	Opening Words	TMC CD #	Published Tape Title & #
2/26/64	238	Obedience is the	98-1	
3/4/64	—		98-3	
3/11/64	—		110-1	
3/18/64	239	OBEDIENCE IS THE SIGN	110-3	
3/25/64	243	ROMANS 5:17-21	110-4	
4/1/64	245	ROMANS 13:1-14	116-1	
4/15/64	249	It is a response	115-1	
4/22/64	250	III. *Wrong Approaches*	115-3	
5/13/64	252	OBEDIENCE: DEFINITION	114-3	
5/20/64	253	PROMPTITUDE	105-1	Obedience: Means of Letting Go (AA2616)
6/3/64	254	*Obedientiae speciale*	105-4	
7/1/64	257	*The Source of Authority*	119-1	
7/8/64	260	4. The superior	119-3	
7/15/64	263	A. *Sins against the Vow*:	120-2	
7/29/64	265	B. *Sins against the Virtue*:	121-3	
8/1/64	—		121-4	
8/5/64	—		122-1	
8/19/64	—		123-2	Vow of Conversion (AA2228)
8/26/64	—		124-1	Vow of Conversion (AA2228)
9/2/64	—		124-4	Conversion in Christ (AA2229)
9/16/64	—		125-3	Conversion in Christ (AA2229)
10/14/64	—		128-1	Becoming Our True Self (AA2230)
10/21/64	—		128-4	
10/28/64	—		129-2	
11/11/64	—		131-2	
11/25/64	274	l. By this vow	132-2	Conversion of Manners (AA2231)
12/2/64	279	(b) Some modern	134-2	Permanent Conversion to God (AA2231)

Date	Page #	Opening Words	TMC CD #	Published Tape Title & #
12/9/64	—		135-1	
5/3/65	—		144-3	
5/10/65	—		145-2	Patience of Conversion (AA2232)
5/17/65	296	The spirit of the vow	147-1	Patience of Conversion (AA2232)
5/31/65	—		148-1	Commitment to Conversion (AA2233)
6/21/65	311	CHASTITY and VIRGINITY	149-2	Symbol of Chastity (AA2132)
6/28/65	369	*The Spirit of Purity*:	149-4	Symbol of Chastity (AA2132)
7/5/65	—		150-2	Uses of Chastity (AA2131)
7/12/65	—		151-1	Authentic Friendship (AA2130)
7/19/65	—		151-4	
7/26/65	346	b) *Particular Friendships*	152-3	Authentic Friendship (AA2130)
8/9/65	337	b) *Distillatio*	153-2	
8/16/65	331	*Insensibility*	154-1	

- Conjectural dates are bracketed.
- Absence of page numbers indicates conference material independent of text.
- All published tapes are those issued by Credence Communications, except #21-3, issued by Electronic Paperbacks.

APPENDIX C

For Further Reading

A. Other Writings by Merton on Topics Treated in *The Life of the Vows*

Basic Principles of Monastic Spirituality. Trappist, KY: Abbey of Gethsemani, 1957.

Cistercian Contemplatives: A Guide to Trappist Life. Trappist, KY: Abbey of Gethsemani, 1948.

Contemplation in a World of Action. Garden City, NY: Doubleday, 1971.

Gethsemani: A Life of Praise. Trappist, KY: Abbey of Gethsemani, 1966.

The Monastic Journey, ed. Brother Patrick Hart. Kansas City: Sheed, Andrews & McMeel, 1977.

Monastic Life at Gethsemani. Trappist, KY: Abbey of Gethsemani, 1965.

Monastic Observances: Initiation into the Monastic Tradition 5, ed. Patrick F. O'Connell, Monastic Wisdom [MW], vol. 25. Collegeville, MN: Cistercian Publications, 2010.

Monastic Peace. Trappist, KY: Abbey of Gethsemani, 1958.

"Monastic Vows: A Memorandum," *The Merton Seasonal*, 36.2 (Summer 2011), 3–5.

The Rule of Saint Benedict: Initiation into the Monastic Tradition 4, ed. Patrick F. O'Connell, MW 19. Collegeville, MN: Cistercian Publications, 2009.

The Silent Life. New York: Farrar, Straus & Cudahy, 1957.

B. Significant Writings by Other Authors on Topics Treated in *The Life of the Vows*

Merkle, Judith A. *A Different Touch: A Study of Vows in Religious Life*. Collegeville, MN: Liturgical Press, 1998.

Roberts, Augustine, ocso. *Centered on Christ: A Guide to Monastic Profession*, third ed., MW 5. Kalamazoo, MI: Cistercian Publications, 2005.

Thurston, Bonnie Bowman. *Religious Vows, the Sermon on the Mount, and Christian Living*. Collegeville, MN: Liturgical Press, 2006.

INDEX

abandon: xviii, 38
abandonment: 97, 112, 156, 180, 214, 233, 287, 290
abbey: 235
Abbo, John A.: 222
abbot: x, lvii, lx, lxiv, 110, 114, 133, 152, 162, 171, 186, 198, 202, 217, 235, 248, 252, 257, 260, 262–63, 270–72, 288, 385, 387, 390, 394–95, 398, 401, 405, 412, 438–39, 445, 447, 452, 462, 467; general: 220, 263, 397; local: 263, 397; will of: lxiv
abdication: lxvi, 246
Abelard, Peter: 161
abilities: 164, 204, 210
abjection: lxi
abnegation: xxiv, lxi, 143–51, 194, 305–6; practice of: 149–50; works of: 305
abode: 464
Abraham: 303–4, 321
absence(s): 287–88, 290, 330
abstention, sexual: 336
abstinence: 230, 333
abundance: 378, 437
abuse(s): 179, 200, 202–4, 208, 262, 372
accidentals: 147, 246, 253, 477
accidents: 339, 350, 477
accommodation: lxiii
accusation: 419
acedia: 448
a Cervia, Eugenio: 182
achievement(s): 473, 477
act(s), animal: 370; ascetical: 184; bad: 40; biological: 370; contingent: 173; creative: 60–61; diverse: 169; divine: 19; ethical: 184; evil: 38; exterior: 155, 262; external: 48, 165, 248, 370; final: 174–75; formal: 237; free: 14, 18, 168–69, 173, 257–58; good: 37, 40, 186–87; human: viii, 10, 12, 14, 16–18, 21, 36, 40, 59, 169, 173–74, 177, 183, 232, 235, 259, 261, 265, 336, 342, 346, 393, 462, 485; illegal: 403; instinctive: 324; intense: 38–39, 327; interior: 262; involuntary: 21, 324; juridical: 151, 181, 397; just: 59; liturgical: 192; material: 379; mechanical: 35, 337; of charity: 35; of choice: 14, 17, 237; of consent: 181; of contemplation: 125; of faith: 86, 253; of God: 61; of justice: 61; of love: 31, 72, 76, 167, 346; of obedience: 170; of passion: 35; of profession: 183; of proprietorship: 387–88, 398; of religion: 155; of sensible appetite: xvii; of soul: xvii, 17–18, 325; of virtue: 54, 92, 184, 186, 330; of will: 18, 26, 35, 155, 169, 172, 176, 180, 234, 327; of worship: xxv, 155, 192; penitential: 105; pious: 36; possible: 169–73; prescribed: 49; public: 165, 192, 237; pure: 102; rational: 174; religious: 68, 163, 183, 185; repeated: 35–37; ritual: 66; sexual: 334, 341, 343; spiritual: 168, 370; supernatural: 16, 168, 307, 329; symbolic: 370; thoughtless: 403; venereal: 340–42, 344–45; voluntary: 16, 18, 52, 177
action(s): xviii, 10, 14, 36, 38, 118, 124, 126, 131, 142, 145, 164, 167, 176–78, 184, 188, 192, 225, 227, 275, 327,

551

pain: 29, 75; cult of: 353
paper: 402
paper clips: 402
parable(s): 33, 170, 322
paradise: 43
parasite: 435
parasitism: 213
parent(s): 45, 138, 223, 247, 337, 385, 390, 415, 483
Paris: 161
parish: 457
parlor: 223
parousia: 71
participation: 28, 407
parties: 417
party, political: 487
Paschasius Radbertus: 237
Passerini, Pietro, OP: 162
passion(s): xvii, xxiii, xxxii, 15, 17–27, 34–35, 37, 39, 41, 55, 84, 88, 105, 115, 159, 162, 168, 176, 247, 272, 279, 313, 324–27, 331–35, 357, 359, 368, 371, 450; carnal: 55; concupiscible: 23; divinized: 26; irascible: 23; principal: 22–23; sexual: 327
passivity: lv, lxi, 240, 482
Pasternak, Boris: xli
pastor(s): 90, 110
paternalism: 415
patience: 86–87, 90, 208, 253, 256, 273, 308, 328, 352, 359–60, 365, 378, 448, 471, 473
patrimony: 398, 401, 409
patronage: 415
pattern: 436; definite: 215; of life: 225
Paul, St.: xxxi, 18, 20, 64, 87, 90, 92, 243, 246, 273, 313, 315, 319, 322–24, 433, 435–36
Paul the Deacon: 280
pay: 399
peace: liii, lxxiii, 18, 22, 25, 43, 86, 90, 92, 100, 112, 114, 142, 149–50, 156, 158, 174, 179, 199, 204–5, 213, 215,

238–39, 243, 302, 305, 307, 311, 330, 338, 346, 351, 358–59, 424, 427, 429, 434, 447, 457, 463; fraternal: 158; kiss of: 364
Pearson, Paul M.: lxxx
peasant, French: 411
peasantry: 440
peculiarities: 209
peculium: 407
pen: 385
penalty: 48
penance(s): xviii, xxx, liii, 17, 41, 48, 67, 82, 119, 130, 140, 152, 193, 203, 230, 232, 239, 260, 266, 286, 302, 331, 344, 359; instruments of: 365; public: 191
pencils: 402
penitence: 151
penitents: 109
pension: 400
Pentecost, Feast of: xli, 435
people, American: 487; chosen: 420–21, 423–25, 434; of God: xxxi
perfect: 115
perfection: x–xi, xvi, xxiii–xxiv, lxxii, 12–13, 16, 19, 38, 54, 58, 63, 70, 84–86, 89, 111, 116, 118–21, 128, 143–44, 149, 154, 158, 174, 184, 188–89, 193, 197, 210, 217, 225–27, 231, 241, 250, 255, 263, 267, 271, 274, 276–77, 282, 288, 292, 294, 296, 312, 365, 409; Christian: 54, 92, 145; divine: 226; exclusive: lxx; inner: 238; life of: 90, 110; moral: x–xi, 145, 190; of being: 10; of charity: 86, 113, 123, 128, 144, 164; of lover: 30; religious: 119, 383, 418; spiritual: 190; state of: xxiii, 110, 112, 114, 116, 127, 159–60, 174
perfume: 340
periodicals: 362
permanence: xviii, 38
permission(s): 166, 171, 186, 200–202, 219–23, 232, 267, 271, 284, 288–90,